P9-EGM-313

The Ethical Life

The Ethical Life

*Fundamental Readings
in Ethics and Moral Problems*

Fourth Edition

RUSS SHAFER-LANDAU
The University of Wisconsin at Madison

New York   Oxford
OXFORD UNIVERSITY PRESS

Oxford University Press is a department of the University of Oxford.
It furthers the University's objective of excellence in research, scholarship,
and education by publishing worldwide. Oxford is a registered trade mark
of Oxford University Press in the UK and certain other countries.

Published in the United States of America by Oxford University Press
198 Madison Avenue, New York, NY 10016, United States of America.

© 2018, 2014, 2012, 2010 by Oxford University Press

For titles covered by Section 112 of the US Higher Education
Opportunity Act, please visit www.oup.com/us/he for the latest
information about pricing and alternate formats.

All rights reserved. No part of this publication may be reproduced,
stored in a retrieval system, or transmitted, in any form or by any means,
without the prior permission in writing of Oxford University Press, or as
expressly permitted by law, by license, or under terms agreed with the
appropriate reproduction rights organization. Inquiries concerning
reproduction outside the scope of the above should be sent to the
Rights Department, Oxford University Press, at the address above.

You must not circulate this work in any other form
and you must impose this same condition on any acquirer.

Library of Congress Cataloging-in-Publication Data

Names: Shafer-Landau, Russ, author.
Title: The ethical life : fundamental readings in ethics and moral problems /
    Russ Shafer-Landau, The University of Wisconsin at Madison.
Description: Fourth edition. | New York : Oxford University Press, [2018]
Identifiers: LCCN 2017006839 | ISBN 9780190631314 (student edition)
Subjects: LCSH: Ethics--Textbooks.
Classification: LCC BJ1012 .E882 2018 | DDC 170—dc23
LC record available at https://lccn.loc.gov/2017006839

9 8 7 6 5 4 3 2 1
Printed by LSC Communications, United States of America

CONTENTS

Preface   ix

A Note on the Companion Volume   xiii

INTRODUCTION   1

PART I   The Good Life

1. *John Stuart Mill*   Hedonism   11
2. *Robert Nozick*   The Experience Machine   21
3. *Chris Heathwood*   Faring Well and Getting What You Want   25
4. *Brad Hooker*   The Elements of Well-Being   37
5. *Susan Wolf*   Happiness and Meaning: Two Aspects of the Good Life   53

PART II   Normative Ethics   *Theories of Right Conduct*

6. *Plato*   Euthyphro   75
7. *Thomas Aquinas*   Natural Law   84
8. *John Stuart Mill*   Utilitarianism   97
9. *Immanuel Kant*   The Good Will and the Categorical Imperative   107
10. *Thomas Hobbes*   Leviathan   120
11. *W. D. Ross*   What Makes Right Acts Right?   131
12. *Aristotle*   Nicomachean Ethics   143
13. *Hilde Lindemann*   What Is Feminist Ethics?   155

PART III   Metaethics   *The Status of Morality*

14. *David Hume*   Moral Distinctions Not Derived from Reason   171
15. *J. L. Mackie*   The Subjectivity of Values   181
16. *Gilbert Harman*   Ethics and Observation   190
17. *Harry Gensler*   Cultural Relativism   199
18. *David Enoch*   Why I Am an Objectivist about Ethics (And Why You Are, Too)   208

PART IV **Moral Problems**

19. *Kwame Anthony Appiah* What Will Future Generations Condemn Us For? 225

POVERTY AND HUNGER

20. *Peter Singer* The Singer Solution to World Poverty 230
21. *Jan Narveson* Feeding the Hungry 238

EUTHANASIA AND A MODEST PROPOSAL

22. *James Rachels* The Morality of Euthanasia 252
23. *John Harris* The Survival Lottery 258

THE MORAL STATUS OF ANIMALS

24. *Alastair Norcross* Puppies, Pigs and People: Eating Meat and Marginal Cases 267
25. *R. G. Frey* Moral Standing, the Value of Lives, and Speciesism 283

THE ENVIRONMENT

26. *Eric A. Posner and Cass R. Sunstein* Climate Change Justice 301
27. *Thomas Hill, Jr.* Ideals of Human Excellence and Preserving Natural Environments 317

ABORTION

28. *Judith Jarvis Thomson* A Defense of Abortion 333
29. *Don Marquis* Why Abortion Is Immoral 346
30. *Philippa Foot* The Problem of Abortion and the Doctrine of the Double Effect 357

THE DEATH PENALTY

31. *Igor Primoratz* Justifying Legal Punishment 370
32. *Stephen Nathanson* An Eye for an Eye? 380

GUNS

33. *Jeff McMahan* Why Gun 'Control' Is Not Enough 390
34. *Michael Huemer* Is There a Right to Own a Gun? 396

THE LEGACY OF RACISM

35. *Chris Lebron* Time for a New Black Radicalism 411
36. *Louis P. Pojman* The Case Against Affirmative Action 417
37. *Daniel M. Hausman* Affirmative Action: Bad Arguments and Some Good Ones 432
38. *Elizabeth Anderson* The Future of Racial Integration 446

DRUGS

39. *Michael Huemer*   America's Unjust Drug War   466

40. *Peter de Marneffe*   Against the Legalization of Drugs   480

COPYRIGHT

41. *Jonathan Trerise*   Why Illegally Downloading Files Is Morally Wrong   496

42. *Tim Anderson and D. E. Wittkower*   Why Legally Downloading Music Is Morally Wrong   508

PREFACE

B rief yet thorough, *The Ethical Life: Fundamental Readings in Ethics and Moral Problems* is a collection of original writings in ethics. Its four parts—The Good Life, Normative Ethics, Meta-ethics, and Moral Problems—serve to introduce readers to each of the major branches of moral philosophy, with readings that have been carefully selected for their engaging style and their accessibility. This book can be usefully read on its own, and is an ideal way to acquaint students with the major themes of moral philosophy through a large selection of primary source material.

Changes to the Fourth Edition

This edition of *The Ethical Life* contains a dozen new selections and two new sections.

Part I now offers Brad Hooker's assessment of different theories of well-being and Susan Wolf's popular paper discussing the relationship between happiness and meaning in life.

Part II now offers selections from two classics: Thomas Aquinas's presentation of natural law theory and John Stuart Mill's exposition of utilitarian ethics.

Part III now includes Gilbert Harman's influential challenge to the objectivity of ethics, a challenge that unfavorably contrasts morality with the natural sciences.

Part IV has seen the largest number of changes. This part now begins with a provocative piece by Kwame Anthony Appiah, who invites us to reflect on the morality of contemporary practices by asking what future generations will condemn us for. There is a new section on copyright law, which contains two commissioned pieces, one by Jonathan Trerise and another by Tim Anderson and D. E. Wittkower. These papers focus specifically on the morality of (il)legally downloading music. There is another new section, this one on gun control, featuring opposing pieces by Jeff McMahan and Michael Huemer. In other selections that are new to this edition, Eric A. Posner and Cass R. Sunstein discuss what justice requires when facing the challenges of climate change, Elizabeth Anderson argues for the importance of racial integration as a social policy, and Peter de Marneffe offers arguments against the legalization of drugs.

Input from students, instructors, and reviewers, plus a mandate to keep the book to the length of previous editions, has also led to having to say goodbye to several pieces from the last edition, many of which are personal favorites of mine. With some sadness, the following articles have been deleted for the fourth edition: Epicurus, "Letter to Menoeceus;" Jean Kazez, "Necessities;" Philippa Foot, "Natural Goodness;" J. J. C. Smart, "Extreme and Restricted Utilitarianism;" A. J. Ayer, "A Critique of Ethics;" John Corvino, "Why Shouldn't Tommy and Jimmy Have Sex?;" Michael Walzer, "Terrorism: A Critique of Excuses;" Alan Dershowitz, "Should the Ticking Bomb Terrorist Be Tortured?;" Paul Taylor, "The Ethics of Respect for Nature;" Michael Sandel, "The Case Against Perfection;" and Julian Savulescu, "Genetic Interventions and the Ethics of Enhancement of Human Beings."

Instructor's Manual and Companion Website

The companion website designed to support this book offers self-quizzes, further reading, and web links to sites of further interest. You can visit the website at: www.oup.com/us/shafer-landau.

In addition, the Instructor's Manual can be accessed on the Oxford University Press Ancillary Resource Center (ARC) at https://arc2.oup-arc.com/access/shafer-landau-ethical-life-4e-instructor-resources. The manual itself has short abstracts of every reading with accompanying essay questions, a computerized test bank, further reading, lecture outlines on PowerPoint slides, and web links to sites of further interest. The ARC is a convenient, instructor-focused single destination for resources to accompany this text. Accessed online through individual user accounts, the ARC provides instructors with access to up-to-date ancillaries at any time while guaranteeing the security of grade-significant resources. In addition, it allows OUP to keep instructors informed when new content becomes available.

The work for these ancillary materials was undertaken by my stellar research assistants Justin Horn, who provided all of the web materials associated with the first two editions, and Ben Schwan, who provided updates associated with the third and this latest edition. I am very grateful for their dedicated efforts in making these first-rate resources.

Learning Management System (LMS) cartridges are available in formats compatible with any LMS in use at your college or university and include the following:

- The Instructor's Manual and Computerized Test Bank
- Student resources from the companion website

Acknowledgments

It has been a lot of fun putting this book together, but it hasn't always been an easy thing to do. By far the most difficult aspect of the project was the winnowing. Ethics is so large a field, with so much that is provocative and interesting within it, yet books must have their page limits, and those limits often forced me to leave a prized piece behind. It has been a real challenge to offer a representative sampling of subject matter and viewpoints within a book of this size. To the extent that I have met with any success, it is owing in large part to the helpful suggestions and kind critical advice I have received from the following philosophers: Kristofer Arca at Miami Dade College, Ben Almassi at College of Lake County, Fidel Arnecillo at CSU–San Bernardino, Ralph Baergen at Idaho State University, Jeffrey Brand-Ballard at George Washington University, Patrick Martin Breen at the College of Staten Island, Adam Briggle at University of North Texas, David Burris at Arizona Western College, Tom Carson at Loyola University Chicago, Charles Comer at Harrisburg Area Community College, Christian Coons at Bowling Green State University, Richard DeGeorge at the University of Kansas, Neil Delaney at the University of Notre Dame, David Detmer at Purdue University Calumet, Tyler Doggett at the University of Vermont, Robert M. Farley at Hillsborough Community College, Andrew Fitz-Gibbon at SUNY Cortland, Amber George at Le Moyne College, Deke Gould at Syracuse University, Christopher Grau at Clemson University, Craig Hanks at Texas State University, Richard Haynes at the University of Florida, Darren Hibbs at Nova Southeastern University, Kelly Heuer at Georgetown University, Richard Hine at the University of Connecticut, John Huss at the University of Akron, Clark Hutton at Volunteer State Community College, Phil Jenkins at Marywood University, Carla Johnson at St. Cloud State University, Keith Korcz at the University of Louisiana at Lafayette, Jacob Krch at University of Wisconsin–Madison, Mark LeBar at Ohio University, Richard Lee at the University of Arkansas, Hilde Lindeman at Michigan State University, Patrick Linden at NYU Polytechnic, Jessica Logue at the University of Portland, Sarah Lublink at Florida Southwestern State College, Eugene Marshall at Wellesley College, Michael McKenna at Florida State University, Brian Merrill at Brigham Young University–Idaho, John Messerly at Shoreline Community College, Christian Miller at Wake Forest University, Richard Momeyer at Miami University of Ohio, Michelle Moon at CSU Channel Islands, Jennifer Morton at CUNY, Mark Murphy at Georgetown University, Nathan Nobis at Morehouse College, Aleksandr Pjevalica at University of Texas–El Paso, David Pereplyotchik at Baruch College, Jamie Phillips at Clarion University of Pennsylvania, Philip Robbins at the University of Missouri, Nathan Rockwood at Virginia Tech, David Sobel at Syracuse University, Stephen Sullivan at Edinboro University, Mark van Roojen at the University of Nebraska–Lincoln, Dave Schmidtz at the University of Arizona, David Shoemaker at Tulane University, Paul Wagner at the University of Houston Clear Lake, Brian Wagoner at Davis and Elkins College, Kit Wellman at Washington University in St. Louis, Jason Zinser at the University of Florida, and Christopher Zurn at the University of Kentucky. I am very grateful for their assistance.

I would also like to acknowledge the terrific support of my editor at Oxford, Robert Miller, and his crack assistant Alyssa Palazzo, who helped shepherd this book through its various stages. I feel very fortunate to have had a chance to work with Robert on this and other projects over the years, and am, as always, grateful for his advice, constant encouragement, open-mindedness, and inspired good sense.

R.S.L.
Madison, Wisconsin

A NOTE ON THE
COMPANION VOLUME

This collection can be used as a self-standing introduction to ethics. It includes readings from each of the major divisions within moral philosophy. Together with the General Introduction, an introduction to each reading, study questions, and all of the supplementary materials available at the book's website, I hope that readers are able to get a very good feel for just how interesting moral philosophy can be.

This collection is designed to serve as a natural partner to *Fundamentals of Ethics* (Oxford University Press), an introduction to moral philosophy that I have written. *Fundamentals* is a textbook, though I hope that it is a bit more lively than such a label implies. Both books offer coverage of the good life, the nature of duty and virtue, and the status of morality. The book you have in your hands also offers extensive coverage of many practical ethical problems, such as abortion, gun control, famine relief, etc. My hope, of course, is that the two books work neatly in tandem. The theories and positions I present and analyze in *Fundamentals* are here represented by some of their finest defenders. For those who are content to get the view directly from the source, this book should do. But if you would like a moral theory or an ethical position placed in a broader context, its main lines of argument laid out clearly and then critically assessed, then a dip into the companion volume might not be a bad idea.

I am very interested in hearing from readers who are willing to offer me their feedback, both positive and negative. Perhaps you have found some pieces dull or uninspired, or some that were especially exciting and challenging. For teachers who are familiar with this terrain, perhaps you've been disappointed at seeing a beloved piece gone missing, or would like to pass along the success of a given selection in sparking conversation. The easiest way to reach me is by email: *RussShaferlandau@gmail.com*. I'd be very pleased to receive your thoughts on how this book might be improved.

R. S. L.

The Ethical Life

INTRODUCTION

M oral philosophy, or ethics—I use the terms interchangeably—is, in its widest application, the study of what we should aspire to in our lives, and of how we should live.

There is no agreed-upon definition of morality, or even of philosophy. We can offer vague (very vague) platitudes, on the order of: philosophy is the love of wisdom; morality is the code that we should live by. It isn't clear to me that we can do *much* better than that. More instructive, I think, is to describe the specific fields within ethics. Through an understanding of these areas, we can better appreciate what moral philosophy is all about.

Nowadays, it is standard to distinguish four different areas of moral philosophy. And (surprise!) the four parts of this book correspond to each of these areas.

The first is known as *value theory*. This is the part of ethics that tries to determine what is valuable in and of itself, what a good life consists in. Is happiness, for instance, the ultimate good? Our first author, the Englishman John Stuart Mill, certainly thinks so. But others are skeptical. These include the late Harvard philosopher Robert Nozick. Perhaps what is most important is simply that we get what we want out of life—no matter what we want? That's what Chris Heathwood argues, in an article that he has written especially for this book. Yet others (represented here by Brad Hooker and Susan Wolf) reject this idea and offer a variety of things (self-determination, moral virtue, happiness, loving relationships, etc.) that are said to be good in their own right.

In Part II we turn to that area of moral philosophy known as *normative ethics*. This large branch of philosophy is devoted to identifying the supreme principle(s) of right action. Many philosophers have sought just a single, fundamental principle that will unify the entire field, that will explain, for instance, why keeping your word, telling the truth, and helping the poor are morally right.

There are many important contenders that seek to fill this role. Consider, for instance, the Divine Command Theory, which tells us that acts are right just because God commands them. The first extended discussion of this view appears in Plato's dialogue *Euthyphro*, a large portion of which is presented here. Socrates, Plato's teacher and mouthpiece in this work, doesn't look too kindly on this view. Though Socrates assumes that there are many gods rather than one, and focuses on what makes actions pious rather than right, the central philosophical concerns about the Divine Command Theory that worry philosophers today are just the ones that Socrates advanced 2,400 years ago.

If God is not the ultimate source of morality, what is? Many have looked to nature—and human nature, in particular—to answer this question. *Natural law theory* takes this idea most seriously, and in one form or another (there are many varieties), it tries to show that moral action is a matter of acting in a way that respects our nature. Thomas Aquinas is the greatest of the natural lawyers; a small selection from his magnum opus, *Summa Theologica*, is reprinted here.

We next turn to *utilitarianism* (presented here by its most elegant defender, John Stuart Mill), which instructs us always to produce the greatest happiness for the greatest number. Utilitarianism focuses on an action's results—did it yield the greatest happiness of all available actions?—to determine its morality. The German philosopher Immanuel Kant, by contrast, tells us that results are morally irrelevant. Acts are right, he says, just because we can use their guiding principles consistently, without involving ourselves in contradiction. This isn't an easy thought to understand, but the basic idea is pretty simple. The essence of morality, Kant thinks, is fairness and justice. Immorality is a matter of making an exception of yourself, of living by rules that, in some sense, cannot possibly serve as the basis of everyone's actions.

Kant's view shares some features with another important normative ethic, the *social contract theory*. Though this theory was briefly discussed as far back as the ancient Greeks, it was not fully developed until well into the sixteenth century. It was brilliantly set forth in the work of Thomas

Hobbes, whose book *Leviathan* is excerpted here. The social contract theory tells us that morality is essentially a cooperative enterprise and that the moral rules are those that self-interested people would obey on the condition that all others do so as well. Both Kantianism and the social contract theory take the natural ethical question—What if everyone did that?—quite seriously, and both use an answer to this question as a foundation of their normative ethical theory.

One thing that all of the theories canvassed so far have in common is that they try to identify a single, supreme moral rule that serves as the ultimate basis of all of our moral duties. But what if there is no such thing? British philosopher W. D. Ross took this question very seriously and argued against the existence of any such moral rule in developing his ethic of *prima facie duties*. Prima facie duties are those that can be outweighed by competing duties. If Ross is right, *every* general duty is like this. We have a standing duty to keep our word, to do justice, to prevent harm, etc. But sometimes these duties conflict with one another. When they do, only one can be our "all-things-considered" duty, the thing we really must do on that particular occasion. The problem, though, is that there is no fixed ranking of the moral principles, and so it can be very difficult to know what to do when they conflict. Sometimes it is more important to prevent harm than to keep our word, but sometimes the reverse is true. The same is true of all conflicts of duty. While Ross thinks that we can know each prima facie moral duty just through careful reflection, things get much more complicated when it comes to knowing what our final, all-things-considered duty is in specific situations.

Aristotle is next. By many accounts, he is the greatest philosopher who ever lived. He developed the first elaborate version of *virtue ethics*, the view that places the virtues at center stage in ethical inquiry. Virtue theorists reject the idea of a single formula that can provide ethical advice for every occasion. They instead tell us to look to virtuous role models and imagine what they would do if they were in our shoes. It is tempting to begin ethical thinking by selecting a standard (such as the utilitarian standard) and saying that a virtue is a steady commitment that tends to produce right action, as measured by that standard. Virtue ethicists turn this on its head and argue that we can understand the nature of right action only by first understanding the virtues.

Some of the most exciting recent work in normative ethics has been done by those who consider morality from the perspective of *feminist ethics*. This is best understood as an approach to ethics, rather than as a single view that is a direct competitor with the normative ethical theories we have briefly looked at thus far. In her selection here, philosopher Hilde Lindemann sketches the distinctive features of a feminist outlook on morality. These include an emphasis on taking the experience of women seriously when developing one's ethical ideas and ideals and eliminating the many ways in which sexist assumptions creep into traditional philosophizing. Lindemann offers a variety of examples and interesting points as a way of introducing us to the large family of feminist approaches to ethics.

We have thus far canvassed those areas of ethics that deal with the good and the right, value theory, and normative ethics. But there is another part of ethics that takes a step back from these debates and asks, more generally, about the *status* of moral views in both areas. Philosophers call this branch of moral theory *metaethics*, and it is the focus of Part III.

Metaethics studies such questions as these: Is morality just a convenient fiction? If not, can moral standards be true? Suppose they are: Does their truth depend on personal opinion, social consensus, God's commands, or something else? If there are genuine moral truths, how can we know them? And do they have any authority over us—is it always rational to be moral, or is it sometimes reasonable to take the immoral path?

I have divided the authors in this section into two camps—those who are skeptical of objective morality and those who defend it. As I understand it, morality is objective just in case there are some moral standards that apply to us regardless of what any human being believes.

Opponents of moral objectivity get the first hearing. The Scottish Enlightenment thinker David Hume starts us off. His criticisms of reason's place in ethics have been extremely influential across the past two and a half centuries, and rightly so. Most of today's important critiques of moral objectivity have their ancestors in one or more of the arguments that Hume provided. Hume thought that if moral claims were objectively true, then we should be able to discover our moral duty just by thinking hard about it. But Hume argues that no amount of careful reasoning could do that. And therefore morality cannot be objective.

Hume did not seek to undermine ethics, but rather to offer a diagnosis of its true nature. J. L. Mackie seeks to go further and show that there are no moral truths. He argues that all of our moral thinking is based on an error. Mackie believes that moral thought starts from the view that morality is objective. He offers some important arguments to try to show that it isn't. He sees morality as a product of human insecurity and imagination, with no real authority over us. If we all do assume that morality is objective, and if Mackie is right about its being (at best) a useful fiction, then morality really is bankrupt.

Last among the critics of moral objectivity is Gilbert Harman. He argues that ethics and the natural sciences are fundamentally different, in a way that isn't flattering to morality. Science can provide us with an objective picture of reality; ethics can't, because there is no objective morality. We can verify scientific claims, because the best explanation of our scientific observations is that they have been caused by real objects, out in the world. By contrast, we cannot test our moral beliefs against the world. We have no external check on our moral opinions, no objective moral facts that might cause us to have the moral opinions we do. Consider two competing hypotheses, designed to account for our moral beliefs: (1) we are caused to have the moral beliefs we do because moral facts somehow impress themselves upon us; or (2) our moral views are the product of social influences and agreements. If Harman is correct, then (2) is by far the better explanation.

We then turn the tables and allow the ethical objectivists to have their say. Harry Gensler starts us off by arguing against cultural relativism, which is the idea that a society's guiding ideals are the ultimate moral standards. Since different societies have different ideals, relativists believe that there is no universal or objective morality. Gensler offers four reasons to oppose relativism. First, it cannot allow for consistent disagreement with one's social code. Second, relativism is a very poor basis for defending tolerance. Third, relativism is a counsel of unthinking conformity. And, finally, relativism is unable to offer any advice about how to act when one is a member of different cultures.

In an article written especially for this book, David Enoch argues that almost all of us, whether we realize it or not, are committed to some form of objectivity about morality. He devises a number of tests to help us see the extent of this commitment. That we are committed to morality's objectivity does not prove that our commitments are correct. But we should assume that they are until such time as we have excellent reason to reject them. Enoch considers a number of arguments designed to show that morality is not in fact objective, and then offers his reasons for rejecting those critiques.

This concludes the section on metaethics, and with it, the first half of this collection.

No philosopher sees his field in just the same way that others do. My take on what really matters in ethics is bound to be personal and, to some degree, not shared by my fellow practitioners. Still, I have aimed in this volume to respect standard divisions within this large field, and have tried to balance selections from classic works with some relatively unfamiliar material that strikes me as important and provocative.

Whether beginners or old pros, each of us improves our moral thinking by being exposed to a variety of viewpoints on the deep questions that interest us. The ideal philosophical introduction, therefore, would present at least the main competitors within the various subfields that make up ethics, thereby giving newcomers a taste of the different perspectives that have shaped debates within this rich area of philosophy. I hope that I have managed some success on this front, but in at least one case, it would have been clearly impossible to achieve this within a reasonable amount of space.

I am thinking here of the last and largest section of the book, Part IV, the one devoted to a variety of *moral problems*. There are far too many interesting moral conundrums to fit them all into a collection of this size. I hope that the topics on offer are compelling, but I recognize that many exciting subjects and insightful articles have been left behind. Short of greatly increasing the size of this collection, I see no way to avoid this, and must hope that the twenty-four offerings available here are of sufficient interest and importance to do what they are meant to do—inspire you to grapple with their puzzles, thought experiments, and arguments and to appreciate a bit of the complexity of the moral issues that take center stage in this part of the book. What you have in this section (and all the others) is just a small sampling of possible positions and supporting arguments. The readings throughout this book are designed to whet your appetite, not to sate it.

There is no theoretical unity to this half of the volume. The authors here represent a variety of different theoretical approaches, and some, as you will see, do not argue directly from any normative theory at all.

This might be surprising, because a time-honored picture of how to argue about moral problems is to claim that you must first identify the correct normative theory, take note of the relevant nonmoral facts, and presto!—out comes your moral verdict. This way of arguing actually happens less often than you may think, which is why the more common term for this sort of moral philosophy, "applied ethics," is a bit misleading. That label implies that all practical moral problems can be solved in a top-down way, by first selecting the proper normative ethic, and then just "applying" it—as if that were a straightforward matter of cranking out its implications.

One reason that philosophers don't always proceed this way is because there is still huge disagreement about which normative ethic is the correct one. And so any philosopher who restricted her arguments to applying a single normative theory would be losing a good deal of her audience—specifically, the large segment of it that disagreed with her normative ethic. As a result, most philosophers who grapple with real-life moral problems begin not with the grand normative theories but rather with more concrete principles (keep your word, don't violate patient confidentiality, avoid imposing unnecessary pain, etc.) or examples that we are already expected to accept. Armed with these, the author then tries to show that a commitment to them implies some specific view about the problem at hand.

The topics covered in this last section are of the first importance: famine relief, euthanasia, animal rights, environmental ethics, abortion, affirmative action, racial integration, drug laws, gun control, and the morality of copyright laws. Are there other topics that deserve a place at the table? Absolutely. But these strike me as being worthy of our attention, and the pieces I have selected all present interesting sets of arguments that deserve careful scrutiny. Some of these pieces do represent pretty direct applications of the normative theories discussed in the second part of this book. In these cases, you can use the arguments contained here as a way of testing those normative theories. In other cases, as I mentioned above, the arguments will be theoretically more free-standing. In any event, I hope that there will be plenty to inspire your interest, curiosity, and, occasionally, your outrage. I have found that each of these reactions can be an excellent catalyst to serious philosophical thinking.

PART I

The Good Life

1

Hedonism

John Stuart Mill

....

John Stuart Mill (1806–1873) was one of the great hedonistic thinkers. In this excerpt from his long pamphlet *Utilitarianism* (1863), Mill defends his complex version of hedonism. Sensitive to criticisms that it counsels us to pursue a life of brutish pleasure, Mill distinguishes between "higher and lower pleasures" and claims, famously, that it is "better to be Socrates dissatisfied, than a fool satisfied." He also offers here his much-discussed "proof" of hedonism, by drawing a parallel between the evidence we have for something's being visible (that all of us see it) and something's being desirable (that all of us desire it). He also argues for the claim that we do and can desire nothing but pleasure, and uses this conjecture as a way of defending the view that pleasure is the only thing that is always worth pursuing for its own sake.

....

The creed which accepts, as the foundation of morals, Utility, or the Greatest-happiness Principle, holds that actions are right in proportion as they tend to promote happiness, wrong as they tend to produce the reverse of happiness. By happiness is intended pleasure and the absence of pain; by unhappiness, pain and the privation of pleasure. To give a clear view of the moral standard set up by the theory, much more requires to be said; in particular, what things it includes in the ideas of pain and pleasure, and to what extent this is left an open question. But these supplementary explanations do not affect the theory of life on which this theory of morality is grounded,—namely, that pleasure, and freedom from pain, are the only things desirable as ends; and that all desirable things (which are as numerous in the utilitarian as in any other scheme) are desirable either for the pleasure inherent in themselves, or as means to the promotion of pleasure and the prevention of pain.

Now, such a theory of life excites in many minds, and among them in some of the most estimable in feeling and purpose, inveterate dislike. To suppose that life has (as they express it) no higher end than pleasure,—no better and nobler object of desire and pursuit,—they designate as utterly mean and groveling; as a doctrine worthy only of swine, to whom the followers of Epicurus were, at a very early period, contemptuously likened: and modern holders of the doctrine are occasionally made the subject of equally polite comparisons by its German, French, and English assailants.

When thus attacked, the Epicureans have always answered, that it is not they, but their accusers, who represent human nature in a degrading light, since the accusation supposes human beings to be capable of no pleasures except those of which swine are capable. If this supposition were true, the charge could not be gainsaid, but would then be no longer an imputation; for, if the sources of pleasure were precisely the same to human beings and to swine, the rule of life which is good enough for the one would be good enough for the other. The comparison of the Epicurean life to that of beasts is felt as degrading, precisely because a beast's pleasures do not satisfy a human being's conceptions of happiness. Human beings have faculties more elevated than the animal appetites; and, when once made conscious of them, do not regard any thing as happiness which does not include their gratification. I do not, indeed, consider the Epicureans to have been by any means faultless in drawing out their scheme of consequences from the utilitarian principle. To do this in any sufficient manner, many Stoic as well as Christian elements require to be included. But there is no known Epicurean theory of life which does not assign to the pleasures of the intellect, of the feeling and imagination, and of the moral sentiments, a much higher value as pleasures than to those of mere sensation. It must be admitted, however, that utilitarian writers in general have placed the superiority of mental over bodily pleasures chiefly in the greater permanency, safety, uncostliness, &c., of the former,—that is, in their circumstantial advantages rather than in their intrinsic nature. And, on all these points, utilitarians have fully proved their case; but they might have taken the other, and, as it may be called, higher ground, with entire consistency. It is quite compatible with the principle of utility to recognize the fact, that some *kinds* of pleasure are more desirable and more valuable than others. It would be absurd, that while, in estimating all other things, quality is considered as well as quantity, the estimation of pleasures should be supposed to depend on quantity alone.

If I am asked what I mean by difference of quality in pleasures, or what makes one pleasure more valuable than another, merely as a pleasure, except its being greater in amount, there is but one possible answer. Of two pleasures, if there be one to which all or almost all who have experience of both give a decided preference, irrespective of any feeling of moral obligation to prefer it, that is the more desirable pleasure. If one of the two is, by those who are competently acquainted with both, placed so far above the other that they prefer it, even though knowing it to be attended with a greater amount of discontent, and would not resign it for any quantity of the other pleasure which their nature is capable of, we are justified in ascribing to the preferred enjoyment a superiority in quality, so far outweighing quantity, as to render it, in comparison, of small account.

Now, it is an unquestionable fact, that those who are equally acquainted with and equally capable of appreciating and enjoying both do give a most marked preference to the manner of existence which employs their higher faculties. Few human creatures would consent to be changed into any of the lower animals, for a promise of the fullest allowance of a beast's pleasures: no intelligent human being would consent to be a fool, no instructed person would be an ignoramus, no person of feeling and conscience would be selfish and base, even though they should be persuaded that the fool, the dunce, or the rascal is better satisfied with his lot than they are with theirs. They would not resign what they possess more than he for the most complete satisfaction of all the desires which they have in common with him. If they ever fancy they would, it is only in cases of unhappiness so extreme, that, to escape from it, they would exchange their lot for almost any other, however undesirable in their own eyes. A being of higher faculties requires more to make him happy, is capable probably of more acute suffering, and certainly accessible to it at more points, than one of an inferior type; but, in spite of these liabilities, he can never really wish to sink into what he feels to be a lower grade of existence. We may give what explanation we please of this unwillingness; we may attribute it to pride, a name which is given indiscriminately to some of the most and to some of the least estimable feelings of which mankind are capable; we may refer it to the love of liberty and personal independence,—an appeal to which was with the Stoics one of the most effective means for the inculcation of it; to the love of power, or to the love of excitement, both of which do really enter into and contribute to it: but its most appropriate appellation is a sense of dignity, which all human beings possess in one form or other, and in some, though by no means in exact, proportion to their higher faculties, and which is so essential a part of the happiness of those in whom it is strong, that nothing which conflicts with it could be, otherwise than momentarily, an object of desire to them. Whoever supposes that this preference takes place at a sacrifice of happiness; that the superior being, in any thing like equal circumstances, is not happier than the inferior— confounds the two very different ideas of happiness and content. It is indisputable, that the being whose capacities of enjoyment are low has the greatest chance of having them fully satisfied; and a highly endowed being will always feel that any happiness which he can look for, as the world is constituted, is imperfect. But he can learn to bear its imperfections, if they are at all bearable; and they will not make him envy the being who is indeed unconscious of the imperfections, but only because he feels not at all the good which those imperfections qualify. It is better to be a human being dissatisfied, than a pig satisfied; better to be Socrates dissatisfied, than a fool satisfied. And if the fool or the pig are of a different opinion, it is because they only know their own side of the question. The other party to the comparison knows both sides.

It may be objected, that many who are capable of the higher pleasures, occasionally, under the influence of temptation, postpone them to the lower. But this is quite compatible with a full appreciation of the intrinsic superiority of the higher. Men often, from infirmity of character, make their election for the nearer good, though they know it to be the less valu-able, and this no less when the choice is between two bodily pleasures than when it is between bodily and mental. They pursue sensual indulgences to the injury of health, though perfectly aware that health is the greater good. It may be further objected, that many who begin with youthful enthusiasm for everything noble, as they advance in years sink into indolence and self-ishness. But I do not believe that those who undergo this very common change voluntarily choose the lower description of pleasures in preference to the higher. I believe, that, before they devote themselves exclusively to the one, they have already become incapable of the other. Capacity for the nobler feelings is in most natures a very tender plant, easily killed, not only by hostile influences, but by mere want of sustenance; and, in the majority of young persons, it speedily dies away if the occupations to which their position in life has devoted them, and the society into which it has thrown them, are not favorable to keeping that higher capacity in exercise. Men lose their high aspirations as they lose their intellectual tastes, because they have not time or opportunity for indulging them; and they addict themselves to inferior pleasures, not because they deliberately prefer them, but because they are either the only ones to which they have access, or the only ones which they are any longer capable of enjoying. It may be questioned whether any one, who has remained equally susceptible to both classes of pleasures, ever knowingly and calmly preferred the lower; though many in all ages have broken down in an ineffectual attempt to combine both.

From this verdict of the only competent judges, I apprehend there can be no appeal. On a question, which is the best worth having of two pleasures, or which of two modes of existence is the most grateful to the feelings, apart from its moral attributes and from its consequences, the judgment of those who are qualified by knowledge of both, or, if they differ, that of the majority among them, must be admitted as final. And there needs be the less hesitation to accept this judgment respecting the quality of pleasures, since there is no other tribunal to be referred to even on the question of quantity. What means are there of determining which is the acutest of two pains, or the intensest of two pleasurable sensations, except the general suffrage of those who are familiar with both? Neither pains nor pleasures are homogeneous, and pain is always heterogeneous with pleasure. What is there to decide whether a particular pleasure is worth purchasing at the cost of particular pain, except the feelings and judgment of the experienced? When, therefore, those feelings and judgment declare the pleasures derived from the higher faculties to be preferable *in kind*, apart from the question of intensity, to those of which the animal nature, disjoined from the higher faculties, is susceptible, they are entitled on this subject to the same regard. . . .

It has already been remarked, that questions of ultimate ends do not admit of proof, in the ordinary acceptation of the term. To be incapable of proof by reasoning is common to all first principles; to the first premises of our knowledge, as well as to those of our conduct. But the former, being matters of fact, may be the subject of a direct appeal to the faculties which judge of fact—namely, our senses, and our internal consciousness. Can an appeal be made to the same faculties on questions of practical ends? Or by what other faculty is cognisance taken of them?

Questions about ends are, in other words, questions of what things are desirable. The utilitarian doctrine is, that happiness is desirable, and the only thing desirable, as an end; all other things being only desirable as means to that end. What ought to be required of this doctrine—what conditions is it requisite that the doctrine should fulfil—to make good its claim to be believed?

The only proof capable of being given that an object is visible, is that people actually see it. The only proof that a sound is audible, is that people hear it: and so of the other sources of our experience. In like manner, I apprehend, the sole evidence it is possible to produce that anything is desirable, is that people do actually desire it. If the end which the utilitarian doctrine proposes to itself were not, in theory and in practice, acknowledged to be an end, nothing could ever convince any person that it was so. No reason can be given why the general happiness is desirable, except that each person, so far as he believes it to be attainable, desires his own happiness. This, however, being a fact, we have not only all the proof which the case admits of, but all which it is possible to require, that happiness is a good: that each person's happiness is a good to that person, and the general happiness, therefore, a good to the aggregate of all persons. Happiness has made out its title as one of the ends of conduct, and consequently one of the criteria of morality.

But it has not, by this alone, proved itself to be the sole criterion. To do that, it would seem, by the same rule, necessary to show, not only that people desire happiness, but that they never desire anything else. Now it is palpable that they do desire things which, in common language, are decidedly distinguished from happiness. They desire, for example, virtue, and the absence of vice, no less really than pleasure and the absence of pain. The desire of virtue is not as universal, but it is as authentic a fact, as the desire of happiness. And hence the opponents of the utilitarian standard deem that they have a right to infer that there are other ends of human action besides happiness, and that happiness is not the standard of approbation and disapprobation.

But does the utilitarian doctrine deny that people desire virtue, or maintain that virtue is not a thing to be desired? The very reverse. It maintains not only that virtue is to be desired, but that it is to be desired disinterestedly, for itself. Whatever may be the opinion of utilitarian moralists as to the original conditions by which virtue is made virtue; however they may believe (as they do) that actions and dispositions are only virtuous because they promote another end than virtue; yet this being granted, and it having been decided, from considerations of this description, what is virtuous, they not only place virtue at the very head of the things which are

good as means to the ultimate end, but they also recognise as a psychological fact the possibility of its being, to the individual, a good in itself, without looking to any end beyond it; and hold, that the mind is not in a right
state, not in a state conformable to Utility, not in the state most conducive
to the general happiness, unless it does love virtue in this manner—as a
thing desirable in itself, even although, in the individual instance, it should
not produce those other desirable consequences which it tends to produce,
and on account of which it is held to be virtue. This opinion is not, in the
smallest degree, a departure from the Happiness principle. The ingredients
of happiness are very various, and each of them is desirable in itself, and
not merely when considered as swelling an aggregate. The principle of utility does not mean that any given pleasure, as music, for instance, or any
given exemption from pain, as for example health, is to be looked upon as
means to a collective something termed happiness, and to be desired on
that account. They are desired and desirable in and for themselves; besides
being means, they are a part of the end. Virtue, according to the utilitarian
doctrine, is not naturally and originally part of the end, but it is capable of
becoming so; and in those who love it disinterestedly it has become so, and
is desired and cherished, not as a means to happiness, but as a part of their
happiness.

   To illustrate this farther, we may remember that virtue is not the only
thing, originally a means, and which if it were not a means to anything
else, would be and remain indifferent, but which by association with what
it is a means to, comes to be desired for itself, and that too with the utmost
intensity. What, for example, shall we say of the love of money? There is
nothing originally more desirable about money than about any heap of
glittering pebbles. Its worth is solely that of the things which it will buy;
the desires for other things than itself, which it is a means of gratifying. Yet
the love of money is not only one of the strongest moving forces of human
life, but money is, in many cases, desired in and for itself; the desire to possess it is often stronger than the desire to use it, and goes on increasing
when all the desires which point to ends beyond it, to be compassed by it,
are falling off. It may, then, be said truly, that money is desired not for the
sake of an end, but as part of the end. From being a means to happiness, it
has come to be itself a principal ingredient of the individual's conception
of happiness. The same may be said of the majority of the great objects of
human life—power, for example, or fame; except that to each of these there
is a certain amount of immediate pleasure annexed, which has at least the
semblance of being naturally inherent in them; a thing which cannot be

said of money. Still, however, the strongest natural attraction, both of power and of fame, is the immense aid they give to the attainment of our other wishes; and it is the strong association thus generated between them and all our objects of desire, which gives to the direct desire of them the intensity it often assumes, so as in some characters to surpass in strength all other desires. In these cases the means have become a part of the end, and a more important part of it than any of the things which they are means to. What was once desired as an instrument for the attainment of happiness, has come to be desired for its own sake. In being desired for its own sake it is, however, desired as part of happiness. The person is made, or thinks he would be made, happy by its mere possession; and is made unhappy by failure to obtain it. The desire of it is not a different thing from the desire of happiness, any more than the love of music, or the desire of health. They are included in happiness. They are some of the elements of which the desire of happiness is made up. Happiness is not an abstract idea, but a concrete whole; and these are some of its parts. And the utilitarian standard sanctions and approves their being so. Life would be a poor thing, very ill provided with sources of happiness, if there were not this provision of nature, by which things originally indifferent, but conducive to, or otherwise associated with, the satisfaction of our primitive desires, become in themselves sources of pleasure more valuable than the primitive pleasures, both in permanency, in the space of human existence that they are capable of covering, and even in intensity.

Virtue, according to the utilitarian conception, is a good of this description. There was no original desire of it, or motive to it, save its conduciveness to pleasure, and especially to protection from pain. But through the association thus formed, it may be felt a good in itself, and desired as such with as great intensity as any other good; and with this difference between it and the love of money, of power, or of fame, that all of these may, and often do, render the individual noxious to the other members of the society to which he belongs, whereas there is nothing which makes him so much a blessing to them as the cultivation of the disinterested love of virtue. And consequently, the utilitarian standard, while it tolerates and approves those other acquired desires, up to the point beyond which they would be more injurious to the general happiness than promotive of it, enjoins and requires the cultivation of the love of virtue up to the greatest strength possible, as being above all things important to the general happiness.

It results from the preceding considerations, that there is in reality nothing desired except happiness. Whatever is desired otherwise than as a means to some end beyond itself, and ultimately to happiness, is desired as itself a part of happiness, and is not desired for itself until it has become so. Those who desire virtue for its own sake, desire it either because the consciousness of it is a pleasure, or because the consciousness of being without it is a pain, or for both reasons united; as in truth the pleasure and pain seldom exist separately, but almost always together, the same person feeling pleasure in the degree of virtue attained, and pain in not having attained more. If one of these gave him no pleasure, and the other no pain, he would not love or desire virtue, or would desire it only for the other benefits which it might produce to himself or to persons whom he cared for. We have now, then, an answer to the question, of what sort of proof the principle of utility is susceptible. If the opinion which I have now stated is psychologically true—if human nature is so constituted as to desire nothing which is not either a part of happiness or a means of happiness, we can have no other proof, and we require no other, that these are the only things desirable. If so, happiness is the sole end of human action, and the promotion of it the test by which to judge of all human conduct; from whence it necessarily follows that it must be the criterion of morality, since a part is included in the whole. . . .

John Stuart Mill: Hedonism

1. Mill claims that "Pleasure, and freedom from pain, are the only things desirable as ends." Are there any examples that can challenge this claim?
2. What does Mill propose as a standard to determine which kinds of pleasure are more valuable than others? Is this a plausible standard?
3. Mill states that it is "Better to be Socrates dissatisfied, than a fool satisfied." What reasons does he give for thinking this?
4. In order to show that an object is visible, it is enough to show that people actually see it. Mill claims, similarly, "The sole evidence it is possible to produce that anything is desirable, is that people do actually desire it." Are visibility and desirability similar in this way?
5. Mill claims that "Each person's happiness is a good to that person." He then concludes from this that "the general happiness" is therefore "a good to the aggregate of all persons." Is this a good argument?

6. According to Mill, "The ingredients of happiness are very various, and each of them is desirable in itself." Does this contradict his earlier claim, given in question 1?

7. At the beginning of this selection, Mill says that pleasure and the absence of pain are the only things desirable as ends. Toward the end he claims that "Happiness is the sole end of human action." Are happiness and pleasure the same thing?

2

The Experience Machine

Robert Nozick

....

In this brief selection from his book *Anarchy, State, and Utopia* (1974), the late Harvard philosopher Robert Nozick (1938–2002) invites us to contemplate a life in which we are placed within a very sophisticated machine that is capable of simulating whatever experiences we find most valuable. Such a life, Nozick argues, cannot be the best life for us, because it fails to make contact with reality. This is meant to show that the good life is not entirely a function of the quality of our inner experiences. Since hedonism measures our well-being in precisely this way, hedonism, says Nozick, must be mistaken.

....

. . . Suppose there were an experience machine that would give you any experience you desired. Superduper neuropsychologists could stimulate your brain so that you would think and feel you were writing a great novel, or making a friend, or reading an interesting book. All the time you would be floating in a tank, with electrodes attached to your brain. Should you plug into this machine for life, preprogramming your life's experiences? If you are worried about missing out on desirable experiences, we can suppose that business enterprises have researched thoroughly the lives of many others. You can pick and choose from their large library or smorgasbord

Anarchy, State, and Utopia, Robert Nozick. Copyright © 1974 Basic Books. Reprinted by permission of Basic Books, a member of Perseus Books Group.

of such experiences, selecting your life's experiences for, say, the next two years. After two years have passed, you will have ten minutes or ten hours out of the tank, to select the experiences of your *next* two years. Of course, while in the tank you won't know that you're there; you'll think it's all actually happening. Others can also plug in to have the experiences they want, so there's no need to stay unplugged to serve them. (Ignore problems such as who will service the machines if everybody plugs in.) Would you plug in? *What else can matter to us, other than how our lives feel from the inside?* Nor should you refrain because of the few moments of distress between the moment you've decided and the moment you're plugged. What's a few moments of distress compared to a lifetime of bliss (if that's what you choose), and why feel any distress at all if your decision *is* the best one?

What does matter to us in addition to our experiences? First, we want to *do* certain things, and not just have the experience of doing them. In the case of certain experiences, it is only because first we want to do the actions that we want the experiences of doing them or thinking we've done them. (But *why* do we want to do the activities rather than merely to experience them?) A second reason for not plugging in is that we want to *be* a certain way, to be a certain sort of person. Someone floating in a tank is an indeterminate blob. There is no answer to the question of what a person is like who has long been in the tank. Is he courageous, kind, intelligent, witty, loving? It's not merely that it's difficult to tell; there's no way he is. Plugging into the machine is a kind of suicide. It will seem to some, trapped by a picture, that nothing about what we are like can matter except as it gets reflected in our experiences. But should it be surprising that what *we are* is important to us? Why should we be concerned only with how our time is filled, but not with what we are?

Thirdly, plugging into an experience machine limits us to a man-made reality, to a world no deeper or more important than that which people can construct. There is no *actual* contact with any deeper reality, though the experience of it can be simulated. Many persons desire to leave themselves open to such contact and to a plumbing of deeper significance.[1] This

---

1. Traditional religious views differ on the *point* of contact with a transcendent reality. Some say that contact yields eternal bliss or Nirvana, but they have not distinguished this sufficiently from merely a *very* long run on the experience machine. Others think it is intrinsically desirable to do the will of a higher being which created us all, though presumably no one would think this if we discovered we had been created as an object of amusement by some superpowerful child from another galaxy or dimension. Still others imagine an eventual merging with a higher reality, leaving unclear its desirability, or where that merging leaves *us*.

clarifies the intensity of the conflict over psychoactive drugs, which some view as mere local experience machines, and others view as avenues to a deeper reality; what some view as equivalent to surrender to the experience machine, others view as following one of the reasons *not* to surrender!

We learn that something matters to us in addition to experience by imagining an experience machine and then realizing that we would not use it. We can continue to imagine a sequence of machines each designed to fill lacks suggested for the earlier machines. For example, since the experience machine doesn't meet our desire to *be* a certain way, imagine a transformation machine which transforms us into whatever sort of person we'd like to be (compatible with our staying us). Surely one would not use the transformation machine to become as one would wish, and thereupon plug into the experience machine![2] So something matters in addition to one's experiences *and* what one is like. Nor is the reason merely that one's experiences are unconnected with what one is like. For the experience machine might be limited to provide only experiences possible to the sort of person plugged in. Is it that we want to make a difference in the world? Consider then the result machine, which produces in the world any result you would produce and injects your vector input into any joint activity. We shall not pursue here the fascinating details of these or other machines. What is most disturbing about them is their living of our lives for us. Is it misguided to search for *particular* additional functions beyond the competence of machines to do for us? Perhaps what we desire is to live (an active verb) ourselves, in contact with reality. (And this, machines cannot do *for* us.) Without elaborating on the implications of this, which I believe connect surprisingly with issues about free will and causal accounts of knowledge, we need merely note the intricacy of the question of what matters *for people* other than their experiences. Until one finds a satisfactory answer, and determines that this answer does not *also* apply to animals, one cannot reasonably claim that only the felt experiences of animals limit what we may do to them.

---

2. Some wouldn't use the transformation machine at all; it seems like *cheating*. But the one-time use of the transformation machine would not remove all challenges; there would still be obstacles for the new us to overcome, a new plateau from which to strive even higher. And is this plateau any the less earned or deserved than that provided by genetic endowment and early childhood environment? But if the transformation machine could be used indefinitely often, so that we could accomplish anything by pushing a button to transform ourselves into someone who could do it easily, there would remain no limits we *need* to strain against or try to transcend. Would there be anything left *to do*? Do some theological views place God outside of time because an omniscient omnipotent being couldn't fill up his days?

Robert Nozick: The Experience Machine

1. Nozick suggests that most people would choose not to plug in to an "experience machine" if given the opportunity. Would you plug in? Why or why not?
2. Hedonists such as Epicurus and Mill claim that pleasure is the only thing worth pursuing for its own sake. If some people would choose not to plug in to the experience machine, does this show that hedonism is false?
3. One reason Nozick gives for not getting into the experience machine is that "We want to *do* certain things, and not just have the experience of doing them." Do some activities have value independent of the experiences they produce? If so, what is an example of such an activity?
4. Nozick claims that "Plugging into the machine is a kind of suicide." What does he mean by this? Do you think he is right?

3

Faring Well and Getting
What You Want

Chris Heathwood

....

Chris Heathwood opens his contribution with a very helpful discussion that distinguishes a number of different concerns we may have when talking about the good life. When we speak of a good life, we may be referring to what it is that makes for a *morally* good life. Or we may be asking about how a person can manifest various nonmoral excellences, such as being a great athlete or musician. In asking about the good life, we might also be wondering about life's meaning, and how we can live a meaningful life (if we can). While these are all interesting topics for reflection, Heathwood focuses elsewhere: he wants to know what it is that, in and of itself, makes our lives go better. What, in other words, is intrinsically good for us?

Objectivists answer this question by presenting a list of things whose possession, all by themselves, is supposed to make us better off. Familiar candidates include pleasure, friendship, knowledge, freedom, and virtue. The idea is that no matter our attitude toward such things, our lives go better to the extent that we have more of these items on the list.

Heathwood rejects all objective views about what is intrinsically good for us. He endorses *subjectivism about welfare*: the view "that something we get in life benefits us when and only when we have an interest in it, or want it, or have some other positive attitude towards it (or it causes us to get something else that we have, or will have, a positive attitude towards)." Heathwood asks us to imagine a scenario in which, for any supposedly objective good, a person feels no attraction to it at all. If a person doesn't like, care about, or want (say) freedom, then how could freedom, in itself, improve her lot in life? If Heathwood is right, the answer is: it can't.

....

The Question of Welfare

One of the greatest and oldest questions we can ask ourselves is, What is the good life? What is the best kind of life for a person to live? What are the things in a life that make it worth choosing over other possible lives one could lead? It's hard to imagine a more important question. However, I want to focus on what I take to be a narrower question, namely, What things in life are ultimately to our *benefit*? Or to put it a few other ways, What things make us *better off*?, What makes a life a good life *for us*?, What is it to *fare well*? Taking our cue from this last expression, let's call this *the question of welfare*. In what follows, I'm going to offer my answer to the question of welfare. But first, let's clarify the question further.

I think that the question of welfare is a narrower question than the question of the good life because there are things that make a life a better kind of life to live without necessarily being of any benefit to the person living it. That it would be beneficial to you is one reason for you to choose a life, but not the only reason. Another reason is that the life would be beneficial to others, or, more generally, would exhibit *moral virtue*. Although it is often in a person's self-interest to do the right thing, sometimes doing good is of no benefit to the do-gooder. Imagine a bystander who saves a child in a flash flood, but loses her life in the process. This praiseworthy deed was of great benefit to the child, but, sadly, not to the hero who did it.

Another way a life can be good without being good *for* the person living it is by manifesting *excellence*. People manifest excellence when they excel at certain worthwhile activities, such as playing the cello, proving interesting mathematical theorems, or mastering Szechuan cooking. As with moral virtue, a life that manifests excellence seems to be in that way better, but an activity's being excellent isn't the same thing as its benefitting the person doing it. Someone might have an amazing talent for basketball, but find the sport boring and repetitive, and claim to "get nothing out of it."

This is likely a case in which manifesting excellence in a certain aspect of life would be of no benefit to the person.

A third value that we should distinguish from welfare is *meaning*. When I ask what things are of ultimate benefit or harm to us, I don't intend to be asking about the meaning of life. Whatever having a meaningful life consists in, I take it that it can vary independently from how well off one is.

There is another important clarification of the question of welfare. If someone asks what things improve the quality of a person's life, he is likely to have in mind the question of what things *tend to cause* a person's life to be improved. He might be wondering, for example, whether all the new technology in our lives really makes us better off; or he might be wondering whether he would have been better off now had he gone to graduate school years ago. These causal questions, while immensely important, are not our question. Our question is rather the question of what things make us better off *in themselves*, independent of any other changes that these things might cause in our lives. In terms philosophers use, we are asking what things are *intrinsically good* for us rather than what things are merely *instrumentally good* for us (i.e., good for us because of what they lead to). The question of intrinsic value has a kind of priority over the question of instrumental value, in that any answer to the question of instrumental value will presuppose, if only implicitly, an answer to the question about intrinsic value.

Preliminary Steps in Answering the Question of Welfare

Now that we have a clearer understanding of the question of welfare, how do we go about answering it? One natural way to begin is to devise a list of things whose presence in our lives seems intuitively to make our lives better. In developing such a list, we should keep in mind the distinction just introduced between intrinsic and instrumental value. Since the question of welfare is the question of intrinsic welfare value, we want to include on the list intuitive *intrinsic* goods only. Consider an example: while medicine can certainly make our lives better, there is no plausibility to the claim that possessing or taking medicine is good *in itself* for us. If medicine benefits us, this is due to the effects that it has on our health. We can also ask, in turn, whether being healthy is an intrinsic or merely an instrumental good. My own view is that bodily health, like medicine, is of merely instrumental value; we'll get to that view shortly.

So what might such a list include? Here are some natural candidates: happiness, knowledge, love, freedom, friendship, the appreciation of beauty, creative activity, being respected. Why think that the presence of such things in themselves makes our lives better? One reason is that these are things that we tend to want or value in our lives, and, moreover, to want or value *for their own sakes*—not merely for their effects. Next, note that such desires *seem reasonable*. These aren't crazy things to want in your life; it makes sense to want them. If it does, what explains this? The view that these things are intrinsically good for us would explain it.

Subjective vs. Objective Theories of Welfare

But now I want to ask a question, consideration of which, I believe, pulls us in the opposite direction—that is, away from the view that all of the items above are intrinsically good for us. It's true that many of us, much of the time, want the above things in our lives, and that we are glad to have them when we get them. But do we want them because it is good to have them, or is it good to have them because we want them? To put the question slightly differently, Do the items on our list above make our lives better only because they are things that we want and are glad to have in our lives, or do these things make our lives better even if we have no interest in them? This question—one of the deepest and most central questions in the philosophy of welfare—is the question of whether welfare is objective or subjective.

Subjectivists hold that something we get in life benefits us when and only when we have an interest in it, or want it, or have some other positive attitude towards it (or it causes us to get something else that we have, or will have, a positive attitude towards). *Objectivists* about welfare deny this, and maintain that at least some of the intrinsically beneficial things in our lives are good for us even if we don't want them, don't like them, don't care about them, and even if they fail to get us anything else that we want or care about. They are good for us "whether we like it or not."

The debate over whether welfare is objective or subjective should not be confused with the debate over whether *morality* is objective or subjective. In my view, morality is pretty clearly objective. It is wrong to light a cat on fire for one's amusement. And the fact that this is wrong does not—as subjectivists about morality would have it—depend upon my or anyone else's negative attitudes towards this kind of act. It's not wrong to light cats on fire because we disapprove of this; rather, we disapprove of it because it's wrong. I feel pretty confident about that. Much less obvious is the notion that a person can be *benefitted*, can have her own interests advanced, when she gets things that she herself in no way wants, things that leave her cold. Indeed, it seems to me that this cannot happen. It seems to me to be a truth about welfare that if something is truly a benefit to someone, it must be something she wants, likes, or cares about, or something that helps her get something she wants, likes, or cares about.

If I am right that this is a truth about welfare, I think that it is probably a foundational truth. That means that there are no deeper truths about welfare from which we can derive it, and hence argue for it. But there are still considerations that can help us to see it. Concrete examples can help do this. Consider the following case:

Charlie wants to improve his quality of life. He has heard that it is philosophers who claim to be experts on this topic, so he looks through some philosophy journals at his library. He finds an article claiming to have discovered the correct account of welfare. It is an objective theory that includes the items on our list above. The paper is in a pretty good journal, so Charlie decides to go about trying to increase his share of some of the items on the list. For example, to increase his freedom, he moves to a state with higher speed limits. Charlie is careful to make sure that the move won't have any detrimental side effects—that it won't cause him to fail to get less of any of the other goods on the list.

After succeeding in increasing his freedom, Charlie finds that he doesn't care about it, that he is completely indifferent to it. Although he is free to drive faster, he never does (he never wants to). Nor does the freedom to drive faster get him anything else that he is interested in. Charlie considers whether he is any better off as a result of the increase in his freedom. He concludes that he is no better off.

Do you agree with Charlie's own assessment of his situation? I do. I feel confident that Charlie is right that his gains in freedom turned out to be of no benefit to him. Note that the objective theory in question implies otherwise. For according to that theory, *freedom itself*—not freedom that you happen to want, but freedom itself—makes your life better. Since (i) this objective theory implies that Charlie's life is going better as a result of this increase in freedom, but (ii) in fact Charlie's life is not going any better as a result of this increase in freedom, the theory must be mistaken.

Importantly, the point here generalizes. For any of the alleged goods on the list, so long as it is an objective putative good—i.e., a putative good that bears no necessary connection to any positive attitudes on the part of the person for whom it is supposed to be good—we could construct a case similar in all relevant respects to Charlie's case. This would be a case in which someone gets the supposed good, but is in no way glad to have it, and is in no way glad to have anything else that it gets her. I believe that we would again feel confident that this person receives no benefit. And the reason we can always construct such a case, I submit, is the idea mentioned earlier: that if something is truly a benefit to someone, it must be something she wants, likes, or cares about, or something that helps her get such a thing. This is why I'm inclined to believe that whereas objectivism is the correct view of morality, subjectivism is the correct view of welfare.

If there are such good reasons to be a subjectivist, why would anyone reject the view? One of the main reasons that some are driven to reject subjectivism about welfare is that, intuitively, it's possible for a person to want, like, or care about getting *the wrong things*. Some pursuits, for example, strike us as pointless or meaningless. What if someone wants never to step on a crack when he walks on the sidewalk? Would his life really be going better for him each time he satisfies this desire?

But the objection may be most forceful when it appeals to pursuits that are positively bad. Consider, to take a real life example, the serial rapist and murderer Ted Bundy. What Bundy wanted most in his life was to inflict pain on innocent strangers, to wield power over them, and to watch them beg, suffer, and die at his own hand. For quite a number of years, Bundy got just what he wanted. According to subjectivism, when it comes to welfare, anything you take an interest in is as good as any other; that is, it doesn't matter what you want, so long as you get it, and so long as your getting it doesn't conflict with your getting other things that you want. Thus, assuming that Bundy wasn't plagued with guilt or regret during his reign of terror, and that he avoided other unwanted side-effects of his lifestyle, subjectivists must say that Bundy benefitted greatly in doing what he did, that he was quite well off, at least before he got caught. Objectivists, by contrast, have the resources to condemn Bundy's behavior, not just morally, but from the point of view of his own self-interest. They can say that Bundy would himself have been better off if he had had, and had achieved, more admirable goals.

Thus we need to ask ourselves a question. Consider the years before Bundy was caught, the years in which he lived just the sort of life he most wanted to live. Were these years good years for Bundy? Did he live a life that was in his interest to live? Was he just as well off as he would have been during these years had he had morally acceptable interests, and success-fully pursued those? Note that our question is not, Did Bundy's lifestyle *make him happy*? Objectivists can agree that it did. Our question is not, Did Bundy *get just what he wanted*? Objectivists agree that he did. Nor should we be distracted by the fact that Bundy's lifestyle led to his eventual ruin. Subjectivists agree that his choices harmed him later on, after he got caught. (Bundy was eventually executed for his crimes.) Rather, our question is, Were the years before he got caught good years for Bundy?

I agree that Bundy was a monster. I condemn what he did in the stron-gest terms. But it strikes me as a false hope to think that Bundy could not have benefitted from doing what he did. Thus, I "bite the bullet" and maintain that Bundy in fact was quite well off before he got caught. To be honest, I don't even think of this as biting a bullet. It strikes me as the genuinely correct verdict. Remember that all we are saying is that Bundy *benefitted*, for a time, from his lifestyle. We are not saying that his lifestyle was morally acceptable or that it was worth emulating. Indeed, the claim that Bundy benefitted from his monstrous lifestyle helps explain some-thing. It helps explain why we find the whole situation so sickening: here is this monster, doing the most unspeakable things, and all the while living large because of it.

The Desire Theory of Welfare

Subjectivists maintain that being well off has to do with the attitudes we have towards what we get in life rather than the nature of the things them-selves. Being benefitted is a matter of having a positive attitude towards things, whatever these things are. Subjectivists often hold that *desire* or *wanting* is the special positive attitude here. Desire may even be an ele-ment in all positive attitudes, attitudes such as liking, preferring, caring about something, or having something as a goal.

According to the desire theory of welfare, human welfare consists in the satisfaction of desire. Whenever what a person wants to be the case is in fact the case, this constitutes a benefit for the person. Whenever a per-son's desires are frustrated, this constitutes a basic harm. The theory recog-nizes no other fundamental sources of benefit and harm. Many other kinds of event—making money, becoming sick, gaining freedom, appreciating beauty—can cause our lives to go better or worse, but only by being things that we want or don't want, or by causing us to get, or fail to get, other things that we want or don't want. *How* good or bad a desire satisfaction or frustration is for its subject, according to the theory, is a function of the strength of the desire; the more deeply we want something to be the case, the better it is for us if it is the case, and the worse it is if it's not. How well things go for us overall in life is determined by the extent to which we get what we want throughout our lives, both on a day-to-day basis and with respect to larger life goals.

We can distinguish two different things we might mean by the term "want." One sense of the term is merely behavioral. If we voluntarily do something, it follows, on the behavioral sense of the term, that it is something we wanted to do. According to a second sense of the term, we count as wanting something only if we are genuinely attracted to it, only if it genuinely appeals to us. Sometimes a person voluntarily does something that holds no appeal for him. On the behavioral sense of the term, it follows that he wanted to do it. But this kind of desire satisfaction does not seem to be of any benefit to the person faced with doing the unappealing thing. Thus I believe that the best version of the desire theory of welfare is one that understands "desire" or "want"— I use these terms interchangeably—in the "genuine attraction" sense mentioned above. Only when we get, or get to do, those things that we are genuinely attracted to or that genuinely appeal to us—the things we "really want"—are we made better off.

What about Pleasure and Happiness?

One of the simplest and oldest theories of human welfare is hedonism, the view that pleasure is the only thing that is intrinsically good for us. Almost everyone accepts that pleasure is an intrinsic welfare good. Hedonism is controversial mainly because it claims that there are no other such goods. How does the desire satisfaction theory of welfare accommodate the value of pleasure?

Whether it can make such an accommodation, and whether it should, depends upon what pleasure is. On one view of the nature of pleasure, pleasure is an indefinable feeling or sensation, in the same general category as the indefinable sensations of seeing red, of the taste of chocolate, or of nausea. If this is what pleasure is, I don't think that pleasure is good in itself for anyone. For imagine a creature who is completely indifferent to this feeling, or even finds it unbearable. It is not plausible to suggest that such a creature would be having a good experience—an experience that is good for it, and makes its life better—when it experiences this indifferent, or even reviled, sensation. Rather, if this view of the nature of pleasure is right, then pleasure's value depends entirely on the creature's wanting it, liking it, or taking an interest in it. It would be just like the taste of chocolate, which (ignoring side effects) is good for a creature to taste when, but only when, the creature wants to be tasting it.

On a competing account of the nature of pleasure, pleasure is a positive attitude, an attitude that one can take up towards things like the chocolate taste one is currently experiencing, the music one is hearing, or the fact that one has gotten a raise. The attitude of being pleased that something is the case is certainly a good state to be in, but it is one that, in my view, ultimately involves desire. Taking pleasure in a chocolate taste sensation just is to be wanting to be experiencing it as you are experiencing it. To be pleased that you have gotten a raise is to want the raise while seeing that you have gotten it. Thus, if pleasure turns out to be a kind of state that is indeed intrinsically valuable, it is a kind of state whose value the desire theory of welfare can recognize, and even explain.

The desire theory can also accommodate the irresistible idea that it's good to be happy. Consider being happy that one has gotten a raise, or that the sun is shining, or that one is living in Barcelona. These are good states to be in. But, just as above, I believe that they are states that essentially involve desire. They involve, respectively, the desire for a raise, the desire that the sun be shining, and the desire to be living in Barcelona. If one gets a raise, and is happy about this, one will necessarily be receiving a desire satisfaction. In this way the value of happiness can be accommodated by the desire theory of welfare.

Refining the Desire Theory

Sometimes our desires are based on ignorance or confused thinking. When they are, it can seem doubtful that satisfying them benefits us. Thus we have a potential problem for the desire theory of welfare, and probably for any subjective theory. To take a simple example, suppose that I have a strong craving for cherry pie, not knowing that I have recently developed a serious allergy to cherries. If I satisfy my desire, I'll need a shot of adrenaline to avoid suffocating to death. Still, in my ignorant state, cherry pie is what I want most. The desire theory of welfare seems to imply, absurdly, that it is most in my interest to have cherry pie.

For this reason, many subjectivists revise the theory so that what determines our welfare is not our actual desires but our *idealized* desires. These are the desires we would have if we knew all the facts, were vividly appreciating them, and were thinking rationally. If I knew, and vividly appreciated, what eating cherry pie would do to me, I would prefer not to have it; the informed desire theory thus does not imply that it would be most in my interest to satisfy my desire for cherry pie.

Subjectivists who are troubled by the problems caused by pointless or immoral desires may hope that the move to idealized desires will help here as well. Perhaps if Ted Bundy had appreciated the effects that his actions would have on his victims, and had been thinking rationally about it, he would not have desired to do the horrible things he did. Perhaps he would have instead wanted the things on the objectivist's list. This is a nice thought, but for it to be true, it would have to be that no one who was fully informed, vividly appreciating the facts, and thinking clearly could have pointless or immoral desires. But surely it's just wishful thinking to believe that.

In any case, the move to ideal desires faces a problem: it begins to abandon the core idea of subjectivism. That idea is simple: what is good for you must be connected to what *you yourself* want, like, or care about—not what someone else wants for you, even if that someone else is an improved version of yourself. If you had full knowledge and appreciation of all of what was possible for you, perhaps you would prefer caviar and experimental music. As it happens, you prefer peanuts and baseball. Surely you benefit when you receive the things you actually want (peanuts and baseball) rather than the things (caviar and experimental music) that you merely would want if you were fully informed and rational. For this reason, I believe that we should regard our actual desires as the ones whose satisfaction directly benefits us.

Fortunately, the problem that motivated the move to idealization—the problem to do with desires based on ignorance—can be solved within the original theory, the theory that appeals to one's actual desires. Recall the case of the allergenic cherry pie. The actual desire theory can say that it is in fact not in my interest to eat the pie. The theory does imply that I'll receive *some* benefit from doing so, but that is plausible—I crave the pie, after all, and I will be very glad to be eating it. But the theory doesn't imply that I'll receive a *net* benefit. For I also have strong desires not to be sent to an emergency room and not to be suffocating. Eating the pie will frustrate these very strong desires. The theory thus delivers the desired result: that overall I'm better off not eating the cherry pie. The move to idealization, which violates the spirit of subjectivism, is not necessary in the first place.

Other objections pose more serious problems for the desire theory and may require that we refine it. Here is one such objection. Suppose that my uncle must go into exile, and I know that I will never see him again. Whenever I think of him, I think of him fondly, hoping very much that he is happy and healthy. As a matter of fact, though I couldn't know this, my uncle *is* happy and healthy. According to the desire theory of welfare, a person benefits whenever a desire of his is satisfied. For a desire to be satisfied, all that is required is that the desired event actually occur; the person need not know this and need derive no satisfaction from it for it to be true that his desire was satisfied. The desire theory thus implies that I am made better off when my uncle achieves happiness and health.

Many (though not all) desire theorists regard this as an unacceptably counterintuitive implication of the theory. They think that I have not been benefitted in the example. I agree, though there is little agreement on how best to handle such a case. One popular solution is to revise the theory so that it counts only desires that are *about one's own life*. My uncle's being happy and healthy is an event in his life, not mine, and thus when it occurs, this revised theory denies that I am benefitted even though I wanted the event to occur. But I believe this restriction excludes too much; it excludes, for example, the desires of fans for their team to win. In my view, the lesson of the exiled uncle is rather that in order to be benefitted, we must *be aware* that the desired event has occurred, or is occurring.

This raises all sorts of issues that we cannot explore here. But I hope I have made a decent case for the ideas that subjectivism is the better approach to welfare, that the desire theory is the way for the subjectivist to go, that the desire theory should appeal to desires in the "genuine attraction" sense of the term, and that your actual rather than ideal desires are plausibly regarded as what determines how well you fare in life.

Chris Heathwood: Faring Well and Getting What You Want

1. Heathwood claims that the meaningfulness of a life can vary independently from how well off the person living it is. To see whether you agree, try to describe an example of (a) a life that you think is meaningful that is not beneficial to the person living it, and (b) a life that is beneficial to the person living it without being a meaningful life.

2. Suppose someone claims that being healthy is intrinsically good for us. Can you think of a way to test whether this is true? Here is one idea: describe a pair of cases that are exactly alike except that in one of the cases, the person involved has greater health than in the other case. It's crucial that there be no other differences between the cases. What do you think this tells us about the intrinsic value of being healthy?

3. Do you agree that Charlie's gains in freedom turned out to be of no benefit to him? If they are of no benefit to him, is that enough to show that objectivism about well-being is mistaken? If not, what more is required?

4. What is an ideal desire as opposed to an actual desire? Which kind of desire does Heathwood think is connected to welfare? Why does he think this?

5. Do you believe that Heathwood benefits when, unbeknownst to him, his exiled uncle achieves happiness and health? Why or why not?

6. According to one version of the desire theory of welfare, a person is benefited just when a desire that is about her own life is satisfied. Is this theory plausible? Explain.

7. Heathwood thinks that our life is a good life for us to the extent that we get what we want, so long as we are aware of it, and so long as this is a want in the "genuine attraction" sense of "want." Are there any cases in which your life goes better for you even though no such want is satisfied? Are there any cases in which such wants are satisfied, but one fails to be benefited as a result?

4

The Elements of Well-Being

Brad Hooker

....

After a brief discussion of the merits of hedonism and the "desire-fulfilment" theory of well-being, Brad Hooker investigates what he takes to be the most plausible version of an objective list view. Such a view endorses the idea that there are several elements of well-being that are non-instrumentally valuable. In other words, these elements make a direct contribution to a person's well-being, regardless of what other improvements in a life they happen to cause. In other words, these elements make a direct contribution to a person's well-being, regardless of what other improvements in a life they happen to cause.

There are two central questions we must ask of any objective list view. Perhaps obviously, the first is this: What *are* the elements of well-being? The second asks how to justify the elements of the list: What arguments can be given for thinking that some things really are elements of well-being while other, perhaps popular, candidates for such elements are best left off the list?

Hooker answers the first question by citing pleasure, friendship, significant achievement, important knowledge, and autonomy. Each of these is a *distinct* good—the value of friendship, for instance, cannot be reduced to the amount of pleasure it causes. And each of these is an *objective* good—each one is good for a person even if he or she fails to affirm its value. On this view, a misanthrope who despises friendship, or a lazy person who denies the value of significant achievement, is making a mistake.

Journal of Practical Ethics, Vol. 3, June 2015, pp. 15–35.

Hooker answers the second question by arguing for a kind of controlled experiment to determine whether something qualifies as an element of well-being. He asks us to imagine two situations that are identical in every respect but one—namely, that there is more of the candidate element. So, for instance, imagine yourself just as you are now. And then imagine things exactly the same, except for one change: you are enjoying more pleasure then you were in the first scenario. If you are no better off in the second case, then pleasure is *not* an element of well-being. But Hooker, like most people, thinks that you *are* better off in the second case than the first. And he thinks that the best explanation of this improvement is that pleasure is an element of well-being.

Interestingly, when Hooker applies this test to living a moral life, he argues that it fails to qualify as the sort of thing that directly makes your life go better. Of course being morally virtuous makes your life *morally* better. And living a moral life often brings with it other valuable things—it is often a path to firmer friendships and significant achievement, for instance. But in two situations where everything is the same except for the fact that in one you are morally admirable and in the other you are not, Hooker argues that you are no better off in the second case than in the first.

....

Clarifications

Like most philosophers, I will take the term 'well-being' to be synonymous with 'welfare,' 'personal good,' and 'individual utility.' Contributions to well-being I refer to as benefits or gains. Subtractions from well-being I refer to as harms, losses, or costs. The elements of well-being are whatever constitutes benefits, that is, contributions to well-being.

Absolutely essential is the distinction between non-instrumental value, which is sometimes called final value, and instrumental value. Examples of things with merely instrumental value are money, medicine, and sleep. This paper focuses on non-instrumental value. When I refer to contributions to well-being, I mean *non-instrumental* contributions, that is, things that are good for us in their own right as opposed to good only because they are means to other things. The main focus of the paper is on the question of what constitutes non-instrumental contributions to a person's well-being. Definitely, all of the values I will be discussing do have instrumental value. But I will be focusing on these values not for their instrumental benefits but as putative elements of well-being.

Hedonism

Hedonism is the theory that well-being consists in pleasures minus pains. Pleasures are experiences found attractive solely because of their experiential quality, rather than for other reasons. Pains are experiences found aversive solely because of their experiential quality, rather than for other reasons.

The focus on experiential quality brings out a defining feature of pleasures and pains, namely that they are *introspectively discernible* (which is not to say that they are *actually* discerned). Imagine someone who fails in the central project of her life but never finds out about this failure. An example might be the amateur sleuth who spent the last five years of her life trying to discover how and why the child Madeleine McCann disappeared. The sleuth died thinking that she had made the crucial discovery that solved the case. But in fact her 'discovery' turned out to be quite mistaken. Because she didn't find out that she failed, her pleasures were what they would have been had her project instead been a success. Hedonists hold that the failure of a life project does not, in itself, reduce the person's welfare. Hedonists think that a person's welfare is determined solely by how this person's life feels from the inside. How her life feels from the inside may depend in part on whether she *believes* her desires have been fulfilled. How her life feels from the inside does not necessarily depend on whether her desires *really* have been fulfilled.

I have contended that introspective discernibility is essential to pleasure and that success in one's projects is not. This is true whether the project is relatively discrete, such as finding out how and why a small child suddenly disappeared, or much more complex and general, such as the goals of having lots of good friends and of being knowledgeable about science, history, and metaphysics and of creating things of enduring value. Consider someone who believes that he has enough good friends and that he is knowledgeable about science, history, and metaphysics and that he has created things of enduring value. This person is likely to feel some satisfaction with his life.

Perhaps this sort of satisfaction is the most important kind of pleasure. Nevertheless, getting this kind of pleasure is possible even if one is deluded about whether one's desires for good friends, for knowledge of science, history, and metaphysics, and for creative success have actually been ful-filled. Feeling satisfied with one's life is compatible with delusion about pretty much everything except whether one feels satisfied with one's life.

Desire-Fulfilment

Another main view of welfare holds that a person's well-being is consti-tuted by the fulfilment of his or her desires, whether or not the person knows the desires have been fulfilled. This view is often called the desire-fulfilment (or preference-satisfaction) theory of well-being.

The main argument in favour of the desire-fulfilment theory over hedonism is that many people's self-interested concern extends beyond their own pleasures and pains, enjoyments and frustrations. For example, many people have stronger self-interested concern for knowing the truth (especially about whether their other desires are fulfilled) than for blissful ignorance.

The main argument against the desire-fulfilment theory is that some desires are so wacky that their fulfilment would not itself constitute a ben-efit for the people who have them (even if whatever associated pleasure these people derived from believing their desires were fulfilled *would* con-stitute a benefit for them). Imagine someone who wants a saucer of mud, or to count all the blades of grass in the lawns along a street, or to turn on as many radios as possible (Anscombe, 1958, p. 70; Rawls, 1971, p. 432; Quinn 1993, p. 236). Suppose this person wants these things *for their own sakes*, i.e., non-instrumentally. Fulfilment of such desires in itself would not be of any benefit to this person, we intuitively think.

Objective List Theory

A third theory of welfare agrees with hedonism that pleasure constitutes a benefit. Where this third theory departs from hedonism is over the ques-tion of whether there is only one element of well-being or more than one. The third theory claims that other things can also constitute benefits—for example, knowledge of important matters, friendship, significant achieve-ment, and autonomy. Derek Parfit (1984, pp. 493–502) dubbed this theory the 'objective list theory,' but often the name is shortened to the 'list theory.' According to this objective list theory, a life contains more welfare to the extent that it contains pleasure, knowledge of important matters, friend-ship, significant achievement, and autonomy. A life full of pleasure and fulfilment of desires for things other than the goods just listed could still be of low quality precisely because it lacked the goods just listed.

What makes one achievement more significant than another? Thomas Hurka (1993, chs. 8–10; 2011, ch. 5) argues persuasively that extended and difficult achievements are more significant than narrow and easy ones. Admittedly, a narrower and less difficult achievement might benefit you more than one that is more extended and difficult, because the narrower one brings you greater pleasure or because it helps develop your friendships or because you learn more from it. In other words, when instrumental as well as intrinsic value is considered, a narrower and less difficult achievement can be on balance more beneficial to you than a wider and more difficult achievement. But when we ignore the instrumental benefits of different achievements, we should conclude that extended and difficult achievements are more significant than narrow and easy ones.

We might likewise follow Hurka (1993, chs. 8–10; 2011, ch. 4) in holding that extended and explanatory knowledge is better than narrow and shallow knowledge. For example, knowledge of the basic truths of physics or biology or metaphysics is more important than knowledge of the batting averages achieved by the middle-ranking players on a particular team in a particular month thirty-three years ago. But knowledge about yourself or things closely connected to you can sometimes constitute a larger benefit to you than would more general knowledge about things with no special connection to you. Knowing important facts about yourself—having self-knowledge—is a more important element of your well-being than knowing general truths about physics or biology or metaphysics or other people. For example, knowing your own failings is more important than knowing other people's failings. On the other hand, knowing that something is true not only of you but also of everyone else would constitute a larger benefit than knowing merely the truth about yourself.

Even more contestable than which kind of achievement or knowledge is most valuable as an element of well-being is the question of exactly what comprises autonomy. Does autonomy consist merely in having one's actions be guided by desires that one desires to have? Or does autonomy consist in having one's decisions be guided by one's own value judgements? Or does autonomy require that one's value judgements be themselves autonomously produced? Or does autonomy require that one's value judgements be at least minimally sensible?

These questions are fascinating but, alas, too difficult to address here. Hence, I must simply assume an answer. This is that someone's life contains autonomy to the extent to which she has a variety of important options to choose among, her choices reflect her value judgements, and her value judgements are at least minimally reflective (i.e., she has at least once considered them rather than merely always accepted them without consideration). If Jack severely constricted Jill's set of important options, or if he controlled her choices by controlling her value judgements, she would lack autonomy. The same would be true if a brain injury or mental illness controlled her value judgements or prevented her from being able to assess them.

Now, how can we ascertain whether any given putative good is an item on the objective list? We must run the following kind of thought experiment. We imagine two possible lives for someone that are as much alike as possible except that one of these lives contains more of some candidate good than the other. We then think about whether the life containing more of the candidate good would be more beneficial to the person living it than the other life. If the correct answer is no, then definitely the candidate good in question is not an element of well-being. On the other hand, if the correct answer is instead that the life with more of the candidate good is more beneficial, then we inquire what is the right explanation of this life's being more beneficial. One possible explanation is that the candidate good in question really is an element of well-being.

Pleasure

Here is an illustrative example. We imagine two possible lives for someone that are as much alike as possible except that one of these lives contains a larger amount of innocent pleasure than the other. We are trying to hold everything equal as much as possible with the single variable being the amount of innocent pleasure in the two possible lives. We then think about whether the life containing the larger amount of innocent pleasure would be more beneficial to the person living it than would be the as similar as possible life with a smaller amount of innocent pleasure. If the correct answer is that the life containing the larger amount of innocent pleasure would *not* be more beneficial to the person living it than would be the as similar as possible life with a smaller amount of innocent pleasure, then innocent pleasure is not an element of well-being. On the other hand, if the correct answer is that the life with a larger amount of innocent pleasure *is* more beneficial, then we need to inquire what is the right explanation of this life's being more beneficial. The explanation that suggests itself is that innocent pleasure is indeed an element of well-being.

For that possible explanation to be correct, rival possible explanations must be mistaken. Perhaps the leading rival possible explanation is that, although by hypothesis the two lives being compared are as much alike as possible with the exception that one includes a larger amount of innocent pleasure than the other, the fact that one of these possible lives contains a larger amount of innocent pleasure brings with it differences in the levels of *other* goods and these differences are what account for the superiority of one possible life to the other. In short, although our thought experiment was supposed to isolate one variable, the rival possible explanation claims that other variables are not only ineliminable but also pivotal.

Here is an example of such a rival explanation. This explanation begins with the proposal that the life with the larger amount of innocent pleasure must also have contained a larger amount of significant achievement or friendship or important knowledge or autonomy, as sources of the extra innocent pleasure. This rival explanation then adds that what makes the life with the larger amount of innocent pleasure more beneficial to the person who lives it than the life with a smaller amount of innocent pleasure is not the extra innocent pleasure but instead the larger amount of significant achievement or friendship or important knowledge or autonomy.

This rival explanation starts from a false supposition—namely, that the life with the larger amount of innocent pleasure *must* also have contained a larger amount of significant achievement or friendship or important knowledge or autonomy, as sources of the extra innocent pleasure. This supposition is false because the extra pleasure might have come from insignificant achievement or unimportant knowledge or false beliefs or the satisfaction of physiological urges. The source of innocent pleasure can be trivial or misconceived or merely physiological. There is no necessity that the source of innocent pleasure is itself something valuable, much less an element of well-being.

We can conclude, then, that innocent pleasure is definitely an element of well-being. This is the best explanation of why a life containing a larger amount of innocent pleasure would be more beneficial to the person living it than another possible life as much as possible like the first one except that this life contains a smaller amount of innocent pleasure.

I am aware that, to many people, the thesis that innocent pleasure is an element of well-being seems completely obvious. However, there are some people who do not find innocent pleasure obviously valuable.

My argument above is aimed at these people. Later in this essay, there is an argument aimed at people who think innocent pleasure is valuable only if obtained in the course of a worthwhile activity.

Significant Achievement

The structure of the argument above can be applied to other candidate elements of well-being. Let us apply it to significant achievement. We imagine two possible lives for someone that are as much alike as possible except that one of these lives contains a larger amount of significant achievement than the other. We are trying to hold everything equal as much as possible with the single variable being the amount of significant achievement in the two possible lives. We then think about whether the life containing the larger amount of significant achievement would be more beneficial to the person living it than the life that contains a smaller amount of significant achievement but is otherwise as similar as possible. If the correct answer is no, then significant achievement is not an element of well-being. However, the correct answer seems to me to be that the life with a larger amount of significant achievement is more beneficial to the person who leads that life than the life that contains a smaller amount of significant achievement but is otherwise as similar as possible.

Now, what is the best explanation of this life's being more beneficial? One possible explanation is that significant achievement is indeed an element of well-being. The rival possible explanation starts from the supposition that the life with the larger amount of significant achievement must also have contained a larger amount of innocent pleasure or friendship or important knowledge or autonomy. From this supposition, the rival explanation infers that what makes the life with the larger amount of significant achievement more beneficial to the person who lives it is not the extra significant achievement but instead the larger amount of pleasure or friendship or important knowledge or autonomy.

Lives containing a larger amount of significant achievements often do also have more pleasure, friendship, important knowledge, or autonomy in them than they would have had if they had contained a smaller amount of significant achievement. But this certainly is not always true. Sometimes people sacrifice pleasure, friendship, and important knowledge for the sake of pursuing significant achievement. Indeed, obsession about a goal can be instrumental to achieving it but at the same time in conflict with obtaining pleasure, alienating to friends and potential friends, and a blinder to information not relevant to the goal. For such reasons, there is no necessity that a larger amount of significant achievement correlates perfectly with a larger amount of pleasure, friendship, or important knowledge. This is especially obvious in cases where the person who made a significant achievement never found out about it, and thus could not have gained lots of pleasure from knowing about the achievement.

So what is the correct explanation of the fact that the life containing the larger amount of significant achievement would be more beneficial to the person living it than the life that is as similar as possible except that it contains a smaller amount of significant achievement? The correct explanation cannot be that the life with the larger amount of significant achievement *must* also have contained a larger amount of innocent pleasure or friendship or important knowledge or autonomy. The correct explanation is instead that significant achievement is an element of well-being.

Important Knowledge

The same kind of argument can be run for concluding that important knowledge is an element of well-being. Imagine that two lives are as much alike as possible except that one of those lives has important knowledge and the other life does not or one life contains a considerably larger amount of important knowledge than the other. The life containing no or a considerably smaller amount of important knowledge is worse for the agent than a life as much as possible like that one except that it contains at least some or a considerably larger amount of important knowledge.

Again, we have to ask, what is the best explanation of the greater benefit in the life with a larger amount of important knowledge? One possible explanation is that important knowledge is indeed an element of well-being. The rival possible explanation starts from the supposition that the life with the larger amount of important knowledge must also have contained a larger amount of innocent pleasure or more friendship or a larger amount of significant achievement or greater autonomy. From this supposition, the rival explanation infers that what makes the life with the larger amount of important knowledge more beneficial to the person who lives it is not the extra important knowledge but instead the greater pleasure or friendship or significant achievement or autonomy.

We should not accept the supposition that the life with the larger amount of important knowledge must also have contained a larger amount of innocent pleasure or friendship or significant achievement or autonomy. Sometimes important knowledge reduces rather than increases innocent pleasure. Sometimes important knowledge harms friendships. Sometimes important knowledge is not a significant achievement because it was not something that was pursued and thus not an achievement at all. Hence the life with the larger amount of important knowledge *might not* also contain greater innocent pleasure or friendship or significant achievement or autonomy.

Thus, the best explanation of the fact that a life containing no or a considerably smaller amount of important knowledge is worse for the agent than a life as much as possible like that one except that it contains a larger amount of important knowledge *cannot* be that the life with the larger amount of important knowledge must also contain greater innocent pleasure or friendship or significant achievement or autonomy. The best explanation must instead be that important knowledge is an element of well-being.

Autonomy

Concerning autonomy, we can try an argument with the same structure as the arguments above. We imagine two possible lives for someone as similar as possible except that one contains more autonomy and the other less. Then we ask which of these two possible lives is more beneficial to the person who lives it. The autonomous life seems better. Since we have imagined that the two lives are as equal as possible in terms of the other elements of well-being, we minimize the extent to which the superiority of the more autonomous life can be explained by the instrumental value of autonomy.

Again, we face the objection that there are multiple, though correlative, variables here. The objection is that, if one possible life contains greater autonomy than another possible life that is otherwise as similar as possible, the possible life with greater autonomy in it *must* also contain greater pleasure or knowledge or friendship or achievement than the other life. From this supposition, the objection infers that the greater pleasure or knowledge or friendship or achievement, and not the greater autonomy, is what makes this life better.

However, it just is not true that if one possible life contains greater autonomy than another life that is otherwise as similar as possible, then the possible life with greater autonomy in it must also contain greater pleasure or knowledge or friendship or achievement. Greater autonomy might lead to some successes but also, of course, to some failures—some missed opportunities for pleasure, some lack of knowledge, some ruined friendships, and some unsuccessful projects. So, on balance, greater autonomy might not lead to greater pleasure or knowledge or friendship or achievement. So there is nothing to prevent our imagining two possible lives that are equal in terms of pleasure, friendship, achievement, and knowledge and yet one of these lives contains more autonomy than the other.

We thus ask which of these two possible lives is more beneficial to the person who lives it. The more autonomous life seems better. Since we have imagined that the two lives are as equal as possible in terms of the other elements of well-being, the best explanation of the superiority of the more autonomous life in this comparison is that autonomy is an element of well-being.

Appreciating Beauty

Experiencing something as beautiful can definitely be instrumental to other benefits. Most obviously, experiencing something as beautiful can produce pleasure, even ecstasy. Experiencing something as beautiful can also lead to other goods, such as love and knowledge. But is experiencing something as beautiful a non-instrumental good such that a life containing such appreciation must be pro tanto better than a life without?

Well, are judgements of beauty like judgements of taste, i.e., merely subjective? Whether a food is delicious or not is merely subjective. For example, if you judge pears to be delicious and I do not, neither of us need be mistaken. If beauty is like deliciousness, then while you can be correct about whether you find something's aesthetic qualities attractive, you cannot be correct about whether these qualities *really* are attractive or about whether they *ought* to attract. If beauty is like deliciousness, then what would make a possible life in which you find more beauty better for you than a possible life in which you find less beauty would be the additional pleasure or friendship that the extra beauty would bring you. If beauty is like deliciousness, then appreciating beauty is not itself an element of well-being.

If beauty is not like deliciousness but is instead an objective value, then you can be correct not merely about whether certain qualities attract you and others but also about whether certain qualities *really* are attractive or about whether they *ought* to attract. In that case, you can have knowledge of aesthetic properties. If this is correct, perhaps we should classify appreciation of beauty as a kind of important knowledge. If appreciation of beauty is a kind of important knowledge, then we have grounds for holding that appreciation of beauty is an element of well-being—under the heading of important knowledge.

Living a Morally Good Life

Let us now turn to the question of whether living a morally good life is an element of well-being. Even if it is not, living a morally good life is of course *morally* good. And living a morally good life might be what there is strongest reason to do even where living a morally good life involves self-sacrifice. We can be interested in the question of whether living a morally good life is an element of well-being even if we are committed to sacrificing our own good either for the sake of benefiting others or because moral restrictions get in the way of doing what is most beneficial to oneself.

Living a morally good life is rewarding in terms of the other elements of well-being. Living a morally good life definitely constitutes a significant achievement. And living a morally good life can bring pleasure and ferment friendship. And knowing what morality requires is important knowledge. But is living a morally good life in itself—not under the heading of achievement, or as an instrument to pleasure or friendship, or in its connection with knowledge—an element of well-being?

This is not a question to which the answer seems to me directly apparent. The best I can do is approach the question indirectly, via what I call the sympathy test.

Suppose we ask ourselves whether we are inclined to feel sympathy for someone whose life lacks a particular property. Sympathy is a judgement-sensitive attitude. Our having sympathy for someone whose life lacks a particular property makes sense only if we judge that a life's lacking that property makes the life less beneficial to the person whose life it is than would be a life as similar as possible except that it has this property. So if we *do* feel sympathy for someone whose life lacks the property, this attitude makes sense only if deep down we think that a life's having that property *is* an element of well-being. And if we do *not* feel sympathy for someone whose life lacks the property, one possible explanation is that deep down we think that a life's having that property is not an element of well-being.

We do feel sympathy for people whose lives lack pleasure, friendships, autonomy, significant achievement, or important knowledge without some sort of compensation in terms of a greater amount of one or more of these other goods. In contrast, we do not feel sympathy for people who fail to live morally good lives. One possible explanation of the absence of sympathy is that deep down we really do not believe that living a morally good life is an element of well-being.

Is the sympathy test a good one? If we do have sympathy for someone, we can legitimately make inferences about our beliefs. To be more specific, if we do feel sympathy for someone whose life lacks a particular property, then we must think that a life's lacking this property makes the life less beneficial to the person whose life it is than would be a life as similar as possible except that it has this property. The limitation of the sympathy test appears in cases where we do not feel sympathy for someone whose life lacks a particular property. Yes, one possible explanation for our lack of sympathy is that we really think that a life's having that property is not an element of well-being. However, another possible explanation is that something else prevents us from feeling sympathy. For example, we might think that the person under consideration deserves a life with lower well-being.

We might initially suspect that feeling sympathy for someone is difficult to combine with the condemnation and blame and indignation that we feel towards those we believe have failed to lead morally good lives. Moral blame is regularly accompanied by a kind of hostility, which can get in the way of sympathy.

And yet, blaming someone does not necessarily get in the way of feeling sympathy for that person. Sometimes we have to blame someone about whom we care very strongly. When we blame someone about whom we care very strongly, the blame *can* be accompanied by sympathy. For example, we might blame ourselves for something but at the same time feel sorry for the harm we have caused to ourselves.

So far in this argument I have assumed that we do not feel sympathy for people who fail to live morally good lives. I have cast suspicion on the attempt to explain this lack of sympathy as an effect of blame for those who fail to live morally good lives. Blame for people who fail to live morally good lives does not always prevent sympathy for them. So I *tentatively* surmise that the best explanation of our lack of sympathy for people who fail to lead morally good lives is that we do not really think that living such a life is a distinct element of well-being. (This conclusion should be tempered by the recognition that living a morally good life can be instrumentally beneficial to the person who lives it and can constitute a significant achievement.)

For Well-Being, Friendship Is More Than a Kind of Achievement

Earlier, I argued that friendship should be listed as a distinct element of well-being. I have just now appealed to the sympathy test to argue that we do not really believe that living a morally good life is a distinct element of well-being, though living a morally good life is a kind of significant achievement, which is an element of well-being. With that conclusion in mind, someone might appeal to the fact that forming and sustaining friendships is also an important kind of achievement, albeit one less multidimensional than living a morally good life.

I do not see how it could plausibly be denied that forming and sustaining friendships is also an important kind of achievement. Here is an example. Imagine someone named Frieda who has found the good in a friend named Markus and forgiven him and sustained her interest in him for decades. This really is an impressive achievement on her part, given how conflicted and moody and self-deluded and intermittently self-destructive Markus is. (In contrast, that he has continued to love her is no achievement on his part, given how breathtakingly easy she is to admire and appreciate.)

Now consider the following argument:

> *Premise 1: Forming and sustaining friendships is like living a morally good life in being an important kind of achievement.*
>
> *Premise 2: Living a moral life is not a distinct element of well-being.*
>
> *Premise 3: If forming and sustaining friendships is like living a morally good life in being an important kind of achievement, and if living a morally good life is not a distinct element of well-being, then forming and sustaining friendships is not a distinct element of well-being.*
>
> *Conclusion: Forming and sustaining friendships is not a distinct element of well-being.*

Since this argument's conclusion does follow from the premises, we should assess the premises. Premise 1 is clearly true. Premise 2 is the conclusion we reached via application of the sympathy test, and so let us accept this premise. Premise 3 presumes that different things that are alike in one relevant respect are also alike in other relevant respects. We should not accept this premise, since different things are sometimes not alike in more than one relevant respect. Rejecting premise 3, we must reject the above argument as unsound.

To show that an argument is unsound is not to show that its conclusion is false. In the case of the above argument, however, I think there is an argument showing that its conclusion is false. In other words, this is an argument to show that forming and sustaining friendships is in fact a distinct element of well-being.

This argument begins with the premise that there is diminishing marginal benefit in each element of well-being (this argument was inspired by Hurka, 1993, pp. 84–96; 2011, pp. 166–74). For example, a life with no achievement but a lot of pleasure would benefit a great deal from gaining a significant achievement. Let us dub this achievement A of size S. Compare a very different life, one with lots of achievement already. This second life would not benefit as much from gaining the same achievement A of the same size S. In other words, the two lives we are comparing each gain an achievement A of size S; but, in the life where this is the *only* significant achievement, achievement A of size S constitutes a large benefit, and, in the life where there were already lots of other achievements, achievement A of size S constitutes a smaller benefit.

The diminishing marginal benefit to a life of its containing more instances of a kind of value of which it already contains a lot is relevant for the following reason. Imagine a life that already contained a lot of achievement but as yet no friendship. Suppose now this life gains one friendship. If friendship were not a distinct element of well-being but instead merely a subcategory of achievement, then a life that already contained a lot of achievement but as yet no friendship would *not benefit much* from the addition of one friendship. However, a life that already had a lot of achievement but as yet no friendship would *benefit hugely* from the addition of one friendship. So friendship is not merely a subcategory of achievement but instead is a distinct element of well-being.

References

Anscombe, E. 1958. *Intention*, Oxford, Blackwell Publishers.
Hurka, T. 1993. *Perfectionism*, Oxford, Clarendon Press.
———2011. *The Best Things in Life*, Oxford, Oxford University Press.
Parfit, D. 1984. *Reasons and Persons*, Oxford, Clarendon Press.
Quinn, W. 1993. *Morality and Action*, Cambridge, Cambridge University Press.
Rawls, J. 1971. *A Theory of Justice*, Cambridge, MA, Harvard University Press.

Brad Hooker: The Elements of Well-Being

1. What is the difference between instrumental and non-instrumental value?
2. Hooker thinks that we can assess the non-instrumental value of something by comparing two situations. Describe his method and apply it to a candidate element of well-being that he does not consider. How does the method fare?
3. What is Hooker's "sympathy test"? Is it a plausible test for whether something qualifies as an element of well-being?
4. Some people deny that autonomy is an element of well-being—they think autonomy is valuable only when it leads to something else that is good. Hooker disagrees. On what ground do you (or don't you) find his argument compelling?
5. Many people think that moral virtue is an element of well-being. Present and assess Hooker's argument against this view.

=== ❧ ===

5

Happiness and Meaning: Two Aspects of the Good Life

Susan Wolf

....

In this wide-ranging essay, Susan Wolf argues that an essential element of a life that is good for the person living it is that her life be *meaningful*. As Wolf defines it, a meaningful life is one where "subjective attraction meets objective attractiveness"—in other words, it is a life lived by someone who derives fulfilment from engagement in objectively worthwhile activities. For Wolf, both elements here are essential to meaningfulness. One can have a great deal of pleasure in one's life without its being meaningful, since those pleasures may be taken in worthless activities. Alternatively, one can be engaged in truly valuable activities but derive no pleasure thereby. In such a case, one's life is meaningless as well.

Wolf does not deny the hedonist's claim that pleasure is an element of well-being. But given the importance she places on living a meaningful life, Wolf does deny that pleasure is the *only* such element. Wolf also takes issue with preference-satisfaction theorists, who claim that something contributes to your well-being when, and only when, it fulfills one of your desires or preferences. It is possible, she thinks, for people to prefer only worthless activities to worthwhile ones. Even if they then get everything they want, their lives will be meaningless, since they are not engaged with things of genuine value.

Social Policy and Philosophy (1997), pp. 207–225 abridged, with notes edited and renumbered.

Once we appreciate the essential role that living a meaningful life plays in well-being, we encounter some difficult questions: How should the balance between happiness and meaningfulness be struck when having to choose between the two? How can we measure (if we can) degrees of meaningfulness in a life? How meaningful must a life be in order for it to qualify as a good one? Wolf concludes her essay by considering such questions and arguing, among other things, that the very notion of self-interest diminishes in importance once we recognize the distinction between happiness and meaning in a life.

. . . .

The topic of self-interest raises large and intractable philosophical questions—most obviously, the question "In what does self-interest consist?" The concept, as opposed to the content of self-interest, however, seems clear enough. Self-interest is interest in one's own good. To act self-interestedly is to act on the motive of advancing one's own good. Whether what one does actually is in one's self-interest depends on whether it actually does advance, or at least, minimize the decline of, one's own good. Though it may be difficult to tell whether a person is motivated by self-interest in a particular instance, and difficult also to determine whether a given act or decision really is in one's self-interest, the meaning of the claims in question seems unproblematic.

My main concern in this essay is to make a point about the content of self-interest. Specifically I shall put forward the view that meaningfulness, in a sense I shall elaborate, is an important element of a good life. It follows, then, that it is part of an enlightened self-interest that one wants to secure meaning in one's life, or, at any rate, to allow and promote meaningful activity within it. Accepting this substantial conception of self-interest, however, carries with it a curious consequence: the concept of self-interest which formerly seemed so clear begins to grow fuzzy. Fortunately, it comes to seem less important as well.

I. Theories of Self-Interest

In *Reasons and Persons*,[1] Derek Parfit distinguishes three sorts of theories about self-interest—hedonistic theories, preference theories, and what he

---

1. Derek Parfit, *Reasons and Persons* (Oxford: Oxford University Press, 1984).

calls "objective-list theories." *Hedonistic theories* hold that one's good is a matter of the felt quality of one's experiences. The most popular theory of self-interest, which identifies self-interest with happiness, and happiness with pleasure and the absence of pain, is a prime example of a hedonistic theory. Noting that some people do not care that much about their own happiness, however—and, importantly, that they do not even regard their own happiness as the exclusive element of their own good—has led some to propose a *preference theory* of self-interest, which would identify a person's good with what the person most wants for herself. Thus, for example, if a person cares more about being famous, even posthumously famous, than about being happy, then a preference theory would accord fame a proportionate weight in the identification of her self-interest. If a person cares more about knowing the truth than about believing what it is pleasant or comfortable to believe, then it is in her self-interest to have the truth, unpleasant as it may be.

A person's preferences regarding herself, however, may be self-destructive or otherwise bizarre, and it may be that some things (including pleasure) are good for a person whether the person prefers them or not. It is not absurd to think that being deceived is bad for a person (and thus that not being deceived is good for a person) whether or not the person in question consciously values this state. Friendship and love may also seem to be things whose goodness explains, rather than results from, people's preferences for them. The plausibility of these last thoughts explains the appeal of *objective-list theories*, according to which a person's good includes at least some elements that are independent of or prior to her preferences and to their effect on the felt quality of her experience. On this view, there are some items, ideally specifiable on an "objective list," whose relevance to a fully successful life are not conditional on the subject's choice.

The view that I shall be advancing, that meaningfulness is an ingredient of the good life, commits one to a version of this last kind of theory, for my claim is that meaningfulness is a nonderivative aspect of a good life—its goodness does not result from its making us happy or its satisfying the preferences of the person whose life it is. Thus, it follows that any theory that takes self-interest to be a wholly subjective matter, either in a sense that identifies self-interest with the subjective quality of a person's experiences or in a sense that allows the standards of self-interest to be set by a person's subjective preferences, must be inadequate. At the same time, it would be a mistake to think that the objective good of a meaningful life is one that is wholly independent of the subject's experience or preferences, as if it could be good for a person to live a meaningful life whether or not it makes her happy or satisfies her preferences. Indeed, as we will see, the very idea that activities can make a life meaningful without the subject's endorsement is a dubious one.

II. Meaning in Life

What is a meaningful life? Spelling it out will constitute the bulk of my essay, for my hope is that once the idea is spelled out, it will be readily agreed that it is an element of a fully successful life.

A meaningful life is, first of all, one that has within it the basis for an affirmative answer to the needs or longings that are characteristically described as needs for meaning. I have in mind, for example, the sort of questions people ask on their deathbeds, or simply in contemplation of their eventual deaths, about whether their lives have been (or are) worth living, whether they have had any point, and the sort of questions one asks when considering suicide and wondering whether one has any reason to go on. These questions are familiar from Russian novels and existentialist philosophy, if not from personal experience. Though they arise most poignantly in times of crisis and intense emotion, they also have their place in moments of calm reflection, when considering important life choices. Moreover, paradigms of what are taken to be meaningful and meaningless lives in our culture are readily available. Lives of great moral or intellectual accomplishment—Gandhi, Mother Teresa, Albert Einstein—come to mind as unquestionably meaningful lives (if any are); lives of waste and isolation—Thoreau's "lives of quiet desperation," typically anonymous to the rest of us, and the mythical figure of Sisyphus—represent meaninglessness.

To what general characteristics of meaningfulness do these images lead us and how do they provide an answer to the longings mentioned above? Roughly, I would say that meaningful lives are lives of active engagement in projects of worth. Of course, a good deal needs to be said in elaboration of this statement. Let me begin by discussing the two key phrases, "active engagement" and "projects of worth."

A person is actively engaged by something if she is gripped, excited, involved by it. Most obviously, we are actively engaged by the things and people about which and whom we are passionate. Opposites of active engagement are boredom and alienation. To be actively engaged in something is not always pleasant in the ordinary sense of the word. Activities in which people are actively engaged frequently involve stress, danger, exertion, or sorrow (consider, for example: writing a book, climbing a mountain, training for a marathon, caring for an ailing friend). However, there is something good about the feeling of engagement: one feels (typically without thinking about it) especially alive.

That a meaningful life must involve "projects of worth" will, I expect, be more controversial, for the phrase hints of a commitment to some sort of objective value. This is not accidental, for I believe that the idea of meaningfulness, and the concern that our lives possess it, are conceptually linked to such a commitment. Indeed, it is this linkage that I want to defend, for I have neither a philosophical theory of what objective value is nor a substantive theory about what has this sort of value. What is clear to me is that there can be no sense to the idea of meaningfulness without a distinction between more and less worthwhile ways to spend one's time, where the test of worth is at least partly independent of a subject's ungrounded preferences or enjoyment.

Consider first the longings or concerns about meaning that people have, their wondering whether their lives are meaningful, their vows to add more meaning to their lives. The sense of these concerns and resolves cannot fully be captured by an account in which what one does with one's life doesn't matter, as long as one enjoys or prefers it. Sometimes people have concerns about meaning despite their knowledge that their lives to date have been satisfying. Indeed, their enjoyment and "active engagement" with activities and values they now see as shallow seems only to heighten the sense of meaninglessness that comes to afflict them. Their sense that their lives so far have been meaningless cannot be a sense that their activities have not been chosen or fun. When they look for sources of meaning or ways to add meaning to their lives, they are searching for projects whose justifications lie elsewhere.

Second, we need an explanation for why certain sorts of activities and involvements come to mind as contributors to meaningfulness while others seem intuitively inappropriate. Think about what gives meaning to your own life and the lives of your friends and acquaintances. Among the things that tend to come up on such lists, I have already mentioned moral and intellectual accomplishments and the ongoing activities that lead to them. Relationships with friends and relatives are perhaps even more important for most of us. Aesthetic enterprises (both creative and appreciative), the cultivation of personal virtues, and religious practices frequently loom large. By contrast, it would be odd, if not bizarre, to think of crossword puzzles, sitcoms, or the kind of computer games to which I am fighting off addiction as providing meaning in our lives, though there is no question that they afford a sort of satisfaction and that they are the objects of choice. Some things, such as chocolate and aerobics class, I choose even at considerable cost to myself (it is irrelevant that these particular choices may be related), so I must find them worthwhile in a sense. But they are not the sorts of things that make life worth living.

"Active engagement in projects of worth," I suggest, answers to the needs an account of meaningfulness in life must meet. If a person is or has been thus actively engaged, then she does have an answer to the question of whether her life is or has been worthwhile, whether it has or has had a point. When someone looks for ways to add meaning to her life, she is looking (though perhaps not under this description) for worthwhile projects about which she can get enthused. The account also explains why some activities and projects but not others come to mind as contributors to meaning in life. Some projects, or at any rate, particular acts, are worthwhile but too boring or mechanical to be sources of meaning. People do not get meaning from recycling or from writing checks to Oxfam and the ACLU. Other acts and activities, though highly pleasurable and deeply involving, like riding a roller coaster or meeting a movie star, do not seem to have the right kind of value to contribute to meaning.

Bernard Williams once distinguished categorical desires from the rest. Categorical desires give us reasons for living—they are not premised on the assumption that we will live. The sorts of things that give meaning to life tend to be objects of categorical desire. We desire them, at least so I would suggest, because we think them worthwhile. They are not worthwhile simply because we desire them or simply because they make our lives more pleasant.

Roughly, then, according to my proposal, a meaningful life must satisfy two criteria, suitably linked. First, there must be active engagement, and second, it must be engagement in (or with) projects of worth. A life is meaningless if it lacks active engagement with anything. A person who is bored or alienated from most of what she spends her life doing is one whose life can be said to lack meaning. Note that she may in fact be performing functions of worth. A housewife and mother, a doctor, or a bus-driver may be competently doing a socially valuable job, but because she is not engaged by her work (or, as we are assuming, by anything else in her life), she has no categorical desires that give her a reason to live. At the same time, someone who *is* actively engaged may also live a meaningless life, if the objects of her involvement are utterly worthless. It is difficult to come up with examples of such lives that will be uncontroversial without being bizarre. But both bizarre and controversial examples have their place. In the bizarre category, we might consider pathological cases: someone whose sole passion in life is collecting rubber bands, or memorizing the dictionary, or making handwritten copies of *War and Peace*. Controversial cases will include the corporate lawyer who sacrifices her private life and health for success along the professional ladder, the devotee of a religious cult, or—an example offered by Wiggins[2] the pig farmer who buys more land to grow more corn to feed more pigs to buy more land to grow more corn to feed more pigs.

We may summarize my proposal in terms of a slogan: "Meaning arises when subjective attraction meets objective attractiveness." The idea is that in a world in which some things are more worthwhile than others, meaning arises when a subject discovers or develops an affinity for one or typically several of the more worthwhile things and has and makes use of the opportunity to engage with it or them in a positive way.

An advantage of the slogan is that it avoids the somewhat misleading reference to "projects." That term is less than ideal in its suggestion of well-defined and goal-oriented tasks. To be sure, many projects do add meaning to life—mastering a field of study, building a house, turning a swamp into a garden, curing cancer—but much of what gives meaning to life consists in ongoing relationships and involvements—with friends, family, the scientific community, with church or ballet or chess. These ongoing strands of life give rise to and are partly constituted by projects—you plan a surprise party for your spouse, coach a little league team, review an article for a journal—but the meaning comes less from the individuated projects than from the larger involvements of which they are parts. The slogan, moreover, is intentionally vague, for if pretheoretical judgments about meaning even approximate the truth, then not only the objects of worth but also the sorts of interaction with them that are capable of contributing to meaning are immensely variable. One can get meaning from creating, promoting, protecting (worthwhile) things, from helping people one loves and people in need, from achieving levels of skill and excellence, from overcoming obstacles, from gaining understanding, and even from just communing with or actively appreciating what is there to be appreciated.

---

2. See David Wiggins, "Truth, Invention, and the Meaning of Life," *Proceedings of the British Academy*, vol. 62 (1976), p. 342.

It is part of our job, if not our natural bent, as philosophers to be skeptical—about the correctness of these pretheoretical judgments, about our ability reliably to distinguish meaningful from meaningless activities, and about the very coherence of the distinction. About the first two worries I am not very concerned. Assuming that the distinctions are coherent and that some activities are more worthwhile than others, our culture-bound, contemporary judgments of which activities are worthwhile are bound to be partly erroneous. History is full of unappreciated geniuses, of artists, inventors, explorers whose activities at their time were scorned, as it is full of models of behavior and accomplishment that later seem to have been overrated. Though we may improve our judgments, both particular and general, by an open-minded, concentrated, and communal effort to examine and articulate the basis for them (a project that strikes me as both worthwhile and intrinsically interesting), the hope or expectation that such scrutiny will yield a reliable method for generally distinguishing worthwhile from worthless activities seems overly optimistic. Why do we respect people who devote themselves to chess more than those who become champions at pinball? Why do we admire basketball stars more than jump-rope champions? What is more worthwhile about writing a book on the philosophy of language than writing one on Nicole Brown Simpson's sex life? It is useful to ask and to answer such questions, so far as we can, both to widen and correct our horizons and to increase our understanding. But our inability to give complete and adequate answers, or to be confident in the details of our assessments, need not be a serious problem. The point of recognizing the distinction, after all, is not to give rankings of meaningful lives. There is no need, in general, to pass judgment on individuals or even on activities in which people want to engage. The point is rather at a more general level to understand the ingredients of our own and others' good, and to get a better idea of the sorts of considerations that provide reasons for living our lives one way rather than another.

The point, which I am in the midst of developing, is that meaningfulness is a nonderivative part of an individual's good, and that meaningfulness consists in active engagement in projects or activities of worth. Though it seems to me that the point and most of its usefulness can stand despite acknowledged difficulties with identifying precisely which projects or activities these are, it would be utterly destroyed if it turned out that there were no such things as projects or activities of worth at all—if it turned out, in other words, as Bentham thought, that pushpin were as good as poetry, not because of some heretofore undiscovered excellences in the game of pushpin, but because the very idea of distinctions in worth is bankrupt or incoherent. If there are no projects of worth (in contrast to other projects), then there are no such things as what I have in mind by more and less meaningful lives, and so it cannot be a part of one's good to live a more meaningful rather than a less meaningful life. If the idea of a worthwhile project is just a fraud or a hoax, then my account of self-interest is undone by it.

Since I have no *theory* of worth by which to prove the coherence of the concept or refute all skeptical challenges, I can only acknowledge the vulnerability of my account of self-interest in this regard. That we do, most of us, believe that some activities and projects are more worthwhile than others, that we regard certain activities as wastes of time (or near wastes of time) and others as inherently valuable, seems undeniable. These beliefs lie behind dispositions to feel proud or disgusted with ourselves for time spent well or badly, and they account for at least some of our efforts to steer our children and our friends toward some activities and away from others. When I try to take up a point of view that denies the distinction between worthwhile and worthless activity, I cannot find it convincing. Still, it is an article of faith that these untheoretical judgments, or some core of them, are philosophically defensible. It is on the assumption that they are defensible that my views about meaningfulness and self-interest are built.

III. Two Challenges

My proposal so far has been that meaningfulness in life arises from engagement in worthwhile activity. I have argued for the plausibility of this account on the grounds that it fits well both with the needs that are typically referred to as needs for meaning and with the concrete judgments of meaningful and meaningless activity that are most commonly made. Before proceeding with an examination of the relation between meaning and self-interest, two challenges to this account of meaning should be answered.

The first objects that, contrary to my claims, my account of meaning fails to meet the requirements I have set up for it. It fails, more particularly, to answer to the needs of at least one type of longing for meaning that members of our species tend to have. Traditional worries about the meaning of life, often set off by reflections on our own mortality and on the indifference of the cosmos in which we occupy so tiny a place, are rarely appeased by the reflection that one can actively engage in projects of worth. At least, they are not appeased by reflection on the availability of the kind of projects I have been talking about, like taking up the cello, writing a novel, volunteering at a child's day-care center or a nursing home. Tolstoy, the publicly acclaimed author of some of the greatest works of literature ever written, the father and spouse of what he described (perhaps inaccurately) as a loving and successful family, could have had no doubt that, relatively speaking, his life was spent in projects as worthwhile as any. Yet he was plagued by the thought that it was all for naught.[3] Nothing he did seemed to save his life from meaninglessness.

Among those who think that meaning in life, or the lack of it, is primarily concerned with facts about the human condition, some disagree not with my general account of meaning but with, if you will, its application. Their position, in other words, shares my view that meaning comes from engagement in projects of worth, but assigns certain facts about the human condition a crucial role in settling whether there are any such projects. If God does not exist, they think, then nothing is any more worthwhile than anything else. Within this group, some believe that God is the only possible standard for judgments of nonsubjective value. If God does not exist, they think, then neither does moral or aesthetic value or any other sort of value that could distinguish some projects as better than others. Others believe that though there may be a difference between great literature and junk, and between virtue and vice, there is no point in bothering about which you occupy yourself with. Nothing lasts forever; the human race will be destroyed; the earth will crash into the sun. Only God, and the promise of an eternal life either for ourselves or for the universe in which our accomplishments have a place, can give a point to our living lives one way rather than another. Only God can make meaningful life so much as a possibility.

My own view about this position is that it expresses an irrational obsession with permanence; but it is enough for the purposes of this essay to note that it does not really challenge the account of meaning I have offered. I have already acknowledged that the usefulness of my account rests on the assumption that the distinction between worthwhile and worthless projects is defensible, and on the assumption that at least a core of our beliefs about what is worthwhile and what is worthless is roughly

---

3. See Leo Tolstoy, "My Confession," in E. D. Klemke, ed., *The Meaning of Life* (New York: Oxford University Press, 1981).

correct. Those who think that God is a necessary grounding for these assumptions and who believe in Him may still find my account of meaning acceptable. Those who think that God is a necessary grounding that unfortunately does not exist will reject my substantive claims about meaning for reasons we have already admitted.

The second challenge to my account of meaningfulness is more directly relevant to the issue of the nature of self-interest. It consists of an alternative subjective account of meaning. According to this position, meaning is not a matter of one's projects in life being worthwhile from some objective point of view. Rather, a person's life is meaningful, one might say, if it is meaningful *to her*, and it is meaningful to her if she thinks or feels it is.

The suggestion that something is meaningful to someone as long as she thinks it is can be of no help to us in developing an account of meaningfulness, for we cannot understand what it would be for someone to think her life meaningful until we have an account of what meaningfulness is. The view I want to discuss, however, is, strictly speaking, more concerned with a feeling or, better, a sense or qualitative character that some of our experiences have. We may use the term "fulfillment" to refer to it. It is pleasant to be or to feel fulfilled or to find an activity or a relationship fulfilling, but it is a pleasure of a specific sort, one that seems closely associated with the thought that our lives or certain activities within them are meaningful. Recognizing this, it may be suggested, gives us all the basis we need for an account of meaning that meets my requirements. We may understand people's longing for meaning as a longing for this particular feeling, a longing which other sorts of pleasure cannot satisfy. We can also explain why some activities characteristically answer the call of meaning better than others. Some yield the feeling of fulfillment while others do not. Chocolate is filling but not fulfilling; it gives pleasure but not of this particular kind. When a person steps back, wondering whether her life has had meaning, or searching for a way to give it more meaning, she may simply be surveying her life for its quotient of fulfillment or looking for ways to increase it.

The very close ties between meaningfulness and fulfillment on which this account of meaning relies are important for understanding both the concept of meaning and its value. That meaningful activity or a meaningful life is at least partly fulfilling is, as this account suggests, a conceptual truth. To *identify* meaningfulness with fulfillment, however, neglects aspects of our use of the terms, and aspects of the experiences that are described by them, that my more objective account of meaningfulness better accommodates.

For one thing, fulfillment is not a brute feeling but one with some cognitive content or concomitant. That certain activities tend to be fulfilling and others not seems connected to features of the relevant activities that make this fact intelligible. There is a fittingness between certain kinds of activities and the potential for fulfillment. When a relationship or a job is fulfilling, there is something about it that makes it so. One feels appreciated or loved, or has the sense of doing good, or finds the challenge of the work rewarding. It is not just that the activities in question meet our expectations, though that is a part of it. Some things are fine but not fulfilling—my relationship with my hairdresser, for example, or my weekly trips to the supermarket.

These considerations suggest that we find things fulfilling only if we can think about them in a certain way. It is difficult precisely to identify a single belief that is always associated with the experience of fulfillment. Still, I propose that there is some association between finding an activity fulfilling and believing, or at least dimly, inarticulately perceiving, there to be something independently worthwhile or good about it.

If we accept the idea that the feeling of fulfillment is necessarily connected with beliefs about its objects—if we accept that an activity or relationship can be fulfilling only if one believes it to be somehow independently good—then we can distinguish two hypotheses about the relationship between meaning and fulfillment. Does meaning come from the experience of fulfillment, no matter what its cause, or is a meaningful life one in which a subject is fulfilled by activities suitable to the experience? The subjective account opts for the former; but the latter seems to square better with our ordinary use of the concept.

We can construct a test case by considering someone whose judgment of an aspect of her life has changed. A woman previously blissfully in love discovers that the man she loved has been using her. She had found the relationship fulfilling before she learned of his deceits. She would have said, had you asked her earlier, that the relationship contributed to the meaningfulness of her life. What would she say now, however, and what should we say about her? No one can take away the feelings of fulfillment she experienced during the period she was deceived; but it seems unlikely that she would say, after the fact, that the relationship truly had given meaning to her life. Indeed, part of what makes this sort of event so sad is that, in addition to the pain that is caused when the deception is discovered, it undermines the value of all the pleasure that came before.

[Consider] cases of addicts or inductees of religious cults whose feelings of contentment are caused, but not justified, by the things that bring them about. Though we should be cautious about passing judgment on the activities that others take to be worthwhile, this is no reason to rule out the possibility that people are sometimes mistaken, that their finding something fulfilling can be wrongly induced, either through the establishment of false factual beliefs (such as belief in a loved one's fidelity or in the divine status of a charismatic leader) or by drugs or electrodes. If, moreover, they are led by such mind-altering means to spend their lives occupied by some equivalent of stone-rolling—watching endless reruns of *Leave It to Beaver* or counting and recounting the number of tiles on the bathroom floor— then it seems to me most in line with ordinary language to describe them as leading meaningless lives, however fulfilled they may feel themselves to be. If, further, such people wake up or snap out of it—if they come to occupy a point of view that devalues their former lives—then their later descriptions would not, I think, grant meaning to the things in which they had found contentment before.

IV. Meaningfulness and Self-Interest

So far I have been occupied with spelling out a conception of what meaningfulness in life is. My point in doing so, in the present context, is to bring it to bear on the idea of self-interest. Meaningfulness seems to me an important ingredient of a good life, and one that is too often either neglected or distorted by contemporary accounts of individual well-being.

Most people—at least most people within a certain group, bounded perhaps by class or education as well as by culture and history—behave in ways that suggest that they are looking for worthwhile things to do with their lives. They actively seek projects or, more typically, happily seize upon activities, from among those to which they are attracted, that they believe to be worthwhile. Explicit thoughts about worth and meaning often occur in connection with major life decisions, in addition to those moments of crisis to which I referred before. Some people decide to have children because they think it will give meaning to their lives. Others decide not to have children because they fear that the attendant responsibilities will deprive them of the time and resources and peace of mind that they need for other things in which they do find meaning. Deliberations about whether to pursue a particular career, or any career, may similarly involve concerns about whether the job is worthwhile, or whether it would demand time and energy that would distract one from what is worthwhile. Even many who do not talk explicitly in terms of meaning or worth make choices that are best explained by reference to them. In other words, our behavior, including some of our speech, seems to reveal a preference for a meaningful life.

We are, however, more apt to explain our choices in terms of fulfillment than meaning. A man opts for the more challenging of two possible careers, even at the cost of stress and insecurity. A woman chooses to work for less pay at a job she believes is morally valuable. People arrange their lives so as to give a few hours a week to Meals on Wheels, or to practicing piano, or to keeping up with their book group, even though it means going with a little less sleep, less flexibility, less straightforward fun. Why? Because, they will say, they find these things fulfilling. They choose to live this way because they regard it as, in some sense, best for them.

Since a meaningful life is necessarily at least partly fulfilling, and since fulfillment is a major component of happiness, a very important reason for taking meaningfulness to be in our interest is that it brings fulfillment with it. It would be misleading, however, to draw from this the conclusion that meaningfulness is an instrumental good for us. To think of meaning as good because it is a means to an independent good of fulfillment would be a mistake.

It is doubtful that fulfillment is an independent good, although feeling fulfilled is pleasant and feeling unfulfilled unpleasant. If fulfillment were an independent good, it would follow that the feeling of fulfillment would be desirable no matter what its cause. It would have to be better to be Sisyphus happy (or, more precisely, Sisyphus fulfilled) than Sisyphus unhappy (unfulfilled), even if this required that Sisyphus was perpetually stoned out of his normal mind. Opinion, however, divides on this matter. Many value fulfillment only on the condition that it be based on appropriate thoughts or perceptions. Moreover, even among those who believe that feeling fulfilled is unconditionally better than the alternative, many would still prefer that these feelings were suitably caused. Better to be Sisyphus happy than Sisyphus unhappy, they may say, but better still not to be Sisyphus at all.

A proponent of a purely hedonistic theory of self-interest may point out that reports of such intuitions prove nothing. People's thinking that justified or appropriate fulfillment is better than unjustified inappropriate fulfillment doesn't make it so. To those who have these intuitions, however, the burden of proof seems to lie with the hedonist. Unless one is committed to a purely hedonistic account of value ahead of time, there seems no reason to doubt that what is principally desirable is getting fulfillment from genuinely fulfilling activities, from activities, that is, whose accompanying feeling of fulfillment comes from the correct perception of their value. There seems no reason to doubt, in other words, that what is principally desirable is living a meaningful life and not living a life that seems or feels meaningful. Insofar as we prefer a truly meaningful life to one that merely seems or feels meaningful, a purely hedonistic theory of self-interest will not account for it.

A preference theory of self-interest, however, would not have to account for it—preference theorists simply accept our preferences and go on to compute our self-interest from there. This suggests an alternative account of the relation between meaning and self-interest. According to preference theories, meaning is important to our well-being if and only if meaning matters to us. Since many of us do want to live meaningful lives— since we think it is better for us if we do—preference theorists will agree that it is in our interest that our lives are meaningful. From their point of view, there is no need to make any more objective claims than that.

From a practical perspective, it matters little whether we accept this theory or a more objective one, particularly if you think, as I do, that the preference for a meaningful life is widespread and deep. If it is accepted as a fact of human nature (even a statistical fact, and even of a culturally created human nature) that people just do care about meaning in their lives, then this gives us reason enough to shape our lives in ways that will encourage not just fulfillment but meaningfulness, and it gives us reason enough to shape our social and political institutions in ways that will increase the opportunities for everyone to live not just happily and comfortably but meaningfully as well.

A preference theory does not, however, seem accurately to reflect the status a meaningful life has for most of us. Most of us, it seems, do not regard our preference for a meaningful life as an ungrounded preference we just happen to have. If we did think so, then we would judge it a matter of indifference whether anyone else had or lacked this preference, and indeed, we would have no reason to want to keep this preference ourselves if we were convinced that we would be better off without it. For most people, however, at least so it seems to me, having a meaningful life is a value and not just a preference. We do not just want our lives to be meaningful, we think it good that we want it. Indeed, our interest and concern for meaning is sometimes mentioned as a mark of our humanity, as an aspect of what raises us above brutes. We think that we would be diminished as a species if we lost the aspiration, or the interest, in living meaningful lives and not just happy ones. Individuals who lack the desire that their lives be meaningful we regard with regret or even pity.

Again it may be noted that our believing something is no proof of its being true, and again I must acknowledge that I have no proof of the value or objective desirability of meaningfulness. At the same time, the claim that a meaningful life is preferable (and not just brutely preferred) to a meaningless one may seem so nearly self-evident as to require no proof. Once one is willing to apply the terms of meaningfulness and meaninglessness at all, it may seem unstable to believe that a life that lacks meaning is no worse than one that possesses it. Even if we can logically distinguish the position that some lives are more meaningful than others from the position which adds that (some) meaningfulness is a good, this latter position seems more natural than one which denies it. Though we may be unable to argue for caring about meaning in a way that would convince someone who doesn't care to begin with, the concern or the desire for meaningful activity is, for those who have it, more rationally coherent with other values and dispositions than its absence would be.

In response to the question "Why care about living a meaningful life rather than a meaningless one?" the answer that I believe best expresses reflective common sense will begin with the connection between meaning and happiness: Nine times out of ten, perhaps ninety-nine times out of a hundred, a meaningful life will be happier than a meaningless one. The feelings of fulfillment one gets from interacting positively and supportively with things or creatures (or "realms") whose love seems deserved are wonderful feelings, worth more, on qualitative grounds alone, than many other sorts of pleasure, and worth the cost of putting up with considerable quantities of pain. Moreover, the awareness, even dim and inarticulate, of a lack of anything that can constitute a source of pride or a source of connection to anything valuable outside of oneself can be awful, making one irritable, restless, and contemptuous of oneself.

Except in an academic philosophical context such as this, it is perhaps unnatural to press further. If we do press further, however, it seems to me that the strength and character of these feelings of pleasure and pain are not best explained as mere quirks of our natural or culturally conditioned psyches. Rather, that we feel so good or so bad in accordance with our sense of connection to value outside ourselves seems to me best explained in terms of an underlying belief that a life is better when it possesses such connections. What precisely is better about it is difficult to say. But perhaps it has to do with our place in the universe: since we are, each of us, occupants in a world full of value independent of our individual selves, living in such a way as to connect positively and supportively with some nonsubjective value harmonizes better with our objective situation than would a life whose chief occupations can be only subjectively defended.

V. The Deconstruction of Self-Interest

I have in this essay been concerned to defend, or rather to elaborate, what I take to be a deeply and widely held view about individual human good, namely, that a fully successful life is, among other things, a meaningful one. Further, I have urged that this claim is distorted if it is understood as an element of either a hedonistic or a preference theory of self-interest. Properly understood, it requires a rejection of both of these sorts of theories.

As a substantive claim, I do not expect that the point that a good life must be meaningful will be surprising. We are not used to thinking very explicitly or very analytically about it, however; and in popular unreflective consciousness, a substantive interest in a meaningful life often sits side by side with assumptions that are incompatible with it. How often have you heard someone say, "What's the point of doing something if it isn't fun, or if you don't enjoy it?" I hear this sentiment expressed quite frequently, despite living on the East Coast. To be fair, such expressions tend to be limited to contexts of self-interest. They are not intended as rejections of the rational authority of moral or legal obligation. Moreover, there is often a point behind such remarks that I would strongly endorse. Against a kind of workaholism and related neurotic obsessions with some forms of success and achievement, it can be useful to step back and reflect in the way these remarks would invoke. Still, the suggestion that there can be no point to things if they are neither duties nor fun is, strictly speaking, both false and dangerous.

Much of what we do would be inexplicable, or at least indefensible, if its justification depended either on its being a duty or, even in the long run, on its maximally contributing to our net fun. Relationships with friends and family, nonobligatory aspects of professional roles, and long-term commitments to artistic, scholarly, or athletic endeavors typically lead us to devote time and energy to things that are difficult and unpleasant, and to forgo opportunities for relaxation and enjoyment. It is arguable that many of these choices advance our happiness (in the broadest sense, our fun) in the long run, but such arguments are at best uncertain, and the thought that they are necessary for the defense of these choices puts a regrettable kind of pressure on the commitments that give rise to them. There is, however, a point—even a self-interested point—to doing things that fall outside the categories both of duty and of fun. One can find a reason, or at least a justifying explanation, for doing something in the fact that the act or activity in question contributes to the meaningfulness of one's life.

Once we have ceased to identify self-interest with happiness, however, other assumptions are also undermined. The concept of self-interest becomes more difficult to work with. Specifically, a conception of self-interest that recognizes the importance of meaning to a good life admits of much greater indeterminacy than the more traditional conceptions. This is partly a function of indeterminacy within the category of meaningfulness itself. Though meaningfulness is not an all-or-nothing concept—some lives are more meaningful than others, a person's life may not have *enough* meaning in it to be satisfactory—there is no well-formed system for making comparative judgments. The meaningfulness of a life may vary depending on how much of it is spent in meaningful activity, on how worthwhile the activities in question are, or on how fully engaged (or attracted) the individual is. In many instances, however, it seems absurd to think there is a correct comparison to be made. Is the life of a great but lonely philosopher more or less meaningful than that of a beloved housekeeper? There seems to be no reason to assume that there is a fact of the matter about this. Moreover, from a self-interested point of view, it is unclear whether, beyond a certain point, it matters whether one's life is more meaningful. A meaningful life is better than a meaningless one, but once it is meaningful enough, there may be no self-interested reason to want, as it were, to squeeze more meaning into it. Finally, the mix between meaning and felt happiness may have no determinate ideal. A person often has to choose between taking a path that would strengthen or expand a part of his or her life that contributes to its meaningfulness (going to graduate school, adopting a child, getting politically involved) and taking an easier or more pleasant road. Once one has accepted a conception of self-interest that recognizes meaningfulness as an independent aspect of one's personal good, one may have to admit that in such cases there may be no answer to the question of what is most in one's self-interest.

Susan Wolf: Happiness and Meaning: Two Aspects of the Good Life

1. How does Wolf define a meaningful life? Do you agree with her definition?
2. The mythical Sisyphus was condemned by the gods to roll a huge boulder up a hill, watch it inevitably fall to the bottom, and then repeat his

efforts—forever. Imagine that this is just the life that Sisyphus prefers for himself and that he is happy with his fate. Why does Wolf think that such a life would nevertheless be meaningless? Do you agree?

3. Wolf identifies both happiness and meaning as elements in a good life. Do you think that there are any others? If so, state and argue for them.

4. Wolf concedes that if nothing were objectively valuable, then her theory would imply that our lives are meaningless. Are you persuaded by her claims and examples to share her view that there are indeed objectively worthwhile activities? Why or why not?

5. Suppose that nothing is objectively valuable and that our lives are therefore (according to Wolf) meaningless. Imagine, though, that we found much of what we did fulfilling and were engaged in our activities in a way that led to a sense of personal satisfaction. How bad for us would it be to lack meaning in our lives?

PART II

Normative Ethics

Theories of Right Conduct

6

Euthyphro

Plato

....

In an early section (omitted here) of this dialogue about the nature
of piety, Socrates bumps into Euthyphro in front of the law courts of
Athens. Socrates is on trial for his life; Euthyphro is there to prosecute
a murderer. It turns out that Euthyphro is prosecuting his own father,
an act that would shock ancient Greek audiences as much as it would
shock us in our own time. When Socrates asks him why he would do
such a thing, Euthyphro replies that he is privy to many secrets of the
gods, and that piety demands that he seek his father's conviction.

Our excerpt picks up at this point. Socrates immediately begs
Euthyphro to reveal the essence of piety, its true nature, so that
Socrates and others may live more pious lives. Euthyphro first provides
some examples of pious actions, but this is not what Socrates is after.
He wants to know what is common to all instances of piety. Euthyphro
then says that piety is what the gods love.

Socrates then asks what has since come to be known as the Euthyphro Question: Are acts pious because the gods love them, or do the
gods love actions because they are pious? We can modify the question
a bit to get the following puzzle: Is an action morally right because God
commands it, or does God command an action because it is right?

Many who think that religion is essential to morality endorse the
first option—God's commands are what make actions right, so that if

From *Five Dialogues*, 2nd ed., trans. G. M. A. Grube, rev. by John Cooper (Indianapolis:
Hackett Publishers, 2002), pp. 7–14.

God does not exist, or does not issue commands, then nothing is morally right. Plato's arguments are designed to cast doubt on this view.

....

SOCRATES: . . . So tell me now, by Zeus, what you just now maintained you clearly knew: what kind of thing do you say that godliness and ungodliness are, both as regards murder and other things; or is the pious not the same and alike in every action, and the impious the opposite of all that is pious and like itself, and everything that is to be impious presents us with one form or appearance insofar as it is impious?

EUTHYPHRO: Most certainly, Socrates.

SOCRATES: Tell me then, what is the pious, and what the impious, do you say?

EUTHYPHRO: I say that the pious is to do what I am doing now, to prosecute the wrongdoer, be it about murder or temple robbery or anything else, whether the wrongdoer is your father or your mother or anyone else; not to prosecute is impious. And observe, Socrates, that I can cite powerful evidence that the law is so. I have already said to others that such actions are right, not to favor the ungodly, whoever they are. These people themselves believe that Zeus is the best and most just of the gods, yet they agree that he bound his father because he unjustly swallowed his sons, and that he in turn castrated his father for similar reasons. But they are angry with me because I am prosecuting my father for his wrongdoing. They contradict themselves in what they say about the gods and about me. . . .

SOCRATES: And do you believe that there really is war among the gods, and terrible enmities and battles, and other such things as are told by the poets, and other sacred stories such as are embroidered by good writers and by representations of which the robe of the goddess is adorned when it is carried up to the Acropolis? Are we to say these things are true, Euthyphro?

EUTHYPHRO: Not only these, Socrates, but, as I was saying just now, I will, if you wish, relate many other things about the gods which I know will amaze you.

SOCRATES: I should not be surprised, but you will tell me these at leisure some other time. For now, try to tell me more clearly what I was asking just now, for, my friend, you did not teach me adequately when

I asked you what the pious was, but you told me that what you are doing now, in prosecuting your father for murder, is pious.

EUTHYPHRO: And I told the truth, Socrates.

SOCRATES: Perhaps. You agree, however, that there are many other pious actions.

EUTHYPHRO: There are.

SOCRATES: Bear in mind then that I did not bid you tell me one or two of the many pious actions but that form itself that makes all pious actions pious, for you agreed that all impious actions are impious and all pious actions pious through one form, or don't you remember?

EUTHYPHRO: I do.

SOCRATES: Tell me then what this form itself is, so that I may look upon it and, using it as a model, say that any action of yours or another's that is of that kind is pious, and if it is not that it is not.

EUTHYPHRO: If that is how you want it, Socrates, that is how I will tell you.

SOCRATES: That is what I want.

EUTHYPHRO: Well then, what is dear to the gods is pious, what is not is impious.

SOCRATES: Splendid, Euthyphro! You have now answered in the way I wanted. Whether your answer is true I do not know yet, but you will obviously show me that what you say is true.

EUTHYPHRO: Certainly.

SOCRATES: Come then, let us examine what we mean. An action or a man dear to the gods is pious, but an action or a man hated by the gods is impious. They are not the same, but quite opposite, the pious and the impious. Is that not so?

EUTHYPHRO: It is indeed.

SOCRATES: And that seems to be a good statement?

EUTHYPHRO: I think so, Socrates.

SOCRATES: We have also stated that the gods are in a state of discord, that they are at odds with each other, Euthyphro, and that they are at enmity with each other. Has that, too, been said?

EUTHYPHRO: It has.

SOCRATES: What are the subjects of difference that cause hatred and anger? Let us look at it this way. If you and I were to differ about numbers as to which is the greater, would this difference make us enemies and angry with each other, or would we proceed to count and soon resolve our difference about this?

EUTHYPHRO: We would certainly do so.

SOCRATES: Again, if we differed about the larger and the smaller, we would turn to measurement and soon cease to differ.

EUTHYPHRO: That is so.

SOCRATES: And about the heavier and the lighter, we would resort to weighing and be reconciled.

EUTHYPHRO: Of course.

SOCRATES: What subject of difference would make us angry and hostile to each other if we were unable to come to a decision? Perhaps you do not have an answer ready, but examine as I tell you whether these subjects are the just and the unjust, the beautiful and the ugly, the good and the bad. Are these not the subjects of difference about which, when we are unable to come to a satisfactory decision, you and I and other men become hostile to each other whenever we do?

EUTHYPHRO: That is the difference, Socrates, about those subjects.

SOCRATES: What about the gods, Euthyphro? If indeed they have differences, will it not be about these same subjects?

EUTHYPHRO: It certainly must be so.

SOCRATES: Then according to your argument, my good Euthyphro, different gods consider different things to be just, beautiful, ugly, good, and bad, for they would not be at odds with one another unless they differed about these subjects, would they?

EUTHYPHRO: You are right.

SOCRATES: And they like what each of them considers beautiful, good, and just, and hate the opposites of these?

EUTHYPHRO: Certainly.

SOCRATES: But you say that the same things are considered just by some gods and unjust by others, and as they dispute about these things they are at odds and at war with each other. Is that not so?

EUTHYPHRO: It is.

SOCRATES: The same things then are loved by the gods and hated by the gods, and would be both god-loved and god-hated.

EUTHYPHRO: It seems likely.

SOCRATES: And the same things would be both pious and impious, according to this argument?

EUTHYPHRO: I'm afraid so.

SOCRATES: So you did not answer my question, you surprising man. I did not ask you what same thing is both pious and impious, and it appears that what is loved by the gods is also hated by them. So it is in no way surprising if your present action, namely punishing your father, may be pleasing to Zeus but displeasing to Cronus and Uranus, pleasing to Hephaestus but displeasing to Hera, and so with any other gods who differ from each other on this subject.

EUTHYPHRO: I think, Socrates, that on this subject no gods would differ from one another, that whoever has killed anyone unjustly should pay the penalty.

SOCRATES: Well now, Euthyphro, have you ever heard any man maintaining that one who has killed or done anything else unjustly should not pay the penalty?

EUTHYPHRO: They never cease to dispute on this subject, both elsewhere and in the courts, for when they have committed many wrongs they do and say anything to avoid the penalty.

SOCRATES: Do they agree they have done wrong, Euthyphro, and in spite of so agreeing do they nevertheless say they should not be punished?

EUTHYPHRO. No, they do not agree on that point.

SOCRATES: So they do not say or do just anything. For they do not venture to say this, or dispute that they must not pay the penalty if they have done wrong, but I think they deny doing wrong. Is that not so?

EUTHYPHRO: That is true.

SOCRATES: Then they do not dispute that the wrongdoer must be punished, but they may disagree as to who the wrongdoer is, what he did, and when.

EUTHYPHRO: You are right.

SOCRATES: Do not the gods have the same experience, if indeed they are at odds with each other about the just and the unjust, as your argument maintains? Some assert that they wrong one another, while others deny it, but no one among gods or men ventures to say that the wrongdoer must not be punished.

EUTHYPHRO: Yes, that is true, Socrates, as to the main point.

SOCRATES: And those who disagree, whether men or gods, dispute about each action, if indeed the gods disagree. Some say it is done justly, others unjustly. Is that not so?

EUTHYPHRO: Yes, indeed.

SOCRATES: Come now, my dear Euthyphro, tell me, too, that I may become wiser, what proof you have that all the gods consider that man to have been killed unjustly who became a murderer while in your service, was bound by the master of his victim, and died in his bonds before the one who bound him found out from the seers what was to be done with him, and that it is right for a son to denounce and to prosecute his father on behalf of such a man. Come, try to show me a clear sign that all the gods definitely believe this action to be right. If you can give me adequate proof of this, I shall never cease to extol your wisdom.

EUTHYPHRO: This is perhaps no light task, Socrates, though I could show you very clearly.

SOCRATES: I understand that you think me more dull-witted than the jury, as you will obviously show them that these actions were unjust and that all the gods hate such actions.

EUTHYPHRO: I will show it to them clearly, Socrates, if only they will listen to me.

SOCRATES: They will listen if they think you show them well. But this thought came to me as you were speaking, and I am examining it, saying to myself: "If Euthyphro shows me conclusively that all the gods consider such a death unjust, to what greater extent have I learned from him the nature of piety and impiety? This action would then, it seems, be hated by the gods, but the pious and the impious were not thereby now defined, for what is hated by the gods has also been shown to be loved by them." So I will not insist on this point; let us assume, if you wish, that all the gods consider this unjust and that they all hate it. However, is this the correction we are making in our discussion, that what all the gods hate is impious, and what they all love is pious, and that what some gods love and others hate is neither or both? Is that how you now wish us to define piety and impiety?

EUTHYPHRO: What prevents us from doing so, Socrates?

SOCRATES: For my part nothing, Euthyphro, but you look whether on your part this proposal will enable you to teach me most easily what you promised.

EUTHYPHRO: I would certainly say that the pious is what all the gods love, and the opposite, what all the gods hate, is the impious.

SOCRATES: Then let us again examine whether that is a sound statement, or do we let it pass, and if one of us, or someone else, merely says that something is so, do we accept that it is so? Or should we examine what the speaker means?

EUTHYPHRO: We must examine it, but I certainly think that this is now a fine statement.

SOCRATES: We shall soon know better whether it is. Consider this: Is the pious being loved by the gods because it is pious, or is it pious because it is being loved by the gods?

EUTHYPHRO: I don't know what you mean, Socrates.

SOCRATES: I shall try to explain more clearly: we speak of something carried and something carrying, of something led and something leading, of something seen and something seeing, and you understand that these things are all different from one another and how they differ?

EUTHYPHRO: I think I do.

SOCRATES: So there is also something loved and—a different thing— something loving.

EUTHYPHRO: Of course.

SOCRATES: Tell me then whether the thing carried is a carried thing because it is being carried, or for some other reason?

EUTHYPHRO: No, that is the reason.

SOCRATES: And the thing led is so because it is being led, and the thing seen because it is being seen?

EUTHYPHRO: Certainly.

SOCRATES: It is not being seen because it is a thing seen but on the contrary it is a thing seen because it is being seen; nor is it because it is something led that it is being led but because it is being led that it is something led; nor is something being carried because it is something carried, but it is something carried because it is being carried. Is what I want to say clear, Euthyphro? I want to say this, namely, that if anything is being changed or is being affected in any way, it is not being changed because it is something changed, but rather it is something changed because it is being changed; nor is it being affected because it is something affected, but it is something affected because it is being affected. Or do you not agree?

EUTHYPHRO: I do.

SOCRATES: Is something loved either something changed or something affected by something?

EUTHYPHRO: Certainly.

SOCRATES: So it is in the same case as the things just mentioned; it is not being loved by those who love it because it is something loved, but it is something loved because it is being loved by them?

EUTHYPHRO: Necessarily.

SOCRATES: What then do we say about the pious, Euthyphro? Surely that it is being loved by all the gods, according to what you say?

EUTHYPHRO: Yes.

SOCRATES: Is it being loved because it is pious, or for some other reason?

EUTHYPHRO: For no other reason.

SOCRATES: It is being loved then because it is pious, but it is not pious because it is being loved?

EUTHYPHRO: Apparently.

SOCRATES: And yet it is something loved and god-loved because it is being loved by the gods?

EUTHYPHRO: Of course.

SOCRATES: Then the god-loved is not the same as the pious, Euthyphro, nor the pious the same as the god-loved, as you say it is, but one differs from the other.

EUTHYPHRO: How so, Socrates?

SOCRATES: Because we agree that the pious is being loved for this reason, that it is pious, but it is not pious because it is being loved. Is that not so?

EUTHYPHRO: Yes.

SOCRATES: And that the god-loved, on the other hand, is so because it is being loved by the gods, by the very fact of being loved, but it is not being loved because it is god-loved.

EUTHYPHRO: True.

SOCRATES: But if the god-loved and the pious were the same, my dear Euthyphro, then if the pious was being loved because it was pious, the god-loved would also be being loved because it was god-loved; and if the god-loved was god-loved because it was being loved by the gods, then the pious would also be pious because it was being loved by the gods. But now you see that they are in opposite cases as being altogether different from each other: the one is such as to be loved because it is being loved, the other is being loved because it is such as to be loved. I'm afraid, Euthyphro, that when you were asked what piety is, you did not wish to make its nature clear to me, but you told me an affect or a quality of it, that the pious has the quality of being loved by all the gods, but you have not yet told me what the pious is.

Plato: Euthyphro

1. What is Euthyphro's first answer to Socrates's question about the nature of piety? Why does Socrates find this answer to be inadequate?

2. In his second attempt to answer Socrates's question, Euthyphro suggests that "what is dear to the gods is pious, what is not is impious." Socrates points out that the gods sometimes disagree (according to the traditional religious views of ancient Greece). Why does this raise a

problem for the view in question? Is there any analogous problem for the monotheistic theory that what God commands is morally right?

3. The most famous question of the dialogue comes when Socrates asks: "Is the pious being loved by the gods because it is pious, or is it pious because it is being loved by the gods?" How does Socrates attempt to explain this question when Euthyphro does not understand? What exactly does the question mean?

4. When Euthyphro suggests that the gods love the pious because it is pious, Socrates responds with the complaint, "you have not yet told me what the pious is." Why does Socrates say this? Is he correct?

5. Suppose Euthyphro were to claim that the pious is pious because it is loved by the gods. What objections might Socrates raise to this proposal?

7

Natural Law

Thomas Aquinas

This is a short excerpt from St. Thomas Aquinas's magnum opus, *Summa Theologica*, which has served as a central basis of Roman Catholic theology since Aquinas wrote it over seven hundred years ago. Here Aquinas offers some of the essentials of his understanding of natural law. The text is difficult for contemporary readers but repays careful study. In it, Aquinas develops his conception of natural law by considering a series of objections to various aspects of it, then offering three sorts of reply: first, one that cites a biblical text in support of his position; second, a general reply that sets the objection in context; and third, a specific reply to each of the objections he considers.

In this selection Aquinas develops his views on natural law by first asking (and answering) the question of whether there is an unchanging, eternal law. He answers affirmatively, arguing that God (whose existence is presupposed throughout this selection) is himself unchanging and eternal, and that since God governs the entire universe by means of various principles (he calls these "dictates of practical reason"), these laws themselves are eternal and unchanging. The natural law is a subset of the eternal laws and is therefore itself eternal and in some respects unchanging. Aquinas divides the natural law into first principles—the fundamental ones that are taken as self-evident axioms and are entirely

From *Summa Theologica*, First Part of the Second Part, Question 91, Articles 1 and 2; Question 94, Articles 2–6. Benziger Brothers edition, 1947. Translated by Fathers of the English Dominican Province.

unchanging—and secondary ones, which might sometimes be difficult to discern and in rare cases admit of change.

Aquinas argues that everyone has God-given, innate knowledge of the basic principles of natural law, though our understanding may be clouded by various things. He then argues that virtuous acts are those prescribed by the natural law. He claims that we are naturally inclined to act in accordance with reason; acting in accordance with reason is always virtuous; and so acting naturally is always virtuous. And acting unnaturally—as, he claims, people do when having intercourse with others of the same sex—is invariably immoral. Aquinas then considers whether natural law might be different for those in different societies or for those of different temperaments. He argues that its general principles are universally binding on all human beings at all times, but allows that certain secondary principles might subtly differ depending on circumstances.

....

Whether There Is an Eternal Law?

Objection 1: It would seem that there is no eternal law. Because every law is imposed on someone. But there was not someone from eternity on whom a law could be imposed: since God alone was from eternity. Therefore no law is eternal.

Objection 2: Further, promulgation is essential to law. But promulgation could not be from eternity: because there was no one to whom it could be promulgated from eternity. Therefore no law can be eternal.

On the contrary, Augustine says (De Lib. Arb. i, 6): "That Law which is the Supreme Reason cannot be understood to be otherwise than unchangeable and eternal."

I answer that a law is nothing else but a dictate of practical reason emanating from the ruler who governs a perfect community. Now it is evident, granted that the world is ruled by Divine Providence . . . , that the whole community of the universe is governed by Divine Reason. Wherefore the very Idea of the government of things in God the Ruler of the universe, has the nature of a law. And since the Divine Reason's conception of things is not subject to time but is eternal, according to Prov. 8:23, therefore it is that this kind of law must be called eternal.

Reply to Objection 1: Those things that are not in themselves, exist with God, inasmuch as they are foreknown and preordained by Him, according to Rm. 4:17: "Who calls those things that are not, as those that are." Accordingly the eternal concept of the Divine law bears the character of an eternal law, in so far as it is ordained by God to the government of things foreknown by Him.

Reply to Objection 2: Promulgation is made by word of mouth or in writing; and in both ways the eternal law is promulgated: because both the Divine Word and the writing of the Book of Life are eternal. But the promulgation cannot be from eternity on the part of the creature that hears or reads.

Whether There Is in Us a Natural Law?

Objection 1: It would seem that there is no natural law in us. Because man is governed sufficiently by the eternal law: for Augustine says (De Lib. Arb. i) that "the eternal law is that by which it is right that all things should be most orderly." But nature does not abound in superfluities as neither does she fail in necessaries. Therefore no law is natural to man.

Objection 2: Further, by the law man is directed, in his acts, to the end. But the directing of human acts to their end is not a function of nature, as is the case in irrational creatures, which act for an end solely by their natural appetite; whereas man acts for an end by his reason and will. Therefore no law is natural to man.

Objection 3: Further, the more a man is free, the less is he under the law. But man is freer than all the animals, on account of his free-will, with which he is endowed above all other animals. Since therefore other animals are not subject to a natural law, neither is man subject to a natural law.

On the contrary, A gloss on Rm. 2:14: "When the Gentiles, who have not the law, do by nature those things that are of the law," comments as follows: "Although they have no written law, yet they have the natural law, whereby each one knows, and is conscious of, what is good and what is evil."

I answer that law, being a rule and measure, can be in a person in two ways: in one way, as in him that rules and measures; in another way, as in that which is ruled and measured, since a thing is ruled and measured, in so far as it partakes of the rule or measure. Wherefore, since all things subject to Divine providence are ruled and measured by the eternal law; it is evident that all things partake somewhat of the eternal law, in so far as, namely, from its being imprinted on them, they derive their respective inclinations to their proper acts and ends. Now among all others, the rational creature is subject to Divine providence in the most excellent way, in so far as it partakes of a share of providence, by being provident both for itself and for others. Wherefore it has a share of the Eternal Reason, whereby it has a natural inclination to its proper act and end: and this participation of the eternal law in the rational creature is called the natural law. Hence the Psalmist: "The light of Thy countenance, O Lord, is signed upon us": thus implying that the light of natural reason, whereby we discern what is good and what is evil, which is the function of the natural law, is nothing else than an imprint on us of the Divine light. It is therefore evident that the natural law is nothing else than the rational creature's participation of the eternal law.

Reply to Objection 1: This argument would hold, if the natural law were something different from the eternal law: whereas it is nothing but a participation thereof.

Reply to Objection 2: Every act of reason and will in us is based on that which is according to nature: for every act of reasoning is based on principles that are known naturally, and every act of appetite in respect of the means is derived from the natural appetite in respect of the last end. Accordingly the first direction of our acts to their end must be in virtue of the natural law.

Reply to Objection 3: Even irrational animals partake in their own way of the Eternal Reason, just as the rational creature does. But because the rational creature partakes thereof in an intellectual and rational manner, therefore the participation of the eternal law in the rational creature is properly called a law, since a law is something pertaining to reason. Irrational creatures, however, do not partake thereof in a rational manner, wherefore there is no participation of the eternal law in them, except by way of similitude.

Whether the Natural Law Contains Several Precepts, or Only One?

Objection 1: It would seem that the natural law contains, not several precepts, but one only. For law is a kind of precept. If therefore there were many precepts of the natural law, it would follow that there are also many natural laws.

Objection 2: Further, the natural law is consequent to human nature. But human nature, as a whole, is one; though, as to its parts, it is manifold.

Therefore, either there is but one precept of the law of nature, on account of the unity of nature as a whole; or there are many, by reason of the number of parts of human nature. The result would be that even things relating to the inclination of the concupiscible faculty belong to the natural law.

Objection 3: Further, law is something pertaining to reason. Now reason is but one in man. Therefore there is only one precept of the natural law.

On the contrary, The precepts of the natural law in man stand in relation to practical matters, as the first principles to matters of demonstration. But there are several first indemonstrable principles. Therefore there are also several precepts of the natural law.

I answer that the precepts of the natural law are to the practical reason, what the first principles of demonstrations are to the speculative reason; because both are self-evident principles. Now a thing is said to be self-evident in two ways: first, in itself; secondly, in relation to us. Any proposition is said to be self-evident in itself, if its predicate is contained in the notion of the subject: although, to one who knows not the definition of the subject, it happens that such a proposition is not self-evident. For instance, this proposition, "Man is a rational being," is, in its very nature, self-evident, since who says "man," says "a rational being": and yet to one who knows not what a man is, this proposition is not self-evident. Hence it is that, as Boethius says (De Hebdom.), certain axioms or propositions are universally self-evident to all; and such are those propositions whose terms are known to all, as, "Every whole is greater than its part," and, "Things equal to one and the same are equal to one another." But some propositions are self-evident only to the wise, who understand the meaning of the terms of such propositions: thus to one who understands that an angel is not a body, it is self-evident that an angel is not circumscriptively in a place: but this is not evident to the unlearned, for they cannot grasp it.

Now a certain order is to be found in those things that are apprehended universally. For that which, before aught else, falls under apprehension, is "being," the notion of which is included in all things whatsoever a man apprehends. Wherefore the first indemonstrable principle is that "the same thing cannot be affirmed and denied at the same time," which is based on the notion of "being" and "not-being": and on this principle all others are based. Now as "being" is the first thing that falls under the apprehension simply, so "good" is the first thing that falls under the apprehension of the practical reason, which is directed to action: since every agent acts for an end under the aspect of good. Consequently the first principle of practical reason is one founded on the notion of good, viz. that "good is that which all things seek after." Hence this is the first precept of law, that "good is to be done and pursued, and evil is to be avoided." All other precepts of the natural law are based upon this: so that whatever the practical reason naturally apprehends as man's good (or evil) belongs to the precepts of the natural law as something to be done or avoided.

Since, however, good has the nature of an end, and evil, the nature of a contrary, hence it is that all those things to which man has a natural inclination, are naturally apprehended by reason as being good, and consequently as objects of pursuit, and their contraries as evil, and objects of avoidance. Wherefore according to the order of natural inclinations, is the order of the precepts of the natural law. Because in man there is first of all an inclination to good in accordance with the nature which he has in common with all substances: inasmuch as every substance seeks the preservation of its own being, according to its nature: and by reason of this inclination, whatever is a means of preserving human life, and of warding off its obstacles, belongs to the natural law. Secondly, there is in man an inclination to things that pertain to him more specially, according to that nature which he has in common with other animals: and in virtue of this inclination, those things are said to belong to the natural law, "which nature has taught to all animals" [Pandect. Just. I, tit. i], such as sexual intercourse, education of offspring and so forth. Thirdly, there is in man an inclination to good, according to the nature of his reason, which nature is proper to him: thus man has a natural inclination to know the truth about God, and to live in society: and in this respect, whatever pertains to this inclination belongs to the natural law; for instance, to shun ignorance, to avoid offending those among whom one has to live, and other such things regarding the above inclination.

Reply to Objection 1: All these precepts of the law of nature have the character of one natural law, inasmuch as they flow from one first precept.

Reply to Objection 2: All the inclinations of any parts whatsoever of human nature, e.g. of the concupiscible and irascible parts, in so far as they are ruled by reason, belong to the natural law, and are reduced to one first precept, as stated above: so that the precepts of the natural law are many in themselves, but are based on one common foundation.

Reply to Objection 3: Although reason is one in itself, yet it directs all things regarding man; so that whatever can be ruled by reason, is contained under the law of reason.

Whether All Acts of Virtue Are Prescribed by the Natural Law?

Objection 1: It would seem that not all acts of virtue are prescribed by the natural law. Because it is essential to a law that it be ordained to the common good. But some acts of virtue are ordained to the private good of the individual, as is evident especially in regards to acts of temperance. Therefore not all acts of virtue are the subject of natural law.

Objection 2: Further, every sin is opposed to some virtuous act. If therefore all acts of virtue are prescribed by the natural law, it seems to follow that all sins are against nature: whereas this applies [only] to certain special sins.

Objection 3: Further, those things which are according to nature are common to all. But acts of virtue are not common to all, since a thing is virtuous in one, and vicious in another. Therefore not all acts of virtue are prescribed by the natural law.

On the contrary, Damascene says (De Fide Orth. iii, 4) that "virtues are natural." Therefore virtuous acts also are a subject of the natural law.

I answer that, We may speak of virtuous acts in two ways: first, under the aspect of virtuous; secondly, as such and such acts considered in their proper species. If then we speak of acts of virtue, considered as virtuous, thus all virtuous acts belong to the natural law. For to the natural law belongs everything to which a man is inclined according to his nature. Now each thing is inclined naturally to an operation that is suitable to it according to its form: thus fire is inclined to give heat. Wherefore, since the rational soul is the proper form of man, there is in every man a natural inclination to act according to reason: and this is to act according to virtue. Consequently, considered thus, all acts of virtue are prescribed by the natural law: since each one's reason naturally dictates to him to act virtuously. But if we speak of virtuous acts, considered in themselves, i.e. in their proper species, then not all virtuous acts are prescribed by the natural law: for many things are done virtuously, to which nature does not incline at first; but which, through the inquiry of reason, have been found by men to be conducive to well-living.

Reply to Objection 1: Temperance is about the natural concupiscences of food, drink and sexual matters, which are indeed ordained to the natural common good, just as other matters of law are ordained to the moral common good.

Reply to Objection 2: By human nature we may mean either that which is proper to man—and in this sense all sins, as being against reason, are also against nature: or we may mean that nature which is common to man and other animals; and in this sense, certain special sins are said to be against nature; thus contrary to sexual intercourse, which is natural to all animals, is unisexual lust, which has received the special name of the unnatural crime.

Reply to Objection 3: This argument considers acts in themselves. For it is owing to the various conditions of men, that certain acts are virtuous for some, as being proportionate and becoming to them, while they are vicious for others, as being out of proportion to them.

Whether the Natural Law Is the Same in All Men?

Objection 1: It would seem that the natural law is not the same in all. For it is stated in the Decretals (Dist. i) that "the natural law is that which is contained in the Law and the Gospel." But this is not common to all men; because, as it is written (Rm. 10:16), "not all obey the gospel." Therefore the natural law is not the same in all men.

Objection 2: Further, "Things which are according to the law are said to be just," as stated in [Aristotle's] Ethic. v. But it is stated in the same book that nothing is so universally just as not to be subject to change in regard to some men. Therefore even the natural law is not the same in all men.

Objection 3: Further, to the natural law belongs everything to which a man is inclined according to his nature. Now different men are naturally inclined to different things; some to the desire of pleasures, others to the desire of honors, and other men to other things. Therefore there is not one natural law for all.

On the contrary, Isidore says (Etym. v, 4): "The natural law is common to all nations."

I answer that, to the natural law belongs those things to which a man is inclined naturally: and among these it is proper to man to be inclined to act according to reason. Now the process of reason is from the common to the proper, as stated in [Aristotle's] Phys. i. The speculative reason, however, is differently situated in this matter, from the practical reason. For, since the speculative reason is busied chiefly with the necessary things, which cannot be otherwise than they are, its proper conclusions, like the universal principles, contain the truth without fail. The practical reason, on the other hand, is busied with contingent matters, about which human actions are concerned: and consequently, although there is necessity in the general principles, the more we descend to matters of detail, the more frequently we encounter defects. Accordingly then in speculative matters truth is the same in all men, both as to principles and as to conclusions: although the truth is not known to all as regards the conclusions, but only as regards the principles which are called common notions. But in matters of action, truth or practical rectitude is not the same for all, as to matters of detail, but only as to the general principles: and where there is the same rectitude in matters of detail, it is not equally known to all.

It is therefore evident that, as regards the general principles whether of speculative or of practical reason, truth or rectitude is the same for all, and is equally known by all. As to the proper conclusions of the speculative reason, the truth is the same for all, but is not equally known to all: thus it is true for all that the three angles of a triangle are together equal to two right angles, although it is not known to all. But as to the proper conclusions of the practical reason, neither is the truth or rectitude the same for all, nor, where it is the same, is it equally known by all. Thus it is right and true for all to act according to reason: and from this principle it follows as a proper conclusion, that goods entrusted to another should be restored to their owner. Now this is true for the majority of cases: but it may happen in a particular case that it would be injurious, and therefore unreasonable, to restore goods held in trust; for instance, if they are claimed for the purpose of fighting against one's country. And this principle will be found to fail the more, according as we descend further into detail, e.g. if one were to say that goods held in trust should be restored with such and such a guarantee, or in such and such a way; because the greater the number of conditions added, the greater the number of ways in which the principle may fail, so that it be not right to restore or not to restore.

Consequently we must say that the natural law, as to general principles, is the same for all, both as to rectitude and as to knowledge. But as to certain matters of detail, which are conclusions, as it were, of those general principles, it is the same for all in the majority of cases, both as to rectitude and as to knowledge; and yet in some few cases it may fail, both as to rectitude, by reason of certain obstacles (just as natures subject to generation and corruption fail in some few cases on account of some obstacle), and as to knowledge, since in some the reason is perverted by passion, or evil habit, or an evil disposition of nature; thus formerly, theft, although it is expressly contrary to the natural law, was not considered wrong among the Germans, as Julius Caesar relates (De Bello Gall. vi).

Reply to Objection 1: The meaning of the sentence quoted is not that whatever is contained in the Law and the Gospel belongs to the natural law, since they contain many things that are above nature; but that what ever belongs to the natural law is fully contained in them. Wherefore Gratian, after saying that "the natural law is what is contained in the Law and the Gospel," adds at once, by way of example, "by which everyone is commanded to do to others as he would be done by."

Reply to Objection 2: The saying of the Philosopher [Aristotle] is to be understood of things that are naturally just, not as general principles, but as conclusions drawn from them, having rectitude in the majority of cases, but failing in a few.

Reply to Objection 3: As, in man, reason rules and commands the other powers, so all the natural inclinations belonging to the other powers must needs be directed according to reason. Wherefore it is universally right for all men, that all their inclinations should be directed according to reason.

Whether the Natural Law Can Be Changed?

Objection 1: It would seem that the natural law can be changed. Because on Ecclus. 17:9, "He gave them instructions, and the law of life," the gloss says: "He wished the law of the letter to be written, in order to correct the law of nature." But that which is corrected is changed. Therefore the natural law can be changed.

Objection 2: Further, the slaying of the innocent, adultery, and theft are against the natural law. But we find these things changed by God: as when God commanded Abraham to slay his innocent son (Gen. 22:2); and when he ordered the Jews to borrow and purloin the vessels of the Egyptians (Ex. 12:35); and when He commanded Osee to take to himself "a wife of fornications" (Osee 1:2). Therefore the natural law can be changed.

Objection 3: Further, Isidore says (Etym. 5:4) that "the possession of all things in common, and universal freedom, are matters of natural law." But these things are seen to be changed by human laws. Therefore it seems that the natural law is subject to change.

On the contrary, It is said in the Decretals (Dist. v): "The natural law dates from the creation of the rational creature. It does not vary according to time, but remains unchangeable."

I answer that, A change in the natural law may be understood in two ways. First, by way of addition. In this sense nothing hinders the natural law from being changed: since many things for the benefit of human life have been added over and above the natural law, both by the Divine law and by human laws.

Secondly, a change in the natural law may be understood by way of subtraction, so that what previously was according to the natural law, ceases to be so. In this sense, the natural law is altogether unchangeable in its first principles: but in its secondary principles, which are certain detailed proximate conclusions drawn from the first principles, the natural law is not changed so that what it prescribes be not right in most cases. But it may be changed in some particular cases of rare occurrence, through some special causes hindering the observance of such precepts.

Reply to Objection 1: The written law is said to be given for the correction of the natural law, either because it supplies what was wanting to the natural law; or because the natural law was perverted in the hearts of some men, as to certain matters, so that they esteemed those things good which are naturally evil; which perversion stood in need of correction.

Reply to Objection 2: All men alike, both guilty and innocent, die the death of nature: which death of nature is inflicted by the power of God on account of original sin, according to 1 Kgs. 2:6: "The Lord killeth and maketh alive." Consequently, by the command of God, death can be inflicted on any man, guilty or innocent, without any injustice whatever. In like manner adultery is intercourse with another's wife; who is allotted to him by the law emanating from God. Consequently intercourse with any woman, by the command of God, is neither adultery nor fornication. The same applies to theft, which is the taking of another's property. For whatever is taken by the command of God, to Whom all things belong, is not taken against the will of its owner, whereas it is in this that theft consists. Nor is it only in human things, that whatever is commanded by God is right; but also in natural things, whatever is done by God, is, in some way, natural.

Reply to Objection 3: A thing is said to belong to the natural law in two ways. First, because nature inclines thereto: e.g. that one should not do harm to another. Secondly, because nature did not bring in the contrary: thus we might say that for man to be naked is of the natural law, because nature did not give him clothes, but art invented them. In this sense, "the possession of all things in common and universal freedom" are said to be of the natural law, because, to wit, the distinction of possessions and slavery were not brought in by nature, but devised by human reason for the benefit of human life. Accordingly the law of nature was not changed in this respect, except by addition.

Whether the Law of Nature Can Be Abolished from the Heart of Man?

Objection 1: It would seem that the natural law can be abolished from the heart of man. Because on Rm. 2:14, "When the Gentiles who have not the law," etc. a gloss says that "the law of righteousness, which sin had blotted out, is graven on the heart of man when he is restored by grace." But the law of righteousness is the law of nature. Therefore the law of nature can be blotted out.

Objection 2: Further, the law of grace is more efficacious than the law of nature. But the law of grace is blotted out by sin. Much more therefore can the law of nature be blotted out.

Objection 3: Further, that which is established by law is made just. But many things are enacted by men, which are contrary to the law of nature. Therefore the law of nature can be abolished from the heart of man.

On the contrary, Augustine says (Confessions ii): "Thy law is written in the hearts of men, which iniquity itself effaces not." But the law which is written in men's hearts is the natural law. Therefore the natural law cannot be blotted out.

I answer that there belong to the natural law, first, certain most general precepts, that are known to all; and secondly, certain secondary and more detailed precepts, which are, as it were, conclusions following closely from first principles. As to those general principles, the natural law, in the abstract, can nowise be blotted out from men's hearts. But it is blotted out in the case of a particular action, in so far as reason is hindered from applying the general principle to a particular point of practice, on account of concupiscence or some other passion. But as to the other, i.e. the secondary precepts, the natural law can be blotted out from the human heart, either by evil persuasions, just as in speculative matters errors occur in respect of necessary conclusions; or by vicious customs and corrupt habits, as among some men, theft, and even unnatural vices, as the Apostle states (Rm. i), were not esteemed sinful.

Reply to Objection 1: Sin blots out the law of nature in particular cases, not universally, except perchance in regard to the secondary precepts of the natural law, in the way stated above.

Reply to Objection 2: Although grace is more efficacious than nature, yet nature is more essential to man, and therefore more enduring.

Reply to Objection 3: This argument is true of the secondary precepts of the natural law, against which some legislators have framed certain enactments which are unjust.

Thomas Aquinas: Natural Law

1. Aquinas believes that acting in accordance with one's natural inclinations is virtuous and that acting contrary to those inclinations is vicious (i.e., exemplifies a vice). What sense of 'natural' is required in order to make these claims as plausible as they can be?
2. Aquinas says that the natural law is a "dictate of practical reason." What do you think he means by this?
3. Aquinas's version of natural law clearly depends on its having been authored by God. Can you think of a way to defend a version of natural law theory that does not depend on divine authorship?
4. Aquinas believes that the general principles of the natural law apply to all human beings at all times. Do you find this view of the fundamental moral principles appealing? Why or why not?
5. What can be said on behalf of Aquinas's claim that the first principles of morality are known by everyone?

8

Utilitarianism

John Stuart Mill

........................,,,,,,,,,,,,, ...

Though written over a hundred and fifty years ago in the form of a long pamphlet, Mill's *Utilitarianism* is the most influential presentation of the doctrine yet to appear. In this excerpt from its second chapter, Mill identifies the essential core of the moral theory, namely, its Greatest Happiness Principle: "actions are right in proportion as they tend to promote happiness, wrong as they tend to produce the reverse of happiness." Mill is keen to say that one's own happiness is no more important than another's—the utilitarian creed insists that a virtuous person will be concerned with the general happiness and align her own interests with those of the larger population to the extent possible.

The discussion here takes the form of replies to a series of objections; along the way, Mill takes the opportunity to identify positive attractions of the view. One objection is that utilitarianism demands too much of us by requiring that we always be motivated to promote the greater good. Mill replies by denying this and distinguishing between the standard of right action—the Greatest Happiness Principle—and the standard by which we assess people's motives and character. An act that yields only avoidable harm is wrong, even though the person who did it tried hard to do good. In such a case we need not blame the person, even though he acted immorally. Mill claims that only a small handful of people are in a position to do good on a large scale; as a

Mill, *Utilitarianism* (1861), ch. 2,

result, most of us would do best not to ordinarily have the Greatest Happiness Principle as our primary motivation.

Indeed, rather than always ask ourselves which of our options will produce the greatest happiness, Mill thinks that we should rely on a battery of familiar moral rules to guide our actions and in most cases don't even need to reflect much in order to know which of our actions is the right one. We will do more good by relying on these familiar rules (e.g., don't lie, don't kill others, keep your promises) than on frequent, direct calculations of utility. But these rules are themselves justified because following them usually leads to increases in happiness or decreases in unhappiness. Further, these rules will sometimes conflict; when they do, Mill touts as a significant advantage of utilitarianism that its Greatest Happiness Principle provides a principled basis for determining how to resolve such conflicts.

....

The creed which accepts as the foundation of morals, Utility, or the Greatest Happiness Principle, holds that actions are right in proportion as they tend to promote happiness, wrong as they tend to produce the reverse of happiness. By happiness is intended pleasure, and the absence of pain; by unhappiness, pain, and the privation of pleasure. To give a clear view of the moral standard set up by the theory, much more requires to be said; in particular, what things it includes in the ideas of pain and pleasure; and to what extent this is left an open question. But these supplementary explanations do not affect the theory of life on which this theory of morality is grounded—namely, that pleasure, and freedom from pain, are the only things desirable as ends; and that all desirable things (which are as numerous in the utilitarian as in any other scheme) are desirable either for the pleasure inherent in themselves, or as means to the promotion of pleasure and the prevention of pain. . . .

[T]he happiness which forms the utilitarian standard of what is right in conduct, is not the agent's own happiness, but that of all concerned. As between his own happiness and that of others, utilitarianism requires him to be as strictly impartial as a disinterested and benevolent spectator. In the golden rule of Jesus of Nazareth, we read the complete spirit of the ethics of utility. To do as you would be done by, and to love your neighbour as yourself, constitute the ideal perfection of utilitarian morality. As the means of making the nearest approach to this ideal, utility would enjoin, first, that laws and social arrangements should place the happiness, or (as speaking practically it may be called) the interest, of every individual, as nearly as possible in harmony with the interest of the whole; and secondly, that education and opinion, which have so vast a power over human character, should so use that power as to establish in the mind of every individual an indissoluble association between his own happiness and the good of the whole; especially between his own happiness and the practice of such modes of conduct, negative and positive, as regard for the universal happiness prescribes; so that not only may he be unable to conceive the possibility of happiness to himself, consistently with conduct opposed to the general good, but also that a direct impulse to promote the general good may be in every individual one of the habitual motives of action, and the sentiments connected therewith may fill a large and prominent place in every human being's sentient existence. If the impugners of the utilitarian morality represented it to their own minds in this, its true character, I know not what recommendation possessed by any other morality they could possibly affirm to be wanting to it; what more beautiful or more exalted developments of human nature any other ethical system can be supposed to foster, or what springs of action, not accessible to the utilitarian, such systems rely on for giving effect to their mandates.

The objectors to utilitarianism cannot always be charged with representing it in a discreditable light. On the contrary, those among them who entertain anything like a just idea of its disinterested character, sometimes find fault with its standard as being too high for humanity. They say it is exacting too much to require that people shall always act from the inducement of promoting the general interests of society. But this is to mistake the very meaning of a standard of morals, and confound the rule of action with the motive of it. It is the business of ethics to tell us what are our duties, or by what test we may know them; but no system of ethics requires that the sole motive of all we do shall be a feeling of duty; on the contrary, ninety-nine hundredths of all our actions are done from other motives, and rightly so done, if the rule of duty does not condemn them. It is the more unjust to utilitarianism that this particular misapprehension should be made a ground of objection to it, inasmuch as utilitarian moralists have gone beyond almost all others in affirming that the motive has nothing to do with the morality of the action, though much with the worth of the agent. He who saves a fellow creature from drowning does what is morally right, whether his motive be duty, or the hope of being paid for his trouble; he who betrays the friend that trusts him, is guilty of a crime, even if his object be to serve another friend to whom he is under greater obligations.

But to speak only of actions done from the motive of duty, and in direct obedience to principle: it is a misapprehension of the utilitarian mode of thought, to conceive it as implying that people should fix their minds upon so wide a generality as the world, or society at large. The great majority of good actions are intended not for the benefit of the world, but for that of individuals, of which the good of the world is made up; and the thoughts of the most virtuous man need not on these occasions travel beyond the particular persons concerned, except so far as is necessary to assure himself that in benefiting them he is not violating the rights, that is, the legitimate and authorised expectations, of any one else. The multiplication of happiness is, according to the utilitarian ethics, the object of virtue: the occasions on which any person (except one in a thousand) has it in his power to do this on an extended scale, in other words to be a public benefactor, are but exceptional; and on these occasions alone is he called on to consider public utility; in every other case, private utility, the interest or happiness of some few persons, is all he has to attend to. Those alone the influence of whose actions extends to society in general, need concern themselves habitually about so large an object. In the case of abstinences indeed—of things which people forbear to do from moral considerations, though the consequences in the particular case might be beneficial—it would be unworthy of an intelligent agent not to be consciously aware that the action is of a class which, if practised generally, would be generally injurious, and that this is the ground of the obligation to abstain from it. The amount of regard for the public interest implied in this recognition is no greater than is demanded by every system of morals, for they all enjoin to abstain from whatever is manifestly pernicious to society.

The same considerations dispose of another reproach against the doctrine of utility, founded on a still grosser misconception of the purpose of a standard of morality, and of the very meaning of the words right and wrong. It is often affirmed that utilitarianism renders men cold and unsympathising; that it chills their moral feelings towards individuals; that it makes them regard only the dry and hard consideration of the consequences of actions, not taking into their moral estimate the qualities from which those actions emanate. If the assertion means that they do not allow their judgment respecting the rightness or wrongness of an action to be influenced by their opinion of the qualities of the person who does it, this is a complaint not against utilitarianism, but against having any standard of morality at all; for certainly no known ethical standard decides an action to be good or bad because it is done by a good or a bad man, still less because done by an amiable, a brave, or a benevolent man, or the contrary. These considerations are relevant, not to the estimation of actions, but of persons; and there is nothing in the utilitarian theory inconsistent with the fact that there are other things which interest us in persons besides the rightness and wrongness of their actions. The Stoics, indeed, with the paradoxical misuse of language which was part of their system, and by which they strove to raise themselves above all concern about anything but virtue, were fond of saying that he who has that has everything; that he, and only he, is rich, is beautiful, is a king. But no claim of this description is made for the virtuous man by the utilitarian doctrine. Utilitarians are quite aware that there are other desirable possessions and qualities besides virtue, and are perfectly willing to allow to all of them their full worth. They are also aware that a right action does not necessarily indicate a virtuous character, and that actions which are blamable, often proceed from qualities entitled to praise. When this is apparent in any particular case, it modifies their estimation, not certainly of the act, but of the agent. I grant that they are, notwithstanding, of opinion, that in the long run the best proof of a good character is good actions; and resolutely refuse to consider any mental disposition as good, of which the predominant tendency is to produce bad conduct. This makes them unpopular with many people; but it is an unpopularity which they must share with every one who regards the distinction between right and wrong in a serious light; and the reproach is not one which a conscientious utilitarian need be anxious to repel.

If no more be meant by the objection than that many utilitarians look on the morality of actions, as measured by the utilitarian standard, with too exclusive a regard, and do not lay sufficient stress upon the other beauties of character which go towards making a human being lovable or admirable, this may be admitted. Utilitarians who have cultivated their moral feelings, but not their sympathies nor their artistic perceptions, do fall into this mistake; and so do all other moralists under the same conditions. What can be said in excuse for other moralists is equally available for them, namely, that, if there is to be any error, it is better that it should be on that side. As a matter of fact, we may affirm that among utilitarians as among adherents of other systems, there is every imaginable degree of rigidity and of laxity in the application of their standard: some are even puritanically rigorous, while others are as indulgent as can possibly be desired by sinner or by sentimentalist. But on the whole, a doctrine which brings prominently forward the interest that mankind have in the repression and prevention of conduct which violates the moral law, is likely to be inferior to no other in turning the sanctions of opinion against such violations. It is true, the question, What does violate the moral law? is one on which those who recognise different standards of morality are likely now and then to differ. But difference of opinion on moral questions was not first introduced into the world by utilitarianism, while that doctrine does supply, if not always an easy, at all events a tangible and intelligible mode of deciding such differences.

It may not be superfluous to notice a few more of the common misapprehensions of utilitarian ethics. . . . We not uncommonly hear the doctrine of utility inveighed against as a godless doctrine. If it be necessary to say anything at all against so mere an assumption, we may say that the question depends upon what idea we have formed of the moral character of the Deity. If it be a true belief that God desires, above all things, the happiness of his creatures, and that this was his purpose in their creation, utility is not only not a godless doctrine, but more profoundly religious than any other. If it be meant that utilitarianism does not recognise the revealed will of God as the supreme law of morals, I answer, that a utilitarian who believes in the perfect goodness and wisdom of God, necessarily believes that whatever God has thought fit to reveal on the subject of morals, must fulfil the requirements of utility in a supreme degree. But others besides utilitarians have been of opinion that the Christian revelation was intended, and is fitted, to inform the hearts and minds of mankind with a spirit which should enable them to find for themselves what is right, and incline them to do it when found, rather than to tell them, except in a very general way, what it is; and that we need a doctrine of ethics, carefully followed out, to interpret to us the will of God. Whether this opinion is correct or not, it is superfluous here to discuss; since whatever aid religion, either natural or revealed, can afford to ethical investigation, is as open to the utilitarian moralist as to any other. He can use it as the testimony of God to the usefulness or hurtfulness of any given course of action, by as good a right as others can use it for the indication of a transcendental law, having no connection with usefulness or with happiness.

Again, Utility is often summarily stigmatised as an immoral doctrine by giving it the name of Expediency, and taking advantage of the popular use of that term to contrast it with Principle. But the Expedient, in the sense in which it is opposed to the Right, generally means that which is expedient for the particular interest of the agent himself; as when a minister sacrifices the interests of his country to keep himself in place. When it means anything better than this, it means that which is expedient for some immediate object, some temporary purpose, but which violates a rule whose observance is expedient in a much higher degree. The Expedient, in this sense, instead of being the same thing with the useful, is a branch of the hurtful. Thus, it would often be expedient, for the purpose of getting over some momentary embarrassment, or attaining some object immediately useful to ourselves or others, to tell a lie. But inasmuch as the cultivation in ourselves of a sensitive feeling on the subject of veracity, is one of the most useful, and the enfeeblement of that feeling one of the most hurtful, things to which our conduct can be instrumental; and inasmuch as any, even unintentional, deviation from truth, does that much towards weakening the trustworthiness of human assertion, which is not only the principal support of all present social well-being, but the insufficiency of which does more than any one thing that can be named to keep back civilisation, virtue, everything on which human happiness on the largest scale depends; we feel that the violation, for a present advantage, of a rule of such transcendant expediency, is not expedient, and that he who, for the sake of a convenience to himself or to some other individual, does what depends on him to deprive mankind of the good, and inflict upon them the evil, involved in the greater or less reliance which they can place in each other's word, acts the part of one of their worst enemies. Yet that even this rule, sacred as it is, admits of possible exceptions, is acknowledged by all moralists; the chief of which is when the withholding of some fact (as of information from a malefactor, or of bad news from a person dangerously ill) would save an individual (especially an individual other than oneself) from great and unmerited evil, and when the withholding can only be effected by denial. But in order that the exception may not extend itself beyond the need, and may have the least possible effect in weakening reliance on veracity, it ought to be recognised, and, if possible, its limits defined; and if the principle of utility is good for anything, it must be good for weighing these conflicting utilities against one another, and marking out the region within which one or the other preponderates.

Again, defenders of utility often find themselves called upon to reply to such objections as this—that there is not time, previous to action, for calculating and weighing the effects of any line of conduct on the general happiness. This is exactly as if any one were to say that it is impossible to guide our conduct by Christianity, because there is not time, on every occasion on which anything has to be done, to read through the Old and New Testaments. The answer to the objection is, that there has been ample time, namely, the whole past duration of the human species. During all that time, mankind have been learning by experience the tendencies of actions; on which experience all the prudence, as well as all the morality of life, are dependent. People talk as if the commencement of this course of experience had hitherto been put off, and as if, at the moment when some man feels tempted to meddle with the property or life of another, he had to begin considering for the first time whether murder and theft are injurious to human happiness. Even then I do not think that he would find the question very puzzling; but, at all events, the matter is now done to his hand.

It is truly a whimsical supposition that, if mankind were agreed in considering utility to be the test of morality, they would remain without any agreement as to what is useful, and would take no measures for having their notions on the subject taught to the young, and enforced by law and opinion. There is no difficulty in proving any ethical standard whatever to work ill, if we suppose universal idiocy to be conjoined with it; but on any hypothesis short of that, mankind must by this time have acquired positive beliefs as to the effects of some actions on their happiness; and the beliefs which have thus come down are the rules of morality for the multitude, and for the philosopher until he has succeeded in finding better. That philosophers might easily do this, even now, on many subjects; that the received code of ethics is by no means of divine right; and that mankind have still much to learn as to the effects of actions on the general happiness, I admit, or rather, earnestly maintain. The corollaries from the principle of utility, like the precepts of every practical art, admit of indefinite improvement, and, in a progressive state of the human mind, their improvement is perpetually going on.

But to consider the rules of morality as improvable, is one thing; to pass over the intermediate generalisations entirely, and endeavour to test each individual action directly by the first principle, is another. It is a strange notion that the acknowledgment of a first principle is inconsistent with the admission of secondary ones. To inform a traveller respecting the place of his ultimate destination, is not to forbid the use of landmarks and direction-posts on the way. The proposition that happiness is the end and aim of morality, does not mean that no road ought to be laid down to that goal, or that persons going thither should not be advised to take one direction rather than another. Men really ought to leave off talking a kind of nonsense on this subject, which they would neither talk nor listen to on other matters of practical concernment. Nobody argues that the art of navigation is not founded on astronomy, because sailors cannot wait to calculate the Nautical Almanack. Being rational creatures, they go to sea with it ready calculated; and all rational creatures go out upon the sea of life with their minds made up on the common questions of right and wrong, as well as on many of the far more difficult questions of wise and foolish. And this, as long as foresight is a human quality, it is to be presumed they will continue to do. Whatever we adopt as the fundamental principle of morality, we require subordinate principles to apply it by; the impossibility of doing without them, being common to all systems, can afford no argument against any one in particular; but gravely to argue as if no such secondary principles could be had, and as if mankind had remained till now, and always must remain, without drawing any general conclusions from the experience of human life, is as high a pitch, I think, as absurdity has ever reached in philosophical controversy.

The remainder of the stock arguments against utilitarianism mostly consist in laying to its charge the common infirmities of human nature, and the general difficulties which embarrass conscientious persons in shaping their course through life. We are told that a utilitarian will be apt to make his own particular case an exception to moral rules, and, when under temptation, will see a utility in the breach of a rule, greater than he will see in its observance. But is utility the only creed which is able to furnish us with excuses for evil doing, and means of cheating our own conscience? They are afforded in abundance by all doctrines which recognise as a fact in morals the existence of conflicting considerations; which all doctrines do, that have been believed by sane persons. It is not the fault of any creed, but of the complicated nature of human affairs, that rules of conduct cannot be so framed as to require no exceptions, and that hardly any kind of action can safely be laid down as either always obligatory or always condemnable. There is no ethical creed which does not temper the rigidity of its laws, by giving a certain latitude, under the moral responsibility of the agent, for accommodation to peculiarities of circumstances; and under every creed, at the opening thus made, self-deception and dishonest casuistry get in. There exists no moral system under which there do not arise unequivocal cases of conflicting obligation. These are the real difficulties, the knotty points both in the theory of ethics, and in the conscientious guidance of personal conduct. They are overcome practically, with greater or with less success, according to the intellect and virtue of the individual; but it can hardly be pretended that any one will be the less qualified for dealing with them, from possessing an ultimate standard to which conflicting rights and duties can be referred. If utility is the ultimate source of moral obligations, utility may be invoked to decide between them when their demands are incompatible. Though the application of the standard may be difficult, it is better than none at all: while in other systems, the moral laws all claiming independent authority, there is no common umpire entitled to interfere between them; their claims to precedence one over another rest on little better than sophistry, and unless determined, as they generally are, by the unacknowledged influence of considerations of utility, afford a free scope for the action of personal desires and partialities. We must remember that only in these cases of conflict between secondary principles is it requisite that first principles should be appealed to. There is no case of moral obligation in which some secondary principle is not involved; and if only one, there can seldom be any real doubt which one it is, in the mind of any person by whom the principle itself is recognised.

John Stuart Mill: Utilitarianism

1. Utilitarianism claims that my happiness is no more important than yours. This kind of impartiality seems highly appealing. But this also appears to prohibit us from giving ourselves or our family priority over the interests of others. Is this appearance correct? Can utilitarianism allow for partiality to oneself or one's family?
2. Mill claims that virtuous people will rarely have the Greatest Happiness Principle in mind when acting. Why does he say this? Is his claim plausible? And is it what a utilitarian really should say?
3. Mill believes that the motives that prompt an action are irrelevant to that action's morality. Is this claim plausible? Why or why not?
4. Many critics of utilitarianism claim that the theory requires that we sacrifice too much for others. Mill counters by saying that only a very few people are in a position to do much good for many others; as a result, most of us are not required to focus our efforts in ways that require significant self-sacrifice. Is Mill's view too rosy, especially now that we are so easily able to learn of how unfortunate others are and are easily able to give to charities that can help improve the lives of those who are less well off than we are?
5. Some have argued that utilitarianism is a godless doctrine. What is Mill's reply to this? Do you find it plausible?

9

The Good Will and the Categorical Imperative

Immanuel Kant

....

Immanuel Kant (1724–1804) was the greatest German philosopher who ever lived. In this excerpt from his *Groundwork of the Metaphysics of Morals*, Kant introduces two key elements of his moral philosophy. According to Kant, the first of these, the *good will*, is the only thing possessed of unconditional value: it is valuable in its own right, in every possible circumstance. The good will is the steady commitment to do our duty for its own sake. Our actions possess moral worth if, but only if, they are prompted by the good will.

The second important element is the *categorical imperative*, Kant's term for a requirement of reason that applies to us regardless of what we care about. Moral requirements are categorical imperatives—we must, for instance, sometimes give help to others in need, even if we don't want to, and even if such help gets us nothing that we care about. Kant believed that moral action is rational action. Each of us has a compelling reason to obey morality, even when doing so only frustrates our deepest desires.

Kant here sets out two tests for morally acceptable action. The first says that actions are morally acceptable only when the principles that inspire them can be acted on by everyone consistently. The second requires us to treat humanity always as an end in itself, and

From *Groundwork of the Metaphysics of Morals*, trans. Mary Gregor (1998). Reprinted with the permission of Cambridge University Press.

never as a mere means. Kant realizes that such formulations are somewhat abstract, and so here offers us a number of illustrations that are meant to help us understand and apply them.

....

The Good Will

It is impossible to think of anything at all in the world, or indeed even beyond it, that could be considered good without limitation except a **good will**. Understanding, wit, judgment and the like, whatever such *talents* of mind may be called, or courage, resolution, and perseverance in one's plans, as qualities of *temperament*, are undoubtedly good and desirable for many purposes, but they can also be extremely evil and harmful if the will which is to make use of these gifts of nature, and whose distinctive constitution is therefore called *character*, is not good. It is the same with *gifts of fortune*. Power, riches, honor, even health and that complete well-being and satisfaction with one's condition called *happiness*, produce boldness and thereby often arrogance as well unless a good will is present which corrects the influence of these on the mind and, in so doing, also corrects the whole principle of action and brings it into conformity with universal ends—not to mention that an impartial rational spectator can take no delight in seeing the uninterrupted prosperity of a being graced with no feature of a pure and good will, so that a good will seems to constitute the indispensable condition even of worthiness to be happy.

Some qualities are even conducive to this good will itself and can make its work much easier; despite this, however, they have no inner unconditional worth but always presuppose a good will, which limits the esteem one otherwise rightly has for them and does not permit their being taken as absolutely good. Moderation in affects and passions, self-control, and calm reflection are not only good for all sorts of purposes but even seem to constitute a part of the *inner* worth of a person; but they lack much that would be required to declare them good without limitation (however unconditionally they were praised by the ancients); for, without the basic principles of a good will they can become extremely evil, and the coolness of a scoundrel makes him not only far more dangerous but also immediately more abominable in our eyes than we would have taken him to be without it.

A good will is not good because of what it effects or accomplishes, because of its fitness to attain some proposed end, but only because of its volition, that is, it is good in itself and, regarded for itself, is to be valued incomparably higher than all that could merely be brought about by it in favor of some inclination and indeed, if you will, of the sum of all inclinations. Even if, by a special disfavor of fortune or by the niggardly provision of a stepmotherly nature, this will should wholly lack the capacity to carry out its purpose—if with its greatest efforts it should yet achieve nothing and only the good will were left (not, of course, as a mere wish but as the summoning of all means insofar as they are in our control)—then, like a jewel, it would still shine by itself, as something that has its full worth in itself. Usefulness or fruitlessness can neither add anything to this worth nor take anything away from it. Its usefulness would be, as it were, only the setting to enable us to handle it more conveniently in ordinary commerce or to attract to it the attention of those who are not yet expert enough, but not to recommend it to experts or to determine its worth. . . .

We have, then, to explicate the concept of a will that is to be esteemed in itself and that is good apart from any further purpose, as it already dwells in natural sound understanding and needs not so much to be taught as only to be clarified—this concept that always takes first place in estimating the total worth of our actions and constitutes the condition of all the rest. In order to do so, we shall set before ourselves the concept of **duty**, which contains that of a good will though under certain subjective limitations and hindrances, which, however, far from concealing it and making it unrecognizable, rather bring it out by contrast and make it shine forth all the more brightly.

I here pass over all actions that are already recognized as contrary to duty, even though they may be useful for this or that purpose; for in their case the question whether they might have been done *from duty* never arises, since they even conflict with it. I also set aside actions that are really in conformity with duty but to which human beings have *no inclination* immediately and which they still perform because they are impelled to do so through another inclination. For in this case it is easy to distinguish whether an action in conformity with duty is done *from duty* or from a self seeking purpose. It is much more difficult to note this distinction when an action conforms with duty and the subject has, besides, an *immediate* inclination to it. For example, it certainly conforms with duty that a shopkeeper not overcharge an inexperienced customer, and where there is a good deal of trade a prudent merchant does not overcharge but keeps a fixed general price for everyone, so that a child can buy from him as well as everyone else. People are thus served *honestly*; but this is not nearly enough for us to believe that the merchant acted in this way from duty and basic principles of honesty; his advantage required it; it cannot be assumed here that he had, besides, an immediate inclination toward his customers, so as from love, as it were, to give no one preference over another in the matter of price. Thus the action was done neither from duty nor from immediate inclination but merely for purposes of self-interest.

On the other hand, to preserve one's life is a duty, and besides everyone has an immediate inclination to do so. But on this account the often anxious care that most people take of it still has no inner worth and their maxim has no moral content. They look after their lives *in conformity with duty* but not *from duty*. On the other hand, if adversity and hopeless grief have quite taken away the taste for life; if an unfortunate man, strong of soul and more indignant about his fate than despondent or dejected, wishes for death and yet preserves his life without loving it, not from inclination or fear but from duty, then his maxim has moral content.

To be beneficent where one can is a duty, and besides there are many souls so sympathetically attuned that, without any other motive of vanity or self-interest they find an inner satisfaction in spreading joy around them and can take delight in the satisfaction of others so far as it is their own work. But I assert that in such a case an action of this kind, however it may conform with duty and however amiable it may be, has nevertheless no true moral worth but is on the same footing with other inclinations, for example, the inclination to honor, which, if it fortunately lights upon what is in fact in the common interest and in conformity with duty and hence honorable, deserves praise and encouragement but not esteem; for the maxim lacks moral content, namely that of doing such actions not from inclination but *from duty*. Suppose, then, that the mind of this philanthropist were overclouded by his own grief, which extinguished all sympathy with the fate of others, and that while he still had the means to benefit others in distress their troubles did not move him because he had enough to do with his own; and suppose that now, when no longer incited to it by any inclination, he nevertheless tears himself out of this deadly insensibility and does the action without any inclination, simply from duty; then the action first has its genuine moral worth.

Still further: if nature had put little sympathy in the heart of this or that man; if (in other respects an honest man) he is by temperament cold and indifferent to the sufferings of others, perhaps because he himself is provided with the special gift of patience and endurance toward his own sufferings and presupposes the same in every other or even requires it; if nature had not properly fashioned such a man (who would in truth not be its worst product) for a philanthropist, would he not still find within himself a source from which to give himself a far higher worth than what a mere good-natured temperament might have? By all means! It is just then that the worth of character comes out, which is moral and incomparably the highest, namely that he is beneficent not from inclination but from duty. . . .

Thus the moral worth of an action does not lie in the effect expected from it and so too does not lie in any principle of action that needs to borrow its motive from this expected effect. For, all these effects (agreeableness of one's condition, indeed even promotion of others' happiness) could have been also brought about by other causes, so that there would have been no need, for this, of the will of a rational being, in which, however, the highest and unconditional good alone can be found. Hence nothing other than the *representation of the law* in itself, *which can of course occur only in a rational being*, insofar as it and not the hoped-for effect is the determining ground of the will, can constitute the preeminent good we call moral, which is already present in the person himself who acts in accordance with this representation and need not wait upon the effect of his action.

But what kind of law can that be, the representation of which must determine the will, even without regard for the effect expected from it, in order for the will to be called good absolutely and without limitation? Since I have deprived the will of every impulse that could arise for it from obeying some law, nothing is left but the conformity of actions as such with universal law, which alone is to serve the will as its principle, that is, *I ought never to act except in such a way that I could also will that my maxim should become a universal law*. Here mere conformity to law as such, without having as its basis some law determined for certain actions, is what serves the will as its principle, and must so serve it, if duty is not to be everywhere an empty delusion and a chimerical concept. Common human reason also agrees completely with this in its practical appraisals and always has this principle before its eyes. Let the question be, for example: may I, when hard pressed, make a promise with the intention not to keep it? Here I easily distinguish two significations the question can have: whether it is prudent or whether it is in conformity with duty to make a false promise. The first can undoubtedly often be the case. I see very well that it is not enough to get out of a present difficulty by means of this subterfuge but that I must reflect carefully whether this lie may later give rise to much greater inconvenience for me than that from which I now extricate myself; and since, with all my supposed *cunning*, the results cannot be so easily foreseen but that once confidence in me is lost this could be far more prejudicial to me than all the troubles I now think to avoid, I must reflect whether the matter might be handled *more prudently* by proceeding on a general maxim and making it a habit to promise nothing except with the intention of keeping it. But it is soon clear to me that such a maxim will still be based only on results feared. To be truthful from duty, however, is something entirely different from being truthful from anxiety about detrimental results, since in the first case the concept of the action in itself already contains a law for me while in the second I must first look about elsewhere to see what effects on me might be combined with it. For, if I deviate from the principle of duty this is quite certainly evil; but if I am unfaithful to my maxim of prudence this can sometimes be very advantageous to me, although it is certainly safer to abide by it. However, to inform myself in the shortest and yet infallible way about the answer to this problem, whether a lying promise is in conformity with duty, I ask myself: would I indeed be content that my maxim (to get myself out of difficulties by a false promise) should hold as a universal law (for myself as well as for others)? and could I indeed say to myself that every one may make a false promise when he finds himself in a difficulty he can get out of in no other way? Then I soon become aware that I could indeed will the lie, but by no means a universal law to lie; for in accordance with such a law there would properly be no promises at all, since it would be futile to avow my will with regard to my future actions to others who would not believe this avowal or, if they rashly did so, would pay me back in like coin; and thus my maxim, as soon as it were made a universal law, would have to destroy itself.

I do not, therefore, need any penetrating acuteness to see what I have to do in order that my volition be morally good. Inexperienced in the course of the world, incapable of being prepared for whatever might come to pass in it, I ask myself only: can you also will that your maxim become a universal law? If not, then it is to be repudiated, and that not because of a disadvantage to you or even to others forthcoming from it but because it cannot fit as a principle into a possible giving of universal law, for which lawgiving reason, however, forces from me immediate respect. Although I do not yet see what this respect is based upon (this the philosopher may investigate), I at least understand this much: that it is an estimation of a worth that far outweighs any worth of what is recommended by inclination, and that the necessity of my action from *pure* respect for the practical law is what constitutes duty, to which every other motive must give way because it is the condition of a will good *in itself,* the worth of which surpasses all else. . . .

The Categorical Imperative

Now, all imperatives command either *hypothetically* or *categorically.* The former represent the practical necessity of a possible action as a means to achieving something else that one wills (or that it is at least possible for one to will). The categorical imperative would be that which represented an action as objectively necessary of itself, without reference to another end.

Since every practical law represents a possible action as good and thus as necessary for a subject practically determinable by reason, all imperatives are formulae for the determination of action that is necessary in accordance with the principle of a will which is good in some way. Now, if the action would be good merely as a means *to something else* the imperative is *hypothetical*; if the action is represented as *in itself* good, hence as necessary in a will in itself conforming to reason, as its principle, *then it is categorical.* . . .

There is one imperative that, without being based upon and having as its condition any other purpose to be attained by certain conduct, commands this conduct immediately. This imperative is **categorical**. It has to do not with the matter of the action and what is to result from it, but with the form and the principle from which the action itself follows; and the essential good in the action consists in the disposition, let the result be what it may. This imperative may be called the imperative **of morality.** . . .

When I think of a *hypothetical* imperative in general I do not know beforehand what it will contain; I do not know this until I am given the condition. But when I think of a *categorical* imperative I know at once what it contains. For, since the imperative contains, beyond the law, only the necessity that the maxim[1] be in conformity with this law, while the law contains no condition to which it would be limited, nothing is left with which the maxim of action is to conform but the universality of a law as such; and this conformity alone is what the imperative properly represents as necessary.

There is, therefore, only a single categorical imperative and it is this: *act only in accordance with that maxim through which you can at the same time will that it become a universal law.*

Now, if all imperatives of duty can be derived from this single imperative as from their principle, then, even though we leave it undecided whether what is called duty is not as such an empty concept, we shall at least be able to show what we think by it and what the concept wants to say.

Since the universality of law in accordance with which effects take place constitutes what is properly called *nature* in the most general sense (as regards its form)—that is, the existence of things insofar as it is determined in accordance with universal laws—the universal imperative of duty can also go as follows: *act as if the maxim of your action were to become by your will a* **universal law of nature.**

We shall now enumerate a few duties in accordance with the usual division of them into duties to ourselves and to other human beings and into perfect and imperfect duties.[2]

(1) Someone feels sick of life because of a series of troubles that has grown to the point of despair, but is still so far in possession of his reason that he can ask himself whether it would not be contrary to his duty to himself to take his own life. Now he inquires whether the maxim of his action could indeed become a universal law of nature. His maxim, however, is: from self-love I make it my principle to shorten my life when its longer duration threatens more troubles than it promises agreeableness. The only further question is whether this principle of self-love could become a universal law of nature. It is then seen at once that a nature

---

1. A maxim is the subjective principle of acting, and must be distinguished from the objective principle, namely the practical law. The former contains the practical rule determined by reason conformably with the conditions of the subject (often his ignorance or also his inclinations), and is therefore the principle in accordance with which the subject acts; but the law is the objective principle valid for every rational being, and the principle in accordance with which he ought to act, i.e., an imperative.

2. I understand here by a perfect duty one that admits no exception in favor of inclination.

whose law it would be to destroy life itself by means of the same feeling whose destination is to impel toward the furtherance of life would contradict itself and would therefore not subsist as nature; thus that maxim could not possibly be a law of nature and, accordingly, altogether opposes the supreme principle of all duty.

(2) Another finds himself urged by need to borrow money. He well knows that he will not be able to repay it but sees also that nothing will be lent him unless he promises firmly to repay it within a determinate time. He would like to make such a promise, but he still has enough conscience to ask himself: is it not forbidden and contrary to duty to help oneself out of need in such a way? Supposing that he still decided to do so, his maxim of action would go as follows: when I believe myself to be in need of money I shall borrow money and promise to repay it, even though I know that this will never happen. Now this principle of self-love or personal advantage is perhaps quite consistent with my whole future welfare, but the question now is whether it is right. I therefore turn the demand of self-love into a universal law and put the question as follows: how would it be if my maxim became a universal law? I then see at once that it could never hold as a universal law of nature and be consistent with itself, but must necessarily contradict itself. For, the universality of a law that everyone, when he believes himself to be in need, could promise whatever he pleases with the intention of not keeping it would make the promise and the end one might have in it itself impossible, since no one would believe what was promised him but would laugh at all such expressions as vain pretenses.

(3) A third finds in himself a talent that by means of some cultivation could make him a human being useful for all sorts of purposes. However, he finds himself in comfortable circumstances and prefers to give himself up to pleasure than to trouble himself with enlarging and improving his fortunate natural predispositions. But he still asks himself whether his maxim of neglecting his natural gifts, besides being consistent with his propensity to amusement, is also consistent with what one calls duty. He now sees that a nature could indeed always subsist with such a universal law, although (as with the South Sea Islanders) the human being should let his talents rust and be concerned with devoting his life merely to idleness, amusement, procreation—in a word, to enjoyment; only he cannot possibly will that this become a universal law or be put in us as such by means of natural instinct. For, as a rational being he necessarily wills that all the capacities in him be developed, since they serve him and are given to him for all sorts of possible purposes.

(4) Yet a *fourth*, for whom things are going well while he sees that others (whom he could very well help) have to contend with great hardships, thinks: what is it to me? let each be as happy as heaven wills or as he can make himself; I shall take nothing from him nor even envy him; only I do not care to contribute anything to his welfare or to his assistance in need! Now, if such a way of thinking were to become a universal law the human race could admittedly very well subsist, no doubt even better than when everyone prates about sympathy and benevolence and even exerts himself to practice them occasionally, but on the other hand also cheats where he can, sells the right of human beings or otherwise infringes upon it. But although it is possible that a universal law of nature could very well subsist in accordance with such a maxim, it is still impossible to will that such a principle hold everywhere as a law of nature. For, a will that decided this would conflict with itself, since many cases could occur in which one would need the love and sympathy of others and in which, by such a law of nature arisen from his own will, he would rob himself of all hope of the assistance he wishes for himself. . . .

If we now attend to ourselves in any transgression of a duty, we find that we do not really will that our maxim should become a universal law, since that is impossible for us, but that the opposite of our maxim should instead remain a universal law, only we take the liberty of making an *exception* to it for ourselves (or just for this once) to the advantage of our inclination. Consequently, if we weighed all cases from one and the same point of view, namely that of reason, we would find a contradiction in our own will, namely that a certain principle be objectively necessary as a universal law and yet subjectively not hold universally but allow exceptions. . . .

Suppose there were something the *existence of which in itself* has an absolute worth, something which as *an end in itself* could be a ground of determinate laws; then in it, and in it alone, would lie the ground of a possible categorical imperative, that is, of a practical law.

Now I say that the human being and in general every rational being *exists* as an end in itself, *not merely as a means* to be used by this or that will at its discretion; instead he must in all his actions, whether directed to himself or also to other rational beings, always be regarded *at the same time as an end*. All objects of the inclinations have only a conditional worth; for, if there were not inclinations and the needs based on them, their object would be without worth. But the inclinations themselves, as sources of needs, are so far from having an absolute worth, so as to make one wish to have them, that it must instead be the universal wish of every rational being to be altogether free from them. Thus the worth of any object *to be acquired* by our action is always conditional. Beings the existence of which rests not on our will but on nature, if they are beings without reason, still have only a relative worth, as means, and are therefore called *things*, whereas rational beings are called *persons* because their nature already marks them out as an end in itself, that is, as something that may not be used merely as a means, and hence so far limits all choice (and is an object of respect). These, therefore, are not merely subjective ends, the existence of which as an effect of our action has a worth *for us*, but rather *objective ends*, that is, beings the existence of which is in itself an end, and indeed one such that no other end, to which they would serve *merely* as means, can be put in its place, since without it nothing of *absolute worth* would be found anywhere; but if all worth were conditional and therefore contingent, then no supreme practical principle for reason could be found anywhere.

If, then, there is to be a supreme practical principle and, with respect to the human will, a categorical imperative, it must be one such that, from the representation of what is necessarily an end for everyone because it is an *end in itself*, it constitutes an *objective* principle of the will and thus can serve as a universal practical law. The ground of this principle is: *rational nature exists as an end in itself*. The human being necessarily represents his own existence in this way; so far it is thus a *subjective* principle of human actions. But every other rational being also represents his existence in this way consequent on just the same rational ground that also holds for me; thus it is at the same time an *objective* principle from which, as a supreme practical ground, it must be possible to derive all laws of the will. The practical imperative will therefore be the following: *So act that you use humanity, whether in your own person or in the person of any other, always at the same time as an end, never merely as a means.* We shall see whether this can be carried out.

To keep to the preceding examples:

First, as regards the concept of necessary duty to oneself, someone who has suicide in mind will ask himself whether his action can be consistent with the idea of humanity *as an end in itself*. If he destroys himself in order to escape from a trying condition he makes use of a person *merely as a means* to maintain a tolerable condition up to the end of life. A human being, however, is not a thing and hence not something that can be used *merely* as a means, but must in all his actions always be regarded as an end in itself. I cannot, therefore, dispose of a human being in my own person by maiming, damaging or killing him. (I must here pass over a closer determination of this principle that would prevent any misinterpretation, e.g., as to having limbs amputated in order to preserve myself, or putting my life in danger in order to preserve my life, and so forth; that belongs to morals proper.)

Second, as regards necessary duty to others or duty owed them, he who has it in mind to make a false promise to others sees at once that he wants to make use of another human being *merely as a means*, without the other at the same time containing in himself the end. For, he whom I want to use for my purposes by such a promise cannot possibly agree to my way of behaving toward him, and so himself contain the end of this action. This conflict with the principle of other human beings is seen more distinctly if examples of assaults on the freedom and property of others are brought forward. For then it is obvious that he who transgresses the rights of human beings intends to make use of the person of others merely as means, without taking into consideration that, as rational beings, they are always to be valued at the same time as ends, that is, only as beings who must also be able to contain in themselves the end of the very same action.

Third, with respect to contingent (meritorious) duty to oneself, it is not enough that the action does not conflict with humanity in our person as an end in itself; it must also *harmonize with it*. Now there are in humanity predispositions to greater perfection, which belong to the end of nature with respect to humanity in our subject; to neglect these might admittedly be consistent with the *preservation* of humanity as an end in itself but not with the *furtherance* of this end.

Fourth, concerning meritorious duty to others, the natural end that all human beings have is their own happiness. Now, humanity might indeed subsist if no one contributed to the happiness of others but yet did not intentionally withdraw anything from it; but there is still only a negative and not a positive agreement with *humanity as an end in itself* unless everyone also tries, as far as he can, to further the ends of others. For, the ends of a subject who is an end in itself must as far as possible be also *my* ends, if that representation is to have its *full* effect in me. . . .

Immanuel Kant: The Good Will and the Categorical Imperative

1. Kant claims that a good will is the only thing that can be considered "good without limitation." What does he mean by this? Do you find this claim plausible?

2. Unlike hedonists, Kant believes that happiness is not always good. What reasons does he give for thinking this? Do you agree with him?

3. What is the difference between doing something "in conformity with duty" and doing something "from duty"? Is Kant correct in saying that only actions done *from duty* have moral worth?

4. Kant claims to have discovered a *categorical imperative*, a moral requirement that we have reason to follow regardless of what we happen to desire. Can people have reasons for action that are completely independent of their desires?

5. According to Kant, it is morally permissible to act on a particular principle (or "maxim") only if "you can at the same time will that it become a universal law." Do you think this is a good test of whether an action is morally permissible? Can you think of any immoral actions that would pass this test, or any morally permissible actions that would fail it?

6. Kant later gives another formulation of the categorical imperative: "So act that you use humanity, whether in your own person or in the person of any other, always at the same time as an end, never merely as a means." What does it mean to treat someone as an end? Are we always morally required to treat humans in this way?

10

Leviathan

Thomas Hobbes

Thomas Hobbes (1588–1679) was the most brilliant of the modern social contract theorists. His theory, important in both ethics and political philosophy, views the basic moral rules of society as ones that rational people would adopt in order to protect their own interests. Without obedience to such rules, the situation deteriorates into a "war of all against all, in which the life of man is solitary, poor, nasty, brutish and short."

Hobbes was an ethical egoist—someone who thinks that our fundamental duty is to look after our own interests—as well as a social contract theorist. Many commentators have found a tension in this combination. See for yourself whether Hobbes succeeded in justifying the basic moral rules by reference to self-interest.

Among the many interesting features in this excerpt from Hobbes's classic *Leviathan* is his discussion of the fool. The fool is someone who allows that breaking one's promises is unjust, but who thinks that it may sometimes be rational to do so anyway. Hobbes resists this idea. He wants to show that it is always rational to do one's duty—to live by the laws of cooperation that would be accepted by free and rational people. His overall view is motivated by the thought that moral duties must provide each of us with excellent reasons to obey them, and that these reasons must ultimately stem from self-interest. As a result, Hobbes's discussion casts fascinating light on the perennial question of why we should be moral.

Of the Natural Condition of Mankind as Concerning Their Felicity and Misery

Nature hath made men so equal in the faculties of body and mind as that, though there be found one man sometimes manifestly stronger in body or of quicker mind than another, yet when all is reckoned together the difference between man and man is not so considerable as that one man can thereupon claim to himself any benefit to which another may not pretend as well as he. For as to the strength of body, the weakest has strength enough to kill the strongest, either by secret machination or by confederacy with others that are in the same danger with himself.

And as to the faculties of the mind, setting aside the arts grounded upon words, and especially that skill of proceeding upon general and infallible rules, called science, which very few have and but in few things, as being not a native faculty born with us, nor attained, as prudence, while we look after somewhat else, I find yet a greater equality amongst men than that of strength. For prudence is but experience, which equal time equally bestows on all men in those things they equally apply themselves unto. That which may perhaps make such equality incredible is but a vain conceit of one's own wisdom, which almost all men think they have in a greater degree than the vulgar; that is, than all men but themselves, and a few others, whom by fame, or for concurring with themselves, they approve. For such is the nature of men that howsoever they may acknowledge many others to be more witty, or more eloquent or more learned, yet they will hardly believe there be many so wise as themselves; for they see their own wit at hand, and other men's at a distance. But this proveth rather that men are in that point equal, than unequal. For there is not ordinarily a greater sign of the equal distribution of anything than that every man is contented with his share.

From this equality of ability ariseth equality of hope in the attaining of our ends. And therefore if any two men desire the same thing, which nevertheless they cannot both enjoy, they become enemies; and in the way to their end (which is principally their own conservation, and sometimes their delectation only) endeavour to destroy or subdue one another. And from hence it comes to pass that where an invader hath no more to fear than another man's single power, if one plant, sow, build, or possess a convenient seat, others may probably be expected to come prepared with forces united to dispossess and deprive him, not only of the fruit of his labour, but also of his life or liberty. And the invader again is in the like danger of another.

And from this diffidence of one another, there is no way for any man to secure himself so reasonable as anticipation; that is, by force, or wiles, to master the persons of all men he can so long till he see no other power great enough to endanger him: and this is no more than his own conservation requireth, and is generally allowed. Also, because there be some that, taking pleasure in contemplating their own power in the acts of conquest, which they pursue farther than their security requires, if others, that otherwise would be glad to be at ease within modest bounds, should not by invasion increase their power, they would not be able, long time, by standing only on their defence, to subsist. And by consequence, such augmentation of dominion over men being necessary to a man's conservation, it ought to be allowed him.

Again, men have no pleasure (but on the contrary a great deal of grief) in keeping company where there is no power able to overawe them all. For every man looketh that his companion should value him at the same rate he sets upon himself, and upon all signs of contempt or undervaluing naturally endeavours, as far as he dares (which amongst them that have no common power to keep them in quiet is far enough to make them destroy each other), to extort a greater value from his contemners, by damage; and from others, by the example.

So that in the nature of man, we find three principal causes of quarrel. First, competition; secondly, diffidence; thirdly, glory.

The first maketh men invade for gain; the second, for safety; and the third, for reputation. The first use violence, to make themselves masters of other men's persons, wives, children, and cattle; the second, to defend them; the third, for trifles, as a word, a smile, a different opinion, and any other sign of undervalue, either direct in their persons or by reflection in their kindred, their friends, their nation, their profession, or their name.

Hereby it is manifest that during the time men live without a common power to keep them all in awe, they are in that condition which is called war; and such a war as is of every man against every man. For war consisteth not in battle only, or the act of fighting, but in a tract of time, wherein the will to contend by battle is sufficiently known: and therefore the notion of time is to be considered in the nature of war, as it is in the nature of weather. For as the nature of foul weather lieth not in a shower or two of rain, but in an inclination thereto of many days together: so the nature of war consisteth not in actual fighting, but in the known disposition thereto during all the time there is no assurance to the contrary. All other time is peace.

Whatsoever therefore is consequent to a time of war, where every man is enemy to every man, the same consequent to the time wherein men live without other security than what their own strength and their own invention shall furnish them withal. In such condition there is no place for industry, because the fruit thereof is uncertain: and consequently no culture of the earth; no navigation, nor use of the commodities that may be imported by sea; no commodious building; no instruments of moving and removing such things as require much force; no knowledge of the face of the earth; no account of time; no arts; no letters; no society; and which is worst of all, continual fear, and danger of violent death; and the life of man, solitary, poor, nasty, brutish, and short.

It may seem strange to some man that has not well weighed these things that Nature should thus dissociate and render men apt to invade and destroy one another: and he may therefore, not trusting to this inference, made from the passions, desire perhaps to have the same confirmed by experience. Let him therefore consider with himself: when taking a journey, he arms himself and seeks to go well accompanied; when going to sleep, he locks his doors; when even in his house he locks his chests; and this when he knows there be laws and public officers, armed, to revenge all injuries shall be done him; what opinion he has of his fellow subjects, when he rides armed; of his fellow citizens, when he locks his doors; and of his children, and servants, when he locks his chests. Does he not there as much accuse mankind by his actions as I do by my words? But neither of us accuse man's nature in it. The desires, and other passions of man, are in themselves no sin. No more are the actions that proceed from those passions till they know a law that forbids them; which till laws be made they cannot know, nor can any law be made till they have agreed upon the person that shall make it.

It may peradventure be thought there was never such a time nor condition of war as this; and I believe it was never generally so, over all the world: but there are many places where they live so now. For the savage people in many places of America, except the government of small families, the concord whereof dependeth on natural lust, have no government at all, and live at this day in that brutish manner, as I said before. Howsoever, it may be perceived what manner of life there would be, where there were no common power to fear, by the manner of life which men that have formerly lived under a peaceful government use to degenerate into a civil war.

But though there had never been any time wherein particular men were in a condition of war one against another, yet in all times kings and persons of sovereign authority, because of their independency, are in continual jealousies, and in the state and posture of gladiators, having their weapons pointing, and their eyes fixed on one another; that is, their forts, garrisons, and guns upon the frontiers of their kingdoms, and continual spies upon their neighbours, which is a posture of war. But because they uphold thereby the industry of their subjects, there does not follow from it that misery which accompanies the liberty of particular men.

To this war of every man against every man, this also is consequent; that nothing can be unjust. The notions of right and wrong, justice and injustice, have there no place. Where there is no common power, there is no law; where no law, no injustice. Force and fraud are in war the two cardinal virtues. Justice and injustice are none of the faculties neither of the body nor mind. If they were, they might be in a man that were alone in the world, as well as his senses and passions. They are qualities that relate to men in society, not in solitude. It is consequent also to the same condition that there be no propriety, no dominion, no mine and thine distinct; but only that to be every man's that he can get, and for so long as he can keep it. And thus much for the ill condition which man by mere nature is actually placed in; though with a possibility to come out of it, consisting partly in the passions, partly in his reason.

The passions that incline men to peace are: fear of death; desire of such things as are necessary to commodious living; and a hope by their industry to obtain them. And reason suggesteth convenient articles of peace upon which men may be drawn to agreement. These articles are they which otherwise are called the laws of nature, whereof I shall speak more particularly in the two following chapters.

Of the First and Second Natural Laws, and of Contracts

The right of nature, which writers commonly call *jus naturale*, is the liberty each man hath to use his own power as he will himself for the preservation of his own nature; that is to say, of his own life; and consequently, of doing anything which, in his own judgement and reason, he shall conceive to be the aptest means thereunto.

By liberty is understood, according to the proper signification of the word, the absence of external impediments; which impediments may oft take away part of a man's power to do what he would, but cannot hinder him from using the power left him according as his judgement and reason shall dictate to him.

A law of nature, *lex naturalis*, is a precept, or general rule, found out by reason, by which a man is forbidden to do that which is destructive of his life, or taketh away the means of preserving the same, and to omit that by which he thinketh it may be best preserved.

And because the condition of man . . . is a condition of war of every one against every one, in which case every one is governed by his own reason, and there is nothing he can make use of that may not be a help unto him in preserving his life against his enemies; it followeth that in such a condition every man has a right to every thing, even to one another's body. And therefore, as long as this natural right of every man to every thing endureth, there can be no security to any man, how strong or wise soever he be, of living out the time which nature ordinarily alloweth men to live. And consequently it is a precept, or general rule of reason: that every man ought to endeavour peace, as far as he has hope of obtaining it; and when he cannot obtain it, that he may seek and use all helps and advantages of war. The first branch of which rule containeth the first and fundamental law of nature, which is: to seek peace and follow it. The second, the sum of the right of nature, which is: by all means we can to defend ourselves.

From this fundamental law of nature, by which men are commanded to endeavour peace, is derived this second law: that a man be willing, when others are so too, as far forth as for peace and defence of himself he shall think it necessary, to lay down this right to all things; and be contented with so much liberty against other men as he would allow other men against himself. For as long as every man holdeth this right, of doing anything he liketh; so long are all men in the condition of war. But if other men will not lay down their right, as well as he, then there is no reason for anyone to divest himself of his: for that were to expose himself to prey, which no man is bound to, rather than to dispose himself to peace. This is that law of the gospel: Whatsoever you require that others should do to you, that do ye to them.

Whensoever a man transferreth his right, or renounceth it, it is either in consideration of some right reciprocally transferred to himself, or for some other good he hopeth for thereby. For it is a voluntary act: and of the voluntary acts of every man, the object is some good to himself. And therefore there be some rights which no man can be understood by any words, or other signs, to have abandoned or transferred. As first a man cannot lay down the right of resisting them that assault him by force to take away his life, because he cannot be understood to aim thereby at any good to himself. The same may be said of wounds, and chains, and imprisonment, both because there is no benefit consequent to such patience, as there is to the patience of suffering another to be wounded or imprisoned, as also because a man cannot tell when he seeth men proceed against him by violence whether they intend his death or not. And lastly the motive and end for which this renouncing and transferring of right is introduced is nothing else but the security of a man's person, in his life, and in the means of so preserving life as not to be weary of it. And therefore if a man by words, or other signs, seem to despoil himself of the end for which those signs were intended, he is not to be understood as if he meant it, or that it was his will, but that he was ignorant of how such words and actions were to be interpreted.

The mutual transferring of right is that which men call contract. . . .

Signs of contract are either express or by inference. Express are words spoken with understanding of what they signify: and such words are either of the time present or past; as, I give, I grant, I have given, I have granted, I will that this be yours: or of the future; as, I will give, I will grant, which words of the future are called promise.

Signs by inference are sometimes the consequence of words; sometimes the consequence of silence; sometimes the consequence of actions; sometimes the consequence of forbearing an action: and generally a sign by inference, of any contract, is whatsoever sufficiently argues the will of the contractor.

Words alone, if they be of the time to come, and contain a bare promise, are an insufficient sign of a free gift and therefore not obligatory. For if they be of the time to come, as, tomorrow I will give, they are a sign I have not given yet, and consequently that my right is not transferred, but remaineth till I transfer it by some other act. . . .

If a covenant be made wherein neither of the parties perform presently, but trust one another, in the condition of mere nature (which is a condition of war of every man against every man) upon any reasonable suspicion, it is void: but if there be a common power set over them both, with right and force sufficient to compel performance, it is not void. For he that performeth first has no assurance the other will perform after, because the bonds of words are too weak to bridle men's ambition, avarice, anger, and other passions, without the fear of some coercive power; which in the condition of mere nature, where all men are equal, and judges of the justness of their own fears, cannot possibly be supposed. And therefore he which performeth first does but betray himself to his enemy, contrary to the right he can never abandon of defending his life and means of living.

But in a civil estate, where there is a power set up to constrain those that would otherwise violate their faith, that fear is no more reasonable; and for that cause, he which by the covenant is to perform first is obliged so to do.

Of Other Laws of Nature

From that law of nature by which we are obliged to transfer to another such rights as, being retained, hinder the peace of mankind, there followeth a third; which is this: that men perform their covenants made; without which covenants are in vain, and but empty words; and the right of all men to all things remaining, we are still in the condition of war.

And in this law of nature consisteth the fountain and original of justice. For where no covenant hath preceded, there hath no right been transferred, and every man has right to everything and consequently, no action can be unjust. But when a covenant is made, then to break it is unjust and the definition of injustice is no other than the not performance of covenant. And whatsoever is not unjust is just.

But because covenants of mutual trust, where there is a fear of not performance on either part (as hath been said in the former chapter), are invalid, though the original of justice be the making of covenants, yet injustice actually there can be none till the cause of such fear be taken away; which, while men are in the natural condition of war, cannot be done. Therefore before the names of just and unjust can have place, there must be some coercive power to compel men equally to the performance of their covenants, by the terror of some punishment greater than the benefit they expect by the breach of their covenant, and to make good that propriety which by mutual contract men acquire in recompense of the universal right they abandon: and such power there is none before the erection of a Commonwealth. And this is also to be gathered out of the ordinary definition of justice in the Schools, for they say that justice is the constant will of giving to every man his own. And therefore where there is no own, that is, no propriety, there is no injustice; and where there is no coercive power erected, that is, where there is no Commonwealth, there is no propriety, all men having right to all things: therefore where there is no Commonwealth, there nothing is unjust. So that the nature of justice consisteth in keeping of valid covenants, but the validity of covenants begins not but with the constitution of a civil power sufficient to compel men to keep them: and then it is also that propriety begins.

The fool hath said in his heart, there is no such thing as justice, and sometimes also with his tongue, seriously alleging that every man's conservation and contentment being committed to his own care, there could be no reason why every man might not do what he thought conduced thereunto: and therefore also to make, or not make; keep, or not keep, covenants was not against reason when it conduced to one's benefit. He does not therein deny that there be covenants; and that they are sometimes broken, sometimes kept; and that such breach of them may be called injustice, and the observance of them justice: but he questioneth whether injustice, taking away the fear of God (for the same fool hath said in his heart there is no God), may not sometimes stand with that reason which dictateth to every man his own good; and particularly then, when it conduceth to such a benefit as shall put a man in a condition to neglect not only the dispraise and revilings, but also the power of other men. The kingdom of God is gotten by violence: but what if it could be gotten by unjust violence? Were it against reason so to get it, when it is impossible to receive hurt by it? And if it be not against reason, it is not against justice: or else justice is not to be approved for good. From such reasoning as this, successful wickedness hath obtained the name of virtue: and some that in all other things have disallowed the violation of faith, yet have allowed it when it is for the getting of a kingdom. And the heathen that believed that Saturn was deposed by his son Jupiter believed nevertheless the same Jupiter to be the avenger of injustice, somewhat like to a piece of law in Coke's Commentaries on Littleton; where he says if the right heir of the crown be attainted of treason, yet the crown shall descend to him, and *eo instante* the attainder be void: from which instances a man will be very prone to infer that when the heir apparent of a kingdom shall kill him that is in possession, though his father, you may call it injustice, or by what other name you will; yet it can never be against reason, seeing all the voluntary actions of men tend to the benefit of themselves; and those actions are most reasonable that conduce most to their ends. This specious reasoning is nevertheless false.

For the question is not of promises mutual, where there is no security of performance on either side, as when there is no civil power erected over the parties promising; for such promises are no covenants: but either where one of the parties has performed already, or where there is a power to make him perform, there is the question whether it be against reason; that is, against the benefit of the other to perform, or not. And I say it is not against reason. For the manifestation whereof we are to consider; first, that when a man doth a thing, which notwithstanding anything can be foreseen and reckoned on tendeth to his own destruction, howsoever some accident, which he could not expect, arriving may turn it to his benefit; yet such events do not make it reasonably or wisely done. Secondly, that in a condition of war, wherein every man to every man, for want of a common power to keep them all in awe, is an enemy, there is no man can hope by his own strength, or wit, to defend himself from destruction without the help of confederates; where every one expects the same defence by the confederation that any one else does: and therefore he which declares he thinks it reason to deceive those that help him can in reason expect no other means of safety than what can be had from his own single power. He, therefore, that breaketh his covenant, and consequently declareth that he thinks he may with reason do so, cannot be received into any society that unite themselves for peace and defence but by the error of them that receive him; nor when he is received be retained in it without seeing the danger of their error; which errors a man cannot reasonably reckon upon as the means of his security: and therefore if he be left, or cast out of society, he perisheth; and if he live in society, it is by the errors of other men, which he could not foresee nor reckon upon, and consequently against the reason of his preservation; and so, as all men that contribute not to his destruction forbear him only out of ignorance of what is good for themselves.

As for the instance of gaining the secure and perpetual felicity of heaven by any way, it is frivolous; there being but one way imaginable, and that is not breaking, but keeping of covenant.

And for the other instance of attaining sovereignty by rebellion; it is manifest that, though the event follow, yet because it cannot reasonably be expected, but rather the contrary, and because by gaining it so, others are taught to gain the same in like manner, the attempt thereof is against reason. Justice therefore, that is to say, keeping of covenant, is a rule of reason by which we are forbidden to do anything destructive to our life, and consequently a law of nature.

Thomas Hobbes: Leviathan

1. At the beginning of the selection, Hobbes argues that all humans are fundamentally equal. In what ways does Hobbes claim that we are equal? Do you agree with him?

2. Hobbes claims that without a government to enforce law and order, we would find ourselves in a "war . . . of every man against every man." What reasons does he give for believing this? Do you think he is right?

3. According to Hobbes, if there were no governments to establish laws, nothing would be just or unjust. Does this seem plausible? Would some actions be unjust even if there were no authority around to punish those who committed them?
4. Hobbes says, "Of the voluntary acts of every man, the object is some good to himself." Is Hobbes correct in thinking that self-interest is what motivates every voluntary action?
5. Hobbes claims that it is always unjust to violate our covenants (or contracts), provided that there is a government with the power to enforce them. He also claims that any action that does not violate a covenant is just. Can you think of any counterexamples to either of these claims?
6. The "fool" claims that it is rational to unjustly break one's covenants in cases where doing so promotes one's self-interest. How does Hobbes respond to this claim? Do you find Hobbes's replies convincing?

11

What Makes Right Acts Right?

W. D. Ross

W. D. Ross (1877–1971) developed a truly novel moral theory in his book *The Right and the Good* (1930), from which this selection is taken. He found something attractive about both utilitarianism and Kantianism, the major theoretical competitors of his day, but found that each had a major flaw. Ross applauded utilitarianism's emphasis on benevolence, but rejected its idea that maximizing goodness is our sole moral duty. Kantianism, on the other hand, preserved the attractive idea that justice is independently important, but erred in claiming that the moral rules that specify such duties are absolute (never to be broken).

Ross created a kind of compromise theory, in which he identified a number of distinct grounds for moral duty (benevolence, fidelity to promises, truth-telling, avoiding harm, gratitude, justice, reparation). Each of these is a basis for a *prima facie duty*—an always-important reason that generates an "all-things-considered" duty, provided that no other reason or set of reasons is weightier in the situation. In other words, it is sometimes acceptable to violate a prima facie duty.

But when? We cannot offer a permanent ranking of these prima facie duties. Sometimes, for instance, it is right to promote the general happiness even if we have to commit an injustice to do so. But at other times, the balance should be struck in the opposite way.

W. D. Ross, "What Makes Right Acts Right?" from *The Right and the Good* (1930), pp. 16–32. By permission of Oxford University Press, Inc.

Ross insisted that these prima facie duties are self-evident. Here he offers some very influential (and controversial) remarks on how we can gain moral knowledge, both of the moral principles themselves and of the correct verdicts to reach in particular cases.

....

The point at issue is that to which we now pass, viz. whether there is any general character which makes right acts right, and if so, what it is. Among the main historical attempts to state a single characteristic of all right actions which is the foundation of their rightness are those made by egoism and utilitarianism. But I do not propose to discuss these, not because the subject is unimportant, but because it has been dealt with so often and so well already, and because there has come to be so much agreement among moral philosophers that neither of these theories is satisfactory. A much more attractive theory has been put forward by Professor Moore: that what makes actions right is that they are productive of more *good* than could have been produced by any other action open to the agent.

This theory is in fact the culmination of all the attempts to base rightness on productivity of some sort of result. The first form this attempt takes is the attempt to base rightness on conduciveness to the advantage or pleasure of the agent. This theory comes to grief over the fact, which stares us in the face, that a great part of duty consists in an observance of the rights and a furtherance of the interests of others, whatever the cost to ourselves may be. Plato and others may be right in holding that a regard for the rights of others never in the long run involves a loss of happiness for the agent, that 'the just life profits a man.' But this, even if true, is irrelevant to the rightness of the act. As soon as a man does an action *because* he thinks he will promote his own interests thereby, he is acting not from a sense of its rightness but from self-interest.

To the egoistic theory hedonistic utilitarianism supplies a much-needed amendment. It points out correctly that the fact that a certain pleasure will be enjoyed by the agent is no reason why he ought to bring it into being rather than an equal or greater pleasure to be enjoyed by another, though, human nature being what it is, it makes it not unlikely that he will try to bring it into being. But hedonistic utilitarianism in its turn needs a correction. On reflection it seems clear that pleasure is not the only thing in life that we think good in itself, that for instance we think the possession of a good character, or an intelligent understanding of the world, as good or better. A great advance is made by the substitution of 'productive of the greatest good' for 'productive of the greatest pleasure.'

Not only is this theory more attractive than hedonistic utilitarianism, but its logical relation to that theory is such that the latter could not be true unless it were true, while it might be true though hedonistic utilitarianism were not. It is in fact one of the logical bases of hedonistic utilitarianism. For the view that what produces the maximum pleasure is right has for its bases the views (1) that what produces the maximum good is right, and (2) that pleasure is the only thing good in itself. If, therefore, it can be shown that productivity of the maximum good is not what makes all right actions right, we shall *a fortiori* have refuted hedonistic utilitarianism.

When a plain man fulfils a promise because he thinks he ought to do so, it seems clear that he does so with no thought of its total consequences, still less with any opinion that these are likely to be the best possible. He thinks in fact much more of the past than of the future. What makes him think it right to act in a certain way is the fact that he has promised to do so—that and, usually, nothing more. That his act will produce the best possible consequences is not his reason for calling it right. What lends colour to the theory we are examining, then, is not the actions (which form probably a great majority of our actions) in which some such reflection as 'I have promised' is the only reason we give ourselves for thinking a certain action right, but the exceptional cases in which the consequences of fulfilling a promise (for instance) would be so disastrous to others that we judge it right not to do so. It must of course be admitted that such cases exist. If I have promised to meet a friend at a particular time for some trivial purpose, I should certainly think myself justified in breaking my engagement if by doing so I could prevent a serious accident or bring relief to the victims of one. And the supporters of the view we are examining hold that my thinking so is due to my thinking that I shall bring more good into existence by the one action than by the other. A different account may, however, be given of the matter, an account which will, I believe, show itself to be the true one. It may be said that besides the duty of fulfilling promises I have and recognize a duty of relieving distress, and that when I think it right to do the latter at the cost of not doing the former, it is not because I think I shall produce more good thereby but because I think it the duty which is in the circumstances more of a duty. This account surely corresponds much more closely with what we really think in such a situation.

If, so far as I can see, I could bring equal amounts of good into being by fulfilling my promise and by helping some one to whom I had made no promise, I should not hesitate to regard the former as my duty. Yet on the view that what is right is right because it is productive of the most good I should not so regard it.

There are two theories, each in its way simple, that offer a solution of such cases of conscience. One is the view of Kant, that there are certain duties of perfect obligation, such as those of fulfilling promises, of paying debts, of telling the truth, which admit of no exception whatever in favour of duties of imperfect obligation, such as that of relieving distress. The other is the view of, for instance, Professor Moore and Dr. Rashdall, that there is only the duty of producing good, and that all 'conflicts of duties' should be resolved by asking 'by which action will most good be produced?' But it is more important that our theory fit the facts than that it be simple, and the account we have given above corresponds (it seems to me) better than either of the simpler theories with what we really think, viz. that normally promise-keeping, for example, should come before benevolence, but that when and only when the good to be produced by the benevolent act is very great and the promise comparatively trivial, the act of benevolence becomes our duty.

In fact the theory of 'ideal utilitarianism,' if I may for brevity refer so to the theory of Professor Moore, seems to simplify unduly our relations to our fellows. It says, in effect, that the only morally significant relation in which my neighbours stand to me is that of being possible beneficiaries by my action. They do stand in this relation to me, and this relation is morally significant. But they may also stand to me in the relation of promisee to promiser, of creditor to debtor, of wife to husband, of child to parent, of friend to friend, of fellow countryman to fellow countryman, and the like; and each of these relations is the foundation of a *prima facie* duty, which is more or less incumbent on me according to the circumstances of the case. When I am in a situation, as perhaps I always am, in which more than one of these *prima facie* duties is incumbent on me, what I have to do is to study the situation as fully as I can until I form the considered opinion (it is never more) that in the circumstances one of them is more incumbent than any other; then I am bound to think that to do this *prima facie* duty is my duty *sans phrase* in the situation.

I suggest '*prima facie* duty' or 'conditional duty' as a brief way of referring to the characteristic (quite distinct from that of being a duty proper) which an act has, in virtue of being of a certain kind (e.g. the keeping of a promise), of being an act which would be a duty proper if it were not at the same time of another kind which is morally significant. Whether an act is a duty proper or actual duty depends on *all* the morally significant kinds it is an instance of.

The phrase '*prima facie* duty' must be apologized for, since (1) it suggests that what we are speaking of is a certain kind of duty, whereas it is in fact not a duty, but something related in a special way to duty. Strictly speaking, we want not a phrase in which duty is qualified by an adjective, but a separate noun. (2) '*Prima*' *facie* suggests that one is speaking only of an appearance which a moral situation presents at first sight, and which may turn out to be illusory; whereas what I am speaking of is an objective fact involved in the nature of the situation, or more strictly in an element of its nature, though not, as duty proper does, arising from its whole nature.

There is nothing arbitrary about these *prima facie* duties. Each rests on a definite circumstance which cannot seriously be held to be without moral significance. Of *prima facie* duties I suggest, without claiming completeness or finality for it, the following division.

1. Some duties rest on previous acts of my own. These duties seem to include two kinds.
   A. Those resting on a promise or what may fairly be called an implicit promise, such as the implicit undertaking not to tell lies which seems to be implied in the act of entering into conversation (at any rate by civilized men), or of writing books that purport to be history and not fiction. These may be called the duties of fidelity.
   B. Those resting on a previous wrongful act. These may be called the duties of reparation.
2. Some rest on previous acts of other men, i.e. services done by them to me. These may be loosely described as the duties of gratitude.
3. Some rest on the fact or possibility of a distribution of pleasure or happiness (or of the means thereto) which is not in accordance with the merit of the persons concerned; in such cases there arises a duty to upset or prevent such a distribution. These are the duties of justice.
4. Some rest on the mere fact that there are beings in the world whose condition we can make better in respect of virtue, or of intelligence, or of pleasure. These are the duties of beneficence.

5. Some rest on the fact that we can improve our own condition in respect of virtue or of intelligence. These are the duties of self-improvement.

6. I think that we should distinguish from (4) the duties that may be summed up under the title of 'not injuring others.' No doubt to injure others is incidentally to fail to do them good; but it seems to me clear that non-maleficence is apprehended as a duty distinct from that of beneficence, and as a duty of a more stringent character.

The essential defect of the 'ideal utilitarian' theory is that it ignores, or at least does not do full justice to, the highly personal character of duty. If the only duty is to produce the maximum of good, the question who is to have the good—whether it is myself, or my benefactor, or a person to whom I have made a promise to confer that good on him, or a mere fellow man to whom I stand in no such special relation—should make no difference to my having a duty to produce that good. But we are all in fact sure that it makes a vast difference.

If the objection be made, that this catalogue of the main types of duty is an unsystematic one resting on no logical principle, it may be replied, first, that it makes no claim to being ultimate. It is a *prima facie* classification of the duties which reflection on our moral convictions seems actually to reveal. And if these convictions are, as I would claim that they are, of the nature of knowledge, and if I have not misstated them, the list will be a list of authentic conditional duties, correct as far as it goes though not necessarily complete. The list of *goods* put forward by the rival theory is reached by exactly the same method—the only sound one in the circumstances—viz. that of direct reflection on what we really think. Loyalty to the facts is worth more than a symmetrical architectonic or a hastily reached simplicity. If further reflection discovers a perfect logical basis for this or for a better classification, so much the better.

It may, again, be objected that our theory that there are these various and often conflicting types of *prima facie* duty leaves us with no principle upon which to discern what is our actual duty in particular circumstances. But this objection is not one which the rival theory is in a position to bring forward. For when we have to choose between the production of two heterogeneous goods, say knowledge and pleasure, the 'ideal utilitarian' theory can only fall back on an opinion, for which no logical basis can be offered, that one of the goods is the greater; and this is no better than a similar opinion that one of two duties is the more urgent. And again, when we consider the infinite variety of the effects of our actions in the way of pleasure, it must surely be admitted that the claim which *hedonism* sometimes makes, that it offers a readily applicable criterion of right conduct, is quite illusory.

I am unwilling, however, to content myself with an *argumentum ad hominem*, and I would contend that in principle there is no reason to anticipate that every act that is our duty is so for one and the same reason. Why should two sets of circumstances, or one set of circumstances, not possess different characteristics, any one of which makes a certain act our *prima facie* duty? When I ask what it is that makes me in certain cases sure that I have a *prima facie* duty to do so and so, I find that it lies in the fact that I have made a promise; when I ask the same question in another case, I find the answer lies in the fact that I have done a wrong. And if on reflection I find (as I think I do) that neither of these reasons is reducible to the other, I must not on any *a priori* ground assume that such a reduction is possible.

It is necessary to say something by way of clearing up the relation between *prima facie* duties and the actual or absolute duty to do one particular act in particular circumstances. If, as almost all moralists except Kant are agreed, and as most plain men think, it is sometimes right to tell a lie or to break a promise, it must be maintained that there is a difference between *prima facie* duty and actual or absolute duty. When we think ourselves justified in breaking, and indeed morally obliged to break, a promise in order to relieve some one's distress, we do not for a moment cease to recognize a *prima facie* duty to keep our promise, and this leads us to feel, not indeed shame or repentance, but certainly compunction, for behaving as we do; we recognize, further, that it is our duty to make up somehow to the promisee for the breaking of the promise. We have to distinguish from the characteristic of being our duty that of tending to be our duty. Any act that we do contains various elements in virtue of which it falls under various categories. In virtue of being the breaking of a promise, for instance, it tends to be wrong; in virtue of being an instance of relieving distress it tends to be right.

Something should be said of the relation between our apprehension of the *prima facie* rightness of certain types of act and our mental attitude towards particular acts. It is proper to use the word 'apprehension' in the former case and not in the latter. That an act, *qua* fulfilling a promise, or *qua* effecting a just distribution of good, or *qua* returning services rendered, or *qua* promoting the good of others, or *qua* promoting the virtue or insight of the agent, is *prima facie* right, is self-evident; not in the sense that it is evident from the beginning of our lives, or as soon as we attend to the proposition for the first time, but in the sense that when we have reached sufficient mental maturity and have given sufficient attention to the proposition it is evident without any need of proof, or of evidence beyond itself. It is self-evident just as a mathematical axiom, or the validity of a form of inference, is evident. The moral order expressed in these propositions is just as much part of the fundamental nature of the universe (and, we may add, of any possible universe in which there were moral agents at all) as is the spatial or numerical structure expressed in the axioms of geometry or arithmetic. In our confidence that these propositions are true there is involved the same trust in our reason that is involved in our confidence in mathematics; and we should have no justification for trusting it in the latter sphere and distrusting it in the former. In both cases we are dealing with propositions that cannot be proved, but that just as certainly need no proof.

Our judgements about our actual duty in concrete situations have none of the certainty that attaches to our recognition of the general principles of duty. A statement is certain, i.e. is an expression of knowledge, only in one or other of two cases: when it is either self-evident, or a valid conclusion from self-evident premises. And our judgements about our particular duties have neither of these characters. (1) They are not self-evident. Where a possible act is seen to have two characteristics, in virtue of one of which it is *prima facie* right, and in virtue of the other *prima facie* wrong, we are (I think) well aware that we are not certain whether we ought or ought not to do it; that whether we do it or not, we are taking a moral risk. We come in the long run, after consideration, to think one duty more pressing than the other, but we do not feel certain that it is so. And though we do not always recognize that a possible act has two such characteristics, and though there may be cases in which it has not, we are never certain that any particular possible act has not, and therefore never certain that it is right, nor certain that it is wrong. For, to go no further in the analysis, it is enough to point out that any particular act will in all probability in the course of time contribute to the bringing about of good or of evil for many human beings, and thus have a *prima facie* rightness or wrongness of which we know nothing. (2) Again, our judgements about our particular duties are not logical conclusions from self-evident premisses. The only possible premisses would be the general principles stating their *prima facie* rightness or wrongness *qua* having the different characteristics they do have; and even if we could (as we cannot) apprehend the extent to which an act will tend on the one hand, for example, to bring about advantages for our benefactors, and on the other hand to bring about disadvantages for fellow men who are not our benefactors, there is no principle by which we can draw the conclusion that it is on the whole right or on the whole wrong. In this respect the judgement as to the rightness of a particular act is just like the judgement as to the beauty of a particular natural object or work of art. A poem is, for instance, in respect of certain qualities beautiful and in respect of certain others not beautiful; and our judgement as to the degree of beauty it possesses on the whole is never reached by logical reasoning from the apprehension of its particular beauties or particular defects. Both in this and in the moral case we have more or less probable opinions which are not logically justified conclusions from the general principles that are recognized as self-evident.

There is therefore much truth in the description of the right act as a fortunate act. If we cannot be certain that it is right, it is our good fortune if the act we do is the right act. This consideration does not, however, make the doing of our duty a mere matter of chance. There is a parallel here between the doing of duty and the doing of what will be to our personal advantage. We never *know* what act will in the long run be to our advantage. Yet it is certain that we are more likely in general to secure our advantage if we estimate to the best of our ability the probable tendencies of our actions in this respect, than if we act on caprice. And similarly we are more likely to do our duty if we reflect to the best of our ability on the *prima facie* rightness or wrongness of various possible acts in virtue of the characteristics we perceive them to have, than if we act without reflection. With this greater likelihood we must be content.

The general principles of duty are obviously not self-evident from the beginning of our lives. How do they come to be so? The answer is, that they come to be self-evident to us just as mathematical axioms do. We find by experience that this couple of matches and that couple make four matches, that this couple of balls on a wire and that couple make four balls: and by reflection on these and similar discoveries we come to see that it is of the nature of two and two to make four. In a precisely similar way, we see the *prima facie* rightness of an act which would be the fulfilment of a particular promise, and of another which would be the fulfilment of another promise, and when we have reached sufficient maturity to think in general terms, we apprehend *prima facie* rightness to belong to the nature of any fulfilment of promise. What comes first in time is the apprehension of the self-evident *prima facie* rightness of an individual act of a particular type. From this we come by reflection to apprehend the self-evident general principle of *prima facie* duty. From this, too, perhaps along with the apprehension of the self-evident *prima facie* rightness of the same act in virtue of its having another characteristic as well, and perhaps in spite of the apprehension of its *prima facie* wrongness in virtue of its having some third characteristic, we come to believe something not self-evident at all, but an object of probable opinion, viz. that this particular act is (not *prima facie* but) actually right.

In what has preceded, a good deal of use has been made of 'what we really think' about moral questions; a certain theory has been rejected because it does not agree with what we really think. It might be said that this is in principle wrong; that we should not be content to expound what our present moral consciousness tells us but should aim at a criticism of our existing moral consciousness in the light of theory. Now I do not doubt that the moral consciousness of men has in detail undergone a good deal of modification as regards the things we think right, at the hands of moral theory. But if we are told, for instance, that we should give up our view that there is a special obligatoriness attaching to the keeping of promises because it is self-evident that the only duty is to produce as much good as possible, we have to ask ourselves whether we really, when we reflect, are convinced that this is self-evident, and whether we really can get rid of our view that promise-keeping has a bindingness independent of productiveness of maximum good. In my own experience I find that I cannot, in spite of a very genuine attempt to do so; and I venture to think that most people will find the same.

I would maintain, in fact, that what we are apt to describe as 'what we think' about moral questions contains a considerable amount that we do not think but know, and that this forms the standard by reference to which the truth of any moral theory has to be tested, instead of having itself to be tested by reference to any theory. I hope that I have in what precedes indicated what in my view these elements of knowledge are that are involved in our ordinary moral consciousness.

It would be a mistake to found a natural science on 'what we really think', i.e. on what reasonably thoughtful and well-educated people think about the subjects of the science before they have studied them scientifically.

For such opinions are interpretations, and often misinterpretations, of sense-experience; and the man of science must appeal from these to sense-experience itself, which furnishes his real data. In ethics no such appeal is possible. We have no more direct way of access to the facts about rightness and goodness and about what things are right or good, than by thinking about them; the moral convictions of thoughtful and well-educated people are the data of ethics just as sense-perceptions are the data of a natural science. Just as some of the latter have to be rejected as illusory, so have some of the former; but as the latter are rejected only when they are in conflict with other more accurate sense-perceptions, the former are rejected only when they are in conflict with other convictions which stand better the test of reflection. The existing body of moral convictions of the best people is the cumulative product of the moral reflection of many generations, which has developed an extremely delicate power of appreciation of moral distinctions; and this the theorist cannot afford to treat with anything other than the greatest respect. The verdicts of the moral consciousness of the best people are the foundation on which he must build; though he must first compare them with one another and eliminate any contradictions they may contain.

W. D. Ross: What Makes Right Acts Right?

1. Ross begins by considering the view that the right action is the one that is "productive of more *good* than could have been produced by any other action open to the agent." What objections does he offer to this view? Do you think they are good ones?

2. Ross also considers Kant's view, according to which there are certain moral rules that must be followed without exception. What does Ross think is wrong with this theory? Do you agree with his criticism?

3. What does Ross mean by "*prima facie* duties," and how do these differ from "duty proper"? How does he think we should use our knowledge of prima facie duties to determine what our duty is in a particular situation?

4. How does Ross think we come to know prima facie duties? Do you find his view plausible?

5. What reasons does Ross give for his claim that we can never be certain about what the right thing to do is in a particular situation? Do you agree with him about this?

6. Ross claims that "the moral convictions of thoughtful and well-educated people are the data of ethics just as sense-perceptions are the data of a natural science." Is beginning with our own moral convictions the best way of doing ethics, or do you think there is a better way?

12

Nicomachean Ethics

Aristotle

....

Aristotle (384–322 BCE) was perhaps the greatest philosopher who ever lived. He worked in a variety of philosophical areas (logic, metaphysics, philosophy of mind, epistemology, ethics, rhetoric), and in each field produced work that exerted an influence across many centuries.

His seminal work in moral philosophy is *Nicomachean Ethics*, believed to be a set of carefully recorded lecture notes taken down by Aristotle's students. In this excerpt, from book 2 of the *Nicomachean Ethics*, Aristotle discusses the nature of virtue, its role in a good human life, and its relation to happiness and to "the golden mean." Aristotle's thoughts on the virtues have served as the basis of almost every version of virtue ethics developed in Western philosophy over the past two millennia.

....

Aristotle, from *Nicomachean Ethics* (1998), trans. W. D. Ross, pp. 28–47. By permission of Oxford University Press.

Moral Virtue

Moral Virtue, How Produced, in What Medium and in What Manner Exhibited

Moral virtue, like the arts, is acquired by repetition of the corresponding acts

VIRTUE, . . . being of two kinds, intellectual and moral, intellectual virtue in the main owes both its birth and its growth to teaching (for which reason it requires experience and time), while moral virtue comes about as a result of habit, whence also its name (ἠθική) is one that is formed by a slight variation from the word 'ἔθος (habit). From this it is also plain that none of the moral virtues arises in us by nature; for nothing that exists by nature can form a habit contrary to its nature. For instance the stone which by nature moves downwards cannot be habituated to move upwards, not even if one tries to train it by throwing it up ten thousand times; nor can fire be habituated to move downwards, nor can anything else that by nature behaves in one way be trained to behave in another. Neither by nature, then, nor contrary to nature do the virtues arise in us; rather we are adapted by nature to receive them, and are made perfect by habit.

Again, of all the things that come to us by nature we first acquire the potentiality and later exhibit the activity (this is plain in the case of the senses; for it was not by often seeing or often hearing that we got these senses, but on the contrary we had them before we used them, and did not come to have them by using them); but the virtues we get by first exercising them, as also happens in the case of the arts as well. For the things we have to learn before we can do them, we learn by doing them, e.g. men become builders by building and lyre-players by playing the lyre; so too we become just by doing just acts, temperate by doing temperate acts, brave by doing brave acts.

These acts cannot be prescribed exactly, but must avoid excess and defect

Since, then, the present inquiry does not aim at theoretical knowledge like the others (for we are inquiring not in order to know what virtue is, but in order to become good, since otherwise our inquiry would have been of no use), we must examine the nature of actions, namely how we ought to do them; for these determine also the nature of the states of character that are produced, as we have said. Now, that we must act according to the right rule is a common principle and must be assumed—it will be discussed later, i.e. both what the right rule is, and how it is related to the other virtues. But this must be agreed upon beforehand, that the whole account of matters of conduct must be given in outline and not precisely, . . . that the accounts we demand must be in accordance with the subject-matter; matters concerned with conduct and questions of what is good for us have no fixity, any more than matters of health. The general account being of this nature, the account of particular cases is yet more lacking in exactness; for they do not fall under any art or precept, but the agents themselves must in each case consider what is appropriate to the occasion, as happens also in the art of medicine or of navigation.

But though our present account is of this nature we must give what help we can. First, then, let us consider this, that it is the nature of such things to be destroyed by defect and excess, as we see in the case of strength and of health (for to gain light on things imperceptible we must use the evidence of sensible things); exercise either excessive or defective destroys the strength, and similarly drink or food which is above or below a certain amount destroys the health, while that which is proportionate both produces and increases and preserves it. So too is it, then, in the case of temperance and courage and the other virtues. For the man who flies from and fears everything and does not stand his ground against anything becomes a coward, and the man who fears nothing at all but goes to meet every danger becomes rash; and similarly the man who indulges in every pleasure and abstains from none becomes self-indulgent, while the man who shuns every pleasure, as boors do, becomes in a way insensible; temperance and courage, then, are destroyed by excess and defect, and preserved by the mean.

But not only are the sources and causes of their origination and growth the same as those of their destruction, but also the sphere of their actualization will be the same; for this is also true of the things which are more evident to sense, e.g. of strength; it is produced by taking much food and undergoing much exertion, and it is the strong man that will be most able to do these things. So too is it with the virtues; by abstaining from pleasures we become temperate, and it is when we have become so that we are most able to abstain from them; and similarly too in the case of courage; for by being habituated to despise things that are fearful and to stand our ground against them we become brave, and it is when we have become so that we shall be most able to stand our ground against them.

Pleasure in doing virtuous acts is a sign that the virtuous
disposition has been acquired: a variety of considerations
show the essential connexion of moral virtue with
pleasure and pain

We must take as a sign of states of character the pleasure or pain that supervenes upon acts; for the man who abstains from bodily pleasures and delights in this very fact is temperate, while the man who is annoyed at it is self-indulgent, and he who stands his ground against things that are terrible and delights in this or at least is not pained is brave, while the man who is pained is a coward. For moral excellence is concerned with pleasures and pains; it is on account of the pleasure that we do bad things, and on account of the pain that we abstain from noble ones. Hence we ought to have been brought up in a particular way from our very youth, as Plato says, so as both to delight in and to be pained by the things that we ought; this is the right education.

We assume, then, that this kind of excellence tends to do what is best with regard to pleasures and pains, and vice does the contrary.

That virtue, then, is concerned with pleasures and pains, and that by the acts from which it arises it is both increased and, if they are done differently, destroyed, and that the acts from which it arose are those in which it actualizes itself—let this be taken as said.

The actions that produce moral virtue are not good in the same
sense as those that flow from it: the latter must
fulfil certain conditions not necessary
in the case of the arts

The question might be asked, what we mean by saying that we must become just by doing just acts, and temperate by doing temperate acts; for if men do just and temperate acts, they are already just and temperate, exactly as, if they do what is in accordance with the laws of grammar and of music, they are grammarians and musicians.

Or is this not true even of the arts? It is possible to do something that is in accordance with the laws of grammar, either by chance or under the guidance of another. A man will be a grammarian, then, only when he has both said something grammatical and said it grammatically; and this means doing it in accordance with the grammatical knowledge in himself.

Again, the case of the arts and that of the virtues are not similar; for the products of the arts have their goodness in themselves, so that it is enough that they should have a certain character, but if the acts that are in accordance with the virtues have themselves a certain character it does not follow that they are done justly or temperately. The agent also must be in a certain condition when he does them; in the first place he must have knowledge, secondly he must choose the acts, and choose them for their own sakes, and thirdly his action must proceed from a firm and unchangeable character. These are not reckoned in as conditions of the possession of the arts except the bare knowledge; but as a condition of the possession of the virtues knowledge has little or no weight, while the other conditions count not for a little but for everything, i.e. the very conditions which result from often doing just and temperate acts.

Actions, then, are called just and temperate when they are such as the just or the temperate man would do; but it is not the man who does these that is just and temperate, but the man who also does them *as* just and temperate men do them. It is well said, then, that it is by doing just acts that the just man is produced, and by doing temperate acts the temperate man; without doing these no one would have even a prospect of becoming good.

Definition of Moral Virtue
The genus of moral virtue: it is a state of character, not a passion, nor a faculty

Next we must consider what virtue is. Since things that are found in the soul are of three kinds—passions, faculties, states of character—virtue must be one of these. By passions I mean appetite, anger, fear, confidence, envy, joy, friendly feeling, hatred, longing, emulation, pity, and in general the feelings that are accompanied by pleasure or pain; by faculties the things in virtue of which we are said to be capable of feeling these, e.g. of becoming angry or being pained or feeling pity; by states of character the things in virtue of which we stand well or badly with reference to the passions, e.g. with reference to anger we stand badly if we feel it violently or too weakly, and well if we feel it moderately; and similarly with reference to the other passions.

Now neither the virtues nor the vices are *passions*, because we are not called good or bad on the ground of our passions, but are so called on the ground of our virtues and our vices, and because we are neither praised nor blamed for our passions (for the man who feels fear or anger is not praised, nor is the man who simply feels anger blamed, but the man who feels it in a certain way), but for our virtues and our vices we *are* praised or blamed.

Again, we feel anger and fear without choice, but the virtues are modes of choice or involve choice. Further, in respect of the passions we are said to be moved, but in respect of the virtues and the vices we are said not to be moved but to be disposed in a particular way.

For these reasons also they are not *faculties*; for we are neither called good or bad, nor praised or blamed, for the simple capacity of feeling the passions; again, we have the faculties by nature, but we are not made good or bad by nature; we have spoken of this before.

If, then, the virtues are neither passions nor faculties, all that remains is that they should be *states of character*.

Thus we have stated what virtue is in respect of its genus.

The differentia of moral virtue: it is a disposition to choose the mean

We must, however, not only describe virtue as a state of character, but also say what sort of state it is. We may remark, then, that every virtue or excellence both brings into good condition the thing of which it is the excellence and makes the work of that thing be done well; e.g. the excellence of the eye makes both the eye and its work good; for it is by the excellence of the eye that we see well. Similarly the excellence of the horse makes a horse both good in itself and good at running and at carrying its rider and at awaiting the attack of the enemy. Therefore, if this is true in every case, the virtue of man also will be the state of character which makes a man good and which makes him do his own work well.

How this is to happen we have stated already, but it will be made plain also by the following consideration of the specific nature of virtue. In everything that is continuous and divisible it is possible to take more, less, or an equal amount, and that either in terms of the thing itself or relatively to us; and the equal is an intermediate between excess and defect. By the intermediate in the object I mean that which is equidistant from each of the extremes, which is one and the same for all men; by the intermediate relatively to us that which is neither too much nor too little—and this is not one, nor the same for all. For instance, if ten is many and two is few, six is the intermediate, taken in terms of the object; for it exceeds and is exceeded by an equal amount; this is intermediate according to arithmetical proportion. But the intermediate relatively to us is not to be taken so; if ten pounds are too much for a particular person to eat and two too little, it does not follow that the trainer will order six pounds; for this also is perhaps too much for the person who is to take it, or too little—too little for Milo, too much for the beginner in athletic exercises. The same is true of running and wrestling. Thus a master of any art avoids excess and defect, but seeks the intermediate and chooses this—the intermediate not in the object but relatively to us.

If it is thus, then, that every art does its work well— by looking to the intermediate and judging its works by this standard (so that we often say of good works of art that it is not possible either to take away or to add anything, implying that excess and defect destroy the goodness of works of art, while the mean preserves it; and good artists, as we say, look to this in their work), and if, further, virtue is more exact and better than any art, as nature also is, then virtue must have the quality of aiming at the intermediate. I mean moral virtue; for it is this that is concerned with passions and actions, and in these there is excess, defect, and the intermediate. For instance, both fear and confidence and appetite and anger and pity and in general pleasure and pain may be felt both too much and too little, and in both cases not well; but to feel them at the right times, with reference to the right objects, towards the right people, with the right motive, and in the right way, is what is both intermediate and best, and this is characteristic of virtue. Similarly with regard to actions also there is excess, defect, and the intermediate. Now virtue is concerned with passions and actions, in which excess is a form of failure, and so is defect, while the intermediate is praised and is a form of success; and being praised and being successful are both characteristics of virtue. Therefore virtue is a kind of mean, since, as we have seen, it aims at what is intermediate.

Again, it is possible to fail in many ways (for evil belongs to the class of the unlimited, as the Pythagoreans conjectured, and good to that of the limited), while to succeed is possible only in one way (for which reason also one is easy and the other difficult—to miss the mark easy, to hit it difficult); for these reasons also, then, excess and defect are characteristic of vice, and the mean of virtue;

For men are good in but one way, but bad in many.

Virtue, then, is a state of character concerned with choice, lying in a mean, i.e. the mean relative to us, this being determined by a rational principle, and by that principle by which the man of practical wisdom would determine it. Now it is a mean between two vices, that which depends on excess and that which depends on defect; and again it is a mean because the vices respectively fall short of or exceed what is right in both passions and actions, while virtue both finds and chooses that which is intermediate. Hence in respect of what it is, i.e. the definition which states its essence, virtue is a mean, with regard to what is best and right an extreme.

But not every action nor every passion admits of a mean; for some have names that already imply badness, e.g. spite, shamelessness, envy, and in the case of actions adultery, theft, murder; for all of these and such-like things imply by their names that they are themselves bad, and not the excesses or deficiencies of them. It is not possible, then, ever to be right with regard to them; one must always be wrong. Nor does goodness or badness with regard to such things depend on committing adultery with the right woman, at the right time, and in the right way, but simply to do any of them is to go wrong. It would be equally absurd, then, to expect that in unjust, cowardly, and voluptuous action there should be a mean, an excess, and a deficiency; for at that rate there would be a mean of excess and of deficiency, an excess of excess, and a deficiency of deficiency. But as there is no excess and deficiency of temperance and courage because what is intermediate is in a sense an extreme, so too of the actions we have mentioned there is no mean nor any excess and deficiency, but however they are done they are wrong; for in general there is neither a mean of excess and deficiency, nor excess and deficiency of a mean.

The above proposition illustrated by reference to particular virtues

We must, however, not only make this general statement, but also apply it to the individual facts. For among statements about conduct those which are general apply more widely, but those which are particular are more true, since conduct has to do with individual cases, and our statements must harmonize with the facts in these cases. We may take these cases from our table. With regard to feelings of fear and confidence courage is the mean; of the people who exceed, he who exceeds in fearlessness has no name (many of the states have no name), while the man who exceeds in confidence is rash, and he who exceeds in fear and falls short in confidence is a coward. With regard to pleasures and pains—not all of them, and not so much with regard to the pains—the mean is temperance, the excess self-indulgence. Persons deficient with regard to the pleasures are not often found; hence such persons also have received no name. But let us call them 'insensible.'

With regard to giving and taking of money the mean is liberality, the excess and the defect prodigality and meanness. In these actions people exceed and fall short in contrary ways; the prodigal exceeds in spending and falls short in taking, while the mean man exceeds in taking and falls short in spending. (At present we are giving a mere outline or summary, and are satisfied with this; later these states will be more exactly determined.) With regard to money there are also other dispositions—a mean, magnificence (for the magnificent man differs from the liberal man; the former deals with large sums, the latter with small ones), an excess, tastelessness and vulgarity, and a deficiency, niggardliness; these differ from the states opposed to liberality, and the mode of their difference will be stated later.

With regard to honour and dishonour the mean is proper pride, the excess is known as a sort of 'empty vanity,' and the deficiency is undue humility; and as we said liberality was related to magnificence, differing from it by dealing with small sums, so there is a state similarly related to proper pride, being concerned with small honours while that is concerned with great. For it is possible to desire honour as one ought, and more than one ought, and less, and the man who exceeds in his desires is called ambitious, the man who falls short unambitious, while the intermediate person has no name. The dispositions also are nameless, except that that of the ambitious man is called ambition. Hence the people who are at the extremes lay claim to the middle place; and we ourselves sometimes call the intermediate person ambitious and sometimes unambitious, and sometimes praise the ambitious man and sometimes the unambitious. The reason of our doing this will be stated in what follows; but now let us speak of the remaining states according to the method which has been indicated.

With regard to anger also there is an excess, a deficiency, and a mean. Although they can scarcely be said to have names, yet since we call the intermediate person good-tempered let us call the mean good temper; of the persons at the extremes let the one who exceeds be called irascible, and his vice irascibility, and the man who falls short an unirascible sort of person, and the deficiency unirascibility.

Characteristics of the Extreme and Mean States: Practical Corollaries

The extremes are opposed to each other and to the mean

There are three kinds of disposition, then, two of them vices, involving excess and deficiency respectively, and one a virtue, viz. the mean, and all are in a sense opposed to all; for the extreme states are contrary both to the intermediate state and to each other, and the intermediate to the extremes; as the equal is greater relatively to the less, less relatively to the greater, so the middle states are excessive relatively to the deficiencies, deficient relatively to the excesses, both in passions and in actions. For the brave man appears rash relatively to the coward, and cowardly relatively to the rash man; and similarly the temperate man appears self-indulgent relatively to the insensible man, insensible relatively to the self-indulgent, and the liberal man prodigal relatively to the mean man, mean relatively to the prodigal. Hence also the people at the extremes push the intermediate man each over to the other, and the brave man is called rash by the coward, cowardly by the rash man, and correspondingly in the other cases.

These states being thus opposed to one another, the greatest contrariety is that of the extremes to each other, rather than to the intermediate; for these are further from each other than from the intermediate, as the great is further from the small and the small from the great than both are from the equal. Again, to the intermediate some extremes show a certain likeness, as that of rashness to courage and that of prodigality to liberality; but the extremes show the greatest unlikeness to each other; now contraries are defined as the things that are furthest from each other, so that things that are further apart are more contrary.

To the mean in some cases the deficiency, in some the excess, is more opposed; e.g. it is not rashness, which is an excess, but cowardice, which is a deficiency, that is more opposed to courage, and not insensibility, which is a deficiency, but self-indulgence, which is an excess, that is more opposed to temperance. This happens from two reasons, one being drawn from the thing itself; for because one extreme is nearer and liker to the intermediate, we oppose not this but rather its contrary to the intermediate. E.g., since rashness is thought liker and nearer to courage, and cowardice more unlike, we oppose rather the latter to courage; for things that are further from the intermediate are thought more contrary to it. This, then, is one cause, drawn from the thing itself; another is drawn from ourselves; for the things to which we ourselves more naturally tend seem more contrary to the intermediate. For instance, we ourselves tend more naturally to pleasures, and hence are more easily carried away towards self-indulgence than towards propriety. We describe as contrary to the mean, then, rather the directions in which we more often go to great lengths; and therefore self-indulgence, which is an excess, is the more contrary to temperance.

The mean is hard to attain, and is grasped by perception, not by reasoning

That moral virtue is a mean, then, and in what sense it is so, and that it is a mean between two vices, the one involving excess, the other deficiency, and that it is such because its character is to aim at what is intermediate in passions and in actions, has been sufficiently stated. Hence also it is no easy task to be good. For in everything it is no easy task to find the middle, e.g. to find the middle of a circle is not for everyone but for him who knows; so, too, anyone can get angry—that is easy—or give or spend money; but to do this to the right person, to the right extent, at the right time, with the right motive, and in the right way, *that* is not for everyone, nor is it easy; wherefore goodness is both rare and laudable and noble.

Hence he who aims at the intermediate must first depart from what is the more contrary to it, as Calypso advises—

Hold the ship out beyond that surf and spray.

For of the extremes one is more erroneous, one less so; therefore, since to hit the mean is hard in the extreme, we must as a second best, as people say, take the least of the evils; and this will be done best in the way we describe.

But we must consider the things towards which we ourselves also are easily carried away; for some of us tend to one thing, some to another; and this will be recognizable from the pleasure and the pain we feel. We must drag ourselves away to the contrary extreme; for we shall get into the intermediate state by drawing well away from error, as people do in straightening sticks that are bent.

Now in everything the pleasant or pleasure is most to be guarded against; for we do not judge it impartially. We ought, then, to feel towards pleasure as the elders of the people felt towards Helen, and in all circumstances repeat their saying; for if we dismiss pleasure thus we are less likely to go astray. It is by doing this, then, (to sum the matter up) that we shall best be able to hit the mean.

But this is no doubt difficult, and especially in individual cases; for it is not easy to determine both how and with whom and on what provocation and how long one should be angry; for we too sometimes praise those who fall short and call them good-tempered, but sometimes we praise those who get angry and call them manly. The man, however, who deviates little from goodness is not blamed, whether he do so in the direction of the more or of the less, but only the man who deviates more widely; for *he* does not fail to be noticed. But up to what point and to what extent a man must deviate before he becomes blameworthy it is not easy to determine by reasoning, any more than anything else that is perceived by the senses; such things depend on particular facts, and the decision rests with perception. So much, then, is plain, that the intermediate state is in all things to be praised, but that we must incline sometimes towards the excess, sometimes towards the deficiency; for so shall we most easily hit the mean and what is right.

Aristotle: Nicomachean Ethics

1. Some philosophers have maintained that people are naturally morally good, while others have held that people are naturally wicked. Aristotle takes a middle ground, saying, "Neither by nature, then, nor contrary to nature do the virtues arise in us." Which view do you think is correct, and why?

2. What do you think Aristotle means when he says that "matters concerned with conduct and questions of what is good for us have no fixity"? Do you agree with this statement?

3. What is the difference, according to Aristotle, between performing virtuous actions and being a virtuous person? Do you agree with him that the latter is more valuable?

4. Aristotle says that virtue is a "mean" between extremes. For instance, the virtue of courage consists of the disposition to feel neither too much nor too little fear, but rather some appropriate amount in between. Is this consistent with his claim that some actions (such as stealing or adultery) are always wrong in all circumstances?

5. What advice does Aristotle give regarding how we should go about seeking the mean between extremes? Do you think this is good advice?

13

═══ ❧ ═══

What Is Feminist Ethics?

Hilde Lindemann

· ·

Hilde Lindemann offers us a brief overview of feminist ethics in this selection. She first discusses the nature of feminism and identifies some of the various ways that people have defined it. Lindemann argues against thinking of feminism as focused primarily on equality, women, or the differences between the sexes. She instead invites us to think of feminism as based on considerations of gender—specifically, considerations to do with the lesser degree of power that women have, largely the world over, as compared with men.

Lindemann proceeds to discuss the sex/gender distinction and to identify the central tasks of feminist ethics: to understand, criticize, and correct the inaccurate gender assumptions that underlie our moral thinking and behavior. An important approach of most feminists is a kind of skepticism about the ability to distinguish political commitments from intellectual ones. Lindemann concludes by discussing this skepticism and its implications for feminist thought.

· ·

Afew years ago, a dentist in Ohio was convicted of having sex with his female patients while they were under anesthesia. I haven't been able to discover whether he had to pay a fine or do jail time,

---

Hilde Lindemann, "What Is Feminist Ethics?" from *An Invitation to Feminist Ethics* (2004), pp. 2–3, 6–16. Reproduced with the permission of The McGraw-Hill Companies.

but I do remember that the judge ordered him to take a course in ethics. And I recall thinking how odd that order was. Let's suppose, as the judge apparently did, that the dentist really and truly didn't know it was wrong to have sex with anesthetized patients (this will tax your imagination, but try to suppose it anyway). Can we expect—again, as the judge apparently did—that on completing the ethics course, the dentist would be a better, finer man?

Hardly. If studying ethics could make you good, then the people who have advanced academic degrees in the subject would be paragons of moral uprightness. I can't speak for all of them, of course, but though the ones I know are nice enough, they're no more moral than anyone else. Ethics doesn't improve your character. Its *subject* is morality, but its relationship to morality is that of a scholarly study to the thing being studied. In that respect, the relationship is a little like the relationship between grammar and language.

Let's explore that analogy. People who speak fluent English don't have to stop and think about the correctness of the sentence "He gave it to *her*." But here's a harder one. Should you say, "He gave it to *her* who must be obeyed?" or "He gave it to *she* who must be obeyed?" To sort this out, it helps to know a little grammar—the systematic, scholarly description of the structure of the language and the rules for speaking and writing in it. According to those rules, the object of the preposition "to" is the entire clause that comes after it, and the subject of that clause is "she." So, even though it sounds peculiar, the correct answer is "He gave it to she who must be obeyed."

In a roughly similar vein, morally competent adults don't have to stop and think about whether it's wrong to have sex with one's anesthetized patients. But if you want to understand whether it's wrong to have large signs in bars telling pregnant women not to drink, or to sort out the conditions under which it's all right to tell a lie, it helps to know a little ethics. The analogy between grammar and ethics isn't exact, of course. For one thing, there's considerably more agreement about what language is than about what morality is. For another, grammarians are concerned only with the structure of language, not with the meaning or usage of particular words. In both cases, however, the same point can be made: You already have to know quite a lot about how to behave—linguistically or morally—before there's much point in studying either grammar or ethics. . . .

What Is Feminism?

What, then, is feminism? As a social and political movement with a long, intermittent history, feminism has repeatedly come into public awareness, generated change, and then disappeared again. As an eclectic body of theory, feminism entered colleges and universities in the early 1970s as a part of the women's studies movement, contributing to scholarship in every academic discipline, though probably most heavily in the arts, social sciences, literature, and the humanities in general. Feminist ethics is a part of the body of theory that is being developed primarily in colleges and universities.

Many people in the United States think of feminism as a movement that aims to make women the social equals of men, and this impression has been reinforced by references to feminism and feminists in the newspapers, on television, and in the movies. But bell hooks has pointed out in *Feminist Theory from Margin to Center* (1984, 18–19) that this way of defining feminism raises some serious problems. Which men do women want to be equal to? Women who are socially well off wouldn't get much advantage from being the equals of the men who are poor and lower class, particularly if they aren't white. hooks's point is that there are no women and men in the abstract. They are poor, black, young, Latino/a, old, gay, able-bodied, upper class, down on their luck, Native American, straight, and all the rest of it. When a woman doesn't think about this, it's probably because she doesn't have to. And that's usually a sign that her own social position is privileged. In fact, privilege often means that there's something uncomfortable going on that others have to pay attention to but you don't. So, when hooks asks which men women want to be equal to, she's reminding us that there's an unconscious presumption of privilege built right in to this sort of demand for equality.

There's a second problem with the equality definition. Even if we could figure out which men are the ones to whom women should be equal, that way of putting it suggests that the point of feminism is somehow to get women to measure up to what (at least some) men already are. Men remain the point of reference; theirs are the lives that women would naturally want. If the first problem with the equality definition is "Equal to *which* men?" the second problem could be put as "Why equal to *any* men?" Reforming a system in which men are the point of reference by allowing women to perform as their equals "forces women to focus on men and address men's conceptions of women rather than creating and developing women's values about themselves," as Sarah Lucia Hoagland puts it in *Lesbian Ethics* (1988, 57). For that reason, Hoagland and some other feminists believe that feminism is first and foremost about women.

But characterizing feminism as about women has its problems too. What, after all, is a woman? In her 1949 book, *The Second Sex*, the French feminist philosopher Simone de Beauvoir famously observed, "One is not born, but becomes a woman. No biological, psychological, or economic fate determines the figure that the human female presents in society: it is civilization as a whole that produces this creature, intermediate between male and eunuch, which is described as feminine" (Beauvoir 1949, 301). Her point is that while plenty of human beings are born female, 'woman' is not a natural fact about them—it's a social invention. According to that invention, which is widespread in "civilization as a whole," man represents the positive, typical human being, while woman represents only the negative, the not-man. She is the Other against whom man defines himself—he is all the things that she is not. And she exists only in relation to him. In a later essay called "One Is Not Born a Woman," the lesbian author and theorist Monique Wittig (1981, 49) adds that because women belong to men sexually as well as in every other way, women are necessarily heterosexual. For that reason, she argued, lesbians aren't women.

But, you are probably thinking, everybody knows what a woman is, and lesbians certainly *are* women. And you're right. These French feminists aren't denying that there's a perfectly ordinary use of the word *woman* by which it means exactly what you think it means. But they're explaining what this comes down to, if you look at it from a particular point of view. Their answer to the question "What is a woman?" is that women are different from men. But they don't mean this as a trite observation. They're saying that 'woman' refers to *nothing but* difference from men, so that apart from men, women aren't anything. 'Man' is the positive term, 'woman' is the negative one, just like 'light' is the positive term and 'dark' is nothing but the absence of light.

A later generation of feminists have agreed with Beauvoir and Wittig that women are different from men, but rather than seeing that difference as simply negative, they put it in positive terms, affirming feminine qualities as a source of personal strength and pride. For example, the philosopher Virginia Held thinks that women's moral experience as mothers, attentively nurturing their children, may serve as a better model for social relations than the contract model that the free market provides. The poet Adrienne Rich celebrated women's passionate nature (as opposed, in stereotype, to the rational nature of men), regarding the emotions as morally valuable rather than as signs of weakness.

But defining feminism as about the positive differences between men and women creates yet another set of problems. In her 1987 *Feminism Unmodified*, the feminist legal theorist Catharine A. MacKinnon points out that this kind of difference, as such, is a symmetrical relationship: If I am different from you, then you are different from me in exactly the same respects and to exactly the same degree. "Men's differences from women are equal to women's differences from men," she writes. "There is an *equality* there. Yet the sexes are not socially equal" (MacKinnon 1987, 37). No amount of attention to the differences between men and women explains why men, as a group, are more socially powerful, valued, advantaged, or free than women. For that, you have to see differences as counting in certain ways, and certain differences being created precisely because they give men *power* over women.

Although feminists disagree about this, my own view is that feminism isn't—at least not directly—about equality, and it isn't about women, and it isn't about difference. It's about power. Specifically, it's about the social pattern, widespread across cultures and history, that distributes power asymmetrically to favor men over women. This asymmetry has been given many names, including the subjugation of women, sexism, male dominance, patriarchy, systemic misogyny, phallocracy, and the oppression of women. A number of feminist theorists simply call it gender, and throughout this book, I will too.

What Is Gender?

Most people think their gender is a natural fact about them, like their hair and eye color: "Jones is 5 foot 8, has red hair, and is a man." But gender is a *norm*, not a fact. It's a prescription for how people are supposed to act; what they must or must not wear; how they're supposed to sit, walk, or stand; what kind of person they're supposed to marry; what sorts of things they're supposed to be interested in or good at; and what they're entitled to. And because it's an *effective* norm, it creates the differences between men and women in these areas.

Gender doesn't just tell women to behave one way and men another, though. It's a *power* relation, so it tells men that they're entitled to things that women aren't supposed to have, and it tells women that they are supposed to defer to men and serve them. It says, for example, that men are supposed to occupy positions of religious authority and women are supposed to run the church suppers. It says that mothers are supposed to take care of their children but fathers have more important things to do. And it says that the things associated with femininity are supposed to take a back seat to the things that are coded masculine. Think of the many tax dollars allocated to the military as compared with the few tax dollars allocated to the arts. Think about how kindergarten teachers are paid as compared to how stockbrokers are paid. And think about how many presidents of the United States have been women. Gender operates through social institutions (like marriage and the law) and practices (like education and medicine) by disproportionately conferring entitlements and the control of resources on men, while disproportionately assigning women to subordinate positions in the service of men's interests.

To make this power relation seem perfectly natural—like the fact that plants grow up instead of down, or that human beings grow old and die—gender constructs its norms for behavior around what is supposed to be the natural biological distinction between the sexes. According to this distinction, people who have penises and testicles, XY chromosomes, and beards as adults belong to the male sex, while people who have clitorises and ovaries, XX chromosomes, and breasts as adults belong to the female sex, and those are the only sexes there are. Gender, then, is the complicated set of cultural meanings that are constructed around the two sexes. Your sex is either male or female, and your gender—either masculine, or feminine—corresponds socially to your sex.

As a matter of fact, though, sex isn't quite so simple. Some people with XY chromosomes don't have penises and never develop beards, because they don't have the receptors that allow them to make use of the male hormones that their testicles produce. Are they male or female? Other people have ambiguous genitals or internal reproductive structures that don't correspond in the usual manner to their external genitalia. How should we classify them? People with Turner's syndrome have XO chromosomes instead of XX. People with Klinefelter's syndrome have three sex chromosomes: XXY. Nature is a good bit looser in its categories than the simple male/female distinction acknowledges. Most human beings can certainly be classified as one sex or the other, but a considerable number of them fall somewhere in between.

The powerful norm of gender doesn't acknowledge the existence of the in betweens, though. When, for example, have you ever filled out an application for a job or a driver's license or a passport that gave you a choice other than M or F? Instead, by basing its distinction between masculine and feminine on the existence of two and only two sexes, gender makes the inequality of power between men and women appear natural and therefore legitimate.

Gender, then, is about power. But it's not about the power of just one group over another. Gender always interacts with other social markers— such as race, class, level of education, sexual orientation, age, religion, physical and mental health, and ethnicity —to distribute power unevenly among women positioned differently in the various social orders, and it does the same to men. A man's social status, for example, can have a great deal to do with the extent to which he's even perceived as a man. There's a wonderful passage in the English travel writer Frances Trollope's *Domestic Manners of the Americans* (1831), in which she describes the exaggerated delicacy of middle-class young ladies she met in Kentucky and Ohio. They wouldn't dream of sitting in a chair that was still warm from contact with a gentleman's bottom, but thought nothing of getting laced into their corsets in front of a male house slave. The slave, it's clear, didn't count as a man—not in the relevant sense, anyway. Gender is the force that makes it matter whether you are male or female, but it always works hand in glove with all the other things about you that matter at the same time. It's one power relation intertwined with others in a complex social system that distinguishes your betters from your inferiors in all kinds of ways and for all kinds of purposes.

Power and Morality

If feminism is about gender, and gender is the name for a social system that distributes power unequally between men and women, then you'd expect feminist ethicists to try to *understand, criticize,* and *correct* how gender operates within our moral beliefs and practices. And they do just that. In the first place, they challenge, on moral grounds, the powers men have over women, and they claim for women, again on moral grounds, the powers that gender denies them. As the moral reasons for opposing gender are similar to the moral reasons for opposing power systems based on social markers other than gender, feminist ethicists also offer moral arguments against systems based on class, race, physical or mental ability, sexuality, and age. And because all these systems, including gender, are powerful enough to *conceal* many of the forces that keep them in place, it's often necessary to make the forces visible by explicitly identifying—and condemning—the various ugly ways they allow some people to treat others. This is a central task for feminist ethics.

Feminist ethicists also produce theory about the moral meaning of various kinds of *legitimate* relations of unequal power, including relationships of dependency and vulnerability, relationships of trust, and relationships based on something other than choice. Parent–child relationships, for example, are necessarily unequal and for the most part unchosen. Parents can't help having power over their children, and while they may have chosen to have children, most don't choose to have the particular children they do, nor do children choose their parents. This raises questions about the responsible use of parental power and the nature of involuntary obligations, and these are topics for feminist ethics. Similarly, when you trust someone, that person has power over you. Whom should you trust, for what purposes, and when is trust not warranted? What's involved in being trustworthy, and what must be done to repair breaches of trust? These too are questions for feminist ethics.

Third, feminist ethicists look at the various forms of power that are required for morality to operate properly at all. How do we learn right from wrong in the first place? We usually learn it from our parents, whose power to permit and forbid, praise and punish, is essential to our moral training. For whom or what are we ethically responsible? Often this depends on the kind of power we have over the person or thing in question. If, for instance, someone is particularly vulnerable to harm because of something I've done, I might well have special duties toward that person. Powerful social institutions—medicine, religion, government, and the market, to take just a few examples—typically dictate what is morally required of us and to whom we are morally answerable. Relations of power set the terms for who must answer to whom, who has authority over whom, and who gets excused from certain kinds of accountability to whom. But because so many of these power relations are illegitimate, in that they're instances of gender, racism, or other kinds of bigotry, figuring out which ones are morally justified is a task for feminist ethics.

Description and Prescription

So far it sounds as if feminist ethics devotes considerable attention to *description*—as if feminist ethicists were like poets or painters who want to show you something about reality that you might otherwise have missed. And indeed, many feminist ethicists emphasize the importance of understanding how social power actually works, rather than concentrating solely on how it ought to work. But why, you might ask, should ethicists worry about how power operates within societies? Isn't it up to sociologists and political scientists to describe how things *are*, while ethicists concentrate on how things *ought* to be?

As the philosopher Margaret Urban Walker has pointed out in *Moral Contexts*, there is a tradition in Western philosophy, going all the way back to Plato, to the effect that morality is something ideal and that ethics, being the study of morality, properly examines only that ideal. According to this tradition, notions of right and wrong as they are found in the world are unreliable and shadowy manifestations of something lying outside of human experience—something to which we ought to aspire but can't hope to reach. Plato's Idea of the Good, in fact, is precisely not of this earth, and only the gods could truly know it. Christian ethics incorporates Platonism into its insistence that earthly existence is fraught with sin and error and that heaven is our real home. Kant too insists that moral judgments transcend the histories and circumstances of people's actual lives, and most moral philosophers of the twentieth century have likewise shown little interest in how people really live and what it's like for them to live that way. "They think," remarks Walker (2001), "that there is little to be learned from what is about what ought to be" (3).

In Chapter Four [omitted here—ed.] we'll take a closer look at what goes wrong when ethics is done that way, but let me just point out here that if you don't know how things are, your prescriptions for how things ought to be won't have much practical effect. Imagine trying to sail a ship without knowing anything about the tides or where the hidden rocks and shoals lie. You might have a very fine idea of where you are trying to go, but if you don't know the waters, at best you are likely to go off course, and at worst you'll end up going down with all your shipmates. If, as many feminists have noted, a crucial fact about human selves is that they are always embedded in a vast web of relationships, then the forces at play within those relationships must be understood. It's knowing how people are situated with respect to these forces, what they are going through as they are subjected to them, and what life is like in the face of them, that lets us decide which of the forces are morally justified. Careful description of how things are is a crucial part of feminist methodology, because the power that puts certain groups of people at risk of physical harm, denies them full access to the good things their society has to offer, or treats them as if they were useful only for other people's purposes is often hidden and hard to see. If this power isn't seen, it's likely to remain in place, doing untold amounts of damage to great numbers of people.

All the same, feminist ethics is *normative* as well as descriptive. It's fundamentally about how things ought to be, while description plays the crucial but secondary role of helping us to figure that out. Normative language is the language of "ought" instead of "is," the language of "worth" and "value," "right" and "wrong," "good" and "bad." Feminist ethicists differ on a number of normative issues, but as the philosopher Alison Jaggar (1991) has famously put it, they all share two moral commitments: "that the subordination of women is morally wrong and that the moral experience of women is worthy of respect" (95). The first commitment—that women's interests ought not systematically to be set in the service of men's—can be understood as a moral challenge to power under the guise of gender. The second commitment—that women's experience must be taken seriously—can be understood as a call to acknowledge how that power operates. These twin commitments are the two normative legs on which any feminist ethics stands. . . .

Morality and Politics

If the idealization of morality goes back over two thousand years in Western thought, a newer tradition, only a couple of centuries old, has split off morality from politics. According to this tradition, which can be traced to Kant and some other Enlightenment philosophers, morality concerns the relations between persons, whereas politics concerns the relations among nation-states, or between a state and its citizens. So, as Iris Marion Young (1990) puts it, ethicists have tended to focus on intentional actions by individual persons, conceiving of moral life as "conscious, deliberate, a rational weighing of alternatives," whereas political philosophers have focused on impersonal governmental systems, studying "laws, policies, the large-scale distribution of social goods, countable quantities like votes and taxes" (149).

For feminists, though, the line between ethics and political theory isn't quite so bright as this tradition makes out. It's not always easy to tell where feminist ethics leaves off and feminist political theory begins. There are two reasons for this. In the first place, while ethics certainly concerns personal behavior, there is a long-standing insistence on the part of feminists that the personal *is* political. In a 1970 essay called "The Personal Is Political," the political activist Carol Hanisch observed that "personal problems are political problems. There are no personal solutions at this time" (204–205). What Hanisch meant is that even the most private areas of everyday life, including such intensely personal areas as sex, can function to maintain abusive power systems like gender. If a heterosexual woman believes, for example, that contraception is primarily her responsibility because she'll have to take care of the baby if she gets pregnant, she is propping up a system that lets men evade responsibility not only for pregnancy, but for their own offspring as well. Conversely, while unjust social arrangements such as gender and race invade every aspect of people's personal lives, "there are no personal solutions," either when Hanisch wrote those words or now, because to shift dominant understandings of how certain groups may be treated, and what other groups are entitled to expect of them, requires concerted political action, not just personal good intentions.

The second reason why it's hard to separate feminist ethics from feminist politics is that feminists typically subject the ethical theory they produce to critical political scrutiny, not only to keep untoward political biases out, but also to make sure that the work accurately reflects their feminist politics. Many nonfeminist ethicists, on the other hand, don't acknowledge that their work reflects their politics, because they don't think it should. Their aim, by and large, has been to develop ideal moral theory that applies to all people, regardless of their social position or experience of life, and to do that objectively, without favoritism, requires them to leave their own personal politics behind. The trouble, though, is that they aren't really leaving their own personal politics behind. They're merely refusing to notice that their politics is inevitably built right in to their theories. (This is an instance of Lindemann's ad hoc rule Number 22: Just because you think you are doing something doesn't mean you're actually doing it.) Feminists, by contrast, are generally skeptical of the idealism nonfeminists favor, and they're equally doubtful that objectivity can be achieved by stripping away what's distinctive about people's experiences or commitments. Believing that it's no wiser to shed one's political allegiances in the service of ethics than it would be to shed one's moral allegiances, feminists prefer to be transparent about their politics as a way of keeping their ethics intellectually honest. . . .

Hilde Lindemann: What Is Feminist Ethics?

1. Near the beginning of her piece, Lindemann claims that studying ethics "doesn't improve your character." Do you think she is right about this? If so, what is the point of studying ethics?
2. What problems does Lindemann raise for the view that feminism is fundamentally about equality between men and women? Can these problems be overcome, or must we admit that feminism is concerned with equality?
3. What is the difference between sex and gender? Why does Lindemann think that gender is essentially about power? Do you think she is right about this?
4. Lindemann claims that feminist ethics is "*normative* as well as descriptive." What does she mean by this? In what ways is feminist ethics more descriptive than other approaches to ethics? Do you see this as a strength or a weakness?
5. What is meant by the slogan "The personal is political"? Do you agree with the slogan?
6. Lindemann claims that one should not set aside one's political views when thinking about ethical issues. What reasons does she give for thinking this? Do you agree with her?

For Further Reading

Baier, Annette. 1994. *Moral Prejudices: Essays on Ethics*. Cambridge, MA: Harvard University Press.

Beauvoir, Simone de. 1949 [1974]. *The Second Sex*. Trans. and ed. H. M. Parshley. New York: Modern Library.

Hanisch, Carol. 1970. "The Personal Is Political." In *Notes from the Second Year*. New York: Radical Feminism.

Hoagland, Sarah Lucia. 1988. *Lesbian Ethics: Toward New Value*. Palo Alto, CA: Institute of Lesbian Studies.

hooks, bell. 1984. *Feminist Theory from Margin to Center*. Boston: South End Press.

Jaggar, Alison. 1991. "Feminist Ethics: Projects, Problems, Prospects." In *Feminist Ethics*, ed. Claudia Card. Lawrence: University Press of Kansas.

MacKinnon, Catharine A. 1987. *Feminism Unmodified.* Cambridge, MA: Harvard University Press.

Plumwood, Val. 2002. *Environmental Culture: The Ecological Crisis of Reason.* London: Routledge.

Walker, Margaret Urban. 2001. "Seeing Power in Morality: A Proposal for Feminist Naturalism in Ethics." In *Feminists Doing Ethics,* ed. Peggy DesAutels and Joanne Waugh. Lanham, MD: Rowman & Littlefield.

———. 2003. *Moral Contexts.* Lanham, MD: Rowman & Littlefield.

Wittig, Monique. 1981. "One Is Not Born a Woman." *Feminist Issues* 1, no. 2.

Young, Iris Marion. 1990. *Justice and the Politics of Difference.* Princeton, NJ: Princeton University Press.

PART III

Metaethics

The Status of Morality

14

Moral Distinctions
Not Derived from Reason

David Hume

....

David Hume (1711–1776) sought to offer a wholly naturalistic account
of the nature and origins of morality. He rejected the idea of eternal moral
truths, graspable by reason alone. He thought that morality is essentially
a way of organizing our emotional responses to a value-free world. In this
excerpt from his first masterpiece, *A Treatise of Human Nature* (1737),
Hume offers several influential arguments against moral rationalism—
the idea that reason is the basis of morality, our primary means of gaining
moral knowledge, and the source of moral motivation. Also included here
is perhaps his most famous claim about morality, namely, that one cannot
derive an *ought* from an *is*. According to Hume, it is impossible to substantiate a claim about what ought to be done, or ought to be the case, solely
from claims about how the world actually is. Since reason is confined to
telling us what is the case, it cannot, by itself, supply us with advice about
our duty, or about which ideals we should aspire to.

....

... It has been observed, that nothing is ever present to the mind but its
perceptions; and that all the actions of seeing, hearing, judging, loving,
hating, and thinking, fall under this denomination. The mind can never
exert itself in any action which we may not comprehend under the term
of *perception*; and consequently that term is no less applicable to those

judgments by which we distinguish moral good and evil, than to every other operation of the mind. To approve of one character, to condemn another, are only so many different perceptions.

Now, as perceptions resolve themselves into two kinds, viz. *impressions* and *ideas*, this distinction gives rise to a question, with which we shall open up our present inquiry concerning morals, *whether it is by means of our ideas or impressions we distinguish betwixt vice and virtue, and pronounce an action blamable or praise-worthy?* This will immediately cut off all loose discourses and declamations, and reduce us to something precise and exact on the present subject.

Those who affirm that virtue is nothing but a conformity to reason; that there are eternal fitnesses and unfitnesses of things, which are the same to every rational being that considers them; that the immutable measure of right and wrong impose an obligation, not only on human creatures, but also on the Deity himself: all these systems concur in the opinion, that morality, like truth, is discerned merely by ideas, and by their juxtaposition and comparison. In order, therefore, to judge of these systems, we need only consider whether it be possible from reason alone, to distinguish betwixt moral good and evil, or whether there must concur some other principles to enable us to make that distinction.

If morality had naturally no influence on human passions and actions, it were in vain to take such pains to inculcate it; and nothing would be more fruitless than that multitude of rules and precepts with which all moralists abound. Philosophy is commonly divided into *speculative* and *practical*; and as morality is always comprehended under the latter division, it is supposed to influence our passions and actions, and to go beyond the calm and indolent judgments of the understanding. And this is confirmed by common experience, which informs us that men are often governed by their duties, and are deterred from some actions by the opinion of injustice, and impelled to others by that of obligation.

Since morals, therefore, have an influence on the actions and affections, it follows that they cannot be derived from reason; and that because reason alone, as we have already proved, can never have any such influence. Morals excite passions, and produce or prevent actions. Reason of itself is utterly impotent in this particular. The rules of morality, therefore, are not conclusions of our reason.

No one, I believe, will deny the justness of this inference; nor is there any other means of evading it, than by denying that principle on which it is founded. As long as it is allowed, that reason has no influence on our passions and actions, it is in vain to pretend that morality is discovered only by a deduction of reason. An active principle can never be founded on an inactive; and if reason be inactive in itself, it must remain so in all its shapes and appearances, whether it exerts itself in natural or moral subjects, whether it considers the powers of external bodies, or the actions of rational beings.

It would be tedious to repeat all the arguments by which I have proved that reason is perfectly inert, and can never either prevent or produce any action or affection. It will be easy to recollect what has been said upon that subject. I shall only recall on this occasion one of these arguments, which I shall endeavour to render still more conclusive, and more applicable to the present subject.

Reason is the discovery of truth or falsehood. Truth or falsehood consists in an agreement or disagreement either to the *real* relations of ideas, or to *real* existence and matter of fact. Whatever therefore is not susceptible of this agreement or disagreement, is incapable of being true or false, and can never be an object of our reason. Now, it is evident our passions, volitions, and actions, are not susceptible of any such agreement or disagreement; being original facts and realities, complete in themselves, and implying no reference to other passions, volitions, and actions. It is impossible, therefore, they can be pronounced either true or false, and be either contrary or conformable to reason.

This argument is of double advantage to our present purpose. For it proves *directly*, that actions do not derive their merit from a conformity to reason, nor their blame from a contrariety to it; and it proves the same truth more *indirectly*, by showing us, that as reason can never immediately prevent or produce any action by contradicting or approving of it, it cannot be the source of moral good and evil, which are found to have that influence. Actions may be laudable or blamable; but they cannot be reasonable or unreasonable: laudable or blamable, therefore, are not the same with reasonable or unreasonable. The merit and demerit of actions frequently contradict, and sometimes control our natural propensities. But reason has no such influence. Moral distinctions, therefore, are not the offspring of reason. Reason is wholly inactive, and can never be the source of so active a principle as conscience, or a sense of morals.

But perhaps it may be said, that though no will or action can be immediately contradictory to reason, yet we may find such a contradiction in some of the attendants of the actions, that is, in its causes or effects. The action may cause a judgment, or may be *obliquely* caused by one, when the judgment concurs with a passion; and by an abusive way of speaking, which philosophy will scarce allow of, the same contrariety may, upon that account, be ascribed to the action. How far this truth or falsehood may be the source of morals, it will now be proper to consider.

It has been observed that reason, in a strict and philosophical sense, can have an influence on our conduct only after two ways: either when it excites a passion, by informing us of the existence of something which is a proper object of it; or when it discovers the connection of causes and effects, so as to afford us means of exerting any passion. These are the only kinds of judgment which can accompany our actions, or can be said to produce them in any manner; and it must be allowed, that these judgments may often be false and erroneous. A person may be affected with passion, by supposing a pain or pleasure to lie in an object which has no tendency to produce either of these sensations, or which produces the contrary to what is imagined. A person may also take false measures for the attaining of his end, and may retard, by his foolish conduct, instead of forwarding the execution of any object. These false judgments may be thought to affect the passions and actions, which are connected with them, and may be said to render them unreasonable, in a figurative and improper way of speaking. But though this be acknowledged, it is easy to observe, that these errors are so far from being the source of all immorality, that they are commonly very innocent, and draw no manner of guilt upon the person who is so unfortunate as to fall into them. They extend not beyond a mistake of *fact*, which moralists have not generally supposed criminal, as being perfectly involuntary. I am more to be lamented than blamed, if I am mistaken with regard to the influence of objects in producing pain or pleasure, or if I know not the proper means of satisfying my desires. No one can ever regard such errors as a defect in my moral character. A fruit, for instance, that is really disagreeable, appears to me at a distance, and, through mistake, I fancy it to be pleasant and delicious. Here is one error. I choose certain means of reaching this fruit, which are not proper for my end. Here is a second error; nor is there any third one, which can ever possibly enter into our reasonings concerning actions. I ask, therefore, if a man in this situation, and guilty of these two errors, is to be regarded as vicious and criminal, however unavoidable they might have been? Or if it be possible to imagine that such errors are the sources of all immorality?

And here it may be proper to observe, that if moral distinctions be derived from the truth or falsehood of those judgments, they must take place wherever we form the judgments; nor will there be any difference, whether the question be concerning an apple or a kingdom, or whether the error be avoidable or unavoidable.

For as the very essence of morality is supposed to consist in an agreement or disagreement to reason, the other circumstances are entirely arbitrary, and can never either bestow on any action the character of virtuous or vicious, or deprive it of that character. To which we may add, that this agreement or disagreement, not admitting of degrees, all virtues and vices would of course be equal.

Should it be pretended, that though a mistake of *fact* be not criminal, yet a mistake of *right* often is; and that this may be the source of immorality: I would answer, that it is impossible such a mistake can ever be the original source of immorality, since it supposes a real right and wrong; that is, a real distinction in morals, independent of these judgments. A mistake, therefore, of right, may become a species of immorality; but it is only a secondary one, and is founded on some other antecedent to it.

As to those judgments which are the *effects* of our actions, and which, when false, give occasion to pronounce the actions contrary to truth and reason; we may observe, that our actions never cause any judgment, either true or false, in ourselves, and that it is only on others they have such an influence. It is certain that an action, on many occasions, may give rise to false conclusions in others; and that a person, who, through a window, sees any lewd behaviour of mine with my neighbour's wife, may be so simple as to imagine she is certainly my own. In this respect my action resembles somewhat a lie or falsehood; only with this difference, which is material, that I perform not the action with any intention of giving rise to a false judgment in another, but merely to satisfy my lust and passion. It causes, however, a mistake and false judgment by accident; and the falsehood of its effects may be ascribed, by some odd figurative way of speaking, to the action itself. But still I can see no pretext of reason for asserting, that the tendency to cause such an error is the first spring or original source of all immorality.

Thus, upon the whole, it is impossible that the distinction betwixt moral good and evil can be made by reason; since that distinction has an influence upon our actions, of which reason alone is incapable. Reason and judgment may, indeed, be the mediate cause of an action, by prompting or by directing a passion; but it is not pretended that a judgment of this kind, either in its truth or falsehood, is attended with virtue or vice. And as to the judgments, which are caused by our judgments, they can still less bestow those moral qualities on the actions which are their causes.

But, to be more particular, and to show that those eternal immutable fitnesses and unfitnesses of things cannot be defended by sound philosophy, we may weigh the following considerations.

If the thought and understanding were alone capable of fixing the boundaries of right and wrong, the character of virtuous and vicious either must lie in some relations of objects, or must be a matter of fact which is discovered by our reasoning. This consequence is evident. As the operations of human understanding divide themselves into two kinds, the comparing of ideas, and the inferring of matter of fact, were virtue discovered by the understanding, it must be an object of one of these operations; nor is there any third operation of the understanding which can discover it. There has been an opinion very industriously propagated by certain philosophers, that morality is susceptible of demonstration; and though no one has ever been able to advance a single step in those demonstrations, yet it is taken for granted that this science may be brought to an equal certainty with geometry or algebra. Upon this supposition, vice and virtue must consist in some relations; since it is allowed on all hands, that no matter of fact is capable of being demonstrated. Let us therefore begin with examining this hypothesis, and endeavour, if possible, to fix those moral qualities which have been so long the objects of our fruitless researches; point out distinctly the relations which constitute morality or obligation, that we may know wherein they consist, and after what manner we must judge of them.

If you assert that vice and virtue consist in relations susceptible of certainty and demonstration, you must confine yourself to those *four* relations which alone admit of that degree of evidence; and in that case you run into absurdities from which you will never be able to extricate yourself. For as you make the very essence of morality to lie in the relations, and as there is no one of these relations but what is applicable, not only to an irrational but also to an inanimate object, it follows that even such objects must be susceptible of merit or demerit. *Resemblance, contrariety, degrees in quality,* and *proportions in quantity and number;* all these relations belong as properly to matter as to our actions, passions, and volitions. It is unquestionable, therefore, that morality lies not in any of these relations, nor the sense of it in their discovery.

Should it be asserted, that the sense of morality consists in the discovery of some relation distinct from these, and that our enumeration was not complete when we comprehended all demonstrable relations under four general heads; to this I know not what to reply, till some one be so good as to point out to me this new relation. It is impossible to refute a system which has never yet been explained. In such a manner of fighting in the dark, a man loses his blows in the air, and often places them where the enemy is not present.

I must therefore, on this occasion, rest contented with requiring the two following conditions of any one that would undertake to clear up this system. *First*, as moral good and evil belong only to the actions of the mind, and are derived from our situation with regard to external objects, the relations from which these moral distinctions arise must lie only betwixt internal actions and external objects, and must not be applicable either to internal actions, compared among themselves, or to external objects, when placed in opposition to other external objects. For as morality is supposed to attend certain relations, if these relations could belong to internal actions considered singly, it would follow, that we might be guilty of crimes in ourselves, and independent of our situation with respect to the universe; and in like manner, if these moral relations could be applied to external objects, it would follow that even inanimate beings would be susceptible of moral beauty and deformity. Now, it seems difficult to imagine that any relation can be discovered betwixt our passions, volitions, and actions, compared to external objects, which relation might not belong either to these passions and volitions, or to these external objects, compared among *themselves*.

But it will be still more difficult to fulfil the *second* condition, requisite to justify this system. According to the principles of those who maintain an abstract rational difference betwixt moral good and evil, and a natural fitness and unfitness of things, it is not only supposed, that these relations, being eternal and immutable, are the same, when considered by every rational creature, but their *effects* are also supposed to be necessarily the same; and it is concluded they have no less, or rather a greater, influence in directing the will of the Deity, than in governing the rational and virtuous of our own species. These two particulars are evidently distinct. It is one thing to know virtue, and another to conform the will to it. In order, therefore, to prove that the measures of right and wrong are eternal laws, *obligatory* on every rational mind, it is not sufficient to show the relations upon which they are founded: we must also point out the connection betwixt the relation and the will; and must prove that this connection is so necessary, that in every well-disposed mind, it must take place and have its influence; though the difference betwixt these minds be in other respects immense and infinite. Now, besides what I have already proved, that even in human nature no relation can ever alone produce any action; besides this, I say, it has been shown, in treating of the understanding, that there is no connection of cause and effect, such as this is supposed to be, which is discoverable otherwise than by experience, and of which we can pretend to have any security by the simple consideration of the objects. All beings in the universe, considered in themselves, appear entirely loose and independent of each other. It is only by experience we learn their influence and connection; and this influence we ought never to extend beyond experience.

Thus it will be impossible to fulfil the *first* condition required to the system of eternal rational measures of right and wrong; because it is impossible to show those relations, upon which such a distinction may be founded: and it is as impossible to fulfil the *second* condition: because we cannot prove *a priori*, that these relations, if they really existed and were perceived, would be universally forcible and obligatory. . . .

Nor does this reasoning only prove, that morality consists not in any relations that are the objects of science; but if examined, will prove with equal certainty, that it consists not in any *matter of fact*, which can be discovered by the understanding. This is the *second* part of our argument; and if it can be made evident, we may conclude that morality is not an object of reason. But can there be any difficulty in proving that vice and virtue are not matters of fact, whose existence we can infer by reason? Take any action allowed to be vicious; wilful murder, for instance. Examine it in all lights, and see if you can find that matter of fact, or real existence, which you call *vice*. In whichever way you take it, you find only certain passions, motives, volitions, and thoughts. There is no other matter of fact in the case. The vice entirely escapes you, as long as you consider the object. You never can find it, till you turn your reflection into your own breast, and find a sentiment of disapprobation, which arises in you, towards this action. Here is a matter of fact; but it is the object of feeling, not of reason. It lies in yourself, not in the object. So that when you pronounce any action or character to be vicious, you mean nothing, but that from the constitution of your nature you have a feeling or sentiment of blame from the contemplation of it. Vice and virtue, therefore, may be compared to sounds, colours, heat, and cold, which, according to modern philosophy, are not qualities in objects, but perceptions in the mind: and this discovery in morals, like that other in physics, is to be regarded as a considerable advancement of the speculative sciences; though, like that too, it has little or no influence on practice. Nothing can

to point out to me this new relation. It is impossible to re
which has never yet been explained. In such a manner
in the dark, a man loses his blows in the air, and often places
the enemy is not present.

I must therefore, on this occasion, rest contented with requ
two following conditions of any one that would undertake to clea
system. *First*, as moral good and evil belong only to the actions of th
and are derived from our situation with regard to external objec
relations from which these moral distinctions arise must lie only be
internal actions and external objects, and must not be applicable e
to internal actions, compared among themselves, or to external obje
when placed in opposition to other external objects. For as morality is su
posed to attend certain relations, if these relations could belong to inte
nal actions considered singly, it would follow, that we might be guilty o
crimes in ourselves, and independent of our situation with respect to the
universe; and in like manner, if these moral relations could be applied to
external objects, it would follow that even inanimate beings would be susceptible of moral beauty and deformity. Now, it seems difficult to imagine
that any relation can be discovered betwixt our passions, volitions, and
actions, compared to external objects, which relation might not belong
either to these passions and volitions, or to these external objects, compared among *themselves*.

But it will be still more difficult to fulfil the *second* condition, requisite to justify this system. According to the principles of those who maintain an abstract rational difference betwixt moral good and evil, and a
natural fitness and unfitness of things, it is not only supposed, that these
relations, being eternal and immutable, are the same, when considered
by every rational creature, but their *effects* are also supposed to be necessarily the same; and it is concluded they have no less, or rather a greater,
influence in directing the will of the Deity, than in governing the rational and virtuous of our own species. These two particulars are evidently
distinct. It is one thing to know virtue, and another to conform the will
to it. In order, therefore, to prove that the measures of right and wrong
are eternal laws, *obligatory* on every rational mind, it is not sufficient to
show the relations upon which they are founded: we must also point out
the connection betwixt the relation and the will; and must prove that this
connection is so necessary, that in every well-disposed mind, it must take
place and have its influence; though the difference betwixt these minds be
in other respects immense and infinite. Now, besides what I have already

be more real, or concern us more, than our own sentiments of pleasure and uneasiness; and if these be favourable to virtue, and unfavourable to vice, no more can be requisite to the regulation of our conduct and behaviour.

I cannot forbear adding to these reasonings an observation, which may, perhaps, be found of some importance. In every system of morality which I have hitherto met with, I have always remarked, that the author proceeds for some time in the ordinary way of reasoning, and establishes the being of a God, or makes observations concerning human affairs; when of a sudden I am surprised to find, that instead of the usual copulations of propositions, *is*, and *is not*, I meet with no proposition that is not connected with an *ought*, or an *ought not*. This change is imperceptible; but is, however, of the last consequence. For as this *ought*, or *ought not*, expresses some new relation or affirmation, it is necessary that it should be observed and explained; and at the same time that a reason should be given, for what seems altogether inconceivable, how this new relation can be a deduction from others, which are entirely different from it. But as authors do not commonly use this precaution, I shall presume to recommend it to the readers; and am persuaded, that this small attention would subvert all the vulgar systems of morality, and let us see that the distinction of vice and virtue is not founded merely on the relations of objects, nor is perceived by reason.

David Hume: Moral Distinctions Not Derived from Reason

1. According to Hume, "reason has no influence on our passions and actions." What does Hume mean by this? Do you think he is right?
2. Hume claims that the rules of morality "are not conclusions of our reason." How does he argue for this? Do you find his argument convincing?
3. Hume admits that "false judgments" may influence our behavior, but argues that the truth of our judgments does not determine whether actions are morally right or wrong. What is his argument for thinking this?
4. According to Hume, to say that an action is wrong is equivalent to saying that "from the constitution of your nature you have a feeling or sentiment of blame from the contemplation of it." Is this a plausible account of what we mean when we say that an action is wrong? Does this imply

that different actions are wrong for different people, depending on how they feel?

5. Hume claims it is "inconceivable" that we can deduce claims about what *ought* to be the case from claims about what *is* the case. What exactly does he mean by this? Do you think there are any counterexamples to this claim?

15

The Subjectivity of Values

J. L. Mackie

J. L. Mackie (1917–1981), who taught for many years at Oxford University, regarded all ethical views as bankrupt. In this excerpt from his book *Ethics: Inventing Right and Wrong* (1977), Mackie outlines the basic ideas and the central motivating arguments for his *error theory*—the view that all positive moral claims are mistaken. All moral talk, as Mackie sees it, is based on a false assumption: that there are objective moral values. This fundamental error infects the entire system of morality. The foundations are corrupt, and so the entire moral edifice must come tumbling down.

Mackie offers a number of important arguments to substantiate his critique of morality. The argument from relativity claims that the extent of moral disagreement is best explained by the claim that there are no objective values. The argument from queerness contends that objective moral values would be objectionably different from any other kind of thing in the universe, possessed of strange powers that are best rejected. Mackie concludes with his account of why so many people, for so long, have fallen into error by succumbing to the temptation to think of morality as objective.

From *Ethics: Inventing Right and Wrong* by J. L. Mackie (Pelican Books, 1977). Copyright © J. L. Mackie, 1977. Reproduced with permission of Penguin Books Ltd.

Moral Scepticism

There are no objective values. This is a bald statement of the thesis of this chapter, but before arguing for it I shall try to clarify and restrict it in ways that may meet some objections and prevent some misunderstanding. . . .

The claim that values are not objective, are not part of the fabric of the world, is meant to include not only moral goodness, which might be most naturally equated with moral value, but also other things that could be more loosely called moral values or disvalues—rightness and wrongness, duty, obligation, an action's being rotten and contemptible, and so on. It also includes non-moral values, notably aesthetic ones, beauty and various kinds of artistic merit. I shall not discuss these explicitly, but clearly much the same considerations apply to aesthetic and to moral values, and there would be at least some initial implausibility in a view that gave the one a different status from the other. . . .

The claim to objectivity, however ingrained in our language and thought, is not self-validating. It can and should be questioned. But the denial of objective values will have to be put forward not as the result of an analytic approach, but as an 'error theory,' a theory that although most people in making moral judgements implicitly claim, among other things, to be pointing to something objectively prescriptive, these claims are all false. It is this that makes the name 'moral scepticism' appropriate.

But since this is an error theory, since it goes against assumptions ingrained in our thought and built into some of the ways in which language is used, since it conflicts with what is sometimes called common sense, it needs very solid support. It is not something we can accept lightly or casually and then quietly pass on. If we are to adopt this view, we must argue explicitly for it. Traditionally it has been supported by arguments of two main kinds, which I shall call the argument from relativity and the argument from queerness. . . .

The Argument from Relativity

The argument from relativity has as its premiss the well-known variation in moral codes from one society to another and from one period to another, and also the differences in moral beliefs between different groups and classes within a complex community. Such variation is in itself merely a truth of descriptive morality, a fact of anthropology which entails neither first order nor second order ethical views. Yet it may indirectly support second order subjectivism: radical differences between first order moral judgements make it difficult to treat those judgements as apprehensions of objective truths. But it is not the mere occurrence of disagreements that tells against the objectivity of values. Disagreement on questions in history or biology or cosmology does not show that there are no objective issues in these fields for investigators to disagree about. But such scientific disagreement results from speculative inferences or explanatory hypotheses based on inadequate evidence, and it is hardly plausible to interpret moral disagreement in the same way. Disagreement about moral codes seems to reflect people's adherence to and participation in different ways of life. The causal connection seems to be mainly that way round: it is that people approve of monogamy because they participate in a monogamous way of life rather than that they participate in a monogamous way of life because they approve of monogamy. Of course, the standards may be an idealization of the way of life from which they arise: the monogamy in which people participate may be less complete, less rigid, than that of which it leads them to approve. This is not to say that moral judgements are purely conventional. Of course there have been and are moral heretics and moral reformers, people who have turned against the established rules and practices of their own communities for moral reasons, and often for moral reasons that we would endorse. But this can usually be understood as the extension, in ways which, though new and unconventional, seemed to them to be required for consistency, of rules to which they already adhered as arising out of an existing way of life. In short, the argument from relativity has some force simply because the actual variations in the moral codes are more readily explained by the hypothesis that they reflect ways of life than by the hypothesis that they express perceptions, most of them seriously inadequate and badly distorted, of objective values.

But there is a well-known counter to this argument from relativity, namely to say that the items for which objective validity is in the first place to be claimed are not specific moral rules or codes but very general basic principles which are recognized at least implicitly to some extent in all society—such principles as provide the foundations of what Sidgwick has called different methods of ethics: the principle of universalizability, perhaps, or the rule that one ought to conform to the specific rules of any way of life in which one takes part, from which one profits, and on which one relies, or some utilitarian principle of doing what tends, or seems likely, to promote the general happiness. It is easy to show that such general principles, married with differing concrete circumstances, different existing social patterns or different preferences, will beget different specific moral rules; and there is some plausibility in the claim that the specific rules thus generated will vary from community to community or from group to group in close agreement with the actual variations in accepted codes.

The argument from relativity can be only partly countered in this way. To take this line the moral objectivist has to say that it is only in these principles that the objective moral character attaches immediately to its descriptively specified ground or subject: other moral judgements are objectively valid or true, but only derivatively and contingently—if things had been otherwise, quite different sorts of actions would have been right. And despite the prominence in recent philosophical ethics of universalization, utilitarian principles, and the like, these are very far from constituting the whole of what is actually affirmed as basic in ordinary moral thought. Much of this is concerned rather with what Hare calls 'ideals' or, less kindly, 'fanaticism.' That is, people judge that some things are good or right, and others are bad or wrong, not because—or at any rate not only because—they exemplify some general principle for which widespread implicit acceptance could be claimed, but because something about those things arouses certain responses immediately in them, though they would arouse radically and irresolvably different responses in others. 'Moral sense' or 'intuition' is an initially more plausible description of what supplies many of our basic moral judgements than 'reason.' With regard to all these starting points of moral thinking the argument from relativity remains in full force.

The Argument from Queerness

Even more important, however, and certainly more generally applicable, is the argument from queerness. This has two parts, one metaphysical, the other epistemological. If there were objective values, then they would be entities or qualities or relations of a very strange sort, utterly different from anything else in the universe. Correspondingly, if we were aware of them, it would have to be by some special faculty of moral perception or intuition, utterly different from our ordinary ways of knowing everything else. These points were recognized by Moore when he spoke of non-natural qualities, and by the intuitionists in their talk about a 'faculty of moral intuition.' Intuitionism has long been out of favour, and it is indeed easy to point out its implausibilities. What is not so often stressed, but is more important, is that the central thesis of intuitionism is one to which any objectivist view of values is in the end committed: intuitionism merely makes unpalatably plain what other forms of objectivism wrap up. Of course the suggestion that moral judgements are made or moral problems solved by just sitting down and having an ethical intuition is a travesty of actual moral thinking. But, however complex the real process, it will require (if it is to yield authoritatively prescriptive conclusions) some input of this distinctive sort, either premises or forms of argument or both. When we ask the awkward question, how we can be aware of this authoritative prescriptivity, of the truth of these distinctively ethical premises or of the cogency of this distinctively ethical pattern of reasoning, none of our ordinary accounts of sensory perception or introspection or the framing and confirming of explanatory hypotheses or inference or logical construction or conceptual analysis, or any combination of these, will provide a satisfactory answer; 'a special sort of intuition' is a lame answer, but it is the one to which the clear-headed objectivist is compelled to resort.

Indeed, the best move for the moral objectivist is not to evade this issue, but to look for companions in guilt. For example, Richard Price argues that it is not moral knowledge alone that such an empiricism as those of Locke and Hume is unable to account for, but also our knowledge and even our ideas of essence, number, identity, diversity, solidity, inertia, substance, the necessary existence and infinite extension of time and space, necessity and possibility in general, power, and causation. If the understanding, which Price defines as the faculty within us that discerns truth, is also a source of new simple ideas of so many other sorts, may it not also be a power of immediately perceiving right and wrong, which yet are real characters of actions?

This is an important counter to the argument from queerness. The only adequate reply to it would be to show how, on empiricist foundations, we can construct an account of the ideas and beliefs and knowledge that we have of all these matters. I cannot even begin to do that here, though I have undertaken some parts of the task elsewhere. I can only state my belief that satisfactory accounts of most of these can be given in empirical terms. If some supposed metaphysical necessities or essences resist such treatment, then they too should be included, along with objective values, among the targets of the argument from queerness.

This queerness does not consist simply in the fact that ethical statements are 'unverifiable.' Although logical positivism with its verifiability theory of descriptive meaning gave an impetus to non-cognitive accounts of ethics, it is not only logical positivists but also empiricists of a much more liberal sort who should find objective values hard to accommodate. Indeed, I would not only reject the verifiability principle but also deny the conclusion commonly drawn from it, that moral judgements lack descriptive meaning. The assertion that there are objective values or intrinsically prescriptive entities or features of some kind, which ordinary moral judgements presuppose, is, I hold, not meaningless but false.

Plato's Forms give a dramatic picture of what objective values would have to be. The Form of the Good is such that knowledge of it provides the knower with both a direction and an overriding motive; something's being good both tells the person who knows this to pursue it and makes him pursue it. An objective good would be sought by anyone who was acquainted with it, not because of any contingent fact that this person, or every person, is so constituted that he desires this end, but just because the end has to-be-pursuedness somehow built into it. Similarly, if there were objective principles of right and wrong, any wrong (possible) course of action would have not-to-be-doneness somehow built into it. Or we should have something like Clarke's necessary relations of fitness between situations and actions, so that a situation would have a demand for such-and-such an action somehow built into it.

The need for an argument of this sort can be brought out by reflection on Hume's argument that 'reason'—in which at this stage he includes all sorts of knowing as well as reasoning—can never be an 'influencing motive of the will.' Someone might object that Hume has argued unfairly from the lack of influencing power (not contingent upon desires) in ordinary objects of knowledge and ordinary reasoning, and might maintain that values differ from natural objects precisely in their power, when known, automatically to influence the will. To this Hume could, and would need to, reply that this objection involves the postulating of value-entities or value-features of quite a different order from anything else with which we are acquainted, and of a corresponding faculty with which to detect them. That is, he would have to supplement his explicit argument with what I have called the argument from queerness.

Another way of bringing out this queerness is to ask, about anything that is supposed to have some objective moral quality, how this is linked with its natural features. What is the connection between the natural fact that an action is a piece of deliberate cruelty—say, causing pain just for fun—and the moral fact that it is wrong? It cannot be an entailment, a logical or semantic necessity. Yet it is not merely that the two features occur together. The wrongness must somehow be 'consequential' or 'supervenient'; it is wrong because it is a piece of deliberate cruelty. But just what *in the world* is signified by this 'because'? And how do we know the relation that it signifies, if this is something more than such actions being socially condemned, and condemned by us too, perhaps through our having absorbed attitudes from our social environment? It is not even sufficient to postulate a faculty which 'sees' the wrongness: something must be postulated which can see at once the natural features that constitute the cruelty, and the wrongness, and the mysterious consequential link between the two. Alternatively, the intuition required might be the perception that wrongness is a higher order property belonging to certain natural properties; but what is this belonging of properties to other properties, and how can we discern it? How much simpler and more comprehensible the situation would be if we could replace the moral quality with some sort of subjective response which could be causally related to the detection of the natural features on which the supposed quality is said to be consequential.

It may be thought that the argument from queerness is given an unfair start if we thus relate it to what are admittedly among the wilder products of philosophical fancy—Platonic Forms, non-natural qualities, self-evident relations of fitness, faculties of intuition, and the like. Is it equally forceful if applied to the terms in which everyday moral judgements are more likely to be expressed—though still, as has been argued in the original work, with a claim to objectivity—'you must do this,' 'you can't do that,' 'obligation,' 'unjust,' 'rotten,' 'disgraceful,' 'mean,' or talk about good reasons for or against possible actions? Admittedly not; but that is because the objective prescriptivity, the element a claim for whose authoritativeness is embedded in ordinary moral thought and language, is not yet isolated in these forms of speech, but is presented along with relations to desires and feelings, reasoning about the means to desired ends, interpersonal demands, the injustice which consists in the violation of what are in the context the accepted standards of merit, the psychological constituents of meanness, and so on. There is nothing queer about any of these, and under cover of them the claim for moral authority may pass unnoticed. But if I am right in arguing that it is ordinarily there, and is therefore very likely to be incorporated almost automatically in philosophical accounts of ethics which systematize our ordinary thought even in such apparently innocent terms as these, it needs to be examined, and for this purpose it needs to be isolated and exposed as it is by the less cautious philosophical reconstructions.

Patterns of Objectification

Considerations of these kinds suggest that it is in the end less paradoxical to reject than to retain the common-sense belief in the objectivity of moral values, provided that we can explain how this belief, if it is false, has become established and is so resistant to criticisms. This proviso is not difficult to satisfy.

On a subjectivist view, the supposedly objective values will be based in fact upon attitudes which the person has who takes himself to be recognizing and responding to those values. If we admit what Hume calls the mind's 'propensity to spread itself on external objects', we can understand the supposed objectivity of moral qualities as arising from what we can call the projection or objectification of moral attitudes. This would be analogous to what is called the 'pathetic fallacy', the tendency to read our feelings into their objects. If a fungus, say, fills us with disgust, we may be inclined to ascribe to the fungus itself a non-natural quality of foulness. But in moral contexts there is more than this propensity at work. Moral attitudes themselves are at least partly social in origin: socially established—and socially necessary—patterns of behaviour put pressure on individuals, and each individual tends to internalize these pressures and to join in requiring these patterns of behaviour of himself and of others. The attitudes that are objectified into moral values have indeed an external source, though not the one assigned to them by the belief in their absolute authority. Moreover, there are motives that would support objectification. We need morality to regulate interpersonal relations, to control some of the ways in which people behave towards one another, often in opposition to contrary inclinations. We therefore want our moral judgements to be authoritative for other agents as well as for ourselves: objective validity would give them the authority required. Aesthetic values are logically in the same position as moral ones; much the same metaphysical and epistemological considerations apply to them. But aesthetic values are less strongly objectified than moral ones; their subjective status, and an 'error theory' with regard to such claims to objectivity as are incorporated in aesthetic judgements, will be more readily accepted, just because the motives for their objectification are less compelling.

But it would be misleading to think of the objectification of moral values as primarily the projection of feelings, as in the pathetic fallacy.

More important are wants and demands. As Hobbes says, 'whatsoever is the object of any man's Appetite or Desire, that is it, which he for his part calleth *Good* '; and certainly both the adjective 'good' and the noun 'goods' are used in non-moral contexts of things because they are such as to satisfy desires. We get the notion of something's being objectively good, or having intrinsic value, by reversing the direction of dependence here, by making the desire depend upon the goodness, instead of the goodness on the desire. And this is aided by the fact that the desired thing will indeed have features that make it desired, that enable it to arouse a desire or that make it such as to satisfy some desire that is already there. It is fairly easy to confuse the way in which a thing's desirability is indeed objective with its having in our sense objective value. The fact that the word 'good' serves as one of our main moral terms is a trace of this pattern of objectification. . . .

J. L. Mackie: The Subjectivity of Values

1. Why does Mackie refer to his view as an "error theory"? What is the "error" that Mackie takes himself to be pointing out?
2. Mackie cites widespread disagreement about morality as evidence for his view that there are no objective moral values. Yet he admits that the existence of scientific disagreement does not suggest that there are no objective scientific truths. Why does Mackie think that ethics is different from science in this regard? Do you think he is right about this?
3. One might object to Mackie's argument from disagreement by noting that some moral prohibitions (against killing innocent people, against adultery, etc.) are widely shared across cultures. Does this show that there is something wrong with the argument from disagreement? How do you think Mackie would respond to such an objection?
4. Mackie claims that objective values, if they existed, would be entities "of a very strange sort, utterly different from anything else in the universe." What feature of moral values would make them so strange? Do you agree with Mackie that the "queerness" of moral properties is a good reason to deny their existence?
5. Mackie suggests that his view is "simpler and more comprehensible" than accepting objective values. In what ways is his view simpler? Is this a good reason to reject the existence of objective values?
6. Mackie thinks that for his error theory to succeed, he must explain how people come to think that there are objective moral values in the first place. How does he attempt to do so? Do you think he is successful?

====== ❧ ======

16

Ethics and Observation

Gilbert Harman

....

In this brief selection from his book *The Nature of Morality* (1977), Gilbert Harman argues that there is a fundamental difference between the claims of ethics and those of the natural sciences. We can verify scientific claims by testing them against the world. We can't do this with moral claims. The reason is that moral facts appear to cause nothing, and without any causal power, it is impossible to detect their presence. This leaves us no choice but to test our moral views exclusively by seeing how well they relate to other beliefs we already hold. But since those further moral beliefs are also unable to be scientifically confirmed, there is no reason to think that moral beliefs can record some independent reality, in the way that true scientific beliefs report facts about the natural world.

Harman's arguments have generated a substantial amount of attention, focusing our thoughts as they do on what seems to be a fundamental difference between scientific claims and moral claims. If there is a moral reality out there, awaiting our discovery, then we should, says Harman, be able to find out about it in the same way we learn about the natural world that science describes. But we can't do that. In a part of the book that is omitted here, Harman relies on the arguments from this selection to support his moral relativism, which insists that morality is a matter of social agreements, with no objective basis.

Gilbert Harman, "Ethics and Observation" from *The Nature of Morality* (1977), pp. 3–10. By permission of Oxford University Press, Inc.

Harman's arguments have been very influential in shaping debates within metaethics over the past few decades. Many have found his ideas compelling. Others have sought to show that ethics is really a kind of natural science, its claims testable "against the world," and so subject to scientific confirmation. Still others have been content to deny that ethics is any kind of science, but have then proceeded to argue that ethics is none the worse for this difference.

....

The Basic Issue

Can moral principles be tested and confirmed in the way scientific principles can? Consider the principle that, if you are given a choice between five people alive and one dead or five people dead and one alive, you should always choose to have five people alive and one dead rather than the other way round. We can easily imagine examples that appear to confirm this principle. Here is one:

> You are a doctor in a hospital's emergency room when six accident victims are brought in. All six are in danger of dying but one is much worse off than the others. You can just barely save that person if you devote all of your resources to him and let the others die. Alternatively, you can save the other five if you are willing to ignore the most seriously injured person.

It would seem that in this case you, the doctor, would be right to save the five and let the other person die. So this example, taken by itself, confirms the principle under consideration. Next, consider the following case.

> You have five patients in the hospital who are dying, each in need of a separate organ. One needs a kidney, another a lung, a third a heart, and so forth. You can save all five if you take a single healthy person and remove his heart, lungs, kidneys, and so forth, to distribute to these five patients. Just such a healthy person is in room 306. He is in the hospital for routine tests. Having seen his test results, you know that he is perfectly healthy and of the right tissue compatibility. If you do nothing, he will survive without incident; the other patients will die, however. The other five patients can be saved only if the person in Room 306 is cut up and his organs distributed. In that case, there would be one dead but five saved.

The principle in question tells us that you should cut up the patient in Room 306. But in this case, surely you must not sacrifice this innocent bystander, even to save the five other patients. Here a moral principle has been tested and disconfirmed in what may seem to be a surprising way.

This, of course, was a "thought experiment." We did not really compare a hypothesis with the world. We compared an explicit principle with our feelings about certain imagined examples. In the same way, a physicist performs thought experiments in order to compare explicit hypotheses with his "sense" of what should happen in certain situations, a "sense" that he has acquired as a result of his long working familiarity with current theory. But scientific hypotheses can also be tested in real experiments, out in the world.

Can moral principles be tested in the same way, out in the world? You can observe someone do something, but can you ever perceive the rightness or wrongness of what he does? If you round a corner and see a group of young hoodlums pour gasoline on a cat and ignite it, you do not need to *conclude* that what they are doing is wrong; you do not need to figure anything out; you can *see* that it is wrong. But is your reaction due to the actual wrongness of what you see or is it simply a reflection of your moral "sense," a "sense" that you have acquired perhaps as a result of your moral upbringing?

Observation

The issue is complicated. There are no pure observations. Observations are always "theory laden." What you perceive depends to some extent on the theory you hold, consciously or unconsciously. You see some children pour gasoline on a cat and ignite it. To really see that, you have to possess a great deal of knowledge, know about a considerable number of objects, know about people: that people pass through the life stages infant, baby, child, adolescent, adult. You must know what flesh and blood animals are, and in particular, cats. You must have some idea of life. You must know what gasoline is, what burning is, and much more. In one sense, what you "see" is a pattern of light on your retina, a shifting array of splotches, although, even that is theory, and you could never adequately describe what you see in that sense. In another sense, you see what you do because of the theories you hold. Change those theories and you would see something else, given the same pattern of light.

Similarly, if you hold a moral view, whether it is held consciously or unconsciously, you will be able to perceive rightness or wrongness, goodness or badness, justice or injustice. There is no difference in this respect between moral propositions and other theoretical propositions. If there is a difference, it must be found elsewhere.

Observation depends on theory because perception involves forming a belief as a fairly direct result of observing something; you can form a belief only if you understand the relevant concepts and a concept is what it is by virtue of its role in some theory or system of beliefs. To recognize a child as a child is to employ, consciously or unconsciously, a concept that is defined by its place in a framework of the stages of human life. Similarly, burning is an empty concept apart from its theoretical connections to the concepts of heat, destruction, smoke, and fire.

Moral concepts—Right and Wrong, Good and Bad, Justice and Injustice—also have a place in your theory or system of beliefs and are the concepts they are because of their context. If we say that observation has occurred whenever an opinion is a direct result of perception, we must allow that there is moral observation, because such an opinion can be a moral opinion as easily as any other sort. In this sense, observation may be used to confirm or disconfirm moral theories. The observational opinions that, in this sense, you find yourself with can be in either agreement or conflict with your consciously explicit moral principles. When they are in conflict, you must choose between your explicit theory and observation. In ethics, as in science, you sometimes opt for theory, and say that you made an error in observation or were biased or whatever, or you sometimes opt for observation, and modify your theory.

In other words, in both science and ethics, general principles are invoked to explain particular cases and, therefore, in both science and ethics, the general principles you accept can be tested by appealing to particular judgments that certain things are right or wrong, just or unjust, and so forth; and these judgments are analogous to direct perceptual judgments about facts.

Observational Evidence

Nevertheless, observation plays a role in science that it does not seem to play in ethics. The difference is that you need to make assumptions about certain physical facts to explain the occurrence of the observations that support a scientific theory, but you do not seem to need to make assumptions about any moral facts to explain the occurrence of the so-called moral observations I have been talking about. In the moral case, it would seem that you need only make assumptions about the psychology or moral sensibility of the person making the moral observation. In the scientific case, theory is tested against the world.

The point is subtle but important. Consider a physicist making an observation to test a scientific theory. Seeing a vapor trail in a cloud chamber, he thinks, "There goes a proton." Let us suppose that this is an observation in the relevant sense, namely, an immediate judgment made in response to the situation without any conscious reasoning having taken place. Let us also suppose that his observation confirms his theory, a theory that helps give meaning to the very term "proton" as it occurs in his observational judgment. Such a confirmation rests on inferring an explanation. He can count his making the observation as confirming evidence for his theory only to the extent that it is reasonable to explain his making the observation by assuming that, not only is he in a certain psychological "set," given the theory he accepts and his beliefs about the experimental apparatus, but furthermore, there really was a proton going through the cloud chamber, causing the vapor trail, which he saw as a proton. (This is evidence for the theory to the extent that the theory can explain the proton's being there better than competing theories can.) But, if his having made that observation could have been equally well explained by his psychological set alone, without the need for any assumption about a proton, then the observation would not have been evidence for the existence of that proton and therefore would not have been evidence for the theory. His making the observation supports the theory only because, in order to explain his making the observation, it is reasonable to assume something about the world over and above the assumptions made about the observer's psychology. In particular, it is reasonable to assume that there was a proton going through the cloud chamber, causing the vapor trail.

Compare this case with one in which you make a moral judgment immediately and without conscious reasoning, say, that the children are wrong to set the cat on fire or that the doctor would be wrong to cut up one healthy patient to save five dying patients. In order to explain your making the first of these judgments, it would be reasonable to assume, perhaps, that the children really are pouring gasoline on a cat and you are seeing them do it. But, in neither case is there any obvious reason to assume anything about "moral facts," such as that it really is wrong to set the cat on fire or to cut up the patient in Room 306. Indeed, an assumption about moral facts would seem to be totally irrelevant to the explanation of your making the judgment you make. It would seem that all we need assume is that you have certain more or less well articulated moral principles that are reflected in the judgments you make, based on your moral sensibility. It seems to be completely irrelevant to our explanation whether your intuitive immediate judgment is true or false.

The observation of an event can provide observational evidence for or against a scientific theory in the sense that the truth of that observation can be relevant to a reasonable explanation of why that observation was made. A moral observation does not seem, in the same sense, to be observational evidence for or against any moral theory, since the truth or falsity of the moral observation seems to be completely irrelevant to any reasonable explanation of why that observation was made. The fact that an observation of an event was made at the time it was made is evidence not only about the observer but also about the physical facts. The fact that you made a particular moral observation when you did does not seem to be evidence about moral facts, only evidence about you and your moral sensibility. Facts about protons can affect what you observe, since a proton passing through the cloud chamber can cause a vapor trail that reflects light to your eye in a way that, given your scientific training and psychological set, leads you to judge that what you see is a proton. But there does not seem to be any way in which the actual rightness or wrongness of a given situation can have any effect on your perceptual apparatus. In this respect, ethics seems to differ from science.

In considering whether moral principles can help explain observations, it is therefore important to note an ambiguity in the word "observation." You see the children set the cat on fire and immediately think, "That's wrong." In one sense, your observation is that what the children are doing is wrong. In another sense, your observation is your thinking that thought. Moral observations might explain observations in the first sense but not in the second sense. Certain moral principles might help to explain why it was *wrong* of the children to set the cat on fire, but moral principles seem to be of no help in explaining *your thinking* that that is wrong. In the first sense of "observation," moral principles can be tested by observation— "That this act is wrong is evidence that causing unnecessary suffering is wrong." But in the second sense of "observation," moral principles cannot clearly be tested by observation, since they do not appear to help explain observations in this second sense of "observation." Moral principles do not seem to help explain your observing what you observe.

Of course, if you are already given the moral principle that it is wrong to cause unnecessary suffering, you can take your seeing the children setting the cat on fire as observational evidence that they are doing something wrong. Similarly, you can suppose that your seeing the vapor trail is observational evidence that a proton is going through the cloud chamber, if you are given the relevant physical theory. But there is an important apparent difference between the two cases. In the scientific case, your making that observation is itself evidence for the physical theory because the physical theory explains the proton, which explains the trail, which explains your observation. In the moral case, your making your observation does not seem to be evidence for the relevant moral principle because that principle does not seem to help explain your observation. The explanatory chain from principle to observation seems to be broken in morality. The moral principle may "explain" why it is wrong for the children to set the cat on fire. But the wrongness of that act does not appear to help explain the act, which you observe, itself. The explanatory chain appears to be broken in such a way that neither the moral principle nor the wrongness of the act can help explain why you observe what you observe.

A qualification may seem to be needed here. Perhaps the children perversely set the cat on fire simply "because it is wrong." Here it may seem at first that the actual wrongness of the act does help explain why they do it and therefore indirectly helps explain why you observe what you observe just as a physical theory, by explaining why the proton is producing a vapor trail, indirectly helps explain why the observer observes what he observes. But on reflection we must agree that this is probably an illusion. What explains the children's act is not clearly the actual wrongness of the act but, rather, their belief that the act is wrong. The actual rightness or wrongness of their act seems to have nothing to do with why they do it.

Observational evidence plays a part in science it does not appear to play in ethics, because scientific principles can be justified ultimately by their role in explaining observations, in the second sense of observation— by their explanatory role. Apparently, moral principles cannot be justified in the same way. It appears to be true that there can be no explanatory chain between moral principles and particular observings in the way that there can be such a chain between scientific principles and particular observings. Conceived as an explanatory theory, morality, unlike science, seems to be cut off from observation.

Not that every legitimate scientific hypothesis is susceptible to direct observational testing. Certain hypotheses about "black holes" in space cannot be directly tested, for example, because no signal is emitted from within a black hole. The connection with observation in such a case is indirect. And there are many similar examples. Nevertheless, seen in the large, there is the apparent difference between science and ethics we have noted. The scientific realm is accessible to observation in a way the moral realm is not.

Ethics and Mathematics

Perhaps ethics is to be compared, not with physics, but with mathematics. Perhaps such a moral principle as "You ought to keep your promises" is confirmed or disconfirmed in the way (whatever it is) in which such a mathematical principle as "5 + 7 = 12" is. Observation does not seem to play the role in mathematics it plays in physics. We do not and cannot perceive numbers, for example, since we cannot be in causal contact with them. We do not even understand what it would be like to be in causal contact with the number 12, say. Relations among numbers cannot have any more of an effect on our perceptual apparatus than moral facts can.

Observation, however, *is* relevant to mathematics. In explaining the observations that support a physical theory, scientists typically appeal to mathematical principles. On the other hand, one never seems to need to appeal in this way to moral principles. Since an observation is evidence for what best explains it, and since mathematics often figures in the explanations of scientific observations, there is indirect observational evidence for mathematics. There does not seem to be observational evidence, even indirectly, for basic moral principles. In explaining why certain observations have been made, we never seem to use purely moral assumptions. In this respect, then, ethics appears to differ not only from physics but also from mathematics.

Gilbert Harman: Ethics and Observation

1. According to Harman, "Observations are always 'theory laden.'" What does he mean by this? Do you think he is correct?
2. Harman claims that ethics differs from science in that "you do not seem to need to make assumptions about any moral facts to explain the occurrence of the so-called moral observations." How does Harman think we can explain moral observations? Is his explanation a good one?
3. Harman says that the rightness or wrongness of actions cannot "have any effect on your perceptual apparatus." Can moral features (such as rightness or wrongness) ever cause anything? If not, is this good reason to conclude that they do not exist?

4. It might be suggested that ethics is similar to mathematics in that neither can be empirically confirmed. What is Harman's argument against this suggestion? How does our evidence for mathematical claims differ from our evidence for ethical claims?

5. Suppose that we accept Harman's assertion that ethical claims cannot be tested by observation. What should we conclude from this? Does this show that moral principles cannot be objectively true?

17

Cultural Relativism

Harry Gensler

....

In this essay, Harry Gensler presents and evaluates the doctrine known as *cultural relativism*. This is the view that social approval is the ultimate measure of morality. Those acts approved of by society are good; those that are socially frowned on are bad.

Cultural relativists believe that morality is like the law, or other social conventions. Just as what is legal varies from society to society, so too does what is moral. There are no objective moral standards that apply universally. Rather, what is right or wrong depends entirely on the customs that have arisen in different societies. Different customs mean different moral standards, none of which is uniquely correct for all people at all times.

Though many people are attracted to relativism because it appears to be soundly based on the fact of wide cultural differences and on the importance of tolerating diverse customs, Gensler argues that relativism is deeply problematic. He cites four reasons that cast doubt on the doctrine.

First, relativism cannot allow for consistent disagreement with one's own social code. So long as a society can make moral mistakes, then its approval is not enough to show that something is morally good.

Second, relativism is a very poor basis for defending tolerance. If a society favors intolerance, as many societies do, then relativism tells us that intolerance within those societies is a good thing.

From *Ethics* by Harry Gensler, copyright © 1998 by Routledge. Reproduced by permission of Taylor and Francis Books UK.

Third, relativism is a counsel of conformity. When trying to morally educate children, relativism tells us to be uncritical of the norms of our society, since they are, by relativist definition, always correct.

Fourth, relativism offers us poor advice about what to do in a situation that is increasingly common. Many of us are members of subcultures situated within larger groups. When we belong to more than one social group, then what do we do if the norms of these groups conflict? Relativism gives us either no advice at all, or conflicting advice.

Gensler concludes by trying to show why considerations that have led many people to relativism are compatible with antirelativist, objective views of ethics.

....

Cultural relativism (CR) says that good and bad are relative to culture. What is "good" is what is "socially approved" in a given culture. Our moral principles describe social conventions and must be based on the norms of our society.

We'll begin by listening to the fictional Ima Relativist explain her belief in cultural relativism. As you read this and similar accounts, reflect on how plausible you find the view and how well it harmonizes with your own thinking. After listening to Ima, we'll consider various objections to CR.

Ima Relativist

My name is Ima Relativist. I've embraced cultural relativism as I've come to appreciate the deeply cultural basis for morality.

I was brought up to believe that morality is about objective facts. Just as snow is white, so also infanticide is wrong. But attitudes vary with time and place. The norms that I was taught are the norms of my own society; other societies have different ones. Morality is a cultural construct. Just as societies create different styles of food and clothing, so too they create different moral codes. I've learned about these in my anthropology class and experienced them as an exchange student in Mexico.

Consider my belief that infanticide is wrong. I was taught this as if it were an objective standard. But it isn't; it's just what my society holds. When I say "Infanticide is wrong," this just means that my society disapproves of it. For the ancient Romans, on the other hand, infanticide was all right. There's no sense in asking which side here is "correct." Their view is true relative to their culture, and our view is true relative to ours. There are no objective truths about right or wrong. When we claim otherwise, we're just imposing our culturally taught attitudes as the "objective truth."

"Wrong" is a relative term. Let me explain what this means. Something isn't "to the left" absolutely, but only "to the left *of*" this or that. Similarly, something isn't "wrong" absolutely, but only "wrong *in*" this or that society. Infanticide might be wrong in one society but right in another.

We can express CR most clearly as a definition: "X is good" means "The majority (of the society in question) approves of X." Other moral terms, like "bad" and "right," can be defined in a similar way. Note the reference to a specific society. Unless otherwise specified, the society in question is that of the person making the judgment. When I say "Hitler acted *wrongly*," I mean "according to the standards of *my* society."

The myth of objectivity says that things can be good or bad "absolutely"—not relative to this or that culture. But how can we know what is good or bad absolutely? How can we argue about this without just presupposing the standards of our own society? People who speak of good or bad absolutely are absolutizing the norms of their own society. They take the norms that they were taught to be objective facts. Such people need to study anthropology, or to live for a time in another culture.

As I've come to believe in cultural relativism, I've grown in my acceptance of other cultures. Like many exchange students, I used to have this "we're right and they're wrong" attitude. I struggled against this. I came to realize that the other side isn't "wrong" but just "different." We have to see others from their point of view; if we criticize them, we're just imposing the standards of our own society. We cultural relativists are more tolerant.

Through cultural relativism I've also come to be more accepting of the norms of my own society. CR gives a basis for a common morality within a culture—a democratic basis that pools everyone's ideas and insures that the norms have wide support. So I can feel solidarity with my own people, even though other groups have different values.

Objections to CR

Ima has given us a clear formulation of an approach that many find attractive. She's thought a lot about morality, and we can learn from her. Yet I'm convinced that her basic perspective on morality is wrong. Ima will likely come to agree as she gets clearer in her thinking.

Let me point out the biggest problem. CR forces us to conform to society's norms—or else we contradict ourselves. If "good" and "socially approved" meant the same thing, then whatever was one would have to be the other. So this reasoning would be valid:

> Such and such is socially approved.
> ∴ Such and such is good.

If CR were true, then we couldn't consistently disagree with the values of our society. But this is an absurd result. We surely can consistently disagree with the values of our society. We can consistently affirm that something is "socially approved" but deny that it is "good." This would be impossible if CR were true.

Ima could bite the bullet (accept the implausible consequence), and say that it *is* self-contradictory to disagree morally with the majority. But this would be a difficult bullet for her to bite. She'd have to hold that civil rights leaders contradicted themselves when they disagreed with accepted views on segregation. And she'd have to accept the majority view on all moral issues—even if she sees that the majority is ignorant.

Suppose that Ima learned that most people in her society approve of displaying intolerance and ridicule toward people of other cultures. She'd then have to conclude that such intolerance is good (even though this goes against her new insights):

> Intolerance is socially approved.
> ∴ Intolerance is good.

She'd have to either accept the conclusion (that intolerance is good) or else reject cultural relativism. Consistency would require that she change at least one of her views.

Here's a bigger bullet for Ima to bite. Imagine that Ima meets a figure skater named Lika Rebel, who is on tour from a Nazi country. In Lika's homeland, Jews and critics of the government are put in concentration camps. The majority of the people, since they are kept misinformed, support these policies. Lika dissents. She says that these policies are supported by the majority but are wrong. If Ima applied CR to this case, she'd have to say something like this to Lika:

> Lika, your word "good" refers to what is approved in your culture.
> Since your culture approves of racism and oppression, you must

accept that these are good. You can't think otherwise. The minority view is always wrong—since what is "good" is by definition what the majority approves.

CR is intolerant toward minority views (which are automatically wrong) and would force Lika to accept racism and oppression as good. These results follow from CR's definition of "good" as "socially approved." Once Ima sees these results, she'll likely give up CR.

Racism is a good test case for ethical views. A satisfying view should give some way to attack racist actions. CR fails at this, since it holds that racist actions are good in a society if they're socially approved. If Lika followed CR, she'd have to agree with a racist majority, even if they're misinformed and ignorant. CR is very unsatisfying here.

Moral education gives another test case for ethical views. If we accepted CR, how would we bring up our children to think about morality? We'd teach them to think and live by the norms of their society—whatever these were. We'd teach conformity. We'd teach that these are examples of correct reasoning:

- "My society approves of A, so A is good."
- "My peer-group society approves of getting drunk on Friday night and then driving home, so this is good."
- "My Nazi society approves of racism, so racism is good."

CR would make us uncritical about the norms of our society. These norms can't be in error—even if they come from stupidity and ignorance. Likewise, the norms of another society (even Lika's Nazi homeland) can't be in error or be criticized. Thus CR goes against the critical spirit that characterizes philosophy.

Moral Diversity

CR sees the world as neatly divided into distinct societies. Each one has little or no moral disagreement, since the majority view determines what is right or wrong in that society. But the world isn't like that. Instead, the world is a confusing mixture of overlapping societies and groups; and individuals don't necessarily follow the majority view.

CR ignores the subgroup problem. We all belong to overlapping groups. I'm part of a specific nation, state, city, and neighborhood. And I'm also part of various family, professional, religious, and peer groups.

These groups often have conflicting values. According to CR, when I say "Racism is wrong" I mean "My society disapproves of racism." But *which* society does this refer to? Maybe most in my national and religious societies disapprove of racism, while most in my professional and family societies approve of it. CR could give us clear guidance only if we belonged to just one society. But the world is more complicated than that. We're all multicultural to some extent.

CR doesn't try to establish common norms *between* societies. As technology shrinks the planet, moral disputes between societies become more important. Nation A approves of equal rights for women (or for other races or religions), but nation B disapproves. What is a multinational corporation that works in both societies to do? Or societies A and B have value conflicts that lead to war. Since CR helps very little with such problems, it gives a poor basis for life in the twenty-first century.

How do we respond to moral diversity between societies? Ima rejects the dogmatic "we're right and they're wrong" attitude. And she stresses the need to understand the other side from their point of view. These are positive ideas. But Ima then says that neither side can be wrong. This limits our ability to learn. If our society can't be wrong, then it can't learn from its mistakes. Understanding the norms of another culture can't then help us to correct errors in our own norms.

Those who believe in objective values see the matter differently. They might say something like this:

> There's a truth to be found in moral matters, but no culture has a monopoly on this truth. Different cultures need to learn from each other. To see the errors and blind spots in our own values, we need to see how other cultures do things, and how they react to what we do. Learning about other cultures can help us to correct our cultural biases and move closer to the truth about how we ought to live.

Objective Values

We need to talk more about the objectivity of values. . . . The objective view (also called moral realism) claims that some things are objectively right or wrong, independently of what anyone may think or feel. Dr Martin Luther King, for example, claimed that racist actions were objectively wrong. The wrongness of racism was a fact. Any person or culture that approved of racism was mistaken. In saying this, King wasn't absolutizing the norms of his society; instead, he disagreed with accepted norms. He appealed to a higher truth about right and wrong, one that didn't depend on human thinking or feeling. He appealed to objective values.

Ima rejects this belief in objective values and calls it "the myth of objectivity." On her view, things are good or bad only relative to this or that culture. Things aren't good or bad objectively, as King thought. But are objective values really a "myth"? Let's examine Ima's reasoning.

Ima had three arguments against objective values. There can't be objective moral truths, she thought, because

1. morality is a product of culture,
2. cultures disagree widely about morality, and
3. there's no clear way to resolve moral differences.

But these arguments fall apart if we examine them carefully.

(1) "Since morality is a product of culture, there can't be objective moral truths." The problem with this reasoning is that a product of culture can express objective truths. Every book is a product of culture; and yet many books express objective truths. So too, a moral code could be a product of culture and yet still express objective truths about how people ought to live.

(2) "Since cultures disagree widely about morality, there can't be objective moral truths." But the mere fact of disagreement doesn't show that there's no truth of the matter, that neither side is right or wrong. Cultures disagree widely about anthropology or religion or even physics. Yet there may still be a truth of the matter about these subjects. So a wide disagreement on moral issues wouldn't show that there's no truth of the matter on moral issues.

We might also question whether cultures differ so deeply about morality. Most cultures have fairly similar norms against killing, stealing, and lying. Many moral differences can be explained as the application of similar basic values to differing situations. The golden rule, "Treat others as you want to be treated," is almost universally accepted across the world. And the diverse cultures that make up the United Nations have agreed to an extensive statement on basic human rights.

(3) "Since there's no clear way to resolve moral differences, there can't be objective moral truths." But there may be clear ways to resolve at least many moral differences. We need a way to reason about ethics that would appeal to intelligent and open-minded people of all cultures—and that would do for ethics what scientific method does for science. . . .

Even if there were no solid way to know moral truths, it wouldn't follow that there are no such truths. There may be truths that we have no solid way of knowing about. Did it rain on this spot 500 years ago today? There's some truth about this, but we'll never know it. Only a small percentage of all truths are knowable. So there could be objective moral truths, even if we had no solid way to know them.

So Ima's attack on objective values fails. But this isn't the end of the matter, for there are further arguments on the issue. The dispute over objective values is important, and we'll talk more about it later. But before leaving this section, let me clarify some related points.

The objective view says that *some* things are objectively right or wrong, independently of what anyone may think or feel; but it still could accept much relativity in other areas. Many social rules clearly are determined by local standards:

- Local law: "Right turns on a red light are forbidden."
- Local rule of etiquette: "Use the fork only in your left hand."

We need to respect such local rules; otherwise, we may hurt people, either by crashing their cars or by hurting their feelings. On the objective view, the demand that we not hurt people is a rule of a different sort—a *moral* rule—and *not* determined by local customs. Moral rules are seen as more authoritative and objective than government laws or rules of etiquette; they are rules that *any* society must follow if it is to survive and prosper. If we go to a place where local standards permit hurting people for trivial reasons, then the local standards are mistaken. Cultural relativists would dispute this. They insist that local standards determine even basic moral principles; so hurting others for trivial reasons would be good if it were socially approved.

Respecting a range of cultural differences doesn't make you a cultural relativist. What makes you a cultural relativist is the claim that *anything* that is socially approved must thereby be good.

Harry Gensler: Cultural Relativism

1. What is Gensler's definition of cultural relativism? What analogies does he use to establish the idea of the relativity of morality? Can you think of other analogies that might convey cultural relativism's central idea?
2. Many people endorse cultural relativism because they think that it naturally supports tolerance toward the moral standards of different

societies. Gensler rejects this thought. Explain how he does so, and then assess his reasoning.

3. Can societies make moral mistakes? If so, can cultural relativism allow for that?

4. What is the correct attitude to have toward one's own society's moral norms? Can cultural relativism support this attitude? Why or why not?

5. Cultures sometimes disagree about morality. Does this support cultural relativism? Gensler denies that it does. Is his reasoning plausible?

Why I Am an Objectivist about Ethics (And Why You Are, Too)

David Enoch

David Enoch claims that almost all of us are committed to the objectivity of ethics. When we reflect on our attitudes toward ethical claims and ethical practices, it is clear that we are assuming that there are correct answers to moral questions, and correct standards of moral evaluation, whose truth and authority do not depend on our beliefs or attitudes about them. In the first half of his paper, Enoch presents three tests that attempt to reveal our commitment to moral objectivity. Even if these tests succeed in their aim—and Enoch thinks that they clearly do—he realizes that this is not enough to prove that morality is objective. For, as he says, religious commitments also aspire to objectivity. And yet this does not show that any religious claim is objectively true (or true at all).

Still, the compelling appearance of objectivity in morality gives us good reason to think that morality is indeed objective—unless, of course, there are even stronger arguments that undermine this appearance. Enoch devotes the second half of his paper to considering a few of the most important of these arguments. Some critics argue that the extent of moral disagreement undermines moral objectivity. Critics also argue that those who defend the existence of objective truths need to provide a way of coming to know them, but that there is no plausible way to gain moral knowledge, if morality is indeed objective. Critics also worry that ethical objectivity supports intolerance and dogmatism.

Enoch carefully presents each criticism and then offers sharp replies to the objections.

....

You may think that you're a moral relativist or subjectivist—many people today seem to. But I don't think you are. In fact, when we start doing metaethics—when we start, that is, thinking philosophically about our moral discourse and practice—thoughts about morality's objectivity become almost irresistible. Now, as is always the case in philosophy, that some thoughts seem irresistible is only the starting point for the discussion, and under argumentative pressure we may need to revise our relevant beliefs. Still, it's important to get the starting points right. So it's important to understand the deep ways in which rejecting morality's objectivity is unappealing. What I want to do, then, is to highlight the ways in which accepting morality's objectivity is appealing, and to briefly address some common worries about it, worries that may lead some to reject—or to think they reject—such objectivity. In the final section, I comment on the (not obvious) relation between the underlying concerns about morality's objectivity and the directions in which current discussion in metaethics are developing. As it will emerge, things are not (even) as simple as the discussion below seems to suggest. This is just one reason why metaethics is so worth doing.

Why Objectivity? Three (Related) Reasons

In the next section we're going to have to say a little more about what objectivity is. But sometimes it's helpful to start by engaging the underlying concerns, and return to more abstract, perhaps conceptual, issues later on.

The Spinach Test

Consider the following joke (which I borrow from Christine Korsgaard): A child hates spinach. He then reports that he's glad he hates spinach. To the question "Why?" he responds: "Because if I liked it, I would have eaten it, and it's yucky!"

In a minute we're going to have to annoyingly ask why the joke is funny. For now, though, I want to highlight the fact that similar jokes are not always similarly funny. Consider, for instance, someone who grew up in the twentieth-century West and who believes that the earth revolves around the sun. Also, she reports to be happy she wasn't born in the Middle Ages, "because had I grown up in the Middle Ages, I would have believed that the earth is in the center of the universe, and that belief is false!"

To my ears, the joke doesn't work in this latter version (try it on your friends!). The response in the earth-revolves-around-the-sun case sounds perfectly sensible, precisely in a way in which the analogous response does not sound sensible in the spinach case.

We need one last case. Suppose someone grew up in the United States in the late twentieth century and rejects any manifestation of racism as morally wrong. He then reports that he's happy that that's when and where he grew up, "because had I grown up in the eighteenth century, I would have accepted slavery and racism. And these things are wrong!" How funny is this third, last version of the joke? To my ears, it's about as (un) funny as the second one, and nowhere nearly as amusing as the first. The response to the question in this last case (why he is happy that he grew up in the twentieth century) seems to me to make perfect sense, and I suspect it makes sense to you too. And this is why there's nothing funny about it.

OK, then, why is the spinach version funny and the others are not? Usually, our attitude towards our own likings and dislikings (when it comes to food, for instance) is that it's all about us. If you don't like spinach, the reason you shouldn't have it is precisely that you don't like it. So if we're imagining a hypothetical scenario in which you do like it, then you no longer have any reason not to eat it. This is what the child in the first example gets wrong: he's holding fixed his dislike for spinach, even in thinking about the hypothetical case in which he likes spinach. But because these issues are all about him and what he likes and dislikes, this makes no sense.

But physics is different: What we want, believe or do—none of this affects the earth's orbit. The fact that the earth revolves around the sun is just not about us at all. So it makes sense to hold this truth fixed even when thinking about hypothetical cases in which you don't believe it. And so it makes sense to be happy that you aren't in the Middle Ages, since you'd then be in a situation in which your beliefs about the earth's orbit would be false (even if you couldn't know that they were). And because this makes sense, the joke isn't funny.

And so we have the spinach test: About any relevant subject matter, formulate an analogue of the spinach joke. If the joke works, this seems to indicate that the subject matter is all about us and our responses, our likings and dislikings, our preferences, and so on. If the joke doesn't work, the subject matter is much more objective than that, as in the astronomy case. And when we apply the spinach test to a moral issue (like the moral status of racism), it seems to fall squarely on the objective side.

(Exercise: Think about your taste in music, and formulate the spinach test for it. Is the joke funny?)

Disagreement and Deliberation

We sometimes engage in all sorts of disagreements. Sometimes, for instance, we may engage in a disagreement about even such silly things as whether bitter chocolate is better than milk chocolate. Sometimes we disagree about such things as whether human actions influence global warming. But these two kinds of disagreement are very different. One way of seeing this is thinking about what it feels like from the inside to engage in such disagreements. In the chocolate case, it feels like stating one's own preference, and perhaps trying to influence the listener into getting his own preferences in line. In the global warming case, though, it feels like trying to get at an objective truth, one that is there anyway, independently of our beliefs and preferences. (Either human actions contribute to global warming, or they don't, right?)

And so another test suggests itself, a test having to do with what it *feels like* to engage in disagreement (or, as we sometimes say, with the *phenomenology* of disagreement).

But now think of some serious moral disagreement—about the moral status of abortion, say. Suppose, then, that you are engaged in such disagreement. (It's important to imagine this from the inside, as it were. Don't imagine looking from the outside at two people arguing over abortion; think what it's like to be engaged in such argument yourself—if not about abortion, then about some other issue you care deeply about.) Perhaps you think that there is nothing wrong with abortion, and you're arguing with someone who thinks that abortion is morally wrong. What does such disagreement feel like? In particular, does it feel more like disagreeing over which chocolate is better, or like disagreeing over factual matters (such as whether human actions contribute to global warming)?

Because this question is a phenomenological one (that is, it's about what something feels like from the inside), I can't answer this question for you. You have to think about what it feels like for you when you are engaged in moral disagreement. But I can say that in my case such moral disagreement feels exactly like the one about global warming—it's about an objective matter of fact, that exists independently of us and our disagreement. It is in no way like disagreeing over the merits of different kinds of chocolate. And I think I can rather safely predict that this is how it feels for you too.

So on the phenomenology-of-disagreement test as well, morality seems to fall on the objective side.

In fact, we may be able to take disagreement out of the picture entirely. Suppose there is no disagreement—perhaps because you're all by yourself trying to make up your mind about what to do next. In one case, you're thinking about what kind of chocolate to get. In another, you're choosing between buying a standard car and a somewhat more expensive hybrid car (whose effect on global warming, if human actions contribute to global warming, is less destructive). Here, too, there's a difference. In the first case, you seem to be asking questions about yourself and what you like more (in general, or right now). In the second case, you need to make up your mind about your own action, of course, but you're asking yourself questions about objective matters of fact that do not depend on you at all—in particular, about whether human actions affect global warming.

Now consider a third case, in which you're trying to make up your mind about having an abortion, or advising a friend who is considering an abortion. So you're wondering whether abortion is wrong. Does it feel like asking about your own preferences or like an objective matter of fact? Is it more like the chocolate case or like the hybrid car case? If, like me, you answer that it's much more like the hybrid car case, then you think, like me, that the phenomenology of deliberation too indicates that morality is objective.

(Exercise: think about your taste in music again. In terms of the phenomenology of disagreement and deliberation, is it on the objective side?)

Would It Still Have Been Wrong If ...?

Top hats are out of fashion. This may be an interesting, perhaps even practically relevant, fact—it may, for instance, give you reason to wear a top hat (if you want to be special) or not to (if not). But think about the following question: Had our fashion practices been very different—had we all worn top hats, thought they were cool, and so on—would it still have been true that top hats are out of fashion? The answer, it seems safe to assume, is "no."

Smoking causes cancer. This is an interesting, practically relevant, fact—it most certainly gives you a reason not to smoke, or perhaps to stop smoking. Now, had our relevant practices and beliefs regarding smoking been different—had we been OK with it, had we not banned it, had we thought smoking was actually quite harmless—would it still have been true that smoking causes cancer? I take it to be uncontroversial that the answer is "yes." The effects of smoking on our health do not depend on our beliefs and practices in anything like the way in which the fashionability of top hats does. Rather, it is an objective matter of fact.

And so we have a third objectivity test, one in terms of the relevant "what if" sentences (or *counterfactuals*, as they are often called), such as "Had our beliefs and practices been very different, would it still have been true that so-and-so?" Let's apply this test to morality.

Gender-based discrimination is wrong. I hope you agree with me on this (if you don't, replace this with a moral judgment you're rather confident in). Would it still have been wrong had our relevant practices and beliefs been different? Had we been all for gender-based discrimination, would that have made gender-based discrimination morally acceptable? Of course, in such a case we would have *believed* that there's nothing wrong with gender-based discrimination. But would it *be* wrong? To me it seems very clear that the answer is "Yes!" Gender-based discrimination is just as wrong in a society where everyone believes it's morally permissible. (This, after all, is why we would want such a society to change, and why, if we are members, we would fight for reform.) The problem in such a society is precisely that its members miss something so important—namely, the wrongness of gender-based discrimination. Had we thought gender-based discrimination was okay, we would have been mistaken. The morality of such discrimination does not depend on our opinion of it. The people in that hypothetical society may accept gender-based discrimination, but that doesn't make such discrimination acceptable.

In this respect too, then, morality falls on the objective side. When it comes to the counterfactual test, moral truths behave more like objective, factual truths (like whether smoking causes cancer) than like purely subjective, perhaps conventional claims (say, that top hats are unfashionable).

(Exercises: Can you see how the counterfactual test relates to the spinach test? And think about your favorite music, the kind of music that you don't just like, but that you think is *good*. Had you not liked it, would it still have been good?)

What's At Issue?

We have, then, three tests for objectivity—the spinach test, the phenomenology-of-disagreement-and-deliberation test, and the counterfactual test. And though we haven't yet said much about what objectivity comes to, these tests test for something that is recognizably in the vicinity of what we're after with our term "objectivity."

Objectivity, like many interesting philosophical terms, can be understood in more than one way. As a result, when philosophers affirm or deny the objectivity of some subject matter, it's not to be taken for granted that they're asserting or denying the same thing. But we don't have to go through a long list of what may be meant by morality's objectivity. It will be more productive, I think, to go about things in a different way. We can start by asking, why does it matter whether morality is objective? If we have a good enough feel for the answer to this question, we can then use it to find the sense of objectivity that we care about.

I suggest that we care about the objectivity of morality for roughly the reasons specified in the previous section. We want morality's objectivity to support our responses in those cases. We want morality's objectivity to vindicate the phenomenology of deliberation and disagreement, and our relevant counterfactual judgments. We want morality's objectivity to explain why the moral analogue of the spinach test isn't funny.

Very well, then, in what sense must morality be objective in order for the phenomenology of disagreement and deliberation and our counterfactual judgments to be justified? The answer, it seems to me, is that a subject matter is objective if the truths or facts in it exist independently of what we think or feel about them.

This notion of objectivity nicely supports the counterfactual test. If a certain truth (say, that smoking causes cancer) doesn't depend on our views about it, then it would have been true even had we not believed it. Not so for truths that do depend on our beliefs, practices, or emotions (such as the truth that top hats are unfashionable). And if moral truths are similarly independent of our beliefs, desires, preferences, emotions, points of view, and so on—if, as is sometimes said, moral truths are *response-independent*—then it's clear why gender-based discrimination would have been wrong even had we approved of it.

Similarly, if it's our responses that make moral claims true, then in a case of disagreement, it seems natural to suppose that both sides may be right. Perhaps, in other words, your responses make it the case that abortion is morally permissible ("for you," in some sense of this very weird phrase?), and your friend's responses make it the case that abortion is morally wrong ("for her"?). But if the moral status of abortion is response-*in*dependent, we understand why moral disagreement feels like factual disagreement—only one of you is right, and it's important to find out who. And of course, the whole point of the spinach test was to distinguish between caring about things just because we care about them (such as not eating spinach, if you find it yucky) and caring about things that seem to us important independently of us caring about them (such as the wrongness of racism).

Another way of making the same point is as follows: Objective facts are those we seek to discover, not those we make true. And in this respect too, when it comes to moral truths, we are in a position more like that of the scientist who tries to discover the laws of nature (which exist independently of her investigations) than that of the legislator (who creates laws).

Now, in insisting that morality is objective in this sense—for instance, by relying on the reasons given in the previous section—it's important to see what has and what has not been established. In order to see this, it may help to draw an analogy with religious discourse. So think of your deeply held religious beliefs, if you have any. (If, like me, you do not, try to think what it's like to be deeply committed to a religious belief, or perhaps think of your commitment to atheism.) And try to run our tests—does it make sense to be happy that you were brought up under the religion in which you deeply believe, even assuming that with a different education you would have believed another religion, or no religion at all? What do you think of the phenomenology of religious deliberation and disagreement? And had you stopped believing, would the doctrines of your faith still have been true?

Now, perhaps things are not obvious here, but it seems to me that for many religious people, religious discourse passes all these objectivity tests. But from this it does not follow that atheism is false, much less that a specific religion is true. When they are applied to some specific religious discourse, the objectivity tests show that such discourse *aspires* to objectivity. In other words, the tests show what the world must be like for the commitments of the discourse to be vindicated: if (say) a Catholic's religious beliefs are to be true, what must be the case is that the doctrines of the Catholic Church hold objectively, that is, response-independently. This leaves entirely open the question whether these doctrines do in fact hold.

Back to morality, then. Here too, what the discussion of objectivity (tentatively) establishes is just something about the *aspirations* of moral discourse: namely, that it aspires to objectivity. If our moral judgments are to be true, it must be the case that things have value, that people have rights and duties, that there are better and worse ways to live our lives—and all of this must hold objectively, that is, response-independently. But establishing that moral discourse *aspires* to objectivity is one thing. Whether *there actually are* objective moral truths is quite another.

And now you may be worried. Why does it matter, you may wonder, what morality's aspirations are, if (for all I've said so far) they may not be met? I want to offer two replies here. First, precisely in order to check whether morality's aspirations are in fact fulfilled, we should understand them better. If you are trying to decide, for instance, whether the commitments of Catholicism are true, you had better understand them first. Second, and more importantly, one of the things we are trying to do here is to gain a better understanding of what we are already committed to. You may recall that I started with the hypothesis that you may think you're a relativist or a subjectivist. But if the discussion so far gets things right (if, that is, morality aspires to this kind of objectivity), and if you have any moral beliefs at all (don't you think that some things are wrong? do we really need to give gruesome examples?), then it follows that you yourself are already committed to morality's objectivity. And this is already an interesting result, at least for you.

That morality aspires in this way to objectivity also has the implication that any full metaethical theory—any theory, that is, that offers a full description and explanation of moral discourse and practice—has to take this aspiration into account. Most likely, it has to accommodate it. Less likely, but still possibly, such a theory may tell us that this aspiration is futile, explaining why even though morality is not objective, we tend to think that it is, why it manifests the marks of objectivity that the tests above catch on, and so on. What no metaethical theory can do, however, is ignore the very strong appearance that morality is objective. I get back to this in the final section, below.

Why Not?

As I already mentioned, we cannot rule out the possibility that under argumentative pressure we're going to have to revise even some of our most deeply held beliefs. Philosophy, in other words, is hard. And as you can imagine, claims about morality's objectivity have not escaped criticism. Indeed, perhaps some such objections have already occurred to you. In this section, I quickly mention some of them, and hint at the ways in which I think they can be coped with. But let me note how incomplete the discussion here is. There are, of course, other objections, objections that I don't discuss here. More importantly, there are many more things to say—on both sides—regarding the objections that I do discuss. The discussion here is meant as an introduction to these further discussions, no more than that. (Have I mentioned that philosophy is hard?)

Disagreement

I have been emphasizing ways in which moral disagreement may motivate the thought that morality is objective. But it's very common to think that something about moral disagreement actually goes the other way. For if there are perfectly objective moral truths, why is there so much disagreement about them? Wouldn't we expect, if there are such objective truths, to see everyone converging on them? Perhaps such convergence cannot be expected to be perfect and quick, but still—why is there so much persistent, apparently irreconcilable disagreement in morality, but not in subject matters whose objectivity is less controversial? If there is no answer to this question, doesn't this count heavily against morality's objectivity?

It is not easy to see exactly what this objection comes to. (Exercise: Can you try and formulate a precise argument here?) It may be necessary to distinguish between several possible arguments. Naturally, different ways of understanding the objection will call for different responses. But there are some things that can be said in general here. First, the objection seems to underrate the extent of disagreement in subject matters whose objectivity is pretty much uncontroversial (think of the causes and effects of global warming again). It may also overrate the extent of disagreement in morality. Still, the requirement to explain the scope and nature of moral disagreements seems legitimate. But objectivity-friendly explanations seem possible.

Perhaps, for instance, moral disagreement is sometimes best explained by noting that people tend to accept the moral judgments that it's in their interest to accept, or that tend to show their lives and practices in good light. Perhaps this is why the poor tend to believe in the welfare state, and the rich tend to believe in property rights.

Perhaps the most important general lesson here is that not all disagreements count against the objectivity of the relevant discourse. So what we need is a criterion to distinguish between objectivity-undermining and non-objectivity-undermining disagreements. And then we need an argument showing that moral disagreement is of the former kind. I don't know of a fully successful way of filling in these details here.

Notice, by the way, that such attempts are going to have to overcome a natural worry about *self-defeat*. Some theories defeat themselves, that is, roughly, fail even by their own lights. Consider, for instance, the theory "All theories are false," or the belief "No belief is justified." (Exercise: Can you think of other self-defeating theories?) Now, disagreement in philosophy has many of the features that moral disagreement seems to have. In particular, so does metaethical disagreement. Even more in particular, so does disagreement about *whether disagreement undermines objectivity*. If moral disagreement undermines the objectivity of moral conclusions, metaethical disagreement seems to undermine the objectivity of metaethical conclusions, including the conclusion that disagreement of this kind undermines objectivity. And this starts to look like self-defeat. So if some disagreement-objection to the objectivity of morality is going to succeed, it must show how moral disagreement undermines the objectivity of morality, but metaethical disagreement does *not* undermine the objectivity of metaethical claims. Perhaps it's possible to do so. But it's not going to be easy.

But How Do We Know?

Even if there are these objective moral truths—for instance, the kind of objective moral truth that both sides to a moral disagreement typically lay a claim to—how can we ever come to know them? In the astronomical case of disagreement about the relative position and motion of the earth and the sun, there are things we can say in response to a similar question— we can talk about perception, and scientific methodology, and progress. Similarly in other subject matters where we are very confident that objective truths await our discovery. Can anything at all be said in the moral case? We do not, after all, seem to possess something worth calling moral perception, a direct perception of the moral status of things. And in the moral case it's hard to argue that we have an established, much less uncontroversial, methodology either. (Whether there is moral progress is, I'm sure you've already realized, highly controversial.)

In other words, what we need is a moral epistemology, an account of how moral knowledge is possible, of how moral beliefs can be more or less justified, and the like. And I do not want to belittle the need for a moral epistemology, in particular an epistemology that fits well with an objectivist understanding of moral judgments. But the objectivist is not without resources here. After all, morality is not the only subject matter where perception and empirical methodology do not seem to be relevant. Think, for instance, of mathematics, and indeed of philosophy. But we do not often doubt the reality of mathematical knowledge. (Philosophical knowledge is a harder case, perhaps. Exercise: Can you see how claiming that we do not have philosophical knowledge may again give rise to a worry about self-defeat?)

Perhaps, then, what is really needed is a general epistemology of the a priori—of those areas, roughly, where the empirical method seems out of place. And perhaps it's not overly optimistic to think that any plausible epistemology of the a priori will vindicate moral knowledge as well.

Also, to say that there is no methodology of doing ethics is at the very least an exaggeration. Typically, when facing a moral question, we do not just stare at it helplessly. Perhaps we're not always very good at morality. But this doesn't mean that we never are. And perhaps at our best, when we employ our best ways of moral reasoning, we manage to attain moral knowledge.

(Exercise: There is no *uncontroversial* method of doing ethics. What, if anything, follows from this?)

Who Decides?

Still, even if moral knowledge is not especially problematic, even if moral disagreement can be explained in objectivity-friendly ways, and even if there are perfectly objective moral truths, what should we do in cases of disagreement and conflict? Who gets to decide what the right way of proceeding is? Especially in the case of intercultural disagreement and conflict, isn't saying something like "We're right and you're wrong about what is objectively morally required" objectionably dogmatic, intolerant, perhaps an invitation to fanaticism?

Well, in a sense, no one decides. In another sense, everyone does. The situation here is precisely as it is everywhere else: no one gets to decide whether smoking causes cancer, whether human actions contribute to global warming, whether the earth revolves around the sun. Our decisions do not make these claims true or false. But everyone gets (roughly speaking) to decide what they are going to believe about these matters. And this is so for moral claims as well.

How about intolerance and fanaticism? If the worry is that people are likely to become dangerously intolerant if they believe in objective morality, then first, such a prediction would have to be established. After all, many social reformers (think, for instance, of Martin Luther King, Jr.) who fought *against* intolerance and bigotry seem to have been inspired by the thought that their vision of equality and justice was objectively correct. Further, even if it's very dangerous for people to believe in the objectivity of their moral convictions, this doesn't mean that morality isn't objective. Such danger would give us reasons not to let people know about morality's objectivity. It would not give us a reason to believe that morality is not objective. (Compare: even if it were the case that things would go rapidly downhill if atheism were widely believed, this wouldn't prove that atheism is false.)

More importantly, though, it's one thing to believe in the objectivity of morality, it's quite another to decide what to do about it. And it's quite possible that the right thing to do, given morality's objectivity, is hardly ever to respond with "I am simply right and you are simply wrong!" or to be intolerant. In fact, if you think that it's wrong to be intolerant, aren't you committed to the objectivity of this very claim? (Want to run the three tests again?) So it seems as if the only way of accommodating the importance of toleration is actually to *accept* morality's objectivity, not to *reject* it.

Conclusion

As already noted, much more can be said—about what objectivity is, about the reasons to think that morality is objective, and about these (and many other) objections to morality's objectivity. Much more work remains to be done.

And one of the ways in which current literature addresses some of these issues may sound surprising, for a major part of the debate *assumes* something like morality's aspiration to objectivity in the sense above, but refuses to infer from such observations quick conclusions about the nature of moral truths and facts. In other words, many metaethicists today deny the most straightforward objectivist view of morality, according to which moral facts are a part of response-independent reality, much like mathematical and physical facts. But they do not deny morality's objectivity— they care, for instance, about passing the three tests above. And so they attempt to show how even on other metaethical views, morality's objectivity can be accommodated. As you can imagine, philosophers disagree about the success (actual and potential) of such accommodation projects.

Naturally, such controversies also lead to attempts to better understand what the objectivity at stake exactly is, and why it matters (if it matters) whether morality is objective. As is often the case, attempts to evaluate answers to a question make us better understand—or wonder about—the question itself.

Nothing here, then, is simple. But I hope that you now see how you are probably a moral objectivist, at least in your intuitive starting point. Perhaps further philosophical reflection will require that you abandon this starting point. But this will be an *abandoning*, and a very strong reason is needed to justify it. Until we get such a conclusive argument against moral objectivity, then, objectivism should be the view to beat.

David Enoch: Why I Am an Objectivist about Ethics (And Why You Are, Too)

1. In what ways does our attitude to morality seem to be different from our attitude to matters of taste?
2. In what ways does our attitude to morality seem to be different from our attitude to matters of convention, like fashion?
3. How can the phenomenon of moral disagreement count against the objectivity of morality?
4. Can the dangerousness of belief in moral objectivity give us reason to believe that morality is not after all objective? If so, how? If not, why not?
5. In what ways do we treat our aesthetic commitments and our moral ones on a par? In what ways do they seem to differ?

PART IV

Moral Problems

19

What Will Future Generations Condemn Us For?

Kwame Anthony Appiah

In this provocative short piece, the distinguished philosopher Kwame Anthony Appiah invites us to reflect on the morality of our current practices by asking what future generations would think of them. He notes that we are puzzled at how our ancestors allowed and even positively supported such practices as slavery, the exclusion of women from the voting rolls, and racist lynchings— practices that nowadays strike us as abhorrent.

The underlying idea behind Appiah's thought experiment is that we may be able to uncover our moral blind spots by reflecting on how future generations will regard us. He identifies three signs that a contemporary practice may draw the condemnation of future generations. First, there are already contemporary arguments leveled against the practice, even if those arguments are currently doing little to sway broad public opinion. Second, defenders of these practices tend not to offer arguments but rather appeals to tradition, necessity, or human nature. Third, supporters of these questionable practices tend to engage in what Appiah calls "strategic ignorance," turning their attention away from the unsavory aspects of the practices that they enjoy or otherwise take for granted.

Appiah identifies four contemporary practices that he thinks exemplify all three of these features and are likely to be the target of future moral condemnation: our prison system, industrial meat production, the institutionalization of the elderly, and our treatment of the environment.

....

Once, pretty much everywhere, beating your wife and children was regarded as a father's duty, homosexuality was a hanging offense, and waterboarding was approved—in fact, invented—by the Catholic Church. Through the middle of the 19th century, the United States and other nations in the Americas condoned plantation slavery. Many of our grandparents were born in states where women were forbidden to vote. And well into the 20th century, lynch mobs in this country stripped, tortured, hanged and burned human beings at picnics.

Looking back at such horrors, it is easy to ask: What were people thinking?

Yet, the chances are that our own descendants will ask the same question, with the same incomprehension, about some of our practices today.

Is there a way to guess which ones? After all, not every disputed institution or practice is destined to be discredited. And it can be hard to distinguish in real time between movements, such as abolition, that will come to represent moral common sense and those, such as prohibition, that will come to seem quaint or misguided. Recall the book-burners of Boston's old Watch and Ward Society or the organizations for the suppression of vice, with their crusades against claret, contraceptives and sexually candid novels.

Still, a look at the past suggests three signs that a particular practice is destined for future condemnation.

First, people have already heard the arguments against the practice. The case against slavery didn't emerge in a blinding moment of moral clarity, for instance; it had been around for centuries.

Second, defenders of the custom tend not to offer moral counterarguments but instead invoke tradition, human nature or necessity. (As in, "We've always had slaves, and how could we grow cotton without them?")

And third, supporters engage in what one might call strategic ignorance, avoiding truths that might force them to face the evils in which they're complicit. Those who ate the sugar or wore the cotton that the slaves grew simply didn't think about what made those goods possible.

That's why abolitionists sought to direct attention toward the conditions of the Middle Passage, through detailed illustrations of slave ships and horrifying stories of the suffering below decks.

With these signs in mind, here are four contenders for future moral condemnation.

Our Prison System

We already know that the massive waste of life in our prisons is morally troubling; those who defend the conditions of incarceration usually do so in non-moral terms (citing costs or the administrative difficulty of reforms); and we're inclined to avert our eyes from the details. Check, check and check.

Roughly 1 percent of adults in this country are incarcerated. We have 4 percent of the world's population but 25 percent of its prisoners. No other nation has as large a proportion of its population in prison; even China's rate is less than half of ours. What's more, the majority of our prisoners are non-violent offenders, many of them detained on drug charges. (Whether a country that was truly free would criminalize recreational drug use is a related question worth pondering.)

And the full extent of the punishment prisoners face isn't detailed in any judge's sentence. More than 100,000 inmates suffer sexual abuse, including rape, each year; some contract HIV as a result. Our country holds at least 25,000 prisoners in isolation in so-called supermax facilities, under conditions that many psychologists say amount to torture.

Industrial Meat Production

The arguments against the cruelty of factory farming have certainly been around a long time; it was Jeremy Bentham, in the 18th century, who observed that, when it comes to the treatment of animals, the key question is not whether animals can reason but whether they can suffer. People who eat factory-farmed bacon or chicken rarely offer a moral justification for what they're doing. Instead, they try not to think about it too much, shying away from stomach-turning stories about what goes on in our industrial abattoirs.

Of the more than 90 million cattle in our country, at least 10 million at any time are packed into feedlots, saved from the inevitable diseases of overcrowding only by regular doses of antibiotics, surrounded by piles of their own feces, their nostrils filled with the smell of their own urine. Picture it—and then imagine your grandchildren seeing that picture. In the European Union, many of the most inhumane conditions we allow are already illegal or—like the sow stalls into which pregnant pigs are often crammed in the United States—will be illegal soon.

The Institutionalized and Isolated Elderly

Nearly 2 million of America's elderly are warehoused in nursing homes, out of sight and, to some extent, out of mind. Some 10,000 for-profit facilities have arisen across the country in recent decades to hold them. Other elderly Americans may live independently, but often they are isolated and cut off from their families. (The United States is not alone among advanced democracies in this. Consider the heat wave that hit France in 2003: While many families were enjoying their summer vacations, some 14,000 elderly parents and grandparents were left to perish in the stifling temperatures.) Is this what Western modernity amounts to—societies that feel no filial obligations to their inconvenient elders?

Sometimes we can learn from societies much poorer than ours. My English mother spent the last 50 years of her life in Ghana, where I grew up. In her final years, it was her good fortune not only to have the resources to stay at home, but also to live in a country where doing so was customary. She had family next door who visited her every day, and she was cared for by doctors and nurses who were willing to come to her when she was too ill to come to them. In short, she had the advantages of a society in which older people are treated with respect and concern.

Keeping aging parents and their children closer is a challenge, particularly in a society where almost everybody has a job outside the home (if not across the country). Yet the three signs apply here as well: When we see old people who, despite many living relatives, suffer growing isolation, we know something is wrong. We scarcely try to defend the situation; when we can, we put it out of our minds. Self-interest, if nothing else, should make us hope that our descendants will have worked out a better way.

The Environment

Of course, most transgenerational obligations run the other way—from parents to children—and of these the most obvious candidate for opprobrium is our wasteful attitude toward the planet's natural resources and ecology. Look at a satellite picture of Russia, and you'll see a vast expanse of parched wasteland where decades earlier was a lush and verdant landscape. That's the Republic of Kalmykia, home to what was recognized in the 1990s as Europe's first man-made desert. Desertification, which is primarily the result of destructive land-management practices, threatens a third of the Earth's surface; tens of thousands of Chinese villages have been overrun by sand drifts in the past few decades.

It's not as though we're unaware of what we're doing to the planet: We know the harm done by deforestation, wetland destruction, pollution, overfishing, greenhouse gas emissions—the whole litany. Our descendants, who will inherit this devastated Earth, are unlikely to have the luxury of such recklessness. Chances are, they won't be able to avert their eyes, even if they want to.

Let's not stop there, though. We will all have our own suspicions about which practices will someday prompt people to ask, in dismay: What were they thinking?

Even when we don't have a good answer, we'll be better off for anticipating the question.

Kwame Anthony Appiah: What Will Future Generations Condemn Us For?

1. Appiah identifies three signs that a practice will be targeted for condemnation by future generations. Do you agree that these are good indicators that something is morally suspect?
2. Can you think of other such signs?
3. Which contemporary practices, other than the four that Appiah mentions, do you think will be the target of future moral criticism?
4. Can you think of good signs that a contemporary practice will earn the *respect* of future generations? If so, what are these signs?
5. Which current practices possess these features and so, to your mind, are likely to earn the respect of future generations?

20

≈ ❧ ≈

The Singer Solution to World Poverty

Peter Singer

....

Peter Singer argues that our ordinary patterns of spending money on ourselves are immoral. Such spending involves the purchase of many things that are not essential to preserving our lives or health. The money we spend on fancy dinners, new clothes, or vacations could instead be sent to relief agencies that save people's lives. We don't know our potential beneficiaries, but that is morally irrelevant. Our decision not to spend money to save their lives is morally inexcusable.

Singer offers us a series of fascinating examples in which people have the opportunity to prevent an innocent person's death but fail to do so. We regard the person in each example as having done something extremely immoral. Singer argues that we who spend money on inessential personal pleasures are no better.

But what if most of the people we know are also failing to give anything to famine relief or aid agencies? That doesn't let us off the hook—it just means that they are also behaving in a deeply immoral way.

Perhaps the money sent overseas will not do as much good as advertised? Singer mentions some very reliable aid agencies (and provides contact information) that will not squander your money. For a couple hundred dollars, you can save a child's life, or purchase a

Reprinted by permission of the author. © Peter Singer, 1999. This article first appeared under the title "The Singer Solution to World Poverty," *New York Times Magazine* (Sept 5, 1999), pp. 60–63.

few new additions to your wardrobe. If Singer is right, then choosing to spend that money on yourself means knowingly allowing an innocent person to die. Given the relatively small sacrifice you would be making if you sent that money overseas, and given the great benefit you would be providing if you did, morality gives you no choice. World poverty could largely be solved if we in the wealthier nations did our moral duty and gave much more than we currently do to those in greatest need.

....

I n the Brazilian film *Central Station*, Dora is a retired schoolteacher who makes ends meet by sitting at the station writing letters for illiterate people. Suddenly she has an opportunity to pocket $1,000. All she has to do is persuade a homeless 9-year-old boy to follow her to an address she has been given. (She is told he will be adopted by wealthy foreigners.) She delivers the boy, gets the money, spends some of it on a television set, and settles down to enjoy her new acquisition. Her neighbor spoils the fun, however, by telling her that the boy was too old to be adopted—he will be killed and his organs sold for transplantation. Perhaps Dora knew this all along, but after her neighbor's plain speaking, she spends a troubled night. In the morning Dora resolves to take the boy back.

Suppose Dora had told her neighbor that it is a tough world, other people have nice new TVs too, and if selling the kid is the only way she can get one, well, he was only a street kid. She would then have become, in the eyes of the audience, a monster. She redeems herself only by being prepared to bear considerable risks to save the boy.

At the end of the movie, in cinemas in the affluent nations of the world, people who would have been quick to condemn Dora if she had not rescued the boy go home to places far more comfortable than her apartment. In fact, the average family in the United States spends almost one-third of its income on things that are no more necessary to them than Dora's new TV was to her. Going out to nice restaurants, buying new clothes because the old ones are no longer stylish, vacationing at beach resorts—so much of our income is spent on things not essential to the preservation of our lives and health. Donated to one of a number of charitable agencies, that money could mean the difference between life and death for children in need.

All of which raises a question: In the end, what is the ethical distinction between a Brazilian who sells a homeless child to organ peddlers and an American who already has a TV and upgrades to a better one—knowing that the money could be donated to an organization that would use it to save the lives of kids in need?

Of course, there are several differences between the two situations that could support different moral judgments about them. For one thing, to be able to consign a child to death when he is standing right in front of you takes a chilling kind of heartlessness; it is much easier to ignore an appeal for money to help children you will never meet. Yet for a utilitarian philosopher like myself—that is, one who judges whether acts are right or wrong by their consequences—if the upshot of the American's failure to donate the money is that one more kid dies on the streets of a Brazilian city, then it is, in some sense, just as bad as selling the kid to the organ peddlers. But one doesn't need to embrace my utilitarian ethic to see that, at the very least, there is a troubling incongruity in being so quick to condemn Dora for taking the child to the organ peddlers while, at the same time, not regarding the American consumer's behavior as raising a serious moral issue.

In his 1996 book, *Living High and Letting Die,* the New York University philosopher Peter Unger presented an ingenious series of imaginary examples designed to probe our intuitions about whether it is wrong to live well without giving substantial amounts of money to help people who are hungry, malnourished or dying from easily treatable illnesses like diarrhea. Here's my paraphrase of one of these examples:

Bob is close to retirement. He has invested most of his savings in a very rare and valuable old car, a Bugatti, which he has not been able to insure. The Bugatti is his pride and joy. In addition to the pleasure he gets from driving and caring for his car, Bob knows that its rising market value means that he will always be able to sell it and live comfortably after retirement. One day when Bob is out for a drive, he parks the Bugatti near the end of a railway siding and goes for a walk up the track. As he does so, he sees that a runaway train, with no one aboard, is running down the railway track. Looking farther down the track, he sees the small figure of a child very likely to be killed by the runaway train. He can't stop the train and the child is too far away to warn of the danger, but he can throw a switch that will divert the train down the siding where his Bugatti is parked. Then nobody will be killed—but the train will destroy his Bugatti. Thinking of his joy in owning the car and the financial security it represents, Bob decides not to throw the switch. The child is killed. For many years to come, Bob enjoys owning his Bugatti and the financial security it represents.

Bob's conduct, most of us will immediately respond, was gravely wrong. Unger agrees. But then he reminds us that we, too, have opportunities to save the lives of children. We can give to organizations like UNICEF or Oxfam America. How much would we have to give one of these organizations to have a high probability of saving the life of a child threatened by easily preventable diseases? (I do not believe that children are more worth saving than adults, but since no one can argue that children have brought their poverty on themselves, focusing on them simplifies the issues.) Unger called up some experts and used the information they provided to offer some plausible estimates that include the cost of raising money, administrative expenses and the cost of delivering aid where it is most needed. By his calculation, $200 in donations would help a sickly 2-year-old transform into a healthy 6-year-old—offering safe passage through childhood's most dangerous years. To show how practical philosophical argument can be, Unger even tells his readers that they can easily donate funds by using their credit card and calling one of these toll-free numbers: (800) 367-5437 for Unicef; (800) 693-2687 for Oxfam America. [http:// supportunicef.org/forms/whichcountry2.html for Unicef and http://www .oxfam.org/eng/donate.htm for Oxfam—PS.]

Now you, too, have the information you need to save a child's life. How should you judge yourself if you don't do it? Think again about Bob and his Bugatti. Unlike Dora, Bob did not have to look into the eyes of the child he was sacrificing for his own material comfort. The child was a complete stranger to him and too far away to relate to in an intimate, personal way. Unlike Dora, too, he did not mislead the child or initiate the chain of events imperiling him. In all these respects, Bob's situation resembles that of people able but unwilling to donate to overseas aid and differs from Dora's situation.

If you still think that it was very wrong of Bob not to throw the switch that would have diverted the train and saved the child's life, then it is hard to see how you could deny that it is also very wrong not to send money to one of the organizations listed above. Unless, that is, there is some morally important difference between the two situations that I have overlooked.

Is it the practical uncertainties about whether aid will really reach the people who need it? Nobody who knows the world of overseas aid can doubt that such uncertainties exist. But Unger's figure of $200 to save a child's life was reached after he had made conservative assumptions about the proportion of the money donated that will actually reach its target.

One genuine difference between Bob and those who can afford to donate to overseas aid organizations but don't is that only Bob can save the child on the tracks, whereas there are hundreds of millions of people who can give $200 to overseas aid organizations. The problem is that most of them aren't doing it. Does this mean that it is all right for you not to do it?

Suppose that there were more owners of priceless vintage cars—Carol, Dave, Emma, Fred, and so on, down to Ziggy—all in exactly the same situation as Bob, with their own siding and their own switch, all sacrificing the child in order to preserve their own cherished car. Would that make it all right for Bob to do the same? To answer this question affirmatively is to endorse follow-the-crowd ethics—the kind of ethics that led many Germans to look away when the Nazi atrocities were being committed. We do not excuse them because others were behaving no better.

We seem to lack a sound basis for drawing a clear moral line between Bob's situation and that of any reader of this article with $200 to spare who does not donate it to an overseas aid agency. These readers seem to be acting at least as badly as Bob was acting when he chose to let the runaway train hurtle toward the unsuspecting child. In the light of this conclusion, I trust that many readers will reach for the phone and donate that $200. Perhaps you should do it before reading further.

Now that you have distinguished yourself morally from people who put their vintage cars ahead of a child's life, how about treating yourself and your partner to dinner at your favorite restaurant? But wait. The money you will spend at the restaurant could also help save the lives of children overseas! True, you weren't planning to blow $200 tonight, but if you were to give up dining out just for one month, you would easily save that amount. And what is one month's dining out, compared to a child's life? There's the rub. Since there are a lot of desperately needy children in the world, there will always be another child whose life you could save for another $200. Are you therefore obliged to keep giving until you have nothing left? At what point can you stop?

Hypothetical examples can easily become farcical. Consider Bob. How far past losing the Bugatti should he go? Imagine that Bob had got his foot stuck in the track of the siding, and if he diverted the train, then before it rammed the car it would also amputate his big toe. Should he still throw the switch? What if it would amputate his foot? His entire leg?

As absurd as the Bugatti scenario gets when pushed to extremes, the point it raises is a serious one: only when the sacrifices become very significant indeed would most people be prepared to say that Bob does nothing wrong when he decides not to throw the switch. Of course, most people could be wrong; we can't decide moral issues by taking opinion polls. But consider for yourself the level of sacrifice that you would demand of Bob, and then think about how much money you would have to give away in order to make a sacrifice that is roughly equal to that. It's almost certainly much, much more than $200. For most middle-class Americans, it could easily be more like $200,000.

Isn't it counterproductive to ask people to do so much? Don't we run the risk that many will shrug their shoulders and say that morality, so conceived, is fine for saints but not for them? I accept that we are unlikely to see, in the near or even medium-term future, a world in which it is normal for wealthy Americans to give the bulk of their wealth to strangers. When it comes to praising or blaming people for what they do, we tend to use a standard that is relative to some conception of normal behavior. Comfortably off Americans who give, say, 10 percent of their income to overseas aid organizations are so far ahead of most of their equally comfortable fellow citizens that I wouldn't go out of my way to chastise them for not doing more. Nevertheless, they should be doing much more, and they are in no position to criticize Bob for failing to make the much greater sacrifice of his Bugatti.

At this point various objections may crop up. Someone may say: "If every citizen living in the affluent nations contributed his or her share I wouldn't have to make such a drastic sacrifice, because long before such levels were reached, the resources would have been there to save the lives of all those children dying from lack of food or medical care. So why should I give more than my fair share?" Another, related, objection is that the Government ought to increase its overseas aid allocations, since that would spread the burden more equitably across all taxpayers.

Yet the question of how much we ought to give is a matter to be decided in the real world—and that, sadly, is a world in which we know that most people do not, and in the immediate future will not, give substantial amounts to overseas aid agencies. We know, too, that at least in the next year, the United States Government is not going to meet even the very modest United Nations-recommended target of 0.7 percent of gross national product; at the moment it lags far below that, at 0.09 percent, not even half of Japan's 0.22 percent or a tenth of Denmark's 0.97 percent.

Thus, we know that the money we can give beyond that theoretical "fair share" is still going to save lives that would otherwise be lost. While the idea that no one need do more than his or her fair share is a powerful one, should it prevail if we know that others are not doing their fair share and that children will die preventable deaths unless we do more than our fair share? That would be taking fairness too far.

Thus, this ground for limiting how much we ought to give also fails. In the world as it is now, I can see no escape from the conclusion that each one of us with wealth surplus to his or her essential needs should be giving most of it to help people suffering from poverty so dire as to be life-threatening. That's right: I'm saying that you shouldn't buy that new car, take that cruise, redecorate the house or get that pricey new suit. After all, a $1,000 suit could save five children's lives.

So how does my philosophy break down in dollars and cents? An American household with an income of $50,000 spends around $30,000 annually on necessities, according to the Conference Board, a nonprofit economic research organization. Therefore, for a household bringing in $50,000 a year, donations to help the world's poor should be as close as possible to $20,000. The $30,000 required for necessities holds for higher incomes as well. So a household making $100,000 could cut a yearly check for $70,000. Again, the formula is simple: whatever money you're spending on luxuries, not necessities, should be given away.

Now, evolutionary psychologists tell us that human nature just isn't sufficiently altruistic to make it plausible that many people will sacrifice so much for strangers. On the facts of human nature, they might be right, but they would be wrong to draw a moral conclusion from those facts. If it is the case that we ought to do things that, predictably, most of us won't do, then let's face that fact head-on. Then, if we value the life of a child more than going to fancy restaurants, the next time we dine out we will know that we could have done something better with our money. If that makes living a morally decent life extremely arduous, well, then that is the way things are. If we don't do it, then we should at least know that we are failing to live a morally decent life—not because it is good to wallow in guilt but because knowing where we should be going is the first step toward heading in that direction.

When Bob first grasped the dilemma that faced him as he stood by that railway switch, he must have thought how extraordinarily unlucky he was to be placed in a situation in which he must choose between the life of an innocent child and the sacrifice of most of his savings. But he was not unlucky at all. We are all in that situation.

Peter Singer: The Singer Solution to World Poverty

1. Was it morally wrong of Bob to refrain from throwing the switch, thus allowing the child to die? Is there any moral difference between Bob's decision and the decision of well-off people to spend money on luxuries rather than the alleviation of poverty?

2. One difference between the case of Bob and the case of someone not giving to charity is that Bob is the only person in a position to prevent the child's death, while many people are in a position to give to charity. Why doesn't Singer think that this is a morally relevant difference? Do you agree with him?

3. How much of our income does Singer think we are morally required to give away? Do you find his standard reasonable?

4. How does Singer respond to the objection that his theory is too demanding, and that people will never make the sacrifices he suggests? Do you find his response convincing?

5. One might respond to Singer's proposals by claiming that instead of individuals contributing money to alleviate world poverty, governments should be responsible for handling such efforts. Why doesn't Singer think that this undermines his view that middle-class people should give large percentages of their income to charity?

21

Feeding the Hungry

Jan Narveson

....

What obligations do we have to those who are starving? If Jan Narveson is right, the answer is usually: none.

Narveson argues that most of us who are well-fed and relatively comfortable in our lives have no duties at all to relieve the suffering of the poor and hungry. If we are responsible for creating the unfortunate situation in which someone else finds himself impoverished, then we *do* owe him relief and support. But those cases aside, Narveson argues that any help we give to the starving is entirely morally optional. We may give if we like, but such assistance is not morally required.

For Narveson, our moral duties are supplied entirely by the demands of justice. And justice requires only two things. First, we must right the wrongs we have done to others. Second, we must respect the liberty of others to do as they please. In other words, we must not "invade" their liberty by (for instance) robbing or beating or killing them. So long as we respect their liberty, and provide compensation where we have wronged others, then we are completely fulfilling the requirements of justice—and so of morality.

Justice is a matter of respecting everyone's rights. Narveson argues that the poor do not have a right to be fed—the needs of others do not automatically give them a right to your assistance. Suppose you are wealthy and I am poor, and I need money for an operation. This does not by itself give me a right to some of your money. So if you refuse to

Reprinted by permission from Jan Narveson, *Moral Matters* (Lewiston, N.Y.: Broadview Press, 1993), pp. 138–150.

help me, then you are not committing an injustice. Of course you are certainly permitted to fund my operation. But that would be charity. And charity is not something that we morally can compel.

For Narveson, we are morally permitted to do anything we like, so long as we do not violate the rights of others. While it would be generous and kind and compassionate of us to feed the hungry, doing so is morally optional, rather than required. It is a matter of charity, not justice.

....

Throughout history it has been the lot of most people to know of others worse off than they, and often enough of others who face starvation. In the contemporary world, television and other mass media enable all of us in the better-off areas to hear about starvation in even the most remote places. What, if any, are our obligations toward victims of starvation?

This can be a rather complex subject in real-world situations. We must begin by distinguishing importantly different cases. For *starve* functions both as a passive verb, indicating something that happens to one, and as an active verb, designating something inflicted by one person on another. In the latter case, starvation is a form of killing, and of course comes under the same strictures that any other method of killing is liable to. But when the problem is plague, crop-failure due to drought, or sheer lack of know-how, there is no obviously guilty party. Then the question is whether we, the amply fed, are guilty parties if we fail to come to the rescue of those victims.

Starvation and Murder

If I lock you in a room with no food and don't let you out, I have murdered you. If group A burns the crops of group B, it has slaughtered the Bs. There is, surely, no genuine *issue* about such cases. It is wrong to kill innocent people, and one way of killing them is as eligible for condemnation by this principle as any other, so far as killing goes. Such cases are happily unusual, and we need say no more about them.

Our interest, then, is in the cases where this is not so, or at least not obviously so. But some writers, such as James Rachels, hold that letting

someone die is morally equivalent to killing them. Or "basically" equivalent. Is this so? Most people do not think so; it takes a subtle philosophical
argument to persuade them of this. The difference between a bad thing
which I intentionally or at least foreseeably brought about, and one which
just happened, through no fault of my own, matters to most of us in practice. Is our view sustainable in principle, too? Suppose the case is one I
could do something about, as when you are starving and my granary is
burgeoning. Does that make a difference?

Duties of Justice and Duties of Charity

Another important question, which has cropped up in some of our other
cases too but is nowhere more clearly relevant than here, is the distinction
between *justice* and *charity*. By justice I here intend those things which we
may, if necessary, be *forced* to do—where our actions can be constrained
by others in order to ensure our performance. Charity, on the other hand,
comes "from the heart": *charity* means, roughly, *caring*, an emotionally-
tinged desire to benefit other people just because they need it.

We should note a special point about this. It is often said that charity
"cannot be compelled." Is this true? In one clear sense, it is. For in this
sense, charity consists *only* of benefits motivated by love or concern. If
instead you regard an act as one that we may forcibly compel people to do,
then you are taking that act to be a case of *justice*. Can it at the same time
be charity? It can if we detach the motive from the act, and define charity simply as doing good for others. The claim that charity in this second
sense cannot be compelled is definitely not true by definition, and is in fact
false. People are frequently compelled to do good for others, especially by
our government, which taxes us in order to benefit the poor, educate the
uneducated, and so on. Whether they *should* be thus compelled is a real
moral question, however, and must not be evaded by recourse to seman-
tics. (Whether those programs produce benefits that outweigh their costs
is a very complex question; but that they do often produce some benefits,
at whatever cost, is scarcely deniable.)

When we ask, then, on which side of the moral divide we should put
feeding the hungry—unenforceable charity, to be left to individual consciences, or enforceable justice, perhaps to be handled by governments—is
a genuine moral issue, and an important one. We are asking whether feeding the hungry is not only something we ought to do but also something

we *must do,* as a matter of justice. It is especially this latter question that concerns us in this chapter.

We should note also the logical possibility that someone might differ so strongly with most of us on this matter as to think it positively *wrong* to feed the hungry. That is a rather extreme view, but it looks rather like the view that some writers, such as Garrett Hardin, defend. However, it is misleading to characterize their view in this way. Hardin thinks that feeding the hungry is an exercise in *misguided* charity, not real charity. In feeding the hungry today, he argues, we merely create a much greater problem tomorrow, for feeding the relatively few now will create an unmanageably large number next time their crops fail, a number we won't be able to feed and who will consequently starve. Thus we actually cause more starvation by feeding people now than we do by not feeding them, hard though that may sound. Hardin, then, is not favouring cruelty toward the weak. The truly charitable, he believes, should be *against* feeding the hungry, at least in some types of cases.

Hardin's argument brings up the need for another distinction, of urgent importance: between *principles* and *policies.* Being in favour of feeding the hungry *in principle* may or may not imply that we should feed the particular persons involved in any specific case. For that may depend on further facts about those cases. For example, perhaps trying to feed *these* hungry people runs into the problem that the government of those hungry people doesn't want you feeding them. If the price of feeding them is that you must go to war, then it may not be the best thing to do. If enormous starvation faces a group in the farther future if the starving among them now are fed now, then a policy of feeding them now may not be recommended by a principle of humanity. And so on. Principles are relatively abstract and may be considered just by considering possibilities; but when it comes to policy pursued in the real world, facts cannot be ignored.

The Basic Issues

Our general question is what sort of moral concerns we have with the starving. The basic question then breaks down into these two: first, is there a *basic duty of justice* to feed the starving? And second, if there isn't, then is there a *basic requirement of charity* that we be disposed to do so, and if so, how strong is that requirement?

Justice and Starvation

Let's begin with the first. Is it *unjust* to let others starve to death? We must distinguish two very different ways in which someone might try to argue for this.

First, there are those who, like Rachels, argue that there is no fundamental distinction between killing and letting die. If that is right, then the duty not to kill is all we need to support the conclusion that there is a duty of justice not to let people starve, and the duty not to kill (innocent) people is uncontroversial. Second, however, some insist that feeding the hungry is a duty of justice even if we don't accept the equivalence of killing and letting-die. They therefore need a different argument, in support of a positive right to be fed. The two different views call for very different discussions.

Starving and Allowing to Starve

Starving and allowing-to-starve are special cases of killing and letting-die. Are they the same, as some *insist*? In *our* discussion of euthanasia, we saw the need for a crucial distinction here: between the view that they are literally indistinguishable, and the view that even though they are logically distinguishable, they are nevertheless morally equivalent. As to the first, the argument for nonidentity of the two is straightforward. When you kill someone, you do an act, *x*, which brings it about that the person is dead *when he would otherwise still be alive*. You induce a *change* (for the worse) in his condition. But when you let someone die, this is not so, for she would have died even if you had, say, been in Australia at the time. How can you be said to be the "cause" of something which would have happened if you didn't exist?

To be sure, we do often attribute causality to human inaction. But the clear cases of such attribution are those where the agent in question had an antecedent *responsibility* to do the thing in question. The geraniums may die because you fail to water them, but to say that you thus *caused* them to die is to imply that you were *supposed* to do so. And of course we may agree that *if* we *have* a duty to feed the poor and we don't feed them, then we are at fault. But the question before us is *whether* we have this duty, and the argument we are examining purports to prove this by showing that even when we do nothing, we still "cause" their deaths. If the argument presupposes that very responsibility, it plainly begs the question rather than giving us a good answer to it. What about the claim that killing and letting die are "morally equivalent"? Here again, there is a danger of begging the question. *If* we have a duty to feed the hungry and we don't, then not doing so might be morally equivalent to killing them, perhaps—though I doubt that any proponent would seriously propose life imprisonment for failing to contribute to the cause of feeding the hungry! But again, the consequence clearly doesn't follow if we don't have that duty, which is in question. Those who think we do not have fundamental duties to take care of each other, but only duties to refrain from killing and the like will deny that they are morally equivalent.

The liberty proponent will thus insist that when Beethoven wrote symphonies instead of using his talents to grow food for the starving, like the peasants he depicted in his Pastorale symphony, he was doing what he had a perfect right to do. A connoisseur of music might go further and hold that he was also *doing the right thing:* that someone with the talents of a Beethoven does more for people by composing great music than by trying to save lives—even if he would have been *successful* in saving those lives, which is not terribly likely anyway!

How do we settle this issue? If we were all connoisseurs, it would be easy: if you know and love great music, you will find it easy to believe that a symphony by Beethoven or Mahler is worth more than prolonging the lives of a few hundred starvelings for another few miserable years. If you are one of those starving persons, your view might be different. (But it might not. Consider the starving artist in his garret, famed in Romantic novels and operas: they lived *voluntarily* in squalor, believing that what they were doing was worth the sacrifice.)

We are not all connoisseurs, nor are most of us starving. Advocates of welfare duties talk glibly as though there were a single point of view ("welfare") that dominates everything else. But it's not true. There are all kinds of points of view, diverse, and to a large extent incommensurable. Uniting them is not as simple as the welfarist or utilitarian may think. It is *not* certain, not obvious, that we "add more to the sum of human happiness" by supporting Oxfam than by supporting the opera. How are we to unite diverse people on these evaluative matters? The most plausible answer, I think, is the point of view that allows different people to live their various lives, by forbidding interference with them. Rather than insisting, with threats to back it up, that I help someone for whose projects and purposes I have no sympathy whatever, let us all agree to respect each other's pursuits. We'll agree to let each person live as that person sees fit, with only our bumpings into each other being subject to public control. To do this, we need to draw a sort of line around each person, and insist that others not cross that line without the permission of the occupant. The rule will be not to forcibly intervene in the lives of others, thus requiring that our relations be mutually agreeable. Enforced feeding of the starving, however, does cross the line, invading the farmer or the merchant, forcing him to part with some of his hard-earned produce and give it without compensation to others. That, says the advocate of liberty, is theft, not charity.

So if someone is starving, we may pity him or we may be indifferent, but the question so far as our *obligations* are concerned is only this: how did he *get* that way? If it was not the result of my previous activities, then I have no obligation to him, and may help him out or not, as I choose. If it was such a result, then of course I must do something. If you live and have long lived downstream from me, and I decide to dam up the river and divert the water elsewhere, then I have deprived you of your water and must compensate you, by supplying you with the equivalent, or else desist. But if you live in the middle of a parched desert and it does not rain, so that you are faced with death from thirst, that is not my doing and I have no compensating to do.

This liberty-respecting idea avoids, by and large, the need to make the sort of utility comparisons essential to the utility or welfare view. If we have no general obligation to manufacture as much utility for others as possible, then we don't have to concern ourselves about measuring that utility. Being free to pursue our own projects, we will evaluate our results as best we may, each in our own way. There is no need to keep a constant check on others to see whether we ought to be doing more for them and less for ourselves.

The Ethics of the Hair Shirt

In stark contrast to the liberty-respecting view stands the idea that we are to count the satisfactions of others as equal in value to our own. If I can create a little more pleasure for some stranger by spending my dollar on him than I would create for myself by spending it on an ice cream cone, I then have a putative *obligation* to spend it on him. Thus I am to continually defer to others in the organization of my activities, and shall be assailed by guilt whenever I am not bending my energies to the relief of those allegedly less fortunate than I. Benefit others, at the expense of yourself—and keep doing it until you are as poor and miserable as those whose poverty and misery you are supposed to be relieving! That is the ethics of the hair shirt.

How should we react to this idea? Negatively, in my view—and, I think, in yours. Doesn't that view really make us the slaves of the (supposedly) less well off? Surely a rule of conduct that permits people to be themselves and to try to live the best and most interesting lives they can is better than one which makes us all, in effect, functionaries in a welfare state? The rule that neither the rich nor the poor ought to be enslaved by the others is surely the better rule. Some, of course, think that the poor are, inherently, the "slaves" of the rich, and the rich inherently their masters. Such is the Marxist line, for instance. It's an important argument, but it's important also to realize that it's simply wrong. The wealthy do not have the right to hold a gun to the head of the nonwealthy and tell them what to do. On the contrary, the wealthy, in countries with reasonably free economies, become wealthy by selling things to others, things that those others voluntarily purchase. This makes the purchaser better off as well as the seller; and of course the employees of the latter become better off in the process of making those things, via their wages. The result of this activity is that there are more goods in the world than there would otherwise be.

This is precisely the opposite of the way the thief makes his money. He expends time and energy depriving someone else, involuntarily, of what his victims worked to produce, rather than devoting his own energies to productive activities. He in consequence leaves the world poorer than it was before he set out on his exploitative ways. The Marxist assimilates the honest accumulator to the thief. Rather than being, as so many seem to think, a profound contribution to social theory, that is a first-rank conceptual error, a failure to appreciate that wealth comes about precisely because of the prohibition of theft, rather than by its wholesale exercise.

Mutual Aid

But the anti-welfarist idea can be taken too far as well. Should people be disposed to assist each other in time of need? Certainly! But the appropriate rule for this is not that each person is duty bound to minister to the poor until he himself is a pauper or near-pauper as well. Rather, the appropriate rule is what the characterization, "in time of need" more nearly suggests. There are indeed emergencies in life when a modest effort by someone will do a great deal for someone else. People who aren't ready to help others are people who deserve to be avoided when they themselves turn to others in time of need.

But this all assumes that these occasions are, in the first place, relatively unusual, and in the second, that the help offered is genuinely of modest cost to the provider. If a stranger on the street asks for directions, a trifling expenditure of time and effort saves him great frustration, and perhaps also makes for a pleasant encounter with another human (which that other human should try to make so, by being polite and saying "thanks!" for example). But if as I walk down the street I am accosted on all sides by similar requests, then I shall never get my day's work done if I can't just say, "Sorry, I've got to be going!" or merely ignore the questioners and walk right on. If instead I must minister to each, then soon there will be nothing to give, since its existence depends entirely on the activities of people who produce it. If the stranger asks me to drive him around town all day looking for a long-lost friend, for instance, then that's going too far. Though of course we should be free to help him out even to that extent, if we are so inclined.

What about parting with the means for making your sweet little daughter's birthday party a memorable one, in order to keep a dozen strangers alive on the other side of the world? Is this something you are morally required to do? Indeed not. She may well *matter* to you more than they. This illustrates again the fact that people do *not* "count equally" for most of us. Normal people care more about some people than others, and build their very lives around those carings. It is both absurd and very arrogant for theorists, talking airily about the equality of all people, to insist on cramming it down our throats—which is how ordinary people do see it.

It is reasonable, then, to arrive at a general understanding that we shall be ready to help when help is urgent and when giving it is not very onerous to us. But a general understanding that we shall help everyone as if they were our spouses or dearest friends is quite another matter. Only a thinker whose heart has been replaced by a calculating machine could suppose that to be reasonable.

Is There a Duty of Charity?

One of the good things we can do in life is to make an effort to care about people about whom we don't ordinarily care or think. This can benefit not only the intended beneficiaries in distant places, but it can also benefit you, by broadening your perspective. There is a place for the enlargement of human sympathies. But then, these are sympathies, matters of the heart; and for such matters, family, friends, colleagues, and co-workers in things are rightly first on your agenda. Why so? First, just because you are you and not somebody else—not, for example, a godlike "impartial observer." But there is another reason of interest, even if you think there is something right about the utilitarian view. This is what amounts to a consideration of *efficiency*. We know ourselves and our loved ones; we do not, by definition, know strangers. We can choose a gift for people we know and love, but are we wise to try to benefit someone of alien culture and diet? If we do a good thing for someone we know well, we make an investment that will be returned as the years go by; but we have little idea of the pay-off from charity for the unknown. Of course, that can be overcome, once in awhile—you might end up pen pals with a peasant in Guatemala, but it would not be wise to count on it.

The tendency and desire to do good for others is a virtue. And it is a *moral* virtue, for we all have an interest in the general acquisition of this quality. Just as anyone can kill anyone else, so anyone can benefit anyone else; and so long as the cost to oneself of participating in the general scheme of helpfulness is low—namely, decidedly less than the return— then it is worth it. But it is not reasonable to take the matter beyond that. In particular, it is not reasonable to become a busybody, or a fanatic like Dickens' character Mrs. Jellyby, who is so busy with her charitable work for the natives in darkest Africa that her own children run around in rags and become the terror of the neighbourhood. Nor is it reasonable to be so concerned for the welfare of distant persons that you resort to armed robbery in your efforts to help them out ("Stick 'em up! I'm collecting for Oxfam!").

Notes on the Real World

If we are persuaded by the above, then as decent human beings we will be concerned about starvation and inclined to do something to help out if we can. This raises two questions. First, what is the situation? Are there lots of people in danger of imminent demise from lack of food? And second, just what should we do about it if there are?

Regarding the first question, one notes that contemporary philosophers and many others talk as though the answer is obviously and overwhelmingly in the affirmative. They write as though people by the million are starving daily. It is of interest to realize that they are, generally speaking, wrong, and in the special cases where there really is hunger, its causes are such as to strikingly affect our answer to the second question.

It turns out that starvation in the contemporary world is *not at all* due to the world's population having outgrown its resources, as Garrett Hardin and so many others seem to think; nor is the world even remotely a "lifeboat," as implied by the title of a famous article by Onora O'Neill ("Lifeboat Earth"). In fact, it has come to be appreciated that the world can support an indefinite number of people, certainly vastly more than there are now. If people have more children, they can be fed, or at least there is no reason why they couldn't be, so far as the actual availability of resources is concerned; nor does anyone in the affluent part of the world need to give up eating meat in order to enable them to do so. In 1970, harbingers of gloom and doom on these matters were reporting that by the 1990s there would be massive starvation in the world unless we got to work right now, clamping birth-control measures on the recalcitrant natives. Now in 1992 there are perhaps a half-billion more people than there were then, and—surprise!—they're all eating, and eating better at that. All, that is, *except* for those being starved at gunpoint by their governments or warring political factions. Meanwhile, Western nations are piling up food surpluses and wondering what to do to keep their farmers from going broke for lack of demand for their burgeoning products.

In fact, all of the incidence of substantial starvation (as opposed to the occasional flood) has been due to politics, not agriculture. In several African countries, in Nicaragua for awhile, in China until not long ago, the regimes in power, propelled by ideology or a desire for cheap votes, imposed artificially low food prices or artificially inefficient agricultural systems, on their people, and thus provided remarkably effective disincentives to their farmers to grow food. Not surprisingly, they responded by not growing it. The cure is to let the farmers farm in peace, and charge whatever they like for their produce; it is astonishing how rapidly they will then proceed to grow food to meet the demand. But the cure isn't to have Western countries send over boatloads of Western wheat. Even if the local government will *let* people have this bounty (they often don't—corrupt officials have been known to go out and privately resell the grain elsewhere instead of distributing it to their starving subjects), providing it indiscriminately hooks them on Western charity instead of enabling them to regain the self-sufficiency they enjoyed in earlier times, before modern Western benefits like "democracy" enabled incompetent local governments to disrupt the food supply.

We must also mention countries with governments that drive people forcibly off their land, burn their crops, and at a minimum steal it from the peasantry, as in Ethiopia and Somalia (at the time of this writing). Governments in those countries have combined such barbarities with the familiar tendency to prevent Western aid from getting to its intended recipients. Nature has nothing to do with starvation in such cases, and improvements in agriculture are not the cure. Improvements in politics are—but will not soon be coming, we may be sure. This means that the would-be charitable person faces a pretty difficult problem when he turns to the second question: What to do? In cases of natural disaster, as when a huge flood inundates the coast of Bangladesh, there will be short-term problems, and charitable agencies are excellent at responding quickly with needed food and medical supplies. Supporting some of those for dealing with such emergencies is likely a good idea. But in many other cases, there is very little that an outside agency can do. Tinpot Marxist dictators are not exactly paradigm cases of sweet reason at work, and only governments normally have the kind of clout that can open doors, even a crack, to the sort of aid we might like to give their beleaguered peoples.

The American Peace Corps and CUSO are two interesting organizations whose enthusiastic volunteers go to third-world communities to try to help them in various ways. To what extent they succeed is very hard to say, especially because the fundamental question of what constitutes "help" is so hard to answer. Do we help a native tribe in Africa that has maintained its way of life for thousands of years when we get their children learning arithmetic and wearing jeans? Or do we only destroy what they have and replace it with something impossible for them to cope with? (As a sobering case in point, the travel-writer Dervla Murphy, in *Muddling Through in Madagascar*, describes how one community was given an efficient modern pump for its communal water supply, which provided lots of clean water and relieved people of long trips to polluted wells. It stopped some years later, by which time the people who installed it had long since gone, and nobody knew how to repair it. But, interestingly, they didn't seem terribly concerned about it and made no effort whatever to get someone to fix it, but simply went back to the old ways, uncomplainingly and inefficiently. Apparently *they* didn't realize how terribly "essential" was this pump. Do we really know better than they? Why are we so sure that we do?)

Helping people who are very different from us is not an easy matter. Did all those missionaries who descended on the hapless Africans in the past centuries do them a lot of good by teaching them Christianity, or by bringing the infant mortality rate way down so that families accustomed to having a manageable number of children surviving to maturity suddenly found themselves with six or seven mouths to feed instead of two? Or by building a road to enable tourists to drive up to the villages and give the natives all sorts of Western diseases for which their immune systems were totally unprepared? There is surely a real question here for thoughtful people. Our efforts could well create disasters for the people we are trying to help, as well as to impose pointless costs on ourselves.

The sober conclusion from all this is that maybe it's better on all counts to spend that money on the opera after all. We are unlikely to act well when we act in ignorance, and when we deal with people vastly different from ourselves, ignorance is almost certain to afflict our efforts.

Summing Up

The basic question of this chapter is whether the hungry have a positive right to be fed. Of course we have a right to feed them if we wish, and they have a negative right to be fed. But may we forcibly impose a duty on others to feed them? We may not. If the fact that others are starving is not our fault, then we do not need to provide for them as a duty of justice. To think otherwise is to suppose that we are, in effect, slaves to the badly off. And so we can in good conscience spend our money on the opera instead of on the poor. Even so, feeding the hungry and taking care of the miserable is a nice thing to do, and is morally recommended. Charity is a virtue. Moreover, starvation turns out to be almost entirely a function of bad governments, rather than nature's inability to accommodate the burgeoning masses. Our charitable instincts can handle easily the problems that are due to natural disaster. We can feed the starving *and* go to the opera!

Jan Narveson: Feeding the Hungry

1. Narveson mentions that there are two ways to argue that it is unjust to let others starve to death. What are they? How does he respond to each? Do you think his response is successful? Why or why not?

2. Under what conditions does Narveson think we are obligated to give to those in need? When does he think it is virtuous to give to those in need? How do facts about the real world affect our obligations and virtues? Do you find his view plausible? Why or why not?

3. Explain Narveson's distinction between justice and charity. When is starvation a matter of justice and when is it a matter of charity? Apply this distinction to another moral issue. Do you think the distinction yields plausible results regarding your issue? Why or why not?

4. Explain what Narveson calls "the ethics of the hair shirt." Why does he think this view is mistaken? Explain one way the hair shirt ethicist might respond. Do you think the response is successful? Why or why not?

5. Explain the "liberty proponent" response to the distinction between starving and allowing to starve. According to the liberty proponent, to what extent is morality up to each individual? Do you find this problematic? Why or why not?

22

═══ ❧ ═══

The Morality of Euthanasia

James Rachels

James Rachels (1941–2003) argues that active euthanasia is sometimes morally permissible. Active euthanasia occurs when someone (typically a medical professional) takes action to deliberately end a patient's life, at the patient's request, for the patient's own good. Rachels argues that considerations of mercy play a vital role in justifying active euthanasia in many cases.

He first considers a utilitarian argument on behalf of active euthanasia, but finds problems with utilitarianism that are weighty enough to undermine this argument. However, Rachels believes that a different version can succeed. In this one, Rachels claims that any action that promotes the best interests of all concerned, and that violates no rights, is morally acceptable. Since, he claims, active euthanasia sometimes satisfies this description, it is sometimes morally acceptable.

The single most powerful argument in support of euthanasia is the argument from mercy. It is also an exceptionally simple argument, at least in its main idea, which makes one uncomplicated point. Terminally ill patients sometimes suffer pain so horrible that it is beyond

From "Euthanasia," in Tom Beauchamp, ed., *Matters of Life and Death*, 2nd ed. (McGraw-Hill, 1986), pp. 49–52.

the comprehension of those who have not actually experienced it. Their suffering can be so terrible that we do not like even to read about it or think about it; we recoil even from the descriptions of such agony. The argument from mercy says euthanasia is justified because it provides an end to *that*.

The great Irish satirist Jonathan Swift took eight years to die, while, in the words of Joseph Fletcher, "His mind crumbled to pieces." At times the pain in his blinded eyes was so intense he had to be restrained from tearing them out with his own hands. Knives and other potential instruments of suicide had to be kept from him. For the last three years of his life, he could do nothing but sit and drool: and when he finally died it was only after convulsions that lasted thirty-six hours.

Swift died in 1745. Since then, doctors have learned how to eliminate much of the pain that accompanies terminal illness, but the victory has been far from complete. So, here is a more modern example.

Stewart Alsop was a respected journalist who died in 1975 of a rare form of cancer. Before he died, he wrote movingly of his experiences as a terminal patient. Although he had not thought much about euthanasia before, he came to approve of it after rooming briefly with someone he called Jack:

> The third night that I roomed with Jack in our tiny double room in the solid-tumor ward of the cancer clinic of the National Institutes of Health in Bethesda, Md., a terrible thought occurred to me.
>
> Jack had a melanoma in his belly, a malignant solid tumor that the doctors guessed was about the size of a softball. The cancer had started a few months before with a small tumor in his left shoulder, and there had been several operations since. The doctors planned to remove the softball-sized tumor, but they knew Jack would soon die. The cancer had metastasized—it had spread beyond control.
>
> Jack was good-looking, about 28, and brave. He was in constant pain, and his doctor had prescribed an intravenous shot of a synthetic opiate—a pain-killer, or analgesic—every four hours. His wife spent many of the daylight hours with him, and she would sit or lie on his bed and pat him all over, as one pats a child, only more methodically, and this seemed to help control the pain. But at night, when his pretty wife had left (wives cannot stay overnight at the NIH clinic) and darkness fell, the pain would attack without pity.
>
> At the prescribed hour, a nurse would give Jack a shot of the synthetic analgesic, and this would control the pain for perhaps two hours or a bit

more. Then he would begin to moan, or whimper, very low, as though he didn't want to wake me. Then he would begin to howl, like a dog.

When this happened, either he or I would ring for a nurse, and ask for a pain-killer. She would give him some codeine or the like by mouth, but it never did any real good—it affected him no more than half an aspirin might affect a man who had just broken his arm. Always the nurse would explain as encouragingly as she could that there was not long to go before the next intravenous shot—"Only about 50 minutes now." And always poor Jack's whimpers and howls would become more loud and frequent until at last the blessed relief came.

The third night of this routine the terrible thought occurred to me. "If Jack were a dog," I thought, "what would be done with him?" The answer was obvious: the pound, and chloroform. No human being with a spark of pity could let a living thing suffer so, to no good end.

The NIH clinic is, of course, one of the most modern and best-equipped hospitals we have. Jack's suffering was not the result of poor treatment in some backward rural facility; it was the inevitable product of his disease, which medical science was powerless to prevent.

I have quoted Alsop at length not for the sake of indulging in gory details but to give a clear idea of the kind of suffering we are talking about. We should not gloss over these facts with euphemistic language or squeamishly avert our eyes from them. For only by keeping them firmly and vividly in mind can we appreciate the full force of the argument from mercy: If a person prefers— and even begs for—death as the only alternative to lingering on *in this kind of torment*, only to die anyway after a while, then surely it is not immoral to help this person die sooner. As Alsop put it, "No human being with a spark of pity could let a living thing suffer so, to no good end."

The Utilitarian Version of the Argument

In connection with this argument, the utilitarians deserve special mention. They argued that actions and social policies should be judged right or wrong *exclusively* according to whether they cause happiness or misery; and they argued that when judged by this standard, euthanasia turns out to be morally acceptable. The utilitarian argument may be elaborated as follows:

(1) Any action or social policy is morally right if it serves to increase the amount of happiness in the world or to decrease the amount of misery. Conversely, an action or social policy is morally wrong if it serves to decrease happiness or to increase misery.

(2) The policy of killing, at their own request, hopelessly ill patients who are suffering great pain would decrease the amount of misery in the world. (An example could be Alsop's friend Jack.)

(3) Therefore, such a policy would be morally right.

The first premise of this argument, (1), states the Principle of Utility, which is the basic utilitarian assumption. Today most philosophers think that this principle is wrong, because they think that the promotion of happiness and the avoidance of misery are not the *only* morally important things. Happiness, they say, is only one among many values that should be promoted: freedom, justice, and a respect for people's rights are also important. To take one example: people *might* be happier if there were no freedom of religion, for if everyone adhered to the same religious beliefs, there would be greater harmony among people. There would be no unhappiness caused within families by Jewish girls marrying Catholic boys, and so forth. Moreover, if people were brainwashed well enough, no one would mind not having freedom of choice. Thus happiness would be increased. But, the argument continues, even if happiness *could* be increased this way, it would not be right to deny people freedom of religion, because people have a right to make their own choices. Therefore, the first premise of the utilitarian argument is unacceptable.

There is a related difficulty for utilitarianism, which connects more directly with the topic of euthanasia. Suppose a person is leading a miserable life—full of more unhappiness than happiness—but does *not* want to die. This person thinks that a miserable life is better than none at all. Now I assume that we would all agree that the person should not be killed; that would be plain, unjustifiable murder. Yet it *would* decrease the amount of misery in the world if we killed this person—it would lead to an increase in the balance of happiness over unhappiness—and so it is hard to see how, on strictly utilitarian grounds, it could be wrong. Again, the Principle of Utility seems to be an inadequate guide for determining right and wrong. So we are on shaky ground if we rely on *this* version of the argument from mercy for a defense of euthanasia.

Doing What Is in Everyone's Best Interests

Although the foregoing utilitarian argument is faulty, it is nevertheless based on a sound idea. For even if the promotion of happiness and avoidance of misery are not the *only* morally important things, they are still very important. So, when an action or a social policy would decrease misery, that is *a* very strong reason in its favor. In the cases of voluntary euthanasia we are now considering, great suffering is eliminated, and since the patient requests it, there is no question of violating individual rights. That is why, regardless of the difficulties of the Principle of Utility, the utilitarian version of the argument still retains considerable force.

I want now to present a somewhat different version of the argument from mercy, which is inspired by utilitarianism but which avoids the difficulties of the foregoing version by not making the Principle of Utility a premise of the argument. I believe that the following argument is sound and proves that active euthanasia *can* be justified:

1. If an action promotes the best interests of *everyone* concerned and violates *no one's* rights, then that action is morally acceptable.
2. In at least some cases, active euthanasia promotes the best interests of everyone concerned and violates no one's rights.
3. Therefore, in at least some cases, active euthanasia is morally acceptable.

It would have been in everyone's best interests if active euthanasia had been employed in the case of Stewart Alsop's friend Jack. First, and most important, it would have been in Jack's own interests, since it would have provided him with an easier, better death, without pain. (Who among us would choose Jack's death, if we had a choice, rather than a quick painless death?) Second, it would have been in the best interests of Jack's wife. Her misery, helplessly watching him suffer, must have been almost unbearable. Third, the hospital staff's best interests would have been served, since if Jack's dying had not been prolonged, they could have turned their attention to other patients whom they could have helped. Fourth, other patients would have benefited, since medical resources would no longer have been used in the sad, pointless maintenance of Jack's physical existence. Finally, if Jack himself requested to be killed, the act would not have violated his rights. Considering all this, how can active euthanasia in this case be wrong? How can it be wrong to do an action that is merciful, that benefits everyone concerned, and that violates no one's rights?

James Rachels: The Morality of Euthanasia

1. Would someone in circumstances like Jack's be better off dead? That is, would dying quickly and painlessly be in his best interest?
2. What are Rachels's objections to the principle of utility? Do you find them convincing?

3. How does Rachels's second argument differ from the utilitarian argument? Do you agree with Rachels that it is a stronger argument?

4. Rachels claims that euthanasia cannot be said to violate anyone's rights, given that the patient requests it. Do you find this claim plausible? Is it possible to do something that violates someone's rights even if he or she consents to it?

5. Rachels claims that (in some cases) active euthanasia promotes the interests of everyone concerned. If our society were to allow active euthanasia, would this be harmful to anyone's interests? Why or why not?

23

The Survival Lottery

John Harris

In this paper, John Harris invites us to consider the merits of a special sort of organ transplant scheme, which he calls the survival lottery. Each year, many thousands of people die because of organ failure and the lack of a suitable donor organ. Harris proposes that we remedy this situation by instituting a lottery among (almost) all citizens. Whenever two or more people are in need of a vital organ, we pick a citizen at random to be vivisected (dissected while alive—though presumably under anesthesia!), so that his or her organs can be distributed to those who need them to survive.

We don't do this with any sort of punitive intent, but rather in order to minimize the number of people who die, through no fault of their own, because of organ failure. True, the organ donor being killed is wholly innocent. But then so are those who are dying for lack of a donor organ.

Harris is well aware that the lottery sounds like outright murder, and he devotes the bulk of the article to presenting, and then countering, a great many objections to it. He acknowledges that there may be problems with making such a system feasible in practice. If these problems could be ironed out, however, Harris thinks that rational and morally enlightened people would endorse this proposal for their own society.

John Harris, "The Survival Lottery" from *Philosophy* 50 (1975), pp. 81–87. Reprinted with the permission of Cambridge University Press.

et us suppose that organ transplant procedures have been perfected; in such circumstances if two dying patients could be saved by organ transplants then, if surgeons have the requisite organs in stock and no other needy patients, but nevertheless allow their patients to die, we would be inclined to say, and be justified in saying, that the patients died because the doctors refused to save them. But if there are no spare organs in stock and none otherwise available, the doctors have no choice, they cannot save their patients and so must let them die. In this case we would be disinclined to say that the doctors are in any sense the cause of their patients' deaths. But let us further suppose that the two dying patients, Y and Z, are not happy about being left to die. They might argue that it is not strictly true that there are no organs which could be used to save them. Y needs a new heart and Z new lungs. They point out that if just one healthy person were to be killed his organs could be removed and both of them be saved. We and the doctors would probably be alike in thinking that such a step, while technically possible, would be out of the question. We would not say that the doctors were killing their patients if they refused to prey upon the healthy to save the sick. And because this sort of surgical Robin Hoodery is out of the question we can tell Y and Z that they cannot be saved, and that when they die they will have died of natural causes and not of the neglect of their doctors. Y and Z do not however agree, they insist that if the doctors fail to kill a healthy man and use his organs to save them, then the doctors will be responsible for their deaths.

Many philosophers have for various reasons believed that we must not kill even if by doing so we could save life. They believe that there is a moral difference between killing and letting die. On this view, to kill A so that Y and Z might live is ruled out because we have a strict obligation not to kill but a duty of some lesser kind to save life. A. H. Clough's dictum "Thou shalt not kill but need'st not strive officiously to keep alive" expresses bluntly this point of view. The dying Y and Z may be excused for not being much impressed by Clough's dictum. They agree that it is wrong to kill the innocent and are prepared to agree to an absolute prohibition against so doing. They do not agree, however, that A is more innocent than they are. Y and Z might go on to point out that the currently acknowledged right of the innocent not to be killed, even where their deaths might give life to others, is just a decision to prefer the lives of the fortunate to those of the unfortunate. A is innocent in the sense that he has done nothing to deserve death, but Y and Z are also innocent in this sense. Why should they be the ones to die simply because they are so unlucky as to have diseased organs?

Why, they might argue, should their living or dying be left to chance when in so many other areas of human life we believe that we have an obligation to ensure the survival of the maximum number of lives possible?

Y and Z argue that if a doctor refuses to treat a patient, with the result that the patient dies, he has killed that patient as sure as shooting, and that, in exactly the same way, if the doctors refuse Y and Z the transplants that they need, then their refusal will kill Y and Z, again as sure as shooting. The doctors, and indeed the society which supports their inaction, cannot defend themselves by arguing that they are neither expected, nor required by law or convention, to kill so that lives may be saved (indeed, quite the reverse) since this is just an appeal to custom or authority. A man who does his own moral thinking must decide whether, in these circumstances, he ought to save two lives at the cost of one, or one life at the cost of two. The fact that so called "third parties" have never before been brought into such calculations, have never before been thought of as being involved, is not an argument against their now becoming so. There are of course, good arguments against allowing doctors simply to haul passers-by off the streets whenever they have a couple of patients in need of new organs. And the harmful side-effects of such a practice in terms of terror and distress to the victims, the witnesses and society generally, would give us further reasons for dismissing the idea. Y and Z realize this and have a proposal, which they will shortly produce, which would largely meet objections to placing such power in the hands of doctors and eliminate at least some of the harmful side-effects.

In the unlikely event of their feeling obliged to reply to the reproaches of Y and Z, the doctors might offer the following argument: they might maintain that a man is only responsible for the death of someone whose life he might have saved, if, in all the circumstances of the case, he ought to have saved the man by the means available. This is why a doctor might be a murderer if he simply refused or neglected to treat a patient who would die without treatment, but not if he could only save the patient by doing something he ought in no circumstances to do—kill the innocent. Y and Z readily agree that a man ought not to do what he ought not to do, but they point out that if the doctors, and for that matter society at large, ought on balance to kill one man if two can thereby be saved, then failure to do so will involve responsibility for the consequent deaths. The fact that Y's and Z's proposal involves killing the innocent cannot be a reason for refusing to consider their proposal, for this would just be a refusal to face the question at issue and so avoid having to make a decision as to what ought to be done in circumstances like these. It is Y's and Z's claim that failure to adopt their plan will also involve killing the innocent, rather more of the innocent than the proposed alternative.

To back up this last point, to remove the arbitrariness of permitting doctors to select their donors from among the chance passers-by outside hospitals, and the tremendous power this would place in doctors' hands, to mitigate worries about side-effects and lastly to appease those who wonder why poor old A should be singled out for sacrifice, Y and Z put forward the following scheme: they propose that everyone be given a sort of lottery number. Whenever doctors have two or more dying patients who could be saved by transplants, and no suitable organs have come to hand through "natural" deaths, they can ask a central computer to supply a suitable donor. The computer will then pick the number of a suitable donor at random and he will be killed so that the lives of two or more others may be saved. No doubt if the scheme were ever to be implemented a suitable euphemism for "killed" would be employed. Perhaps we would begin to talk about citizens being called upon to "give life" to others. With the refinement of transplant procedures such a scheme could offer the chance of saving large numbers of lives that are now lost. Indeed, even taking into account the loss of the lives of donors, the numbers of untimely deaths each year might be dramatically reduced, so much so that everyone's chance of living to a ripe old age might be increased. If this were to be the consequence of the adoption of such a scheme, and it might well be, it could not be dismissed lightly. It might of course be objected that it is likely that more old people will need transplants to prolong their lives than will the young, and so the scheme would inevitably lead to a society dominated by the old. But if such a society is thought objectionable, there is no reason to suppose that a program could not be designed for the computer that would ensure the maintenance of whatever is considered to be an optimum age distribution throughout the population.

Suppose that inter-planetary travel revealed a world of people like ourselves, but who organized their society according to this scheme. No one was considered to have an absolute right to life or freedom from interference, but everything was always done to ensure that as many people as possible would enjoy long and happy lives. In such a world a man who attempted to escape when his number was up or who resisted on the grounds that no one had a right to take his life, might well be regarded as a murderer. We might or might not prefer to live in such a world, but the morality of its inhabitants would surely be one that we could respect. It would not be obviously more barbaric or cruel or immoral than our own.

Y and Z are willing to concede one exception to the universal application of their scheme. They realize that it would be unfair to allow people who have brought their misfortune on themselves to benefit from the lottery. There would clearly be something unjust about killing the abstemious B so that W (whose heavy smoking has given him lung cancer) and X (whose drinking has destroyed his liver) should be preserved to overindulge again.

What objections could be made to the lottery scheme? A first straw to clutch at would be the desire for security. Under such a scheme we would never know when we would hear *them* knocking at the door. Every post might bring a sentence of death, every sound in the night might be the sound of boots on the stairs. But, as we have seen, the chances of actually being called upon to make the ultimate sacrifice might be slimmer than is the present risk of being killed on the roads, and most of us do not lie trembling a-bed, appalled at the prospect of being dispatched on the morrow. The truth is that lives might well be more secure under such a scheme.

If we respect individuality and see every human being as unique in his own way, we might want to reject a society in which it appeared that individuals were seen merely as interchangeable units in a structure, the value of which lies in its having as many healthy units as possible. But of course Y and Z would want to know why A's individuality was more worthy of respect than theirs.

Another plausible objection is the natural reluctance to play God with men's lives, the feeling that it is wrong to make any attempt to re-allot the life opportunities that fate has determined, that the deaths of Y and Z would be "natural," whereas the death of anyone killed to save them would have been perpetrated by men. But if we are able to change things, then to elect not to do so is also to determine what will happen in the world.

Neither does the alleged moral differences between killing and letting die afford a respectable way of rejecting the claims of Y and Z. For if we really want to counter proponents of the lottery, if we really want to answer Y and Z and not just put them off, we cannot do so by saying that the lottery involves killing and object to it for that reason, because to do so would, as we have seen, just beg the question as to whether the failure to save as many people as possible might not also amount to killing.

To opt for the society which Y and Z propose would be then to adopt a society in which saintliness would be mandatory. Each of us would have to recognize a binding obligation to give up his own life for others when called upon to do so. In such a society anyone who reneged upon this duty would be a murderer. The most promising objection to such a society, and indeed to any principle which required us to kill A in order to save Y and Z, is, I suspect, that we are committed to the right of self-defence. If I can kill A to save Y and Z then he can kill me to save P and Q, and it is only if I am prepared to agree to this that I will opt for the lottery or be prepared to agree to a man's being killed if doing so would save the lives of more than one other man. Of course there is something paradoxical about basing objections to the lottery scheme on the right of self-defence since, *ex hypothesi*, each person would have a better chance of living to a ripe old age if the lottery scheme were to be implemented. None the less, the feeling that no man should be required to lay down his life for others makes many people shy away from such a scheme, even though it might be rational to accept it on prudential grounds, and perhaps even mandatory on utilitarian grounds. Again, Y and Z would reply that the right of self-defence must extend to them as much as to anyone else; and while it is true that they can only live if another man is killed, they would claim that it is also true that if they are left to die, then someone who lives on does so over their dead bodies.

It might be argued that the institution of the survival lottery has not gone far to mitigate the harmful side-effects in terms of terror and distress to victims, witnesses and society generally, that would be occasioned by doctors simply snatching passers-by off the streets and disorganizing them for the benefit of the unfortunate. Donors would after all still have to be procured, and this process, however it was carried out, would still be likely to prove distressing to all concerned. The lottery scheme would eliminate the arbitrariness of leaving the life and death decisions to the doctors, and remove the possibility of such terrible power falling into the hands of any individuals, but the terror and distress would remain. The effect of having to apprehend presumably unwilling victims would give us pause. Perhaps only a long period of education or propaganda could remove our abhorrence. What this abhorrence reveals about the rights and wrongs of the situation is however more difficult to assess. We might be inclined to say that only monsters could ignore the promptings of conscience so far as to operate the lottery scheme. But the promptings of conscience are not necessarily the most reliable guide. In the present case Y and Z would argue that such promptings are mere squeamishness, an over-nice self-indulgence that costs lives. Death, Y and Z would remind us, is a distressing experience whenever and to whomever it occurs, so the less it occurs the better. Fewer victims and witnesses will be distressed as part of the side-effects of

the lottery scheme than would suffer as part of the side-effects of not instituting it.

Lastly, a more limited objection might be made, not to the idea of
killing to save lives, but to the involvement of "third parties." Why, so the
objection goes, should we not give X's heart to Y or Y's lungs to X, the
same number of lives being thereby preserved and no one else's life set at
risk? Y's and Z's reply to this objection differs from their previous line of
argument. To amend their plan so that the involvement of so called "third
parties" is ruled out would, Y and Z claim, violate their right to equal concern and respect with the rest of society. They argue that such a proposal
would amount to treating the unfortunate who need new organs as a class
within society whose lives are considered to be of less value than those of
its more fortunate members. What possible justification could there be for
singling out one group of people whom we would be justified in using as
donors but not another? The idea in the mind of those who would propose
such a step must be something like the following: since Y and Z cannot
survive, since they are going to die in any event, there is no harm in putting their names into the lottery, for the chances of their dying cannot
thereby be increased and will in fact almost certainly be reduced. But this
is just to ignore everything that Y and Z have been saying. For if their lottery scheme is adopted they are not going to die anyway—their chances of
dying are no greater and no less than those of any other participant in the
lottery whose number may come up. This ground for confining selection
of donors to the unfortunate therefore disappears. Any other ground must
discriminate against Y and Z as members of a class whose lives are less
worthy of respect than those of the rest of society.

It might more plausibly be argued that the dying who cannot themselves be saved by transplants, or by any other means at all, should be the
priority selection group for the computer programme. But how far off must
death be for a man to be classified as "dying"? Those so classified might
argue that their last few days or weeks of life are as valuable to them (if
not more valuable) than the possibly longer span remaining to others. The
problem of narrowing down the class of possible donors without discriminating unfairly against some sub-class of society is, I suspect, insoluble.

Such is the case for the survival lottery. Utilitarians ought to be in
favour of it, and absolutists cannot object to it on the ground that it involves
killing the innocent, for it is Y's and Z's case that any alternative must also
involve killing the innocent. If the absolutist wishes to maintain his objection he must point to some morally relevant difference between positive

and negative killing. This challenge opens the door to a large topic with a whole library of literature, but Y and Z are dying and do not have time to explore it exhaustively. In their own case the most likely candidate for some feature which might make this moral difference is the malevolent intent of Y and Z themselves. An absolutist might well argue that while no one intends the deaths of Y and Z, no one necessarily wishes them dead, or aims at their demise for any reason, they do mean to kill A (or have him killed). But Y and Z can reply that the death of A is no part of their plan, they merely wish to use a couple of his organs, and if he cannot live without them . . . *tant pis!* None would be more delighted than Y and Z if artificial organs would do as well, and so render the lottery scheme otiose.

One form of absolutist argument perhaps remains. This involves taking an Orwellian stand on some principle of common decency. The argument would then be that even to enter into the sort of "macabre" calculations that Y and Z propose displays a blunted sensibility, a corrupted and vitiated mind. Forms of this argument have recently been advanced by Noam Chomsky (*American Power and the New Mandarins*) and Stuart Hampshire (*Morality and Pessimism*). The indefatigable Y and Z would of course deny that their calculations are in any sense "macabre," and would present them as the most humane course available in the circumstances. Moreover they would claim that the Orwellian stand on decency is the product of a closed mind, and not susceptible to rational argument. Any reasoned defence of such a principle must appeal to notions like respect for human life, as Hampshire's argument in fact does, and these Y and Z could make conformable to their own position.

Can Y and Z be answered? Perhaps only by relying on moral intuition, on the insistence that we do feel there is something wrong with the survival lottery and our confidence that this feeling is prompted by some morally relevant difference between our bringing about the death of A and our bringing about the deaths of Y and Z. Whether we could retain this confidence in our intuitions if we were to be confronted by a society in which the survival lottery operated, was accepted by all, and was seen to save many lives that would otherwise have been lost, it would be interesting to know.

There would of course be great practical difficulties in the way of implementing the lottery. In so many cases it would be agonizingly difficult to decide whether or not a person had brought his misfortune on himself. There are numerous ways in which a person may contribute to his predicament, and the task of deciding how far, or how decisively, a person is himself responsible for his fate would be formidable. And in those cases where we can be confident that a person is innocent of responsibility for his predicament, can we acquire this confidence in time to save him? The lottery scheme would be a powerful weapon in the hands of someone willing and able to misuse it. Could we ever feel certain the lottery was safe from unscrupulous computer programmers? Perhaps we should be thankful that such practical difficulties make the survival lottery an unlikely consequence of the perfection of transplants. Or perhaps we should be appalled.

It may be that we would want to tell Y and Z that the difficulties and dangers of their scheme would be too great a price to pay for its benefits. It is as well to be clear, however, that there is also a high, perhaps an even higher, price to be paid for the rejection of the scheme. That price is the lives of Y and Z and many like them, and we delude ourselves if we suppose that the reason why we reject their plan is that we accept the sixth commandment.

John Harris: The Survival Lottery

1. What exactly is a survival lottery, and how would it work? Do you think it would be morally permissible to institute one?
2. Some people might object to Harris's proposal by claiming that it is never morally permissible to kill innocent people. Why doesn't Harris think this is a good objection? Do you find his criticisms of this objection convincing?
3. Another objection to the survival lottery claims that any such policy would cause widespread terror, since anyone could be selected to have his or her organs harvested. Is this a good objection? How does Harris respond?
4. Harris allows one exception to the universal application of the survival lottery. What is the exception? Do you agree that these individuals should be excluded from the lottery?
5. Some might think that instituting a survival lottery amounts to "playing God." What does it mean to "play God"? Is it always wrong to do so?
6. What "practical difficulties" does Harris think we would face if we tried to institute a survival lottery? Could these difficulties be overcome?

24

Puppies, Pigs and People: Eating Meat and Marginal Cases

Alastair Norcross

....

Alastair Norcross opens his provocative piece with a fictional scenario that is both outrageous and meant to make a very serious philosophical point. As he sees it, current practices of factory farming are deeply immoral. One might think that meat-eaters are exempt from blame, though, since for the most part they are not the ones who are actually perpetrating the harms to animals on the factory farms that process the great majority of animal products. Norcross rejects this thought. As he sees it, meat-eaters—at least those who know of the cruelty of the treatment of factory-farmed animals—are fully blameworthy for their indulgence. The good they get from eating meat—primarily the gustatory pleasure they get from eating meat—is far outweighed by the awful suffering of the animals when confined and killed on factory farms.

Norcross considers a wide variety of replies to his charge. These include the claim that individual meat-eaters are off the moral hook because their purchases are so insignificant that they cannot affect the practices on factory farms. Another reply is that meat-eaters do not intend to harm animals, but only foresee animal harm as a result of contemporary farming practices. Norcross extensively criticizes both replies.

Alastair Norcross, "Puppies, Pigs and People: Eating Meat and Marginal Cases," from *Philosophical Perspectives* 18 (2004), pp. 229–234, 239–244.

He then introduces a very popular argument in the literature on animal welfare: the argument from marginal cases. This argument says that we must treat animals and so-called "marginal" human beings as equals, since such humans have mental lives that are no more developed than those of the animals that are killed and eaten for food. He considers several replies to this argument, and finds fault with each of them. If we are unwilling to cruelly confine, prematurely kill, and eat "marginal" human beings, then we should be equally reluctant to do such things to animals.

Norcross concludes with a discussion of the difference between being a moral agent (i.e., someone who can respond to moral reasons and control her behavior by means of such reasons) and a moral patient (i.e., a being to whom we owe duties, even if that being lacks rights or lacks the cognitive powers needed to be a moral agent). Norcross argues that animals qualify as moral patients, even if, because of their diminished or nonexistent rationality, they cannot qualify as moral agents. We therefore owe them duties of respect, which protect them against the current practices involved in factory farming.

....

1. Fred's Basement

Consider the story of Fred, who receives a visit from the police one day. They have been summoned by Fred's neighbors, who have been disturbed by strange sounds emanating from Fred's basement. When they enter the basement they are confronted by the following scene: Twenty-six small wire cages, each containing a puppy, some whining, some whimpering, some howling. The puppies range in age from newborn to about six months. Many of them show signs of mutilation. Urine and feces cover the bottoms of the cages and the basement floor. Fred explains that he keeps the puppies for twenty-six weeks, and then butchers them while holding them upside-down. During their lives he performs a series of mutilations on them, such as slicing off their noses and their paws with a hot knife, all without any form of anesthesia. Except for the mutilations, the puppies are never allowed out of the cages, which are barely big enough to hold them at twenty-six weeks. The police are horrified, and promptly charge Fred with animal abuse. As details of the case are publicized, the public is outraged. Newspapers are flooded with letters demanding that Fred be severely punished. There are calls for more severe penalties for animal abuse. Fred is denounced as a vile sadist.

Finally, at his trial, Fred explains his behavior, and argues that he is blameless and therefore deserves no punishment. He is, he explains, a great lover of chocolate. A couple of years ago, he was involved in a car accident, which resulted in some head trauma. Upon his release from hospital, having apparently suffered no lasting ill effects, he visited his favorite restaurant and ordered their famous rich dark chocolate mousse. Imagine his dismay when he discovered that his experience of the mousse was a pale shadow of its former self. The mousse tasted bland, slightly pleasant, but with none of the intense chocolaty flavor he remembered so well. The waiter assured him that the recipe was unchanged from the last time he had tasted it, just the day before his accident. In some consternation, Fred rushed out to buy a bar of his favorite Belgian chocolate. Again, he was dismayed to discover that his experience of the chocolate was barely even pleasurable. Extensive investigation revealed that his experience of other foods remained unaffected, but chocolate, in all its forms, now tasted bland and insipid. Desperate for a solution to his problem, Fred visited a renowned gustatory neurologist, Dr. T. Bud. Extensive tests revealed that the accident had irreparably damaged the godiva gland, which secretes cocoamone, the hormone responsible for the experience of chocolate. Fred urgently requested hormone replacement therapy. Dr. Bud informed him that, until recently, there had been no known source of cocoamone, other than the human godiva gland, and that it was impossible to collect cocoamone from one person to be used by another. However, a chance discovery had altered the situation. A forensic veterinary surgeon, performing an autopsy on a severely abused puppy, had discovered high concentrations of cocoamone in the puppy's brain. It turned out that puppies, who don't normally produce cocoamone, could be stimulated to do so by extended periods of severe stress and suffering. The research, which led to this discovery, while gaining tenure for its authors, had not been widely publicized, for fear of antagonizing animal welfare groups. Although this research clearly gave Fred the hope of tasting chocolate again, there were no commercially available sources of puppy-derived cocoamone. Lack of demand, combined with fear of bad publicity, had deterred drug companies from getting into the puppy torturing business. Fred appeals to the court to imagine his anguish, on discovering that a solution to his severe deprivation was possible, but not readily available. But he wasn't inclined to sit around bemoaning his cruel fate. He did what any chocolate lover would do. He read the research, and set up his own cocoamone collection lab in his basement. Six months of intense puppy suffering, followed by a brutal death, produced enough cocoamone to last him a week, hence the twenty-six cages. He isn't a sadist or an animal abuser, he explains. If there were a method of collecting cocoamone without torturing puppies, he would gladly employ it. He derives no pleasure from the suffering of the puppies itself. He sympathizes with those who are horrified by the pain and misery of the animals, but the court must realize that human pleasure is at stake. The puppies, while undeniably cute, are mere animals. He admits that he would be just as healthy without chocolate, if not more so. But this isn't a matter of survival or health. His life would be unacceptably impoverished without the experience of chocolate.

End of story. Clearly, we are horrified by Fred's behavior, and unconvinced by his attempted justification. It is, of course, unfortunate for Fred that he can no longer enjoy the taste of chocolate, but that in no way excuses the imposition of severe suffering on the puppies. I expect near universal agreement with this claim (the exceptions being those who are either inhumanly callous or thinking ahead, and wish to avoid the following conclusion, to which such agreement commits them). No decent person would even contemplate torturing puppies merely to enhance a gustatory experience. However, billions of animals endure intense suffering every year for precisely this end. Most of the chicken, veal, beef, and pork consumed in the US comes from intensive confinement facilities, in which the animals live cramped, stress-filled lives and endure unanaesthetized mutilations. The vast majority of people would suffer no ill health from the elimination of meat from their diets. Quite the reverse. The supposed benefits from this system of factory farming, apart from the profits accruing to agribusiness, are increased levels of gustatory pleasure for those who claim that they couldn't enjoy a meat-free diet as much as their current meat-filled diets. If we are prepared to condemn Fred for torturing puppies merely to enhance his gustatory experiences, shouldn't we similarly condemn the millions who purchase and consume factory-raised meat? Are there any morally significant differences between Fred's behavior and their behavior?

2. Fred's Behavior Compared with Our Behavior

The first difference that might seem to be relevant is that Fred tortures the puppies himself, whereas most Americans consume meat that comes from animals that have been tortured by others. But is this really relevant? What if Fred had been squeamish and had employed someone else to torture the puppies and extract the cocoamone? Would we have thought any better of Fred? Of course not.

Another difference between Fred and many consumers of factory-raised meat is that many, perhaps most, such consumers are unaware of the treatment of the animals, before they appear in neatly wrapped packages on supermarket shelves. Perhaps I should moderate my challenge, then. If we are prepared to condemn Fred for torturing puppies merely to enhance his gustatory experiences, shouldn't we similarly condemn those who purchase and consume factory-raised meat, in full, or even partial, awareness of the suffering endured by the animals? While many consumers are still blissfully ignorant of the appalling treatment meted out to meat, that number is rapidly dwindling, thanks to vigorous publicity campaigns waged by animal welfare groups. Furthermore, any meat-eating readers of this article are now deprived of the excuse of ignorance.

Perhaps a consumer of factory-raised animals could argue as follows: While I agree that Fred's behavior is abominable, mine is crucially different. If Fred did not consume his chocolate, he would not raise and torture puppies (or pay someone else to do so). Therefore Fred could prevent the suffering of the puppies. However, if I did not buy and consume factory-raised meat, no animals would be spared lives of misery. Agribusiness is much too large to respond to the behavior of one consumer. Therefore I cannot prevent the suffering of any animals. I may well regret the suffering inflicted on animals for the sake of human enjoyment. I may even agree that the human enjoyment doesn't justify the suffering. However, since the animals will suffer no matter what I do, I may as well enjoy the taste of their flesh.

There are at least two lines of response to this attempted defense. First, consider an analogous case. You visit a friend in an exotic location, say Alabama. Your friend takes you out to eat at the finest restaurant in Tuscaloosa. For dessert you select the house specialty, "Chocolate Mousse à la Bama," served with a small cup of coffee, which you are instructed to drink before eating the mousse. The mousse is quite simply the most delicious dessert you have ever tasted. Never before has chocolate tasted so rich and satisfying. Tempted to order a second, you ask your friend what makes this mousse so delicious. He informs you that the mousse itself is ordinary, but the coffee contains a concentrated dose of cocoamone, the newly discovered chocolate-enhancing hormone. Researchers at Auburn

University have perfected a technique for extracting cocoamone from the brains of freshly slaughtered puppies, who have been subjected to lives of pain and frustration. Each puppy's brain yields four doses, each of which is effective for about fifteen minutes, just long enough to enjoy one serving of mousse. You are, naturally, horrified and disgusted. You will certainly not order another serving, you tell your friend. In fact, you are shocked that your friend, who had always seemed to be a morally decent person, could have both recommended the dessert to you and eaten one himself, in full awareness of the loathsome process necessary for the experience. He agrees that the suffering of the puppies is outrageous, and that the gain in human pleasure in no way justifies the appalling treatment they have to endure. However, neither he nor you can save any puppies by refraining from consuming cocoamone. Cocoamone production is now Alabama's leading industry, so it is much too large to respond to the behavior of one or two consumers. Since the puppies will suffer no matter what either of you does, you may as well enjoy the mousse.

If it is as obvious as it seems that a morally decent person, who is aware of the details of cocoamone production, couldn't order Chocolate Mousse à la Bama, it should be equally obvious that a morally decent person, who is aware of the details of factory farming, can't purchase and consume factory-raised meat. If the attempted excuse of causal impotence is compelling in the latter case, it should be compelling in the former case. But it isn't.

The second response to the claim of causal impotence is to deny it. Consider the case of chickens, the most cruelly treated of all animals raised for human consumption, with the possible exception of veal calves. In 1998, almost 8 billion chickens were slaughtered in the US, almost all of them raised on factory farms. Suppose that there are 250 million chicken eaters in the US, and that each one consumes, on average, 25 chickens per year (this leaves a fair number of chickens slaughtered for nonhuman consumption, or for export). Clearly, if only one of those chicken eaters gave up eating chicken, the industry would not respond. Equally clearly, if they all gave up eating chicken, billions of chickens (approximately 6.25 billion per year) would not be bred, tortured, and killed. But there must also be some number of consumers, far short of 250 million, whose renunciation of chicken would cause the industry to reduce the number of chickens bred in factory farms. The industry may not be able to respond to each individual's behavior, but it must respond to the behavior of fairly large numbers. Suppose that the industry is sensitive to a reduction in demand for chicken equivalent to 10,000 people becoming vegetarians.

(This seems like a reasonable guess, but I have no idea what the actual numbers are, nor is it important.) For each group of 10,000 who give up chicken, a quarter of a million fewer chickens are bred per year. It appears, then, that if you give up eating chicken, you have only a one in ten thousand chance of making any difference to the lives of chickens, unless it is certain that fewer than 10,000 people will ever give up eating chicken, in which case you have no chance. Isn't a one in ten thousand chance small enough to render your continued consumption of chicken blameless? Not at all. . . . A one in ten thousand chance of saving 250,000 chickens per year from excruciating lives is morally and mathematically equivalent to the certainty of saving 25 chickens per year. We commonly accept that even small risks of great harms are unacceptable. That is why we disapprove of parents who fail to secure their children in car seats or with seat belts, who leave their small children unattended at home, or who drink or smoke heavily during pregnancy. Or consider commercial aircraft safety measures. The chances that the oxygen masks, the lifejackets, or the emergency exits on any given plane will be called on to save any lives in a given week, are far smaller than one in ten thousand. And yet we would be outraged to discover that an airline had knowingly allowed a plane to fly for a week with non-functioning emergency exits, oxygen masks, and lifejackets. So, even if it is true that your giving up factory-raised chicken has only a tiny chance of preventing suffering, given that the amount of suffering that would be prevented is in inverse proportion to your chance of preventing it, your continued consumption is not thereby excused.

But perhaps it is not even true that your giving up chicken has only a tiny chance of making any difference. Suppose again that the poultry industry only reduces production when a threshold of 10,000 fresh vegetarians is reached. Suppose also, as is almost certainly true, that vegetarianism is growing in popularity in the US (and elsewhere). Then, even if you are not the one, newly converted vegetarian, to reach the next threshold of 10,000, your conversion will reduce the time required before the next threshold is reached. The sooner the threshold is reached, the sooner production, and therefore animal suffering, is reduced. Your behavior, therefore, does make a difference. Furthermore, many people who become vegetarians influence others to become vegetarian, who in turn influence others, and so on. It appears, then, that the claim of causal impotence is mere wishful thinking, on the part of those meat lovers who are morally sensitive enough to realize that human gustatory pleasure does not justify inflicting extreme suffering on animals.

Perhaps there is a further difference between the treatment of Fred's puppies and the treatment of animals on factory farms. The suffering of the puppies is a necessary means to the production of gustatory pleasure, whereas the suffering of animals on factory farms is simply a by-product of the conditions dictated by economic considerations. Therefore, it might be argued, the suffering of the puppies is *intended as a means* to Fred's pleasure, whereas the suffering of factory raised animals is merely *foreseen* as a side-effect of a system that is a means to the gustatory pleasures of millions. The distinction between what is intended, either as a means or as an end in itself, and what is 'merely' foreseen is central to the Doctrine of Double Effect. Supporters of this doctrine claim that it is sometimes permissible to bring about an effect that is merely foreseen, even though the very same effect could not permissibly be brought about if intended. (Other conditions have to be met in order for the Doctrine of Double Effect to judge an action permissible, most notably that there be an out-weighing good effect.) Fred acts impermissibly, according to this line of argument, because he intends the suffering of the puppies as a means to his pleasure. Most meat eaters, on the other hand, even if aware of the suffering of the animals, do not intend the suffering.

In response to this line of argument, I could remind the reader that Samuel Johnson said, or should have said, that the Doctrine of Double Effect is the last refuge of a scoundrel. I won't do that, however, since nei-ther the doctrine itself, nor the alleged moral distinction between intend-ing and foreseeing can justify the consumption of factory-raised meat. The Doctrine of Double Effect requires not merely that a bad effect be foreseen and not intended, but also that there be an outweighing good effect. In the case of the suffering of factory-raised animals, whatever good could plausibly be claimed to come out of the system clearly doesn't outweigh the bad. Furthermore, it would be easy to modify the story of Fred to render the puppies' suffering 'merely' foreseen. For example, suppose that the cocoamone is produced by a chemical reaction that can only occur when large quantities of drain-cleaner are forced down the throat of a conscious, unanaesthetized puppy. The consequent appalling suffering, while not itself a means to the production of cocoamone, is nonetheless an unavoidable side-effect of the means. In this variation of the story, Fred's behavior is no less abominable than in the original.

One last difference between the behavior of Fred and the behavior of the consumers of factory-raised meat is worth discussing, if only because it is so frequently cited in response to the arguments of this paper. Fred's behavior is abominable, according to this line of thinking, because it involves the suffering of *puppies*. The behavior of meat-eaters, on the other hand, 'merely' involves the suffering of chickens, pigs, cows, calves, sheep, and the like. Puppies (and probably dogs and cats in general) are morally different from the other animals. Puppies *count* (morally, that is), whereas the other animals don't, or at least not nearly as much.

So, what gives puppies a higher moral status than the animals we eat? Presumably there is some morally relevant property or properties possessed by puppies but not by farm animals. Perhaps puppies have a greater degree of rationality than farm animals, or a more finely developed moral sense, or at least a sense of loyalty and devotion. The problems with this kind of approach are obvious. It's highly unlikely that any property that has even an outside chance of being ethically relevant is both possessed by puppies and not possessed by any farm animals. For example, it's probably true that most puppies have a greater degree of rationality (whatever that means) than most chickens, but the comparison with pigs is far more dubious. Besides, if Fred were to inform the jury that he had taken pains to acquire particularly stupid, morally obtuse, disloyal and undevoted puppies, would they (or we) have declared his behavior to be morally acceptable? Clearly not.

I have been unable to discover any morally relevant differences between the behavior of Fred, the puppy torturer, and the behavior of the millions of people who purchase and consume factory-raised meat, at least those who do so in the knowledge that the animals live lives of suffering and deprivation. If morality demands that we not torture puppies merely to enhance our own eating pleasure, morality also demands that we not support factory farming by purchasing factory-raised meat. . . .

3. Humans' Versus Animals' Ethical Status—The Rationality Gambit

For the purposes of this discussion, to claim that humans have a superior ethical status to animals is to claim that it is morally right to give the interests of humans greater weight than those of animals in deciding how to behave. Such claims will often be couched in terms of rights, such as the rights to life, liberty or respect, but nothing turns on this terminological matter. One may claim that it is generally wrong to kill humans, but not animals, because humans are rational, and animals are not. Or one may claim that the suffering of animals counts less than the suffering of humans (if at all), because humans are rational, and animals are not. . . .

What could ground the claim of superior moral status for humans? Just as the defender of a higher moral status for puppies than for farm animals needs to find some property or properties possessed by puppies but not by farm animals, so the defender of a higher moral status for humans needs to find some property or properties possessed by humans but not by other animals. The traditional view, dating back at least to Aristotle, is that rationality is what separates humans, both morally and metaphysically, from other animals.

One of the most serious challenges to the traditional view involves a consideration of what philosophers refer to as 'marginal cases.' Whatever kind and level of rationality is selected as justifying the attribution of superior moral status to humans will either be lacking in some humans or present in some animals. To take one of the most commonly-suggested features, many humans are incapable of engaging in moral reflection. For some, this incapacity is temporary, as is the case with infants, or the temporarily cognitively disabled. Others who once had the capacity may have permanently lost it, as is the case with the severely senile or the irreversibly comatose. Still others never had and never will have the capacity, as is the case with the severely mentally disabled. If we base our claims for the moral superiority of humans over animals on the attribution of such capacities, won't we have to exclude many humans? Won't we then be forced to the claim that there is at least as much moral reason to use cognitively deficient humans in experiments and for food as to use animals? Perhaps we could exclude the only temporarily disabled, on the grounds of potentiality, though that move has its own problems. Nonetheless, the other two categories would be vulnerable to this objection.

I will consider two lines of response to the argument from marginal cases. The first denies that we have to attribute different moral status to marginal humans, but maintains that we are, nonetheless, justified in attributing different moral status to animals who are just as cognitively sophisticated as marginal humans, if not more so. The second admits that, strictly speaking, marginal humans are morally inferior to other humans, but proceeds to claim pragmatic reasons for treating them, at least usually, *as if* they had equal status.

As representatives of the first line of defense, I will consider arguments from three philosophers, Carl Cohen, Alan White, and David Schmidtz. First, Cohen:

> [the argument from marginal cases] fails; it mistakenly treats an essential feature of humanity as though it were a screen for sorting humans. The capacity for moral judgment that distinguishes humans from animals is

not a test to be administered to human beings one by one. Persons who are unable, because of some disability, to perform the full moral functions natural to human beings are certainly not for that reason ejected from the moral community. The issue is one of kind. . . . What humans retain when disabled, animals have never had.[1]

Alan White argues that animals don't have rights, on the grounds that they cannot intelligibly be spoken of in the full language of a right. By this he means that they cannot, for example, claim, demand, assert, insist on, secure, waive, or surrender a right. This is what he has to say in response to the argument from marginal cases:

> Nor does this, as some contend, exclude infants, children, the feeble-minded, the comatose, the dead, or generations yet unborn. Any of these may be for various reasons empirically unable to fulfill the full role of right-holder. But . . . they are logically possible subjects of rights to whom the full language of rights can significantly, however falsely, be used. It is a misfortune, not a tautology, that these persons cannot exercise or enjoy, claim, or waive, their rights or do their duty or fulfil their obligations.[2]

David Schmidtz defends the appeal to typical characteristics of species, such as mice, chimpanzees, and humans, in making decisions on the use of different species in experiments. He also considers the argument from marginal cases:

> Of course, some chimpanzees lack the characteristic features in virtue of which chimpanzees command respect as a species, just as some humans lack the characteristic features in virtue of which humans command respect as a species. It is equally obvious that some chimpanzees have cognitive capacities (for example) that are superior to the cognitive capacities of some humans. But whether every human being is superior to every chimpanzee is beside the point. The point is that we can, we do, and we should make decisions on the basis of our recognition that mice, chimpanzees, and humans are relevantly different *types*. We can have it both ways after all. Or so a speciesist could argue.[3]

---

1. Carl Cohen, "The Case for the Use of Animals in Biomedical Research," *The New England Journal of Medicine*, vol. 315, 1986.
2. Alan White, *Rights*, (OUP 1984). Reprinted in *Animal Rights and Human Obligations*, 2nd edition, Tom Regan and Peter Singer (eds.) (Prentice Hall, 1989), 120.
3. David Schmidtz, "Are All Species Equal?," *Journal of Applied Philosophy*, Vol. 15, no. 1 (1998), 61, my emphasis.

There is something deeply troublesome about the line of argument that runs through all three of these responses to the argument from marginal cases. A particular feature, or set of features is claimed to have so much moral significance that its presence or lack can make the difference to whether a piece of behavior is morally justified or morally outrageous. But then it is claimed that the presence or lack of the feature in any *particular* case is not important. The relevant question is whether the presence or lack of the feature is *normal*. Such an argument would seem perfectly preposterous in most other cases. Suppose, for example, that ten famous people are on trial in the afterlife for crimes against humanity. On the basis of conclusive evidence, five are found guilty and five are found not guilty. Four of the guilty are sentenced to an eternity of torment, and one is granted an eternity of bliss. Four of the innocent are granted an eternity of bliss, and one is sentenced to an eternity of torment. The one innocent who is sentenced to torment asks why he, and not the fifth guilty person, must go to hell. Saint Peter replies, "Isn't it obvious Mr. Ghandi? You are male. The other four men—Adolph Hitler, Joseph Stalin, George W. Bush, and Richard Nixon—are all guilty. Therefore the normal condition for a male defendant in this trial is guilt. The fact that you happen to be innocent is irrelevant. Likewise, of the five female defendants in this trial, only one was guilty. Therefore the normal condition for female defendants in this trial is innocence. That is why Margaret Thatcher gets to go to heaven instead of you."

As I said, such an argument is preposterous. Is the reply to the argument from marginal cases any better? Perhaps it will be claimed that a biological category such as a species is more 'natural,' whatever that means, than a category like 'all the male (or female) defendants in this trial.' Even setting aside the not inconsiderable worries about the conventionality of biological categories, it is not at all clear why this distinction should be morally relevant. What if it turned out that there were statistically relevant differences in the mental abilities of men and women? Suppose that men were, on average, more skilled at manipulating numbers than women, and that women were, on average, more empathetic than men. Would such differences in what was 'normal' for men and women justify us in preferring an innumerate man to a female math genius for a job as an accountant, or an insensitive woman to an ultra-sympathetic man for a job as a counselor? I take it that the biological distinction between male and female is just as real as that between human and chimpanzee.

A second response to the argument from marginal cases is to concede that cognitively deficient humans really do have an inferior moral status to normal humans. Can we, then, use such humans as we do animals? I know of no-one who takes the further step of advocating the use of marginal humans for food. . . . How can we advocate this second response while blocking the further step? Mary Anne Warren suggests that "there are powerful practical and emotional reasons for protecting non-rational human beings, reasons which are absent in the case of most non-human animals."[4] It would clearly outrage common human sensibilities, if we were to raise retarded children for food or medical experiments. Here is Steinbock in a similar vein:

> I doubt that anyone will be able to come up with a concrete and morally relevant difference that would justify, say, using a chimpanzee in an experiment rather than a human being with less capacity for reasoning, moral responsibility, etc. Should we then experiment on the severely retarded? Utilitarian considerations aside, we feel a special obligation to care for the handicapped members of our own species, who cannot survive in this world without such care . . . In addition, when we consider the severely retarded, we think, 'That could be me.' It makes sense to think that one might have been born retarded, but not to think that one might have been born a monkey. . . . Here we are getting away from such things as 'morally relevant differences' and are talking about something much more difficult to articulate, namely, the role of feeling and sentiment in moral thinking.[5]

This line of response clearly won't satisfy those who think that marginal humans really do deserve equal moral consideration with other humans. It is also a very shaky basis on which to justify our current practices. What outrages human sensibilities is a very fragile thing. Human history is littered with examples of widespread acceptance of the systematic mistreatment of some groups who didn't generate any sympathetic response from others. That we do feel a kind of sympathy for retarded humans that we don't feel for dogs is, if true, a contingent matter. To see

4. Warren, op. cit. 483, Mary Anne Warren, "Difficulties with the Strong Animal Rights Position," *Between the Species* 2, no. 4, 1987. Reprinted in *Contemporary Moral Problems*, 5th edition, James E. White (ed.) (West, 1997), 482.

5. Steinbock, op. cit. 469–470. Bonnie Steinbock, "Speciesism and the Idea of Equality," *Philosophy* 53, no. 204 (April 1978). Reprinted in *Contemporary Moral Problems*, 5th edition, James E. White (ed.) (West, 1997) 467–468.

just how shaky a basis this is for protecting retarded humans, imagine that a new kind of birth defect (perhaps associated with beef from cows treated with bovine growth hormone) produces severe mental retardation, green skin, and a complete lack of emotional bond between parents and child. Furthermore, suppose that the mental retardation is of the same kind and severity as that caused by other birth defects that don't have the other two effects. It seems likely that denying moral status to such defective humans would not run the same risks of outraging human sensibilities as would the denial of moral status to other, less easily distinguished and more loved defective humans. Would these contingent empirical differences between our reactions to different sources of mental retardation justify us in ascribing different direct moral status to their subjects? The only difference between them is skin color and whether they are loved by others. Any theory that could ascribe moral relevance to differences such as these doesn't deserve to be taken seriously.

Finally, perhaps we could claim that the practice of giving greater weight to the interests of all humans than of animals is justified on evolutionary grounds. Perhaps such differential concern has survival value for the species. Something like this may well be true, but it is hard to see the moral relevance. We can hardly justify the privileging of human interests over animal interests on the grounds that such privileging serves human interests!

6. Agent and Patient—the Speciesist's Central Confusion

Although the argument from marginal cases certainly poses a formidable challenge to any proposed criterion of full moral standing that excludes animals, it doesn't, in my view, constitute the most serious flaw in such attempts to justify the status quo. The proposed criteria are all variations on the Aristotelian criterion of rationality. But what is the moral relevance of rationality? Why should we think that the possession of a certain level or kind of rationality renders the possessor's interests of greater moral significance than those of a merely sentient being? In Bentham's famous words "The question is not, Can they reason? nor Can they talk? But, Can they suffer?"[6]

What do defenders of the alleged superiority of human interests say in response to Bentham's challenge? Some, such as Carl Cohen, simply reiterate

---

6. Jeremy Bentham, *Introduction to the Principles of Morals and Legislation,* (Various) chapter 17.

the differences between humans and animals that they claim to carry moral significance. Animals are not members of moral communities, they don't engage in moral reflection, they can't be moved by moral reasons, *therefore* (?) their interests don't count as much as ours. Others, such as Steinbock and Warren, attempt to go further. Here is Warren on the subject:

> Why is rationality morally relevant? It does not make us "better" than other animals or more "perfect." . . . But it is morally relevant insofar as it provides greater possibilities for cooperation and for the nonviolent resolution of problems.[7]

Warren is certainly correct in claiming that a certain level and kind of rationality is morally relevant. Where she, and others who give similar arguments, go wrong is in specifying what the moral relevance amounts to. If a being is incapable of moral reasoning, at even the most basic level, if it is incapable of being moved by moral reasons, claims, or arguments, then it cannot be a moral agent. It cannot be subject to moral obligations, to moral praise or blame. Punishing a dog for doing something "wrong" is no more than an attempt to alter its future behavior.

All this is well and good, but what is the significance for the question of what weight to give to animal interests? That animals can't be moral *agents* doesn't seem to be relevant to their status as moral *patients*. Many, perhaps most, humans are both moral agents and patients. Most, perhaps all, animals are only moral patients. Why would the lack of moral agency give them diminished status as moral patients? Full status as a moral patient is not some kind of reward for moral agency. I have heard students complain in this regard that it is *unfair* that humans bear the burdens of moral responsibility, and don't get enhanced consideration of their interests in return. This is a very strange claim. Humans are subject to moral obligations, because they are the kind of creatures who *can* be. What grounds moral agency is simply different from what grounds moral standing as a patient. It is no more unfair that humans and not animals are moral agents, than it is unfair that real animals and not stuffed toys are moral patients.

. . . It seems that any attempt to justify the claim that humans have a higher moral status than other animals by appealing to some version of rationality as the morally relevant difference between humans and animals will fail on at least two counts. It will fail to give an adequate answer to the argument from marginal cases, and, more importantly, it will fail to make

---

7. Warren, op. cit. 482.

the case that such a difference is morally relevant to the status of animals as moral patients as opposed to their status as moral agents.

I conclude that our intuitions that Fred's behavior is morally impermissible are accurate. Furthermore, given that the behavior of those who knowingly support factory farming is morally indistinguishable, it follows that their behavior is also morally impermissible.

Alastair Norcross: Puppies, Pigs and People: Eating Meat and Marginal Cases

1. Do you agree that Fred acts immorally in the case that Norcross describes? If so, what exactly is it about Fred's behavior that is morally objectionable? If not, why not?
2. Some might claim that eating meat from factory farms is relevantly different from Fred's behavior because individual consumers are powerless to change the factory-farming system, whereas Fred is fully in control of the puppies. How does Norcross respond to this claim?
3. Another disanalogy between Fred's behavior and that of most meat-eaters is that Fred *intends* to make the puppies suffer, while most consumers of meat don't intend to make any animals suffer. Does this disanalogy undermine Norcross's argument? Why or why not?
4. What is the "argument from marginal cases" and what is it supposed to show? What do you think is the strongest objection to the argument?
5. What is the difference between being a moral agent and being a moral patient? Why does Norcross think that nonhuman animals are moral patients? Do you agree with him?

25

Moral Standing, the Value of Lives, and Speciesism

R. G. Frey

Raymond Frey defends a view that he calls the unequal value thesis—the idea that human life is more valuable than animal life. Some philosophers have charged that this is a version of "speciesism," which is the view that being a member of the species *Homo sapiens* by itself makes human beings more important than other animals. One of the goals of Frey's article is to show that we can defend the unequal value thesis without relying on speciesist assumptions.

Frey denies that species membership is by itself a morally important trait. Being human is not what makes most us more valuable than any other kind of animal. Rather, our lives are valuable just in proportion to their quality: the higher the quality of life, the greater the value of that life. Frey tells us that the quality of life is itself a function of its capacity for enrichment. You and I have this capacity to a very high degree—we can make all sorts of complicated plans, take pleasure in a huge variety of activities, develop deep and complex relationships with others. When we compare the capacity for enriching our lives with that capacity as possessed, say, by a rabbit, it becomes clear that our capacity for an enriched life far outstrips the rabbit's. So our lives are more valuable than a rabbit's (and that of any other animal we know of).

To reinforce the point that this is not a kind of speciesism, Frey invites us to compare the life of a normal adult human being with that

From *Between the Species*, http://digitalcommons.calpoly.edu/bts/

of an elderly patient fully in the grips of Alzheimer's disease. Surely, he says, the former life is more valuable than the latter. Late-stage Alzheimer's patients have far less capacity to enrich their lives than do you and I. Thus Frey judges that their lives are less valuable than ours. It is also the case, according to Frey, that the lives of some animals are *more* valuable than the lives of some humans, since some human beings have a lower quality of life than that of some animals.

Frey thinks that our moral duties to others depend in large part on the value of their lives. As a result, he thinks that, ordinarily, when we must choose between conducting experiments on animals or on humans, we are right to make animals our test subjects, since they usually possess lives of lesser value. But not always. So, morally speaking, we must sometimes conduct tests on humans and spare the animals.

....

I.

Those who concern themselves with the moral considerability of animals may well be tempted to suppose that their work is finished, once they successfully envelop animals within the moral community. Yet, to stop there is never *per se* to address the issue of the value of animal life and so never to engage the position that I, and others, hold on certain issues. Thus, I am a restricted vivisectionist; not because I think animals are outside the moral community but because of views I hold about the value of their lives. Again, I think it is permissible to use animal parts in human transplants, not because I think animals lack moral standing but because I think animal life is less valuable than human life.

I have written of views that I hold; the fact is, I think, that the vast majority of people share my view of the differing value of human and animal life. This view we might capture in the form of three propositions:

1. Animal life has some value;
2. Not all animal life has the same value;
3. Human life is more valuable than animal life.

Very few people today would seem to believe that animal life is without value and that, therefore, we need not trouble ourselves morally about taking it. Equally few people, however, would seem to believe that all animal life has the same value. Certainly, the lives of dogs, cats, and chimps are very widely held to be more valuable than the lives of mice, rats, and worms, and the legal protections we accord these different creatures, for example, reflect this fact. Finally, whatever value we take the lives of dogs and cats to have, most of us believe human life to be more valuable than animal life. We believe this, moreover, even as we oppose cruelty to animals and acknowledge value—in the case of some animals, considerable value—to their lives. I shall call this claim about the comparative value of human and animal life the unequal value thesis. A crucial question, obviously, is whether we who hold this thesis can defend it.

Many "animal rightists" themselves seem inclined to accept something like the unequal value thesis. With respect to the oft-cited raft example, in which one can save a man or a dog but not both, animal rightists often concede that, other things being equal, one ought to save the man. To be sure, this result only says something about our intuitions and about those *in extremis*; yet, what it is ordinarily taken to say about them—that we take human life to be more valuable than animal life—is not something we think in extreme circumstances only. Our intuitions about the greater value of human life seem apparent in and affect all our relations with animals, from the differences in the ways we regard, treat, and even bury humans and animals to the differences in the safeguards for their protection that we construct and the differences in penalties we exact for violation of those safeguards.

In a word, the unequal value thesis seems very much a part of the approach that most of us adopt towards animal issues. We oppose cruelty to animals as well as humans, but this does not lead us to suppose that the lives of humans and animals have the same value. Nor is there any entailment in the matter: one can perfectly consistently oppose cruelty to all sentient creatures without having to suppose that the lives of all such creatures are equally valuable.

We might note in passing that if this is right about our intuitions, then it is far from clear that it is the defender of the unequal value thesis who must assume the burden of proof in the present discussion. Our intuitions about pain and suffering are such that if a theorist today suggested that animal suffering did not count morally, then he would quickly find himself on the defensive. If I am right about our intuitions over the comparative value of human and animal life, why is the same not true in the case of the theorist who urges or assumes that these lives are of equal value? If, over suffering, our intuitions force the exclusion of the pains of animals to be defended, why, over the value of life, do they not force an *equal* value thesis to be defended?

Where pain and suffering are the central issue, most of us tend to think of the human and animal cases in the same way; thus, cruelty to a child and cruelty to a dog are wrong and wrong for the same reason. Pain is pain; it is an evil, and the evidence suggests that it is as much an evil for dogs as for humans. Furthermore, autonomy or agency (or the lack thereof) does not seem a relevant factor here, since the pains of non-autonomous creatures count as well as the pains of autonomous ones. Neither the child nor the dog is autonomous, at least in any sense that captures why autonomy is such an immensely important value; but the pains of both child and dog count and affect our judgments of rightness and wrongness with respect to what is done to them.

Where the value of life is the central issue, however, we do not tend to think of the human and animal cases alike. Here, we come down in favor of humans, as when we regularly experiment upon and kill animals in our laboratories for (typically) human benefit; and a main justification reflective people give for according humans such advantage invokes directly a difference in value between human and animal life. Autonomy or agency is now, moreover, of the utmost significance, since the exercise of autonomy by normal adult humans is one of the central ways they make possible further, important dimensions of value to their lives.

Arguably, even the extended justification of animal suffering in, say, medical research may make indirect appeal to the unequal value thesis. Though pain remains an evil, the nature and size of some benefit determine whether its infliction is justified in the particular cases. Nothing precludes this benefit from accruing to human beings, and when it does, we need an independent defence of the appeal to benefit in this kind of case. For the appeal is typically invoked in cases where those who suffer are those who benefit, as when we go to the dentist, and in the present instance human beings are the beneficiaries of animal suffering. Possibly the unequal value thesis can provide the requisite defence: what justifies the infliction of pain, if anything does, is the appeal to benefit; but what justifies use of the appeal in those cases where humans are the beneficiaries of animal suffering is, arguably, that human life is more valuable than animal life. Thus, while the unequal value thesis cannot alter the character of pain, which remains an evil, and cannot directly, independently of benefit, justify the infliction of pain, it can, the suggestion is, anchor a particular use of the appeal to benefit.

More broadly, I think a presumption, not in favor of, but against the use of animals in medical/scientific research would be desirable. Its intended effect would be to force researchers as a matter of routine to argue in depth a case for animal use. Such a presumption coheres with my earlier remarks. The unequal value thesis in no way compels its adherents to deny that animal lives have value; the destruction or impairment of such lives, therefore, needs to be argued for, which a presumption against use of animals would force researchers to do.

Clearly, a presumption against use is not the same thing as a bar; I allow, therefore, that researchers can make a case. That they must do so, that they must seek to justify the destruction or impairment of lives that have value, is the point.

II.

How might we defend the unequal value thesis? At least the beginnings of what I take to be the most promising option in this regard can be briefly sketched.

Pain is one thing, killing is another, and what makes killing wrong—a killing could be free of pain and suffering—seems to be the fact that it consists in the destruction of something of value. That is, killing and the value of life seem straightforwardly connected, since it is difficult to understand why taking a particular life would be wrong if it had no value. If few people consider animal life to be without value, equally few, I think, consider it to have the same value as normal (adult) human life. They need not be speciesists as a result: in my view, normal (adult) human life is of a much higher quality than animal life, not because of species, but because of richness; and the value of a life is a function of its quality.

Part of the richness of our lives involves activities that we have in common with animals but there are as well whole dimensions to our lives—love, marriage, educating children, jobs, hobbies, sporting events, cultural pursuits, intellectual development and striving, etc.—that greatly expand our range of absorbing endeavors and so significantly deepen the texture of our lives. An impoverished life for *us* need not be one in which food or sex or liberty is absent; it can equally well be a life in which these other dimensions have not taken root or have done so only minimally. When we look back over our lives and regret that we did not make more of them, we rarely have in mind only the kinds of activities that we share with animals; rather, we think much more in terms of precisely these other dimensions of our lives that equally go to make up a rich, full life.

The lives of normal (adult) humans betray a variety and richness that the lives of rabbits do not; certainly, we do not think of ourselves as constrained to live out our lives according to some (conception of a) life

deemed appropriate to our species. Other conceptions of a life for ourselves are within our reach, and we can try to understand and appreciate
them and to choose among them. Some of us are artists, others educators,
still others mechanics; the richness of our lives is easily enhanced through
developing and molding our talents so as to enable us to live out these
conceptions of the good life. Importantly, also, we are not condemned to
embrace in our lifetimes only a single conception of such a life; in the sense
intended, the artist can choose to become an educator and the educator a
mechanic. We can embrace at different times different conceptions of how
we want to live.

Choosing among conceptions of the good life and trying to live out
such a conception are not so intellectualized a set of tasks that only an
elite few can manage them. Some reflection upon the life one wants to
live is necessary, and some reflection is required in order to organize
one's life to live out such a conception; but virtually all of us manage to
engage in this degree of reflection. (One of the tragic aspects of Alzheimer's
disease is how it undoes a person in just this regard, once it has reached
advanced stages.) Even an uneducated man can see the choice between
the army and professional boxing as one that requires him to sit down
and ponder what he wants to do, whether he has the talents to do it,
and what his other, perhaps conflicting desires come to in strength.
Even an habitual street person, if free long enough from the influence
of drink or drugs to be capable of addressing himself to the choice, can
see the life the Salvation Army holds out before him as different in certain respects, some appealing, others perhaps not, from his present life.
Choosing how one will live one's life can often be a matter of simply
focussing upon these particulars and trying to gauge one's desires with
respect to them.

Now, in the case of the rabbit the point is not that the activities which
enrich an adult human's life are different from those which enrich its life;
it is that the scope or potentiality for enrichment is truncated or severely
diminished in the rabbit's case. The quality of a life is a function of its richness, which is a function of its scope or potentiality for enrichment; the
scope or potentiality for enrichment in the rabbit's case never approaches
that of the human. Nothing we have ever observed about rabbits, nothing we know of them, leads us to make judgments about the variety and
richness of their life in anything even remotely comparable to the judgments we make in the human case. To assume as present in the rabbit's life
dimensions that supply the full variety and richness of ours, only that these

dimensions are hidden from us, provides no real answer, especially when the evidence we have about their lives runs in the other direction.

Autonomy is an important part of the human case. By exercising our autonomy we can mold our lives to fit a conception of the good life that we have decided upon for ourselves; we can then try to live out this conception, with all the sense of achievement, self-fulfillment, and satisfaction that this can bring. Some of us pursue athletic or cultural or intellectual endeavors; some of us are good with our hands and enjoy mechanical tasks and manual labor; and all of us see a job—be it the one we have or the one we should like to have—as an important part of a full life. (This is why unemployment affects more than just our incomes.) The emphasis is upon agency: we can *make* ourselves into repairmen, pianists, and accountants; by exercising our autonomy, we can *impose* upon our lives a conception of the good life that we have for the moment embraced. We can then try to live out this conception, with the consequent sense of fulfillment and achievement that this makes possible. Even failure can be part of the picture: a woman can try to make herself into an Olympic athlete and fail; but her efforts to develop and shape her talents and to take control of and to mold her life in the appropriate ways can enrich her life. Thus, by exercising our autonomy and trying to live out some conception of how we want to live, we make possible further, important dimensions of value to our lives.

We still share certain activities with rabbits, but no mere record of those activities would come anywhere near accounting for the richness of our lives. What is missing in the rabbit's case is the same scope or potentiality for enrichment; and lives of less richness have less value.

The kind of story that would have to be told to make us think that the rabbit's life *was* as rich as the life of a normal (adult) human is one that either postulates in the rabbit potentialities and abilities vastly beyond what we observe and take it to have, or lapses into a rigorous scepticism. By the latter, I mean that we should have to say either that we know nothing of the rabbit's life (and so can know nothing of that life's richness and quality) or that what we know can never be construed as adequate for grounding judgments about the rabbit's quality of life. But the real puzzle is how this recourse to scepticism is supposed to make us think that a rabbit's life is as varied and rich as a human's life. If I can know nothing of the rabbit's life, presumably because I do not live that life and so cannot experience it from the inside, then how do I know that the rabbit's life is as rich as a human's life? Plainly, if I cannot know this, I must for the argument's sake assume it. But why should I do this? Nothing I observe and experience leads me to assume it; all the evidence I have about rabbits and humans seems to run entirely in the opposite direction. So, why make this assumption? Most especially, why assume animal lives are as rich as human lives, when we do not even assume, or so I suggest below, that all *human* lives have the same richness?

III.

Agency matters to the value of a life, and animals are not agents. Thus, we require some argument to show that their lack of agency notwithstanding, animals have lives of roughly equal richness and value to the lives of normal (adult) humans. The view that they are members of the moral community will not supply it, the demand is compatible with acknowledging that not all life has the same value; and as we shall see, the argument from the value of the lives of defective humans will not supply it. Any *assumption* that they have lives of equal richness and value to ours seems to run up against, quite apart from the evidence we take ourselves to have about the lives of animals, the fact that, as we shall see, not all human lives have the same richness and value.

Most importantly, it will not do to claim that the rabbit's life is as valuable as the normal (adult) human's life because it is the only life each has. This claim does not as yet say that the rabbit's life has any particular value. If the rabbit and man are dead, they have no life which they can carry on living, at some quality or other; but this *per se* does not show that the lives of the man and the rabbit have a particular value as such, let alone that they have the same value. Put differently, both creatures must be alive in order to have a quality of life, but nothing at all in this shows that they have the same richness and quality of life and, therefore, value of life I am not disputing that animals can have *a* quality of life and that their lives, as a result, can have value; I am disputing that the richness, quality, and value of their lives is that of normal (adult) humans.

IV.

Not all members of the moral community have lives of equal value. Human life is more valuable than animal life. That is our intuition, and as I have assumed, we must defend it. How we defend it is, however, a vitally important affair. For I take the charge of speciesism—the attempt to justify either different treatment or the attribution of a different value of life by appeal to species membership—very seriously. In my view, if a defence of the unequal value thesis is open to that charge, then it is no defence at all.

As a result, one's options for grounding the unequal value thesis become limited; no ground will suffice that appeals, either in whole or in part, to species membership. Certainly, some ways of trying to differentiate the value of human from animal life in the past seem pretty clearly to be speciesist. But not all ways are; the important option set out above—one that construes the value of a life as a function of its quality, its quality as a function of its richness, and its richness as a function of its capacity of enrichment—does not use species membership to determine the value of lives. Indeed, it quite explicitly allows for the possibility that some animal life may be more valuable than some human life.

To see this, we have only to realize that the claim that not all members of the moral community have lives of equal value encompasses not only animals but also some humans. Some human lives have less value than others. An infant born without a brain, or any very severely handicapped infant, seems a case in point, as does an elderly person fully in the grip of Alzheimer's disease or some highly degenerative brain, nervous, or physiological disorder. In other words, I think we are compelled to admit that some human life is of a much lower quality and so value than normal (adult) human life. (This is true as well of infants generally, though readers may think that, unlike the cases of seriously defective infants and adults, some argument from potentiality may be adduced to place them in a separate category. The fact remains, however, that the lives of normal (adult) humans betray a variety and richness that the lives of animals, defective humans, and infants do not.)

Accordingly, we must understand the unequal value thesis to claim that normal (adult) human life is more valuable than animal life. If we justify this claim by appeal to the quality and richness of normal (adult) human life and if we at the same time acknowledge that some human life is of a much lower quality and value than normal (adult) human life, then it seems quite clear that we are not using species membership to determine the value of a life.

Moreover, because some human lives fall drastically below the quality of life of normal (adult) human life, we must face the prospect that the lives of some perfectly healthy animals have a higher quality and greater value than the lives of some humans. And we must face this prospect, with all the implications it may have for the use of these unfortunate humans by others, at least if we continue to justify the use of animals in medical/scientific research by appeal to the lower quality and value of their lives.

What justifies the medical/scientific use of perfectly healthy rabbits instead of humans with a low quality of life? If, for example, experiments on retinas are suggested, why use rabbits or chimps instead of defective humans with otherwise excellent retinas? I know of nothing that cedes human life of any quality, however low, greater value than animal life of any quality, however high. If, therefore, we are going to justify medical/scientific uses of animals by appeal to the value of their lives, we open up directly the possibility of our having to envisage the use of humans of a lower quality of life in preference to animals of a higher quality of life. It is important to bear in mind as well that other factors then come under consideration, such as (i) the nature and size of benefit to be achieved, (ii) the side-effects that any decision to use humans in preference to animals may evoke, (iii) the degree to which education and explanation can dissipate any such negative side-effects, and (iv) the projected reliability of animal results for the human case (as opposed to the projected reliability of human results for the human case). All these things may, in the particular case, work in favor of the use of humans.

The point, of course, is not that we *must* use humans; it is that we cannot invariably use animals in preference to humans, if appeal to the quality and value of lives is the ground we give for using animals. The only way we could justifiably do this is if we could cite something that always, no matter what, cedes human life greater value than animal life. I know of no such thing.

Always in the background, of course, are the benefits that medical/scientific research confers: if we desire to continue to obtain these benefits, are we prepared to pay the price of the use of defective humans? The answer, I think, must be positive, at least until the time comes when we no longer have to use either humans or animals for research purposes. Obviously, this deliberate use of some of the weakest members of our society is distasteful to contemplate and is not something, in the absence of substantial benefit, that we could condone; yet, we presently condone the use of perfectly healthy animals on an absolutely massive scale, and benefit is the justification we employ.

I remain a vivisectionist, therefore, because of the benefits medical/scientific research can bestow. Support for vivisection, however, exacts a cost: it forces us to envisage the use of defective humans in such research. Paradoxically, then, to the extent that one cannot bring oneself to envisage and consent to their use, to that extent, in my view, the case for anti-vivisectionism becomes stronger.

V.

The fact that not even all human life has the same value explains why some argument from marginal cases, one of the most common arguments in support of an equal value thesis, comes unstuck. Such an argument would only be possible if human life of a much lower quality were ceded equal value with normal (adult) human life. In that case, the same concession could be requested for animal life, and an argument from marginal or defective humans could get underway. On the account of the value of a life set out above, however, the initial concession is not made; it is not true that defective human life has the same quality and value as normal (adult) human life. Nor is this result unfamiliar to us today; it is widely employed in much theoretical and practical work in medical ethics.

This leaves the argument from marginal cases to try to force the admission of the equal value of human and animal life. Tom Regan has long relied upon this argument; in a recent article Regan wonders what could be the basis for the view that human life is more valuable than animal life and moves at once to invoke the argument from marginal cases to dispel any such possibility:

> What could be the basis of our having more inherent value than animals? Their lack of reason, or autonomy, or intellect? Only if we are willing to make the same judgment in the case of humans who are similarly deficient. But it is not true that some humans—the retarded child, for example, or the mentally deranged—have less inherent value than you or I.[1]

Regan provides no argument for this claim (and, for that matter, no analysis of "inherent value"), but it seems at least to involve, if not to depend upon, our agreeing that human life of any quality, however low, has the same value as normal (adult) human life. I can see no reason whatever to accept this. Some human lives are so very deficient in quality that we

---

1. Tom Regan, "The Case for Animal Rights," in Peter Singer (ed.), *In Defence of Animals* (Oxford: Basil Blackwell, 1985), p. 23. This article mirrors some central claims of Regan's book of the same name.

would not wish those lives upon anyone, and there are few lengths to which we would not go in order to avoid such lives for ourselves and our loved ones. I can see little point in pretending that lives which we would do everything we could to avoid are of equal value to those normal (adult) human lives that we are presently living.

So far as I can see, the quality of some lives can plummet so disastrously that those lives can cease to have much value at all, can cease to be lives, that is, that are any longer worth living. I acknowledge the difficulty in determining in many cases when a life is no longer worth living; in other cases, however, such as an elderly person completely undone by Alzheimer's disease or an infant born with no or only half a brain, the matter seems far less problematic.

VI.

Is an involved defence of the unequal value thesis, however, really necessary? Is there not a much more direct and uncomplicated defence readily to hand? I have space for only a few words on several possibilities in this regard.

The defence of the unequal value thesis that I have begun to sketch, whether in its positive or negative aspect, does not make reference to religion; yet, it is true that certain religious beliefs seem to favor the thesis. The doctrine of the sanctity of life has normally been held with respect to human life alone; the belief in human dominion over the rest of creation has traditionally been held to set humans apart; and the belief that humans but not animals are possessed of an immortal soul seems plainly to allude to a further dimension of significance to human life. I am not myself religious, however, and I do not adopt a religious approach to questions about the value of lives. Any such approach would seem to tie one's defence of the unequal value thesis to the adequacy of one's theological views, something which a non-religious person can scarcely endorse. I seek a defence of the unequal value thesis, whatever the status of God's existence or the adequacy of this or that religion or religious doctrine. I do not prejudge the issue of whether a religious person can accept a quality-of-life defence of the sort I have favored; my point is simply that that defence does not rely upon theological premises.

It may be asked, however, why we need anything quite so sophisticated as a *defence* of the unequal value thesis at all. Why can we not just express a preference for our own kind and be done with the matter? After all, when a father gives a kidney to save his daughter's life, we perfectly well understand why he did not choose to give the kidney to a stranger *in preference to* his daughter. This "natural bias" we do not condemn and do not take to point to a moral defect in the father. Why, therefore, is not something similar possible in the case of our interaction with animals? Why, that is, can we not appeal to a natural bias in favor of members of our own species? There are a number of things that can be said in response, only several of which I shall notice here.

There is the problem, if one takes the charge of speciesism seriously, of how to articulate this bias in favor of members of our species in such a way as to avoid that charge. Then there is the problem of how to articulate this preference for our own kind in such a way as to exclude interpretations of "our own kind" that express preferences for one's own race, gender, or religion. Otherwise, one is going to let such preferences do considerable work in one's moral decision-making. I do not wish to foreclose all possibilities in these two cases, however; it may well be that a preference for our own kind *can* be articulated in a way that avoids these and some other problems.

Even so, I believe that there is another and deeper level of problem that this preference for our own kind encounters. On the one hand, we can understand the preference to express a bond we feel with members of our own species *over and above* the bond that we (or most of us) feel with ("higher") animals. Such a bond, if it exists, poses no direct problem, if its existence is being used to explain, for example, instances of behavior where we obviously exhibit sympathy for human beings. (We must be careful not to *under-value* the sympathy most people exhibit towards animals, especially domesticated ones.) On the other hand, we can understand this preference for our own kind to express the claim that we stand in a special moral relationship to members of our own species. This claim does pose a problem, since, if we systematically favor humans over animals on the basis of it, it does considerable moral work, work, obviously, that would not be done if the claim were rejected.

I cannot see that species membership is a ground for holding that we stand in a special moral relationship to our fellow humans. The father obviously stands in such a relationship to his daughter, and his decision to marry and to have children is how he comes to have or to stand in that relationship. But how, through merely being born, does one come to stand in a special moral relationship to humans generally? Typically, I can step in and out of special moral relationships; in the case of species member-ship, that is not true. In that case, so long as I live, nothing can change my relationship to others, so long as they live. If this were true, my morality would to an extent no longer express my view of myself at large in a world filled with other people but would be something foisted upon me simply through being born.

Since we do not choose our species membership, a special moral rela-tionship I am supposed to stand in to humans generally would lie outside my control; whereas it is precisely the voluntary nature of such relation-ships that seems most central to their character. And it is precisely because of this voluntary nature, of, as it were, our ability to take on and shed such relationships, that these relationships can be read as expressing *my* view of myself at large in a world filled with other people.

We often do stand in special moral relationships to others; but mere species membership would have us stand in such a relationship to all others. There is something too sweeping about this, as if birth alone can give the rest of human creation a moral hold over me. In a real sense, such a view would sever me from my morality; for my morality would no longer consist in expressions of how I see myself interacting with others and how I choose to interact with them. My own choices and decisions have no effect upon species membership and so on a moral relationship that I am supposed to stand in to each and every living, human being. Such a view is at odds not only with how we typically understand special moral relation-ships but also with how we typically understand our relationship to our own morality.

VII.

It may well be tempting, I suppose, to try to develop another sense of "speciesism" and to hold that a position such as mine is speciesist in that sense. I have space here for only a few comments on one such sense.

If to be a *direct* speciesist is to discriminate among the value of lives solely on the basis of species membership, as it is, for example, for Peter Singer, then I am not, as I have tried to show, a direct speciesist. But am I not, it might be suggested, an *indirect* speciesist, in that, in order to determine the quality and value of a life, I use human-centred criteria as if they were appro-priate for assessing the quality and value of all life? Thus, for instance, when

I emphasize cultural and artistic endeavors, when I emphasize autonomy and mental development and achievement, when I emphasize making choices, directing one's life, and selecting and living out conceptions of the good life, the effect is to widen the gulf between animals and humans by using human-centred criteria for assessing the quality and value of a life as if they were appropriate to appreciating the quality and value of animal life. And this will not do; for it amounts to trying to judge animals and animal lives by human standards. What one should do, presumably, is to judge the quality and value of animal life by criteria appropriate to each separate species of animals.

I stress again that the argument of this paper is not about whether rabbits have lives of value (I think that they do) but rather about whether they have lives of equal value to normal (adult) human life. It is unclear to me how the charge of indirect speciesism addresses this argument.

We must distinguish this charge of an indirect speciesism from the claim, noted earlier, that we can know nothing of animal lives and so nothing about their quality and value; indeed, the two claims may conflict. The point behind the speciesism charge is that I am not using criteria appropriate to a species of animal for assessing its quality of life, which presumably means that there *are* appropriate criteria available for selection. Knowledge of appropriate criteria seems to require that we know something of an animal's life, in order to make the judgment of appropriateness. Yet, the whole point behind the lack of knowledge claim is that we can know nothing of an animal's life, nothing of how it experiences the world, nothing, in essence, about how well or how badly its life is going. It would seem, therefore, as if the two views can conflict.

The crucial thing here about both claims, however, is this: both are advanced against my defence of the unequal value thesis and on behalf of the equality of value of human and animal life without it being in any wise clear how they show this equality.

The ignorance claim would seem to have it that, because we can know nothing of the animal case, we must assume that animal and human life have the same value. But why should we fall in with this assumption? The ignorance claim would have us start from the idea, presumably, that all life, irrespective of its level of development and complexity, has the same value; but why should we start from that particular idea? Surely there must be some reason for thinking all life whatever has the same value. It is this reason that needs to be stated and assessed.

The indirect speciesist claim would seem to have it that, were we only to select criteria for assessing the quality and value of life appropriate to animals' species, we must agree that animal and human life are of equal value. The temptation is to inquire after what these criteria might be in rabbits, but any such concern must be firmly understood in the light of the earlier discussion of the richness of our lives. What the unequal value thesis represents is our quest to gain some understanding of (i) the capacities of animals and humans, (ii) the differences among these various capacities, (iii) the complexity of lives, (iv) the role of agency in this complexity, and (v) the way agency enables humans to add further dimensions of value to their lives. The richness of our lives encompasses these multi-faceted aspects of our being and is a function of them. The point is not that a rabbit may not have a keener sense of smell than we do and may not derive intense, pleasurable sensations through that sense of smell; it is that we have to believe that something like this, augmented, perhaps, by other things we might say in the rabbit's case of like kind, suffices to make the rabbit's life as rich and as full as ours. If one thinks of our various capacities and of the different levels on which they operate, physical, mental, emotional, imaginative, then pointing out that rabbits can have as pleasurable sensations as we do in certain regards does not meet the point.

When we say of a woman that she has "tasted life to the full," we do not make a point about (or solely about) pleasurable sensations; we refer to the different dimensions of our being and to the woman's attempt to develop these in herself and to actualize them in the course of her daily life. And an important aspect in all this is what agency means to the woman: in the sense intended, she is not condemned to live the life that all of her ancestors have lived; she can mold and shape her life to "fit" her own conception of how she should live, thereby enabling her to add further dimensions of value to her life. It is this diversity and complexity in us that needs to be made good in the rabbit's case and that no mere catalogue of its pleasures through the sense of smell seems likely to accomplish.

Again, it is not that the rabbit cannot do things that we are unable to do and not that it has capacities which we lack; what has to be shown is how this sort of thing, given how rabbits behave and live out their days, so enriches their lives that the quality and value of them approach those of humans. And what *is* one going to say in the rabbit's case that makes good the role agency plays in ours? The absence of agency from a human life is a terrible thing; it deeply impoverishes a life and forestalls completely

I emphasize cultural and artistic endeavors, when I emphasize
and mental development and achievement, when I emphasize
choices, directing one's life, and selecting and living out conceptio
good life, the effect is to widen the gulf between animals and hun
using human-centred criteria for assessing the quality and value of a
if they were appropriate to appreciating the quality and value of anim
And this will not do; for it amounts to trying to judge animals and an
lives by human standards. What one should do, presumably, is to ju
the quality and value of animal life by criteria appropriate to each separ
species of animals.

I stress again that the argument of this paper is not about whethe
rabbits have lives of value (I think that they do) but rather about whether
they have lives of equal value to normal (adult) human life. It is unclear to
me how the charge of indirect speciesism addresses this argument.

We must distinguish this charge of an indirect speciesism from the
claim, noted earlier, that we can know nothing of animal lives and so nothing about their quality and value; indeed, the two claims may conflict. The
point behind the speciesism charge is that I am not using criteria appropriate to a species of animal for assessing its quality of life, which presumably
means that there *are* appropriate criteria available for selection. Knowledge of appropriate criteria seems to require that we know something of
an animal's life, in order to make the judgment of appropriateness. Yet, the
whole point behind the lack of knowledge claim is that we can know nothing of an animal's life, nothing of how it experiences the world, nothing,
in essence, about how well or how badly its life is going. It would seem,
therefore, as if the two views can conflict.

The crucial thing here about both claims, however, is this: both are
advanced against my defence of the unequal value thesis and on behalf of
the equality of value of human and animal life without it being in any wise
clear how they show this equality.

The ignorance claim would seem to have it that, because we can know
nothing of the animal case, we must assume that animal and human life
have the same value. But why should we fall in with this assumption? The
ignorance claim would have us start from the idea, presumably, that all
life, irrespective of its level of development and complexity, has the same
value; but why should we start from that particular idea? Surely there must
be some reason for thinking all life whatever has the same value. It is this
reason that needs to be stated and assessed.

one's making one's life into the life one wants to live. Yet, this must be the natural condition of rabbits. It is this gulf that agency creates, the gulf between living out the life appropriate to one's species and living out a life one has chosen for oneself and has molded and shaped accordingly, that is one of the things that it is difficult to understand what rabbits can do to overcome.

VIII.

In sum, I think the unequal value thesis is defensible and can be defended even as its adherent takes seriously the charge of speciesism. And it is the unequal value thesis that figures centrally in the justification of our use of animals in medical and scientific research. If as I have done here, we assume that the thesis must be defended, then the character of that defence, I think, requires that *if* we are to continue to use animals for research purposes, then we must begin to envisage the use of some humans for those same purposes. The cost of holding the unequal value thesis, and most of us, I suggest, do hold it, is to realize that, upon a quality of life defence of it, it encompasses the lives of some humans as well as animals. I cannot at the moment see that any other defence of it both meets the charge of speciesism and yet does indeed amount to a defence.

R. G. Frey: Moral Standing, the Value of Lives, and Speciesism

1. Explain Frey's unequal value thesis. What implications does it have for how we should treat nonhuman animals? What implications does it have for how we should treat other humans? Do you think any of these implications are problematic? Why or why not?
2. What, according to Frey, makes a life valuable? What reasons does he give in support of his account? Do you find the account plausible? Support your answer.
3. Explain the distinction between direct speciesism and indirect speciesism. Why might direct speciesist views be problematic? Why might indirect speciesist views be problematic? Does Frey's view qualify as one or the other? Why or why not?
4. According to Frey, what makes a being worthy of moral consideration? Which (if any) animals are members of the moral community? In

virtue of what are animals' lives more or less valuable than humans' lives? Do you agree with Frey's criteria? Why or why not?

5. Frey refers to himself as a "restricted vivisectionist." Explain what he means by this. Under what conditions does he think that animal experimentation is morally permissible? Under what conditions does he think that human experimentation is morally permissible? Do you think there is a relevant difference between the two that Frey has failed to appreciate? Explain your answer.

26

═══ ❧ ═══

Climate Change Justice

Eric A. Posner and Cass R. Sunstein

....

Climate change is already having a substantial impact on countries around the world and will almost certainly lead to great suffering for large portions of the population over the coming decades. In addition to the very practical issues of how best to forestall or manage such change, there are also issues about what justice demands of the wealthier nations whose actions have been largely responsible for causing climate change. Legal scholars Eric Posner and Cass Sunstein divide such issues into two sorts: those concerning distributive justice and those that have to do with corrective justice.

Distributive justice is a matter of justly distributing resources and opportunities. Many argue that wealthy nations are required by justice to drastically reduce their greenhouse gas emissions so as to protect the citizens of poorer countries who will suffer from the effects of such emissions. Posner and Sunstein raise a variety of questions about this claim. First, they point out that climate change is not an unmitigated disaster—many millions of people who currently live in very cold climates will benefit in a variety of ways when their lands become warmer. That said, they accept, at least for the purpose of argument, that the harms of climate change will greatly outweigh these benefits. Even so, they ask whether the money spent on lowering emissions might instead be better spent as a direct grant to the poorer countries whose future populations are likely to suffer so greatly from climate change. They also worry that offering aid to poorer countries fails to benefit

Georgetown Law Review, vol. 96 (2008), pp. 1565–1612. This article has been abridged.

the poor in wealthy nations while also benefiting the wealthy who are citizens of the poorer nations receiving aid.

Posner and Sunstein allow that justice might demand that wealthy nations greatly lower their emissions if doing so is required in order to avoid a worldwide catastrophe. Whether that is so, though, depends on what the risks actually are—a matter on which they take no stand. It's also the case that lowering emissions may better serve justice than giving direct aid to poorer countries if ineffective or corrupt rulers govern those countries, but even here Posner and Sunstein raise serious questions about what justice requires in such situations.

Corrective justice is a matter of righting wrongs, correcting for past injustices. Wealthier nations have emitted far more greenhouse gases than have poorer ones, and so have done much more to harm the planet. As a result, the argument goes, wealthier nations must repair the damage their harmful emissions have (and will have) caused those in poorer nations.

Posner and Sunstein identify three problems for this argument. First, there is the worry that many of those who are responsible for having caused the relevant harms are now dead, and many others who live in wealthy nations support policies that will substantially reduce greenhouse emissions. So it may be hard to determine who should be asked to pay the costs required to correct for environmental harms. Second, the identity of the victims of climate change is very difficult to discern, since most of the harm will occur decades or centuries from now and most of the victims of such harm have not yet been born. Third, claims of corrective justice rest on showing that the wrongdoer has actually caused the victim's harm. Even if we can settle who has perpetrated the wrong and who has suffered the harm, establishing the causal link between the actions of citizens of wealthy nations and the suffering of citizens in poorer countries will be extremely hard.

....

Climate Change and Distributive Justice

To separate issues of distributive justice from those of corrective justice, and to clarify intuitions, let us begin with a risk of natural calamity that does not involve human action at all.

The Asteroid

Imagine that India faces a serious new threat of some kind—say, a threat of a collision with a large asteroid. Imagine too that the threat will not materialize for a century. Imagine finally that the threat can be eliminated, today, at a cost. India would be devastated by having to bear that cost now; as a practical matter, it lacks the resources to do so. But if the world acts as a whole, it can begin to build technology that will allow it to divert the asteroid, thus ensuring that it does not collide with India a century hence. The cost is high, but it is lower than the discounted benefit of eliminating the threat. If the world delays, it might also be able to eliminate the threat or reduce the damage if it comes to fruition. But many scientists believe that the best approach, considering relevant costs and benefits, is to start immediately to build technology that will divert the asteroid.

Are wealthy nations, such the United States, obliged to contribute significant sums of money to protect India from the asteroid? On grounds of distributive justice, it is tempting to think so. But if we reach that conclusion, how is the case different from one in which India contends, now, that it would be able to prevent millions of premature deaths from disease and malnutrition if the United States gave it (say) some small fraction of its Gross Domestic Product? If one nation is threatened by malaria or a tsunami, other nations might well agree that it is appropriate to help; it is certainly generous and in that sense commendable to assist those in need. But even generous nations do not conventionally think that a threatened nation has an entitlement to their assistance. For those who believe that there is such an entitlement, the puzzle remains: Why is there an entitlement to help in avoiding future harm from an asteroid, rather than current harms from other sources?

The problem of the asteroid threat does have a significant difference from that of climate change, whose adverse effects are not limited to a single nation. To make the analogy closer, assume that all nations are threatened by the asteroid in the sense that it is not possible to project where the collision will occur; scientists believe that each nation faces a risk. But the risk is not identical. Because of its adaptive capacity, its location, its technology, and a range of other factors, assume that the United States is less vulnerable to serious damage than (for example) India and the nations of Africa and Europe. Otherwise the problem is the same. Under plausible assumptions, the world will certainly act to divert the asteroid, and it seems clear that the United States will contribute substantial resources for that purpose. Suppose that all nations favor an international agreement that requires contributions to a general fund, but, because it is less vulnerable, the United States believes that the fund should be smaller than the fund favored by the more vulnerable nations of Africa and Europe, and by India. From the standpoint of domestic self-interest, then, those nations with the most to lose will naturally seek a larger fund than those nations facing lower risks.

At first glance, it might seem intuitive to think that the United States should accept the proposal for the larger fund simply because it is so wealthy. If resources should be redistributed from rich to poor on the ground that redistribution would increase overall welfare or promote fairness, the intuition appears sound. But there is an immediate problem: If redistribution from rich nations to poor nations is *generally* desirable, it is not at all clear that it should take the particular form of a deal in which the United States joins an agreement that is not in its interest. Other things being equal, the more sensible kind of redistribution would be a cash transfer, so that poor nations can use the money as they see fit. Perhaps India would prefer to spend the money on education, or on AIDS prevention, or on health care generally. If redistribution is what is sought, a generous deal with respect to the threat of an asteroid collision seems a crude way of achieving it.

Analytically, that deal has some similarities to housing assistance for poor people when recipients might prefer to spend the money on food or health care. If redistribution is desirable, housing assistance is better than nothing, but it remains puzzling why wealthy nations should be willing to protect poor nations from the risks of asteroid collisions (or climate change), while not being willing to give them resources with which they can set their own priorities. Indeed, a generous deal with respect to the asteroid threat may be worse than housing assistance as a redistributive strategy because, by hypothesis, many of the beneficiaries of the deal are in rich nations and are not poor at all—a point to which we will return.

There is a second difficulty. We have stipulated that the asteroid will not hit the earth for another 100 years. If the world takes action now, it will be spending current resources for the sake of future generations, which are likely to be much richer. The current poor citizens of poor nations are probably much poorer than will be the *future* poor citizens of those nations. If the goal is to help the poor, it is odd for the United States to spend significant resources to help posterity while neglecting the present. Thus far, then, the claim that the United States should join what it believes to be an unjustifiably costly agreement to divert the asteroid is doubly puzzling. Poor nations would benefit more from cash transfers, and the current poor have a stronger claim to assistance than the future (less) poor.

From the standpoint of distributional justice, there is a third problem. Nations are not people; they are collections of people, ranging from very rich to very poor. Wealthy countries, such as the United States, have many poor people, and poor countries, such as India, have many rich people. If the United States is paying a lot of money to avert the threat of an asteroid collision, it would be good to know whether that cost is being paid, in turn, by wealthy Americans or by poor Americans. Suppose, for example, that greenhouse gas reductions lead to a significant increase in the cost of energy. Any such increase—from either carbon taxes or cap-and-trade—would be regressive, in the sense that it would hit poor people harder than wealthy people, who spend a smaller portion of the income on energy costs. But if the concern is to help people who need help, such a tax is hard to defend.

If redistribution is our goal, it would also be good to know whether the beneficiaries are mostly rich or mostly poor. Many of the beneficiaries of actions to reduce a worldwide risk are in wealthy nations, and so it should be clear that the class of those who are helped will include many people who are not poor at all. Because the median member of wealthy nations is wealthier than the median member of poor nations, it is plausible to think that if wealthy nations contribute a disproportionately high amount to the joint endeavor, the distributive effects will be good. For example, the Americans who are asked to make the relevant payments are, on average, wealthier than the Indians who are paying less. But asking Americans to contribute more to a joint endeavor is hardly the best way of achieving the goal of transferring wealth from the rich to the poor.

Climate Change: From Whom to Whom?

In terms of distributive justice, the problem of climate change is closely analogous to the asteroid problem. From that problem, three general questions emerge. First, why should redistribution take the form of an in kind benefit, rather than a general grant of money that poor nations could use as they wish? Second, why should rich nations help poor nations in the future, rather than poor nations now? Third, if redistribution is the goal, why should it take the form of action by rich nations that would hurt many poor people in those nations and benefit many rich people in poor nations? To sharpen these questions, suppose that an international agreement to cut greenhouse gas emissions would cost the United States $325 billion. If distributive justice is the goal, should the United States spend $325 billion on climate change, or instead on other imaginable steps to help people who are in need? If the goal is to assist poor people, perhaps there would be far better means than emissions reductions.

In fact, the argument from distributive justice runs into an additional problem in the context of climate change. No one would gain from an asteroid collision, but millions of people would benefit from climate change. Many people die from cold, and to the extent that warming reduces cold, it will save lives. Warming will also produce monetary benefits in many places, such as Russia, due to increases in agricultural productivity. Indeed, many millions of poor people in such countries may benefit from climate change. Some of them will live when they would otherwise die from extreme cold. In China, many millions of people living in rural areas continue to be extremely poor despite the increasing prosperity of the nation as a whole. These people are among the poorest in the world. For at least some of these people, climate change could well provide benefits by increasing the productivity of their land.

In addition, many millions of poor people would be hurt by the cost of emissions reductions. They would bear that cost in the form of higher energy bills, lost jobs, and increased poverty. Recall too that industrialized and relatively wealthy European nations have been found to be at greater risk than the relatively poorer China.

It follows that purely as an instrument of redistribution, emission reductions on the part of the United States are quite crude. True, a suitably designed emissions control agreement would almost certainly help poor people more than it would hurt them, because disadvantaged people in sub-Saharan Africa and India are at such grave risk. And true, an agreement in which the United States pays more than its self-interest dictates might well be better, from the standpoint of distributive justice, than the status quo, or than an agreement that would simply require all nations to scale back their emissions by a specified amount. But there is a highly imperfect connection between distributive goals on the one hand and requiring wealthy countries to pay for emissions reductions on the other.

To see the problem more concretely, suppose that Americans (and the same could be said about citizens in other wealthy countries) are willing to devote a certain portion, X, of their national income to helping people living in poor countries. The question is, How is X best spent? If X is committed to emissions controls, then X is being spent to benefit wealthy Europeans as well as impoverished Indians, and X is also being spent to harm some or many impoverished people living in China and Russia by denying them the benefit of increased agricultural productivity that warming will bring. And if all of X is spent on global emissions control, then none of X is being spent to purchase malaria nets or to distribute AIDS drugs—which are highly effective ways of helping poor people who are alive today rather than poor people who will be alive in 100 years.

Two Counterarguments

There are two tempting counterarguments. The first involves the risk of catastrophe. The second involves the fact that cash transfers will go to governments that may be ineffective or corrupt.

Catastrophe

On certain assumptions about the science, greenhouse gas cuts are necessary to prevent a catastrophic loss of life. Suppose, by way of imperfect analogy, that a genocide is occurring in some nation. For multiple reasons, it would not be sensible to say that rich countries should give money to such a nation, rather than acting to prevent the genocide. Or suppose that a nation is threatened by a natural disaster that would wipe out millions of lives; if other nations could eliminate the harms associated with such a disaster, it would be hard to object that they should offer cash payments instead. One reason is that if many lives are at risk, and if they can be saved through identifiable steps, taking those steps would seem to be the most effective response to the problem, and cash transfers would have little or no advantage.

Suppose that climate change threatens to create massive losses of life in various countries. In light of the risk of catastrophe, perhaps emissions reductions are preferable to other redistributive strategies. The catastrophic scenario is a way of saying that the future benefits of cuts could be exceptionally high rather than merely high. If poor people in poor nations face a serious risk of catastrophe, then greenhouse gas abatement *could* turn out to be the best way to redistribute wealth (or, more accurately, welfare) to people who would otherwise die in the future.

Ultimately the strength of the argument turns on the extent of the risk. To the extent that the risk of catastrophe is not low, and to the extent that it is faced mostly by people living in difficult or desperate conditions, the argument from distributive justice does gain a great deal of force. To the extent that the catastrophic scenario remains highly unlikely, the argument is weakened. We cannot exclude the possibility that the argument is correct; it depends on the scientific evidence for the truly catastrophic scenarios.

Ineffective or Corrupt Governments

We have emphasized that development aid is likely to be more effective than greenhouse gas restrictions as a method of helping poor people in poor nations. A legitimate response is that cutting greenhouse gas emissions bypasses the governments of poor states more completely than other forms of development aid do. This might be counted as a virtue because the governments of many poor states are either inefficient or corrupt (or both), and partly for that reason, ordinary development aid has not been very effective.

But here too there are counterarguments. As we have stressed, this form of redistribution does not help existing poor people at all; it can, at best, help poor people in future generations. And it is far from clear that donor states can avoid the pathologies of development aid by, in effect, transferring resources to the future rather than to the present, or by transferring resources directly to the people rather than to corrupt governments. Benefits received by individuals can be expropriated, or taxed away, by governments that do not respect the rule of law. This is just as true for the future as for the present. If abatement efforts today result in higher crop yields in Chad in 100 years than would otherwise occur, Chadians might be better off, of course, but it is also possible that a future authoritarian government would expropriate these gains for itself, or that they would be squandered as a result of bad economic policy, or that in the meantime Chad has become a completely different place that does best by importing food from elsewhere.

Even more important, the claim that emissions reductions avoid corruption overlooks the fact that emissions abatement does not occur by itself but must take place through the activity of governments, including those in developing countries. In cap-and-trade systems, for example, the government of a poor country would be given permits that it could then sell to industry, raising enormous sums of money that the government could spend however it chose. Corrupt governments would spend this money badly, perhaps using it to finance political repression, while also possibly accepting bribes from local industry that chooses not to buy permits, in return for non-enforcement of the country's treaty obligations. To be sure, significant emissions reductions by wealthy nations would directly benefit poor nations.

Notwithstanding the complexities here, the basic point remains: in principle, greenhouse gas cuts do not seem to be the most direct or effective means of helping poor people or poor nations. We cannot exclude the possibility that the more direct methods are inferior, for example because it is not feasible to provide that direct aid; but it would remain necessary to explain why a crude form of redistribution is feasible when a less crude form is not.

Corrective Justice

Climate change differs from our asteroid example in another way. In the asteroid example, no one can be blamed for the appearance of the asteroid and the threat that it poses to India (or the world). But many people believe that by virtue of its past actions and policies, the United States, along with other developed nations, is particularly to blame for the problem of climate change. In the international arena, the argument that the United States has an obligation to devote significant resources to reducing greenhouse gas emissions is not solely and perhaps not even mainly an argument about distributive justice. The argument also rests on moral intuitions about corrective justice—about wrongdoers and their victims.

The Basic Argument

Corrective justice arguments are backward-looking, focused on wrongful behavior that occurred in the past. Even though China is now the world's leading greenhouse gas emitter, the United States has been the largest emitter historically and thus has the greater responsibility for the stock of greenhouse gases in the atmosphere. Of course, a disproportionate share of the stock of greenhouse gases can be attributed to other long-industrialized countries as well, such as Germany and Japan, and so what we say here about the United States can be applied, *mutatis mutandi*, to those other countries. The emphasis on the United States is warranted by the fact that the United States has contributed more to the existing stock than any other nation (nearly 30%).

In the context of climate change, the corrective justice argument is that the United States wrongfully harmed the rest of the world—especially low-lying states and others that are most vulnerable to global warming—by emitting greenhouse gases in vast quantities. On a widespread view, corrective justice requires that the United States devote significant resources to remedying the problem—perhaps by paying damages, agreeing to extensive emissions reductions, or participating in a climate pact that is not in its self-interest. India, for example, might be thought to have a moral claim against the United States—one derived from the principles of corrective justice—and on this view the United States has an obligation to provide a compensatory remedy to India. (Because India is especially vulnerable to climate change, we use that nation as a placeholder for those at particular risk.)

This argument enjoys a great deal of support in certain circles and seems intuitively correct. The apparent simplicity of the argument, however, masks some serious difficulties. We shall identify a large number of problems here, and the discussion will be lamentably complex. The most general point, summarizing the argument as a whole, is that the climate change problem poorly fits the corrective justice model because the consequence of tort-like thinking would be to force many people who have not acted wrongfully to provide a remedy to many people who have not been victimized. Some of the problems we identify could be reduced if it were possible to trace complex causal chains with great precision; unfortunately, legal systems lack the necessary tools to do so.

The Wrongdoer Identity Problem

The current stock of greenhouse gases in the atmosphere is a result of the behavior of people living in the past. Much of it is due to the behavior of people who are dead. The basic problem for corrective justice is that dead wrongdoers cannot be punished or held responsible for their behavior, or forced to compensate those they have harmed. At first glance, holding Americans today responsible for the activities of their ancestors is not fair or reasonable on corrective justice grounds, because current Americans are not the relevant wrongdoers; they are not responsible for the harm.

Indeed, many Americans today do not support the current American energy policy and already make some sacrifices to reduce the greenhouse gas emissions that result from their behavior. They avoid driving, they turn down the heat in their homes, and they support electoral candidates who advocate greener policies. Holding these people responsible for the wrongful activities of people who lived in the past seems perverse. An approach that emphasized corrective justice would attempt to be more finely tuned, focusing on particular actors, rather than Americans as a class, which would appear to violate deeply held moral objections to collective responsibility. The task would be to distinguish between the contributions of those who are living and those who are dead.

The most natural and best response to this point is to insist that all or most Americans today benefit from the greenhouse gas emitting activities of Americans living in the past, and therefore it would not be wrong to require Americans today to pay for abatement measures. This argument is familiar from debates about slave reparations, where it is argued that Americans today have benefited from the toil of slaves 150 years ago. To the extent that members of current generations have gained from past wrongdoing, it may well make sense to ask them to make compensation to those harmed as a result. On one view, compensation can work to restore the status quo ante, that is, to put members of different groups, and citizens of different nations, in the position that they would have occupied if the wrongdoing had not occurred.

In the context of climate however, this argument runs into serious problems. The most obvious difficulty is empirical. It is true that many Americans benefit from past greenhouse-gas-emissions, but how many benefit, and how much do they benefit? Many Americans today are, of course, immigrants or children of immigrants, and so not the descendants of greenhouse-gas-emitting Americans of the past. Such people may nonetheless gain from past emissions, because they enjoy the kind of technological advance and material wealth that those emissions made possible. But have they actually benefited, and to what degree? Further, not all Americans inherit the wealth of their ancestors, and even those who do would not necessarily have inherited less if their ancestors' generations had not engaged in the greenhouse-gas-emitting activities. The idea of corrective justice, building on the tort analogy, does not seem to fit the climate change situation.

Suppose that these various obstacles could be overcome and that we could trace, with sufficient accuracy, the extent to which current Americans have benefited from past emissions. As long as the costs are being toted up, the benefits should be as well, and used to offset the requirements of corrective justice. We have noted that climate change is itself anticipated to produce benefits for many nations, both by increasing agricultural productivity and by reducing extremes of cold. And if past generations of Americans have imposed costs on the rest of the world, they have also conferred substantial benefits. American industrial activity has produced products that were consumed in foreign countries, for example, and has driven technological advances from which citizens in other countries have gained. Many of these benefits are positive externalities, for which Americans have not been fully compensated. To be sure, many citizens in, say, India have not much benefited from those advances, just as many citizens of the United States have not much benefited from them. But what would the world, or India, look like if the United States had engaged in 10% of its level of greenhouse gas emissions, or 20%, or 40%? For purposes of corrective justice, a proper accounting would seem to be necessary, and it presents formidable empirical and conceptual problems.

In the context of slave reparations, the analogous points have led to interminable debates, again empirical and conceptual, about historical causation and difficult counterfactuals. But-for causation arguments, used in standard legal analysis and conventional for purposes of conventional justice, present serious and perhaps insuperable problems when applied historically. We can meaningfully ask whether an accident would have occurred if the driver had operated the vehicle more carefully, but conceptual and empirical questions make it difficult to answer the question whether and to what extent white Americans today would have been worse off if there had been no slavery—and difficult too to ask whether Indians would be better off today if Americans of prior generations had not emitted greenhouse gases. What kind of a question is that? In this hypothetical world of limited industrialization in the United States, India would be an entirely different country, and the rest of the world would be unrecognizably different as well.

Proponents of slave reparations have sometimes appealed to principles of corporate liability. Corporations can be immortal, and many corporations today benefited from the slave economy in the nineteenth century. Corporations are collectivities, not individuals, yet they can be held liable for their actions, which means that shareholders today are "punished" (in the sense of losing share value) as a result of actions taken by managers and employees long before the shareholders obtained their ownership interest. If innocent shareholders can be made to pay for the wrongdoing of employees who are long gone, why can't citizens be made to pay for the wrongful actions of citizens who lived in the past?

The best answer is that corporate liability is most easily justified on grounds other than corrective justice. Shareholder liability can be defended on the basis of consent or (in our view most plausibly) on the welfarist ground that corporate liability deters employees from engaging in wrongdoing on behalf of the corporate entity. A factor that distinguishes corporate liability is that purchasing shares is a voluntary activity and one does so with the knowledge that the share price will decline if a past legal violation comes to light, and this is reflected in the share price at the time of purchase. (One also benefits if an unknown past action enhances the value of the company.) But because the corporate form itself is a fiction, and the shareholders today are different from the wrongdoers yesterday, corporate liability cannot be grounded in corrective justice. Thus, it provides no analogy on behalf of corrective justice for the climate change debate.

The Victim/Claimant Identity Problem

As usually understood, corrective justice requires an identity between the victim and the claimant: the person who is injured by the wrongdoer must be the same as the person who has a claim against the wrongdoer. In limited circumstances, a child or other dependent might inherit that claim, but usually one thinks of the dependent as having a separate claim, deriving from the wrongdoer's presumed knowledge that by harming the victim she also harms the victim's dependents.

Who are the victims of climate change? Most of them live in the future. Thus, their claims have not matured. To say that future Indians might have a valid claim against Americans today, or Americans of the past, is not the same as saying that Americans today have a duty to help Indians today. To be sure, some people are now harmed by climate change. In addition, people living in low-lying islands or coastal regions can plausibly contend that a particular flood or storm has some probabilistic relationship with climate change—but from the standpoint of corrective justice, this group presents its own difficulties (a point to which we will return shortly). What remains plausible is the claim that future Indians would have corrective justice claims against current and past Americans.

A successful abatement program would, of course, benefit many people living in the future, albeit by preventing them from becoming victims in the first place or reducing the magnitude of their injury, rather than compensating them for harm. One might justify the abatement approach on welfarist grounds: perhaps the welfare benefits for people living in the future exceed the welfare losses to people living today. One could also make an argument that people living today have a nonwelfarist obligation to refrain from engaging in actions today that harm people in the future. The point for present purposes is that both arguments are forward-looking: the obligation, whether welfarist or nonwelfarist, is not based on past actions, and thus a nation's relative contribution to the current greenhouse gas stock in the atmosphere would not be a relevant consideration in the design of the greenhouse gas abatement program, as we have been arguing. By contrast, the corrective justice argument is that the United States should contribute the most to abatement efforts because it has caused the most damage to the carbon-absorbing capacity of the atmosphere.

The argument that we owe duties to the future, on welfarist or other grounds, seems right, but as a basis for current abatement efforts, it runs into a complication. Suppose that activities in the United States that produce greenhouse gases (a) do harm people in the future by contributing to climate change, but also (b) benefit people in the future by amassing capital on which they can draw to reduce poverty and illness and to protect against a range of social ills. Supposing, as we agree, that present generations are obliged not to render future generations miserable, it is necessary to ask whether current activities create benefits that are equivalent to, or higher than, costs for those generations. As our discussion of distributive justice suggests, it is possible that greenhouse gas abatement programs—as opposed to, say, research and development or promoting economic growth in poor countries—are not the best way to ensure that the appropriate level of intergenerational equity is achieved.

The Causation Problem

Corrective justice requires that the wrongdoing cause the harm. In ordinary person-to-person encounters, this requirement is straightforward. But in the context of climate change, causation poses formidable challenges, especially when we are trying to attribute particular losses to a warmer climate.

To see why, consider a village in India that is wiped out by a monsoon. One might make a plausible argument that the flooding was more likely than it would otherwise have been, as a result of rising sea levels caused by climate change. But it might well be impossible to show that greenhouse gas emissions in the United States "caused" the flooding, in the sense that they were a necessary and sufficient condition, and difficult even to show that they even contributed to it. If the flooding was in a probabilistic sense the result of greenhouse gas activities around the world, its likelihood was also increased by complex natural phenomena that are poorly understood. And to the extent that the United States was involved, much of the contribution was probably due to people who died years ago.

Causation problems are not fatal to corrective justice claims, but they significantly weaken them. In tort law, courts are occasionally willing to assign liability according to market share when multiple firms contribute to a harm—for example, pollution or dangerous products whose provenance cannot be traced. Perhaps scientific and economic studies could find, with sufficient accuracy, aggregate national losses. And it would be plausible to understand corrective justice, in this domain, in probabilistic terms, with the thought that victims should receive "probabilistic recoveries," understood as the fraction of their injury that is probabilistically connected with climate change. It is unclear, however, that statistical relationships can be established with sufficient clarity to support a claim sounding in corrective justice.

Conclusion

Our narrow goal has been to investigate considerations of distributive justice and corrective justice. If the United States wants to use its wealth to help to protect India or Africa or impoverished people generally, there can be no reason for complaint. The question remains, however, what is the best way to help disadvantaged people around the world. It is plausible that protecting other countries from genocide or poverty or famine is such a way. It is far from clear that greenhouse gas restrictions on the part of the United States are the best way to help the most disadvantaged citizens of the world.

It is tempting to treat climate change as a kind of tort, committed by the United States against those who are most vulnerable. But we have seen that principles of corrective justice have an awkward relationship to the problem of climate change. Many of the relevant actors are long dead, and a general transfer from the United States to those in places especially threatened by climate change is not an apt way of restoring some imagined status quo. In this context, the idea of corrective justice is a metaphor, and a highly imperfect one.

Eric A. Posner and Cass R. Sunstein: Climate Change Justice

1. Formulate in your own words the best version of an argument from distributive justice to support the conclusion that wealthy nations are morally required to drastically reduce their greenhouse gas emissions.
2. Formulate in your own words the best version of an argument from corrective justice to support the conclusion that wealthy nations are morally required to drastically reduce their greenhouse gas emissions.
3. Posner and Sunstein identify several worries for an argument from distributive justice. Which of these do you find least compelling, and why?

4. Some scientists claim that devastating climate change is now inevitable. Suppose they are right. What, if anything, does this do to affect the merits of arguments from distributive or corrective justice?

5. Much of the ethical concern about climate change is focused on the impact such change will have on people who won't be born for at least another century. Such people don't exist, and, as a general matter, we lack duties to beings or things that don't exist. What implications do these claims have for climate change justice?

27

Ideals of Human Excellence and Preserving Natural Environments

Thomas Hill, Jr.

....

According to Thomas Hill, Jr., the standard moral theories have difficulty explaining what is wrong with the destruction of the environment. Utilitarianism runs into trouble, because it is possible that overall happiness is maximized when cutting down a virgin forest or bulldozing a field to make way for suburban homes. Kantian and rights-based moral theories have just as much trouble here, because it is very difficult to defend the idea that plants or ecosystems—incapable of reasoning, asserting claims, or even feeling anything—are possessed of rights. Contractarian theories are just as vulnerable on this score. If our basic duties are owed only to our fellow members of the social contract, then plants and ecosystems will again be left out in the cold.

These concerns lead Hill to consider an alternative way of understanding our ethical relations with the environment. Rather than focusing on the question of whether we have any duties directly toward the environment, Hill invites us to consider a virtue ethical approach, which places primary emphasis on the sort of person we should try to become. He argues that those who fail to treat the environment with respect are almost certainly going to be less than fully virtuous. They will fail to be admirable in a number of ways, and will exemplify a variety of vices. In particular, those who are indifferent to the value of nature

---

Thomas Hill, Jr., "Ideals of Human Excellence and Preserving Natural Environments" from *Environmental Ethics* 5 (1983), pp. 211–224.

will almost certainly be ignorant and self-important. They will lack proper humility, and will either fail to have a well-developed sense of beauty, or will be insufficiently grateful for the good things in life. Thus even if we can't defend the claim that nature has rights, or that we owe nature anything, there is still excellent reason to respect and preserve natural environments. For if we don't, we will fall short of plausible ideals of human excellence.

....

I

A wealthy eccentric bought a house in a neighborhood I know. The house was surrounded by a beautiful display of grass, plants, and flowers, and it was shaded by a huge old avocado tree. But the grass required cutting, the flowers needed tending, and the man wanted more sun. So he cut the whole lot down and covered the yard with asphalt. After all it was his property and he was not fond of plants.

It was a small operation, but it reminded me of the strip mining of large sections of the Appalachians. In both cases, of course, there were reasons for the destruction, and property rights could be cited as justification. But I could not help but wonder, "What sort of person would do a thing like that?"

Many Californians had a similar reaction when a recent governor defended the leveling of ancient redwood groves, reportedly saying, "If you have seen one redwood, you have seen them all."

Incidents like these arouse the indignation of ardent environmentalists and leave even apolitical observers with some degree of moral discomfort. The reasons for these reactions are mostly obvious. Uprooting the natural environment robs both present and future generations of much potential use and enjoyment. Animals too depend on the environment; and even if one does not value animals for their own sakes, their potential utility for us is incalculable. Plants are needed, of course, to replenish the atmosphere quite aside from their aesthetic value. These reasons for hesitating to destroy forests and gardens are not only the most obvious ones, but also the most persuasive for practical purposes. But, one wonders, is there nothing more behind our discomfort? Are we concerned solely about the potential use and enjoyment of the forests, etc., for ourselves, later generations, and perhaps animals? Is there not something else which disturbs us when we witness the destruction or even listen to those who would defend it in terms of cost/benefit analysis?

Imagine that in each of our examples those who would destroy the environment argue elaborately that, even considering future generations of human beings and animals, there are benefits in "replacing" the natural environment which outweigh the negative utilities which environmentalists cite. No doubt we could press the argument on the facts, trying to show that the destruction is shortsighted and that its defenders have underestimated its potential harm or ignored some pertinent rights or interests. But is this all we could say? Suppose we grant, for a moment, that the utility of destroying the redwoods, forests, and gardens is equal to their potential for use and enjoyment by nature lovers and animals. Suppose, further, that we even grant that the pertinent human rights and animal rights, if any, are evenly divided for and against destruction. Imagine that we also concede, for argument's sake, that the forests contain no potentially useful endangered species of animals and plants. Must we then conclude that there is no further cause for moral concern? Should we then feel morally indifferent when we see the natural environment uprooted?

II

Suppose we feel that the answer to these questions should be negative. Suppose, in other words, we feel that our moral discomfort when we confront the destroyers of nature is not fully explained by our belief that they have miscalculated the best use of natural resources or violated rights in exploiting them. Suppose, in particular, we sense that part of the problem is that the natural environment is being viewed exclusively as a natural resource. What could be the ground of such a feeling? That is, what is there in our system of normative principles and values that could account for our remaining moral dissatisfaction?

Some may be tempted to seek an explanation by appeal to the interests, or even the rights, of plants. After all, they may argue, we only gradually came to acknowledge the moral importance of all human beings, and it is even more recently that consciences have been aroused to give full weight to the welfare (and rights?) of animals. The next logical step, it may be argued, is to acknowledge a moral requirement to take into account the interests (and rights?) of plants. The problem with the strip miners, redwood cutters, and the like, on this view, is not just that they ignore the

welfare and rights of people and animals: they also fail to give due weight
to the survival and health of the plants themselves.

The temptation to make such a reply is understandable if one assumes
that all moral questions are exclusively concerned with whether *acts* are
right or wrong, and that this, in turn, is determined entirely by how the
acts impinge on the rights and interests of those directly affected. On this
assumption, if there is cause for moral concern, some right or interest
has been neglected; and if the rights and interests of human beings and
animals have already been taken into account, then there must be some
other pertinent interests, for example, those of plants. A little reflection
will show that the assumption is mistaken; but, in any case, the conclusion
that plants have rights or morally relevant interests is surely untenable. We
do speak of what is "good for" plants, and they can "thrive" and also be
"killed." But this does not imply that they have "interests" in any morally
relevant sense. Some people apparently believe that plants grow better if
we talk to them, but the idea that the plants suffer and enjoy, desire and
dislike, etc., is clearly outside the range of both common sense and scientific belief. The notion that the forests should be preserved to avoid *hurting*
the trees or because they have a *right* to life is not part of a widely shared
moral consciousness, and for good reason.

Another way of trying to explain our moral discomfort is to appeal to
certain religious beliefs. If one believes that all living things were created
by a God who cares for them and entrusted us with the use of plants and
animals only for limited purposes, then one has a reason to avoid careless
destruction of the forests, etc., quite aside from their future utility. Again,
if one believes that a divine force is immanent in all nature, then too one
might have reason to care for more than sentient things. But such arguments require strong and controversial premises, and, I suspect, they will
always have a restricted audience.

Early in this century, due largely to the influence of G. E. Moore,
another point of view developed which some may find promising.[1] Moore
introduced, or at least made popular, the idea that certain states of affairs
are intrinsically valuable—not just valued, but valuable, and not necessarily because of their effects on sentient beings. . . . The intrinsic goodness
of something, he thought, was an objective, nonrelational property of the

---

1. G. E. Moore, *Principia Ethica* (Cambridge: Cambridge University Press, 1903); *Ethics* (London:
H. Holt, 1912).

thing, like its texture or color, but not a property perceivable by sense perception or detectable by scientific instruments. In theory at least, a single tree thriving alone in a universe without sentient beings, and even without God, could be intrinsically valuable. . . . The survival of a forest might have worth beyond its worth *to* sentient beings.

Even if we try to . . . think in Moore's terms, it is far from obvious that everyone would agree that the existence of forests, etc., is intrinsically valuable. The test, says Moore, is what we would say when we imagine a universe with just the thing in question, without any effects or accompaniments, and then we ask, "Would its existence be better than its nonexistence?" Be careful. Moore would remind us, not to construe this question as, "Would you *prefer* the existence of that universe to its nonexistence?" The question is, "Would its existence have the objective, nonrelational property, intrinsic goodness?"

Now even among those who have no worries about whether this really makes sense, we might well get a diversity of answers. Those prone to destroy natural environments will doubtless give one answer, and nature lovers will likely give another. When an issue is as controversial as the one at hand, intuition is a poor arbiter.

The problem, then, is this. We want to understand what underlies our moral uneasiness at the destruction of the redwoods, forests, etc., even apart from the loss of these as resources for human beings and animals. But I find no adequate answer by pursuing the questions, "Are rights or interests of plants neglected?" "What is God's will on the matter?" and "What is the intrinsic value of the existence of a tree or forest?" My suggestion, which is in fact the main point of this paper, is that we look at the problem from a different perspective. That is, let us turn for a while from the effort to find reasons why certain *acts* destructive of natural environments are morally wrong to the ancient task of articulating our ideals of human excellence. Rather than argue directly with destroyers of the environment who say, "Show me why what I am doing is *immoral*," I want to ask, "What sort of person would want to do what they propose?" The point is not to skirt the issue with an *ad hominem*, but to raise a different moral question, for even if there is no convincing way to show that the destructive acts are wrong (independently of human and animal use and enjoyment), we may find that the willingness to indulge in them reflects the absence of human traits that we admire and regard as morally important.

This strategy of shifting questions may seem more promising if one reflects on certain analogous situations. Consider, for example, the Nazi who asks, in all seriousness, "Why is it wrong for me to make lampshades out of human skin—provided, of course, I did not myself kill the victims to get the skins?" We would react more with shock and disgust than with indignation, I suspect, because it is even more evident that the question reveals a defect in the questioner than that the proposed act is itself immoral. Sometimes we may not regard an act wrong at all though we see it as reflecting something objectionable about the person who does it. Imagine, for example, one who laughs spontaneously to himself when he reads a newspaper account of a plane crash that kills hundreds. Or, again, consider an obsequious grandson who, having waited for his grandmother's inheritance with mock devotion, then secretly spits on her grave when at last she dies. Spitting on the grave may have no adverse consequences and perhaps it violates no rights. The moral uneasiness which it arouses is explained more by our view of the agent than by any conviction that what he did was immoral. Had he hesitated and asked, "Why shouldn't I spit on her grave?" it seems more fitting to ask him to reflect on the sort of person he is than to try to offer reasons why he should refrain from spitting.

III

What sort of person, then, would cover his garden with asphalt, strip mine a wooded mountain, or level an irreplaceable redwood grove? Two sorts of answers, though initially appealing, must be ruled out. The first is that persons who would destroy the environment in these ways are either shortsighted, underestimating the harm they do, or else are too little concerned for the well-being of other people. Perhaps too they have insufficient regard for animal life. But these considerations have been set aside in order to refine the controversy. Another tempting response might be that we count it a moral virtue, or at least a human ideal, to love nature. Those who value the environment only for its utility must not really love nature and so in this way fall short of an ideal. But such an answer is hardly satisfying in the present context, for what is at issue is *why* we feel moral discomfort at the activities of those who admittedly value nature only for its utility. That it is ideal to care for nonsentient nature beyond its possible use is really just another way of expressing the general point which is under controversy.

What is needed is some way of showing that this ideal is connected with other virtues, or human excellences, not in question. To do so is difficult and my suggestions, accordingly, will be tentative and subject to qualification. The main idea is that, though indifference to nonsentient nature does not *necessarily* reflect the absence of virtues, it often signals the absence of certain traits which we want to encourage because they are, in most cases, a natural basis for the development of certain virtues. It is often thought, for example, that those who would destroy the natural environment must lack a proper appreciation of their place in the natural order, and so must either be ignorant or have too little humility. Though I would argue that this is not necessarily so, I suggest that, given certain plausible empirical assumptions, their attitude may well be rooted in ignorance, a narrow perspective, inability to see things as important apart from themselves and the limited groups they associate with, or reluctance to accept themselves as natural beings. Overcoming these deficiencies will not guarantee a proper moral humility, but for most of us it is probably an important psychological preliminary. Later I suggest, more briefly, that indifference to nonsentient nature typically reveals absence of either aesthetic sensibility or a disposition to cherish what has enriched one's life and that these, though not themselves moral virtues, are a natural basis for appreciation of the good in others and gratitude.

Consider first the suggestion that destroyers of the environment lack an appreciation of their place in the universe. Their attention, it seems, must be focused on parochial matters, on what is, relatively speaking, close in space and time. They seem not to understand that we are a speck on the cosmic scene, a brief stage in the evolutionary process, only one among millions of species on Earth, and an episode in the course of human history. Of course, they know that there are stars, fossils, insects, and ancient ruins; but do they have any idea of the complexity of the processes that led to the natural world as we find it? Are they aware how much the forces at work within their own bodies are like those which govern all living things and even how much they have in common with inanimate bodies? Admittedly scientific knowledge is limited and no one can master it all; but could one who had a broad and deep understanding of his place in nature really be indifferent to the destruction of the natural environment?

This first suggestion, however, may well provoke a protest from a sophisticated anti-environmentalist. "Perhaps *some* may be indifferent to nature from ignorance," the critic may object, "but I have studied astronomy, geology, biology, and biochemistry, and I still unashamedly regard the nonsentient environment as simply a resource for our use. It should not be wasted, of course, but what should be preserved is decidable by weighing long-term costs and benefits." "Besides," our critic may continue, "as philosophers you should know the old Humean formula, 'You cannot derive an *ought* from an *is*.' All the facts of biology, biochemistry, etc., do not entail that I ought to love nature or want to preserve it. What one understands is one thing; what one values is something else. Just as nature lovers are not necessarily scientists, those indifferent to nature are not necessarily ignorant."

Although the environmentalist may concede the critic's logical point, he may well argue that, as a matter of fact, increased understanding of nature tends to heighten people's concern for its preservation. If so, despite the objection, the suspicion that the destroyers of the environment lack deep understanding of nature is not, in most cases, unwarranted, but the argument need not rest here.

The environmentalist might amplify his original idea as follows: "When I said that the destroyers of nature do not appreciate their place in the universe, I was not speaking of intellectual understanding alone, for, after all, a person can *know* a catalog of facts without ever putting them together and seeing vividly the whole picture which they form. To see oneself as just one part of nature is to look at oneself and the world from a certain perspective which is quite different from being able to recite detailed information from the natural sciences. What the destroyers of nature lack is this perspective, not particular information."

Again our critic may object, though only after making some concessions: "All right," he may say, "*some* who are indifferent to nature may lack the cosmic perspective of which you speak, but again there is no *necessary* connection between this failing, if it is one, and any particular evaluative attitude toward nature. In fact, different people respond quite differently when they move to a wider perspective. When I try to picture myself vividly as a brief, transitory episode in the course of nature, I simply get depressed. Far from inspiring me with a love of nature, the exercise makes me sad and hostile. . . ." In sum, the critic may object, "Even if one should try to see oneself as one small transitory part of nature, doing so does not dictate any particular normative attitude. Some may come to love nature, but others are moved to live for the moment; some sink into sad resignation; others get depressed or angry. So indifference to nature is not necessarily a sign that a person fails to look at himself from the larger perspective."

The environmentalist might respond to this objection in several ways. He might, for example, argue that even though some people who see themselves as part of the natural order remain indifferent to nonsentient nature, this is not a common reaction. Typically, it may be argued, as we become more and more aware that we are parts of the larger whole we come to value the whole independently of its effect on ourselves. Thus, despite the possibilities the critic raises, indifference to nonsentient nature is still in most cases a sign that a person fails to see himself as part of the natural order.

If someone challenges the empirical assumption here, the environmentalist might develop the argument along a quite different line. The initial idea, he may remind us, was that those who would destroy the natural environment fail to *appreciate* their place in the natural order. "Appreciating one's place" is not simply an intellectual appreciation. It is also an attitude, reflecting what one values as well as what one knows. When we say, for example, that both the servile and the arrogant person fail to *appreciate* their place in a society of equals, we do not mean simply that they are ignorant of certain empirical facts, but rather that they have certain objectionable attitudes about their importance relative to other people. Similarly, to fail to appreciate one's place in nature is not merely to lack knowledge or breadth of perspective, but to take a certain attitude about what matters. A person who *understands* his place in nature but still views nonsentient nature merely as a resource takes the attitude that nothing is *important* but human beings and animals. Despite first appearances, he is not so much like the pre-Copernican astronomers who made the intellectual error of treating the Earth as the "center of the universe" when they made their calculations. He is more like the racist who, though well aware of other races, treats all races but his own as insignificant.

So construed, the argument appeals to the common idea that awareness of nature typically has, and should have, a humbling effect. The Alps, a storm at sea, the Grand Canyon, towering redwoods, and "the starry heavens above" move many a person to remark on the comparative insignificance of our daily concerns and even of our species, and this is generally taken to be a quite fitting response. What seems to be missing, then, in those who understand nature but remain unmoved is a proper humility.[2] Absence of proper humility is not the same as selfishness or egoism, for one can be devoted to self-interest while still viewing one's own pleasures and projects as trivial and unimportant. And one can have an exaggerated

---

2. By "*proper* humility" I mean that sort and degree of humility that is a morally admirable character trait. How precisely to define this is, of course, a controversial matter; but the point for present purposes is just to set aside obsequiousness, false modesty, underestimation of one's abilities, and the like.

view of one's own importance while grandly sacrificing for those one views as inferior. Nor is the lack of humility identical with belief that one has power and influence, for a person can be quite puffed up about himself while believing that the foolish world will never acknowledge him. The humility we miss seems not so much a belief about one's relative effectiveness and recognition as an attitude which measures the importance of things independently of their relation to oneself or to some narrow group with which one identifies. A paradigm of a person who lacks humility is the self-important emperor who grants status to his family because it is *his*, to his subordinates because *he* appointed them, and to his country because *he* chooses to glorify it. Less extreme but still lacking proper humility is the elitist who counts events significant solely in proportion to how they affect his class. The suspicion about those who would destroy the environment, then, is that what they count important is too narrowly confined insofar as it encompasses only what affects beings who, like us, are capable of feeling.

This idea that proper humility requires recognition of the importance of nonsentient nature is similar to the thought of those who charge meat eaters with "species-ism." In both cases it is felt that people too narrowly confine their concerns to the sorts of beings that are most like them. But, however intuitively appealing, the idea will surely arouse objections from our nonenvironmentalist critic. "Why," he will ask, "do you suppose that the sort of humility I *should* have requires me to acknowledge the importance of nonsentient nature aside from its utility? You cannot, by your own admission, argue that nonsentient nature *is* important, appealing to religious or intuitionist grounds. And simply to assert, without further argument, that an ideal humility requires us to view nonsentient nature as important for its own sake begs the question at issue. If proper humility is acknowledging the relative importance of things as one should, then to show that I must lack this you must first establish that one *should* acknowledge the importance of nonsentient nature."

Though some may wish to accept this challenge, there are other ways to pursue the connection between humility and response to nonsentient nature. For example, suppose we grant that proper humility requires only acknowledging a due status to sentient beings. We must admit, then, that it is logically possible for a person to be properly humble even though he viewed all nonsentient nature simply as a resource. But this logical possibility may be a psychological rarity. It may be that, given the sort of beings we are, we would never learn humility before persons without develop-ing the general capacity to cherish, and regard important, many things for their own sakes. The major obstacle to humility before persons is self-importance, a tendency to measure the significance of everything by its relation to oneself and those with whom one identifies. The processes by which we overcome self-importance are doubtless many and complex, but it seems unlikely that they are exclusively concerned with how we relate to other people and animals. Learning humility requires learning to feel that something matters besides what will affect oneself and one's circle of associates. What leads a child to care about what happens to a lost hamster or a stray dog he will not see again is likely also to generate concern for a lost toy or a favorite tree where he used to live. Learning to value things for their own sake, and to count what affects them important aside from their utility, . . . is necessary to the development of humility and it seems likely to take place in experiences with nonsentient nature as well as with people and animals. If a person views all nonsentient nature merely as a resource, then it seems unlikely that he has developed the capacity needed to overcome self-importance.

IV

This last argument, unfortunately, has its limits. It presupposes an empirical connection between experiencing nature and overcoming self-importance, and this may be challenged. Even if experiencing nature promotes humility before others, there may be other ways people can develop such humility in a world of concrete, glass, and plastic. If not, perhaps all that is needed is limited experience of nature in one's early, developing years; mature adults, having overcome youthful self-importance, may live well enough in arti-ficial surroundings. More importantly, the argument does not fully cap-ture the spirit of the intuition that an ideal person stands humbly before nature. That idea is not simply that experiencing nature tends to foster proper humility before other people; it is, in part, that natural surroundings encourage and are appropriate to an ideal sense of oneself as part of the natural world. Standing alone in the forest, after months in the city, is not merely good as a means of curbing one's arrogance before others; it rein-forces and fittingly expresses one's acceptance of oneself as a natural being.

Previously we considered only one aspect of proper humility, namely, a sense of one's relative importance with respect to other human beings.

Another aspect, I think, is a kind of *self-acceptance*. This involves acknowl-edging, in more than a merely intellectual way, that we are the sort of crea-tures that we are. Whether one is self-accepting is not so much a matter of how one attributes *importance* comparatively to oneself, other people, animals, plants, and other things as it is a matter of understanding, facing squarely, and responding appropriately to who and what one is, e.g., one's powers and limits, one's affinities with other beings and differences from them, one's unalterable nature and one's freedom to change. Self-acceptance is not merely intellectual awareness, for one can be intellectually aware that one is growing old and will eventually die while nevertheless behaving in a thousand foolish ways that reflect a refusal to acknowledge these facts. On the other hand, self-acceptance is not passive resignation, for refusal to pursue what one truly wants within one's limits is a failure to accept the freedom and power one has. Particular behaviors, like dying one's gray hair and dressing like those twenty years younger, do not *necessarily* imply lack of self-acceptance, for there could be reasons for acting in these ways other than the wish to hide from oneself what one really is. One fails to accept oneself when the patterns of behavior and emotion are rooted in a desire to disown and deny features of oneself, to pretend to oneself that they are not there. This is not to say that a self-accepting person makes no value judgments about himself, that he likes all facts about himself, wants equally to develop and display them; he can, and should feel remorse for his past misdeeds and strive to change his current vices. The point is that he does not disown them, pretend that they do not exist or are facts about something other than himself. Such pretense is incompatible with proper humility because it is seeing oneself as better than one is.

Self-acceptance of this sort has long been considered a human excel-lence, under various names, but what has it to do with preserving nature? There is, I think, the following connection. As human beings we are part of nature, living, growing, declining, and dying by natural laws similar to those governing other living beings; despite our awesomely distinc-tive human powers, we share many of the needs, limits, and liabilities of animals and plants. These facts are neither good nor bad in them-selves, aside from personal preference and varying conventional values. To say this is to utter a truism which few will deny, but to accept these facts, as facts about oneself, is not so easy—or so common. Much of what naturalists deplore about our increasingly artificial world reflects, and encourages, a denial of these facts, an unwillingness to avow them with equanimity. . . .

My suggestion is not merely that experiencing nature causally promotes such self-acceptance, but also that those who fully accept themselves as part of the natural world lack the common drive to disassociate themselves from nature by replacing natural environments with artificial ones. A storm in the wilds helps us to appreciate our animal vulnerability, but, equally important, the reluctance to experience it may *reflect* an unwillingness to accept this aspect of ourselves. The person who is too ready to destroy the ancient redwoods may lack humility, not so much in the sense that he exaggerates his importance relative to others, but rather in the sense that he tries to avoid seeing himself as one among many natural creatures.

V

My suggestion so far has been that, though indifference to nonsentient nature is not itself a moral vice, it is likely to reflect either ignorance, a self-importance, or a lack of self-acceptance which we must overcome to have proper humility. A similar idea might be developed connecting attitudes toward nonsentient nature with other human excellences. For example, one might argue that indifference to nature reveals a lack of either an aesthetic sense or some of the natural roots of gratitude.

When we see a hillside that has been gutted by strip miners or the garden replaced by asphalt, our first reaction is probably, "How ugly!" The scenes assault our aesthetic sensibilities. We suspect that no one with a keen sense of beauty could have left such a sight. Admittedly not everything in nature strikes us as beautiful, or even aesthetically interesting, and sometimes a natural scene is replaced with a more impressive architectural masterpiece. But this is not usually the situation in the problem cases which environmentalists are most concerned about. More often beauty is replaced with ugliness.

At this point our critic may well object that, even if he does lack a sense of beauty, this is no moral vice. His cost/benefit calculations take into account the pleasure others may derive from seeing the forests, etc., and so why should he be faulted?

Some might reply that, despite contrary philosophical traditions, aesthetics and morality are not so distinct as commonly supposed. Appreciation of beauty, they may argue, is a human excellence which morally ideal persons should try to develop. But, setting aside this controversial position, there still may be cause for moral concern about those who have no aesthetic response to nature. Even if aesthetic sensibility is not itself

a moral virtue, many of the capacities of mind and heart which it presupposes may be ones which are also needed for an appreciation of other
people. Consider, for example, curiosity, a mind open to novelty, the ability to look at things from unfamiliar perspectives, empathetic imagination, interest in details, variety, and order, and emotional freedom from
the immediate and the practical. All these, and more, seem necessary to
aesthetic sensibility, but they are also traits which a person needs to be
fully sensitive to people of all sorts. The point is not that a moral person
must be able to distinguish beautiful from ugly people; the point is rather
that unresponsiveness to what is beautiful, awesome, dainty, dumpy, and
otherwise aesthetically interesting in nature probably reflects a lack of the
openness of mind and spirit necessary to appreciate the best in human
beings.

The anti-environmentalist, however, may refuse to accept the charge
that he lacks aesthetic sensibility. If he claims to appreciate seventeenth-
century miniature portraits, but to abhor natural wildernesses, he will
hardly be convincing. Tastes vary, but aesthetic sense is not *that* selective.
He may, instead, insist that he *does* appreciate natural beauty. He spends
his vacations, let us suppose, hiking in the Sierras, photographing wild-
flowers, and so on. He might press his argument as follows: "I enjoy natural beauty as much as anyone, but I fail to see what this has to do with
preserving the environment independently of human enjoyment and use.
Nonsentient nature is a resource, but one of its best uses is to give us pleasure. I take this into account when I calculate the costs and benefits of preserving a park, planting a garden, and so on. But the problem you raised
explicitly set aside the desire to preserve nature as a means to enjoyment.
I say, let us enjoy nature fully while we can, but if all sentient beings were
to die tomorrow, we might as well blow up all plant life as well. A redwood
grove that no one can use or enjoy is utterly worthless."

The attitude expressed here, I suspect, is not a common one, but it represents a philosophical challenge. The beginnings of a reply may be found
in the following. When a person takes joy in something, it is a common
(and perhaps natural) response to come to cherish it. To cherish something is not simply to be happy with it at the moment, but to care for it for
its own sake. This is not to say that one necessarily sees it as having feelings
and so wants it to feel good; nor does it imply that one judges the thing to
have Moore's intrinsic value. One simply wants the thing to survive and
(when appropriate) to thrive, and not simply for its utility. We see this

attitude repeatedly regarding mementos. They are not simply valued as a means to remind us of happy occasions; they come to be valued for their own sake. Thus, if someone really took joy in the natural environment, but was prepared to blow it up as soon as sentient life ended, he would lack this common human tendency to cherish what enriches our lives. While this response is not itself a moral virtue, it may be a natural basis of the virtue we call "gratitude." People who have no tendency to cherish things that give them pleasure may be poorly disposed to respond gratefully to persons who are good to them. Again the connection is not one of logical necessity, but it may nevertheless be important. A nonreligious person unable to "thank" anyone for the beauties of nature may nevertheless feel "grateful" in a sense; and I suspect that the person who feels no such "gratitude" toward nature is unlikely to show proper gratitude toward people.

Suppose these conjectures prove to be true. One may wonder what is the point of considering them. Is it to disparage all those who view nature merely as a resource? To do so, it seems, would be unfair, for, even if this attitude typically stems from deficiencies which affect one's attitudes toward sentient beings, there may be exceptions and we have not shown that their view of nonsentient nature is itself blameworthy. But when we set aside questions of blame and inquire what sorts of human traits we want to encourage, our reflections become relevant in a more positive way. The point is not to insinuate that all anti-environmentalists are defective, but to see that those who value such traits as humility, gratitude, and sensitivity to others have reason to promote the love of nature.

Thomas Hill, Jr.: Ideals of Human Excellence and Preserving Natural Environments

1. Why does Hill think it is sometimes difficult to explain what is wrong with destroying the environment in terms of rights and welfare? What alternative framework does he propose for looking at the issue?
2. Hill presents several examples of acts which may not necessarily be immoral, but which would clearly reveal a defect in any person who performed them. Do you find his examples convincing? Is harming the environment relevantly similar to these actions?
3. Hill suggests that many environmentally destructive actions might be performed as a result of ignorance. How does he argue for this claim, and how might an "anti-environmentalist" respond?

4. What exactly is *humility*, and why does Hill claim that those who are unmoved by nature lack it? Do you agree with him?
5. What connection, if any, is there between self-acceptance and preserving nature? Can a person fully accept himself or herself while at the same time destroying natural environments?

28

A Defense of Abortion

Judith Jarvis Thomson

....

In this article, Judith Thomson does what very few pro-choice advocates have been willing to do—namely, to grant, for the purposes of argument, that the fetus is as much a moral person as you or I. Still, she argues, being a person does not, by itself, entitle you to use someone else's resources, even if those resources are needed in order to preserve your life. Thus even if we grant that the fetus is a person, that is not enough to show that the fetus is entitled to the continued use of the mother's "resources" (her body). A pregnant woman has a right to bodily autonomy, and that right, in many cases, morally prevails over any rights possessed by a fetus.

Thomson uses a number of thought experiments to defend this claim. The most famous of these involves a world-class violinist. Suppose that you wake up one morning and find yourself connected to a transfusion machine that is providing life support for this musician. He surely has a right to life. But Thomson says that you would be within your rights to remove yourself from the apparatus—even knowing that, by doing this, he will die. The violinist, of course, is meant to be a stand-in for the fetus. According to Thomson, although it would be awfully nice of pregnant women to continue carrying their fetuses to term, they are not usually morally required to do so.

Judith Jarvis Thomson, "A Defense of Abortion" from *Philosophy and Public Affairs* 1 (1971), pp. 47–66. Copyright © 1971 *Philosophy and Public Affairs*. Reproduced with permission of Blackwell Publishing Ltd.

Thomson anticipates a variety of objections to this example, and provides further examples to support her view that women usually have a moral right to seek and obtain an abortion.

....

Most opposition to abortion relies on the premise that the fetus is a human being, a person, from the moment of conception. The premise is argued for, but, as I think, not well. Take, for example, the most common argument. We are asked to notice that the development of a human being from conception through birth into childhood is continuous; then it is said that to draw a line, to choose a point in this development and say "before this point the thing is not a person, after this point it is a person" is to make an arbitrary choice, a choice for which in the nature of things no good reason can be given. It is concluded that the fetus is, or anyway that we had better say it is, a person from the moment of conception. But this conclusion does not follow. Similar things might be said about the development of an acorn into an oak tree, and it does not follow that acorns are oak trees, or that we had better say they are. Arguments of this form are sometimes called "slippery slope arguments"—the phrase is perhaps self-explanatory—and it is dismaying that opponents of abortion rely on them so heavily and uncritically.

I am inclined to agree, however, that the prospects for "drawing a line" in the development of the fetus look dim. I am inclined to think also that we shall probably have to agree that the fetus has already become a human person well before birth. Indeed, it comes as a surprise when one first learns how early in its life it begins to acquire human characteristics. By the tenth week, for example, it already has a face, arms and legs, fingers and toes; it has internal organs, and brain activity is detectable. On the other hand, I think that the premise is false, that the fetus is not a person from the moment of conception. A newly fertilized ovum, a newly implanted clump of cells, is no more a person than an acorn is an oak tree. But I shall not discuss any of this. For it seems to me to be of great interest to ask what happens if, for the sake of argument, we allow the premise. How, precisely, are we supposed to get from there to the conclusion that abortion is morally impermissible? Opponents of abortion commonly spend most of their time establishing that the fetus is a person, and hardly any time explaining the step from there to the impermissibility of abortion. Perhaps they think the step too simple and obvious to require much comment. Or perhaps instead they are simply being economical in argument. Many of those who defend abortion rely on the premise that the fetus is not a person, but only a bit of tissue that will become a person at birth; and why pay out more arguments than you have to? Whatever the explanation, I suggest that the step they take is neither easy nor obvious, that it calls for closer examination than it is commonly given, and that when we do give it this closer examination we shall feel inclined to reject it.

I propose, then, that we grant that the fetus is a person from the moment of conception. How does the argument go from here? Something like this, I take it. Every person has a right to life. So the fetus has a right to life. No doubt the mother has a right to decide what shall happen in and to her body; everyone would grant that. But surely a person's right to life is stronger and more stringent than the mother's right to decide what happens in and to her body, and so outweighs it. So the fetus may not be killed; an abortion may not be performed.

It sounds plausible. But now let me ask you to imagine this. You wake up in the morning and find yourself back to back in bed with an unconscious violinist. A famous unconscious violinist. He has been found to have a fatal kidney ailment, and the Society of Music Lovers has canvassed all the available medical records and found that you alone have the right blood type to help. They have therefore kidnapped you, and last night the violinist's circulatory system was plugged into yours, so that your kidneys can be used to extract poisons from his blood as well as your own. The director of the hospital now tells you, "Look, we're sorry the Society of Music Lovers did this to you—we would never have permitted it if we had known. But still, they did it, and the violinist now is plugged into you. To unplug you would be to kill him. But never mind, it's only for nine months. By then he will have recovered from his ailment, and can safely be unplugged from you." Is it morally incumbent on you to accede to this situation? No doubt it would be very nice of you if you did, a great kindness. But do you *have* to accede to it? What if it were not nine months, but nine years? Or longer still? What if the director of the hospital says, "Tough luck, I agree, but you've now got to stay in bed, with the violinist plugged into you, for the rest of your life. Because remember this. All persons have a right to life, and violinists are persons. Granted you have a right to decide what happens in and to your body, but a person's right to life outweighs your right to decide what happens in and to your body. So you cannot ever be unplugged from him." I imagine you would regard this as outrageous, which suggests that something really is wrong with that plausible-sounding argument I mentioned a moment ago.

In this case, of course, you were kidnapped; you didn't volunteer for the operation that plugged the violinist into your kidneys. Can those who oppose abortion on the ground I mentioned make an exception for a pregnancy due to rape? Certainly. They can say that persons have a right to life only if they didn't come into existence because of rape; or they can say that all persons have a right to life, but that some have less of a right to life than others, in particular, that those who came into existence because of rape have less. But these statements have a rather unpleasant sound. Surely the question of whether you have a right to life at all, or how much of it you have, shouldn't turn on the question of whether or not you are the product of a rape. And in fact the people who oppose abortion on the ground I mentioned do not make this distinction, and hence do not make an exception in case of rape.

Nor do they make an exception for a case in which the mother has to spend the nine months of her pregnancy in bed. They would agree that would be a great pity, and hard on the mother; but all the same, all persons have a right to life, the fetus is a person, and so on. I suspect, in fact, that they would not make an exception for a case in which, miraculously enough, the pregnancy went on for nine years, or even the rest of the mother's life.

Some won't even make an exception for a case in which continuation of the pregnancy is likely to shorten the mother's life; they regard abortion as impermissible even to save the mother's life. Such cases are nowadays very rare, and many opponents of abortion do not accept this extreme view. All the same, it is a good place to begin: a number of points of interest come out in respect to it.

1. Let us call the view that abortion is impermissible even to save the mother's life "the extreme view." I want to suggest first that it does not issue from the argument I mentioned earlier without the addition of some fairly powerful premises. Suppose a woman has become pregnant, and now learns that she has a cardiac condition such that she will die if she carries the baby to term. What may be done for her? The fetus, being a person, has a right to life, but as the mother is a person too, so has she a right to life. Presumably they have an equal right to life. How is it supposed to come out that an abortion may not be performed? If mother and child have an equal right to life, shouldn't we perhaps flip a coin? Or should we add to the mother's right to life her right to decide what happens in and

to her body, which everybody seems to be ready to grant—the sum of her rights now outweighing the fetus' right to life?

The most familiar argument here is the following. We are told that performing the abortion would be directly killing[1] the child, whereas doing nothing would not be killing the mother, but only letting her die. Moreover, in killing the child, one would be killing an innocent person, for the child has committed no crime, and is not aiming at his mother's death. And then there are a variety of ways in which this might be continued. (1) But as directly killing an innocent person is always and absolutely impermissible, an abortion may not be performed. Or, (2) as directly killing an innocent person is murder, and murder is always and absolutely impermissible, an abortion may not be performed. Or, (3) as one's duty to refrain from directly killing an innocent person is more stringent than one's duty to keep a person from dying, an abortion may not be performed. Or, (4) if one's only options are directly killing an innocent person or letting a person die, one must prefer letting the person die, and thus an abortion may not be performed.

Some people seem to have thought that these are not further premises which must be added if the conclusion is to be reached, but that they follow from the very fact that an innocent person has a right to life. But this seems to me to be a mistake, and perhaps the simplest way to show this is to bring out that while we must certainly grant that innocent persons have a right to life, the theses in (1) through (4) are all false. Take (2), for example. If directly killing an innocent person is murder, and thus is impermissible, then the mother's directly killing the innocent person inside her is murder, and thus is impermissible. But it cannot seriously be thought to be murder if the mother performs an abortion on herself to save her life. It cannot seriously be said that she *must* refrain, that she *must* sit passively by and wait for her death. Let us look again at the case of you and the violinist. There you are, in bed with the violinist, and the director of the hospital says to you, "It's all most distressing, and I deeply sympathize, but you see this is putting an additional strain on your kidneys, and you'll be dead within the month. But you *have* to stay where you are all the same. Because unplugging you would be directly killing an innocent violinist, and that's murder, and that's impermissible." If anything in the

---

1. The term "direct" in the arguments I refer to is a technical one. Roughly, what is meant by "direct killing" is either killing as an end in itself, or killing as a means to some end, for example, the end of saving someone else's life.

world is true, it is that you do not commit murder, you do not do what is impermissible, if you reach around to your back and unplug yourself from that violinist to save your life.

The main focus of attention in writings on abortion has been on what a third party may or may not do in answer to a request from a woman for an abortion. This is in a way understandable. Things being as they are, there isn't much a woman can safely do to abort herself. So the question asked is what a third party may do, and what the mother may do, if it is mentioned at all, is deduced, almost as an afterthought, from what it is concluded that third parties may do. But it seems to me that to treat the matter in this way is to refuse to grant to the mother that very status of person which is so firmly insisted on for the fetus. For we cannot simply read off what a person may do from what a third party may do. Suppose you find yourself trapped in a tiny house with a growing child. I mean a very tiny house, and a rapidly growing child—you are already up against the wall of the house and in a few minutes you'll be crushed to death. The child on the other hand won't be crushed to death; if nothing is done to stop him from growing he'll be hurt, but in the end he'll simply burst open the house and walk out a free man. Now I could well understand it if a bystander were to say, "There's nothing we can do for you. We cannot choose between your life and his, we cannot be the ones to decide who is to live, we cannot intervene." But it cannot be concluded that you too can do nothing, that you cannot attack it to save your life. However innocent the child may be, you do not have to wait passively while it crushes you to death. Perhaps a pregnant woman is vaguely felt to have the status of house, to which we don't allow the right of self-defense. But if the woman houses the child, it should be remembered that she is a person who houses it.

I should perhaps stop to say explicitly that I am not claiming that people have a right to do anything whatever to save their lives. I think, rather, that there are drastic limits to the right of self-defense. If someone threatens you with death unless you torture someone else to death, I think you have not the right, even to save your life, to do so. But the case under consideration here is very different. In our case there are only two people involved, one whose life is threatened, and one who threatens it. Both are innocent: the one who is threatened is not threatened because of any fault, the one who threatens does not threaten because of any fault. For this reason we may feel that we bystanders cannot intervene. But the person threatened can.

In sum, a woman surely can defend her life against the threat to it posed by the unborn child, even if doing so involves its death. And this shows not merely that the theses in (1) through (4) are false; it shows also that the extreme view of abortion is false, and so we need not canvass any other possible ways of arriving at it from the argument I mentioned at the outset.

2. The extreme view could of course be weakened to say that while abortion is permissible to save the mother's life, it may not be performed by a third party, but only by the mother herself. But this cannot be right either. For what we have to keep in mind is that the mother and the unborn child are not like two tenants in a small house which has, by an unfortunate mistake, been rented to both: the mother *owns* the house. The fact that she does adds to the offensiveness of deducing that the mother can do nothing from the supposition that third parties can do nothing. But it does more than this: it casts a bright light on the supposition that third parties can do nothing. Certainly it lets us see that a third party who says "I cannot choose between you" is fooling himself if he thinks this is impartiality. If Jones has found and fastened on a certain coat, which he needs to keep him from freezing, but which Smith also needs to keep him from freezing, then it is not impartiality that says "I cannot choose between you" when Smith owns the coat. Women have said again and again "This body is *my* body!" and they have reason to feel angry, reason to feel that it has been like shouting into the wind. . . .

3. Where the mother's life is not at stake, the argument I mentioned at the outset seems to have a much stronger pull. "Everyone has a right to life, so the unborn person has a right to life." And isn't the child's right to life weightier than anything other than the mother's own right to life, which she might put forward as ground for an abortion?

This argument treats the right to life as if it were unproblematic. It is not, and this seems to me to be precisely the source of the mistake.

For we should now, at long last, ask what it comes to, to have a right to life. In some views having a right to life includes having a right to be given at least the bare minimum one needs for continued life. But suppose that what in fact *is* the bare minimum a man needs for continued life is something he has no right at all to be given? If I am sick unto death, and the only thing that will save my life is the touch of Henry Fonda's cool hand on my fevered brow, then all the same, I have no right to be given the touch of Henry Fonda's cool hand on my fevered brow. It would be frightfully nice of him to fly in from the West Coast to provide it. It would be less nice, though no doubt well meant, if my friends flew out to the West Coast and carried Henry Fonda back with them. But I have no right at all against anybody that he should do this for me. Or again, to return to the story I told earlier, the fact that for continued life that violinist needs the continued use of your kidneys does not establish that he has a right to be given the continued use of your kidneys. He certainly has no right against you that *you* should give him continued use of your kidneys. For nobody has any right to use your kidneys unless you give him such a right; and nobody has the right against you that you shall give him this right—if you do allow him to go on using your kidneys, this is a kindness on your part, and not something he can claim from you as his due. Nor has he any right against anybody else that *they* should give him continued use of your kidneys. Certainly he had no right against the Society of Music Lovers that they should plug him into you in the first place. And if you now start to unplug yourself, having learned that you will otherwise have to spend nine years in bed with him, there is nobody in the world who must try to prevent you, in order to see to it that he is given something he has a right to be given.

Some people are rather stricter about the right to life. In their view, it does not include the right to be given anything, but amounts to, and only to, the right not to be killed by anybody. But here a related difficulty arises. If everybody is to refrain from killing that violinist, then everybody must refrain from doing a great many different sorts of things. Everybody must refrain from slitting his throat, everybody must refrain from shooting him—and everybody must refrain from unplugging you from him. But does he have a right against everybody that they shall refrain from unplugging you from him? To refrain from doing this is to allow him to continue to use your kidneys. It could be argued that he has a right against us that *we* should allow him to continue to use your kidneys. That is, while he had no right against us that we should give him the use of your kidneys, it might be argued that he anyway has a right against us that we shall not now intervene and deprive him of the use of your kidneys. I shall come back to third-party interventions later. But certainly the violinist has no right against you that *you* shall allow him to continue to use your kidneys. As I said, if you do allow him to use them, it is a kindness on your part, and not something you owe him.

The difficulty I point to here is not peculiar to the right to life. It reappears in connection with all the other natural rights; and it is something which an adequate account of rights must deal with. For present purposes it is enough just to draw attention to it. But I would stress that I am not arguing that people do not have a right to life—quite to the contrary, it seems to me that the primary control we must place on the acceptability of an account of rights is that it should turn out in that account to be a truth that all persons have a right to life. I am arguing only that having a right to life does not guarantee having either a right to be given the use of or a right to be allowed continued use of another person's body—even if one needs it for life itself. So the right to life will not serve the opponents of abortion in the very simple and clear way in which they seem to have thought it would.

4. There is another way to bring out the difficulty. In the most ordinary sort of case, to deprive someone of what he has a right to is to treat him unjustly. Suppose a boy and his small brother are jointly given a box of chocolates for Christmas. If the older boy takes the box and refuses to give his brother any of the chocolates, he is unjust to him, for the brother has been given a right to half of them. But suppose that, having learned that otherwise it means nine years in bed with that violinist, you unplug yourself from him. You surely are not being unjust to him, for you gave him no right to use your kidneys, and no one else can have given him any such right. But we have to notice that in unplugging yourself, you are killing him; and violinists, like everybody else, have a right to life, and thus in the view we were considering just now, the right not to be killed. So here you do what he supposedly has a right you shall not do, but you do not act unjustly to him in doing it.

The emendation which may be made at this point is this: the right to life consists not in the right not to be killed, but rather in the right not to be killed unjustly. This runs a risk of circularity, but never mind: it would enable us to square the fact that the violinist has a right to life with the fact that you do not act unjustly toward him in unplugging yourself, thereby killing him. For if you do not kill him unjustly, you do not violate his right to life, and so it is no wonder you do him no injustice.

But if this emendation is accepted, the gap in the argument against abortion stares us plainly in the face: it is by no means enough to show that the fetus is a person, and to remind us that all persons have a right to life—we need to be shown also that killing the fetus violates its right to life, i.e., that abortion is unjust killing. And is it?

I suppose we may take it as a datum that in a case of pregnancy due to rape the mother has not given the unborn person a right to the use of her body for food and shelter. Indeed, in what pregnancy could it be supposed that the mother has given the unborn person such a right? It is not as if there were unborn persons drifting about the world, to whom a woman who wants a child says "I invite you in."

But it might be argued that there are other ways one can have acquired a right to the use of another person's body than by having been invited to use it by that person. Suppose a woman voluntarily indulges in intercourse, knowing of the chance it will issue in pregnancy, and then she does become pregnant; is she not in part responsible for the presence, in fact the very existence, of the unborn person inside her? No doubt she did not invite it in. But doesn't her partial responsibility for its being there itself give it a right to the use of her body? If so, then her aborting it would be more like the boy's taking away the chocolates, and less like your unplugging yourself from the violinist—doing so would be depriving it of what it does have a right to, and thus would be doing it an injustice.

And then, too, it might be asked whether or not she can kill it even to save her own life: If she voluntarily called it into existence, how can she now kill it, even in self-defense?

The first thing to be said about this is that it is something new. Opponents of abortion have been so concerned to make out the independence of the fetus, in order to establish that it has a right to life, just as its mother does, that they have tended to overlook the possible support they might gain from making out that the fetus is *dependent* on the mother, in order to establish that she has a special kind of responsibility for it, a responsibility that gives it rights against her which are not possessed by any independent person—such as an ailing violinist who is a stranger to her.

On the other hand, this argument would give the unborn person a right to its mother's body only if her pregnancy resulted from a voluntary act, undertaken in full knowledge of the chance a pregnancy might result from it. It would leave out entirely the unborn person whose existence is due to rape. Pending the availability of some further argument, then, we would be left with the conclusion that unborn persons whose existence is due to rape have no right to the use of their mothers' bodies, and thus that aborting them is not depriving them of anything they have a right to and hence is not unjust killing.

And we should also notice that it is not at all plain that this argument really does go even as far as it purports to. For there are cases and cases, and the details make a difference. If the room is stuffy, and I therefore open a window to air it, and a burglar climbs in, it would be absurd to say, "Ah, now he can stay, she's given him a right to the use of her house—for she is partially responsible for his presence there, having voluntarily done what enabled him to get in, in full knowledge that there are such things as burglars, and that burglars burgle." It would be still more absurd to say this if I had had bars installed outside my windows, precisely to prevent burglars from getting in, and a burglar got in only because of a defect in the bars. It remains equally absurd if we imagine it is not a burglar who climbs in, but an innocent person who blunders or falls in. Again, suppose it were like this: people-seeds drift about in the air like pollen, and if you open your windows, one may drift in and take root in your carpets or upholstery. You don't want children, so you fix up your windows with fine mesh screens, the very best you can buy. As can happen, however, and on very, very rare occasions does happen, one of the screens is defective; and a seed drifts in and takes root. Does the person-plant who now develops have a right to the use of your house? Surely not—despite the fact that you voluntarily opened your windows, you knowingly kept carpets and upholstered furniture, and you knew that screens were sometimes defective. Someone may argue that you are responsible for its rooting, that it does have a right to your house, because after all you *could* have lived out your life with bare floors and furniture, or with sealed windows and doors. But this won't do—for by the same token anyone can avoid a pregnancy due to rape by having a hysterectomy, or anyway by never leaving home without a (reliable!) army.

It seems to me that the argument we are looking at can establish at most that there are *some* cases in which the unborn person has a right to the use of its mother's body, and therefore *some* cases in which abortion is unjust killing. There is room for much discussion and argument as to precisely which, if any. But I think we should sidestep this issue and leave it open, for at any rate the argument certainly does not establish that all abortion is unjust killing.

5. There is room for yet another argument here, however. We surely must all grant that there may be cases in which it would be morally indecent to detach a person from your body at the cost of his life. Suppose you learn that what the violinist needs is not nine years of your life, but only one hour: all you need do to save his life is to spend one hour in that bed with him. Suppose also that letting him use your kidneys for that one hour would not affect your health in the slightest. Admittedly you were kidnapped. Admittedly you did not give anyone permission to plug him into you. Nevertheless it seems to me plain you *ought* to allow him to use your kidneys for that hour—it would be indecent to refuse.

Again, suppose pregnancy lasted only an hour, and constituted no threat to life or health. And suppose that a woman becomes pregnant as a result of rape. Admittedly she did not voluntarily do anything to bring about the existence of a child. Admittedly she did nothing at all which would give the unborn person a right to the use of her body. All the same it might well be said, as in the newly emended violinist story, that she *ought* to allow it to remain for that hour—that it would be indecent in her to refuse. . . .

6. My argument will be found unsatisfactory on two counts by many of those who want to regard abortion as morally permissible. First, while I do argue that abortion is not impermissible, I do not argue that it is always permissible. There may well be cases in which carrying the child to term requires only Minimally Decent Samaritanism[2] of the mother, and this is a standard we must not fall below. I am inclined to think it a merit of my account precisely that it does *not* give a general yes or a general no. It allows for and supports our sense that, for example, a sick and desperately frightened fourteen-year-old schoolgirl, pregnant due to rape, may *of course* choose abortion, and that any law which rules this out is an insane law. And it also allows for and supports our sense that in other cases resort to abortion is even positively indecent. It would be indecent in the woman to request an abortion, and indecent in a doctor to perform it, if she is in her seventh month, and wants the abortion just to avoid the nuisance of postponing a trip abroad. The very fact that the arguments I have been drawing attention to treat all cases of abortion, or even all cases of abortion in which the mother's life is not at stake, as morally on a par ought to have made them suspect at the outset.

Secondly, while I am arguing for the permissibility of abortion in some cases, I am not arguing for the right to secure the death of the unborn child. It is easy to confuse these two things in that up to a certain point in the life of the fetus it is not able to survive outside the mother's body; hence removing it from her body guarantees its death. But they are importantly different. I have argued that you are not morally required to spend nine months in bed, sustaining the life of that violinist; but to say this is by no means to say that if, when you unplug yourself, there is a miracle and he survives, you then have a right to turn round and slit his throat. You may detach yourself even if this costs him his life; you have no right to be guaranteed his death, by some other means, if unplugging yourself does not kill him. There are some people who will feel dissatisfied by this feature of my argument. A woman may be utterly devastated by the thought

---

2. Meeting a standard of minimally decent treatment towards those in need.—Ed.

of a child, a bit of herself, put out for adoption and never seen or heard of again. She may therefore want not merely that the child be detached from her, but more, that it die. Some opponents of abortion are inclined to regard this as beneath contempt—thereby showing insensitivity to what is surely a powerful source of despair. All the same, I agree that the desire for the child's death is not one which anybody may gratify, should it turn out to be possible to detach the child alive.

At this place, however, it should be remembered that we have only been pretending throughout that the fetus is a human being from the moment of conception. A very early abortion is surely not the killing of a person, and so is not dealt with by anything I have said here.

Judith Jarvis Thomson: A Defense of Abortion

1. Thomson's first thought experiment is the case of the violinist. Do you agree that it would be permissible to unplug yourself from the violinist? What conclusions about abortion should we draw from this thought experiment?
2. What is the "extreme view"? What are Thomson's objections to the view? Do you find her objections compelling?
3. Thomson claims that the notion of a "right to life" cannot be interpreted as a right to "the bare minimum one needs for continued life." Why does she claim this? What, according to Thomson, does having a right to life amount to? Do you agree with her about this?
4. Why doesn't Thomson think that abortion always involves unjust killing? What does the justice of abortion depend on, according to Thomson?
5. Under what conditions (if any) do you think a woman grants a fetus the right to use her body?

29

Why Abortion Is Immoral

Don Marquis

In this article, Don Marquis argues, from entirely secular premises, to the conclusion that abortion is, in most circumstances, a form of murder. He does this by first trying to explain why it is immoral to kill people like you and me. After canvassing a few popular but mistaken options, he arrives at his answer. Such killing is immoral because it deprives us of a future of value.

Human fetuses—most of them, at least—also share this feature. And therefore it is ordinarily wrong to kill human fetuses. And so abortion is usually immoral. Marquis considers a variety of objections to his view, and concludes his article by trying to show how each of them can be met.

T he view that abortion is, with rare exceptions, seriously immoral has received little support in the recent philosophical literature. No doubt most philosophers affiliated with secular institutions of higher education believe that the anti-abortion position is either a symptom of irrational religious dogma or a conclusion generated by seriously confused philosophical argument. The purpose of this essay is to undermine this general belief. This essay sets out an argument that purports to

Don Marquis, "Why Abortion Is Immoral" from *Journal of Philosophy* 86 (1989), pp. 183–202. Used by permission of Don Marquis and *The Journal of Philosophy*.

show, as well as any argument in ethics can show, that abortion is, except possibly in rare cases, seriously immoral, that it is in the same moral category as killing an innocent adult human being. . . .

I.

A sketch of standard anti-abortion and pro-choice arguments exhibits how those arguments possess certain symmetries that explain why partisans of those positions are so convinced of the correctness of their own positions, why they are not successful in convincing their opponents, and why, to others, this issue seems to be unresolvable. An analysis of the nature of this standoff suggests a strategy for surmounting it.

Consider the way a typical anti-abortionist argues. She will argue or assert that life is present from the moment of conception or that fetuses look like babies or that fetuses possess a characteristic such as a genetic code that is both necessary and sufficient for being human. Anti-abortionists seem to believe that (1) the truth of all of these claims is quite obvious, and (2) establishing any of these claims is sufficient to show that abortion is morally akin to murder.

A standard pro-choice strategy exhibits similarities. The pro-choicer will argue or assert that fetuses are not persons or that fetuses are not rational agents or that fetuses are not social beings. Pro-choicers seem to believe that (1) the truth of any of these claims is quite obvious, and (2) establishing any of these claims is sufficient to show that an abortion is not a wrongful killing.

In fact, both the pro-choice and the anti-abortion claims do seem to be true, although the "it looks like a baby" claim is more difficult to establish the earlier the pregnancy. We seem to have a standoff. How can it be resolved?

As everyone who has taken a bit of logic knows, if any of these arguments concerning abortion is a good argument, it requires not only some claim characterizing fetuses, but also some general moral principle that ties a characteristic of fetuses to having or not having the right to life or to some other moral characteristic that will generate the obligation or the lack of obligation not to end the life of a fetus. Accordingly, the arguments of the anti-abortionist and the pro-choicer need a bit of filling in to be regarded as adequate.

Note what each partisan will say. The anti-abortionist will claim that her position is supported by such generally accepted moral principles as "It is always prima facie seriously wrong to take a human life" or "It is always prima facie seriously wrong to end the life of a baby." Since these are generally accepted moral principles, her position is certainly not obviously wrong. The pro-choicer will claim that her position is supported by such plausible moral principles as "Being a person is what gives an individual intrinsic moral worth" or "It is only seriously prima facie wrong to take the life of a member of the human community." Since these are generally accepted moral principles, the pro-choice position is certainly not obviously wrong. Unfortunately, we have again arrived at a standoff.

Now, how might one deal with this standoff? The standard approach is to try to show how the moral principles of one's opponent lose their plausibility under analysis. It is easy to see how this is possible. On the one hand, the anti-abortionist will defend a moral principle concerning the wrongness of killing which tends to be broad in scope in order that even fetuses at an early stage of pregnancy will fall under it. The problem with broad principles is that they often embrace too much. In this particular instance, the principle "It is always prima facie wrong to take a human life" seems to entail that it is wrong to end the existence of a living human cancer-cell culture, on the grounds that the culture is both living and human. Therefore, it seems that the anti-abortionist's favored principle is too broad.

On the other hand, the pro-choicer wants to find a moral principle concerning the wrongness of killing which tends to be narrow in scope in order that fetuses will *not* fall under it. The problem with narrow principles is that they often do *not* embrace enough. Hence, the needed principles such as "It is prima facie seriously wrong to kill only persons" or "It is prima facie wrong to kill only rational agents" do not explain why it is wrong to kill infants or young children or the severely retarded or even perhaps the severely mentally ill. Therefore, we seem again to have a standoff. The anti-abortionist charges, not unreasonably, that pro-choice principles concerning killing are too narrow to be acceptable; the pro-choicer charges, not unreasonably, that anti-abortionist principles concerning killing are too broad to be acceptable. . . .

All this suggests that a necessary condition of resolving the abortion controversy is a more theoretical account of the wrongness of killing. After all, if we merely believe, but do not understand, why killing adult human beings such as ourselves is wrong, how could we conceivably show that abortion is either immoral or permissible?

II.

In order to develop such an account, we can start from the following unproblematic assumption concerning our own case: it is wrong to kill *us*. Why is it wrong? Some answers can be easily eliminated. It might be said that what makes killing us wrong is that a killing brutalizes the one who kills. But the brutalization consists of being inured to the performance of an act that is hideously immoral; hence, the brutalization does not explain the immorality. It might be said that what makes killing us wrong is the great loss others would experience due to our absence. Although such hubris is understandable, such an explanation does not account for the wrongness of killing hermits, or those whose lives are relatively independent and whose friends find it easy to make new friends.

A more obvious answer is better. What primarily makes killing wrong is neither its effect on the murderer nor its effect on the victim's friends and relatives, but its effect on the victim. The loss of one's life is one of the greatest losses one can suffer. The loss of one's life deprives one of all the experiences, activities, projects, and enjoyments that would otherwise have constituted one's future. Therefore, killing someone is wrong, primarily because the killing inflicts (one of) the greatest possible losses on the victim. To describe this as the loss of life can be misleading, however. The change in my biological state does not by itself make killing me wrong. The effect of the loss of my biological life is the loss to me of all those activities, projects, experiences, and enjoyments which would otherwise have constituted my future personal life. These activities, projects, experiences, and enjoyments are either valuable for their own sakes or are means to something else that is valuable for its own sake. Some parts of my future are not valued by me now, but will come to be valued by me as I grow older and as my values and capacities change. When I am killed, I am deprived both of what I now value which would have been part of my future personal life, but also what I would come to value. Therefore, when I die, I am deprived of all of the value of my future. Inflicting this loss on me is ultimately what makes killing me wrong. This being the case, it would seem that what makes killing *any* adult human being prima facie seriously wrong is the loss of his or her future.[1]

---

1. I have been most influenced on this matter by Jonathan Glover, *Causing Death and Saving Lives* (New York: Penguin, 1977), ch. 3; and Robert Young, "What Is So Wrong with Killing People?" *Philosophy*, LIV, 210 (1979): 515–528.

How should this rudimentary theory of the wrongness of killing be evaluated? It cannot be faulted for deriving an 'ought' from an 'is,' for it does not. The analysis assumes that killing me (or you, reader) is prima facie seriously wrong. The point of the analysis is to establish which natural property ultimately explains the wrongness of the killing, given that it is wrong. A natural property will ultimately explain the wrongness of killing, only if (1) the explanation fits with our intuitions about the matter and (2) there is no other natural property that provides the basis for a better explanation of the wrongness of killing. This analysis rests on the intuition that what makes killing a particular human or animal wrong is what it does to that particular human or animal. What makes killing wrong is some natural effect or other of the killing. Some would deny this. For instance, a divine-command theorist in ethics would deny it. Surely this denial is, however, one of those features of divine-command theory which renders it so implausible.

The claim that what makes killing wrong is the loss of the victim's future is directly supported by two considerations. In the first place, this theory explains why we regard killing as one of the worst of crimes. Killing is especially wrong, because it deprives the victim of more than perhaps any other crime. In the second place, people with AIDS or cancer who know they are dying believe, of course, that dying is a very bad thing for them. They believe that the loss of a future to them that they would otherwise have experienced is what makes their premature death a very bad thing for them. A better theory of the wrongness of killing would require a different natural property associated with killing which better fits with the attitudes of the dying. What could it be?

The view that what makes killing wrong is the loss to the victim of the value of the victim's future gains additional support when some of its implications are examined. In the first place, it is incompatible with the view that it is wrong to kill only beings who are biologically human. It is possible that there exists a different species from another planet whose members have a future like ours. Since having a future like that is what makes killing someone wrong, this theory entails that it would be wrong to kill members of such a species. Hence, this theory is opposed to the claim that only life that is biologically human has great moral worth, a claim which many anti-abortionists have seemed to adopt. This opposition, which this theory has in common with personhood theories, seems to be a merit of the theory.

In the second place, the claim that the loss of one's future is the wrong-making feature of one's being killed entails the possibility that the futures of some actual nonhuman mammals on our own planet are sufficiently like ours that it is seriously wrong to kill them also. Whether some animals do have the same right to life as human beings depends on adding to the account of the wrongness of killing some additional account of just what it is about my future or the futures of other adult human beings which makes it wrong to kill us. No such additional account will be offered in this essay. Undoubtedly, the provision of such an account would be a very difficult matter. Undoubtedly, any such account would be quite controversial. Hence, it surely should not reflect badly on this sketch of an elementary theory of the wrongness of killing that it is indeterminate with respect to some very difficult issues regarding animal rights.

In the third place, the claim that the loss of one's future is the wrong-making feature of one's being killed does not entail, as sanctity of human life theories do, that active euthanasia is wrong. Persons who are severely and incurably ill, who face a future of pain and despair, and who wish to die will not have suffered a loss if they are killed. It is, strictly speaking, the value of a human's future which makes killing wrong in this theory. This being so, killing does not necessarily wrong some persons who are sick and dying. Of course, there may be other reasons for a prohibition of active euthanasia, but that is another matter. Sanctity-of-human-life theories seem to hold that active euthanasia is seriously wrong even in an individual case where there seems to be good reason for it independently of public policy considerations. This consequence is most implausible, and it is a plus for the claim that the loss of a future of value is what makes killing wrong that it does not share this consequence.

In the fourth place, the account of the wrongness of killing defended in this essay does straightforwardly entail that it is prima facie seriously wrong to kill children and infants, for we do presume that they have futures of value. Since we do believe that it is wrong to kill defenseless little babies, it is important that a theory of the wrongness of killing easily account for this. Personhood theories of the wrongness of killing, on the other hand, cannot straightforwardly account for the wrongness of killing infants and young children. Hence, such theories must add special ad hoc accounts of the wrongness of killing the young. The plausibility of such ad hoc theories seems to be a function of how desperately one wants such theories to work. The claim that the primary wrong-making feature of a killing is the loss to the victim of the value of its future accounts for the wrongness of killing young children and infants directly; it makes the wrongness of such acts as obvious as we actually think it is. This is a further merit of this theory. Accordingly, it seems that this value of a future-like-ours theory of the wrongness of killing shares strengths of both sanctity-of-life and personhood accounts while avoiding weaknesses of both. In addition, it meshes with a central intuition concerning what makes killing wrong.

The claim that the primary wrong-making feature of a killing is the loss to the victim of the value of its future has obvious consequences for the ethics of abortion. The future of a standard fetus includes a set of experiences, projects, activities, and such which are identical with the futures of adult human beings and are identical with the futures of young children. Since the reason that is sufficient to explain why it is wrong to kill human beings after the time of birth is a reason that also applies to fetuses, it follows that abortion is prima facie seriously morally wrong.

This argument does not rely on the invalid inference that, since it is wrong to kill persons, it is wrong to kill potential persons also. The category that is morally central to this analysis is the category of having a valuable future like ours; it is not the category of personhood. The argument to the conclusion that abortion is prima facie seriously morally wrong proceeded independently of the notion of person or potential person or any equivalent. Someone may wish to start with this analysis in terms of the value of a human future, conclude that abortion is, except perhaps in rare circumstances, seriously morally wrong, infer that fetuses have the right to life, and then call fetuses "persons" as a result of their having the right to life. Clearly, in this case, the category of person is being used to state the *conclusion* of the analysis rather than to generate the *argument* of the analysis. . . .

Of course, this value of a future-like-ours argument, if sound, shows only that abortion is prima facie wrong, not that it is wrong in any and all circumstances. Since the loss of the future to a standard fetus, if killed, is, however, at least as great a loss as the loss of the future to a standard adult human being who is killed, abortion, like ordinary killing, could be justified only by the most compelling reasons. The loss of one's life is almost the greatest misfortune that can happen to one. Presumably abortion could be justified in some circumstances, only if the loss consequent on failing to abort would be at least as great. Accordingly, morally permissible abortions will be rare indeed unless, perhaps, they occur so early in pregnancy that a fetus is not yet definitely an individual. Hence, this argument should be taken as showing that abortion is presumptively very seriously wrong, where the presumption is very strong—as strong as the presumption that killing another adult human being is wrong.

III.

How complete an account of the wrongness of killing does the value of a future-like-ours account have to be in order that the wrongness of abortion is a consequence? This account does not have to be an account of the necessary conditions for the wrongness of killing. Some persons in nursing homes may lack valuable human futures, yet it may be wrong to kill them for other reasons. Furthermore, this account does not obviously have to be the sole reason killing is wrong where the victim did have a valuable future. This analysis claims only that, for any killing where the victim did have a valuable future like ours, having that future by itself is sufficient to create the strong presumption that the killing is seriously wrong.

One way to overturn the value of a future-like-ours argument would be to find some account of the wrongness of killing which is at least as intelligible and which has different implications for the ethics of abortion. . . .

One move of this sort is based upon the claim that a necessary condition of one's future being valuable is that one values it. Value implies a valuer. Given this one might argue that, since fetuses cannot value their futures, their futures are not valuable to them. Hence, it does not seriously wrong them deliberately to end their lives.

This move fails, however, because of some ambiguities. Let us assume that something cannot be of value unless it is valued by someone. This does not entail that my life is of no value unless it is valued by me. I may think, in a period of despair, that my future is of no worth whatsoever, but I may be wrong because others rightly see value—even great value—in it. Furthermore, my future can be valuable to me even if I do not value it. This is the case when a young person attempts suicide, but is rescued and goes on to significant human achievements. Such young people's futures are ultimately valuable to them, even though such futures do not seem to be valuable to them at the moment of attempted suicide. A fetus's future can be valuable to it in the same way. Accordingly, this attempt to limit the anti-abortion argument fails.

Another similar attempt to reject the anti-abortion position is based on Tooley's claim that an entity cannot possess the right to life unless it has the capacity to desire its continued existence. It follows that, since fetuses lack the conceptual capacity to desire to continue to live, they lack the right to life. Accordingly, Tooley concludes that abortion cannot be seriously prima facie wrong.[2] . . .

One might attempt to defend Tooley's basic claim on the grounds that, because a fetus cannot apprehend continued life as a benefit, its continued life cannot be a benefit or cannot be something it has a right to or cannot be something that is in its interest. This might be defended in terms of the general proposition that, if an individual is literally incapable of caring about or taking an interest in some X, then one does not have a right to X or X is not a benefit or X is not something that is in one's interest.

Each member of this family of claims seems to be open to objections. As John C. Stevens[3] has pointed out, one may have a right to be treated with a certain medical procedure (because of a health insurance policy one has purchased), even though one cannot conceive of the nature of the procedure. And, as Tooley himself has pointed out, persons who have been indoctrinated, or drugged, or rendered temporarily unconscious may be literally incapable of caring about or taking an interest in something that is in their interest or is something to which they have a right, or is something that benefits them. Hence, the Tooley claim that would restrict the scope of the value of a future-like-ours argument is undermined by counterexamples. . . .[4]

IV.

In this essay, it has been argued that the correct ethic of the wrongness of killing can be extended to fetal life and used to show that there is a strong presumption that any abortion is morally impermissible. If the ethic of killing adopted here entails, however, that contraception is also seriously immoral, then there would appear to be a difficulty with the analysis of this essay.

But this analysis does not entail that contraception is wrong. Of course, contraception prevents the actualization of a possible future of value. Hence, it follows from the claim that futures of value should be maximized that contraception is prima facie immoral. This obligation to maximize does not exist, however; furthermore, nothing in the ethics of

---

2. Michael Tooley, *Abortion and Infanticide* (New York: Oxford University Press, 1984), pp. 46–47.
3. "Must the Bearer of a Right Have the Concept of That to Which He Has a Right?" *Ethics*, xcv, 1 (1984): 68–74.
4. See Tooley again in *Abortion and Infanticide*, pp. 47–49.

killing in this paper entails that it does. The ethics of killing in this essay would entail that contraception is wrong only if something were denied a human future of value by contraception. Nothing at all is denied such a future by contraception, however.

Candidates for a subject of harm by contraception fall into four categories: (1) some sperm or other, (2) some ovum or other, (3) a sperm and an ovum separately, and (4) a sperm and an ovum together. Assigning the harm to some sperm is utterly arbitrary, for no reason can be given for making a sperm the subject of harm rather than an ovum. Assigning the harm to some ovum is utterly arbitrary, for no reason can be given for making an ovum the subject of harm rather than a sperm. One might attempt to avoid these problems by insisting that contraception deprives both the sperm and the ovum separately of a valuable future like ours. On this alternative, too many futures are lost. Contraception was supposed to be wrong, because it deprived us of one future of value, not two. One might attempt to avoid this problem by holding that contraception deprives the combination of sperm and ovum of a valuable future like ours. But here the definite article misleads. At the time of contraception, there are hundreds of millions of sperm, one (released) ovum and millions of possible combinations of all of these. There is no actual combination at all. Is the subject of the loss to be a merely possible combination? Which one? This alternative does not yield an actual subject of harm either. Accordingly, the immorality of contraception is not entailed by the loss of a future-like-ours argument simply because there is no nonarbitrarily identifiable subject of the loss in the case of contraception.

Don Marquis: Why Abortion Is Immoral

1. Marquis begins by criticizing some common arguments on both sides of the abortion issue. Do his criticisms succeed in refuting the common arguments? Why or why not?
2. What, according to Marquis, is wrong with killing adult humans? Is his theory the best account of what is wrong with such killing?
3. Marquis claims that abortion is wrong for the same reason that killing adult humans is wrong. Are there any differences between the two that would justify abortion?
4. One might object to Marquis's claim that fetuses have a valuable future by pointing out that fetuses do not have the cognitive capacities to value

anything. How does Marquis respond to this objection? Do you find his response convincing?

5. Marquis admits that his theory would be problematic if it led to the view that contraception is seriously morally wrong. How does he argue that his theory does not do this? Do you think he succeeds?

30

The Problem of Abortion and the Doctrine of the Double Effect

Philippa Foot

....

In this article, Philippa Foot (1920–2010) introduces and discusses the merits of the ethical principle known as the doctrine of double effect. The doctrine states that, under certain conditions, it is permitted to cause harm if the harm is merely foreseen, rather than directly intended. Foot offers a variety of fascinating cases to explore the difference between foresight and intention. Many of these cases have become classic examples within moral philosophy, none more so than the Trolley Problem.

The Trolley Problem has generated many variations, but the central case is simple. There is a runaway trolley; you can either allow it to continue on its way, or switch it to a spur. Why would you do either? Well, there are five people on the track ahead, and only one on the spur. All six are innocent. Intuitively, it seems at least permissible, and many think it required, to pull the lever that will send the trolley to the spur. From this example, you might infer that whenever we have to choose between saving a greater and a lesser number of innocent lives, we ought to save the greater number. But, as Foot shows, such a claim is deeply problematic.

In its most general formulation, the challenge is to explain precisely why it is only sometimes, and not always, morally acceptable to

---

Philippa Foot, "The Problem of Abortion and the Doctrine of the Double Effect" from *Oxford Review* 5 (1967), pp. 5–15. Reprinted by permission of the Principal and Fellows of Somerville College Oxford.

minimize harm. The doctrine of double effect has been introduced to do the needed explaining, but Foot finds the doctrine flawed. She concludes with a presentation of her own solution, and an application of it to the issue of abortion.

....

One of the reasons why most of us feel puzzled about the problem of abortion is that we want, and do not want, to allow to the unborn child the rights that belong to adults and children. When we think of a baby about to be born it seems absurd to think that the next few minutes or even hours could make so radical a difference to its status; yet as we go back in the life of the foetus we are more and more reluctant to say that this is a human being and must be treated as such. No doubt this is the deepest source of our dilemma, but it is not the only one. For we are also confused about the general question of what we may and may not do where the interests of human beings conflict. We have strong intuitions about certain cases; saying, for instance, that it is all right to raise the level of education in our country, though statistics allow us to predict that a rise in the suicide rate will follow, while it is not all right to kill the feeble-minded to aid cancer research. It is not easy, however, to see the principles involved, and one way of throwing light on the abortion issue will be by setting up parallels involving adults or children once born. So we will be able to isolate the "equal rights" issue, and should be able to make some advance.

I shall not, of course, discuss all the principles that may be used in deciding what to do where the interests or rights of human beings conflict. What I want to do is to look at one particular theory, known as the "doctrine of the double effect" which is invoked by Catholics in support of their views on abortion but supposed by them to apply elsewhere. As used in the abortion argument this doctrine has often seemed to non-Catholics to be a piece of complete sophistry. . . . And yet this principle has seemed to some non-Catholics as well as to Catholics to stand as the only defence against decisions on other issues that are quite unacceptable. It will help us in our difficulty about abortion if this conflict can be resolved.

The doctrine of the double effect is based on a distinction between what a man foresees as a result of his voluntary action and what, in the strict sense, he intends. He intends in the strictest sense both those things that he aims at as ends and those that he aims at as means to his ends. The latter may be regretted in themselves but nevertheless desired for the sake of the end, as we may intend to keep dangerous lunatics confined for the sake of our safety. By contrast a man is said not strictly, or directly, to intend the foreseen consequences of his voluntary actions where these are neither the end at which he is aiming nor the means to this end. Whether the word "intention" should be applied in both cases is not of course what matters: Bentham spoke of "oblique intention," contrasting it with the "direct intention" of ends and means, and we may as well follow his terminology. Everyone must recognize that some such distinction can be made, though it may be made in a number of different ways, and it is the distinction that is crucial to the doctrine of the double effect. The words "double effect" refer to the two effects that an action may produce: the one aimed at, and the one foreseen but in no way desired. By "the doctrine of the double effect" I mean the thesis that it is sometimes permissible to bring about by oblique intention what one may not directly intend. Thus the distinction is held to be relevant to moral decision in certain difficult cases. It is said for instance that the operation of hysterectomy involves the death of the foetus as the foreseen but not strictly or directly intended consequence of the surgeon's act, while other operations kill the child and count as the direct intention of taking an innocent life, a distinction that has evoked particularly bitter reactions on the part of non-Catholics. If you are permitted to bring about the death of the child, what does it matter how it is done? The doctrine of the double effect is also used to show why in another case, where a woman in labour will die unless a craniotomy operation is performed, the intervention is not to be condoned. There, it is said, we may not operate, but must let the mother die. We foresee her death but do not directly intend it, whereas to crush the skull of the child would count as direct intention of its death.

This last application of the doctrine has been queried by Professor Hart on the ground that the child's death is not strictly a means to saving the mother's life and should logically be treated as an unwanted but foreseen consequence by those who make use of the distinction between direct and oblique intention. To interpret the doctrine in this way is perfectly reasonable given the language that has been used; it would, however, make nonsense of it from the beginning. A certain event may be desired under one of its descriptions, unwanted under another, but we cannot treat these as two different events, one of which is aimed at and the other not. And even if it be argued that there are here two different events—the crushing of the child's skull and its death—the two are obviously much too close for an application of the doctrine of the double effect. To see how odd it would be to apply the principle like this we may consider the story, well known to philosophers, of the fat man stuck in the mouth of the cave. A party of potholers have imprudently allowed the fat man to lead them as they make their way out of the cave, and he gets stuck, trapping the others behind him. Obviously the right thing to do is to sit down and wait until the fat man grows thin; but philosophers have arranged that flood waters should be rising within the cave. Luckily (luckily?) the trapped party have with them a stick of dynamite with which they can blast the fat man out of the mouth of the cave. Either they use the dynamite or they drown. In one version the fat man, whose head is *in* the cave, will drown with them; in the other he will be rescued in due course. Problem: may they use the dynamite or not? Later we will find parallels to this example. Here it is introduced for light relief and because it will serve to show how ridiculous one version of the doctrine of the double effect would be. For suppose that the trapped explorers were to argue that the death of the fat man might be taken as a merely foreseen consequence of the act of blowing him up. ("We didn't want to kill him . . . only to blow him into small pieces" or even " . . . only to blast him out of the mouth of the cave.") I believe that those who use the doctrine of the double effect would rightly reject such a suggestion, though they will, of course, have considerable difficulty in explaining where the line is to be drawn. What is to be the criterion of "closeness" if we say that anything very close to what we are literally aiming at counts as if part of our aim?

Let us leave this difficulty aside and return to the arguments for and against the doctrine, supposing it to be formulated in the way considered most effective by its supporters, and ourselves bypassing the trouble by taking what must on any reasonable definition be clear cases of "direct" or "oblique" intention.

The first point that should be made clear, in fairness to the theory, is that no one is suggesting that it does not matter what you bring about as long as you merely foresee and do not strictly intend the evil that follows. We might think, for instance, of the (actual) case of wicked merchants selling, for cooking, oil they knew to be poisonous and thereby killing a number of innocent people, comparing and contrasting it with that of some unemployed gravediggers, desperate for custom, who got hold of this same oil and sold it (or perhaps *they* secretly gave it away) in order to create orders for graves. They strictly (directly) intend the deaths they cause, while the merchants could say that it was not part of their *plan* that anyone should die. In morality, as in law, the merchants, like the grave-diggers, would be considered as murderers; nor are the supporters of the doctrine of the double effect bound to say that there is the least difference between them in respect of moral turpitude. What they are committed to is the thesis that *sometimes* it makes a difference to the permissibility of an action involving harm to others that this harm, although foreseen, is not part of the agent's direct intention. An end such as earning one's living is clearly not such as to justify *either* the direct or oblique intention of the death of innocent people, but in certain cases one is justified in bringing about knowingly what one could not directly intend.

It is now time to say why this doctrine should be taken seriously in spite of the fact that it sounds rather odd, that there are difficulties about the distinction on which it depends, and that it seemed to yield one sophistical conclusion when applied to the problem of abortion. The reason for its appeal is that its opponents have often *seemed* to be committed to quite indefensible views. Thus the controversy has raged around examples such as the following. Suppose that a judge or magistrate is faced with rioters demanding that a culprit be found for a certain crime and threatening otherwise to take their own bloody revenge on a particular section of the community. The real culprit being unknown, the judge sees himself as able to prevent the bloodshed only by framing some innocent person and having him executed. Beside this example is placed another in which a pilot whose aeroplane is about to crash is deciding whether to steer from a more to a less inhabited area. To make the parallel as close as possible it may rather be supposed that he is the driver of a runaway tram which he can only steer from one narrow track on to another; five men are working on one track and one man on the other; anyone on the track he enters is bound to be killed. In the case of the riots the mob have five hostages, so that in both the exchange is supposed to be one man's life for the lives of five. The question is why we should say, without hesitation, that the driver should steer for the less occupied track, while most of us would be appalled at the idea that the innocent man could be framed. It may be suggested that the special feature of the latter case is that it involves the corruption of justice, and this is, of course, very important indeed. But if we remove that special feature, supposing that some private individual is to kill an innocent person and pass him off as the criminal, we still find ourselves horrified by the idea. The doctrine of the double effect offers us a way out of the difficulty, insisting that it is one thing to steer towards someone foreseeing that you will kill him and another to aim at his death as part of your plan.

Moreover there is one very important element of good in what is here insisted. In real life it would hardly ever be certain that the man on the narrow track would be killed. Perhaps he might find a foothold on the side of the tunnel and cling on as the vehicle hurtled by. The driver of the tram does not then leap off and brain him with a crowbar. The judge, however, needs the death of the innocent man for his (good) purposes. If the victim proves hard to hang he must see to it that he dies another way. To choose to execute him is to choose that this evil *shall come about,* and this must therefore count as a *certainty* in weighing up the good and evil involved. The distinction between direct and oblique intention is crucial here, and is of great importance in an uncertain world. Nevertheless this is no way to defend the doctrine of the double effect. For the question is whether the difference between aiming at something and obliquely intending it is *in itself* relevant to moral decisions; not whether it is important when correlated with a difference of certainty in the balance of good and evil. Moreover we are particularly interested in the application of the doctrine of the double effect to the question of abortion, and no one can deny that in medicine there are sometimes certainties so complete that it would be a mere quibble to speak of the "probable outcome" of this course of action or that. It is not, therefore, with a merely philosophical interest that we should put aside the uncertainty and scrutinize the examples to test the doctrine of the double effect. Why can we not argue from the case of the steering driver to that of the judge?

Another pair of examples poses a similar problem. We are about to give to a patient who needs it to save his life a massive dose of a certain drug in short supply. There arrive, however, five other patients each of whom could be saved by one-fifth of that dose. We say with regret that we cannot spare our whole supply of the drug for a single patient, just as we should say that we could not spare the whole resources of a ward for one dangerously ill individual when ambulances arrive bringing in the victims of a multiple crash. We feel bound to let one man die rather than many if that is our only choice. Why then do we not feel justified in killing people in the interests of cancer research or to obtain, let us say, spare parts for grafting on to those who need them? We can suppose, similarly, that several dangerously ill people can be saved only if we kill a certain individual and make a serum from his dead body. (These examples are not over fanciful considering present controversies about prolonging the life of mortally ill patients whose eyes or kidneys are to be used for others.) Why cannot we argue from the case of the scarce drug to that of the body needed for medical purposes? Once again the doctrine of the double effect comes up with an explanation. In one kind of case but not the other we aim at the death of the innocent man.

A further argument suggests that if the doctrine of the double effect is rejected this has the consequence of putting us hopelessly in the power of bad men. Suppose for example that some tyrant should threaten to torture five men if we ourselves would not torture one. Would it be our duty to do so, supposing we believed him, because this would be no different from choosing to rescue five men from his torturers rather than one? If so anyone who wants us to do something we think wrong has only to threaten that otherwise he himself will do something we think worse. A mad murderer, known to keep his promises, could thus make it our duty to kill some innocent citizen to prevent him from killing two. From this conclusion we are again rescued by the doctrine of the double effect. If we refuse, we foresee that the greater number will be killed but we do not intend it: it is he who intends (that is strictly or directly intends) the death of innocent persons; we do not.

At one time I thought that these arguments in favour of the doctrine of the double effect were conclusive, but I now believe that the conflict should be solved in another way. The clue that we should follow is that the strength of the doctrine seems to lie in the distinction it makes between what we do (equated with direct intention) and what we allow (thought of as obliquely intended). Indeed it is interesting that the disputants tend to argue about whether we are to be held responsible for what we allow as we are for what we do. Yet it is not obvious that this is what they should be discussing, since the distinction between what one does and what one allows to happen is not the same as that between direct and oblique intention. To see this one has only to consider that it is possible *deliberately* to allow something to happen, aiming at it either for its own sake or as part of one's plan for obtaining something else. So one person might want another person dead, and deliberately allow him to die. And again one may be said to do things that one does not aim at, as the steering driver would kill the man on the track. Moreover there is a large class of things said to be brought about rather than either done or allowed, and either kind of intention is possible. So it is possible to *bring about* a man's death by getting him to go to sea in a leaky boat, and the intention of his death may be either direct or oblique.

Whatever it may, or may not, have to do with the doctrine of the double effect, the idea of *allowing* is worth looking into in this context. I shall leave aside the special case of giving permission, which involves the idea of authority, and consider the two main divisions into which cases of allowing seem to fall. There is firstly the allowing which is forbearing to prevent. For this we need a sequence thought of as somehow already in train, and something that the agent could do to intervene. (The agent must be able to intervene, but does not do so.) So, for instance, he could warn someone, but *allows* him to walk into a trap. He could feed an animal but *allows* it to die for lack of food. He could stop a leaking tap but *allows* the water to go on flowing. This is the case of allowing with which we shall be concerned, but the other should be mentioned. It is the kind of allowing which is roughly equivalent to *enabling*, the root idea being the removal of some obstacle which is, as it were, holding back a train of events. So someone may remove a plug and *allow* water to flow; open a door and *allow* an animal to get out; or give someone money and *allow* him to get back on his feet.

The first kind of allowing requires an omission, but there is no other general correlation between omission and allowing, commission and bringing about or doing. An actor who fails to turn up for a performance will generally spoil it rather than allow it to be spoiled. I mentioned the distinction between omission and commission only to not set it aside.

Thinking of the first kind of allowing (forebearing to prevent), we should ask whether there is any difference, from the moral point of view, between what one does or causes and what one merely allows. It seems clear that on occasions one is just as bad as the other, as is recognized in both morality and law. A man may murder his child or his aged relatives, by allowing them to die of starvation as well as by giving poison; he may also be convicted of murder on either account. In another case we would, however, make a distinction. Most of us allow people to die of starvation in India and Africa, and there is surely something wrong with us that we do; it would be nonsense, however, to pretend that it is only in law that we make a distinction between allowing people in the underdeveloped countries to die of starvation and sending them poisoned food. There is worked into our moral system a distinction between what we owe people in the form of aid and what we owe them in the way of noninterference. Salmond, in his *Jurisprudence*, expressed as follows the distinction between the two.

> A positive right corresponds to a positive duty, and is a right that he on whom the duty lies shall do some positive act on behalf of the person entitled. A negative right corresponds to a negative duty, and is a right

that the person bound shall refrain from some act which would operate to the prejudice of the person entitled. The former is a right to be positively benefited; the latter is merely a right not to be harmed.[1]

As a general account of rights and duties this is defective, since not all are so closely connected with benefit and harm. Nevertheless for our purposes it will do well. Let us speak of negative duties when thinking of the obligation to refrain from such things as killing or robbing, and of the positive duty, e.g., to look after children or aged parents. It will be useful, however, to extend the notion of positive duty beyond the range of things that are strictly called duties, bringing acts of charity under this heading. These are owed only in a rather loose sense, and some acts of charity could hardly be said to be owed at all, so I am not following ordinary usage at this point.

Let us now see whether the distinction of negative and positive duties explains why we see differently the action of the steering driver and that of the judge, of the doctors who withhold the scarce drug and those who obtain a body for medical purposes, of those who choose to rescue the five men rather than one man from torture and those who are ready to torture the one man themselves in order to save five. In each case we have a conflict of duties, but what kind of duties are they? Are we, in each case, weighing positive duties against positive, negative against negative, or one against the other? Is the duty to refrain from injury, or rather to bring aid?

The steering driver faces a conflict of negative duties, since it is his duty to avoid injuring five men and also his duty to avoid injuring one. In the circumstances he is not able to avoid both, and it seems clear that he should do the least injury he can. The judge, however, is weighing the duty of not inflicting injury against the duty of bringing aid. He wants to rescue the innocent people threatened with death but can do so only by inflicting injury himself. Since one does not *in general* have the same duty to help people as to refrain from injuring them, it is not possible to argue to a conclusion about what he should do from the steering driver case. It is interesting that, even where the strictest duty of positive aid exists, this still does not weigh as if a negative duty were involved. It is not, for instance, permissible to commit a murder to bring one's starving children food. If the choice is between inflicting injury on one or many there seems only one rational course of action; if the choice is between aid to some at the cost of injury to others, and refusing to inflict the injury to bring the

---

1. J. Salmond, *Jurisprudence*, 11th edition, p. 283.

aid, the whole matter is open to dispute. So it is not inconsistent of us to think that the driver must steer for the road on which only one man stands while the judge (or his equivalent) may not kill the innocent person in order to stop the riots. Let us now consider the second pair of examples, which concern the scarce drug on the one hand and on the other the body needed to save lives. Once again we find a difference based on the distinction between the duty to avoid injury and the duty to provide aid. Where one man needs a massive dose of the drug and we withhold it from him in order to save five men, we are weighing aid against aid. But if we consider killing a man in order to use his body to save others, we are thinking of doing him injury to bring others aid. In an interesting variant of the model, we may suppose that instead of killing someone we deliberately let him die. (Perhaps he is a beggar to whom we are thinking of giving food, but then we say "No, they need bodies for medical research.") Here it does seem relevant that in allowing him to die we are aiming at his death, but presumably we are inclined to see this as a violation of negative rather than positive duty. If this is right, we see why we are unable in either case to argue to a conclusion from the case of the scarce drug.

In the examples involving the torturing of one man or five men, the principle seems to be the same as for the last pair. If we are bringing aid (rescuing people about to be tortured by the tyrant), we must obviously rescue the larger rather than the smaller group. It does not follow, however, that we would be justified in inflicting the injury, or getting a third person to do so, in order to save the five. We may therefore refuse to be forced into acting by the threats of bad men. To refrain from inflicting injury ourselves is a stricter duty than to prevent other people from inflicting injury, which is not to say that the other is not a very strict duty indeed.

So far the conclusions are the same as those at which we might arrive following the doctrine of the double effect, but in others they will be different, and the advantage seems to be on the side of the alternative. Suppose, for instance, that there are five patients in a hospital whose lives could be saved by the manufacture of a certain gas, but that this inevitably releases lethal fumes into the room of another patient whom for some reason we are unable to move. His death, being of no use to us, is clearly a side effect, and not directly intended. Why then is the case different from that of the scarce drug, if the point about that is that we foresaw but did not strictly intend the death of the single patient? Yet it surely is different. The relatives of the gassed patient would presumably be successful if they sued the hospital and the whole story came out. We may find it particularly revolting that someone should be *used* as in the case where he is killed or allowed to die in the interest of medical research, and the fact of *using* may even determine what we would decide to do in some cases, but the principle seems unimportant compared with our reluctance to bring such injury for the sake of giving aid.

My conclusion is that the distinction between direct and oblique intention plays only a quite subsidiary role in determining what we say in these cases, while the distinction between avoiding injury and bringing aid is very important indeed. I have not, of course, argued that there are no other principles. For instance it clearly makes a difference whether our positive duty is a strict duty or rather an act of charity: feeding our own children or feeding those in far away countries. It may also make a difference whether the person about to suffer is one thought of as uninvolved in the threatened disaster, and whether it is his presence that constitutes the threat to the others. In many cases we find it very hard to know what to say, and I have not been arguing for any general conclusion such as that we may never, whatever the balance of good and evil, bring injury to one for the sake of aid to others, even when this injury amounts to death. I have only tried to show that even if we reject the doctrine of the double effect we are not forced to the conclusion that the size of the evil must always be our guide.

Let us now return to the problem of abortion, carrying out our plan of finding parallels involving adults or children rather than the unborn. We must say something about the different cases in which abortion might be considered on medical grounds.

First of all there is the situation in which nothing that can be done will save the life of child and mother, but where the life of the mother can be saved by killing the child. This is parallel to the case of the fat man in the mouth of the cave who is bound to be drowned with the others if nothing is done. Given the certainty of the outcome, as it was postulated, there is no serious conflict of interests here, since the fat man will perish in either case, and it is reasonable that the action that will save someone should be done. It is a great objection to those who argue that the direct intention of the death of an innocent person is never justifiable that the edict will apply even in this case. The Catholic doctrine on abortion must here conflict with that of most reasonable men. Moreover we would be justified in performing the operation whatever the method used, and it is neither a necessary nor a good justification of the special case of hysterectomy that the child's death is not directly intended, being rather a foreseen consequence of what is done. What difference could it make as to how the death is brought about?

Secondly we have the case in which it is possible to perform an operation which will save the mother and kill the child or kill the mother and save the child. This is parallel to the famous case of the shipwrecked mariners who believed that they must throw someone overboard if their boat was not to founder in a storm, and to the other famous case of the two sailors, Dudley and Stephens, who killed and ate the cabin boy when adrift on the sea without food. Here again there is no conflict of interests so far as the decision to act is concerned; only in deciding whom to save. Once again it would be reasonable to act, though one would respect someone who held back from the appalling action either because he preferred to perish rather than do such a thing or because he held on past the limits of reasonable hope. In real life the certainties postulated by philosophers hardly ever exist, and Dudley and Stephens were rescued not long after their ghastly meal. Nevertheless if the certainty were absolute, as it might be in the abortion case, it would seem better to save one than none. Probably we should decide in favour of the mother when weighing her life against that of the unborn child, but it is interesting that, a few years later, we might easily decide it the other way.

The worst dilemma comes in the third kind of example where to save the mother we must kill the child, say by crushing its skull, while if nothing is done the mother will perish but the child can be safely delivered after her death. Here the doctrine of the double effect has been invoked to show that we may not intervene, since the child's death would be directly intended while the mother's would not. On a strict parallel with cases not involving the unborn we might find the conclusion correct though the reason given was wrong. Suppose, for instance, that in later life the presence of a child was certain to bring death to the mother. We would surely not think ourselves justified in ridding her of it by a process that involved its death. For in general we do not think that we can kill one innocent person to rescue another, quite apart from the special care that we feel is due to children once they have prudently got themselves born. What we would be prepared to do when a great many people were involved is another matter, and this is probably the key to one quite common view of abortion on the part of those who take quite seriously the rights of the unborn child. They probably feel that if *enough* people are involved one must be sacrificed, and they think of the mother's life against the unborn child's life as if it were many against one. But of course many people do not view it like this at all, having no inclination to accord to the foetus or unborn child anything like ordinary human status in the matter of rights. I have not been arguing for or against these points of view but only trying to discern some of the currents that are pulling us back and forth. The levity of the examples is not meant to offend.

Philippa Foot: Abortion and the Doctrine of Double Effect

1. What is the doctrine of double effect? Why does Foot think that the doctrine should be taken seriously?
2. What kinds of cases is the doctrine of double effect supposed to explain? Do you think the doctrine offers the correct moral verdict in these cases?
3. According to Foot, some have suggested that rejecting the doctrine of double effect would have "the consequence of putting us hopelessly in the power of bad men." What reason is there to believe this? Do you find the claim plausible?
4. What alternative to the doctrine of double effect does Foot offer? Does her theory succeed in explaining the cases that the doctrine of double effect was supposed to explain?
5. What advantages does Foot believe her theory has over the doctrine of double effect? Which theory do you think is better?
6. What conclusions does Foot draw about the morality of abortion? What other considerations, besides those Foot discusses, are relevant to the question of when (if ever) abortion is morally permissible?

31

===== ❧ =====

Justifying Legal Punishment

Igor Primoratz

....

In this excerpt from his book *Justifying Legal Punishment* (1989), Igor Primoratz defends the retributivist idea that a punishment is justified only if it gives a criminal his just deserts. But what do criminals deserve? Primoratz argues for the following principle: criminals deserve to be deprived of the same value that they deprived their victims of. Primoratz regards all human beings as possessed of lives of equal moral worth, and also believes that nothing is as valuable as human life. So murderers deserve to die. Since justice is a matter of giving people what they deserve, it follows that justice demands that murderers be executed.

Primoratz considers the most popular arguments of the opposing camp, and finds problems for each of them. Opponents claim that capital punishment violates a murderer's right to life; that killing murderers is contradictory; that capital punishment is disproportionally harsh; that the innocent are inevitably going to be executed; and that systematic discrimination undermines any chance at moral legitimacy. Primoratz carefully considers each objection and offers his replies. In the end, he thinks that justice requires the death penalty, that justice is the supreme legal virtue, and that none of the objections is strong enough to undermine the case for capital punishment. Therefore the state ought to execute convicted murderers.

....

From Igor Primoratz, *Justifying Legal Punishment* (Amherst, Humanity Books, 1989), pp. 158–159, 161–166. Copyright © 1989 by Igor Primoratz. All rights reserved. Reprinted with permission of the publisher.

... According to the retributive theory, consequences of punishment, however important from the practical point of view, are irrelevant when it comes to its justification; *the* moral consideration is its justice. Punishment is morally justified insofar as it is meted out as retribution for the offense committed. When someone has committed an offense, he deserves to be punished: it is just, and consequently justified, that he be punished. The offense is the sole ground of the state's right and duty to punish. It is also the measure of legitimate punishment: the two ought to be proportionate. So the issue of capital punishment within the retributive approach comes down to the question, Is this punishment ever proportionate retribution for the offense committed, and thus deserved, just, and justified?

The classic representatives of retributivism believed that it was, and that it was the only proportionate and hence appropriate punishment, if the offense was *murder*—that is, criminal homicide perpetrated voluntarily and intentionally or in wanton disregard of human life. In other cases, the demand for proportionality between offense and punishment can be satisfied by fines or prison terms; the crime of murder, however, is an exception in this respect, and calls for the literal interpretation of the *lex talionis*. The uniqueness of this crime has to do with the uniqueness of the value which has been deliberately or recklessly destroyed. We come across this idea as early as the original formulation of the retributive view—the biblical teaching on punishment: "You shall accept no ransom for the life of a murderer who is guilty of death; but he shall be put to death."[1] The rationale of this command—one that clearly distinguishes the biblical conception of the criminal law from contemporaneous criminal law systems in the Middle East—is that man was not only created *by* God, like every other creature, but also, alone among all the creatures, *in the image of God*:

> That man was made in the image of God ... is expressive of the peculiar and supreme worth of man. Of all creatures, Genesis 1 relates, he alone possesses this attribute, bringing him into closer relation to God than all the rest and conferring upon him the highest value. ... This view of the uniqueness and supremacy of human life ... places life beyond the reach of other values. The idea that life may be measured in terms of money or other property ... is excluded. Compensation of any kind is ruled out. The guilt of the murderer is infinite because the

---

1. Numbers 35.31 (R S V.).

murdered life is invaluable; the kinsmen of the slain man are not competent to say when he has been paid for. An absolute wrong has been committed, a sin against God which is not subject to human discussion. . . . Because human life is invaluable, to take it entails the death penalty.[2]

This view that the value of human life is not commensurable with other values, and that consequently there is only one truly equivalent punishment for murder, namely death, does not necessarily presuppose a theistic outlook. It can be claimed that, simply because we have to be alive if we are to experience and realize any other value at all, there is nothing equivalent to the murderous destruction of a human life except the destruction of the life of the murderer. Any other retribution, no matter how severe, would still be less than what is proportionate, deserved, and just. As long as the murderer is alive, no matter how bad the conditions of his life may be, there are always at least *some* values he can experience and realize. This provides a plausible interpretation of what the classical representatives of retributivism as a philosophical theory of punishment, such as Kant and Hegel, had to say on the subject.[3]

It seems to me that this is essentially correct. With respect to the larger question of the justification of punishment in general, it is the retributive theory that gives the right answer. Accordingly, capital punishment ought to be retained where it obtains, and reintroduced in those jurisdictions that have abolished it, although we have no reason to believe that, as a means of deterrence, it is any better than a very long prison term. It ought to be retained, or reintroduced, for one simple reason: that justice be done in cases of murder, that murderers be punished according to their deserts.

There are a number of arguments that have been advanced against this rationale of capital punishment. . . .

---

2. M. Greenberg, "Some Postulates of Biblical Criminal Law," in J. Goldin (ed.), *The Jewish Expression* (New York: Bantam, 1970), pp. 25–26. (Post-biblical Jewish law evolved toward the virtual abolition of the death penalty, but that is of no concern here.)

3. "There is no *parallel* between death and even the most miserable life, so that there is no equality of crime and retribution [in the case of murder] unless the perpetrator is judicially put to death" (I. Kant, "The Metaphysics of Morals," *Kant's Political Writings*, ed. H. Reiss, trans. H. B. Nisbet [Cambridge: Cambridge University Press, 1970], p. 156). "Since life is the full compass of a man's existence, the punishment [for murder] cannot simply consist in a 'value,' for none is great enough, but can consist only in taking away a second life" (G. W. F. Hegel, *Philosophy of Right*, trans. T. M. Knox [Oxford: Oxford University Press, 1965], p. 247).

[One] abolitionist argument . . . simply says that capital punishment is illegitimate because it violates the right to life, which is a fundamental, absolute, sacred right belonging to each and every human being, and therefore ought to be respected even in a murderer.

If any rights are fundamental, the right to life is certainly one of them; but to claim that it is absolute, inviolable under any circumstances and for any reason, is a different matter. If an abolitionist wants to argue his case by asserting an absolute right to life, she will also have to deny moral legitimacy to taking human life in war, revolution, and self-defense. This kind of pacifism is a consistent but farfetched and hence implausible position.

I do not believe that the right to life (nor, for that matter, any other right) is absolute. I have no general theory of rights to fall back upon here; instead, let me pose a question. Would we take seriously the claim to an absolute, sacred, inviolable right to life—coming from the mouth of a *confessed murderer?* I submit that we would not, for the obvious reason that it is being put forward by the person who confessedly denied another human being this very right. But if the murderer cannot plausibly claim such a right for himself, neither can *anyone else* do that in his behalf. This suggests that there is an element of reciprocity in our general rights, such as the right to life or property. I can convincingly claim these rights only so long as I acknowledge and respect the same rights of others. If I violate the rights of others, I thereby lose the same rights. If I am a murderer, I have no *right* to live.

Some opponents of capital punishment claim that a criminal law system which includes this punishment is contradictory, in that it prohibits murder and at the same time provides for its perpetration: "It is one and the same legal regulation which prohibits the individual from murdering, while allowing the state to murder. . . . This is obviously a terrible irony, an abnormal and immoral logic, against which everything in us revolts."[4]

This seems to be one of the more popular arguments against the death penalty, but it is not a good one. If it were valid, it would prove too much. Exactly the same might be claimed of other kinds of punishment: of prison terms, that they are "contradictory" to the legal protection of liberty; of fines, that they are "contradictory" to the legal protection of property. Fortunately enough, it is not valid, for it begs the question at issue. In order to be able to talk of the state as "murdering" the person it executes, and to claim that there is "an abnormal and immoral logic" at work here,

---

4. S. V. Vulović, *Problem smrtne kazne* (Belgrade: Geca Kon, 1925), pp. 23–24.

which thrives on a "contradiction," one has to use the word "murder" in the very same sense—that is, in the usual sense, which implies the idea of the *wrongful* taking the life of another—both when speaking of what the murderer has done to the victim and of what the state is doing to him by way of punishment. But this is precisely the question at issue: whether capital punishment *is* "murder," whether it is wrongful or morally justified and right.

The next two arguments attack the retributive rationale of capital punishment by questioning the claim that it is only this punishment that satisfies the demand for proportion between offense and punishment in the case of murder. The first points out that any two human lives are different in many important respects, such as age, health, physical and mental capability, so that it does not make much sense to consider them equally valuable. What if the murdered person was very old, practically at the very end of her natural life, while the murderer is young, with most of his life still ahead of him, for instance? Or if the victim was gravely and incurably ill, and thus doomed to live her life in suffering and hopelessness, without being able to experience almost anything that makes a human life worth living, while the murderer is in every respect capable of experiencing and enjoying things life has to offer? Or the other way round? Would not the death penalty in such cases amount either to taking a more valuable life as a punishment for destroying a less valuable one, or *vice versa*? Would it not be either too much, or too little, and in both cases disproportionate, and thus unjust and wrong, from the standpoint of the retributive theory itself?

Any plausibility this argument might appear to have is the result of a conflation of differences between, and value of, human lives. No doubt, any two human lives are *different* in innumerable ways, but this does not entail that they are not *equally valuable*. I have no worked-out general theory of equality to refer to here, but I do not think that one is necessary in order to do away with this argument. The modern humanistic and democratic tradition in ethical, social, and political thought is based on the idea that all human beings are equal. This finds its legal expression in the principle of equality of people under the law. If we are not willing to give up this principle, we have to stick to the assumption that, all differences notwithstanding, any two human lives, *qua* human lives, are equally valuable. If, on the other hand, we allow that, on the basis of such criteria as age, health, or mental or physical ability, it can be claimed that the life of one person is more or less valuable than the life of another, and we admit such claims in the sphere of law, including criminal law, we shall thereby give up the principle of equality of people under the law. In all consistency, we shall not be able to demand that property, physical and personal integrity, and all other rights and interests of individuals be given equal consideration in courts of law either—that is, we shall have to accept systematic discrimination between individuals on the basis of the same criteria across the whole field. I do not think anyone would seriously contemplate an overhaul of the whole legal system along these lines.

The second argument having to do with the issue of proportionality between murder and capital punishment draws our attention to the fact that the law normally provides for a certain period of time to elapse between the passing of a death sentence and its execution. It is a period of several weeks or months; in some cases it extends to years. This period is bound to be one of constant mental anguish for the condemned. And thus, all things considered, what is inflicted on him is disproportionately hard and hence unjust. It would be proportionate and just only in the case of "a criminal who had warned his victim of the date at which he would inflict a horrible death on him and who, from that moment onward, had confined him at his mercy for months."[5]

The first thing to note about this argument is that it does not support a full-fledged abolitionist stand; if it were valid, it would not show that capital punishment is *never* proportionate and just, but only that it is *very rarely* so. Consequently, the conclusion would not be that it ought to be abolished outright, but only that it ought to be restricted to those cases that would satisfy the condition cited above. Such cases do happen, although, to be sure, not very often; the murder of Aldo Moro, for instance, was of this kind. But this is not the main point. The main point is that the argument actually does not hit at capital punishment itself, although it is presented with that aim in view. It hits at something else: a particular way of carrying out this punishment, which is widely adopted in our time. Some hundred years ago and more, in the Wild West, they frequently hanged the man convicted to die almost immediately after pronouncing the sentence. I am not arguing here that we should follow this example today; I mention this piece of historical fact only in order to show that the interval between sentencing someone to death and carrying out the sentence is not a *part* of capital punishment itself. However unpalatable we might find those Wild West hangings, whatever objections we might want

---

5. A. Camus, "Reflections on the Guillotine," *Resistance, Rebellion and Death*, trans. J. O'Brien (London: Hamish Hamilton, 1961), p. 143.

to voice against the speed with which they followed the sentencing, surely we shall not deny them the *description* of "executions." So the implication of the argument is not that we ought to do away with capital punishment altogether, nor that we ought to restrict it to those cases of murder where the murderer had warned the victim weeks or months in advance of what he was going to do to her, but that we ought to reexamine the procedure of carrying out this kind of punishment. We ought to weigh the reasons for having this interval between the sentencing and executing, against the moral and human significance of the repercussions such an interval inevitably carries with it.

These reasons, in part, have to do with the possibility of miscarriages of justice and the need to rectify them. Thus we come to the argument against capital punishment which, historically, has been the most effective of all: many advances of the abolitionist movement have been connected with discoveries of cases of judicial errors. Judges and jurors are only human, and consequently some of their beliefs and decisions are bound to be mistaken. Some of their mistakes can be corrected upon discovery; but precisely those with most disastrous repercussions—those which result in innocent people being executed—can never be rectified. In all other cases of mistaken sentencing we can revoke the punishment, either completely or in part, or at least extend compensation. In addition, by exonerating the accused we give moral satisfaction. None of this is possible after an innocent person has been executed; capital punishment is essentially different from all other penalties by being completely irrevocable and irreparable. Therefore, it ought to be abolished.

A part of my reply to this argument goes along the same lines as what I had to say on the previous one. It is not so far-reaching as abolitionists assume; for it would be quite implausible, even fanciful, to claim that there have *never* been cases of murder which left no room whatever for reasonable doubt as to the guilt and full responsibility of the accused. Such cases may not be more frequent than those others, but they do happen. Why not retain the death penalty at least for them?

Actually, this argument, just as the preceding one, does not speak out against capital punishment itself, but against the existing procedures for trying capital cases. Miscarriages of justice result in innocent people being sentenced to death and executed, even in the criminal-law systems in which greatest care is taken to ensure that it never comes to that. But this does not stem from the intrinsic nature of the institution of capital punishment; it results from deficiencies, limitations, and imperfections of the criminal law procedures in which this punishment is meted out. Errors of justice do not demonstrate the need to do away with capital punishment; they simply make it incumbent on us to do everything possible to improve even further procedures of meting it out.

To be sure, this conclusion will not find favor with a diehard abolitionist. "I shall ask for the abolition of Capital Punishment until I have the infallibility of human judgement demonstrated to me," that is, as long as there is even the slightest possibility that innocent people may be executed because of judicial errors, Lafayette said in his day.[6] Many an opponent of this kind of punishment will say the same today. The demand to do away with capital punishment altogether, so as to eliminate even the smallest chance of that ever happening—the chance which, admittedly, would remain even after everything humanly possible has been done to perfect the procedure, although then it would be very slight indeed—is actually a demand to give a privileged position to murderers as against all other offenders, big and small. For if we acted on this demand, we would bring about a situation in which proportionate penalties would be meted out for all offenses, *except* for murder. Murderers would not be receiving the only punishment truly proportionate to their crimes, the punishment of death, but some other, lighter, and thus disproportionate penalty. All other offenders would be punished according to their deserts; only murderers would be receiving less than *they* deserve. In all other cases justice would be done in full; only in cases of the gravest of offenses, the crime of murder, justice would not be carried out in full measure. It is a great and tragic miscarriage of justice when an innocent person is mistakenly sentenced to death and executed, but systematically giving murderers advantage over all other offenders would also be a grave injustice. Is the fact that, as long as capital punishment is retained, there is a possibility that over a number of years, or even decades, an injustice of the first kind may be committed, unintentionally and unconsciously, reason enough to abolish it altogether, and thus end up with a system of punishments in which injustices of the second kind are perpetrated daily, consciously, and inevitably?

There is still another abolitionist argument that actually does not hit out against capital punishment itself, but against something else. Figures are sometimes quoted which show that this punishment is much more often meted out to the uneducated and poor than to the educated, rich,

---

6. Quoted in E. R. Calvert, *Capital Punishment in the Twentieth Century* (London: G. P. Putnam's Sons, 1927), p. 132.

and influential people; in the United States, much more often to blacks than to whites. These figures are adduced as a proof of the inherent injustice of this kind of punishment. On account of them, it is claimed that capital punishment is not a way of doing justice by meting out deserved punishment to murderers, but rather a means of social discrimination and perpetuation of social injustice.

I shall not question these findings, which are quite convincing, and anyway, there is no need to do that in order to defend the institution of capital punishment. For there seems to be a certain amount of discrimination and injustice not only in sentencing people to death and executing them, but also in meting out other penalties. The social structure of the death rows in American prisons, for instance, does not seem to be basically different from the general social structure of American penitentiaries. If this argument were valid, it would call not only for abolition of the penalty of death, but for doing away with other penalties as well. But it is not valid; as Burton Leiser has pointed out,

> . . . this is not an argument, either against the death penalty or against any other form of punishment. It is an argument against the unjust and inequitable distribution of penalties. If the trials of wealthy men are less likely to result in convictions than those of poor men, then something must be done to reform the procedure in criminal courts. If those who have money and standing in the community are less likely to be charged with serious offenses than their less affluent fellow citizens, then there should be a major overhaul of the entire system of criminal justice. . . . But the maldistribution of penalties is no argument against any particular form of penalty.[7]

Igor Primoratz: Justifying Legal Punishment

1. Retributivists such as Primoratz hold that the punishment of a crime ought to be proportional to the offense. Do you find such a view plausible? Are there any other morally relevant considerations when considering how someone should be punished?
2. Primoratz argues that the only punishment proportional to the offense of murder is the death penalty. What reasons does he give for thinking this? Do you think he is correct?

---

7. B. M. Leiser, *Liberty, Justice and Morals: Contemporary Value Conflicts* (New York: Macmillan, 1973), p. 225.

3. Some argue that capital punishment violates the right to life. Primoratz responds that the right to life is not "absolute." What does he mean by this, and how does he argue for it? Do you agree with him?

4. How does Primoratz respond to the objection that the death penalty is hypocritical because it involves killing people for the offense of killing other people? Do you find his response convincing?

5. Many people object to the death penalty on the grounds that it sometimes results in innocent people being executed, and is often applied in a discriminatory way. Why doesn't Primoratz think these concerns justify abolishing the death penalty? Do you agree?

32

An Eye for an Eye?

Stephen Nathanson

In this excerpt from his book *An Eye for an Eye?* (1987), Stephen Nathanson argues against the classic retributivist principle of punishment: *lex talionis*. This principle tells us to treat criminals just as they treated their victims—an eye for an eye, a tooth for a tooth. Nathanson finds two major problems for *lex talionis*. First, it advises us to commit highly immoral actions—raping a rapist, for instance, or torturing a torturer. Second, it is impossible to apply in many cases of deserved punishment—for instance, the principle offers no advice about what to do with drunk drivers, air polluters, embezzlers, or spies.

Retributivists might replace *lex talionis* with a principle of proportional punishment, according to which increasingly bad crimes must be met with increasingly harsher punishment. This proposal is plausible, says Nathanson, but it offers no justification for the death penalty. All it tells us is that the worst crimes ought to be met with the harshest punishments. But it says nothing about how harsh those punishments should be.

Nathanson concludes by discussing the symbolism of abolishing the death penalty, and claims that we express a respect for each person's inalienable rights by refraining from depriving a murderer of his life.

"An Eye for an Eye?" from *An Eye for an Eye?* by Stephen Nathanson (1987). Reprinted with permission of Rowman & Littlefield.

S uppose we ... try to determine what people deserve from a strictly moral point of view. How shall we proceed?

The most usual suggestion is that we look at a person's actions because what someone deserves would appear to depend on what he or she does. A person's actions, it seems, provide not only a basis for a moral appraisal of the person but also a guide to how he should be treated. According to the *lex talionis* or principle of "an eye for an eye," we ought to treat people as they have treated others. What people deserve as recipients of rewards or punishments is determined by what they do as agents.

This is a powerful and attractive view, one that appears to be backed not only by moral common sense but also by tradition and philosophical thought. The most famous statement of philosophical support for this view comes from Immanuel Kant, who linked it directly with an argument for the death penalty. Discussing the problem of punishment, Kant writes,

> What kind and what degree of punishment does legal justice adopt as its principle and standard? None other than the principle of equality the principle of not treating one side more favorably than the other. Accordingly, any undeserved evil that you inflict on someone else among the people is one that you do to yourself. If you vilify, you vilify yourself; if you steal from him, you steal from yourself; if you kill him, you kill yourself. Only the law of retribution (*jus talionis*) can determine exactly the kind and degree of punishment.[1]

Kant's view is attractive for a number of reasons. First, it accords with our belief that what a person deserves is related to what he does. Second, it appeals to a moral standard and does not seem to rely on any particular legal or political institutions. Third, it seems to provide a measure of appropriate punishment that can be used as a guide to creating laws and instituting punishments. It tells us that the punishment is to be identical with the crime. Whatever the criminal did to the victim is to be done in turn to the criminal.

In spite of the attractions of Kant's view, it is deeply flawed. When we see why, it will be clear that the whole "eye for an eye" perspective must be rejected.

---

1. Kant, *Metaphysical Elements of Justice*, translated by John Ladd (Indianapolis: Bobbs-Merrill, 1965), p. 101.

Problems with the Equal Punishment Principle

. . . [Kant's view] does not provide an adequate criterion for determining appropriate levels of punishment.

. . . We can see this, first, by noting that for certain crimes, Kant's view recommends punishments that are not morally acceptable. Applied strictly, it would require that we rape rapists, torture torturers, and burn arsonists whose acts have led to deaths. In general, where a particular crime involves barbaric and inhuman treatment, Kant's principle tells us to act barbarically and inhumanly in return. So, in some cases, the principle generates unacceptable answers to the question of what constitutes appropriate punishment.

This is not its only defect. In many other cases, the principle tells us nothing at all about how to punish. While Kant thought it obvious how to apply his principle in the case of murder, his principle cannot serve as a general rule because it does not tell us how to punish many crimes. Using the Kantian version or the more common "eye for an eye" standard, what would we decide to do to embezzlers, spies, drunken drivers, airline hijackers, drug users, prostitutes, air polluters, or persons who practice medicine without a license? If one reflects on this question, it becomes clear that there is simply no answer to it. We could not in fact design a system of punishment simply on the basis of the "eye for an eye" principle.

In order to justify using the "eye for an eye" principle to answer our question about murder and the death penalty, we would first have to show that it worked for a whole range of cases, giving acceptable answers to questions about amounts of punishment. Then, having established it as a satisfactory general principle, we could apply it to the case of murder. It turns out, however, that when we try to apply the principle generally, we find that it either gives wrong answers or no answers at all. Indeed, I suspect that the principle of "an eye for an eye" is no longer even a principle. Instead, it is simply a metaphorical disguise for expressing belief in the death penalty. People who cite it do not take it seriously. They do not believe in a kidnapping for a kidnapping, a theft for a theft, and so on. Perhaps "an eye for an eye" once was a genuine principle, but now it is merely a slogan. Therefore, it gives us no guidance in deciding whether murderers deserve to die.

In reply to these objections, one might defend the principle by saying that it does not require that punishments be strictly identical with crimes.

Rather, it requires only that a punishment produce an amount of suffering in the criminal which is equal to the amount suffered by the victim. Thus, we don't have to hijack airplanes belonging to airline hijackers, spy on spies, etc. We simply have to reproduce in them the harm done to others.

Unfortunately, this reply really does not solve the problem. It provides no answer to the first objection, since it would still require us to behave barbarically in our treatment of those who are guilty of barbaric crimes. Even if we do not reproduce their actions exactly, any action which caused equal suffering would itself be barbaric. Second, in trying to produce equal amounts of suffering, we run into many problems. Just how much suffering is produced by an airline hijacker or a spy? And how do we apply this principle to prostitutes or drug users, who may not produce any suffering at all? We have rough ideas about how serious various crimes are, but this may not correlate with any clear sense of just how much harm is done.

Furthermore, the same problem arises in determining how much suffering a particular punishment would produce for a particular criminal. People vary in their tolerance of pain and in the amount of unhappiness that a fine or a jail sentence would cause them. Recluses will be less disturbed by banishment than extroverts. Nature lovers will suffer more in prison than people who are indifferent to natural beauty. A literal application of the principle would require that we tailor punishments to individual sensitivities, yet this is at best impractical. To a large extent, the legal system must work with standardized and rather crude estimates of the negative impact that punishments have on people.

The move from calling for a punishment that is identical to the crime to favoring one that is equal in the harm done is no help to us or to the defense of the principle. "An eye for an eye" tells us neither what people deserve nor how we should treat them when they have done wrong.

Proportional Retributivism

The view we have been considering can be called "equality retributivism," since it proposes that we repay criminals with punishments equal to their crimes. In the light of problems like those I have cited, some people have proposed a variation on this view, calling not for equal punishments but rather for punishments which are *proportional* to the crime. In defending such a view as a guide for setting criminal punishments, Andrew von Hirsch writes:

> If one asks how severely a wrongdoer deserves to be punished, a familiar principle comes to mind: Severity of punishment should be commensurate with the seriousness of the wrong. Only grave wrongs merit severe penalties; minor misdeeds deserve lenient punishments. Disproportionate penalties are undeserved—severe sanctions for minor wrongs or vice versa. This principle has variously been called a principle of "proportionality" or "just deserts"; we prefer to call it commensurate deserts.[2]

Like Kant, von Hirsch makes the punishment which a person deserves depend on that person's actions, but he departs from Kant in substituting proportionality for equality as the criterion for setting the amount of punishment.

In implementing a punishment system based on the proportionality view, one would first make a list of crimes, ranking them in order of seriousness. At one end would be quite trivial offenses like parking meter violations, while very serious crimes such as murder would occupy the other. In between, other crimes would be ranked according to their relative gravity. Then a corresponding scale of punishments would be constructed, and the two would be correlated. Punishments would be proportionate to crimes so long as we could say that the more serious the crime was, the higher on the punishment scale was the punishment administered.

This system does not have the defects of equality retributivism. It does not require that we treat those guilty of barbaric crimes barbarically. This is because we can set the upper limit of the punishment scale so as to exclude truly barbaric punishments. Second, unlike the equality principle, the proportionality view is genuinely general, providing a way of handling all crimes. Finally, it does justice to our ordinary belief that certain punishments are unjust because they are too severe or too lenient for the crime committed.

The proportionality principle does, I think, play a legitimate role in our thinking about punishments. Nonetheless, it is no help to death penalty advocates, because it does not require that murderers be executed. All

---

2. *Doing Justice* (New York: Hill & Wang, 1976), p. 66; reprinted in *Sentencing*, edited by H. Gross and A. von Hirsch (Oxford University Press, 1981), p. 243. For a more recent discussion and further defense by von Hirsch, see his *Past or Future Crimes* (New Brunswick, N.J.: Rutgers University Press, 1985).

that it requires is that if murder is the most serious crime, then murder should be punished by the most severe punishment on the scale. The principle does not tell us what this punishment should be, however, and it is quite compatible with the view that the most severe punishment should be a long prison term.

This failure of the theory to provide a basis for supporting the death penalty reveals an important gap in proportional retributivism. It shows that while the theory is general in scope, it does not yield any *specific* recommendations regarding punishment. It tells us, for example, that armed robbery should be punished more severely than embezzling and less severely than murder, but it does not tell us how much to punish any of these. This weakness is, in effect, conceded by von Hirsch, who admits that if we want to implement the "commensurate deserts" principle, we must supplement it with information about what level of punishment is needed to deter crimes.[3] In a later discussion of how to "anchor" the punishment system, he deals with this problem in more depth, but the factors he cites as relevant to making specific judgments (such as available prison space) have nothing to do with what people deserve. He also seems to suggest that a range of punishments may be appropriate for a particular crime. This runs counter to the death penalty supporter's sense that death alone is appropriate for some murderers.[4]

Neither of these retributive views, then, provides support for the death penalty. The equality principle fails because it is not in general true that the appropriate punishment for a crime is to do to the criminal what he has done to others. In some cases this is immoral, while in others it is impossible. The proportionality principle may be correct, but by itself it cannot determine specific punishments for specific crimes. Because of its flexibility and open-endedness, it is compatible with a great range of different punishments for murder.[5] . . .

3. Von Hirsch, *Doing Justice*, pp. 93–94. My criticisms of proportional retributivism are not novel. For helpful discussions of the view, see Hugo Bedau, "Concessions to Retribution in Punishment," in *Justice and Punishment*, edited by J. Cederblom and W. Blizek (Cambridge, Mass.: Ballinger, 1977), and M. Golding, *Philosophy of Law* (Englewood Cliffs, N.J.: Prentice Hall, 1975), pp. 98–99.

4. See von Hirsch, *Past or Future Crimes*, ch. 8.

5. For more positive assessments of these theories, see Jeffrey Reiman, "Justice, Civilization, and the Death Penalty," *Philosophy and Public Affairs* 14 (1985): 115–48; and Michael Davis, "How to Make the Punishment Fit the Crime," *Ethics* 93 (1983).

The Symbolism of Abolishing the Death Penalty

What is the symbolic message that we would convey by deciding to renounce the death penalty and to abolish its use?

I think that there are two primary messages. The first is the most frequently emphasized and is usually expressed in terms of the sanctity of human life, although I think we could better express it in terms of respect for human dignity. One way we express our respect for the dignity of human beings is by abstaining from depriving them of their lives, even if they have done terrible deeds. In defense of human well-being, we may punish people for their crimes, but we ought not to deprive them of everything, which is what the death penalty does.

If we take the life of a criminal, we convey the idea that by his deeds he has made himself worthless and totally without human value. I do not believe that we are in a position to affirm that of anyone. We may hate such a person and feel the deepest anger against him, but when he no longer poses a threat to anyone, we ought not to take his life.

But, one might ask, hasn't the murderer forfeited whatever rights he might have had to our respect? Hasn't he, by his deeds, given up any rights that he had to decent treatment? Aren't we morally free to kill him if we wish?

These questions express important doubts about the obligation to accord any respect to those who have acted so deplorably, but I do not think that they prove that any such forfeiture has occurred. Certainly, when people murder or commit other crimes, they do forfeit some of the rights that are possessed by the law-abiding. They lose a certain right to be left alone. It becomes permissible to bring them to trial and, if they are convicted, to impose an appropriate—even a dreadful—punishment on them.

Nonetheless, they do not forfeit all their rights. It does not follow from the vileness of their actions that we can do anything whatsoever to them. This is part of the moral meaning of the constitutional ban on cruel and unusual punishments. No matter how terrible a person's deeds, we may not punish him in a cruel and unusual way. We may not torture him, for example. His right not to be tortured has not been forfeited. Why do these limits hold? Because this person remains a human being, and we think that there is something in him that we must continue to respect in spite of his terrible acts.

One way of seeing why those who murder still deserve some consideration and respect is by reflecting again on the idea of what it is to *deserve* something. In most contexts, we think that what people deserve depends on what they have done, intended, or tried to do. It depends on features that are qualities of individuals. The best person for the job deserves to be hired. The person who worked especially hard deserves our gratitude. We can call the concept that applies in these cases *personal* desert.

There is another kind of desert, however, that belongs to people by virtue of their humanity itself and does not depend on their individual efforts or achievements. I will call this impersonal kind of desert *human* desert. We appeal to this concept when we think that everyone deserves a certain level of treatment no matter what their individual qualities are. When the signers of the Declaration of Independence affirmed that people had inalienable rights to "life, liberty, and the pursuit of happiness," they were appealing to such an idea. These rights do not have to be earned by people. They are possessed "naturally," and everyone is bound to respect them.

According to the view that I am defending, people do not lose all of their rights when they commit terrible crimes. They still deserve some level of decent treatment simply because they remain living, functioning human beings. This level of moral desert need not be earned, and it cannot be forfeited. This view may sound controversial, but in fact everyone who believes that cruel and unusual punishment should be forbidden implicitly agrees with it. That is, they agree that even after someone has committed a terrible crime, we do not have the right to do anything whatsoever to him.

What I am suggesting is that by renouncing the use of death as a punishment, we express and reaffirm our belief in the inalienable, unforfeitable core of human dignity.

Why is this a worthwhile message to convey? It is worth conveying because this belief is both important and precarious. Throughout history, people have found innumerable reasons to degrade the humanity of one another. They have found qualities in others that they hated or feared, and even when they were not threatened by these people, they have sought to harm them, deprive them of their liberty, or take their lives from them. They have often felt that they had good reasons to do these things, and they have invoked divine commands, racial purity, and state security to support their deeds.

These actions and attitudes are not relics of the past. They remain an awful feature of the contemporary world. By renouncing the death penalty, we show our determination to accord at least minimal respect even to those whom we believe to be personally vile or morally vicious. This is, perhaps, why we speak of the *sanctity* of human life rather than its value or worth. That which is sacred remains, in some sense, untouchable, and its value is not dependent on its worth or usefulness to us. Kant expressed this ideal of respect in the famous second version of the Categorical Imperative: "So act as to treat humanity, whether in thine own person or in that of any other, in every case as an end withal, never as a means only." . . .

When the state has a murderer in its power and could execute him but does not, this conveys the idea that even though this person has done wrong and even though we may be angry, outraged, and indignant with him, we will nonetheless control ourselves in a way that he did not. We will not kill him, even though we could do so and even though we are angry and indignant. We will exercise restraint, sanctioning killing only when it serves a protective function.

Why should we do this? Partly out of a respect for human dignity. But also because we want the state to set an example of proper behavior. We do not want to encourage people to resort to violence to settle conflicts when there are other ways available. We want to avoid the cycle of violence that can come from retaliation and counter-retaliation. Violence is a contagion that arouses hatred and anger, and if unchecked, it simply leads to still more violence. The state can convey the message that the contagion must be stopped, and the most effective principle for stopping it is the idea that only defensive violence is justifiable. Since the death penalty is not an instance of defensive violence, it ought to be renounced.

We show our respect for life best by restraining ourselves and allowing murderers to live, rather than by following a policy of a life for a life. Respect for life and restraint of violence are aspects of the same ideal. The renunciation of the death penalty would symbolize our support of that ideal.

Stephen Nathanson: An Eye for an Eye?

1. Nathanson rejects the principle of *lex talionis*, according to which we ought to treat criminals as they have treated others. What reasons does he give for rejecting this principle? Do you find his reasons convincing?

2. Nathanson considers the following modification of the principle of *lex talionis*: "a punishment [should] produce an amount of suffering in the criminal which is equal to the amount suffered by the victim." Do you

think this is a plausible principle? What objections does Nathanson offer to the principle?

3. What is the principle of proportional retributivism? Why doesn't Nathanson think that this principle supports the death penalty? Do you agree with him?

4. What symbolic message does Nathanson think that abolishing the death penalty would convey? Is this a good reason to abolish the death penalty?

5. Are there any reasons for supporting the death penalty that Nathanson does not consider? If so, are these reasons ever strong enough to justify sentencing someone to death?

33

≡≡ ❧ ≡≡

Why Gun 'Control' Is Not Enough

Jeff McMahan

Jeff McMahan argues for a near-complete ban on gun ownership. Well-trained police and military officials are the only ones who ought to be allowed to own a gun. For all others—that is, for all private citizens—guns are not to be controlled, but banned.

McMahan's case is both positive and negative. The positive argument is that private gun ownership creates a much more dangerous environment for everyone; the more private citizens who have guns, the more the power of the police declines. And when police power declines, people become more vulnerable and so have greater incentive to get a gun to protect themselves. But when most people have guns, everyone becomes less secure compared to a situation in which no one but police officers have guns.

The negative element of McMahan's case amounts to a critique of the two major reasons that gun advocates have offered on behalf of private gun ownership. The first is that guns provide a lot of recreational value, in the form of target shooting and hunting. While McMahan is open to the idea of allowing hunters to own single-chamber shotguns for hunting purposes, he denies that the value of target shooting justifies gun ownership, since enthusiasts could rent guns whose use is restricted to licensed shooting ranges. The second reason gun advocates have offered is that gun ownership is the best means of self-defense, and our right to self-defense justifies a right to own a gun. McMahan counters that the need for guns to defend oneself arises

New York Times *Opinionator* blog, December 19, 2012, http://opinionator.blogs.nytimes.com /2012/12/19/why-gun-control-is-not-enough/?_r=0 primarily because we allow people to have guns in the first place—if we banned all private gun ownership, then we would all live in much safer environments, and so have less need for a gun for self-defense.

McMahan concludes by rebutting a few familiar pro-gun arguments. The first is that a gun ban is impractical, because of existing political opposition. But McMahan argues that gun advocates cannot press this argument in good faith, since it is only their opposition that stands in the way of such a ban. The second argument is that a ban on gun ownership is impractical in that it will not end gun violence. He agrees that such a ban will not be wholly effective but argues that this is hardly a compelling reason not to enforce the ban. After all, we have laws against murder, though we know in advance that having such a law will not prevent all murders. A third argument is that prohibiting private gun ownership is no different from drug or alcohol prohibition, which have been gross failures. McMahan believes, however, that there is a relevant difference, since millions of people need or crave drugs and alcohol and will engage in such consumption regardless of a legal prohibition, whereas the desire for a gun is primarily driven by a desire for self-defense, and, as already indicated, there would be far less need for a gun for self-defense purposes if private citizens were prohibited from having guns in the first place.

....

Americans are finally beginning to have a serious discussion about guns. One argument we're hearing is the central pillar of the case for private gun ownership: that we are all safer when more individuals have guns because armed citizens deter crime and can defend themselves and others against it when deterrence fails. Those who don't have guns, it's said, are free riders on those who do, as the criminally disposed are less likely to engage in crime the more likely it is that their victim will be armed.

There's some sense to this argument, for even criminals don't like being shot. But the logic is faulty, and a close look at it leads to the conclusion that the United States should ban private gun ownership entirely, or almost entirely.

One would think that if widespread gun ownership had the robust deterrent effects that gun advocates claim it has, our country would be freer of crime than other developed societies. But it's not. When most citizens are armed, as they were in the Wild West, crime doesn't cease.

Instead, criminals work to be better armed, more efficient in their use of guns ("quicker on the draw"), and readier to use them. When this happens, those who get guns may be safer than they would be without them, but those without them become progressively more vulnerable.

Gun advocates have a solution to this: the unarmed must arm themselves. But when more citizens get guns, further problems arise: people who would once have got in a fistfight instead shoot the person who provoked them; people are shot by mistake or by accident.

And with guns so plentiful, any lunatic or criminally disposed person who has a sudden and perhaps only temporary urge to kill people can simply help himself to the contents of Mom's gun cabinet. Perhaps most important, the more people there are who have guns, the less effective the police become. The power of the citizens and that of the police approach parity. The police cease to have even a near-monopoly on the use of force.

To many devotees of the Second Amendment, this is precisely the point. As former Congressman Jay Dickey, Republican of Arkansas, said in January 2011, "We have a right to bear arms because of the threat of government taking over the freedoms we have." The more people there are with guns, the less able the government is to control them. But if arming the citizenry limits the power of the government, it does so by limiting the power of its agents, such as the police. Domestic defense becomes more a matter of private self-help and vigilantism and less a matter of democratically controlled, public law enforcement. Domestic security becomes increasingly "privatized."

There is, of course, a large element of fantasy in Dickey's claim. Individuals with handguns are no match for a modern army. It's also a delusion to suppose that the government in a liberal democracy such as the United States could become so tyrannical that armed insurrection, rather than democratic procedures, would be the best means of constraining it. This is not Syria; nor will it ever be. Shortly after Dickey made his comment, people in Egypt rose against a government that had suppressed their freedom in ways far more serious than requiring them to pay for health care. Although a tiny minority of Egyptians do own guns, the protesters would not have succeeded if those guns had been brought to Tahrir Square. If the assembled citizens had been brandishing Glocks in accordance with the script favored by Second Amendment fantasists, the old regime would almost certainly still be in power and many Egyptians who're now alive would be dead.

For the police to remain effective in a society in which most of those they must confront or arrest are armed, they must, like criminals, become better armed, more numerous, and readier to fire. But if they do that, guns won't have produced a net reduction in the power of the government but will only have generated enormous private and public expenditures, leaving the balance of power between armed citizens and the state as it was before, the unarmed conspicuously worse off, and everyone poorer except the gun industry. The alternative to maintaining the balance of power is to allow it to shift in favor of the armed citizenry and away from the police, again making unarmed citizens—including those who refuse on principle to contribute to the erosion of collective security by getting a gun—the greatest losers overall.

The logic is inexorable: as more private individuals acquire guns, the power of the police declines, personal security becomes more a matter of self-help, and the unarmed have an increasing incentive to get guns, until everyone is armed. When most citizens then have the ability to kill anyone in their vicinity in an instant, everyone is less secure than they would be if no one had guns other than the members of a democratically accountable police force.

The logic of private gun possession is thus similar to that of the nuclear arms race. When only one state gets nuclear weapons, it enhances its own security but reduces that of others, which have become more vulnerable. The other states then have an incentive to get nuclear weapons to try to restore their security. As more states get them, the incentives for others increase. If eventually all get them, the potential for catastrophe—whether through irrationality, misperception, or accident—is great. Each state's security is then much lower than it would be if none had nuclear weapons.

Gun advocates and criminals are allies in demanding that guns remain in private hands. They differ in how they want them distributed. Criminals want guns for themselves but not for their potential victims. Others want them for themselves but not for criminals. But while gun control can do a little to restrict access to guns by potential criminals, it can't do much when guns are to be found in every other household. Either criminals and non-criminals will have them or neither will. Gun advocates prefer for both rather than neither to have them.

But, as with nuclear weapons, we would all be safer if no one had guns— or, rather, no one other than trained and legally constrained police officers. Domestic defense would then be conducted the way we conduct national defense. We no longer accept, as the authors of the now obsolete

Second Amendment did, that "a well-regulated militia" is "necessary to the security of a free state." Rather than leaving national defense to citizens' militias, we now, for a variety of compelling reasons, cede the right of national defense to certain state-authorized professional institutions: the Army, Navy, and so on. We rightly trust these forces to protect us from external threats and not to become instruments of domestic repression. We could have the same trust in a police force designed to protect us from domestic threats.

A prohibition of private ownership would not mean that no one could shoot guns. Guns for target shooting could be rented under security arrangements at the range. And there's perhaps scope for debate about private possession of single chamber shotguns for hunting.

Gun advocates will object that a prohibition of private gun ownership is an impossibility in the United States. But this is not an objection they can press in good faith, for the only reason that a legal prohibition could be impossible in a democratic state is that a majority oppose it. If gun advocates ceased to oppose it, a prohibition would be possible.

They will next argue that even if there were a legal prohibition, it could not be enforced with anything approaching complete effectiveness. This is true. As long as some people somewhere have guns, some people here can get them. Similarly, the legal prohibition of murder cannot eliminate murder. But the prohibition of murder is more effective than a policy of "murder control" would be.

Guns are not like alcohol and drugs, both of which we have tried unsuccessfully to prohibit. Many people have an intense desire for alcohol or drugs that is independent of what other people may do. But the need for a gun for self-defense depends on whether other people have them and how effective the protection and deterrence provided by the state are. Thus, in other Western countries in which there are fewer guns, there are correspondingly fewer instances in which people need guns for effective self-defense.

Gun advocates sometimes argue that a prohibition would violate individuals' rights of self-defense. Imposing a ban on guns, they argue, would be tantamount to taking a person's gun from her just as someone is about to kill her. But this is a defective analogy. Although a prohibition would deprive people of one effective means of self-defense, it would also ensure that there would be far fewer occasions on which a gun would be necessary or even useful for self-defense. For guns would be forbidden not just to those who would use them for defense but also to those who would use them for aggression. Guns are only one means of self-defense and self-defense is only one means of achieving security against attack. It is the right to security against attack that is fundamental. A policy that unavoidably deprives a person of one means of self-defense but on balance substantially reduces her vulnerability to attack is therefore respectful of the more fundamental right from which the right of self-defense is derived.

In other Western countries, per capita homicide rates, as well as rates of violent crime involving guns, are a fraction of what they are in the United States. The possible explanations of this are limited. Gun advocates claim it has nothing to do with our permissive gun laws or our customs and practices involving guns. If they are right, should we conclude that Americans are simply inherently more violent, more disposed to mental derangement, and less moral than people in other Western countries? If you resist that conclusion, you have little choice but to accept that our easy access to all manner of firearms is a large part of the explanation of why we kill each at a much higher rate than our counterparts elsewhere. Gun advocates must search their consciences to determine whether they really want to share responsibility for the perpetuation of policies that make our country the homicide capital of the developed world.

Jeff McMahan: Why Gun 'Control' Is Not Enough

1. Given the political climate in the United States, many think that a gun ban is impractical, and hence unjustified. Present McMahan's reply to this concern and assess its merits.
2. Suppose that a gun-free society is much safer than a gun-filled society. This by itself does not suffice to show that societies should institute a ban on guns. What further assumptions are required in order to get from the initial supposition to the conclusion that a society ought to institute a ban on private gun ownership?
3. McMahan claims that the logic of private gun ownership is "inexorable." Can you clearly state just what this logic is, and why McMahan is concerned about it?
4. How (if at all) do the arguments McMahan offers apply to the question of whether we should allow people to own hunting rifles?
5. Consider McMahan's discussion of the analogy between drug and alcohol prohibition and the prohibition of private gun ownership. Do you find his discussion persuasive? Why or why not?

34

Is There a Right to Own a Gun?

Michael Huemer

Michael Huemer argues that individuals have a powerful right to own a gun and that gun control laws that seek to prevent law-abiding citizens from owning a gun are immoral. Huemer allows that gun rights might sometimes be overridden—i.e., they are not *absolute*—though this is a very small concession, as he believes that no right is absolute. He claims that we have a powerful right to own guns that derives from our fundamental right to liberty: we have a moral right to do whatever we want, so long as we do not violate the rights of others. So we have a moral right to own a gun, so long as we do not use it to violate the rights of others.

According to Huemer, the right to own a gun is significant for two reasons. First, guns are the source of a great deal of recreational value, through target shooting, hunting, etc. Second, and more importantly, guns can be vital means of self-defense. This last consideration leads Huemer to review the statistics on gun crime and crime prevention and to argue that since the right to self-defense is an important right, and since a firearms prohibition would be a significant violation of that right, such a prohibition amounts to a serious rights violation.

Since Huemer allows that any right might possibly be overridden, he then considers whether the right to own a gun might be overridden by the harms caused by guns. To do this he reviews some oft-cited

Social Theory and Practice vol. 29 (2003). This selection has been abridged and its notes have been edited and renumbered.

statistical arguments against gun ownership and finds that they are more problematic than people have recognized. He then discusses the benefits, which lie primarily in the use of guns to prevent crime. Finally, he argues that because the right to own a gun is so morally important, the costs of gun ownership would have to be much greater than the benefits in order to justify a firearms prohibition. Though he admits that calculation of costs and benefits is difficult, he argues that the benefits probably outweigh the costs, and so the right to own a gun—at least on the part of law-abiding citizens—is not in fact outweighed.

....

1. Introduction

Gun control supporters often assume that the acceptability of gun control laws turns on whether they increase or decrease crime rates. The notion that such laws might violate rights, independently of whether they decrease crime rates, is rarely entertained. Nor are the interests of gun owners in keeping and using guns typically given great weight. . . .

I believe these attitudes are misguided. I contend that individuals have a prima facie right to own firearms, that this right is weighty and protects important interests, and that it is not overridden by utilitarian considerations. In support of the last point, I shall argue that the harms of private gun ownership are probably less than the benefits, and that in any case, these harms would have to be many times greater than the benefits in order for the right to own a gun to be overridden. . . .

2. Preliminary Remarks about Rights

2.2 *What Sort of Right Is the Right to Own a Gun?*

First, I distinguish between *fundamental* and *derivative* rights. A right is derivative when it derives at least some of its weight from its relationship to another, independent right. A right is fundamental when it has some force that is independent of other rights. On these definitions, it is possible for a right to be both fundamental and derivative. Derivative rights are usually related to fundamental rights as means to the protection or enforcement of the latter, though this need not be the only way in which a right may be derivative. I claim that the right to own a gun is both fundamental and derivative; however, it is in its *derivative* aspect—as derived from the right of self-defense—that it is most important.

Second, I distinguish between *absolute* and *prima facie* rights. An absolute right is one with overriding importance, such that no considerations can justify violating it. A prima facie right is one that must be given some weight in moral deliberation but that can be overridden by sufficiently important countervailing considerations. Thus, if it would be permissible to steal for sufficiently important reasons—say, to save someone's life—then property rights are not absolute but at most prima facie. It is doubtful whether any rights are absolute. At any rate, I do not propose any absolute rights; I argue only that there is a strong prima facie right to own a gun. . . .

3. Is There a Prima Facie Right to Own a Gun?

Given the presumption in favor of liberty, there is at least a prima facie right to own a gun, unless there are positive grounds . . . for denying such a right. Are there such grounds?

(i) Begin with the principle that one lacks a right to do things that harm others, treat others as mere means, or use others without their consent. It is difficult to see how owning a gun could itself be said to do any of those things, even though owning a gun makes it easier for one to do those things if one chooses to. But we do not normally prohibit activities that merely *make it easier* for one to perform a wrong but require a separate decision to perform the wrongful act.

(ii) Consider the principle that one lacks a right to do things that impose unacceptable, though unintended, risks on others. Since life is replete with risks, to be plausible, the principle must use some notion of *excessive* risks. But the risks associated with normal ownership and recreational use of firearms are minimal. While approximately 77 million Americans now own guns,[1] the accidental death rate for firearms has fallen dramatically during the last century, and is now about .3 per 100,000 population. For comparison, the average citizen is nineteen times more likely to die as a result of an accidental fall, and fifty times

---

1. Surveys indicate that about half of American men and a quarter of women own guns. See Harry Henderson, *Gun Control* (New York: Facts on File, 2000), p. 231; John Lott, *More Guns, Less Crime*, 2nd ed. (Chicago: University of Chicago Press, 2000), pp. 37, 41.

more likely to die in an automobile accident, than to die as a result of a firearms accident.[2]

(iii) Some may think that the firearms accident statistics miss the point: the real risk that gun ownership imposes on others is the risk that the gun owner or someone else will "lose control" during an argument and decide to shoot his opponent. Nicholas Dixon argues: "In 1990, 34.5% of all murders resulted from domestic or other kinds of argument. Since we are all capable of heated arguments, we are all, in the wrong circumstances, capable of losing control and killing our opponent."[3] In response, we should first note the invalidity of Dixon's argument. Suppose that 34.5% of people who run a 4-minute mile have black hair, and that I have black hair. It does not follow that I am capable of running a 4-minute mile. It seems likely that only very atypical individuals would respond to heated arguments by killing their opponents. Second, Dixon's . . . claims are refuted by the empirical evidence. In the largest seventy-five counties in the United States in 1988, over 89% of adult murderers had prior criminal records as adults.[4] This reinforces the common sense view that normal people are extremely unlikely to commit a murder, even if they have the means available. So gun ownership does not typically impose excessive risks on others.

(iv) Consider the idea that individuals lack a right to engage in activities that reasonably appear to evince an intention to harm or impose unacceptable risks on others. This principle does not apply here, as it is acknowledged on all sides that only a tiny fraction of America's 77 million gun owners plan to commit crimes with guns.

(v) It might be argued that the *total social cost* of private gun ownership is significant, that the state is unable to identify in advance those persons who are going to misuse their weapons, and that the state's only viable method of significantly reducing that social cost is therefore to prevent even noncriminal citizens from owning guns. But this is not an argument against the existence of a *prima facie* right to own a gun. It

2. National Safety Council, *Injury Facts, 1999 Edition* (Itasca, Ill.: National Safety Council, 1999), pp. 8–9.

3. Dixon, "Why We Should Ban Handguns," p. 266. Similarly, Jeff McMahan (unpublished comments on this paper, 7 January 2002) writes that "most [murders] occur when a perfectly ordinary person is pushed over a certain emotional threshold by an unusual concatenation of events."

4. Lott, *More Guns*, p. 8.

is just an argument for overriding any such right. In general, the fact that restricting an activity has beneficial consequences does not show that no weight at all should be assigned to the freedom to engage in it; it simply shows that there are competing reasons against allowing the activity. (Compare: suppose that taking my car from me and giving it to you increases total social welfare. It would not follow that I have no claim at all on my car.)

It is difficult to deny the existence of at least a *prima facie* right to own a gun. But this says nothing about the *strength* of this right, nor about the grounds there may be for overriding it. Most gun control advocates would claim, not that there is not even a prima facie right to own a gun, but that the right is a minor one, and that the harms of private gun ownership, in comparison, are very large.

4. Is the Right to Own a Gun Significant?

I shall confine my consideration of gun control to the proposal to ban all private firearms ownership. This would violate the prima facie right to own a gun. I contend that the rights violation would be very serious, owing both to the importance of gun ownership in the lives of firearms enthusiasts, and to the relationship between the right to own a gun and the right of self-defense.

4.1. The Recreational Value of Guns

The recreational uses of guns include target shooting, various sorts of shooting competitions, and hunting. In debates over gun control, participants almost never attach any weight to this recreational value— perhaps because that value initially appears minor compared with the deaths caused or prevented by guns. The insistence that individuals have a right to engage in their chosen forms of recreation may seem frivolous in this context. But it is not. . . .

One might claim that the value of the lives that could be saved by anti-gun laws is simply *much greater* than the recreational value of firearms. It is not obvious that this is correct, *even if* gun control would significantly reduce annual gun-related deaths. Many gun owners appear to derive enormous satisfaction from the recreational use of firearms, and it is no exaggeration to say that for many, recreational shooting is a way of life. Furthermore, there are a great many gun owners. At a rough estimate, the number of gun owners is two thousand times greater than the number of annual firearms-related deaths.[5] Even if we assume optimistically that a substantial proportion of recreational gun users could and would substitute other forms of recreation, we should conclude that the net utility of gun control legislation is greatly overestimated by those who discount the recreational value of guns. For obvious reasons, the utility resulting from recreational use of firearms is not easy to quantify, nor to compare with the value of the lives lost to firearms violence. Yet this is no reason for ignoring the former, as partisans in the gun control debate often do.

But our present concern is not chiefly utilitarian. The argument here is that gun enthusiasts' prima facie right to own guns is significant in virtue of the central place that such ownership plays in their chosen lifestyle. A prohibition on firearms ownership would constitute a major interference in their plans for their own lives.... [T]his suffices to show that such a prohibition would be a serious rights violation.

4.2. *The Right of Self-Defense*

The main argument on the gun rights side goes like this:

1. The right of self-defense is an important right.
2. A firearms prohibition would be a significant violation of the right of self-defense.
3. Therefore, a firearms prohibition would be a serious rights violation.

The strength of the conclusion depends upon the strength of the premises: the more important the right of self-defense is, and the more serious gun control is as a violation of that right, the more serious a rights violation gun control is.

I begin by arguing that the right of self-defense is extremely weighty. Consider this scenario:

Example 1: A killer breaks into a house, where two people—"the victim" and "the accomplice"—are staying. (The "accomplice" need have no prior

---

5. Annual firearms deaths in America, including suicides, are close to 35,000 (Henderson, *Gun Control*, p. 225). Approximately 77 million Americans own guns (ibid., p. 231; Lott, *More Guns*, pp. 37, 41), though most are probably not enthusiasts. This gives a 2200:1 ratio. 46% of gun-owners surveyed report hunting or recreation as their main reason for keeping a gun (Henderson, *Gun Control*, p. 234).

interaction with the killer.) As the killer enters the bedroom where the victim is hiding, the accomplice enters through another door and proceeds, for some reason, to hold the victim down while the killer stabs him to death.

In this scenario, the killer commits what may be the most serious kind of rights violation possible. What about the accomplice who holds the victim down? Most would agree that his crime is, if not equivalent to murder, something close to murder in degree of wrongness, even though he neither kills nor injures the victim. Considered merely as the act of holding someone down for a few moments, the accomplice's action seems a minor rights violation. What makes it so wrong is that it prevents the victim from either defending himself or fleeing from the killer—that is, it violates the right of self-defense. (To intentionally and forcibly prevent a person from exercising a right is to violate that right.) We may also say that the accomplice's crime was that of assisting in the commission of a murder—this is not, in my view, a competing explanation of the wrongness of his action, but rather an elaboration on the first explanation. Since the right of self-defense is a derivative right, serving to protect the right to life among other rights, violations of the right of self-defense will often cause or enable violations of the right to life.

It is common to distinguish *killing* from *letting die*. In this example, we see a third category of action: *preventing the prevention of a death*. This is distinct from killing, but it is not merely letting die, because it requires positive action. The example suggests that preventing the prevention of a death is about as serious a wrong as killing. In any case, the fact that serious violations of the right of self-defense are morally comparable to murder serves to show that the right of self-defense must be a very weighty right.

. . . .

We turn to premise 2, that gun prohibition is serious as a violation of the right of self-defense. Consider:

Example 2: As in example 1, except that the victim has a gun by the bed, which he would, if able, use to defend himself from the killer. As the killer enters the bedroom, the victim reaches for the gun. The accomplice grabs the gun and runs away, with the result that the killer then stabs his victim to death.

The accomplice's action in this case seems morally comparable to his action in example 1. Again, he has intentionally prevented the victim from defending himself, thereby in effect assisting in the murder. The arguments from the criteria for the seriousness of rights violations are the same.

The analogy between the accomplice's action in this case and a general firearms prohibition should be clear. A firearms ban would require confiscating the weapons that many individuals keep for self-defense purposes, with the result that some of those individuals would be murdered, robbed, raped, or seriously injured. If the accomplice's action in example 2 is a major violation of the right of self-defense, then gun prohibition seems to be about equally serious as a violation of the right of self-defense.

Consider some objections to this analogy. First, it might be said that in the case of a gun ban, the government would have strong reasons for confiscating the guns, in order to save the lives of others, which (we presume) is not true of the accomplice in example 2. This, I think, would amount to arguing that the self-defense rights of noncriminal gun owners are overridden by the state's need to protect society from criminal gun owners. I deal with this suggestion in §5 below.

Second, it might be argued that example 2 differs from a gun ban in that the murder is *imminent* at the time the accomplice takes the gun away. But this seems to be morally irrelevant. For suppose that the accomplice, knowing that someone is coming to kill the victim tomorrow (while the victim does not know this), decides to take the victim's gun away from him today, again resulting in his death. This would not make the accomplice's action more morally defensible than it is in example 2.

A third difference might be that, whereas we assume that in example 2 the accomplice knows that the victim is going to be killed or seriously injured, the state does not know that its anti-gun policy will result in murders and injuries to former gun owners. This, however, is surely not true. Although the state may claim that the lives saved by a gun ban would *outnumber* the lives cost, one cannot argue that no lives will be cost at all, unless one claims implausibly that guns are never used in self-defense against life-threatening attacks. Some will think the former claim is all that is needed to justify a gun ban; this would return us to the first objection.

Fourth, it may be observed that in example 2, there is a specific, identifiable victim: the accomplice knows who is going to die as a result of his gun confiscation. In contrast, a gun-banning government cannot identify any specific individuals who are going to be killed as a result of its gun ban, even though it can predict that *some* people will be. But this seems morally irrelevant. Consider:

Example 3: An "accomplice" ties up a family of five somewhere in the wilderness where he knows that wolves roam. He has good reason to believe that a pack of wolves will happen by and eat one or two of the family members (after which they will be satiated), but he doesn't know which ones will be eaten. He leaves them for an hour, during which time the mother of the family is eaten by the wolves.

In this case, the fact that the accomplice did not know who would die as a result of his action does not mitigate his guilt. Likewise, it is unclear how the state's inability to predict who will become the victims of its anti-gun policy would mitigate the state's responsibility for their deaths or injury.

Fifth, the victims of a gun ban would presumably have sufficient forewarning of the coming ban to take alternative measures to protect themselves, unlike the victim in example 2. Unfortunately, statistics from the National Crime Victimization Survey indicate that such alternative means of self-protection would be relatively ineffective—individuals who defend themselves with a gun are less likely to be injured and far less likely to have the crime completed against them than are persons who take any other measures.[6] Consequently, though the present consideration seems to mitigate the state's culpability, it does not remove it. The situation is analogous to one in which the accomplice, rather than taking away the victim's only means of defending himself against the killer, merely takes away the victim's *most effective* means of self-defense, with the result that the victim is killed. Here, the accomplice's action is less wrong than in example 2, but it is still very wrong.

Since gun prohibition is a significant violation of an extremely weighty right, we must conclude that it is a very serious rights violation. The above examples initially suggest that it is on a par with the commission of (multiple) murders, robberies, rapes, and assaults—although the consideration of the preceding paragraph may show that it is somewhat less wrong than that. The point here is not that would-be gun banners are as blameworthy

---

6. Gary Kleck, *Targeting Guns: Firearms and Their Control* (New York: Aldine de Gruyter, 1997), pp. 170–74, 190; Lawrence Southwick, "Self-Defense with Guns: The Consequences," *Journal of Criminal Justice* 28 (2000): 351–70.

as murderers and other violent criminals (since the former do not *know* that their proposals are morally comparable to murder and have different motives from typical murderers). The point is just to assess the strength of the reasons against taking the course of action that they propose.

5. Are Gun Rights Overridden?

I have argued that there is a strong prima facie right to own a gun. Nevertheless, firearms prohibition might be justified, if the reasons for prohibition were strong enough to override that right. To determine whether this is the case, we consider three questions: First, how great are the harms of private gun ownership? Second, how great are the benefits? Third, what must the cost/benefit ratio be like, for the right to own a gun to be overridden? I shall argue, first, that the harms of private gun owner-ship have been greatly exaggerated; second, that the benefits of private gun ownership are large and in fact greater than the harms; and third, that the harms would have to be many times greater than the benefits in order to override the right to own a gun. . . .

5.1. *The Case Against Guns*

5.1.1. *The 43-to-1 Statistic*

One prominent argument claims that a gun kept in the home is 43 times more likely to be used in a suicide, criminal homicide, or accidental death than it is to kill an intruder in self-defense.[7] This statistic is commonly repeated with various modifications; for instance, LaFollette mischarac-terizes the statistic as follows:

> For every case where someone in a gun-owning household uses a gun *to successfully stop a life-threatening attack*, nearly forty-three people in similar households will die from a gunshot.[8]

The problem with LaFollette's characterization, which evinces the statis-tic's tendency to mislead, is that Kellerman and Reay made no estimate of the frequency with which guns are used to stop attacks, life-threatening or otherwise; they only considered cases in which someone was *killed*. Survey

---

7. Arthur Kellerman and Donald Reay, "Protection or Peril? An Analysis of Firearm-Related Deaths in the Home," *New England Journal of Medicine* 314 (1986): 1557–60.
8. Hugh LaFollette, "Gun Control," *Ethics* 110 (2000): 263–81, p. 276 (emphasis added).

data indicate that only a tiny minority of defensive gun uses involve shooting, let alone killing, the criminal; normally, threatening a criminal with a gun is sufficient. To assess the benefits of guns, one would have to examine the frequency with which guns prevent crimes, rather than the frequency with which they kill criminals.

A second problem is that 37 of Kellerman and Reay's 43 deaths were suicides. Available evidence is unclear on whether reduced availability of guns would reduce the suicide rate or whether it would only result in substitution into different methods. In addition, philosophically, it is doubtful that the restriction of gun ownership for the purpose of preventing suicides would fall within the prerogatives of a liberal state, even if such a policy would be effective. One cause for doubt is that such policies infringe upon the rights of gun owners (both the suicidal ones and the nonsuicidal majority) without protecting anyone else's rights. Another cause for doubt, from a utilitarian perspective, is that one cannot assume that individuals who decide to kill themselves have overall happy or pleasant lives; therefore, one should not assume that the prevention of suicide, through means other than improving would-be victims' level of happiness, increases utility, rather than decreasing it. For these reasons, the suicides should be omitted from the figures. . . .

5.1.2. International Comparisons

A second type of argument often used by gun-control proponents relies on comparisons of homicide rates between the United States and other industrialized democracies, such as Canada, Great Britain, Sweden, and Australia. The United States is found to have vastly higher homicide rates, and it is argued that this is due largely to the high gun-ownership rates in the U.S.

Skeptics suggest that the United States has a number of unique cultural factors that influence the murder rate and that invalidate such cross-country comparisons. Some find this claim more plausible than do others. Fortunately, we need not rely on intuitions. Instead, we can test the claim empirically, by examining data within the United States, across jurisdictions with varying gun laws and gun ownership rates and over time periods with changing gun laws and gun ownership rates—this would effectively control for the cultural factors allegedly affecting the murder rate. When we do this, we find that (i) jurisdictions with stricter gun laws tend to have higher crime rates, (ii) shifts to more permissive gun laws tend to be followed by drops in crime rates, (iii) areas with higher gun ownership rates have lower crime rates, and (iv) historically, crime rates have fluctuated with no discernible pattern as the civilian gun stock has increased drastically.[9]

I do not claim to have *proved* that gun laws cause increased crime or that civilian gun ownership fails to do so. Nor do I deny that there is any evidence on the gun control advocates' side. What I am claiming at this point is that the evidence presented by gun control advocates fails to make a very convincing case for the net harmfulness of private gun ownership. The casual comparisons between countries discussed here typically use only a handful of data points, exclude many countries from consideration, and make no attempt to control statistically for any other factors that might affect crime rates. In contrast, far more rigorous studies are available to the other side, as we shall see presently. Thus, at a minimum, one cannot claim justified belief that gun prohibition would be beneficial overall.

5.2. *The Benefits of Guns*

5.2.1. *Frequency of Defensive Gun Uses*

Guns are used surprisingly often by private citizens in the United States for self-defense purposes. . . . Probably among the more reliable [surveys] is Kleck and Gertz's 1993 national survey, which obtained an estimate of 2.5 million annual defensive gun uses, excluding military and police uses and excluding uses against animals. Gun users in 400,000 of these cases believe that the gun certainly or almost certainly saved a life.[10] While survey respondents almost certainly overestimated their danger, if even one tenth of them were correct, the number of lives saved by guns each year would exceed the number of gun homicides and suicides. For the

---

9. On (i) and (ii), see §5.2.1 below and Kopel, "Peril or Protection?" p. 308. On (iii), see Lott, *More Guns*, p. 114. Lott's figures for the correlation between gun ownership and crime rates include controls for arrest rates, income, population density, and other variables. On (iv), see Don Kates, Henry Schaffer, John Lattimer, George Murray, and Edwin Cassem, "Guns and Public Health: Epidemic of Violence or Pandemic of Propaganda?" *Tennessee Law Review* 62 (1995): 513–96, pp. 571–74.

10. Gary Kleck and Marc Gertz, "Armed Resistance to Crime: The Prevalence and Nature of Self-Defense with a Gun," *Journal of Criminal Law and Criminology* 86 (1995): 150–87.

purposes of Kleck and Gertz's study, a "defensive gun use" requires respondents to have actually seen a person (as opposed, for example, to merely hearing a suspicious noise in the yard) whom they believed was committing or attempting to commit a crime against them, and to have at a minimum threatened the person with a gun, but not necessarily to have fired the gun. Kleck's statistics imply that defensive gun uses outnumber crimes committed with guns by a ratio of about 3:1. . . .

5.3. Why a Gun Ban Must Have Much Greater Benefits than Harms to Be Justified

In order to be justified as a case of the overriding of prima facie rights, gun prohibition would have to save many times as many lives as it cost, for:

1. It is wrong to murder a person, even to prevent several other killings. (premise)
2. A violation of a person or group's right of self-defense, predictably resulting in the death of one of the victims, is morally comparable to murder. (premise)
3. If it is wrong to commit a murder to prevent several killings, then it is wrong to commit a rights violation comparable to murder to prevent several killings. (premise)
4. Therefore, it is wrong to violate a person or group's right of self-defense, predictably resulting in the death of one of the victims, even to prevent several killings. (from 1, 2, 3)
5. Therefore, it is wrong to violate a group of people's right of self-defense, predictably resulting in the deaths of many of the victims, even to prevent several times as many killings. (from 4)
6. Gun prohibition would violate a group of people's right of self-defense, predictably resulting in the deaths of many of the victims. (premise)
7. Therefore, gun prohibition is wrong, even if it would prevent several times as many killings as it contributed to. (from 5, 6)

Similar arguments can be made concerning other rights—including, for example, the right to engage in one's chosen form of recreation—the general point of which would be that the overriding of a right for consequentialist reasons requires a benefit not merely greater, but *very much* greater than the harm to the rights-bearer. For simplicity, however, I focus only on how the argument works with the right of self-defense.

Consequentialists reject premise (1). But virtually all who accept the notion of rights would accept (1). Consider this well-worn example[11]:

Example 4: You are a judge in a legal system in which judges render ver dicts of guilt or innocence. You have a defendant on trial for a crime that has caused considerable public outrage. During the course of the trial, it becomes clear to you that the defendant is innocent. However, the public overwhelmingly believes him guilty. As a result, you believe that if the defendant is acquitted, there will be riots, during which several people will be (unjustly) killed and many others injured. Assume that the crime in question carries a mandatory death sentence. Should you convict the defendant?

Most people, including virtually all who believe in rights, say the answer is no. If this is the correct answer, then we must conclude that it is wrong to violate one person's rights (in particular, his right to life) even if doing so would prevent several rights violations of comparable seriousness. This is because rights function as *agent-centered constraints*: each individual is enjoined from violating rights, himself, rather than being enjoined to cause a reduction in the total number of rights violations in the world. Something like premise (1) is essential for distinguishing a rights-based moral theory from a consequentialist theory.

Premise (2) was supported by the argument of §4.2.

Premise (3) is supported by the idea that the requirements for overriding a prima facie right are proportional to the seriousness of the rights violation that would be involved. Even if this assumption does not hold in general, it is plausible that it applies to this case, that is, that *if* it is unjustified to kill a person in order to save several lives, and *if* a particular violation of the right of self-defense is morally on a par with killing a person, then it is also wrong to commit that violation of the right of self-defense in order to save several lives. It is difficult to see why the right of self-defense should work differently, by way of being much easier to override, from the right to life.

Step (5) is a reasonable inference from (4). Suppose that the judge in example 4 opts for conviction, acting wrongly. Suppose he is faced with similar situations four more times throughout his career, each time acting

---

11. H. J. McCloskey, "An Examination of Restricted Utilitarianism," *Philosophical Review* 66 (1957): 466–85, pp. 468–69. I have slightly modified the example.

in the same wrongful manner. Presumably, the whole *series* of actions, consisting in sum of his killing *five* people unjustly in order to save several times that many people, is also wrong. Now consider one more modification: suppose that instead of coming at different times throughout his career, the same five innocent defendants had all come to him in a single, collective trial, that he gave a collective verdict convicting all of them, and that this action saved the same number of other people. Presumably the judge's action is still wrong. It is for this sort of reason that we should accept the inference from (4) to (5).

Premise (6) is supported by the arguments of §5.2.

Finally, (7) follows from (5) and (6). Given the extremely serious nature of gun prohibition as a rights violation, very severe strictures apply to any attempt to justify it morally—strictures similar to those that would apply to justifying a policy that killed many innocent people to achieve some social goal. . . .

Michael Huemer: Is There a Right to Own a Gun?

1. Huemer believes that there is a prima facie right to own a gun. What does this mean? He thinks it fairly easy to establish the existence of this right—how does he do this?
2. Supporters of firearms prohibitions often claim that the presence of guns leads to greater harm—more crimes are committed, and many of those that are committed impose more harm than there would be if guns were not on the scene. What is the best reply to this worry that Huemer might offer? How successful is it?
3. Huemer believes that utilitarian considerations are of only minor importance in determining the permissibility of firearms prohibitions. Do you find this claim plausible? If so, why? If not, why not?
4. Consider the various analogies that Huemer uses when claiming that considerations of self-defense provide the central argument for gun rights. Assess whether these analogies provide the support that Huemer believes they do.
5. Imagine a largely gun-free society and one, like the United States, where guns are prevalent. What is gained and lost in each? Can this thought experiment justify any claims about what the law governing gun ownership ought to be in actual societies?

35

≡≡ ❧ ≡≡

Time for a New Black Radicalism
Chris Lebron

. . . .

Chris Lebron argues that the persistence of racism in the United States calls for the development of a new black radicalism. Such a political movement requires, in his words, "the explicit intention to use strong, nonconventional and unsanctioned means to effect systemic change by either disrupting the status quo or reinstating a preferred previous status quo." Lebron is not advocating a return to earlier, better times—he thinks that African Americans have never enjoyed anything remotely like social equality in the United States. In order to stand a better chance of enjoying a social status at least much closer to one that whites have long enjoyed, Lebron argues that a new version of black radicalism is required.

After criticizing three popular reasons for believing that radical social movements are morally problematic, Lebron explains a psychological dynamic that has long characterized the black community, that of shifting between rage and despair and trying to locate a rational basis for hope in the prospects of racial equality. Lebron argues that such a basis can be provided only through a form of unified political activism guided by a central leadership. Further, he questions whether the passive, non-violent resistance that characterized Martin Luther King, Jr.'s campaign of social activism is appropriate for our times. Lebron does not seek to answer this question but to raise the possibility that King's program, effective as it was for his era, may no longer be an effective tool in the search for real racial justice in the United States.

. . . .

New York Times *Opininator* blog, June 22, 2015, http://opinionator.blogs.nytimes.com/2015/06/22/time-for-a-new black-radicalism/?_r=0

H ere are two statements:

1. *The Negro must love the white man, because the white man needs his love to remove his tensions, insecurities and fears.*
2. *You do too much singing. Today it is time to stop singing, and start swinging.*

Which of the above is emblematic of black radicalism? The answer is not as clear-cut as many of us might think.

The first statement was made by Martin Luther King Jr. in support of his much lauded and widely known strategy of nonviolent resistance.

King's call comes from his 1958 account of the Montgomery, Ala., bus boycott, "Stride Toward Freedom." In it, he articulated what he saw as an essential form of communal love that had its roots in New Testament Christianity but one that King felt was best described by the ancient Greek word "agape," a redeeming love that "springs from the need of the other person." Certainly, the families of the murdered congregationalists of Emanuel African Methodist Episcopal Church, in Charleston, S.C., were practicing that sort of love last week when they publicly forgave Dylann Roof, the young white supremacist who committed those murders.

The second statement was made in a characteristically biting tone by Malcolm X some six years after King's, in a 1964 speech in Detroit, known as "The Ballot or the Bullet," urging a more active resistance in the face of the government's repeated failure to protect black people's rights and lives. It was clearly directed at those who still affirmed King's program of nonviolent resistance, and raised the possibility that the continuation of that government failure might require blacks to take up arms.

Today, as we face a seemingly endless number of black lives being unjustifiably threatened, damaged and lost, and the resulting emotional cycle among black Americans of rage-despair-hope, it seems urgent that we ask again whether now is the time to make black radicalism central to black politics and activism. And if so, what should it demand of American citizens?

By radicalism I mean the explicit intention to use strong, nonconventional and unsanctioned means to effect systemic change by either disrupting the status quo or reinstating a preferred previous status quo. If the convention in a capitalist society is for the tech industry to charge for all services and you offer yours for free on the principle that "knowledge wants to be free," you are a radical; if you're a state legislator who cuts against the separation of church and state by lobbying to make the Bible the official book of the state, you are a radical.

It would be a disservice to the diverse tradition of black thought and activism to present the black radicalism monolithically, but we can identify a central motivation across its various iterations: to secure for blacks, against the history of white supremacy and the persistent racial oppression it has spawned, a degree of respect and dignity by means that directly confront and reconfigure both the discourse of and policies around racial justice. This is typically done with an eye toward not merely rationally persuading white Americans, but to intentionally unsettle and dislodge them from the comforts of white privilege.

We don't typically assign the term "radical" to people like the computer programmer or the legislator described above, for a number of reasons. First, radicalism, especially in the political sphere, is thought to necessarily entail violence. Second, radicalism is often used as a substitute for "fundamentalism." Lastly, radicalism is thought to represent (some form of) insurgency as a way of life or lifestyle. This last reason when combined with the first is what makes the idea of radicalism, especially black radicalism, alarming to many Americans. Yet it turns out that all of these reasons for treating radicalism as a dangerous doctrine are wrong.

It is important to begin by challenging the claim that radicalism and fundamentalism are interchangeable. Fundamentalism is an ideology and all ideologies share one critical flaw. They begin with a basic proposition (for example, the lives of all nonbelievers in religion X are expendable) and assert that proposition as a true statement about the world and then proceed to interpret all evidence in the light of that purported truth; thus ideology short circuits effective means of assessing the reality of social, economic and political situations. Radicalism, in contrast, is significantly (but not entirely) post hoc—it is inherently pragmatic and arises in response to real threats, actual slights, suffered deprivations and obvious oppression.

When we take radicalism to be the same kind of thing as fundamentalism, it is a short step to the third charge—that radicalism is a way of life. This is clearly mistaken. Radicalism responds to real conditions of oppression that bring it into being, thus, seeks to eliminate the very conditions that make its existence necessary.

If one accepts these two clarifications, it also becomes clear that it is a mistake to think that radicalism is necessarily bound up with violence. Yes, it can be. America's founding fathers brought two nations into open warfare in the name of freedom—to disrupt the status quo imposed from without by Britain. This is a form of radicalism represented by Malcolm X. When he exhorted black Americans to stop singing and start swinging, he openly affirmed the legitimacy of violent self-defense against white supremacy and its murderous practitioners. Malcolm certainly sought to disrupt the status quo of white supremacy by unsanctioned means. But what of King teaching that blacks must love whites in order to ease their insecurities and fears? You should accept this as black radicalism as well.

The more obvious radical aspect of King's teaching has to do with the use of nonviolence as a doctrine of insurgent political action. While today political marches in the name of racial justice are common, in the middle of the 20th century large scale protests cut directly against the prevailing sentiment that blacks had no right to express themselves politically and publicly. King's challenge to various police forces to exact violence on a passive gathering sought to effectively and strongly disrupt a white supremacist status quo.

But here is another aspect: King's teachings also sought to disrupt the status quo *within the black community*, where despair risked deactivating the will to political action and rage compelled increasing numbers of black youth to begin considering taking up arms. King always held that passive resistance was the strategy of the truly strong person at a time when the black status quo had reason to view white Americans only as enemies, as undeserving of blacks' love.

In a manner unsettlingly resonant with the heart of the civil rights era, blacks today continue to find themselves moving between rage and despair. Rage at the abuses that should have ended when the slaves were freed, despair because the claim that black lives matter was dismissed up to and beyond the signing of the Civil Rights Act. This leaves hope, a disposition taken up when one thinks the expression of rage and despair might have compelled one's oppressors to finally act with a sense of justice. Have the many decades of expressing rage and despair done its work making space for hope?

As things stand, there is no rational space for *mere* hope—recent events in the light of the facts of history discourage naïveté. A truly intelligent hope leaves little to chance and encourages conviction and action to better secure a preferred future—in our case, a racially just America. It seems to me the way to hope today lies in the promise of a resurgent black radical politics.

Systemic racial inequality is a daily fact of American life. There is no shortage of news of vigilantes and police literally getting away with murdering blacks; white supremacist ideologies still thrive, and at times produce awful consequences, as we saw in the Charleston massacre. And that is just the overtly grim news. When we add to that the persistent racial inequalities in income, housing, education, medical care and employment, there is no denying that the withholding from black Americans of resources, opportunity and basic sympathy is the status quo in America. It is an unjust status quo, thus it must be disturbed, disrupted. The hope here, then, would focus on a future wherein blacks' needs, aspirations, and basic humanity are not only beyond question, but recognized as having equal importance and worth as whites'.

However, maybe you are more concerned with this question: *Which* flavor of black radicalism should be embraced—Malcolm's or Martin's? In a society in which blacks must insist and remind their fellow citizens that *black lives matter*, that really is the question, isn't it? Maybe we should turn to history as our guide.

Blacks have tried for more than 150 years, since the Emancipation Proclamation was signed, to reasonably engage American institutions and whites with a very uneven, and in important respects, failed record of adequate responsiveness. It can be difficult to imagine what else one can say to get what one is owed after so long. But we should accept at least two propositions. First, that any resurgent black radical politics must also be a unified politics, one that values central leadership coupled with an explicit program of action. The protests and movements in response to the past year's abuse of black citizens have shown that local and spontaneous protests can be effective, but also limited in scope—they have not led to adequate action at the level of national politics. Even when local protests have persisted in places like Ferguson, Mo., they tend to quickly fall from the American public's view, and thus their conscience.

Second, some 50 years after King, maybe blacks should not desire his second coming. Though he is consistently invoked by leaders at every political level, it seems to me that the days of sitting at the lunch counter and enduring inhumane abuses must be left to history. Rather, black Americans have tragically earned the right to ask a question more appropriately radical for our present moment: Where is the love *for us*?

It is time that blacks not be expected nor expect of themselves to set the standard for goodness and upstanding character in a society that regularly treats them cruelly. When I ask, *where is the love*, I am really asking you to tell me in return, to speak by your actions and take responsibility for the kind of radicalism it is now appropriate for blacks to take up: Should we heed Martin's counsel and open our arms in embrace or should we be wary of yet another painful and bloody era of speaking and acting in bad faith, and as Malcolm advised, close our fists?

Chris Lebron: Time for a New Black Radicalism

1. How does Lebron characterize radicalism? Does his characterization tally with your understanding of what radicalism is?
2. Must radicalism be violent? If radicalism is a plausible response to oppression, is violence ever a justified element of a radical response? If so, when? If not, why not?
3. Lebron claims that black radical activism "is typically done with an eye toward not merely rationally persuading white Americans, but to intentionally unsettle and dislodge them from the comforts of white privilege." Why does he think such actions are warranted? Do you agree or disagree with his assessment?
4. Lebron enumerates and rejects three popular reasons for thinking radicalism a dangerous doctrine. Present these reasons and assess his critique of them.
5. Lebron claims that "the way to hope today lies in the promise of a resurgent black radical politics." Explain what he means by this and assess the merits of his claim.
6. Lebron writes that "some 50 years after King, maybe blacks should not desire his second coming." Explain what Lebron means by this and assess the merits of his claim.

====== ❧ ======

36

The Case Against Affirmative Action

Louis P. Pojman

....

Louis Pojman argues that strong affirmative action (AA) policies are never morally justified. He makes his case by seeking to undermine pro-AA arguments and then offering some criticisms of AA programs.

Of the familiar arguments in favor of AA, Pojman highlights the following. First, we all need good role models, and AA will ensure that women and minorities, who are the primary beneficiaries of these policies, will have this need fulfilled. Second, women and African Americans have been the victims of terrible historical injustices, and this justifies AA as a form of compensation for these harms. Third, today's white males, while obviously not participating in (say) the enslavement of Africans and African Americans, nevertheless enjoy a variety of undeserved benefits as a result of this legacy of oppression, and AA can serve as a form of leveling the playing field. Fourth, diversity in the workforce, business world, and college campuses is important in its own right and serves a variety of important social goals, and AA is an effective way to ensure diversity in these areas. Finally, the existing social and economic inequalities between men and women, and between whites and minorities, must be the result not of any inherent inferiority on the part of women and minorities, but rather of unequal opportunities and discrimination. AA will enhance opportunities for these traditionally disadvantaged groups and thus reduce a legacy of discrimination.

Pojman finds fault with each of these arguments. He then introduces two arguments of his own to show why AA is immoral. First, Pojman claims that AA is itself a form of unjust discrimination against young white males. As he sees it, all discrimination against innocent people is immoral, no matter its target. Second, Pojman thinks that social and economic benefits ought to be distributed according to merit, rather than to skin color, sex, or gender. But AA violates this principle of merit and is therefore unjustified.

....

In this essay I set forth . . . arguments against Strong Affirmative Action, which I define as preferential treatment, discriminating in favor of members of under-represented groups, which have been treated unjustly in the past, against innocent people. I distinguish this from Weak Affirmative Action, which simply seeks to promote equal opportunity to the goods and offices of a society. I do not argue against this policy. I argue against Strong Affirmative Action, attempting to show that two wrongs don't make a right. This form of Affirmative Action, as it is applied against White males, is both racist and sexist. . . . It is the policy that is currently being promoted under the name of Affirmative Action, so I will use that term or "AA" for short throughout this essay to stand for this version of affirmative action. I will not argue for or against the principle of Weak Affirmative Action. Indeed, I think it has some moral weight. Strong Affirmative Action has none, or so I will argue. . . .

I. A Critique of Arguments for Affirmative Action

1. The Need for Role Models

This argument is straightforward. We all have need of role models, and it helps to know that others like us can be successful. We learn and are encouraged to strive for excellence by emulating our heroes and "our kind of people" who have succeeded.

In the first place, it's not clear that role models of one's own racial or sexual type are necessary (let alone sufficient) for success. One of my heroes was Gandhi, an Indian Hindu; another was my grade school science teacher, Miss DeVoe, and another Martin Luther King, behind whom I marched in Civil Rights demonstrations. More important than having role models of one's "own type" is having genuinely good people, of whatever race or gender, to emulate. Our common humanity should be a sufficient basis for us to see the possibility of success in people of virtue and merit.

To yield to the demand, however tempting it may be to do so, for "role-models-just-like-us" is to treat people like means not ends. It is to elevate morally irrelevant particularity over relevant traits, such as ability and integrity. We don't need people exactly like us to find inspiration. As Steve Allen once quipped, "If I had to follow a role model exactly, I would have become a nun."

Furthermore, even if it is of some help to people with low self-esteem to gain encouragement from seeing others of their particular kind in successful positions, it is doubtful whether this need is a sufficient reason to justify preferential hiring or reverse discrimination. What good is a role model who is inferior to other professors or physicians or business personnel? The best way to create role models is not to promote people because of race or gender but because they are the best qualified for the job. It is the violation of this fact that is largely responsible for the widespread whisper in the medical field (at least in New York) "Never go to a Black physician under 40" (referring to the fact that AA has affected the medical system during the past twenty years). Fight the feeling how I will, I cannot help wondering on seeing a Black or woman in a position of honor, "Is she in this position because she merits it or because of Affirmative Action?" Where Affirmative Action is the policy, the "figment of pigment" creates a stigma of undeservedness, whether or not it is deserved.

Finally, entertain this thought experiment. Suppose we discovered that tall handsome white males somehow made the best role models for the most people, especially poor people. Suppose even large numbers of minority people somehow found inspiration in their sight. Would we be justified in hiring tall handsome white males over better qualified short Hispanic women, who were deemed less role-model worthy?

2. The Compensation Argument

The argument goes like this: blacks have been wronged and severely harmed by whites. Therefore white society should compensate blacks for the injury caused them. Reverse discrimination in terms of preferential hiring, contracts, and scholarships is a fitting way to compensate for the past wrongs.

This argument actually involves a distorted notion of compensation. Normally, we think of compensation as owed by a specific person A to another person B whom A has wronged in a specific way C. For example, if I have stolen your car and used it for a period of time to make business profits that would have gone to you, it is not enough that I return your car. I must pay you an amount reflecting your loss and my ability to pay. If I have only made $5,000 and only have $10,000 in assets, it would not be possible for you to collect $20,000 in damages—even though that is the amount of loss you have incurred.

Sometimes compensation is extended to groups of people who have been unjustly harmed by the greater society. For example, the United States government has compensated the Japanese-Americans who were interred during the Second World War, and the West German government has paid reparations to the survivors of Nazi concentration camps. But here a specific people have been identified who were wronged in an identifiable way by the government of the nation in question.

On the face of it, demands by blacks for compensation does not fit the usual pattern. Perhaps Southern states with Jim Crow laws could be accused of unjustly harming blacks, but it is hard to see that the United States government was involved in doing so. Much of the harm done to blacks was the result of private discrimination, not state action. So the Germany/US analogy doesn't hold. Furthermore, it is not clear that all blacks were harmed in the same way or whether some were unjustly harmed or harmed more than poor whites and others (e.g. short people). Finally, even if identifiable blacks were harmed by identifiable social prac- tices, it is not clear that most forms of Affirmative Action are appropriate to restore the situation. The usual practice of a financial payment seems more appropriate than giving a high level job to someone unqualified or only minimally qualified, who, speculatively, might have been better qualified had he not been subject to racial discrimination. If John is the star tailback of our college team with a promising professional future, and I accidentally (but culpably) drive my pick-up truck over his legs, and so cripple him, John may be due compensation, but he is not due the tailback spot on the football team.

Still, there may be something intuitively compelling about com- pensating members of an oppressed group who are minimally qualified. Suppose that the Hatfields and the McCoys are enemy clans and some youths from the Hatfields go over and steal diamonds and gold from the McCoys, distributing it within the Hatfield economy. Even though we do not know which Hatfield youths did the stealing, we would want to restore the wealth, as far as possible, to the McCoys. One way might be to tax the Hatfields, but another might be to give preferential treatment in terms of scholarships and training programs and hiring to the McCoys.

This is perhaps the strongest argument for Affirmative Action, and it may well justify some weaker versions of AA, but it is doubtful whether it is sufficient to justify strong versions with quotas and goals and time tables in skilled positions. There are at least two reasons for this. First, we have no way of knowing how many people of any given group would have achieved some given level of competence had the world been different. This is especially relevant if my objections to the Equal Results Argument (#5 below) are correct. Secondly, the normal criterion of competence is a strong prima facie consideration when the most important positions are at stake. There are three reasons for this: (1) treating people according to their merits respects them as persons, as ends in themselves, rather than as means to social ends (if we believe that individuals possess a dignity which deserves to be respected, then we ought to treat that individual on the basis of his or her merits, not as a mere instrument for social policy); (2) society has given people expectations that if they attain certain levels of excellence they will be awarded appropriately and (3) filling the most important positions with the best qualified is the best way to insure efficiency in job-related areas and in society in general. These reasons are not absolutes. They can be overridden. But there is a strong presumption in their favor so that a burden of proof rests with those who would override them.

At this point we get into the problem of whether innocent non-blacks should have to pay a penalty in terms of preferential hiring of blacks. We turn to that argument.

3. The Argument for Compensation from Those Who Innocently Benefitted from Past Injustice

Young White males as innocent beneficiaries of unjust discrimination against blacks and women have no grounds for complaint when society seeks to level the tilted field. They may be innocent of oppressing blacks, other minorities, and women, but they have unjustly benefitted from that oppression or discrimination. So it is perfectly proper that less qualified women and blacks be hired before them.

The operative principle is: He who knowingly and willingly benefits from a wrong must help pay for the wrong. Judith Jarvis Thomson puts it this way. "Many [white males] have been direct beneficiaries of policies which have down-graded blacks and women . . . and even those who did not directly benefit . . . had, at any rate, the advantage in the competition which comes of the confidence in one's full membership [in the community], and of one's right being recognized as a matter of course."[1] That is, white males obtain advantages in self-respect and self-confidence deriving from a racist/sexist system which denies these to blacks and women.

Here is my response to this argument: As I noted in the previous section, compensation is normally individual and specific. If A harms B regarding x, B has a right to compensation from A in regards to x. If A steals B's car and wrecks it, A has an obligation to compensate B for the stolen car, but A's son has no obligation to compensate B. Furthermore, if A dies or disappears, B has no moral right to claim that society compensate him for the stolen car—though if he has insurance, he can make such a claim to the insurance company. Sometimes a wrong cannot be compensated, and we just have to make the best of an imperfect world.

Suppose my parents, divining that I would grow up to have an unsurpassable desire to be a basketball player, bought an expensive growth hormone for me. Unfortunately, a neighbor stole it and gave it to little Michael, who gained the extra 13 inches—my 13 inches—and shot up to an enviable 6 feet 6 inches. Michael, better known as Michael Jordan, would have been a runt like me but for his luck. As it is he profited from the injustice, and excelled in basketball, as I would have done had I had my proper dose.

Do I have a right to the millions of dollars that Jordan made as a professional basketball player—the unjustly innocent beneficiary of my growth hormone? I have a right to something from the neighbor who stole the hormone, and it might be kind of Jordan to give me free tickets to the Bulls' basketball games, and perhaps I should be remembered in his will. As far as I can see, however, he does not owe me anything, either legally or morally.

Suppose further that Michael Jordan and I are in high school together and we are both qualified to play basketball, only he is far better than I. Do I deserve to start in his position because I would have been as good as he is had someone not cheated me as a child? Again, I think not. But if being the lucky beneficiary of wrong-doing does not entail that Jordan (or the coach) owes me anything in regards to basketball, why should it be a reason to engage in preferential hiring in academic positions or highly coveted jobs? If minimal qualifications are not adequate to override

1. Judith Jarvis Thomson, "Preferential Hiring" in Marshall Cohen, Thomas Nagel and Thomas Scanlon, eds, *Equality and Preferential Treatment* (Princeton: Princeton University Press, 1977).

excellence in basketball, even when the minimality is a consequence of wrongdoing, why should they be adequate in other areas?

4. The Diversity Argument

It is important that we learn to live in a pluralistic world, learning to get along with those of other races and cultures, so we should have fully integrated schools and employment situations. We live in a shrinking world and need to appreciate each other's culture and specific way of looking at life. Diversity is an important symbol and educative device. . . . Thus preferential treatment is warranted to perform this role in society.

Once again, there is some truth in these concerns. Diversity of ideas challenges us to scrutinize our own values and beliefs, and diverse customs have aesthetic and moral value, helping us to appreciate the novelty and beauty in life. Diversity may expand our moral horizons. But, again, while we can admit the value of diversity, it hardly seems adequate to override the moral requirement to treat each person with equal respect. Diversity for diversity's sake is moral promiscuity, since it obfuscates rational distinctions, undermines treating individuals as ends, treating them, instead as mere means (to the goals of social engineering), and, furthermore, unless those hired are highly qualified, the diversity factor threatens to become a fetish. At least at the higher levels of business and the professions, competence far outweighs considerations of diversity. I do not care whether the group of surgeons operating on me reflect racial or gender balance, but I do care that they are highly qualified. Neither do most football or basketball fans care whether their team reflects ethnic and gender diversity, but whether they are the best combination of players available. And likewise with airplane pilots, military leaders, business executives, and, may I say it, teachers and university professors. One need not be a white male to teach, let alone, appreciate Shakespeare, nor need one be Black to teach, let alone appreciate, Alice Walker's *Color Purple*.

There may be times when diversity may seem to be "crucial" to the well-being of a diverse community, such as a diverse police force. Suppose that White policemen overreact to young Black males and the latter group distrust White policemen. Hiring more less qualified Black policemen, who would relate better to these youth, may have overall utilitarian value. But such a move, while we might make it as a lesser evil, could have serious consequences in allowing the demographic prejudices to dictate social policy. A better strategy would be to hire the best police, that is, those who can perform in disciplined, intelligent manner, regardless of their race. A White policeman must be able to arrest a Black burglar, even as a Black policeman must be able to arrest a White rapist. The quality of the policeman or woman, not their race or gender, is what counts.

On the other hand, if the Black policeman, though lacking formal skills of the White policeman, really is able to do a better job in the Black community, this might constitute a case of merit, not Affirmative Action. This is similar to the legitimacy of hiring Chinese men to act as undercover agents in Chinatown.

5. The Equal Results Argument

Some philosophers and social scientists hold that human nature is roughly identical, so that on a fair playing field the same proportion from every race and ethnic group and both genders would attain to the highest positions in every area of endeavor. It would follow that any inequality of results itself is evidence for inequality of opportunity.

History is important when considering governmental rules . . . because low scores by blacks can be traced in large measure to the legacy of slavery and racism: segregation, poor schooling, exclusion from trade unions, malnutrition, and poverty have all played their roles. Unless one assumes that blacks are naturally less able to pass the test, the conclusion must be that the results are themselves socially and legally constructed, not a mere given for which law and society can claim no responsibility.

The conclusion seems to be that genuine equality eventually requires equal results. Obviously blacks have been treated unequally throughout US history, and just as obviously the economic and psychological effects of that inequality linger to this day, showing up in lower income and poorer performance in school and on tests than whites achieve. Since we have no reason to believe that differences in performance can be explained by factors other than history, equal results are a good benchmark by which to measure progress made toward genuine equality. . . .

However, [proponents of Strong AA] fail even to consider studies that suggest that there are innate differences between races, sexes, and groups. If there are genetic differences in intelligence and temperament within families, why should we not expect such differences between racial groups and the two genders? Why should the evidence for this be completely discounted?

[Their] reasoning is as follows: Since we don't know for certain whether groups proportionately differ in talent, we should presume that they are equal in every respect. So we should presume that if we were living in a just society, there would be roughly proportionate representation in every field (e.g., equal representation of doctors, lawyers, professors, carpenters, air-plane pilots, basketball players, and criminals). Hence, it is only fair—productive of justice—to aim at proportionate representation in these fields.

But the logic is flawed. Under a situation of ignorance we should not presume equality or inequality of representation—but conclude that we don't know what the results would be in a just society. Ignorance doesn't favor equal group representation any more than it favors unequal group representation. It is neutral between them.

Consider this analogy. Suppose that you were the owner of a National Basketball Association team. Suppose that I and other frustrated White basketball players bring a class-action suit against you and all the other owners, claiming that you have subtly and systematically discriminated against White and Asian basketball players who make up less than 20% of the NBA players. When you respond to our charges that you and your owners are just responding to individual merit, we respond that the discrimination is a function of deep prejudice against White athletes, especially basketball players, who are discouraged in every way from competing on fair terms with Blacks who dominate the NBA. You would probably wish that the matter of unequal results was not brought up in the first place, but once it has been, would you not be in your rights to defend yourself by producing evidence, showing that average physiological differences exist between Blacks and Whites and Asians, so that we should not presume unjust discrimination?

Similarly, the proponents of the doctrine of equal results open the door to a debate over average ability in ethnic, racial and gender groups. The proponent of equal or fair opportunity would just as soon downplay this feature in favor of judging people as individuals by their merit (hard though that may be). But if the proponent of AA insists on the Equal Results Thesis, we are obliged to examine the Equal Abilities Thesis, on which it is based—the thesis that various ethnic and gender groups all have the same distribution of talent on the relevant characteristic. With regard to cognitive skills we must consult the best evidence we have on average group differences. We need to compare average IQ scores, SAT scores, standard personality testing, success in academic and professional areas and the like. If the evidence shows that group differences are non-existent, the AA proponent may win, but if the evidence turns out to be against the Equal Abilities Thesis, the AA proponent loses.

Consider for a start that the average white and Asian scores 195 points higher on the SAT tests and that on virtually all IQ tests for the past seven or eight decades the average Black IQ is 85 as opposed to the average White and Asian IQ at over 100, or that males and females differ significantly on cognitive ability tests. Females outperform males in reading comprehension, perceptual speed, and associative memory (ratios of 1.4 to 2.2), but males typically outnumber females among high scoring individuals in mathematics, science and social science (by a ratio of 7.0 in the top 1% of overall mathematics distribution).[2] The results of average GRE, LSAT, MCAT scores show similar patterns or significant average racial difference. The Black scholar Glenn Loury notes, "In 1990 black high school seniors from families with annual incomes of $70,000 or more scored an average of 855 on the SAT, compared with average scores of 855 and 879 respectively for Asian-American and white seniors whose families had incomes between $10,000 and 20,000 per year."[3] Note, we are speaking about statistical averages. There are brilliant and retarded people in each group.

When such statistics are discussed many people feel uncomfortable and want to drop the subject. Perhaps these statistics are misleading, but then we need to look carefully at the total evidence. The proponent of equal opportunity would urge us to get beyond racial and gender criteria in assignment of offices and opportunities and treat each person, not as an average white or Black or female or male, but as a person judged on his or her own merits.

Furthermore, on the logic of [Strong AA proponent Albert] Mosley and company, we should take aggressive AA against Asians and Jews since they are over-represented in science, technology, and medicine, and we should presume that Asians and Jews are no more talented than average. So that each group receives its fair share, we should ensure that 12% of the philosophers in the United States are Black, reduce the percentage of Jews from an estimated 15% to 2%—firing about 1,300 Jewish philosophers. The fact that Asians are producing 50% of Ph.D.s in science and math in this country and blacks less than 1% clearly shows, on this reasoning, that we are providing special secret advantages to Asians. By this logic, we should reduce the quota of Blacks in the NBA to 12%.

---

2. Larry Hedges and Amy Nowell, "Sex Differences in Mental Test Scores, Variability, and Numbers of High-Scoring Individuals," *Science* vol. 269 (July 1995), pp. 41–45.
3. Glenn Loury, "Getting Involved: An Appeal for Greater Community Participation in the Public Schools," *Washington Post Education Review* (August 6, 1995).

But why does society have to enter into this results game in the first place? Why do we have to decide whether all difference is environmental or genetic? Perhaps we should simply admit that we lack sufficient evidence to pronounce on these issues with any certainty—but if so, should we not be more modest in insisting on equal results?

We have considered [five] arguments for Affirmative Action and have found no compelling case for Strong AA and only one plausible argument (a version of the compensation argument) for Weak AA. We must now turn to the arguments against Affirmative Action to see whether they fare any better.

II. Arguments Against Affirmative Action

Affirmative Action Requires Discrimination Against a Different Group

Weak Affirmative Action weakly discriminates against new minorities, mostly innocent young white males, and Strong Affirmative Action strongly discriminates against these new minorities. As I argued in I. 4, this discrimination is unwarranted, since, even if some compensation to blacks were indicated, it would be unfair to make innocent white males bear the whole brunt of the payments.

Recently I had this experience. I knew a brilliant philosopher, with outstanding publications in first level journals, who was having difficulty getting a tenure-track position. For the first time in my life I offered to make a phone call on his behalf to a university to which he had applied. When I got the Chair of the Search Committee, he offered that the committee was under instructions from the Administration to hire a woman or a Black. They had one of each on their short-list, so they weren't even considering the applications of White males. At my urging he retrieved my friend's file, and said, "This fellow looks far superior to the two candidates we're interviewing, but there's nothing I can do about it." Cases like this come to my attention regularly. In fact, it is poor white youth who become the new pariahs on the job market. The children of the wealthy have no trouble getting into the best private grammar schools and, on the basis of superior early education, into the best universities, graduate schools, managerial and professional positions. Affirmative Action simply shifts injustice, setting Blacks, Hispanics, Native Americans, Asians and women against young white males, especially ethnic and poor white males.

It makes no more sense to discriminate in favor of a rich Black or female who had the opportunity of the best family and education available against a poor White, than it does to discriminate in favor of White males against Blacks or women. It does little to rectify the goal of providing equal opportunity to all. . . .

Respect for persons entails that we treat each person as an end in him or herself, not simply as a means to be used for social purposes. What is wrong about discrimination against Blacks is that it fails to treat Black people as individuals, judging them instead by their skin color not their merit. What is wrong about discrimination against women is that it fails to treat them as individuals, judging them by their gender, not their merit. What is equally wrong about Affirmative Action is that it fails to treat White males with dignity as individuals, judging them by both their race and gender, instead of their merit. Strong Affirmative Action is both racist and sexist.

An Argument from the Principle of Merit

Traditionally, we have believed that the highest positions in society should be awarded to those who are best qualified. The Koran states that "A ruler who appoints any man to an office, when there is in his dominion another man better qualified for it, sins against God and against the State." Rewarding excellence both seems just to the individuals in the competition and makes for efficiency. Note that one of the most successful acts of racial integration, the Brooklyn Dodgers' recruitment of Jackie Robinson in the late 40s, was done in just this way, according to merit. If Robinson had been brought into the major league as a mediocre player or had batted .200 he would have been scorned and sent back to the minors where he belonged.

As I mentioned earlier, merit is not an absolute value, but there are strong prima facie reasons for awarding positions on its basis, and it should enjoy a weighty presumption in our social practices.

In a celebrated article Ronald Dworkin says that "Bakke had no case" because society did not owe Bakke anything. That may be, but then why does it owe anyone anything? Dworkin puts the matter in Utility terms, but if that is the case, society may owe Bakke a place at the University of California/Davis, for it seems a reasonable rule-utilitarian principle that achievement should be rewarded in society. We generally want the best to have the best positions, the best qualified candidate to win the political office, the most brilliant and competent scientist to be chosen for the most challenging research project, the best qualified pilots to become commercial pilots, only the best soldiers to become generals. Only when little is at stake do we weaken the standards and content ourselves with sufficiency (rather than excellence)—there are plenty of jobs where "sufficiency" rather than excellence is required. Perhaps we have even come to feel that medicine or law or university professorships are so routine that they can be performed by minimally qualified people—in which case AA has a place.

Note! No one is calling for quotas or proportional representation of underutilized groups in the National Basketball Association where blacks make up 80% of the players. But, surely, if merit and merit alone reigns in sports, should it not be valued at least as much in education and industry?

The case for meritocracy has two pillars. One pillar is a deontological argument which holds that we ought to treat people as ends and not merely means. By giving people what they deserve as individuals, rather than as members of groups, we show respect for their inherent worth. If you and I take a test, and you get 95% of the answers correct and I only get 50% correct, it would be unfair to you to give both of us the same grade, say an A, and even more unfair to give me a higher grade A+ than your B+. Although I have heard cases where teachers have been instructed to "race norm" in grading (giving Blacks and Hispanics higher grades for the same numerical scores), most proponents of Affirmative Action stop short of advocating such a practice. But, I would ask them, what's really the difference between taking the overall average of a White and a Black and "race norming" it? If teachers shouldn't do it, why should administrators?

The second pillar for meritocracy is utilitarian. In the end, we will be better off by honoring excellence. We want the best leaders, teachers, policemen, physicians, generals, lawyers, and airplane pilots that we can possibly produce in society. So our program should be to promote equal opportunity, as much as is feasible in a free market economy, and reward people according to their individual merit.

Conclusion

Let me sum up my discussion. The goal of the Civil Rights movement and of moral people everywhere has been justice for all, including equal opportunity. The question is: how best to get there. Civil Rights legislation removed the legal barriers, opening the way towards equal opportunity, but it did not tackle the deeper causes that produce differential results. Weak Affirmative Action aims at encouraging minorities in striving for the highest positions without unduly jeopardizing the rights of majorities. The problem of Weak Affirmative Action is that it easily slides into Strong Affirmative Action where quotas, "goals and time-tables," "equal results"—in a word, reverse discrimination—prevails and is forced onto groups, thus promoting mediocrity, inefficiency, and resentment. Furthermore, Affirmative Action aims at the higher levels of society—universities and skilled jobs—but if we want to improve our society, the best way to do it is to concentrate on families, children, early education, and the like, so all are prepared to avail themselves of opportunity. Affirmative Action, on the one hand, is too much, too soon and on the other hand, too little, too late.

Louis P. Pojman: The Case Against Affirmative Action

1. Explain Pojman's distinction between "Strong Affirmative Action" and "Weak Affirmative Action." Then, explain one of the two arguments *against* Affirmative Action. Do you think this argument applies equally well to Strong and Weak Affirmative action? Explain and defend your response.

2. In your own words, explain the *compensation argument* in favor of Affirmative Action. Under what conditions do you think compensation is owed? Why does Pojman think that Strong Affirmative Action cannot be justified on the grounds that it compensates for past injustices? Do you agree with his assessment? Why or why not?

3. Explain Pojman's example involving Michael Jordan and the expensive growth hormone. What lesson does Pojman draw from this example? How does it apply to the moral permissibility of Strong Affirmative Action? Do you think the example shows what Pojman intends it to show? Explain and defend your answer.

4. In your own words, explain the *equal results argument*. Why might someone find such an argument plausible? How does Pojman respond to this argument? Do you find his response satisfying? Why or why not?

5. Reconstruct Pojman's argument for the conclusion that Strong Affirmative Action is just as wrong as discrimination against minorities. Do you think Pojman has captured all of the wrong-making features of racial discrimination? Do you think Strong Affirmative Action is genuinely analogous to racial discrimination? Explain and defend your response.

6. What are the two pillars of the case for meritocracy? Explain how each supports Pojman's position against Strong Affirmative Action. Do you think that when it comes to important positions we should always select the candidate who is best qualified? Do you think that any other considerations might be important? Explain and defend your response.

≡≡ ❦ ≡≡

37

Affirmative Action: Bad Arguments and Some Good Ones

Daniel M. Hausman

....

In this paper, Daniel Hausman sets himself two goals. First, he wants to reveal the flaws of some popular arguments for and against policies of preferential hiring and admissions (PHA). Second, he offers an argument in favor of PHA that he believes is successful in showing that the practice can be justified.

Many people favor or oppose PHA on the basis of their view of its results. But, as Hausman notes, the actual results of PHA programs are difficult to determine and are highly disputed. Hausman does not take a stand, for instance, on whether PHA has actually improved or damaged the self-esteem of minorities, reduced or increased prejudice, etc. The evidence, he thinks, is inconclusive. But we can still assess the merits of arguments for and against PHA even in the absence of such evidence.

One classic argument opposing PHA claims that it is "racism in reverse." Hausman rejects this line of reasoning, pointing out that PHA is not grounded in assumptions of racial inferiority or racial hatred, and that it is not designed to oppress, humiliate, and exclude. Hausman also rejects arguments against PHA that assume that it is morally wrong in hiring or admissions to take into account anything other than the applicant's qualifications.

On the other side, defenders of PHA often rely on arguments from rectification or reparation to make their case. Many defenders think that harms should be rectified (remedied); racist acts are harmful; so they must be rectified, and PHA will do a good job of that. Hausman agrees that harms should be remedied, but by those who have actually done the harm. The harms of slavery, for instance, can no longer be rectified by those who perpetrated them, so this is a poor basis on which to justify PHA.

Arguments from reparations fare no better. Reparations are compensation owed by the government for wrongs that it has done or permitted. Hausman agrees that the U.S. and state governments were indeed responsible for many racist harms. But he offers a variety of reasons for thinking that PHA is not a good way of correcting for those harms.

Hausman concludes with an argument in favor of PHA. Ensuring equality of opportunity is a fundamental government responsibility. Hausman argues that PHA will help to advance this important goal. PHA won't by itself solve all of the problems that our long legacy of racism has created. But it will to some degree level a playing field that unjustly favors white males.

....

ffirmative action has many aspects. Some, such as requiring that job openings be advertised so that minorities can learn of them, are not controversial. Other aspects, such as preferential hiring and admissions (PHA), with which this essay is concerned, are hotly disputed. PHA takes minority status to increase an applicant's chance of getting a job or getting admitted to a university. Though the policy favors applicants with minority status, it does not imply that minority status should determine hiring or admission all by itself. (Nobody is proposing hiring blind bus drivers because they are minorities.) The idea is to favor otherwise qualified applicants who belong to disadvantaged groups. Because the pool of qualified minority applicants is often small, the direct benefits of PHA are also rather small. To limit the discussion, I shall focus in this essay largely on preferential hiring and admissions of African Americans, because they have a special history of slavery and oppression—even though the greatest beneficiaries of PHA have in fact been women.

There are many arguments defending preferential hiring and admissions and many criticizing it. Many of these arguments depend crucially on facts about the consequences. So, for example, critics have argued that PHA harms those it intends to benefit by undermining their self-confidence or by putting them in positions beyond their abilities in which they are bound to fail. Critics have also argued that those favored by PHA are often incompetent, and PHA thus undermines the credentials of beneficiaries, incites racism, and diminishes economic efficiency. Defenders argue that PHA has changed the American population's conception of what minorities and women can aspire to and that PHA has lessened racial disparities. These arguments would be powerful if their factual premises were true. But it is hard to know what the effects of PHA have been, and there is little evidence supporting any of these claims about the consequences of PHA. Heartwarming tales of successes of recipients of PHA and horror stories of harms and abuses are not serious evidence.[1]

The most prominent arguments do not rely on controversial factual premises. Critics argue that PHA is racism in reverse: discrimination is wrong, regardless of whether it is directed against or for African Americans. Defenders argue that PHA helps to rectify past injustices committed against African Americans. These are the arguments one most often hears. But they are not good arguments. Defenders and critics should stop making them.

"Racism in Reverse"

If it was morally impermissible to exclude African Americans from universities and jobs on the basis of their race, how can it be morally permissible to exclude whites on the basis of their race? Lisa Newton, a philosopher at Fairfield University, enunciates this criticism as follows: "The quota system, as employed by the University of California's medical school at Davis or any similar institution, is unjust, for all the same reasons that the discrimination it attempts to reverse is unjust."[2] Louis Pojman writes in this volume that PHA is a racist policy.

Let us formulate this argument precisely. The word "discrimination" causes confusion, because it has both a neutral and a negative sense. In the neutral sense, discrimination is simply drawing distinctions, which may be a good or a bad thing to do. An admissions office does nothing wrong

---

1. There have been serious investigations of the effects, which I cannot summarize here. In my view, the results have been inconclusive.
2. *National Forum* 58.1 (Winter 1978), pp. 22–23.

when it discriminates (in this sense) among candidates on the basis of factors such as test scores and high school grade averages. In the negative sense, discrimination consists in drawing distinctions unjustly. In the neutral sense, PHA obviously involves discriminating among candidates. Does it also discriminate in the negative sense—that is, unjustly? To avoid confusing the two meanings, it is best to avoid the word "discrimination" altogether, and ask instead whether the distinctions PHA draws among candidates are unjust.

Why might it be unjust to allow an applicant's race to influence hiring or admissions? Perhaps injustice lies simply in allowing race to influence choices. But it not always wrong to take race into account. A director making a movie of the life of Martin Luther King commits no injustice in refusing to consider white actors for the lead role. Refusing to hire a white short-order cook is, on the other hand, harder to justify. What's the difference? The answer seems to be that race is relevant to playing Martin Luther King, while it is not relevant to frying eggs.

One way to capture the racism in reverse argument is as follows:

1. It is wrong in hiring or admissions to take into account anything other than the applicant's qualifications.
2. PHA takes the applicant's race into account.
3. Race is almost always not a qualification.
4. Thus, PHA is almost always wrong.

I hope the reader agrees that this is a good way to formulate the racism in reverse argument, because I am trying to get at the truth rather than to win points in a political debate by misrepresenting the critic's position.

Crucial to this argument is the notion of a "qualification." A qualification is any fact about an applicant that is relevant to how successfully the applicant can promote the legitimate goals of the organization to which the applicant is applying. For example, high school class rank and ACT scores are qualifications, because they are correlated with academic performance in college. Running the 100-meter dash in under ten seconds is also a qualification for admission if the success of its athletic teams is among the legitimate goals of a university. For universities without sports teams, like those in Europe, it is not a qualification. The race of applicants would be relevant to a university devoted to white racial supremacy, but the promotion of racial supremacy is not a legitimate goal. Since, as the Martin Luther King movie example illustrates, race is sometimes a qualification, this argument does not conclude that PHA is always wrong, just that it is almost always wrong. On the view that this argument makes precise, what was wrong with the exclusion and special hurdles faced by African Americans during the Jim Crow era was that their prospects were not determined exclusively by their qualifications.

The argument formulated above is a valid argument. The conclusion follows logically from the premises. To assert all three of the premises and at the same time deny the conclusion is to contradict oneself. Constructing valid arguments can be very helpful. If those whom you are trying to persuade grant the premises, then, on pain of contradiction, they must accept the conclusion. Alternatively, if those you are attempting to persuade reject the conclusion, then they must reject at least one of the premises.

Let us examine whether the argument is also sound—that is, whether as well as being valid, all its premises are true. Premise 2 is obviously true: preferential hiring and admission of African Americans takes race into account. Premise 3 in contrast is debatable, because diversity among students and employees arguably serves legitimate goals of universities and some firms. Among the objectives of universities is to train business and political leaders who can interact with and understand people from many different backgrounds. Diversity within the student body serves this purpose.

More can be said about premise 3 and the importance of diversity, but let us focus on premise 1, which says that hiring and admissions should depend exclusively on qualifications. Premise 1 may seem plausible. It apparently explains why the racist exclusion of African Americans from schools, unions, and many professions was wrong: those exclusions were not based on qualifications. But premise 1 is false, and it does not correctly identify what was wrong with racist exclusions of African Americans. Consider three examples of hiring or admissions that depend on more than just qualifications:

- Case 1: Veterans are given preferences on civil service examinations and in college admissions.
- Case 2: An owner of a small grocery store hires his teenage daughter (rather than a more responsible teenager) to deliver groceries after school because he wants to keep an eye on her.
- Case 3: My father, who owned his own small company, often hired ex-convicts rather than applicants without criminal records because he thought that people who had served their time deserved a second chance. He did not hire ex-convicts because he had any illusions that they would be better workers.

Are the hiring or admissions policies in these three examples wrong?

Before answering, it is important to set aside unrelated reasons why the conduct may be wrong. Suppose, for example, that instead of owning his own company, my father was the personnel officer in a corporation, and he was instructed to hire the most qualified employees. If he then hired less qualified ex-cons because of his concern about their plight, he would be failing in his duties to the company that pays his salary. His actions would be wrong, because they violated company policy, whether or not it is permissible to take factors other than qualifications into account. If instead he had instructions to give preferences to ex-cons and refused to follow them, he would be equally at fault. Second, if the grocery store owner were to put out a sign saying "Help wanted. I shall hire whoever is most qualified," and he then hired his daughter even though he knew there were more qualified applicants, he would be acting wrongly. The wrong consists in deceiving the applicants, not in taking into account his personal relationship to his daughter.

There is no defensible general principle that requires hiring and admissions to depend only on qualifications. It is not automatically wrong to take into account a veteran's past service to the nation when providing education or hiring, even when having patrolled the streets of Baghdad or losing a limb is not a qualification. I'm proud of my father's hiring, even though it was not based only on qualifications. If PHA is wrong, it is not because it takes into account factors other than qualifications.

If it is sometimes acceptable to take factors other than qualifications into account, does that mean that it was okay to exclude blacks from universities, from unions, from neighborhoods, swimming pools, even bathrooms? Of course not! Those policies were despicable, but what explains those wrongs is not that they took factors other than qualifications into account. Consider segregated bathrooms, which are of no economic importance and superficially appear to treat the races equally. (I was with my father almost sixty years ago, when he was thrown out of a "whites only" bathroom in Florida.) What's wrong with having separate bathrooms for different races? Is it only that the bathrooms for whites were nicer? If the bathrooms had been equally nice and the restrictions had been symmetrical, with whites not allowed into the "colored only" bathrooms as blacks were not allowed into the "whites only" bathroom, how could the policy be unjust or harmful to blacks?

Social context is crucial. In a racist black nation where there was a widespread view that contact with whites was defiling, segregated bathrooms would be a racist insult to whites. In the U.S., segregated bathrooms, hotels, train cars, and so forth were a humiliating insult to blacks, not to whites. In 1941, when Marian Anderson, the great African-American contralto, gave a concert at Lawrence University, she could not spend the night in Appleton, Wisconsin, where I used to live. In the 1940s, Appleton did not allow African Americans to reside within city limits. Fortunately, Anderson could stay in a hotel in a nearby town. The inconvenience was not enormous, but the insult was. Think about how it feels to be treated as if you were "unclean"— as if mere contact was defiling.

As these examples suggest, the mistreatment of African Americans that constituted Jim Crow consisted in their systematic denigration by white society, which resulted in their poverty, oppression, and exclusion. It relied on intimidation, beatings, humiliation, and murder. It was deeply wrong because of how it treated African Americans, not because it picked its victims by their race. If those mistreated were chosen not because of their skin color but via lottery and then marked as inferior, perhaps with a tattoo on their foreheads, the mistreatment would be no less repugnant and unjust.

In contrast, preferential hiring and admissions policies—whatever their virtues or vices—are not grounded in hatred of whites. PHA does not denigrate or oppress whites, or exclude them from the mainstream of American life. The admissions offices at universities are not full of white-hating racists out to keep whites from soiling their universities. Lisa Newton is wrong: PHA is not unjust "for all the same reasons that the discrimination it attempts to reverse is unjust." If PHA is unjust, it is not for any of the reasons that racial discrimination against blacks is unjust.

The failure of this common criticism of preferential hiring and admissions does not mean that PHA is fair or advisable. There may be other and better criticisms. But there is no moral prohibition on taking factors other than qualification into account in hiring and admissions, and in any case race is sometimes a qualification. PHA is not reverse racism.

Rectification, Reparations, and PHA

The main argument in defense of PHA fares no better. It maintains that PHA is a good way of rectifying past injustices perpetrated against African Americans. Rectification is a familiar idea. If my neighbor, Henry, were to steal my bicycle, justice would require that Henry give it back to me and compensate me for the inconvenience. When rights have been violated, justice requires that, as far as possible, the injustice be "rectified"—that the world be restored to how it would have been if there had been no injustice. African Americans have over the past centuries been the victims of incalculable injustices. They were enslaved, kidnapped, beaten, raped, tortured, and murdered and, after the Civil War brought slavery to an end, African Americans suffered more than a century of lynching, peonage, and relegation to the status of second-class citizens. Though racism persists, things are obviously better now. But these past injustices have not been rectified. Accordingly, many argue that PHA is justified as a form of rectification.

One might state the core of their argument as follows:

1. Those who commit injustices owe their victims damages.
2. Massive injustices have been perpetrated against African Americans.
3. Thus, those who committed these injustices owe damages to their African-American victims.

If intended to justify PHA, this argument has three problems. First, to rectify past injustice, one needs to identify the perpetrators of injustices and the victims of injustices and to determine the magnitude of the damages the perpetrators should pay to the victims. With respect to slavery, both perpetrators and victims are long dead. Descendants of victims of crimes may have claims to particular goods stolen from parents or grandparents, but their claims are limited. Children are not responsible for their parents' and grandparents' crimes, and members of a race are not responsible for injustices committed by other members of their race. How could PHA constitute the compensation that perpetrators of past injustices owe to their victims?

Second, rectification of an injustice is designed to restore people and their circumstances to that condition that would have obtained if no injustice had been done. Rectification in this sense for the wrongs of slavery is impossible. There is no way to know how the world would have been if there had been no slavery. Life in this country would have been utterly different. Few of our parents or more distant ancestors would have met, and consequently only a small portion of contemporary Americans would have existed in a hypothetical world without slavery. How can we possibly envision how things would have been under circumstances so different that they do not even contain the same people?

Third, identifying those who should pay compensation and those to whom compensation is owed would lead to a divisive inquiry into the virtues and vices of our ancestors, when they came to the United States, whether they conserved or squandered ill-gotten gains, and so forth. This is not a road that those who hope to improve race relations should want to follow.

Although widely misunderstood, invoking reparations rather than rectification solves the problem of identifying the responsible party. Reparations are a form of compensation provided by the government (and hence ultimately taxpayers) to acknowledge and partly to rectify past injustices perpetrated or permitted by the government. For example, the U.S. government provided $20,000 in reparations to Japanese-Americans who were interned during World War II, or to their immediate descendants. The funds were raised through taxation of all Americans, including Japanese-Americans. There was no distinction between those people who may have profited from the internment and the great majority who did not benefit from it, because reparations are a civic responsibility for a civic wrong, rather than a personal responsibility for personal wrongs. Because government at all levels perpetrated injustices toward African Americans and acquiesced in many other injustices that could and should have been prevented, it bears a great responsibility for past injustices toward African Americans.

Conceptualizing PHA as the paying of reparations rather than as rectifying individual injustices should thus in principle avoid divisive inquiries into the vices of our ancestors. But public discussion tramples subtle distinctions, and, unfortunately, proponents and critics misunderstand reparations and turn discussion of the issue into acrimonious finger pointing concerning the intergenerational transmission of personal guilt. A few years ago David Horowitz placed advertisements criticizing reparations in a number of college newspapers. These advertisements led to violent protests by those concerned about the disadvantages that African Americans must deal with. Among Horowitz's ten reasons to oppose reparations were: (1) we cannot identify the descendants of the perpetrators of the crimes of slavery; (2) few Americans owned slaves, and (3) most Americans have no clear connection to slavery. Since reparations are a civic responsibility for the wrongs government caused or permitted, these claims are irrelevant, but neither Horowitz nor most of his readers appear to have understood that. Supporters of reparations are just as confused. For example, in an op-ed piece in the *New York Times* (April 23, 2010), Henry Lewis Gates takes the most vexing problem of reparations to be "how to parcel out blame to those directly involved in the capture and sale of human beings for immense economic gain," and he believes that historical research now makes it possible "to publicly attribute responsibility and culpability where they truly belong, to white people and black people."

Even if reparations did not cause such confusions, other problems with rectification apply equally to reparations. How much should be paid? To whom should reparations be paid? Though there are powerful reasons to diminish the huge racial disparities that divide our nation, those policies should not be regarded as reparations. The risks of misunderstanding, the problems in identifying the recipients, and the problems in determining how much should be paid are reasons not to invoke reparations to justify policies that diminish racial disparities.

Furthermore, even if reparations could be ascertained without provoking confused racial animosity, preferential hiring and admissions policies are not a defensible way of paying reparations. PHA does not focus on those who have been most harmed by past injustices, and it does not distribute the costs of paying reparations in a justifiable way. It unfairly imposes the cost of reparations—a civic responsibility—entirely on non-minority college applicants and job seekers, who bear no more responsibility for past injustices than anyone else. These costs, like the benefits PHA provide, are generally small, but it is still unjust both to make one group in society pay all the costs and arbitrarily to benefit just one group. If PHA were only one of a set of programs whose costs were distributed throughout the population, this objection would not be cogent. But apart from PHA, public policy does little to address racial disparities.

I am not arguing that Americans should forget past injustices. Without understanding the past, how could we understand the present and know what to do about it? Moreover, the fact that the problems of the present arose through past injustices creates a special obligation to address them. But it is impossible to undo the past or rectify old and large-scale injustices. We have no idea what would constitute rectification, and could not carry it out if we did. Although we need to look to the past for understanding, our moral concern should focus on the future. How can we free it of racism and of the disparities that racism has caused?

Preferential Admissions and Equal Opportunity

The other major arguments that do not depend on factual knowledge of details of the consequences of PHA invoke the value of equal opportunity. Critics maintain that equal opportunity condemns PHA. Defenders maintain that PHA promotes equal opportunity. Obviously, both cannot be right.

Consider an analogy. Suppose that in the local elementary school there are two first-grade and two second-grade classes. One of the first-grade teachers is excellent, and one is terrible. One of the second-grade teachers is also excellent, and one is terrible. The socioeconomic status of the families in this community is uniform, and the children have had similar preschool experiences. The school board assigns students to first-grade teachers by lottery on the grounds that the fairest policy gives every student an equal chance at a good first-grade experience.

There is disagreement, however, about how to assign children to the second-grade teachers. Some school board members argue that every child should have one good and one bad teacher. Those children who had the good first-grade teacher should get the bad second-grade teacher and vice versa. These board members say, "If every child has both a good teacher and a bad teacher, then the children's schooling and overall future opportunities will be as close to equal as we can make them." Other school board members argue for a second lottery. They say, "Why should students be punished for having had a good teacher in first grade? Equal opportunity demands that every child should have an equal chance of having a good second-grade teacher."

This analogy is helpful in several regards. First, it explains why it can appear that PHA both promotes and impedes equal opportunity. If one is thinking narrowly about the chance of getting a good second-grade teacher, then a second lottery equalizes opportunity, just as (if there were no racism) the absence of PHA would equalize the chances of being hired or admitted of otherwise equally qualified applicants of different races. On the other hand, if one is concerned with opportunities over a lifetime, insuring that every child has one good teacher and one bad one promotes equality of opportunity, just as PHA does (on the assumption that the opportunities and resources available previously to black applicants have, on average, been worse than those available to white applicants). Those concerned with equal opportunity should be concerned with lifetime opportunities, not opportunities to acquire one or another immediate benefit or burden. Because of past inequalities and continued racism, PHA lessens inequalities in opportunity.

The school analogy also makes clear that PHA does not punish white applicants, just as assigning children who had the good first-grade teacher to the bad second-grade teacher does not punish them. These kids have done nothing wrong. Indeed, it may be that nobody has done anything wrong. The policy of making sure that each student has one good and one bad teacher is not a way of rectifying in second grade an injustice done in first grade, because no injustice has been done. The justification for the second-grade teacher assignments is to provide children with similar overall opportunities, not to restore children to where they would have been if they had not previously been treated unjustly. In the case of PHA, unlike the elementary school analogy, some of the past inequalities in opportunity have been the result of injustices, but the point is to diminish inequality rather than to rectify injustice.

It is important to distinguish between compensation as rectifying injustice and compensation as equalizing opportunity. The former does not justify PHA, because, as I argued earlier, it is unfair to impose the costs of reparations or rectification on white applicants, since reparations are a social responsibility, and rectification is the responsibility of individual wrongdoers. By contrast, equalizing opportunity can justify PHA, because it is not unjust to diminish the chances of applicants whose prospects have on average been inflated by previous inequalities. The relevant question for a rejected white applicant is not "With my qualifications, would I have been admitted or hired if there were no PHA policy?" Nor is it "With my qualifications, would I have been admitted or hired if I were black?" The relevant question is "If the qualifications of all the applicants (including me) had not been skewed by past inequalities in opportunity and if there were no continuing racism, would I have been admitted or hired?"

Given previous inequalities and continuing discrimination, PHA brings us on average closer to equal opportunity.[3] Like the children who had the good first-grade teacher, white applicants on average have had previous advantages. PHA diminishes these inequalities and counteracts some of the continued racist discrimination in hiring.

This argument assumes that the opportunities for black applicants have been in fact on average worse than the opportunities for white applicants. But there can be no serious doubt about its truth. According to the Pew Research Center, the median wealth of African Americans in 2009

---

3. For example, in one study mailed applications with common African-American names were only half as likely to get callbacks as applications with names that are not associated with African Americans. See "Are Emily and Greg More Employable than Lakisha and Jamal? A Field Experiment on Labor Market Discrimination" by Marianne Bertrand and Sendhil Mullainathan (2004) (http://www.economics.harvard.edu/faculty/mullainathan/files/emilygreg.pdf).

was one-twentieth that of whites. There is no plausible explanation of inequalities in outcomes that are this enormous other than unequal opportunities, and such large inequalities in outcomes obviously translate into inequalities in opportunity. A far higher percentage of black children live in poverty and in single-parent homes. On average the parents of African-American children are likely to have had less education, and the schools African-American children attend typically have worse facilities, lower-paid teachers, and larger class sizes. Some black applicants are highly privileged and many white applicants have grown up in dire circumstances, but on average, black applicants have had to cope with greater poverty, more difficult environments, and worse schooling. Their opportunities have been on average considerably worse, and they face the additional burden of continued discrimination.[4] PHA does a little to lessen these inequalities in opportunity. Valuing equal opportunity (not equal results) is a reason to support it, not to oppose it.

Conclusions

This essay has focused on the most popular arguments concerning PHA. Their popularity does not reflect well on the subtlety of public discourse, because they are not good arguments. PHA is not racism in reverse. It is not racist. It does not aim to denigrate, exclude, oppress, or punish whites. The main argument in defense of PHA is just as weak. PHA is not justified as a form of rectification or of reparations. Reparations and rectification are impractical, racially divisive, and incapable of justifying a policy that imposes costs arbitrarily on only one segment of the population.

As we have seen, there are good arguments to be made in defense of PHA as promoting diversity and equal opportunity, but it could turn out that other consequences of PHA are so harmful that there is good reason to abandon the policies. If we knew the effects of PHA on racial animosity, on the self-conception and status of the minorities it aims to benefit, and on the extent to which they and others are successful, we would be in a better position to reach a definite conclusion concerning whether PHA is beneficial. But we do not know its effects well enough.

One other consideration should be mentioned. Preferential hiring and admissions policies are more or less the only social policies in the United

---

4. This conclusion does not rest on the silly view that all differences in outcomes among members of different social groups result from differences in opportunities.

States that acknowledge the special handicaps disadvantaged minorities face and, in a small way, concretely aim to lessen them. Disadvantaged minorities would inevitably see the abandonment of PHA, without putting something substantial in its place, as white America turns its back on a disgracefully unjust situation. The deck is stacked, and white America gets to shuffle the cards. Will it do anything about the poor hands that minorities have been dealt?

Daniel M. Hausman: Affirmative Action: Bad Arguments and Some Good Ones

1. Why isn't it racist for schools to offer preferential admissions to blacks and Hispanics? What's the difference between not admitting someone because they are black or Hispanic and not admitting someone because they are white?

2. If what was wrong with slavery and "Jim Crow" laws was not their racial basis, then what was wrong with them?

3. Suppose that the United States government were to pay reparations to the descendants of slaves. Why should people who are not descended from slave holders (such as recent immigrants) have to pay taxes to support paying these reparations?

4. What is the point of the parable of the two first-grade and two second-grade classes? Is it a good analogy to the circumstances in which preferential hiring or admissions might be called for?

5. What other arguments can you think of supporting or criticizing preferential hiring and admissions? Can you provide logically valid formulations of these arguments?

38

The Future of Racial Integration
Elizabeth Anderson

....

Elizabeth Anderson argues for the importance of racial integration as an ideal that should govern the development of our social and legal policies. She begins by identifying four stages of integration: (1) formal desegregation, which occurs when explicitly racist laws and social policies are abolished; (2) spatial integration, which occurs when members of all races are able to share public spaces on terms of equality; (3) formal social integration, which requires that members of different races fully cooperate with well-defined social roles that are not themselves racially identified; and (4) informal social integration, which occurs when members of different races engage with one another on the basis of trust, intimacy, familiarity, and ease. Anderson focuses her article on conditions in the United States, where only the first stage of integration has been largely achieved.

To make her case for racial integration, Anderson describes the many different kinds of harms that racial segregation imposes, mostly on members of minority groups. Failures of integration threaten the dignity of racial minorities, impose huge costs in terms of unequal social and economic opportunities, and undermine our democratic institutions, whose success is based on cooperative decision-making by equal citizens.

Anderson argues that these failures generate a moral obligation to foster racial integration in our society. Four reasons explain this moral obligation. First, citizens are entitled to social institutions that treat

From Lawrence Thomas, ed., *Contemporary Debates in Social Philosophy* (Blackwell, 2008), pp. 229–240. This selection has been abridged.

them with respect, rather than demean their dignity. Second, societies have a duty to ensure that a citizen's racial identity is not a pervasive liability when trying to make use of social and economic opportunities and public goods. Third, citizens are entitled to real, effective participation in democratic decision-making. Finally, public institutions in the United States bear a great deal of responsibility for past racial injustices and for many of the current racial disparities in opportunities, and so are morally required to remedy the harms they have done.

Anderson then critiques anti-integrationist arguments from both the political right and left. On the right, opponents of racial integration argue that current failures of integration are largely the result of voluntary self-segregation on the part of black citizens, rather than of racist attitudes and practices on the part of white citizens. On the left, Anderson distinguishes three strands of identity politics that deny the importance of racial integration. According to the first, proponents argue that racial self-segregation is required in order for black citizens to develop psychologically mature and healthy racial identities. The second asserts that such self-segregation fosters mutual aid and the building of a distinctive racial culture that implies no animosity toward white majority citizens. In a third model, self-segregated communities, such as those represented by all-black college houses, help to generate knowledge from racially distinctive perspectives, knowledge of just the sort needed to counter racism. Anderson allows that there are valid points to each of these arguments but denies that they are sufficient to justify anti-integrationist practices.

. . . .

Racial integration was once the rallying cry of the civil rights movement. Today, a half-century after *Brown v. Board of Education* declared public school segregation unconstitutional, integration is barely mentioned as an issue in the major media or by politicians. Conservatives tend to argue that whites now welcome integration and that current patterns of segregation are due to the voluntary choices of minority groups to stay apart. As if to confirm this argument, many activists on the Left express disillusionment with integration and defend the virtues of self-segregation. It is time to put integration back on the public agenda, and to reorient policies from voting rights and housing to affirmative action toward integrationist goals.

1. The State of Integration Today

Racial integration consists in the full inclusion and participation as equals of the members of all races in all aspects of social interaction, especially in the main institutions of society that define its opportunities for recognition, educational and economic advancement, access to public goods, and political influence. It takes place in four stages: (1) formal desegregation, (2) spatial integration, (3) formal social integration, and (4) informal social integration. Formal desegregation consists in the abolition of laws and policies enforcing separation of public facilities and accommodations on racial grounds. Spatial integration consists in the common use of facilities and public spaces on terms of equality by substantial numbers of all races. A spatially integrated neighborhood may still be socially segregated, in that neighbors of different races may not interact in neighborly ways—welcome them to the neighborhood, engage in small talk, do small favors for one another. Similarly, a school may be spatially but not socially integrated if students of different races attend different "tracked" classes, participate in different school clubs, sit apart at the lunch table, and, in residential schools, inhabit different halls or dormitories. As Glenn Loury has stressed (2002: 95–6), even when people observe anti-discrimination laws, and so avoid "discrimination in contract," they may still practice "discrimination in contact," which often amounts to the shunning of marginalized groups by avoiding neighborly, collegial, or friendly relationships with them.

   Social integration requires genuine cooperation on terms of racial equality. It can be formal or informal. Formal social integration occurs when members of different races fully cooperate in accordance with institutionally defined social roles, and all races occupy all roles in enough numbers that roles are not racially identified. It happens when white privates obey orders issued to them by black lieutenants, with the same degree of alacrity as they would have had the orders been issued by white lieutenants. It happens when white students and Latino students cooperate as equal lab partners, or as members of the school football team. Informal social integration involves forms of cooperation, ease, welcome, trust, affiliation, and intimacy that go beyond the official requirements of organizationally defined roles. It happens when members of different races form friendships, date, marry, bear children, or adopt different race children. At school and at work, it happens when members of different races share conversations at the lunch table, hobnob over the coffee break, and play together at recess.

I call these "stages" of integration because they are ordered by degree of difficulty, and attaining the easier ones is typically a prerequisite to substantial attainment of the harder ones. Measured by these stages, how far have Americans gone up the ladder of integration? The first stage, formal desegregation, has largely been attained. This was the signal achievement of the civil rights movement. It immediately enabled spatial integration of public accommodations—the common use by all races of restaurants, buses, hotels, drinking fountains, restrooms, and other facilities generally open to the public.

But formal desegregation did not bring about spatial integration in neighborhoods, and only partially achieved it in public schools and workplaces. Even in the workplace, however, social integration is far from complete. Even when blacks have "made it" to managerial and professional positions, they still report high levels of discriminatory and disrespectful treatment.

Informal social integration lags far behind formal social integration. Only 1.9 percent of married couples and 4.3 percent of unmarried cohabiting couples are interracial. Asians have the highest rate of interracial coupling, at 19 percent, followed by Hispanics at 18 percent, and blacks at 5 percent (Fields and Casper 2001: 15). Racially mixed families, in which at least one parent is of a different race from at least one child, are more common: 17 percent of adoptees are of a different race from at least one of their parents. Here again, Asian children are most integrated with other-race households, black children by far the least (Kreider 2003: 13, 14). Informal social integration, especially of blacks, is a largely unfinished agenda.

2. The Harms of Segregation

Notwithstanding dramatic progress in integration since the Jim Crow era, substantial levels of segregation, especially of blacks, and especially at later stages, remain. Should we care? I think we must. Integration is needed to realize three types of goods: dignity, socioeconomic opportunity for marginalized racial groups, and democracy for us all. Each stage of integration has its own role to play in advancing these goods.

2.1 Dignity

Racial segregation by law or policy has a fundamental expressive point: to constitute the excluded group as an untouchable caste. Formal desegregation is therefore necessary to remove the dignitary harm entailed by official segregation. But it is not sufficient. Habits of racial aversion, conceits of racial superiority, and stigmatizing fears of disorder stemming from inter-racial contact persist for generations after their official props have been removed. If, as a result of entrenched residential, school, and workplace segregation, dominant groups have hardly any contact with marginalized ones, how are they to learn more respectful habits of interracial interaction? Habits cannot be taught like a creed. They can only be learned by practice. Spatial integration provides the opportunities needed for practicing the first stage of respectful interaction: extending the common courtesies of civil society to other races—observing queues, yielding the right of way, manifesting the demeanor and bearing of one who accepts the sharing of public facilities with other races as a matter of course. The demands of respect go beyond those of bare civility, however. They include a readiness to welcome others as eligible equal partners in cooperative projects. Formal social integration is needed to learn and express such respect.

It might be thought that the demands of respect fall short of informal social integration. Can't people get along respectfully without being more intimately involved? The answer depends on what is keeping them apart. If it is just a lack of personal chemistry, no disrespect is involved. But the causes of informal social segregation in the US are inextricable from racial stigma. About 12 percent of whites openly reject integration with blacks (Patterson 1997: 47). This factor should not be exaggerated, however. The main problem is not the small hard core of self-avowed racists, but the mismatch between whites' sincerely avowed beliefs and their habits of the heart. Conscious beliefs are the first, easiest, and most superficial thing to change, because they are most fully under our rational control, and most responsive to arguments and evidence. Such beliefs often have relatively weak connections to our feelings, unconscious habits, and somatic responses. To change the latter takes steady practice and a transformation of the conditions that trigger them.

Multiple independent lines of evidence point to a systematic mismatch between whites' conscious non-racist beliefs and their unconscious aversive attitudes toward blacks. Survey research has consistently found a dramatic gap between whites' support for antiracist principles and their opposition to doing anything that would put these principles into practice. Experiments show that people who avow antiracist beliefs nevertheless help blacks less than whites, especially when the blacks occupy higher-status social roles (Gaertner and Dovidio 1986). They also favor whites over blacks when their relative qualifications are ambiguous (Dovidio and Gaertner 2000).

Psychological tests demonstrate pervasive unconscious associations of blacks with negative attributes, even on the part of people who explicitly reject racist beliefs and behavior. Such associations are correlated with negative social interactions with blacks (McConnell and Leibold 2001).

This evidence suggests that, while lack of social integration need not in principle express disrespect for others, the particular antipathy whites display toward social integration with blacks does express stigmatizing attitudes toward blacks. The social segregation of blacks therefore manifests a dignitary harm to blacks. Policies aimed at facilitating social integration in settings conducive to reducing prejudice would reduce this harm.

2.2 Socioeconomic Opportunity

Spatial segregation has profound material implications. Predominantly black neighborhoods are isolated from areas of job growth. This "spatial mismatch" of residence and jobs causes high unemployment in urban black neighborhoods, and high commuting costs for employed residents of poor and middle-class black neighborhoods. It also deprives black neighborhoods of commercial property and hence of a decent tax base. Residents of black neighborhoods therefore pay higher taxes for public services than their equal-income counterparts in predominantly white neighborhoods. Consulting firms advise banks, retailers, and chain restaurants to avoid black neighborhoods, even when their middle-class status indicates a high density of spending power per block. Thus, black neighborhoods enjoy relatively poor shopping, restaurants, and other commercial services (Cashin 2004: 117–23).

White flight tends to suppress demand for houses in neighborhoods with many blacks, leading to low housing appreciation. This deprives blacks of home investment opportunities, the chief source of middle-class wealth. Low housing values limit blacks' access to the credit they need to start businesses. Racial segregation also leads the black middle class to be far more integrated with lower classes than the white middle class. In fragmented metropolitan areas, the black middle class therefore carries a higher burden of taxation for local public services to the poor than the white middle class, leaving even less money to support the kinds of public services that the middle class demands—for example, decent parks, well-maintained streets, and good schools. The black middle class is also less able to escape crime, even when moving to the suburbs.

The black poor suffer additional disadvantages when they are spatially segregated and hence live in neighborhoods with concentrated poverty.

Segregation multiplies and spreads the effects of unemployment by filling poor blacks' social networks with people who have been similarly shut out of job opportunities. Concentrated poverty depresses the prospects of local businesses. It also depresses children's school performance: poor children do better in middle-class schools than in schools where most of their peers are poor (Brooks-Gunn et al. 1993).

Social segregation produces disadvantages over and above spatial segregation. It isolates marginalized groups from the mostly white social networks that govern access to jobs. Moreover, access to opportunities for human development is a function not simply of where one lives but of who one knows, both formally and informally. Discrimination in contact generates "development bias" in disadvantaged communities segregated from the mainstream. If the people in one's community have suffered disadvantages in the acquisition of human capital, one will tend to inherit those same disadvantages (Borjas 1992; Loury 2002: 99–104).

Every organization works through informal as well as formal channels. Managers, for instance, typically have particularly trusted subordinates, whose advice they especially solicit and rely on. Such informal relationships provide critical opportunities for the development and demonstration of highly valued but objectively unmeasurable personal traits, such as loyalty, judgment, and leadership. Even when blacks assume the privileges and responsibilities of their formal titles, they are still often shut out from these informal relationships. Consequently, they tend to be confined to narrow, highly formalized paths to promotion, based on objective criteria such as degrees earned and years of experience, while whites enjoy additional access to informal paths to promotion based on mentoring and impressionistic criteria (Wilson et al. 1999).

Competence in interracial interaction is a two-way street. Disadvantaged racial groups suffer from others' lack of interracial skills. When white teachers and managers feel uncomfortable around blacks and Latinos, instinctively take the side of white students and employees in conflicts, and otherwise manifest unconscious racial aversion, they are rarely the ones to suffer. Whites can acquire interracial interpersonal skills only through practice, which requires that they be socially integrated with other racial groups.

Social integration of dominant and subordinate groups in institutionally supported cooperative settings works to reduce dominant group prejudice and incompetence in interracial interaction. This is known as the "contact hypothesis." It has been updated and confirmed in light of recent research on unconscious biases (Gaertner and Dovidio 2000; Dovidio et al. 2001; Wright et al. 1997). Thus, while social segregation is a major cause of continuing black disadvantage, social integration is a cure.

2.3 Democracy

Segregation harms us all, by undermining democracy. Democracy is a form of collective self-governance based on discussion among equal citizens. Democratic discussion involves reciprocal claim-making, in light of which citizens from all walks of life, through their representatives, work out the rules for living together and decide which collective projects to pursue. The legitimacy of decisions in a democracy depends on their responsiveness to the reasonable concerns of all. This discussion takes place in civil society as well as in the institutions of government. Segregation undermines democratic discussion in both domains.

Consider first civil society, the spaces in which citizens come together to communicate and thereby shape the contours of public opinion. For this process to work democratically, citizens from all walks of life need to share their experiences and concerns, to work out a sense of the problems they share that need a collective response, and what those responses might look like. Political opinions drawn up in ignorance of or indifference to the interests, needs, and concerns of others are defective from a democratic point of view. This is why the "capacity to regard oneself from the perspective of the other . . . is the foundation of the critical interaction necessary for active and effective citizenship" (Post 1998: 23). Segregation obstructs the development and exercise of this capacity. Racial segregation and stigmatization put people of different races in different walks of life: their life circumstances and prospects, the ways they and others view them, are different in politically significant ways. Yet spatial segregation prevents these citizens from different walks of life from communicating; social segregation makes them averse to and awkward in interaction.

The same difficulties arise for discussions among the representatives who occupy political offices. Spatial segregation, exacerbated by racial and partisan gerrymandering of legislative districts, produces a large group of overwhelmingly white districts, along with a handful of majority black, Latino, and integrated districts. Since the residents of the overwhelmingly white districts don't benefit from public spending in the other districts, the ordinary competition among districts for public goods acquires a racial cast. The same lack of benefit means that segregated blacks are less able to find coalition partners of other races (Massey and Denton

1993: 154–5). Even when politics is not overtly racially divisive, it is still likely to be racially negligent, in the sense that policies may be developed and advanced without significant responsiveness to the impact of those policies on racially segregated groups. A politician in an overwhelmingly white district is free to advance policies that have a grossly differential negative impact on disadvantaged racial groups, without being held to account for the costs imposed on other racial groups, and possibly without even knowing the costs.

3. The Imperative of Integration

We have seen that racial integration is needed to undo the dignitary, socio-economic, and democratic harms of segregation. Promoting integration is not simply a good thing; it is an obligation. This is so for four reasons. First, citizens are entitled to the social bases of self-respect—that is, to social arrangements that recognize rather than demean their dignity. Second, citizens are entitled to a basic structure of society that satisfies at least the following weak principle of racial equality of opportunity: that their racial status not constitute a pervasive liability in gaining access to socio-economic opportunity and publicly provided goods. Third, citizens are entitled to effective inclusion in democratic discussion, so that democratic processes are actually responsive to the reasonable articulated concerns and claims of people from all walks of life. Since segregation undermines all three entitlements, society has an obligation to undo it.

These reasons would provide a compelling case for the state and other central institutions to promote integration, even if segregation had been produced by purely private choices. A fourth reason for holding these institutions responsible for promoting integration is that they created segregation through systematic historical wrongdoing. Current patterns of residential and school segregation are largely the product of a century of concerted unconstitutional social engineering by all levels of government: state policies promoting racially exclusive zoning and racial covenants, underwriting mortgages only in all-white neighborhoods, redlining black and integrated neighborhoods to discourage banks from making loans there, locating public housing exclusively in dominantly black neighborhoods, destroying thriving black business districts in the name of urban renewal, deliberately driving highways between black and white neighborhoods to reinforce residential segregation, and locating public schools so as to encourage segregated settlement patterns (Massey and Denton

1993: 17–59). Wrongdoers are obligated not merely to cease engaging in such practices, but to remedy the continuing effects of their past wrongdoing. This is not a matter of compensating for past wrongs, but of dismantling a mechanism—segregation—put in place by past illegal state action that continues to perpetuate injustice.

Given the compelling interest in promoting integration, how is this interest to be advanced? Critics of integration imagine that it must proceed by interfering with freedom of association and destroying black institutions (MacDonald 2000: 212; Young 2000: 216, 226). This confuses means with ends. Of course, informal social integration cannot be forced; this would violate people's rights to freedom of association and be self-defeating besides. But integration can be facilitated, by creating more occasions for interracial cooperation in settings conducive to reducing prejudice.

The integrationist agenda proceeds on four fronts: political, residential, educational, and economic. Political integration aims to redraw political boundaries and powers so that different racial groups share public resources and services, and work together to solve their problems. They urge the formation of cross-border metropolitan regional authorities to deal cooperatively with issues such as public transportation, urban sprawl, and regional planning (Cashin 2004). Political integrationists also urge that state and federal legislative districts be drawn, where possible, to include substantial numbers of each racial group. The aim is to insure that politics proceeds on the basis of interracial engagement, and that politicians, even in majority white districts, have to compete for minority votes and so listen seriously to the concerns of members of disadvantaged racial groups.

On the residential front, the integrationist agenda includes, but looks beyond, vigorous enforcement of housing discrimination laws. For example, the zoning power currently enables municipalities to prohibit the construction of housing affordable to the poor and working class. Because this power is used most frequently by towns close to concentrations of poor blacks, the class-exclusionary zoning power functions as an effective proxy for racial exclusion. From an integrationist point of view, it is high time that the class-exclusionary zoning power be sharply limited, both for the sake of blacks and Latinos and for the sake of the poor of all races.

At selective schools and at work, affirmative action is a primary tool of racial integration. Because work settings enforce cooperation among their participants, they bring about significant formal social integration, which creates a bridge to informal social integration and interracial civic engagement. In selective schools, affirmative action aims to produce a racially integrated and hence democratically responsive and legitimate elite.

The integrationist rationale for affirmative action differs from the standard compensatory and diversity rationales in several ways. The compensatory rationale is backward-looking, and focuses on delivering benefits to the targets of affirmative action preferences, conceived as victims of past discrimination. Integrationist affirmative action is forward-looking: it aims to dismantle current obstacles to racial equality and democracy, and views the targets of affirmative action as agents of this mission rather than victims. While not neglecting the benefits that targets receive from affirmative action, the integrationist perspective stresses the benefits these agents bring to others: expanding the social networks, human capital, and access to employment and professional services of their less integrated same-race associates; stimulating awareness of racial disadvantage and enabling the development of competence in interracial interaction on the part of racially isolated whites doing their part to realize the promise of democracy, especially in constituting a competent, legitimate, representative elite. The integrationist perspective thereby avoids a standard objection to compensatory affirmative action: the mismatch between those targeted for preferences and those most victimized by discrimination.

The integrationist rationale shares with the diversity rationale a forward-looking focus on the ways affirmative action targets bring benefits to others. Unlike the diversity rationale, it does not confine its vision to the ways diversity advances the internal educational mission of schools, but looks to its effects in the wider world. It also resists the capture of affirmative action by identity politics operating under the guise of multiculturalism. It thereby avoids many standard objections to diversity-based affirmative action: that it amounts to a racial spoils system, conflates race with culture, places grossly excessive weight on race compared to other dimensions of diversity, and unjustifiably uses race as a proxy for the diversity features, such as political ideology, that really matter. When racial integration rather than diversity is the goal, the relevance of racial means to achieving it is evident; indeed, race-based selection is inherently the most narrowly tailored means to integration. Moreover, integration raises not merely differences in rationale but in the implementation of affirmative action. Where the diversity rationale tends to favor the preservation and celebration of racial group differences, integration favors conditions that bring people together across racial divides. As I shall discuss later, this means that integrationists look skeptically upon the voluntarily segregated college residential halls that were established by the partisans of identity politics.

4. The Ordeal of Integration (I): Conservative Views

The dramatic costs to disadvantaged racial groups and to democracy of racial segregation make a compelling case for adopting racial integration as a major political imperative. Racial integration is an indispensable means to promoting the dignity of marginalized racial groups, advancing their access to the goods enjoyed in other neighborhoods, developing their social and human capital, enhancing everyone's competence in interracial interaction, reducing racial prejudice, and realizing democracy.

Despite the harms of segregation and the benefits of integration, a surprising confluence of opinion between conservatives and left wing advocates of identity politics has arisen to rationalize segregation and resist active pro-integration policies. Their views highlight some problems with integration that must be addressed. Their recommendations, however, misunderstand the dynamics of racial segregation and integration, and neglect the material and social conditions for the realization of their own professed goals.

Consider first the conservative view, exemplified by Stephan and Abigail Thernstrom (1997). Their position reflects a pattern typical of white opinion in America: support in principle for racial integration, combined with resolute opposition to any active policies for achieving this end. It rests on two arguments: that segregation is due to voluntary black self-segregation, and that attempts to actively promote integration are self-defeating.

The idea that black segregation is voluntary grounds the Thernstroms' complacency about integration. They argue that most whites are willing to accept substantial numbers of blacks in their neighborhoods. If whites avoid neighborhoods with many blacks, this is because these neighborhoods have other undesirable qualities, such as high crime and low-income neighbors. Since this aversion is based on color-blind considerations, whites' avoidance of neighborhoods with many blacks does not reflect racial antipathy. The Thernstroms infer that any segregation that exists today is the result of voluntary black self-segregation (1997: 220–31). Indeed, few blacks are willing to be the first entrants into an all-white neighborhood, and most prefer a neighborhood that is evenly divided between blacks and whites, or one with a predominance of blacks.

The Thernstroms' interpretation of white preferences fails to grasp the changed character of white antipathy for blacks, from overt hatred to unconscious stigmatization. While most whites do not feel hatred for individual blacks, they still hold demeaning stereotypical views about settings in which blacks are numerous or visibly increasing (Ellen 2000). "There goes the neighborhood." This is not a color-blind attitude, nor is it innocent. Such racial profiling of neighborhoods helps create the very conditions—declining property values in "blackening" neighborhoods, with cascading negative consequences—that "justify" it.

Nevertheless, the Thernstroms are right to claim that black self-segregation is a factor in the perpetuation of spatial segregation. But *why* do blacks prefer self-segregation to being pioneers in nearly all-white communities? Is this due to racial solidarity, or fear of an unwelcome reception from whites? Many blacks express pride in controlling their own communities and feel more at home in black majority neighborhoods. The obverse of this is that they *don't* feel at home in majority white neighborhoods. Many blacks who work in majority white settings report "integration fatigue," a response to the constant stresses of exposure to the conscious and unconscious racial prejudice, aversion, and interracial incompetence of whites. To them, going back home to a majority black neighborhood, where they will be welcomed wholeheartedly, their dignity will not be affronted, and their right to be there will be taken for granted, is a blessed refuge from the strains and humiliations of integration. By contrast, commuting back home to an overwhelmingly white neighborhood, where their children may be shunned by some of the neighbors, or suspected as hoodlums by the local police, where a small but hard core of neighbors may actively express hostility to their presence, and most of the others may be cordial but distant, hardly provides the same comfort and affirmation.

Conservatives observe high levels of racial conflict (Rothman et al. 2003) and self-segregation on more racially integrated campuses, and infer from these facts that "socially engineered" integration doesn't work. Indeed, they argue that it is self-defeating, in that it arouses racial discord and resentment (Schuck 2003). Integrationists argue that racial conflict and self-segregation are symptoms of habits established in students' prior segregated lives. Given that most students come from segregated backgrounds, it is no wonder that their interactions at first are marred by stereotypes and prejudice, that they are relatively incompetent at respectful interracial interaction, and that they self-segregate at first, out of habit and comfort, when they enter an integrated setting. The question is whether experience with integration enables them to *learn* how to manage inter-racial interactions in more positive ways.

This can be tested. If the conservative argument is right, then racial conflict would drive out positive experiences of interracial interaction, and people's tendencies to self-segregate would be stable or increase over time. If the integrationist argument is right, then integration in settings of institu-tionalized support for cooperation increases opportunities for both negative *and positive* interracial interaction. Over time, people learn to better manage interracial relationships, and thereby lead more integrated lives. Studies con-sistently confirm the integrationist hypothesis. Students who attend more racially integrated schools lead more racially integrated lives after graduation: they have more racially diverse co-workers, neighbors, and friends than stu-dents who attend less diverse schools (Braddock et al. 1994; Gurin 1999: 133).

The facts of unconscious racial stigma and the dynamics of racial inter-action highlight the unreality of conservative insistence on "color-blind" policies. On the Thernstroms' view, racial discord is caused by race con-sciousness (1997: 539). Any policy, such as affirmative action, that height-ens race consciousness, is therefore self-defeating. Such a view could make sense only on the supposition that beliefs, habits, and attitudes don't exist if we aren't aware of them. Once we acknowledge that mental states reside at various levels of consciousness, the call for conscious color-blindness effectively amounts to a call to let unconscious racial biases operate unop-posed by conscious policies that might change them.

5. The Ordeal of Integration (II): Identity Politics in the Twenty-first Century

If conservatives have been complacent about integration, many on the Left actively promote racial self-segregation. In contrast with conservatives, they do so in recognition of the persistence of unjust racial inequality. The question is whether their prescriptions are up to the task of advanc-ing racial justice. What's missing from their defenses of black and Latino self-segregation, I'll argue, is a clear understanding of the negative conse-quences of white segregation that this entails, as well as a gross undervalu-ation of the importance of forging *racially integrated* collective identities: forms of collective self-understanding, of who "we" are, that take for granted that "we" includes people of all races. Let's consider three models of self-segregation advanced by the Left. Call them the "identity develop-ment," "benign ethnocentrism," and "epistemological" models.

Beverly Tatum is a leading theorist of the identity development model of self-segregation. She argues that self-segregation is needed for individuals to develop psychologically healthy and mature racial identities. Black self-segregation emerges among children as a way to cope with racism and negative images of blacks. Blacks turn to one another for a sympathetic rather than a dismissive ear in discussing negative encounters with whites, to forge more positive black identities than those prevalent in mainstream culture, and to share their experiences of interpersonal racism and learn how to deal with it (Tatum 1997: 54–74).

Iris Young advances a different model of self-segregation, based on benign ethnocentrism, a kind of morally innocent in-group affinity. On this model, a social subgroup can legitimately prefer affiliating with "their own," without implying any antipathy toward outgroups. Residential "clustering" by race is morally permissible

> when its purpose is mutual aid and culture building among those who have affinity with one another, as long as the process of clustering does not exclude some people from access to benefits and opportunities. Such a clustering desire based on lifestyles or comfort is not wrong even when acted on by privileged or formerly privileged groups . . . if it can be distinguished from the involuntary exclusion of others and the preservation of privilege. (Young 2000: 217)

Integration, Young argues, focuses on the wrong issues. The mere fact that neighborhoods are racially identifiable is no cause for concern. What matters is the equal allocation of benefits to different areas, not the equal allocation of racial groups to different areas.

Aimee MacDonald (2000) defends an epistemological model of self-segregation in the course of defending racial program houses on college campuses. Racial self-segregation provides a locus for the generation of knowledge from racially distinctive perspectives, knowledge that is needed to counter racism. Because race defines people's social locations, their opportunities, and the ways people perceive and treat them, people experience the social world differently in virtue of the ways they are racially classified. Arriving at an understanding of how this is so requires people to come to grips with their racial identities, which in turn requires that people of the same race share their experiences and work together to interpret them as a basis for antiracist action.

Taken together, the arguments of Tatum, Young, and MacDonald offer a powerful account of the benefits of self-segregation. *I happily acknowledge that these benefits exist*, or, in Young's idealized case of benign ethnocentrism, which abstracts from the fact that ethnocentrism in today's world is inextricable from outgroup antipathy and responses to it, might exist. Yet none of their accounts is grounded in a realistic appraisal of the material and social conditions for advancing racial equality. To achieve racial equality, blacks need to change, whites need to change, and we need to change. All of these changes can happen only through racial integration. Let us recall why.

Young imagines a world in which racial equality can be achieved by moving resources to the people, rather than moving people to the resources. We could imagine this strategy working if disadvantaged racial groups lacked only material resources. But, as we have seen, people's access to advantages is mediated not simply by impersonal allocative rules, but through social, including personal, relationships. To some degree, affirmative action functions for blacks and Latinos as a formal substitute for the informal social connections that enable whites to get ahead. But it is a fantasy to suppose that the substitute is or ever could be perfect, especially at higher rungs of the occupational ladder, where people need to prove themselves through more intangible criteria, such as trust, that develop and become salient through personal relationships. Moreover, as Patterson and Loury stress, blacks need experience in integrated settings to acquire the skills needed to manage and lead racially integrated, majority white institutions. This is a matter of acquiring human capital, not of assimilation. Integration does not assume that the habits learned and deployed at work or in other integrated settings replace those that prevail in other settings. Racial equality therefore requires that blacks and Latinos change, in that they acquire forms of human and social capital that can be obtained only through social integration.

When blacks and Latinos self-segregate, whites are of necessity racially isolated. Tatum argues that all-white groups can work out positive antiracist white identities for themselves, without having to ask blacks and Latinos to take up the burden of helping them deal with their prejudices (Tatum 1997: 90–113). Yet whites have to be made aware of their own racial privilege for this to happen. Tatum and Young acknowledge that it is hard for whites to become aware of this if they are isolated from blacks and Latinos.

No doubt, among whites eager to have a non-racist identity, the opinions they express in an all-white group could be managed by a skilled psychologist of race relations, such as Tatum herself. The real difficulty lies deeper than people's conscious opinions. To focus on their beliefs about racial privilege or their quest for a non-racist self-understanding is to imagine that acquiring a politically correct consciousness is what whites need to be able to treat blacks and Latinos as equals. Yet we have seen that what most urgently needs to change are people's unconscious habits of interracial interaction and perception. And the fundamental way to change these is to practice respectful interaction in settings that promote interracial cooperation. Whites need this practice more than anyone else, since they have the least experience in integrated settings.

Racial equality cannot be achieved without interracial interaction. To achieve this, we need to generate practical knowledge of how to work together on terms of equality. Only by working and thinking *together* can *we* work out mutually respectful and cooperative habits of interaction. To be sure, MacDonald is right to point out that blacks and Latinos at times need to talk among themselves to work out strategies for coping with the stresses of integration. But she is wrong to suppose that the possibilities for generating such knowledge would be under threat by closing down racial program housing. Self-segregation is the default position of black, white, and Latino Americans. Black and Latino students will find one another and work out racially defined identities and epistemological perspectives without needing to be housed together. The most scarce, important, and difficult community of meaning we need to construct is that of a racially integrated "us." And this community cannot be achieved if black and Latino students institutionalize their self-segregation.

MacDonald's epistemological argument can also be questioned on its own terms, to the extent that it focuses on the *preservation* of racially exclusive communities of meaning. There is no point in preserving the races, understood as social positions in a racialized social hierarchy. But there may be a point in preserving cultural meanings and practices that are independent of racism and the struggle against it. This is why MacDonald, like Young, shifts from a structural account of race to a cultural account. It is no doubt true that cultural meanings and practices that originated in black and Latino communities have immeasurably enriched American culture. But only a spurious association of culture with blood or ancestry can support the thought that racial self-segregation is needed to preserve or develop diverse cultural meanings and practices, even those that originated among segregated groups. Whites and Asians can, and do, play jazz. No group "owns" any particular cultural practice or has any particular entitlement to exclusive development rights to it. In a free and democratic society, culture is part of the commons and is no racial group's intellectual property. The demand to "preserve" particular cultural communities of meaning freezes culture in racialized cubicles, prevents its free appropriation by racial others and, most importantly, prevents its free development by an integrated "us."

The idea that institutionalized self-segregation is needed to preserve epistemic diversity is equally spurious. It makes sense only against a background assumption that integration is the same as assimilation and cultural homogenization, or that it presumes the fixity of mainstream culture. To the contrary, integration is a constant generator of new cultural diversities and epistemic perspectives, just as cross-pollination constantly generates novel combinations of genes in plants. And far from presuming that mainstream culture should remain static, integration aims to *change* it, especially to the extent that it embodies unconscious racial stereotypes and prejudices.

I conclude that the integrated "us," not the self-segregated racial group, is the critical agent of racial justice that most urgently awaits deeper and richer construction. This is consistent with affirming that "effective resistance to racial domination requires that the black victims of that domination organize and motivate themselves to collective action through the systematic practice of pro-black discrimination in contact" (Loury 2002: 97). My point is that neither justice nor democracy can be realized if the self-segregated racial group is celebrated as a more worthy site of identity and emotional investment than the integrated "us," as multiculturalists would have it. Identity politics, in the form of ethnoracial nationalism, was no doubt a necessary moment in the struggle for racial equality (Patterson 1997: 65–6). But it is time to strike a new balance between moments of self-segregation and of integration, decidedly in favor of the racially inclusive "us."

References

Borjas, George J. (1992) "Ethnic Capital and Intergenerational Mobility," *Quarterly Journal of Economics* 107: 123–50.

Braddock, J. H., Dawkins, M. P., and Trent, W. (1994) "Why Desegregate? The Effect of School Desegregation on Adult Occupational Desegregation of African Americans, Whites, and Hispanics," *International Journal of Contemporary Sociology* 31: 273–83,

Brooks-Gunn, Jeanne, Duncan, Greg J., Klebanov, Pamela Kato, and Sealan, Naomi (1993) "Do Neighborhoods Influence Child and Adolescent Development?" *American Journal of Sociology* 99: 353–95.

Cashin, Sheryll (2004) *The Failures of Integration: How Race and Class Are Undermining the American Dream* (New York: Public Affairs).

Dovidio, John, and Gaertner, Samuel (2000) "Aversive Racism and Selection Decisions: 1989 and 1999," *Psychological Science* 11(4): 315–19.

Dovidio, John, Gaertner, Samuel, and Kawakami, Kerry (2001) "Intergroup Contact: The Past, Present, and the Future," *Group Processes & Intergroup Relations* 6(1): 5–20.

Ellen, Ingrid Gould (2000) *Sharing America's Neighborhoods: The Prospects for Stable Racial Integration* (Cambridge, MA: Harvard University Press).

Fields, Jason, and Casper, Lynne (2001) *America's Families and Living Arrangements: March 2000.* Current Population Reports, P20–537. Washington, DC: US Census Bureau: <http://www.census.gov/prod/2001pubs/p20-537.pdf>.

Gaertner, Samuel, and Dovidio, John (1986) "The Aversive Form of Racism," in John Dovidio and Samuel Gaertner, eds., *Prejudice, Discrimination, and Racism* (New York: Academic Press).

Gaertner, S. L., and Dovidio, John (2000) *Reducing Intergroup Bias: The Common Ingroup Identity Model* (Philadelphia: Psychology Press).

Gurin, Patricia (1999) Expert Report of Patricia Gurin. "The Compelling Need for Diversity in Higher Education." *Gratz et al. v. Bollinger et al.*, No. 97–75321 (E. D. Mich.) *Grutter et al. v. Bollinger, et al.*, No. 97–75928 (E. D. Mich.) (Ann Arbor: University of Michigan).

Kreider, Rose (2003) *Adopted Children and Stepchildren: 2000.* Census 2000 Special Reports, CENSR-5RV(Washington, DC: US Census Bureau):<http://www.census.gov/prod/2003pubs/censr-6.pdf>.

Loury, Glenn (2002) *The Anatomy of Racial Inequality* (Cambridge, MA: Harvard University Press).

MacDonald, Aimee (2000) "Racial Authenticity and White Separatism: The Future of Racial Program Housing on College Campuses," in Paula Moya, ed., *Reclaiming Identity: Realist Theory and the Predicament of Postmodernism* (Berkeley and Los Angeles: University of California Press).

Massey, Douglas, and Denton, Nancy (1993) *American Apartheid* (Cambridge, MA: Harvard University Press).

McConnell, Allen, and Leibold, Jill (2001) "Relations Among the Implicit Association Test, Discriminatory Behavior, and Explicit Measures of Racial Attitudes," *Journal of Experimental Social Psychology* 37(5): 435–42.

Patterson, Orlando (1997) *The Ordeal of Integration: Progress and Resentment in America's "Racial" Crisis* (Washington, DC: Civitas/Counterpoint).

Post, Robert (1998) "Introduction: After *Bakke*," in Robert Post and Michael Rogin, eds., *Race and Representation: Affirmative Action* (New York: Zone Books).

Rothman, Stanley, Lipset, Seymour Martin, and Nevitte, Neil (2003) "Racial Diversity Reconsidered," *The Public Interest* (Spring).

Schuck, Peter (2003) *Diversity in America: Keeping Government at a Safe Distance* (Cambridge, MA: Belknap Press).

Tatum, Beverly (1997) *"Why Are All the Black Kids Sitting Together in the Cafeteria?" and Other Conversations About Race* (New York: Basic Books).

Thernstrom, Stephen, and Thernstrom, Abigail (1997) *America in Black and White: One Nation, Indivisible* (New York: Simon and Schuster).

Wilson, George, Sakura-Lemessy, Ian, and West, Jonathan P. (1999) "Reaching the Top: Racial Differences in Mobility Paths to Upper-Tier Occupations," *Work and Occupations* 26: 165–86.

Wright, Stephen C., Aron, Arthur, McLaughlin-Volpe, Tracy, and Ropp, Stacy A. (1997) "The Extended Contact Effect: Knowledge of Cross-Group Friendships and Prejudice," *Journal of Personality and Social Psychology* 73: 73–90.

Young, Iris Marion (2000) *Inclusion and Democracy* (Oxford: Oxford University Press).

Elizabeth Anderson: The Future of Racial Integration

1. Do you think that Anderson has accurately identified the stages of racial integration? If so, give your assessment of where your community stands with regard to her four stages.

2. Anderson offers a distinctive rationale for policies of affirmative action. What is it, and how plausible is it?

3. Anderson presents one politically conservative argument against racial integration. Reconstruct that argument and critically assess Anderson's replies to it.

4. Anderson presents three politically liberal arguments against racial integration. Reconstruct one of those arguments and then critically assess Anderson's reply to it.

5. Do you think that racial integration is valuable for its own sake, valuable only as a means to some further valuable situation, or neither? Defend your answer.

39

America's Unjust Drug War

Michael Huemer

Michael Huemer argues that the recreational use of drugs, including cocaine and heroin, ought to be legal, and that the long-standing U.S. policy of criminalizing their possession and sale is morally unjustified. He presents, and then seeks to rebut, what he regards as the two most prominent arguments for their criminalization.

The first argument is that drugs are very harmful to those who use them, and the prevention of such harm justifies the state in criminalizing drug use. The second is that drug use reliably causes harm to third parties, and since the state's mission is to prevent such harm, the state is again justified in outlawing drug use. Huemer agrees that there are some cases in which drug use does threaten others (such as when one drives while under the influence), and agrees that such activity ought to be prohibited. But, he argues, this represents a small minority of cases—in all other situations, drug use ought to be legally permitted.

Huemer then turns from criticizing prohibitionist arguments, and offers a positive argument for decriminalization. This argument claims that we have a natural moral right—i.e., one that exists independently of its recognition by society—to use our bodies as we please, so long as we do not violate the rights of others in doing so. Unusual exceptions aside, we do not violate another's rights when we use drugs. Therefore

Michael Huemer, "America's Unjust Drug War" from *The New Prohibition*, ed. Bill Masters (Accurate Press, 2004), pp. 133–144. Reprinted with the permission of Michael Huemer.

we have a moral right to use drugs. Huemer thinks that the govern
ment thus violates our moral rights when it prohibits most drug use.
....

S hould the recreational use of drugs such as marijuana, cocaine, heroin, and LSD, be prohibited by law? *Prohibitionists* answer yes. They usually argue that drug use is extremely harmful both to drug users and to society in general, and possibly even immoral, and they believe that these facts provide sufficient reasons for prohibition. *Legalizers* answer no. They usually give one or more of three arguments: First, some argue that drug use is not as harmful as prohibitionists believe, and even that it is sometimes beneficial. Second, some argue that drug prohibition "does not work," in other words, it is not very successful in preventing drug use and/or has a number of very bad consequences. Lastly, some argue that drug prohibition is unjust or violates rights.

I won't attempt to discuss all these arguments here. Instead, I will focus on what seem to me the three most prominent arguments in the drug legalization debate: first, the argument that drugs should be outlawed because of the harm they cause to drug users; second, the argument that they should be outlawed because they harm people other than the user; and third, the argument that drugs should be legalized because drug prohibition violates rights. I shall focus on the moral/philosophical issues that these arguments raise, rather than medical or sociological issues. I shall show that the two arguments for prohibition fail, while the third argument, for legalization, succeeds.

I. Drugs and Harm to Users

The first major argument for prohibition holds that drugs should be prohibited because drug use is extremely harmful to the users themselves, and prohibition decreases the rate of drug abuse. This argument assumes that the proper function of government includes preventing people from harming themselves. Thus, the argument is something like this:

1. Drug use is very harmful to users.
2. The government should prohibit people from doing things that harm themselves.
3. Therefore, the government should prohibit drug use.

Obviously, the second premise is essential to the argument; if I believed that drug use was very harmful, but I did *not* think that the government should prohibit people from harming themselves, then I would not take this as a reason for prohibiting drug use. But premise (2), if taken without qualification, is extremely implausible. Consider some examples of things people do that are harmful (or entail a risk of harm) to themselves: smoking tobacco, drinking alcohol, eating too much, riding motorcycles, having unprotected or promiscuous sex, maintaining relationships with inconsiderate or abusive boyfriends and girlfriends, maxing out their credit cards, working in dead-end jobs, dropping out of college, moving to New Jersey, and being rude to their bosses. Should the government prohibit all of these things?[1] Most of us would agree that the government should not prohibit *any* of these things, let alone all of them. And this is not merely for logistical or practical reasons; rather, we think that controlling those activities is not the business of government.

Perhaps the prohibitionist will argue, not that the government should prohibit *all* activities that are harmful to oneself, but that it should prohibit activities that harm oneself in a certain way, or to a certain degree, or that also have some other characteristic. It would then be up to the prohibitionist to explain how the self-inflicted harm of drug use differs from the self-inflicted harms of the other activities mentioned above. Let us consider three possibilities.

(1) One suggestion would be that drug use also harms people other than the user; we will discuss this harm to others in section II. If, as I will contend, neither the harm to drug users nor the harm to others justifies prohibition, then there will be little plausibility in the suggestion that the combination of harms justifies prohibition. Of course, one could hold that a certain threshold level of total harm must be reached before prohibition of an activity is justified, and that the combination of the harm of drugs to users and their harm to others passes that threshold even though neither kind of harm does so by itself. But if, as I will contend, the "harm to users" and "harm to others" arguments both fail because it is not the government's business to apply criminal sanctions to prevent the kinds of harms in question, *then* the combination of the two harms will not make a convincing case for prohibition.

---

1. Douglas Husak (*Legalize This! The Case for Decriminalizing Drugs*, London: Verso, 2002, pages 7, 101–103) makes this sort of argument. I have added my own examples of harmful activities to his list.

(2) A second suggestion is that drug use is generally *more* harmful than the other activities listed above. But there seems to be no reason to believe this. As one (admittedly limited) measure of harmfulness, consider the mortality statistics. In the year 2000, illicit drug use directly or indirectly caused an estimated 17,000 deaths in the United States.[2] By contrast, tobacco caused an estimated 435,000 deaths.[3] Of course, more people use tobacco than use illegal drugs,[4] so let us divide by the number of users: tobacco kills 4.5 people per 1000 at-risk persons per year; illegal drugs kill 0.66 people per 1000 at-risk persons per year.[5] Yet almost no one favors outlawing tobacco and putting smokers in prison. On a similar note, obesity caused an estimated 112,000 deaths in the same year (due to increased incidence of heart disease, strokes, and so on), or 1.8 per 1000

2. Ali Mokdad, James Marks, Donna Stroup, and Julie Gerberding, "Actual Causes of Death in the United States, 2000," *Journal of the American Medical Association* 291, no. 10, 2004: 1238–45, p. 1242. The statistic includes estimated contributions of drug use to such causes of death as suicide, homicide, motor vehicle accidents, and HIV infection.

3. Mokdad et al., p. 1239; the statistic includes estimated effects of secondhand smoke. The Centers for Disease Control provides an estimate of 440,000 ("Annual Smoking-Attributable Mortality, Years of Potential Life Lost, and Economic Costs—United States, 1995–1999," *Morbidity and Mortality Weekly Report* 51, 2002: 300–303, http://www.cdc.gov/mmwr/PDF/wk/mm5114.pdf, page 300).

4. James Inciardi ("Against Legalization of Drugs" in Arnold Trebach and James Inciardi, *Legalize It? Debating American Drug Policy*, Washington, D.C.: American University Press, 1993, pp. 161, 165) makes this point, accusing drug legalizers of "sophism." He does not go on to calculate the number of deaths per user, however.

5. I include both current and former smokers among "at risk persons." The calculation for tobacco is based on Mokdad et al.'s report (p. 1239) that 22.2% of the adult population were smokers and 24.4% were former smokers in 2000, and the U.S. Census Bureau's estimate of an adult population of 209 million in the year 2000 ("Table 2: Annual Estimates of the Population by Sex and Selected Age Groups for the United States: April 1, 2000 to July 1, 2007 [NC-EST2007-02]," release date May 1, 2008, http://www.census.gov/popest/national/asrh/NC-EST2007/NC-EST2007-02.xls). The calculation for illicit drugs is based on the report of the Office of National Drug Control Policy (hereafter, ONDCP) that, in the year 2000, 11% of persons aged 12 and older had used illegal drugs in the previous year ("Drug Use Trends," October 2002, http://www.whitehousedrugpolicy.gov/publications/factsht/druguse/), and the U.S. Census Bureau's report of a population of about 233 million Americans aged 12 and over in 2000 ("Table 1: Annual Estimates of the Population by Sex and Five-Year Age Groups for the United States: April 1, 2000 to July 1, 2007 [NC-EST2007-01]," release date May 1, 2008, http://www.census.gov/popest/national/asrh/NC-EST2007/NC-EST2007-02.xls). Interpolation was applied to the Census Bureau's "10 to 14" age category to estimate the number of persons aged 12 to 14. In the case of drugs, if "at risk persons" are considered to include only those who admit to having used illegal drugs in the past month, then the death rate is 1.2 per 1000 at-risk persons.

at-risk persons.[6] Health professionals have warned about the pandemic of obesity, but no one has yet called for imprisoning obese people.

There are less tangible harms of drug use—harms to one's general quality of life. These are difficult to quantify. But compare the magnitude of the harm to one's quality of life that one can bring about by, say, dropping out of high school, working in a dead-end job for several years, or marrying a jerk—these things can cause extreme and lasting detriment to one's well-being. And yet no one proposes jailing those who drop out, work in bad jobs, or make poor marriage decisions. The idea of doing so would seem ridiculous, clearly beyond the state's prerogatives.

(3) Another suggestion is that drug use harms users *in a different way* than the other listed activities. What sorts of harms do drugs cause? First, illicit drugs may worsen users' health and, in some cases, entail a risk of death. But many other activities—including the consumption of alcohol, tobacco, and fatty foods; sex; and (on a broad construal of "health") automobiles—entail health risks, and yet almost no one believes those activities should be criminalized.

Second, drugs may damage users' relationships with others—particularly family, friends, and lovers—and prevent one from developing more satisfying personal relationships.[7] Being rude to others can also have this effect, yet no one believes you should be put in jail for being rude. Moreover, it is very implausible to suppose that people should be subject to criminal sanctions for ruining their personal relationships. I have no general theory of what sort of things people should be punished for, but consider the following example: suppose that I decide to break up with my girlfriend, stop calling my family, and push away all my friends. I do this for no good reason—I just feel like it. This would damage my personal relationships as much as anything could. Should the police now arrest me and put me in jail? If not, then why should they arrest me for doing something that only has a *chance* of indirectly bringing about a

---

6. Based on 112,000 premature deaths caused by obesity in 2000 (Katherine Flegal, Barry Graubard, David Williamson, and Mitchell Gail, "Excess Deaths Associated With Underweight, Overweight, and Obesity," *Journal of the American Medical Association* 293, no. 15, 2005: 1861–7), a 30.5% obesity rate among U.S. adults in 2000 (Allison Hedley, Cynthia Ogden, Clifford Johnson, Margaret Carroll, Lester Curtin, and Katherine Flegal, "Prevalence of Overweight and Obesity Among U.S. Children, Adolescents, and Adults, 1999–2002," *Journal of the American Medical Association* 291, no. 23, 2004: 2847–2850) and a U.S. adult population of 209 million in 2000 (U.S. Census Bureau, "Table 2," *op. cit.*).

7. Inciardi, pp. 167, 172.

similar result? The following seems like a reasonable political principle: If it would be wrong (because not part of the government's legitimate functions) to punish people for *directly bringing about* some result, then it would also be wrong to punish people for doing some other action on the grounds that the action has a *chance* of bringing about that result indirectly. If the state may not prohibit me from *directly cutting off* my relationships with others, then the fact that my drug use *might have the result* of damaging those relationships does not provide a good reason to prohibit me from using drugs.

Third, drugs may harm users' financial lives, costing them money, causing them to lose their jobs or not find jobs, and preventing them from getting promotions. The same principle applies here: if it would be an abuse of government power to prohibit me from directly bringing about those sorts of negative financial consequences, then surely the fact that drug use might indirectly bring them about is not a good reason to prohibit drug use. Suppose that I decide to quit my job and throw all my money out the window, for no reason. Should the police arrest me and put me in prison?

Fourth and finally, drugs may damage users' moral character, as James Q. Wilson believes:

> [I]f we believe—as I do—that dependency on certain mind-altering drugs *is* a moral issue and that their illegality rests in part on their immorality, then legalizing them undercuts, if it does not eliminate altogether, the moral message. That message is at the root of the distinction between nicotine and cocaine. Both are highly addictive; both have harmful physical effects. But we treat the two drugs differently not simply because nicotine is so widely used as to be beyond the reach of effective prohibition, but because its use does not destroy the user's essential humanity. Tobacco shortens one's life, cocaine debases it. Nicotine alters one's habits, cocaine alters one's soul. The heavy use of crack, unlike the heavy use of tobacco, corrodes those natural sentiments of sympathy and duty that constitute our human nature and make possible our social life.[8]

In this passage, Wilson claims that the use of cocaine (a) is immoral, (b) destroys one's humanity, (c) alters one's soul, and (d) corrodes one's sense of sympathy and duty. One problem with Wilson's argument is the

---

8. James Q. Wilson, "Against the Legalization of Drugs," *Commentary* 89, 1990: 21–8, p. 26.

lack of evidence supporting claims (a)–(d). Before we put people in prison for corrupting their souls, we should require some objective evidence that their souls are in fact being corrupted. Before we put people in prison for being immoral, we should require some argument showing that their actions are in fact immoral. Perhaps Wilson's charges of immorality and corruption all come down to the charge that drug users lose their sense of sympathy and duty—that is, claims (a)–(c) all rest upon claim (d). It is plausible that *heavy* drug users experience a decreased sense of sympathy with others and a decreased sense of duty and responsibility. Does this provide a good reason to prohibit drug use?

Again, it seems that one should not prohibit an activity on the grounds that it may indirectly cause some result, unless it would be appropriate to prohibit the direct bringing about of that result. Would it be appropriate, and within the legitimate functions of the state, to punish people for being unsympathetic and undutiful, or for behaving in an unsympathetic and undutiful way? Suppose that Howard—though not a drug user—doesn't sympathize with others. When people try to tell Howard their problems, he just tells them to quit whining. Friends and coworkers who ask Howard for favors are rudely rebuffed. Furthermore—though he does not harm others in ways that would be against our current laws—Howard has a poor sense of duty. He doesn't bother to show up for work on time, nor does he take any pride in his work; he doesn't donate to charity; he doesn't try to improve his community. All around, Howard is an ignoble and unpleasant individual. Should he be put in jail?

If not, then why should someone be put in jail merely for doing something that would have a *chance* of causing them to become like Howard? If it would be an abuse of governmental power to punish people for being jerks, then the fact that drug use may cause one to become a jerk is not a good reason to prohibit drug use.

II. Drugs and Harm to Others

Some argue that drug use must be outlawed because drug use harms the user's family, friends, and coworkers, and/or society in general. A report produced by the Office of National Drug Control Policy states:

> Democracies can flourish only when their citizens value their freedom and embrace personal responsibility. Drug use erodes the individual's capacity to pursue both ideals. It diminishes the individual's capacity to operate effectively in many of life's spheres—as a student, a parent, a

spouse, an employee—even as a coworker or fellow motorist. And, while some claim it represents an expression of individual autonomy, drug use is in fact inimical to personal freedom, producing a reduced capacity to participate in the life of the community and the promise of America.[9]

At least one of these alleged harms—dangerous driving—*is* clearly the business of the state. For this reason, I entirely agree that people should be prohibited from driving while under the influence of drugs. But what about the rest of the alleged harms?

Return to our hypothetical citizen Howard. Imagine that Howard—again, for reasons having nothing to do with drugs—does not value freedom, nor does he embrace personal responsibility. It is unclear exactly what this means, but, for good measure, let us suppose that Howard embraces a totalitarian political ideology and denies the existence of free will. He constantly blames other people for his problems and tries to avoid making decisions. Howard is a college student with a part-time job. However, he is a terrible student and worker. He hardly ever studies and frequently misses assignments, as a result of which he gets poor grades. As mentioned earlier, Howard comes to work late and takes no pride in his work. Though he does nothing against our current laws, he is an inattentive and inconsiderate spouse and parent. Nor does he make any effort to participate in the life of his community, or the promise of America. He would rather lie around the house, watching television and cursing the rest of the world for his problems. In short, Howard does all the bad things to his family, friends, coworkers, and society that the ONDCP says *may* result from drug use. And most of this is voluntary.

Should Congress pass laws against what Howard is doing? Should the police then arrest him, and the district attorney prosecute him, for being a loser?

Once again, it seems absurd to suppose that we would arrest and jail someone for behaving in these ways, undesirable as they may be. Since drug use only has a *chance* of causing one to behave in each of these ways, it is even more absurd to suppose that we should arrest and jail people for drug use on the grounds that drug use has these potential effects.

---

9. NDCP, *National Drug Control Strategy 2003*, Washington, D.C.: Government Printing Office, http://www.whitehousedrugpolicy.gov/publications/policy/03ndcs/, pp. 1–2.

III. The Injustice of Drug Prohibition

Philosopher Douglas Husak has characterized drug prohibition as the greatest injustice perpetrated in the United States since slavery.[10] This is no hyperbole. If the drug laws are unjust, then America has over half a million people unjustly imprisoned.[11]

Why think the drug laws are *unjust*? Husak's argument invokes a principle with which few could disagree: it is unjust for the state to punish people without having a good reason for doing so.[12] We have seen the failure of the most common proposed rationales for drug prohibition. If nothing better is forthcoming, then we must conclude that prohibitionists have no rational justification for punishing drug users. We have deprived hundreds of thousands of people of basic liberties and subjected them to severe hardship conditions, for no good reason.

This is bad enough. But I want to say something stronger: it is not merely that we are punishing people for no good reason. We are punishing people for exercising their natural rights. Individuals have a right to use drugs. This right is neither absolute nor exceptionless; suppose, for example, that there existed a drug which, once ingested, caused a significant proportion of users, without any further free choices on their part, to attack other people without provocation. I would think that stopping the use of this drug would be the business of the government. But no existing drug satisfies this description. Indeed, though I cannot take time to delve into the matter here, I think it is clear that the drug *laws* cause far more crime than drugs themselves do.

The idea of a right to use drugs derives from the idea that individuals own their own bodies. That is, a person has the right to exercise control

---

10. Husak, *Legalize This!*, p. 2.

11. In 2006, there were approximately 553,000 people in American prisons and jails whose most serious offense was a drug offense. This included 93,751 federal inmates (U.S. Department of Justice, "Prisoners in 2006," December 2007, http://www.ojp.usdoj.gov/bjs/pub/pdf/p06 .pdf, p. 9). State prisons held another 269,596 drug inmates, based on the 2006 state prison population of 1,377,815 ("Prisoners in 2006," p. 2) and the 2004 rate of 19.57% of state prisoners held on drug charges ("Prisoners in 2006," p. 24). Local jails held another 189,204 drug inmates, based on the 2006 local jail population of 766,010 ("Prisoners in 2006," p. 3) and the 2002 rate of 24.7% of local inmates held on drug charges (U.S. Department of Justice, "Profile of Jail Inmates 2002," published July 2004, revised October 12, 2004, http://www.ojp.usdoj.gov/bjs/pub/pdf/ pji02.pdf, p. 1). In all cases, I have used the latest statistics available as of this writing.

12. Husak, *Legalize This!*, p. 15. See his chapter 2 for an extended discussion of various proposed rationales for drug prohibition, including many issues that I lack space to discuss here.

over his own body—including the right to decide how it should be used, and to exclude others from using it—in a manner similar to the way one may exercise control over one's (other) property. This statement is somewhat vague; nevertheless, we can see the general idea embodied in common sense morality. Indeed, it seems that if there is *anything* one would have rights to, it would be one's own body. This explains why we think others may not physically attack you or kidnap you. It explains why we do not accept the use of unwilling human subjects for medical experiments, even if the experiments are beneficial to society—the rest of society may not decide to use your body for its own purposes without your permission. It explains why some believe that women have a right to an abortion—and why some others do not. The former believe that a woman has the right to do what she wants with her own body; the latter believe that the fetus is a distinct person, and a woman does not have the right to harm *its* body. Virtually no one disputes that, *if* a fetus is merely a part of the woman's body, *then* a woman has a right to choose whether to have an abortion; just as virtually no one disputes that, *if* a fetus is a distinct person, then a woman lacks the right to destroy it. Almost no one disputes that persons have rights over their own bodies but not over others' bodies.

The right to control one's body cannot be interpreted as implying a right to use one's body in *every* conceivable way, any more than we have the right to use our property in every conceivable way. Most importantly, we may not use our bodies to harm others in certain ways, just as we may not use our property to harm others. But drug use seems to be a paradigm case of a legitimate exercise of the right to control one's own body. Drug consumption takes place in and immediately around the user's own body; the salient effects occur *inside* the user's body. If we consider drug use merely as altering the user's own body and mind, it is hard to see how anyone who believes in rights at all could deny that it is protected by a right, for: (a) it is hard to see how anyone who believes in rights could deny that individuals have rights over their own bodies and minds, and (b) it is hard to see how anyone who believes in such rights could deny that drug use, considered merely as altering the user's body and mind, is an example of the exercise of one's rights over one's own body and mind.

Consider two ways a prohibitionist might object to this argument. First, a prohibitionist might argue that drug use does not *merely* alter the user's own body and mind, but also harms the user's family, friends, co-workers, and society. I responded to this sort of argument in section II. Not just *any* way in which an action might be said to "harm" other people makes the action worthy of criminal sanctions. Here we need not try to state a general criterion for what sorts of harms make an action worthy of criminalization; it is enough to note that there are some kinds of "harms" that virtually no one would take to warrant criminal sanctions, and that these include the "harms" I cause to others by being a poor student, an incompetent worker, or an apathetic citizen.[13] That said, I agree with the prohibitionists at least this far: no one should be permitted to drive or operate heavy machinery while under the influence of drugs that impair their ability to do those things; nor should pregnant mothers be permitted to ingest drugs, if it can be proven that those drugs cause substantial risks to their babies (I leave open the question of what the threshold level of risk should be, as well as the empirical questions concerning the actual level of risk created by illegal drugs). But, in the great majority of cases, drug use does not harm anyone in any *relevant* ways—that is, ways that we normally take to merit criminal penalties—and should not be outlawed.

Second, a prohibitionist might argue that drug use fails to qualify as an exercise of the user's rights over his own body, because the individual is not truly acting freely in deciding to use drugs. Perhaps individuals only use drugs because they have fallen prey to some sort of psychological compulsion, because drugs exercise a siren-like allure that distorts users' perceptions, because users don't realize how bad drugs are, or something of that sort. The exact form of this objection doesn't matter; in any case, the prohibitionist faces a dilemma. If users do not freely choose to use drugs, then it is unjust to *punish* them for using drugs. For if users do not choose freely, then they are not morally responsible for their decision, and it is unjust to punish a person for something he is not responsible for. But if users *do* choose freely in deciding to use drugs, then this choice is an exercise of their rights over their own bodies.

I have tried to think of the best arguments prohibitionists could give, but in fact prohibitionists have remained puzzlingly silent on this issue. When a country goes to war, it tends to focus on how to win, sparing little thought for the rights of the victims in the enemy country. Similarly, one effect of America's declaring "war" on drug users seems to have been that prohibitionists have given almost no thought to the rights of drug users. Most either ignore the issue or mention it briefly only to dismiss it without

13. Husak (*Drugs and Rights*, Cambridge University Press, 1992, pp. 166–168), similarly, argues that no one has a *right* that I be a good neighbor, proficient student, and so on, and that only harms that violate rights can justify criminal sanctions.

argument.[14] In an effort to discredit legalizers, the Office of National Drug Control Policy produced the following caricature—

> The easy cynicism that has grown up around the drug issue is no accident. Sowing it has been the deliberate aim of a decades-long campaign by proponents of legalization, critics whose mantra is "nothing works," and whose central insight appears to be that they can avoid having to propose the unmentionable—a world where drugs are ubiquitous and where use and addiction would skyrocket— if they can hide behind the bland management critique that drug control efforts are "unworkable."[15]

apparently denying the existence of the central issues I have discussed in this essay. It seems reasonable to assume that an account of the state's right to forcibly interfere with individuals' decisions regarding their own bodies is not forthcoming from these prohibitionists.

IV. Conclusion

Undoubtedly, the drug war has been disastrous in many ways that others can more ably describe—in terms of its effects on crime, on police corruption, and on other civil liberties, to name a few. But more than that, the drug war is morally outrageous in its very conception. If we are to call ours a free society, we cannot deploy force to deprive people of their liberty and property for whimsical reasons. The exercise of such coercion requires a powerful and clearly-stated rationale. Most of the reasons that have been proposed in the case of drug prohibition would be considered feeble if advanced in other contexts. Few would take seriously the suggestion that people should be imprisoned for harming their own health, being poor students, or failing to share in the American dream. It is still less credible that we should imprison people for an activity that only *may* lead to those consequences. Yet these and other, similarly weak arguments form the core of prohibition's defense.

Prohibitionists are likewise unable to answer the argument that individuals have a right to use drugs. Any such answer would have to deny

---

14. See Inciardi for an instance of ignoring and Daniel Lungren ("Legalization Would Be a Mistake" in Timothy Lynch, ed., *After Prohibition*, Washington, D.C.: Cato Institute, 2000, page 180) for an instance of unargued dismissal. Wilson (p. 24) addresses the issue, if at all, only by arguing that drug use makes users worse parents, spouses, employers, and co-workers. This fails to refute the contention that individuals have a right to use drugs.

15. ONDCP, *National Drug Control Strategy 2002*, p. 3.

either that persons have rights of control over their own bodies, or that consuming drugs constituted an exercise of those rights. We have seen that the sort of harms drug use allegedly causes to society do not make a case against its being an exercise of the user's rights over his own body. And the claim that drug users can't control their behavior or don't know what they are doing renders it even more mysterious why one would believe drug users deserve to be punished for what they are doing.

I will close by responding to a query posed by prohibition-advocate James Inciardi:

> The government of the United States is not going to legalize drugs any-time soon, if ever, and certainly not in this [the 20th] century. So why spend so much time, expense, and intellectual and emotional effort on a quixotic undertaking? . . . [W]e should know by now that neither politicians nor the polity respond positively to abrupt and drastic strategy alterations.[16]

The United States presently has 553,000 people unjustly imprisoned. Inciardi may—tragically—be correct that our government has no intention of stopping its flagrant violations of the rights of its people any time soon. Nevertheless, it remains the duty of citizens and of political and social theorists to identify the injustice, and not to tacitly assent to it. Imagine a slavery advocate, decades before the Civil War, arguing that abolitionists were wasting their breath and should move on to more productive activities, such as arguing for incremental changes in the way slaves are treated, since the southern states had no intention of ending slavery any time soon. The institution of slavery is a black mark on our nation's history, but our history would be even more shameful if no one at the time had spoken against the injustice.

Is this comparison overdrawn? I don't think so. The harm of being unjustly imprisoned is qualitatively comparable (though it usually ends sooner) to the harm of being enslaved. The increasingly popular scapegoating and stereotyping of drug users and sellers on the part of our nation's leaders is comparable to the racial prejudices of previous generations. Yet very few seem willing to speak on behalf of drug users. Perhaps the unwillingness of those in public life to defend drug users' rights stems from the negative image we have of drug users and the fear of being associated with them. Yet these attitudes remain baffling. I have used illegal drugs myself.

---

16. Inciardi, p. 205.

I know of many decent and successful individuals who have used illegal drugs. Nearly half of all Americans over the age of 11 have used illegal drugs—including at least two United States Presidents, one Vice-President, one Speaker of the House, and one Supreme Court Justice.[17] But now leave aside the absurdity of recommending criminal sanctions for all these people. My point is this: if we are convinced of the injustice of drug prohibition, then—even if our protests should fall on deaf ears—we can not remain silent in the face of such a large-scale injustice in our own country. And, fortunately, radical social reforms *have* occurred, more than once in our history, in response to moral arguments.

Michael Huemer: America's Unjust Drug War

1. Huemer admits that using drugs can be harmful to the user, but points out that alcohol, tobacco, unhealthy food, and unsafe sex can also be harmful. Is there any morally relevant difference between the harms caused by drugs and the harms caused by these other activities?
2. Huemer invokes the following principle: "if it would be wrong to punish people for *directly bringing about* some result, then it would also be wrong to punish people for doing some other action on the grounds that the action has a *chance* of bringing about that result indirectly." Do you find this principle plausible? Why or why not?
3. Consider Huemer's case involving Howard. Should Howard be punished for acting the way he does? If not, does it follow that we should not punish drug users?
4. Do individuals have a right to use drugs? What is Huemer's argument for thinking that they do? Do you find it convincing?
5. Suppose that we accept Huemer's contention that we ought to legalize recreational drug use. Does it follow that all of those currently in prison for drug-related offenses have been unjustly imprisoned?

---

17. In 2006, 45% of Americans aged 12 and over reported having used at least one illegal drug (U.S. Department of Health and Human Services, "National Survey on Drug Use and Health," 2006, Table 1.1B, http://www.oas.samhsa.gov/NSDUH/2k6NSDUH/tabs/Sect1peTabs1to46 .htm). Bill Clinton, Al Gore, Newt Gingrich and Clarence Thomas have all acknowledged past drug use (reported by David Phinney, "Dodging the Drug Question," ABC News, August 19, 1999, http://abcnews.go.com/sections/politics/DailyNews/prez_questions990819.html). George W. Bush has refused to state whether he has ever used illegal drugs. Barack Obama has admitted to cocaine and marijuana use (*Dreams from My Father*, New York: Random House, 2004, p. 93).

40

Against the Legalization of Drugs

Peter de Marneffe

....

Peter de Marneffe argues for a moderate position on the sale and use of drugs. On the one hand, he believes that drug *use* ought to be decriminalized. According to de Marneffe, people have a moral right to self-sovereignty—a right to do as they please, so long as their actions do not harm or wrong others—that entitles them to put into their bodies anything they like, so long as this does not involve violating the rights of others. The right to self-sovereignty implies that people have a moral right to use drugs, so long as such use is not likely to lead to drug users violating the rights of others. And if they have a moral right to use drugs, then it is wrong of the government to criminalize such use.

On the other hand, the government does have the moral authority to criminalize the manufacture and sale of substantial amounts of drugs. And, according to de Marneffe, the government is fully justified in using that authority to criminalize such behavior. The argument against drug legalization is simple: if the sale and manufacture of drugs is legalized, then many more people will abuse drugs, or abuse them more often than they currently do. Such abuse has terrible consequences. Governments should do what they can to reduce the terrible consequences that beset their citizens. So governments should make the manufacture and sale of drugs illegal.

From Andrew I. Cohen and Christopher Heath Wellman, eds., *Contemporary Debates in Applied Ethics*, 2nd ed. (Blackwell, 2013), pp. 346–357.

De Marneffe devotes the bulk of his article to presenting and then replying to a variety of objections to his proposal. These include the objection that such governmental prohibitions are ineffective; that they are objectionably paternalistic; that they violate the rights of drug users; that they have led to the many problems of the so-called War on Drugs; that they have immoral effects on imprisoned youth; that they lead to and reinforce racial discrimination; that they only increase the amount of violence in society; that they foster the corruption of government officials in the foreign countries where drugs are manufactured; that it is inconsistent to legally allow the sale and manufacture of cigarettes and alcohol while prohibiting the sale and manufacture of other drugs; that if drugs ought to be illegal then so too should the sale and manufacture of unhealthy foods; and, finally, that there is no scientific proof that drug abuse would increase with the legalization of drugs.

....

Introduction

By the *legalization of drugs* I mean the removal of criminal penalties for the manufacture, sale, and possession of large quantities of recreational drugs, such as marijuana, cocaine, heroin, and methamphetamine. In this chapter, I present an argument against drug legalization in this sense. But I do not argue against *drug decriminalization*, by which I mean the removal of criminal penalties for recreational drug use and the possession of small quantities of recreational drugs. Although I am against drug legalization, I am for drug decriminalization. So one of my goals here is to explain why this position makes sense as a matter of principle.

The argument against drug legalization is simple. If drugs are legalized, they will be less expensive and more available. If drugs are less expensive and more available, drug use will increase, and with it, proportionately, drug abuse. So if drugs are legalized, there will be more drug abuse. By *drug abuse* I mean drug use that is likely to cause harm.

Ineffectiveness Objection

A common objection is that drug laws do not work. The imagined proof is that people still use drugs even though they are illegal. But this is a bad argument. People are still murdered even though murder is illegal, and we do not conclude that murder laws do not work or that they ought to be repealed. This is because we think these laws work well enough in reducing murder rates to justify the various costs of enforcing them. So even if drug laws do not eliminate drug abuse, they might likewise reduce it by enough to justify their costs.

Why should we think that drug laws reduce drug abuse? For one thing, our general knowledge of human psychology and economic behavior provides a good basis for predicting that drug use will increase if drugs are legalized. People use drugs because they enjoy them. If it is easier and less expensive to do something enjoyable, more people will do it and those who do it already will do it more often. Laws against the manufacture and sale of drugs make drugs less available, because they prohibit their sale in convenient locations, such as the local drug or liquor or grocery store, and more expensive, because the retail price of illegal drugs reflects the risk to manufacturers and sellers of being arrested and having their goods confiscated. So if drugs are legalized, the price will fall and they will be easier to get. "Hey honey, feel like some heroin tonight?" "Sure, why not stop at Walgreens on the way home from picking up the kids?"

The claim that drug laws reduce drug abuse is also supported by the available empirical evidence. During Prohibition it was illegal to manufacture, sell, and transport "intoxicating liquors" (but not illegal to drink alcoholic beverages or to make them at home for one's own use). During this same period, deaths from cirrhosis of the liver and admissions to state hospitals for alcoholic psychosis declined dramatically compared to the previous decade (Warburton, 1932, pp. 86, 89). Because cirrhosis and alcoholic psychosis are highly correlated with heavy drinking, this is good evidence that Prohibition reduced heavy drinking substantially. Recent studies of alcohol consumption also conclude that heavy drinking declines with increases in price and decreases in availability (Edwards et al., 1994; Cook, 2007). Further evidence that drug use is correlated with availability is that the use of controlled psychoactive drugs is significantly higher among physicians and other health care professionals (who have much greater access to these drugs) than it is among the general population (Goode, 2012, pp. 454–455), and that veterans who reported using heroin in Vietnam, where it was legal, reported not using it on returning to the USA, where it was illegal (Robins et al., 1974).

For all these reasons it is a safe bet that drug abuse would increase if drugs were legalized, and it is hard to find an expert on drug policy who denies this. This alone, however, does not settle whether laws against drugs are a good policy because we do not know by how much drug abuse would increase if drugs were legalized and we do not know how much harm would result from this increase in drug abuse. It is important to recognize, too, that drug laws also cause harm by creating a black market, which fosters violence and government corruption, and by sending people to prison. It is possible that the harms created by drug laws outweigh their benefits in reducing drug abuse. I will say more about this possibility below, but first I address some philosophical objections to drug laws.

Paternalism Objection

One objection is that drug laws are paternalistic: they limit people's liberty for their own good. A related objection is that drug laws are moralistic: they impose the view that drug use is wrong on everyone, including those who think it is good. It is true that drug use can be harmful, but most people who use drugs do not use them in a way that harms someone or that creates a significant risk of harm. This is true even of so-called "hard drugs" such as heroin and cocaine. Is it not wrong for the government to prohibit us from doing something we enjoy if it causes no harm?

To oppose drug legalization, however, is to oppose the removal of penalties for the *commercial manufacture* and *sale* and *possession of large quantities* of drugs; it is not to support criminal penalties for the use or possession of small quantities of drugs. To oppose drug legalization is therefore not to hold that anyone should be prohibited from doing something they enjoy for their own good, or that the government should impose the controversial view that drug use is wrong on everyone.

Violation of Rights Objection

A more fundamental objection to drug laws is that they violate our rights. I believe there is some truth to this. So I want to explain why it makes sense to oppose drug legalization even though some drug laws do violate our rights.

Each of us has a right of self-sovereignty: a moral right to control our own minds and bodies. Laws that prohibit people from using drugs or from possessing small quantities of them violate this right because the choice to use drugs involves an important form of control over our minds and bodies, and recreational drug use does not usually harm anyone or pose a serious risk of harm. The choice to use drugs involves an important form of control over our minds partly because recreational drug use is a form of mood control, which is an important aspect of controlling our minds. There are also perceptual experiences that we can have only as the result of using certain drugs, such as LSD, and certain kinds of euphoria that we can experience only as the result of using certain drugs, such as heroin. The choice to put a drug into one's body—to snort it, smoke it, inject it, or ingest it—is also an important form of control over one's body. Because we have a right to control our own minds and bodies, the government is justified in prohibiting us from using a drug only if the choice to use this drug is likely to harm someone, which is not true of most recreational drug use. Laws that prohibit us from using recreational drugs therefore violate our right of self-sovereignty and for this reason should be repealed.

The choice to manufacture or sell drugs, in contrast, does not involve an important form of control over one's own mind or body—no more than the choice to manufacture or sell any commercial product does. These are choices to engage in a commercial enterprise for profit, and may therefore be regulated or restricted for reasons of public welfare, just as any other commercial enterprise may be. One might think that there is something "hypocritical" or "inconsistent" about prohibiting the manufacture and sale of drugs and not prohibiting their possession and use, but this is confused. If one opposes drug legalization on the ground that the government should do whatever it can to reduce drug abuse, regardless of whether it violates anyone's rights, then it would be inconsistent to oppose drug criminalization. But it is not inconsistent to oppose drug criminalization if one opposes drug legalization on the ground that the government should do whatever it can to reduce drug abuse consistent with respect for individual rights. This is because it makes sense to hold that whereas drug criminalization violates the right of self-sovereignty, non-legalization does not (de Marneffe, 2013).

Some might argue that non-legalization violates the right of self-sovereignty too, because it is not possible to use drugs if no one is legally permitted to sell them. But this is obviously false because people still use drugs even though selling them is illegal. Although this fact is sometimes cited to demonstrate the futility of drug control, ironically it makes drug control easier to justify. If drug non-legalization really did make it impossible to use drugs, and so to have the unique experiences they provide, this policy would arguably violate the right of self-sovereignty on this ground. But drug control laws do not make drug use impossible; they only increase the price and reduce the availability of drugs. This is no more a violation of self-sovereignty than a decision by the local supermarket not to carry a certain food or to double its price.

High Costs of the Drug War Objection

Laws against the manufacture and sale of drugs might of course still be a bad policy even if they do not violate the right of self-sovereignty. This is because these laws have costs, and these costs might outweigh the benefits of these laws in reducing drug abuse. Laws against the manufacture and sale of drugs create a black market, which fosters violence, because when disputes arise in an illegal trade the disputants cannot go to the legal system for resolution. The black market also fosters government corruption, because those in an illegal trade must pay government officials for protection from arrest and confiscation. Drug laws also cost money to enforce, which might be better spent in other ways. Finally, drug laws result in some people being arrested and imprisoned and being left with criminal records. It is certainly possible that these costs outweigh the benefits of drug control in reducing drug abuse.

It is important to understand, though, that drug control policy need not be as costly as the so-called War on Drugs, which is current US policy. So even if the War on Drugs is too costly, as critics maintain, it does not follow that drugs should be legalized. The case against drug legalization rests on the assumption that the benefits of drug control in reducing drug abuse are sufficient to justify the costs of drug control *once these costs are reduced as much as possible consistent with effective drug control*. By *effective* drug control, I mean a policy that reduces drug abuse substantially compared to the amount of drug abuse that would exist if drugs were legalized. I do not mean a policy that eliminates drug abuse altogether. It is no more possible to eliminate drug abuse than it is to eliminate crime. But just as effective crime control is still possible, effective drug control is possible too. And if it is possible to have effective drug control without the high costs of the War on Drugs, then the benefits of prohibiting the manufacture and sale of drugs are more likely to justify the costs.

One compelling objection to the War on Drugs is to the sentencing rules for drug law violations, which require judges to impose long prison terms for drug trafficking offenses. Critics rightly argue that mandatory sentences and long prison terms for selling drugs are morally indefensible. These are not, however, necessary features of effective drug control policy. They are not features of European drug control policy, for example. So it makes sense to oppose harsh mandatory penalties while also opposing drug legalization.

Drug control works primarily by increasing price and reducing availability, which can be accomplished by reliably enforcing laws against the manufacture and sale of drugs with moderate penalties. Where it is illegal to manufacture and sell drugs, most business persons avoid the drug trade because they do not want to be arrested and have their goods confiscated. This reduces supply, which increases price. Where it is illegal to sell drugs, stores that aim to retain their licenses also do not sell them, which reduces availability. Heavy penalties no doubt drive the price up even higher and decrease availability even more by increasing the risks of drug trafficking—but the biggest increases in price and the biggest reductions in availability come simply from the illegality of the trade itself together with reliable enforcement of laws against manufacture and sale (Kleiman et al., 2011, pp. 48–50). If effective drug control does not require harsh mandatory penalties, then the fact that such penalties are unjustifiable is not a good argument for drug legalization.

Effect on Imprisoned Youths Objection

Another objection to US drug control policy is that it results in many young people being arrested, imprisoned, and left with criminal records, who would otherwise not suffer these misfortunes. Some might retort that if a person chooses to deal drugs illegally, he cannot legitimately complain about the foreseeable consequences of his choice. But this response is inadequate because by making drugs illegal the government creates a hazard that otherwise would not exist. By making the manufacture and sale of drugs illegal, the government creates a lucrative illegal market, and the money-making opportunities that this market creates are attractive, especially to young people who lack a college education or special training, because they can make much more money by dealing drugs than by doing anything else. When the government creates a system of penalties for manufacturing and selling drugs it therefore creates a hazard; it creates a tempting opportunity to make money and then imposes penalties for making money in this way.

In general, the government has an obligation to reduce the risk to individuals of being harmed by the hazards it creates. When the government tests weapons, for example, it must take care that people do not wander into the testing areas. Bright signs are not enough; it must also build fences and monitor against trespass. The government also has an obligation to help young people avoid the worst consequences of their willingness to take unwise risks. It has an obligation to require teenagers to wear helmets when they ride a motorcycle, for example. So when the government creates the hazard of imprisonment by making the manufacture and sale of drugs illegal, it must guard against the likelihood of imprisonment, and it must take special care to reduce this likelihood for young people who commonly lack a proper appreciation of the negative impact that conviction and imprisonment will have on their lives. For all these reasons, the government must structure drug laws so that young people have an adequate opportunity to avoid being imprisoned for drug offenses, and to avoid acquiring a criminal record. This means, among other things, that no one should be arrested for a drug offense prior to receiving an official warning; no penalty for a first conviction should involve prison time; initial jail or prison sentences should be short and subject to judicial discretion; and imprisonment for subsequent convictions should increase in length only gradually and also be subject to judicial discretion.

Racial Discrimination Objection

A related objection to the War on Drugs is that those imprisoned for drug offenses in the USA are disproportionately black inner city males (Alexander, 2012). This objection would be addressed to some degree by the changes in sentencing policy just proposed, but one might predict that any effective drug control policy would result in the same sort of disproportionality, which some might see as an argument for drug legalization. However, it also is important to consider the potential negative impact of drug legalization on inner city communities. Drug legalization will result in a substantial increase in drug abuse. Drug abuse commonly leads parents to neglect their children, and to neglect their own health and jobs, which harms their children indirectly. Drug abuse also distracts teenagers from their schoolwork, interferes with the development of a sense of responsibility, and makes young people less likely to develop the skills necessary for acquiring good jobs as adults. If drugs are legalized, there will therefore be more child neglect as a result and more truancy by teenagers. This is likely to have an even more devastating impact on the life prospects of young people in non-affluent inner city communities than it has on the life prospects of young people in affluent suburbs. I suspect this is the primary reason why many inner city community leaders oppose drug legalization.

It is true that incarcerating large numbers of inner city youths for drug offenses also has a negative impact on inner city communities. A man who is in jail cannot be present as a parent or make money to support his children, and a person with a criminal record has a harder time finding a decent job. These consequences alone would warrant drug legalization if there were no downside. If we assume, however, that drug legalization would result in a substantial increase in child neglect and adolescent truancy, then legalization does not seem like a good way to improve the life prospects of inner city youth overall. It seems better to maintain laws against the manufacture and sale of drugs, and reduce the number of those who are convicted and imprisoned for drug offenses. This would be consistent with effective drug control because the number of dealers in prison could be reduced dramatically without making drugs noticeably cheaper or easier to get (Kleiman et al., 2011, p. 203).

Increase in Violence Objection

Another objection to US drug control policy is that it has increased violence in other countries, particularly Mexico. Americans enjoy using drugs and are willing to pay for them. Because it is illegal to manufacture and sell drugs in the USA, American drug control policy creates opportunities for people south of the border to get rich by making drugs and selling them wholesale to retailers north of the border. Because those in the drug trade use violence to control market share and to intimidate law enforcement, US drug laws result in violence. If drugs were legalized in the USA, the recreational drug market would presumably be taken over by large US drug, liquor, and food companies and it would not be possible for anyone in Mexico to get rich by selling illegal drugs to Americans, which would eliminate the associated violence there.

Drug legalization, however, is not the only way to reduce drug-related violence abroad. Here are some alternative strategies:

- The USA might legalize the private production of marijuana for personal use (the way it was legal during Prohibition to make alcoholic beverages at home). Because much of the Mexican drug trade is in marijuana, this would reduce its profitability, and so presumably the associated violence.

- The USA might also concentrate its drug enforcement efforts in Mexico on the most violent drug trafficking organizations, as opposed to concentrating on the biggest and most profitable organizations, which would create incentives for those in the Mexican drug trade to be less violent.

- The USA might also ease border control at entry points not on the US-Mexico border. The violence in Mexico is created partly by the fact that it is the primary conduit of cocaine from South and Central America to North America. If the USA were to loosen border control in Florida, fewer drugs would travel through Mexico. Because the USA imports so many goods, it is not possible to stop drugs from coming into this country. Some would cite this as proof that drug control is futile, but this conclusion is unwarranted because border controls still raise the retail price of drugs substantially, which results in less drug abuse (Kleiman et al., 2011, pp. 162–163). The suggestion here is that a general policy of border control is consistent with US law enforcement experimenting with different border control policies with an eye to reducing violence abroad (Kleiman et al., 2011, p. 170).

None of these proposals would eliminate drug-related violence in Mexico, but it is unrealistic to think that criminal violence in Mexico would be eliminated by drug legalization in the USA. After all, what will career criminals in Mexico do once they cannot make money via the drug trade? Presumably they will turn to other criminal activities, such as kidnapping, extortion, and human trafficking, which also involve violence.

Corruption of Foreign Governments Objection

Another objection to US drug control policy is that it fosters the corruption of foreign governments. Because those in the foreign drug trade need protection from arrest, prosecution, and confiscation of assets, because they are willing to pay government officials to look the other way, and because some government officials are willing to accept this payment, the drug trade increases government corruption. If drugs were legalized in the USA, this would destroy the illegal market abroad, which would remove an important contributing factor in government corruption.

It is naive, though, to think that US drug control policy is the primary cause of government corruption abroad. Although we associate police corruption with drug trafficking, the latter tends to flourish where government officials are already corrupt (Kleiman et al., 2011, p. 177). [A] foreign police force that is not fully professionalized will be susceptible to financial corruption regardless of whether the USA legalizes drugs.

The Inconsistency Objection

Another argument against drug laws is that it is hypocritical or inconsistent for our government to prohibit the manufacture and sale of heroin, cocaine, and methamphetamine while permitting the manufacture and sale of alcohol and cigarettes. Drinking and smoking cause far more harm than other kinds of recreational drug use. This is partly because there is so much more drinking and smoking, which is partly because the manufacture and sale of alcohol and cigarettes are legal. But drinking and smoking are also inherently more harmful than other forms of drug use. Drinking alcohol is correlated much more highly with violence, property crime, and accidental injury than the use of heroin is, and a regular user of heroin who uses it safely—in moderate doses with clean equipment—does not face any significant health risk as a result, whereas cigarette smoking is known to cause heart and lung disease. So it can seem that if the government is justified in prohibiting the manufacture and sale of heroin, it must also be justified in prohibiting the manufacture and sale of alcohol and cigarettes.

This would be a good objection to drug laws if laws against the manufacture and sale of alcoholic beverages and cigarettes were wrong in principle, but it is hard to see why they would be. After all, drinking and smoking cause a lot of harm and neither policy would violate the right of self-sovereignty discussed above, because a law that prohibits only the manufacture and sale of a drug does not prohibit its possession or make its use impossible. Of course, the suggestion that alcohol prohibition might be justified is commonly dismissed with the incantation that Prohibition was a disastrous failure, but historians agree that Prohibition succeeded in substantially reducing heavy drinking, and it would have been even more effective had its enforcement been adequately funded and had it been administered from the outset by law enforcement professionals instead of by political appointees (Okrent, 2010, pp. 134–145, 254–261). Prohibition did fail politically, but so did Reconstruction and the Equal Rights

Amendment. The fact that a policy is rejected or abandoned does not show that it was wrong in principle. Finally, it is worth noting that alcohol prohibition still exists in some parts of this country, on Indian reservations, for example, and that these policies make sense as part of an effort to reduce alcoholism and the harms associated with it.

It is not necessary, though, to advocate alcohol prohibition in order to defend other drug laws, because there are relevant differences between them. For one thing, the institution of alcohol prohibition now is likely not to reduce heavy drinking by as much as drug non-legalization reduces drug abuse. Drinking is widely accepted and a part of normal social rituals, in a way that heroin, cocaine, and methamphetamine use is not. This means that alcohol prohibition now would not work in tandem with a strong social stigma, which would presumably reduce its effectiveness in reducing alcohol abuse. It is possible, too, that in an environment of social acceptance, sharply increasing the excise taxes on alcoholic beverages would achieve almost as much as prohibition in reducing the harms caused by heavy drinking with none of the costs of prohibition (though it is worth noting here that liquor industry lobbying has been more effective in preventing excise tax increases than it was in preventing Prohibition). There are also important ways in which instituting alcohol prohibition now would be more burdensome than continuing with drug non-legalization. Many people have built their lives around the alcoholic beverage industry. If alcohol were now prohibited, many of these people would lose their jobs, and many companies, restaurants and bars would go out of business, which would be a serious hardship for owners and employees. In contrast, people who go into the drug trade do so knowing that it is illegal. So the burden on them of maintaining drug laws is not as great as the burden that alcohol prohibition would impose on those who have built their lives around the liquor trade on the assumption that the manufacture and sale of alcohol will remain legal. Ironically, it is drug *legalization* that would burden those in the illegal drug trade, in much the same way as Prohibition burdened those in the legal liquor trade: by depriving them of their livelihood.

There are also important differences between illicit drugs and cigarettes. Drug legalization, I assume, would result in a substantial increase in drug abuse, which, I assume, would also result in a substantial increase in child neglect and adolescent truancy, which would have a substantial negative impact on the life prospects of many young people. Cigarette smoking, in contrast, does not make someone a worse parent or a worse student or employee. Furthermore, because heavy smoking typically has a negative impact on a person's life only toward the end when he or she is older, smoking as a young person is less likely than adolescent drug abuse to have a negative impact on the *kind* of life a person has. Finally, although psychologically challenging, it is quite possible to quit smoking as an adult and so to reduce the long-term health consequences of starting to smoke as a teenager—much easier than it is to reverse the long-term negative consequences of having had inadequate parenting or having failed out of high school as the result of drug abuse. Given these differences between the consequences of smoking and drug abuse, one can consistently oppose the legalization of drugs for the reasons I have given here without advocating prohibiting the manufacture and sale of cigarettes.

In explaining above how one might consistently oppose the legalization of drugs without advocating alcohol prohibition, I observed that drinking is so widespread and socially accepted that alcohol prohibition is likely to reduce heavy drinking by less than drug abuse is reduced by laws against the manufacture and sale of illicit drugs. This same point might now be given as an argument for legalizing marijuana: marijuana use is so widespread and socially accepted that laws against the manufacture and sale of marijuana do not do very much to reduce it. It might also be argued that legalizing marijuana would not result in a dramatic increase in drug abuse because marijuana is less subject to abuse than other drugs (including alcohol). Finally, legalizing marijuana in the USA would dramatically reduce the drug trade in Mexico, which would result in a corresponding reduction in violence and government corruption there. Should not marijuana be legalized, then, even if other drugs should not be?

In this chapter I am arguing against the view that the manufacture and sale of *all* drugs should be legalized; I am not arguing that there is *no* drug that should be legalized. Suppose that marijuana legalization would not result in a substantial increase in drug abuse. Suppose that most of those who would use marijuana if it were legalized are already using it and using it almost as much as they want to. Or suppose that marijuana use itself is harmless and does not lead to the use of more harmful drugs. If either of these things is true, then marijuana should be legalized. It is also possible, though, that, as a result of legalization, many more young people would use marijuana than do now, and that a sizable fraction of them would use it in ways that interfere with their education or employment, and that a sizable fraction of them would go on to abuse more harmful drugs who would otherwise never have tried them. Because I am not sure that these things would not happen, I do not support legalizing marijuana. With more information, though, I might change my mind. So it is important to make clear that whether a drug should be legalized depends on the consequences of legalizing it, and not on whether any *other* drug should be legalized. Hence, even if marijuana should be legalized, it would not follow that heroin, cocaine, and methamphetamine should be legalized too.

Unhealthy Foods Objection

Another argument against drug laws is that if the government is justified in prohibiting us from putting a drug into our bodies for our own good, then it is also justified in prohibiting us from putting unhealthy foods into our bodies for our own good. The suggestion that the government is entitled to control what we eat strikes many of us as outrageous. Why is it not likewise outrageous for the government to prohibit us from using recreational drugs?

For the reasons given above, I think it is. Laws that prohibit us from using drugs—or drinking alcohol or smoking cigarettes—violate our right of self-sovereignty in the same way that laws that prohibit us from eating high fat or high sugar foods would. However, just as laws that prohibit the manufacture and sale of drugs do not violate our self-sovereignty, laws that regulate the sale of fatty or sugary foods do not either. So if the government prohibits fast food restaurants from selling humongous hamburgers, or prohibits convenience stores from selling sugary soda in giant cups, or prohibits vending machines in schools from stocking items with high fat or sugar content, no one's right of self-sovereignty is violated. Whether these policies are a good idea is a separate question, but if they are a bad idea, it is not because they violate anyone's rights.

No Scientific Proof Objection

In arguing against drug legalization, I assume that drug abuse would increase substantially if drugs were legalized. Some might now object that there is no proof of this, and this is true, but there is also no proof that murder rates will rise if murder is decriminalized. That is, this assumption is not warranted by any set of controlled laboratory experiments or randomized field trials. Should murder therefore be decriminalized? Obviously not. Some might say that the freedom to murder is not a very important liberty, so the standard of proof need not be so high. But most of us also support on the basis of assumptions for which there is no scientific proof policies that do impinge on important liberties. For example, many of us support restrictions on campaign contributions on the assumption that unrestricted contributions would result in more political corruption. But there is no scientific proof of this, and restrictions on campaign contributions impinge on the important freedom of political speech. Many of us also support immigration laws on the assumption that unrestricted immigration would lower our quality of life. But there is also no scientific proof of this, and freedom of movement is also an important liberty. Should we withdraw our support for these policies just because we support them on the basis of scientifically unproven assumptions? I think not. In general we are justified in supporting a legal restriction for a reason if two conditions are met: (a) this reason would justify this restriction if it was based on true assumptions, and (b) we are warranted by the available evidence in believing that the relevant assumptions are true. So if we are warranted by the available evidence in believing that drug abuse will increase if drugs are legalized, then we are justified in making this assumption for the purpose of evaluating drug control policy. And we are warranted in making this assumption—by what we know about patterns of alcohol and drug consumption and more generally about human psychology and economic behavior.

Conclusion

If drug abuse would increase substantially if drugs were legalized, and laws that prohibit the manufacture and sale of drugs do not violate our right of self-sovereignty, and effective drug control requires only moderate penalties reliably and conscientiously enforced, then it makes sense to oppose drug legalization. This, in essence, is the argument I have made here. In evaluating drug policy, it is important, too, to consider how public policy would be shaped if drugs were legalized. Beer, liquor, and cigarette companies already do as much as they can to prevent the government from adopting policies that would reduce drinking and smoking and so their associated harms. They do as much as they can to prevent increases in excise taxes, which increase the price of alcohol and cigarettes, and so reduce their sales, and so smoking and drinking. They do as much as they can to prevent restrictions on the hours and locations of the sale of alcohol and cigarettes. They do as much as they can to prevent licensing and rationing policies, which would reduce the amount of alcohol consumed by problem drinkers. And they do as much as they can to make their products attractive through advertising, particularly to young people. We should expect that if drugs are legalized, drug companies will behave in the same way: that they will do everything they can to prevent the enactment of laws that restrict the marketing and sale of heroin, cocaine, and methamphetamine, and that they will do everything they can to market these drugs successfully, particularly to young people, who will be their most profitable market. Because drug use is currently stigmatized, drug companies are unlikely to be as successful as liquor companies in preventing sound public policy, at least initially. But if we envision a world in which legal drug companies are legally trying to persuade consumers to buy recreational drugs from legal vendors and legally trying to prevent any socially responsible legislation that reduces their legal sales, it is hard to envision a world that does not have much more drug abuse.

References

Alexander, M. (2012) *The New Jim Crow: Mass Incarceration in the Age of Colorblindness*. New York: New Press.

Cook, P. J. (2007) *Paying the Tab: The Economics of Alcohol Policy*. Princeton, NJ: Princeton University Press.

de Marneffe, P. (2013) Vice laws and self-sovereignty. *Criminal Law and Philosophy* 7: 29–41.

Edwards, G., Anderson, P., Babor, T. F. et al. (1994) *Alcohol Policy and the Public Good*. New York: Oxford University Press.

Goode, E. (2012) *Drugs in American Society*, 8th ed. New York: McGraw-Hill.

Kleiman, M.A.R. et al. (2011) *Drugs and Drug Policy: What Everyone Needs to Know*. New York: Oxford University Press.

Okrent, D. (2010) *Last Call: The Rise and Fall of Prohibition*. New York: Scribner.

Robins, L. N. et al. (1974) Drug use by U.S. army in Vietnam: a follow-up on their return home. *American Journal of Epidemiology* 99: 235–249.

Warburton, C. (1932) *The Economic Results of Prohibition*. New York: Columbia University Press.

Peter de Marneffe: Against the Legalization of Drugs

1. Is it consistent to favor drug decriminalization while also urging that the sale and manufacture of drugs be illegal? Why or why not?
2. Reconstruct the argument from self-sovereignty in support of drug decriminalization. Is that argument sound?
3. Is there another objection to the criminalization of the sale and manufacture of drugs that de Marneffe has failed to consider and that you find compelling? If so, what is it?
4. De Marneffe has considered eleven objections to his argument. Are any of these objections stronger than he supposes? If so, which ones?

41

——— ❧ ———

Why Illegally Downloading Files Is Morally Wrong

Jonathan Trerise

....

Jonathan Trerise presents a simple argument designed to show that illegally downloading files is in most cases immoral. Such downloading is an instance of either directly stealing from or breaking a contract with authors, artists, or their legal representatives (such as a record company or book publisher); stealing and breaking contracts is almost always morally wrong; therefore, illegally downloading files is almost always morally wrong. There may be extreme situations where sacrificing the strong moral duty not to steal or break a contract is permitted, so this moral prohibition on illegally downloading is not absolute. But exceptions will likely be quite rare.

After developing this argument, Trerise considers a number of potential objections. One is that many consumers pay artists in other ways, for instance, by buying tickets to their performances. But this doesn't license a person to steal or break a contract, says Trerise. A second challenge is that many wealthy artists won't be harmed by a single instance of illegal downloading. In response, Trerise notes that most artists aren't rich. But even for those who are, it is still wrong to steal from them or break a contract with them, even if they won't be much harmed as a result. A third objection concedes that illegal downloading is wrong, but denies that its harm is that substantial. Trerise replies that the extent of the harms is often unknown and may in fact

---

This article was commissioned for the fourth edition of *The Ethical Life*.

be substantial, but even when it isn't, this objection grants his main point—namely, that illegal downloading is immoral after all.

A fourth concern is that the wrongness of illegally downloading files depends on the legitimacy of the current copyright system—and that system is in fact deeply flawed. Trerise replies by saying that the merits of the current system are irrelevant—the wrong one does by illegal downloading is that of breaking a contract, and that is immoral even if the contractual system (in this case, that which regulates copyright) is imperfect. A fifth challenge alleges that (nearly) everyone is engaged in illegal downloading, and so it cannot be wrong after all. Trerise, in reply, argues that actions can be wrong even if widely done. It would be wrong to kill or to cheat on one's taxes even if many people were perpetrating such deeds.

A sixth objection asserts that the current system of copyright is excessively overprotective of the intellectual property rights of creators, and so illegal downloading is unobjectionable, since it is targeting a corrupt area of the law. Trerise responds by claiming that the current system may well be overprotective. Still, this does not license stealing or contract-breaking. People need significant protection of their ideas, both for its own sake and for the sake of spurring innovation. So long as some form of copyright protection is justified, illegal downloading will violate the rights of authors and artists and so is wrong, absent some very powerful moral reason to download files that do not belong to you.

Finally, someone might argue that the current copyright system is so corrupt that the contracts it imposes are unfair and so are not morally binding in the first place. Trerise regards this as the most powerful objection to his thesis. He allows that some practices are inherently immoral (such as slavery) and that no contracts made within them are morally binding. But the recording industry, while far from ideal in its treatment of artists, is not inherently immoral, and so consumers are not morally free to violate the terms of the contracts that the industry dictates for use of its recordings. The same applies to book publishers and to other copyright holders.

....

S uppose your friend Lars has just written a piece of music he's proud of and wants to show you. But, for whatever reason—he's persnickety, protective, or just not comfortable with its release yet—he doesn't want you to share it with anyone else. This is especially relevant as you have an eidetic memory when it comes to music—you hear it once, you can play it or transcribe it without error. Or you carry excellent recording devices around with you. It doesn't matter; either way, you could copy and reproduce the song with ease, and Lars is very careful before playing it to you. He asks you to agree not to record, copy, or share it with anyone without his permission. You agree, and, after he plays it for you, you write down the notes and start to play it for other friends. (Or, you play what you recorded for them.)

It seems clear that you've acted immorally and have wronged Lars. He asked you not to do something, you agreed not to do it, and you did it anyway. Note that you did not try to profit from his work. Nor did you remove something from his possession. Still, you've wronged him. (Had you, say, sold his song for a profit, it would seem your action would be worse.) And the situation remains the same even if Lars wasn't your friend. Though the wrong in the case as originally described includes the wrong of disloyalty, your action would be wrong even if Lars were not your friend. You've broken a promise or contract. These actions are wrong no matter what your relationship is with Lars.

The above is, I think, the kind of wrong that is often involved in illegally downloading music and other files. I'm not saying that it's wrong *because* it's illegal. I'm also not saying that there's never justification for illegal downloading. But, in the normal case, downloading illegal files such as music and movies is wrong for just the same kind of reason that your action in the above case is wrong. In downloading illegal files one has broken a promise or contract. This is the simple statement of the thesis I shall defend.

In doing so, I will be providing the basics of a defense of *copyright*. Copyright is legal protection for the expression of ideas as embodied in music, film, literature and other works of art. When one illegally downloads files, one has violated copyright. This paper then constitutes a basic *moral* defense of the *legal* institution of copyright protection. If the following argument is correct—that illegal downloading is morally wrong because it represents broken contracts—it is then only a short step to a *presumptive* (that is, a strong but not absolute) defense of copyright. So, assuming the soundness of the coming argument for the immorality of illegal downloading, how is copyright justified? Basically, since our legal system rightly enforces contracts in general, the legal system's enforcement of copyright as the simple maintenance, regulation, and enforcement of contracts is basically unproblematic. Of course many details will need to be sorted out. But if the argument of this paper is sound, then a legal institution of copyright is presumptively justified. And that means that, absent some very compelling justification, illegally downloading files is morally wrong.

After a basic defense of my thesis, I shall explore various challenges to the argument. Though I reject these challenges, some of them do indicate that our work on developing morally justified copyright protection is not yet finished.

Here, then, is *the main argument for the immorality of illegal downloading:*

1. Breaking contracts is morally wrong unless there's an overriding moral reason to do so.
2. Illegally downloading music and other files is the breaking of a contract.
3. There is normally no overriding moral reason to illegally download music and other files.
4. Therefore, illegally downloading music and other files is normally morally wrong.

As the argument is logically valid—that is, guaranteed to yield a true conclusion if all premises are true—we need only ensure that the premises are true in order to ensure the truth of the conclusion. Premise 1 is clearly true: breaking contracts is ordinarily morally wrong. Though there are exceptional cases where doing such things is morally acceptable, such actions require an overriding moral reason. All plausible ethical theories will agree on premise 1.

Premise 3 is also true. Though there are unusual circumstances in which illegal downloading is, all things considered, the morally right thing to do, these cases are relatively rare. In most cases there is no such overriding moral reason that would justify illegal downloading. The circumstances would indeed have to be rather extreme. Suppose, for example, Joseph is incredibly moved by Maya Angelou's *I Know Why the Caged Bird Sings*. He was able to read it in an unprecedented month of access to a library. This book—every word of it—is part of what motivates him to move beyond his tragically poor and disadvantaged circumstances (which include, importantly, a general lack of access to books and other media). Luckily, through the charity of others, he has a digital device where he could download the book for free (he has no money to purchase the book). Here is a case where there may be overriding moral reason for Joseph to break a contract that requires him not to download the book. It should be obvious, however, that this is an extreme case. Similar cases are certainly possible, but also rare, and do not represent the lion's share of instances of illegal downloading.

Premise 2 is where the action is. Now, it seems to me clear that when one illegally downloads music, one breaks a contract. Suppose a songwriter does not freely release her music. Usually she (or her proxy, say, a producer at a record company) attaches conditions on the purchase and use of the music, in particular through user agreements on something like iTunes or on the packaging of a CD. These conditions usually require that the purchaser not copy, share, or sell the music in question. This is a contract that the purchaser signs by going through with the purchase. If purchasers do not want to fulfill the terms of the contract, they do not have to enter into it in the first place—but then they would not be able to enjoy the item. Once people make a purchase, they've made a contract. Copying, sharing, or selling the music after that would thus constitute the breaking of a contract. It is possible that, upon purchase, the consumer made a false promise or false contract in that they never intended to fulfill their end of the agreement in the first place, but this is still morally problematic.

Of course not all possession of illegally downloaded material comes in this way. Some downloading happens through third-party websites that illegally make files available for free download, while some others happen through the use of software that illegally "rips" files from websites that legally have the files. In the first kind of case, the downloading party may not have signed any contract, but they are in possession of stolen material, and so they avoid the wrong of contract-breaking only by engaging in the wrong of being in possession of stolen material. In the second kind of case, the illegal use of software to copy protected material is akin to the copying of material from a CD that has the respect of the copyright as a condition of its purchase. The material is made available only on the understanding that it will not be copied without permission. That is, a contract has been made. While there may be other kinds of illegal downloading, it seems likely that they will exhibit one of these wrongs: either stealing, being in the possession of stolen material, or the breaking of a contract.

Setting aside the cases of stealing, then, the basic wrong that occurs in a violation of copyright is the same as the basic wrong in your treatment of Lars in the example conveyed at the beginning of the paper. Even if you haven't stolen anything from Lars, you've made a contract and then broken it. These are actions which are normally wrong, and thus the violation of copyright—through the downloading of illegal files from the Internet—is also normally wrong. So the more nuanced statement of my thesis is this:

even when simple stealing or being in the possession of stolen material has not occurred, the downloading of illegal files is (exceptional cases aside) still morally wrong, as it is a violation of a contract.

In the remainder of this paper, I will present seven challenges to the main argument. After the third challenge they get successively more interesting and meaningful. Still, I conclude that none of them shows the argument to be problematic. They do, however, indicate that there is a variety of issues that we need to be concerned with in justifying the legal institution of copyright and developing its details.

Challenge #1: I Pay the Artist in Other Ways

Many people are quick to point out, rightly, that most musicians, for example, do not make much on the sale of their album. They make pennies on the dollar at best, while the production company makes the lion's share. Hence, many readers might think that, as long as they support the musicians in other ways—say, by attending a live concert, where musicians make a much greater share of the profits—this permits their illegal downloading. This point (like others in this paper) easily applies to other works of art beyond music.

The problem with this challenge is that it says nothing about the argument itself; that is, it does not show any aspect of the argument to be problematic. Hence the argument stands. At most, this consideration tells us something important about how musicians make money. It cannot show that illegal downloading is permissible. It simply changes the subject. In fact the response is an arrogant one; those who would compensate an artist in one way rather than another just assume that their way of compensating the artist is the right way, no matter what the artist thinks.

Challenge #2: It's Not Wrong to Break Contracts with Rich Artists or Powerful Production Companies since It Doesn't Harm Them

This challenge says that the people who are supposedly wronged by illegal downloading—generally, powerful production companies—actually are not harmed since they stand to lose very little by such downloading. Some people have thought this because high profile defenders of their copyrights, such as the bands Metallica and Talking Heads, are financially quite well off. We don't owe the rich and powerful the same moral respect (to not break contracts) that we normally owe others.

Put as explicitly as that, however, this seems implausible. While we may owe *more* to people to who are suffering (in poverty, for example), it seems strange to think that we owe *less* to those who are financially well-off. I don't have any more of a right to kill you because you're rich than if you were poor. Perhaps we feel worse for a poor person who has his money stolen than we do if the same thing happens to someone who is rich, but this is quite different from saying that the theft from the rich person is morally permissible. It may be *less* wrong to rob from the rich than from the poor, but even that may seem odd to many readers, and it is still *wrong*. We still owe basic moral duties to rich people, no matter how much worse we feel when poor people are treated wrongly. Further, it is implausible to assume that most artists whose music is illegally downloaded are rich. And, even if they were, little harm does not equal no harm; lost profits still harm producers as well as artists. Even if the main harms are done to wealthy producers, this doesn't eliminate the harm, and of course a producer's lost profits can end up hurting other, unestablished artists whom producers will be less willing to take a risk on. So challenge #2 seems implausible.

Challenge #3: Ok, Maybe It's Wrong, But It's Not That Big of a Deal

This challenge concedes that illegal downloading is wrong, but appeals to the widely accepted notion that some wrongs are relatively insignificant. Like white lies or taking office supplies from work, these actions are technically wrong but we don't care too much about them. Illegal downloading is certainly not on the level of murder and rape, for instance. This challenge gains some traction when we see that, while musicians and production companies have had some reduced profits in this era of rampant illegal downloading, they're still profiting from the sale of their music. Using alternative business models, the music industry has moved on and continues to be successful in the digital age.

This challenge overstates its case. Though it is no doubt true that there will be cases of illegal downloading—perhaps many—where little damage is done, it would take carefully collected evidence to establish that such downloading causes no significant harm. The harm is not as obvious or as grave as the harm of murder. Still, the harms that come from illegal downloading may be quite real and very serious. Record companies, facing a reduction in profits, may not take risks on unproven artists, given the chance that the companies may not recoup their investment in them.

This poses the risk of significant harm to poor artists. Further, as more and more people commit this supposedly insignificant wrong, the wrong gains in magnitude. Finally, this challenge at the very least concedes the wrongness of illegal downloading, which means it's not much of a challenge to my thesis.

Challenge #4: *Our System* Is the Problem, Not Copyright in the General Way You're Portraying It

This challenge grants me the soundness of the main argument, but points out that it does not on its own justify the *current American copyright system*. And, importantly, when people illegally download, they are violating the laws within the current American system. Thus in order to show that people do wrong when they illegally download, the argument would have to show two things: that those who download have broken a contract with the current American system of copyright, *and* that this system is morally legitimate.

While noting problems with the current American copyright system is important for many purposes, it's irrelevant to the main argument. To discuss the details of the American copyright system is a distraction from the point of the argument, which focuses on the breaking of contracts, period. No matter what system one is working within, these actions are wrong, unless there's an overriding moral reason to commit them. But this challenge offers no such overriding reason. It might, however, be thought that the system is so corrupt that any contracts made within it are not morally binding at all. This is a more important criticism, and thus I turn to it later in challenge #7.

Challenge #5: But Everybody Does It!

The "everybody does it" response to a criticism of any specific behavior is usually dismissed, and often with good reason. If everyone committed murder, that would not justify it. Still, I think there's a bit more to this kind of response than meets the eye. The basic idea is that sometimes the behavior of so many people across so many social classes might be a signal that the behavior in question really isn't a big deal. In this case, it might indicate that people are tired of outmoded ways of life, signaling *through* their behavior that it's time to change and grow with the times. In any case, it's a fact that not nearly everyone *does* commit heinous acts like murder, and so it means something important when so few people take the illegality of downloading seriously. Furthermore, one might think that one has "no moral duty to play the sucker" and be disadvantaged when so many others are taking advantage of the system.

While this objection has some force, I still think it fails as a challenge to the main argument. To propose another example perhaps less extreme than the one about murder, many people do cheat on their taxes. The fact that so many people do this does not entail that they are justified in doing so, and clearly does not show that widespread violation of the tax code is permissible. (There may be other reasons that would justify cheating on one's taxes, but the fact that others do so is not one of those reasons.) So, although the fact that many people do it is meaningful, it does not make the action in question justified. It just means we need to give careful thought to *why* so many people are doing something that is illegal (and, if I am right, immoral). That a great many people are breaking their contracts doesn't by itself permit one to do so, at least without significant further argument. This is not to say one has to be made into a sucker; after all, one can avoid immorally breaking such a contract by not entering it in the first place.

Challenge #6: We Have a Problematic Culture of Over-Protection of Ideas

This critique (and the next one) poses the greatest challenge to copyright laws. While our ability to (re)produce works of art has increased exponentially, works that are freely available to the public have not. Artists (or their proxies) take pains to prevent the active sharing and dissemination of their ideas. This is not only unfortunate for the size of the public domain, but it also isn't good for the future of ideas. We need old ideas to produce new ideas. We need people from all sectors of society, all over the world, to be able to see what's out there to generate their own new and brilliant pieces of art. Since so many people value sharing less and less (or since they are prevented from doing so), we stand to suffer as a whole.

This concern is real and deserves to be taken very seriously. Still we must ask what it has to do with the main argument. Yes, sharing ideas matters. Yes, there should be a significant public domain. And yes, we as a culture should promote the free exchange of ideas. But I should still be able to make a contract to keep something secret. This is all the main argument says, and so it seems that illegal downloading is still unjustifiable. Exactly what the *extent* of copyright law should be remains an open question, as we, socially, are trying to strike a balance between the need to protect an artist's work and the public's need for accessible ideas. But so long as we think that people do have significant rights to protect their ideas, the main argument stands. One is not morally permitted to illegally download *because* our culture is over-protective. Even if current copyright law allows too much protection for artists and their work (as I believe it does), the proper solution to over-protection is somewhat less protection, rather than no protection at all.

Challenge #7: The Supposed 'Contracts' Involved in Copyright Are *Unfair,* and Unfair Contracts Are No Contracts at All

In most contracting situations, the contractors have the ability to *negotiate.* They can rework parts of the contract that are less than ideal into something more favorable. You might think that, if the terms are unfavorable, then the contract would not be agreed to. However, parties to a contract often feel some pressure to take less than favorable terms. In other cases, the terms of the contract are less than fully clear.

This challenge, then, expresses the worry that the contracting situation in questions of copyright is possibly unfair. The overwhelming majority of transactions concerning music, for example, are *not* akin to the contracting situation present in the example that started this paper. In that situation, there's a person there, offering to show you his work, under certain terms. You have the opportunity to negotiate with him. If you don't, and you break those terms, you've clearly committed a wrong in breaking a contract. However, when one buys a CD, for example, one has no control over the terms of the deal. You either accept the terms or you don't receive the product, end of story. Furthermore, one may not be able to understand exactly what the terms of the contract are. The worry, then, is that the main argument's second premise is false; illegal downloading of files is not like breaking contracts. The argument thus employs a false analogy.

This is perhaps the most interesting challenge to the main argument. I am indeed troubled by practices involving vague and/or non-negotiable contracts. We need to figure out how to restrain such practices. There's more to say about this, but the main response to the challenge is this: even if it's true that these contracts are problematic in various ways, that doesn't mean that we are morally free to violate such a contract. The person whose rights we violate might be (and probably is) completely innocent of wrongdoing. Such people are probably engaging in a practice that, reasonably, has never struck them as unfair. Hence it seems wrong to treat them this way simply because they are a part of this process we consider unfair.

To help see this, remember my note in the first challenge about the fact that the record industry does not generally pay musicians very well. Most artists make very little from the sale of an album. It's at least plausible to suggest that, following this fact, the way the music industry is set up is so problematic that whatever contracting takes place in the context of that industry is no morally binding contract at all. Since musicians are taken advantage of, it might be thought that one does not need to abide by a contract that is a part of this unjust system.

Again, while I am troubled by how musicians (and customers) are treated by the record industry, this does not yet justify the breaking of contracts that take place in the context of that industry. It is true that some industries are themselves so morally problematic that any contract that takes place within them is not morally binding at all. For example, a contract regarding the holding of slaves I take to be so obviously repugnant as to be no contract at all. Clearly the recording industry—and the contracts that take place within its context—is nothing like this. It would take sophisticated arguments to show that the recording industry's contracts are morally sufficiently close to the slave trade to make it clear that the contracts within the industry are, like those involved in slavery, not morally binding at all. I am friendly to the idea that the contracts in the music industry are not *as* morally binding as contracts in a fully moral business, but, without further argument, that is not enough to show that contracts in the music industry are not morally binding. Until such arguments appear, we are right to think that those who make contracts in and with the music industry are morally required to obey the terms of those contracts.

Conclusion

Downloading illegal music and other files is ordinarily wrong. There can be occasional exceptions (think of the earlier example of Joseph and his passion for *I Know Why the Caged Bird Sings*). But most cases of illegal downloading occur because downloaders do not want to pay for what they want access to. The argument here is that these actions are wrong, and they're wrong for the same reason that breaking contracts is wrong. Though there are challenges to this argument, they are insufficient to change the fact that the illegal downloading of files from the Internet is immoral. The fact that the music industry has various morally troubling contracts is indeed of real concern, but these concerns are not sufficient to show that it is morally acceptable to illegally download an artist's work.

Finally, we have many options to obtain these files without payment—there are numerous artistic items that are publicly available, a variety of files that people don't protect ("found" ideas), as well as numerous methods of obtaining free forms of artistic entertainment. These methods often provide even the poorest of us with access to valuable art forms which we can enjoy without at the same time violating the rights of the artists who have produced them.[1]

Jonathan Trerise: Why Illegally Downloading Files Is Morally Wrong

1. Some argue that since (nearly) everyone illegally downloads files, then it is not wrong to do so. Trerise replies that murder and tax evasion would still be wrong even if most people committed these deeds. Are there some actions that are ordinarily wrong but are such that, if everyone did them, they would no longer be wrong? If so, provide some examples, and then examine whether illegal downloading is more like these examples than the ones that Trerise considers.

2. If a system is corrupt, then contracts made within it are not morally binding. The copyright system is corrupt. Therefore, contracts made within it are not morally binding. Critically assess this argument.

3. Trerise argues for his main thesis by introducing an analogy with a musician named Lars. Is this analogy a good one, or are there relevant differences between the moral duty you owe to Lars and the moral duty that consumers owe to recording and publishing companies?

4. Trerise considers seven objections to his main argument. Can you think of an eighth that might be more powerful that those he has discussed?

5. The harm imposed by any single instance of illegal downloading is probably extremely small. Does this make a difference to the morality of such downloading? Why or why not?

---

1   I thank Russ Shafer-Landau, David Killoren, and Tony Doyle for their careful comments on this paper.

Why Legally Downloading Music Is Morally Wrong

Tim Anderson and D. E. Wittkower

....

Anderson and Wittkower argue for the surprising thesis that *legally* downloading music is immoral. However, they also think that *illegally* downloading music is immoral, though for quite different reasons. This obviously puts the music consumer in a bind—one that the authors do not seek to solve within this article.

In the preceding article, Jonathan Trerise makes a case for why illegally downloading music (and other) files is immoral. This seems to imply that the moral path is to legally download such files, by paying for them in exchange for the use of the file. But Anderson and Wittkower reject that suggestion. Their opposition stems from their appraisal of the current copyright system as deeply immoral. They argue that it treats artists immorally, hinders the development of culture, makes too much of it inaccessible, and renders art a commodity to be passively appreciated, rather than actively engaged in.

But if both legally and illegally downloading music files are immoral, what is a music lover to do? Anderson and Wittkower suggest that we must work to alter current music industry practices and copyright laws so that they are more morally defensible. Once these reforms are in place, then legally downloading files will no longer be so morally problematic, since it will not amount to supporting a morally corrupt set of

---

This article was commissioned for the fourth edition of *The Ethical Life*.

practices. In addition to working for such reforms, we ought to offer direct support to artists, by (for example) purchasing tickets to their shows or buying recordings whose rights are controlled by the artists themselves.

....

W e've all done it. We certainly have, and we will again. But paying for and legally downloading music is morally wrong.

Buying music from labels or retailers in our current intellectual property rights regime and copyright-based industry context (1) fails to appropriately support artists, (2) acts against artists' autonomy, (3) hinders the development and accessibility of culture, and (4) reinforces a relationship to art, music, creation, and creativity which is commodified rather than active, and thereby stifles human potential by diminishing the quality of life in our societies. In other words, paying into the copyright industries, as they currently exist, means being complicit in undermining everything that copyright law is meant to promote, and thus means being complicit in acting against the explicit intention of the constitutional basis of copyright law in the United States.

These are serious moral claims, and we hope that after going through arguments for these four interconnected claims, you'll agree that buying and legally downloading music contributes to significant problems. After making this case, though, it's another question entirely what to *do* about it! Rather than spring this on you at the end of this essay, we'll tell you up front: we don't think *illegally* downloading music is a moral alternative.

What are we supposed to do then? One option is to refrain from supporting existing legal systems of retail and distribution. In this scenario one would listen only to live music or to recordings that have been properly "copylefted" with Creative Commons licenses, or works that are in the public domain. However, this option sets an impractically high moral standard that would effectively restrict listening to a very exacting and non-popular repertoire. It's also kind of beside the point. As Lierre Kieth argues in *Earth at Risk*, "the task of an activist is not to navigate around systems of oppression with as much personal integrity as possible, it's to dismantle those systems." Similarly, if you agree with our arguments, your conclusion should not be that it is morally obligatory to refrain from buying music. While it's good to seek out ways of fixing or avoiding the many problems existing systems of retail and subscription generate, it is even more important to seek out ways to support reform and replacement of these systems. In concrete terms, we recommend (a) engaging in direct support of artists whose work you care about, including going to shows, buying recordings directly from them, or crowdfunding their work; and (b) supporting pro-artist, pro-art, and pro-public reform in copyright law. Ethical music consumers could exert tremendous power if they demanded that their music, like their coffee, be part of a certified Fair Trade system of production, distribution, and payment that was transparent and ethical.

1. Buying Music in the Current Market Fails to Appropriately Support Artists

In the past the system of record production involved labels, distributors, and retailers. Like book publishing, the expenses accrued because of a necessary "value chain"—those linkages that connected producers with advertisers and shops that brought value to records and books by making them known and available to the general public. These significant investments were required: the total expenses of recording, pressing, distributing, and housing discs and artwork could not be avoided. These upfront costs were huge and very risky. Indeed, few artists or authors could have tried to find an audience if they had had to pay for printing and distribution by themselves, and to do so up front, prior to any sales. In this system, publishers and labels shouldered this risk and used the profits of successful titles to both defray the costs of failure and to fund the publication of new works. Under this system, it clearly benefited the public to ensure that publishers could make a robust profit, since these profits funded cultural research and development. The argument was that a label that barely survived couldn't afford to take risks with new musical styles and artists. On the other hand, a publisher awash in funds was more likely to help create and support a diverse and inclusive cultural ecosystem of new musical expressions.

However, in the last twenty years the significant material infrastructure that justified this system has eroded to the point where many artists no longer need these expenditures. It is no longer necessary to press great numbers of CDs and LPs. With the arrival of multiple online listening and distribution platforms, the need for a system of trucks, warehouses and physical retailers has disappeared, and the cost of getting the music into the hands of consumers has plummeted. At the same time, recording and production have radically cheapened as well, with ever-cheaper high-quality hardware and cheap or free software like GarageBand and Audacity. Indeed, even the cost of promotion is decreasing, as more and more artists take to social media as a means of getting the word out about upcoming releases and tours.

This does not mean that labels and publishers have gone away. They will continue to retain their role as gatekeepers, particularly to multinational markets where the many legal and cultural issues key to distributing and performing may be too much for the average musicians to negotiate. It's much more difficult to access large consumer markets without the logistical machinery of a major label.

Yet the question at hand is not about supporting a now-unnecessary and costly system, but rather finding sustainable alternatives. Because of the many tools and practices that did not exist even 15 years ago, most artists today will simply never need the services that labels and retailers can provide. Indeed, today only a small percentage of the most famous musicians are able to earn enough from selling downloads and CDs to make a secure living for themselves and their families. Even in the past, the label system was considered suspicious by some of its greatest successes. For example, Prince once compared the label-contract system to slavery and indentured servitude. If this system of investment and distribution is no longer necessary for most artists, then reflexively supporting these systems is problematic at best and, at worst, unjustifiable, due to the way it allocates an excess of resources to intermediaries rather than artists.

But even labels themselves have changed. For example, the relatively long-term support and nurturing of emerging artists—one of the forms of support that the label system once offered musicians—is no longer the norm. Indeed, labels expect others, particularly artists themselves, to make these vital investments. Digital streams and piracy have also forced labels to rethink what products they are willing to finance. Major labels used to make all of their money from their investment in records. Now new contract agreements, called "360 deals," demand percentages from every moneymaking aspect of a musician's career, including merchandise and live performances. As the saying goes, labels are no longer investing in bands so much as they are investing in brands.

This is why many musicians give away downloads. Those not in 360 agreements make their money playing shows and selling t-shirts. Knowing full well that when the marginal cost of reproduction—the amount it costs to make each copy of each album—is zero, many musicians see downloads as calling cards that are better exchanged for fans' emails. Musicians would often rather have a means of contacting audiences to let them know when they are preparing to tour or when they have a new piece of merchandise to sell than place their bets on minimal royalty statements. It is possible that musicians could make a lot of money in the current copyright industries. Yet as it stands, what the best systems are in this new atmosphere remains unclear, particularly as legal streaming alternatives and their very small per-stream-residual rates are quickly outpacing the option of purchased downloads and their wider margins as a consumer choice. The problem is that we have yet to see what new systems work best for musicians.

2. Buying Music in the Current Market Acts Against Artists' Autonomy

The first thing that one has to realize about the label system is that its support comes on the basis of substantial commercial considerations. When a label invests in a musician it is not necessarily investing in their music. Rather, labels wish to produce commercially oriented goods for exchange. Historically, this has meant that objects like records and CDs were produced for a marketplace. In all cases what labels perceived as the limits of a marketplace often compromised what and how much a musician could produce. Artists could be gently coaxed or forced to produce music in styles outside their strong preferences simply for the sake of sales. In some cases, musicians such as Prince, who produced substantially more music than the typical artist, would not see their works released for fear that the label would oversaturate a market.

Perhaps the most substantial restrictions placed on artists have come in the arena of promotions and marketing. In some cases, artists as weighty and influential as Johnny Cash and LL Cool J criticized their labels for not promoting works they firmly believed in. OK GO's own elaborate videos were restricted from being easily shared by fans by their then-label, EMI-Capitol, because the company wanted to use the promotions as an income stream. Amanda Palmer ran into substantial problems with her label when an executive asked her to cut a few shots from a promotional video because he thought she looked fat. As we will discuss later, in the cases of Amanda Palmer and OK GO, both have been able to secure some form of independence and have become responsible for their careers' successes and mistakes.

3. Buying Music in the Current Market Hinders the Development and Accessibility of Culture

Constitutional law scholar Lawrence Lessig estimates that only 2% of the books published between 1923 and 1942 (the first twenty years still covered by copyright law) are commercially viable and remain in print today. In other words, 98%, the overwhelming majority of written culture produced in those eventful twenty years, is basically inaccessible. Worse, its influence and value is likely to be lost because its circulation has been made illegal. Many works, in fact the majority of works, no longer have a presence in the marketplace because publishers no longer bother to seek profits from them, and others are prevented from distributing them by laws that guarantee publishers' exclusive rights to do so.

One of the sources of this problem is the length of time that rights holders can claim an exclusive right to their intellectual properties. Whether they be song lyrics, patents, or logos, Article I, Section 8, Clause 8 of the US Constitution grants Congress the ability "To promote the Progress of Science and useful Arts, by securing for limited Times to Authors and Inventors the exclusive Right to their respective Writings and Discoveries." In essence, copyright protection is an incentive for more creativity: by securing an exclusive property right for authors and inventors, they are incentivized to create and innovate. However, in the US context, the optimal duration of the exclusive copyright protection has always been unclear. Article 1 does not provide any guidance as to the ideal length of a copyright. Initially, the duration of the exclusive right lasted just 14 years. Today, under the extreme protections of copyright authorized by the Sonny Bono Copyright Term Extension Act of 1998 (CTEA)—often called the "Mickey Mouse Protection Act," as it was passed by the US Congress just before the character Mickey Mouse would have entered the public domain—authors are granted their lifetime plus 70 years; corporations who commission works are granted exclusive rights to that work for 95 years. What this has meant is that an environment exists where a great deal of creative and cultural work is kept from public use in order to protect publishers' profits. Other artists who might wish to access, remix, work with, or even listen to and be inspired by a song or record may not be able to do so because (and despite the fact that) companies owning rights over these works have decided that it is not worth their while to keep these works in the marketplace. Worse yet, if the systematic extension of copyright continues, as one can expect from a Congress sub-ject to heavy industry lobbying pressures, songs and records may effec-tively continue to remain inaccessible to many potential consumers in perpetuity.

To be clear, we do believe that the authors of songs and records should be compensated if they wish to place them in a marketplace. We worry that in an atmosphere where songs and compositions are limited by how and who can share and profit from them, a majority of cultural works will simply become lost and forgotten. If we continue to deny the public the opportunity to harvest the creative wealth of previous works, those works will lie fallow and slowly become irrelevant. Imagine what would happen if every classroom had to pay substantial fees to a corporation when its students were assigned to read Shakespeare or Homer. Simply put, some authors and their ideas contain values that exist beyond the needs of a marketplace. Subjected to the demands of a market, teachers may look elsewhere for cheaper and less valuable works to utilize in educating their students. Just as we believe that the lessons of the Bard and Odys-seus should be accessible to all, we believe that there must be a critical examination of the system that effectively supports and promotes songs and records only insofar as they are private property and not as part of our cultural heritage and inheritance.

This last point can be seen clearly in comparison to patent law. Pat-ents are granted for a term of 20 years. This is meant to strike a balance between inventors' (and corporations') interests and the interests of con-sumers, with an eye to maximally benefiting the public. If the patent term is shorter, it reduces the incentive that inventors and corporations have to invest in innovative technologies, pharmaceuticals, and so on, and this may slow the progress of science and technology. If the patent term is longer, this means that inventors and corporations can sequester the technology and charge monopoly prices for longer. The result is that it takes longer for other innovators and corporations to be able to create more affordable generic versions to benefit more users and to be able to build on the patented invention to create new and further innovations. Innovation is slowed and public benefit is lessened if the term is either too long or too short. We are skeptical that 20 years is the right balance for patents—four or five years might be more appropriate, given the rapid pace of technological development—but it is far more reasonable than the 95 years of artificial monopoly guaranteed to copyrighted works under the CTEA.

The balance with copyright is similar to that with patents: if we want cultural development and innovation, we need to ensure that artists and creators can make a living when they produce valuable work that benefits the public. But we also need to ensure that work enters the public domain when it is still relevant, so that other artists and creators can learn from, rework, and build upon it. The current copyright industrial environment utterly fails to strike the proper balance among these interests; indeed, it fails to effectively support *either* end of the "copyright bargain." As we discussed above, it does not support artists appropriately, and it *also* fails to return work to the public domain while it is still relevant, instead withholding it until (in most cases) it becomes not only irrelevant, but lost altogether.

The possible values of creative reuse and remix are easy to underestimate, since the examples we usually see are very limited, due to our restrictive intellectual property laws. We might think of the use of samples in rap and hip-hop. Think instead about the huge cultural wealth that Disney has appropriated and masterfully transformed—traditional fairy tales and public domain short stories that form the basis of *Snow White and the Seven Dwarfs* (based on the Brothers Grimm story), *Cinderella* (based on Charles Perrault's story), *Alice in Wonderland* (Lewis Carroll), *Peter Pan* (J. M. Barrie), *Sleeping Beauty* (Charles Perrault/Brothers Grimm), *The Little Mermaid* (Hans Christian Andersen), *Beauty and the Beast* (Jeanne-Marie Leprince de Beaumont), *Aladdin* (The Arabian Nights), *Mulan* (木蘭辭), *The Princess and the Frog* (Brothers Grimm), *Tangled* (Brothers Grimm), and *Frozen* (Hans Christian Andersen). Disney has creatively and masterfully reworked and reimagined its public domain cultural inheritance, but has not replenished the well—others do not have the rights to similarly reimagine and rework Disney's cultural contributions.

To get a good idea of the first steps of what this reimagining and reworking would look like in the realm of music, beyond the short samples which can be used legally, search for Girl Talk's *All Day*, or DJ Dangermouse's *Grey Album*, a remix of Jay Z's *Black Album* and the Beatles' *White Album*. These works are blatantly copyright-infringing, but remain widely accessible, for two reasons. First, the artists created these works outside of the copyright industries and without seeking profits. Second, their popular and critical reception has been so positive that labels seem to have determined it not to be in their best interest to bring a suit against these artists, even though they clearly have the right to do so.

4. Buying Music in the Current Market Reinforces a Relationship to Art, Music, Creation, and Creativity That Is Commodified Rather Than Active, Stifling Human Potential and Diminishing the Quality of Life in Our Societies

We live in a unique moment in the history of our species' relation to music. Until very recently, with the availability of technologies of recording and replay, music was almost entirely part of humans' lives when they themselves were participating in making it. Music was created in communities and families, and drumming, singing and playing was a part of work, play, and praise, rather than an object of more passive enjoyment as an audience—with the exception of aristocrats who had or could attend parlor performances, concerts, or operas. It was only in the 20th century, along with the rise of music industries and their accompanying modes of production and distribution, that most of the music most humans ever heard—at least in advanced industrial societies—became something that was done largely by specialists. Singing and playing music have become, for us, newly a matter of choice and study rather than everyday parts of family and community life.

Along with this shift from participation to spectatorship, not unlike the move away from playing active games with one another to the spectacle of spectator sports, what used to be simply matters of our own cultures and histories became an object of production in what Theodor Adorno and Max Horkheimer termed "The Culture Industry." "Culture" is no longer predominantly who we are and how we keep our diverse traditions alive through the generations. Instead, culture is predominantly envisioned as a mass-produced, marketed good, through which we are encouraged to identify ourselves. Thus, we talk of music and identities in terms of distinct genres. Whether listeners love country music, are hip-hop fans, jazz aficionados, or self-described punks, each segment is researched and addressed by companies as a group whose members have their own meaningful taste culture and identity. Indeed, with some exceptions—for example, the context of religious practice—we no longer sing and play the songs of our ancestors. Instead, we purchase, listen to, play, and sing works produced by profit-centered, market-oriented industries.

This represents a massive and wholesale squandering of our cultural inheritances. It is one that threatens a mass extinction of cultural memory and traditions. We stand to lose how our cultures participate in the creation of music and the unique joys communities generate in how they create musical beauty and a sense of belonging and meaning. The experience of choral singing, to use an example many readers will have at least some familiarity with, is a transcendent and deeply powerful experience. Choir members often report that their musical practices create bonds of care and connection with others. We believe that this has not been completely eradicated. However, we worry that seemingly interminable copyright laws could restrict future community expressions if, in the near future, a group must raise capital, hire lawyers, and pay for permission any time it seeks to record and release its interpretation of a 20th century repertoire piece. It is because a choir does not need to go through such machinations that they have the ability to choose from composers from Byrd to Palestrina to both perform and record. It strikes us as absurd that in the relatively near future of 2060 a similar choir may not be similarly free to choose compositions from composers such as McCartney or Strayhorn. We worry that allowing art to remain a private good for unprecedented amounts of time not only restricts music, writing, and other forms of cultural production to specialists, but further restricts cultural production only to those specialists who can afford to access a controlled, privatized, industrially-produced repertoire of cultural expressions.

This, of course, applies equally well to illegal and legal downloading: either way, we are consuming the products of the culture industry rather than participating in and furthering our own cultures by creating music from within our own communities, motivated by our own expressive needs and intentions, and building up and strengthening our communities through this collective creation and heritage. Illegal downloading has at least the virtue of not materially contributing to the culture industry's profitability, but only at the expense of creating a freerider problem—it is predicated on others' having paid into the system, and does nothing to contribute to an alternative.

For those without enough interest to become participants in music making, a better compromise is to participate as an active audience member rather than a passive consumer. Go to shows! The experience of a crowd moved by music's emotional communication creates bonds and meaning for us in a way that standing among hundreds of others, each with her own set of earbuds, cannot.

What Are We Supposed to Do?

We hope to have convinced you that you should have serious and significant moral concerns about legally downloading music in our current legal and industrial environment—that legally buying or streaming music, in most cases, fails to properly support and nurture artists and creators and instead supports a system of cultural production that stifles innovation and diminishes creativity and cultural development. Illegal downloading, as we've also noted, is not a clearly preferable alternative, as it also doesn't support artists and does little or nothing to replace the system of cultural production with anything that might be any better. What, then, ought we to do?

In the fourth argument above we have already indicated some positive actions that can be taken. In short: Consume less, participate more, understand your restrictions, and resist. The best way to do this is to simply make music. Whether you play covers or produce original content, the more you do so, the more you will begin to feel these limitations, understand the injustice of their restraints, and begin to become more critical of these systems and less dependent upon them. The next step is to become politically active. In the United States, activist groups such as Creative Commons, the Electronic Frontier Foundation, and the Future of Music Coalition are open to your participation as they search to create more just, less restrictive systems that better support musicians.

If you are a fan, engage in direct support of artists whose work you care about. Go to their shows. Go to their websites. Buy as directly from them as possible. Ask and find out what kind of engagement and support they want from you. The beauty of the Internet and its many peer-to-peer capacities is that the need of intermediation has drastically lessened. Meet them where they are. Finally, respect their own judgments about how they want to create music and what relationship they want to have with fans.

For example, the relatively new practice of crowdfunding capital to create and distribute work is a kind of direct support that many artists are increasingly interested in. It can allow artists to create through a much more direct engagement with their audiences, it avoids the intermediaries of labels, and allows for a less constrained mode of production and distribution. As such, more and more artists are finding that crowdfunding better supports them financially as well as creatively. By no means is it perfect, though. Not every artist wants the responsibility of connecting with potential backers or feels comfortable asking for money. However, this option has allowed a freer form of expression for those artists who prefer to take on these tasks themselves and who are willing to accept the risk of losing time or face in this uncertain process.

Finally, we believe that these points are moot without lobbying for the reform of the industry in a continual search for more just legal structures. Many artists and listeners believe that current copyright laws are excessive, and are implemented in ways that benefit corporations at the expense of artists. Of course, it is the industry rather than musicians that have the ear of our legislators, but as artists gain more power through technological development, new efforts like Tidal and Kickstarter are beginning to shift the balance of power. As fans we should seek to support artists' reforms and to help to find a fairer, freer way of creating and enjoying music.

Tim Anderson and D. E. Wittkower: Why Legally Downloading Music Is Morally Wrong

1. Legally paying for downloaded music violates no one's rights; if a practice violates no one's rights, then it is morally acceptable, so legally paying for downloaded music is morally acceptable. How would Anderson and Wittkower reply to this argument?

2. Suppose you live where you are unable to easily travel to see your favorite bands. What morally acceptable options do Anderson and Wittkower offer if you want to listen to your favorite music?

3. There are a lot of injustices in the world and only a finite amount of time for any given individual to try to reform them. So people must choose their battles. Suppose that you are fighting injustice of one kind or another but decide that spending your time on trying to reform copyright law and the music industry is not your top priority. Do you think that this gives you an exemption from the arguments offered by Anderson and Wittkower? Why or why not?

4. What are the competing values at play in copyright law? How do you think the balance ought to be struck between them?

5. Anderson and Wittkower rely on an analogy between patent law and copyright law. Explain this analogy. Is it a good one, or are there relevant differences between the two that might undermine their argument?